Rick Steves ®

PORTUGAL

CONTENTS

Post-Pandemic Travels: Expect a Warm Welcome...and a Few Changes
Research for this guidebook was limited by the COVID-19 outbreak, and the long-term impact of the crisis on our recommended destinations is unclear. Some details in this book will change for post-pandemic travelers. Now more than ever, it's smart to reconfirm specifics as you plan and travel. As always, you can find major updates at RickSteves.com/update.

Welcome to Rick Steves' Europe

Travel is intensified living—maximum thrills per minute and one of the last great sources of legal adventure. Travel is freedom. It's recess, and we need it.

I discovered a passion for European travel as a teen and have been sharing it ever since—through my bus tours, public television and radio shows, and travel guidebooks. Over the years, I've taught millions of travelers how to best enjoy Europe's block-buster sights—and experience "Back Door" discoveries that most tourists miss.

This book offers a balanced mix of Portugal's big-city sights and small-town and rural des-tinations. It's selective: Rather than listing dozens of Algarve beach towns, I recommend only the best ones: Salema, Lagos, and Tavira. And it's in-depth: My self-guided sight tours and city walks provide insight into the country's vibrant history and today's living, breathing culture.

I advocate traveling simply and smartly. Take advantage of my money- and time-saving tips on sight-seeing, transportation, and more. Try local, characteristic alternatives to expensive hotels and restaurants. In many ways, spending more money only builds a thicker wall between you and what you traveled so far to see.

We visit Portugal to experience it—to become temporary locals. Thoughtful travel engages us with the world, as we learn to appreciate other cultures and new ways to measure quality of life.

Judging by the positive feedback I receive from readers, this book will help you enjoy a fun, affordable, and rewarding vacation—whether it's your first trip or your tenth.

Boa viagem! Happy travels!

Rick Steves

PORTUGAL

The Atlantic was the source of Portugal's seafaring wealth long ago, and remains the draw for tourists today. Buoyed by fresh seafood, hardworking fisherfolk, and miles of sunny coastline, the country's maritime spirit lives on.

Perched on the Atlantic on the far edge of Europe, Portugal preserves a salty, traditional culture. Gnarled fishermen still mend their nets, and rustically clad women sell fish and produce in markets. Wherever you go, you're never far from the sea.

But you'll also experience modern, urban Portugal—with rejuvenated cityscapes, upscale boutiques, and a surging cuisine scene—especially in the culturally rich capital of Lisbon and the second city of Porto. The cities have a worldly buzz: You can munch barnacles bought from a street vendor on a breezy tiled square, or sit down with gastronomic pilgrims for a feast in foodie heaven.

Portugal seems somewhere just beyond Europe—and the pace of life is noticeably slower. While membership in the European Union has brought sweeping changes here, the traditional economy is still based on fishing, cork, wine, textiles, and tourism.

From a traveler's perspective, Portugal is greater than the sum of its parts. The country has few blockbuster sights. Its cities—while increasingly revitalized—still come with rough edges. Even its ritziest coastal towns are humble, lacking major attractions. And yet the country offers a heady mix—of warmhearted people, vivid culture, dramatic viewpoints, terraced

Celebrating history: Monument to the Discoveries (Lisbon) and Monastery of Santa Maria (Batalha)

vineyards, and (of course) sun-drenched beaches—that makes traveling here a delight.

Portugal is one of Europe's first modern nation-states. Long before Spain famously expelled its North African Muslim rulers in 1492, Portugal bucked the Moors, establishing its present-day borders (unchanged now for 800 years). Alonso Henriques, who helped chase out the Moors, was officially recognized as the country's first king in 1179.

Several centuries later, Portugal became one of the world's richest nations during its Age of Discovery (1400-1600). Explorers such as Vasco da Gama discovered new trade routes and lands to colonize. To this day, Portugal is ethnically diverse, inhabited by many people from its former colonies in Brazil, Africa, and Asia.

The bounty from Portugal's colonies financed an explosion of the arts back home. The finest architecture from the country's Golden Age is in Lisbon, represented by Belém's tower and monastery (in a style called "Manueline," after King Manuel I). Other great monasteries—with grand tombs and restful tiled cloisters—are north of Lisbon, in Batalha and Alcobaça. Portugal peaked with the wealth harvested from its colonies. As its empire faded, so did the country's power and affluence.

Saudade—a deep, yearning nostalgia for something you love but that's forever gone—is a characteristic emotion of the

Bom Apetite!

Portuguese cuisine is sightseeing for your palate—flavored with ingredients and spices originally brought from countries spanning its 15th-century trade routes, including Africa, the Far East, India, and Brazil. One example is piri-piri sauce, made from crushed African chiles—equally delicious on chicken, shrimp, and pork.

You can eat well in mom-and-pop restaurants for about €10, especially outside Lisbon. Bars and cafés are handy for quick snacks. Note that appetizers brought to the table before you've ordered are not free—the mini buffet of olives, bread, and other tasty temptations are usually about €1 each. (If you don't want them, ignore them. Later you can have them taken away.)

The Portuguese are among the world's biggest seafood eaters. Boiled gooseneck barnacles, called *percebes*, are a salty delicacy (fresh April-Sept). They're sold on coastal town streets and in bars as munchies. To eat them, just twist, rip, and bite. They're expensive because they're so dangerous to harvest—they grow on rocky promontories in narrow inlets where the waves and currents are fierce.

Seek out fish soup (*sopa de peixe*), shellfish soup (*sopa de mariscos*), and *bacalhau à Brás,* a sort of cod frittata with potatoes, onions, and herbs. For a seafood blowout, look for *cataplana* (a feast from the sea, simmered in a copper pot). Or, simpler and cheaper, dine on grilled sardines (*sardinhas grelhadas*). For a mix of surf and turf, *carne de porco à Alentejana* is an interesting combination of pork and clams—and Portugal's unique contribution to world cuisine. *Bacalhau*—codfish that's ▶▶▶

Sample the culinary pleasures of Portugal: barnacles (a bar snack good with beer), tasty seafood stew, and versatile cod. Codfish (bacalhau) is dried, then rehydrated, to make many different dishes.

▶▶▶ dried, salted, and then re-hydrated and served a reputed 365 different ways—is the national dish. It's a soupy culture, and the standard is *caldo verde*—a tasty garlic-infused kale-and-potato soup usually topped with a slice of sausage.

Like their Spanish neighbors, the Portuguese use plenty of olive oil, produce delicious cheeses (such as the top-quality *Serra da Estrela*), and love *presunto*, their air-cured ham (*porco preto*—from black ibérico pigs in Alentejo—is tops).

Try regional specialties wherever you go. The Alentejo region (Évora) has a rustic, hearty cuisine heavy on pork and red wine. In Beira (Coimbra), specialties include suckling pig *(leitão)* and baby goat *(cabrito)*. In Porto, a specialty to sample—or perhaps avoid—is *tripas à moda do Porto,* a thick stew of tripe, chicken, beans, and vegetables. Porto's beloved gut-bomb, the *francesinha* sandwich, is stuffed with pork, sausages, and cheese, grilled, topped with more melted cheese and often a fried egg, then drenched with spicy sauces.

Pair your cuisine with regional wines, and for dessert seek out local pastries, such as a white-bean tart *(pastel de feijão)* in Nazaré, or a sweet, eggy pastry *(pastel de Tentúgal)* in Coimbra. A national favorite is the custard tart, *pastel de nata* (called *pastel de Belém* in Lisbon's fancy suburb of the same name). You'll also find heavenly concoctions made from egg yolk and sugar, such as *barriga de freiras* (nuns' belly) and *papo de anjo* (angel's double chin). ■

Portuguese enjoy the best air-cured ham, Porto's gooey francesinha *sandwiches, and Lisbon's warm custard tarts, sprinkled with cinnamon and powdered sugar.*

Portuguese people. These days, Portugal is small…"just us and the Atlantic Ocean," they say. Poets and artists see *saudade* in melancholy people, well-worn yet still ornate buildings, lampposts, fado songs, and even in port wine.

Along with Spain in the 20th century, Portugal suffered through fascist-style rule longer than the rest of Europe: From 1932 to 1974, Portugal endured the repressive regime of António de Oliveira Salazar and his successor Marcelo Caetano—the longest dictatorship in Western European history. This put the country in an economic hole that it's still struggling to emerge from. When Portugal became part of the European Union (just 12 years after the end of the dictatorship), it was Western Europe's poorest country.

The EU spurred great investment in Portugal, helping to bring its economy up to speed. But that money came with strings attached, and—especially following the Great Recession—Portugal found itself struggling to repay EU loans. It's proved challenging to maintain generous social services, keep taxes reasonable, and reduce unemployment. Poverty still exists, particularly in rural areas, but overall, the country is more prosperous than a generation ago. Prices remain low— Portugal is one of the most affordable places to travel in Western Europe.

For a small country, Portugal has many iconic symbols. *Azulejos,* the colorful, typically blue-hued tiles that seem to

Enjoying a café stop (framed by azulejo *tilework); a Nazaré sunset*

9

A trolley ride in Lisbon; a cork harvest in the Alentejo heartland

decorate every surface, are a Portuguese art form you'll never tire of seeing. They are as practical in this hot climate (for their cooling properties) as they are beautiful. Only Portugal offers haunting fado music, capturing the sorrowful feeling of *saudade* in song. The country's heartland—the arid Alentejo—cultivates cork trees to produce that famously versatile material.

To make good use of all those corks, northern Portugal produces the fortified, aged wine called port. And lovably rickety old trolleys trundle footsore commuters and visitors up and down the hills of Lisbon and Porto. While seemingly clichéd, these are all authentic slices of Portuguese life—each with its own backstory, which proud locals love to tell.

All over Portugal, you'll see the country's mascot: the Rooster of Barcelos, with colorful designs on his black body and a proud red pompadour. Inspired by the legend of a rooster who came back from the dead to prove the innocence of an unjustly accused man, it symbolizes justice and good luck—and is a souvenir-stand staple.

If your idea of good travel includes friendly locals (who generally speak English), a rich culture, affordable prices, a thriving urban scene, seaside resort towns, and fresh seafood with chilled white wine on a beach at sunset...you've chosen the right destination.

Portugal's Top Destinations

There's so much to see in Portugal and so little time. This overview breaks the country's top destinations into must-see sights (to help first-time travelers plan their trip) and worth-it sights (for those with extra time or special interests). I've also suggested a minimum number of days to allow per destination.

Atlantic Ocean

SPAIN

Douro

DOURO VALLEY

PORTO   *Douro*

COIMBRA

NAZARÉ & CENTRAL PORTUGAL

SINTRA

LISBON

ÉVORA

THE ALGARVE

100 Kilometers
100 Miles

PLACES COVERED IN THIS BOOK

▲▲▲ Must See
▲▲ Try Hard to See
▲ Worthwhile

MUST-SEE DESTINATIONS

With limited time, prioritize Portugal's biggest city and its southern coast. If you have just a week for Portugal, these destinations will fill your time wonderfully.

▲▲▲Lisbon (allow 2-3 days)

Portugal's lively, hilly port and capital city has fascinating, distinctive neighborhoods: the flat downtown Baixa, flanked by the hill-topping Bairro Alto (with lots of cafés) and the castle-capping Alfama (the old sailors' quarter, with Mediterranean views). The city's neighborhoods—dotted with museums, inviting eateries, and squares grand and small—are connected by historic trolleys and mosaic sidewalks. The soundtrack of the night is a mix of happy eaters and soulful fado.

The nearby suburb of Belém, just a trolley ride away, is home to the 16th-century Monastery of Jerónimos, maritime and coach museums, the Monument to the Discoveries, and the namesake, custard tarts—*pastel de Belém.*

▲▲▲The Algarve (2 days)

The country's southern coast is strung with villages, historic sights, and sandy beaches with seascapes.

My favorite destination on the coast is the fishing village of Salema, with the region's best beach and easygoing restaurant scene. Nearby is the historic "end of the road"—Cape Sagres— where Henry the Navigator founded his school and organized far-ranging expeditions.

The party town of Lagos is the transit hub of the coast, with beaches and boat tours. The river-straddling village of Tavira, with a fun beach island a boat ride away, makes a pleasant stop between Lagos and Spain.

Monastery of Jerónimos (opposite); lunch in Lisbon's Alfama; world map at Monument to the Discoveries; seafront dining in Salema; Algarve beach

WORTH-IT DESTINATIONS

You can weave any of these destinations—rated ▲ or ▲▲—
into your itinerary. It's easy to add some destinations based on
proximity (if you're going to Lisbon, Sintra is next door), but
some out-of-the-way places can merit the journey, depending
on your time and interests.

▲▲Sintra (half-day)
Formerly an aristocratic retreat, the town is famous for its
fairy-tale castles dotting the hilly terrain. Sintra makes a great
day trip by train from Lisbon.

▲▲Évora (1 day)
Encircled by medieval walls, this college town is riddled
with history, from a prehistoric stone circle (nearby), ancient
Roman temple, 12th-century cathedral, medieval chapel of
bones, and 16th-century university, to a lively market street
dating from Roman times.

▲▲Nazaré & Central Portugal (2 days)
Nazaré, a traditional fishing village turned small-town Atlantic
resort, makes an ideal beach break. It's also a jumping off point
for day trips to the monastery at Batalha, the Fátima pilgrimage site, Portugal's largest church in Alcobaça, the Knights
Templar complex in Tomar, and the cute, touristy walled town
of Óbidos.

▲▲Coimbra (1 day)
Portugal's Oxford bustles with students from its prestigious
university; the historic section is open to visit. The Arab-flavored
old town is fun to explore by day and the place to go at night,
especially for fado, sung here by young men.

Sintra's Pena Palace (opposite); Évora evening scene; pilgrim at Fátima; fado performance in Coimbra; Nazaré beach fun

▲▲Porto (1-2 days)

Portugal's gritty but up-and-coming second city hosts steep and picturesque neighborhoods, a scenic riverfront, lively shopping streets, port-wine tastings, and boat tours of the Douro Valley.

▲Douro Valley (1 day)

The pretty terraced valley—the birthplace of port wine—is lined with ample countryside *quintas* (farms with vineyards), offering tastings and accommodations.

Riverfront perch in Porto; port wine tasting tour in Porto; the origin of port wine—terraced vineyards in the Douro Valley

Planning Your Trip

To plan your trip, you'll need to design your itinerary—choosing where and when to go, how you'll travel, and how many days to spend at each destination. For my best general advice on sightseeing, accommodations, restaurants, and more, see the Practicalities chapter.

DESIGNING AN ITINERARY

As you read this book and learn your options...

Choose your top destinations.

My recommended itinerary (see the sidebar on the next page) gives you an idea of how much you can reasonably see in two weeks, but you can adapt it to fit your own interests and time frame.

If you love what big cities have to offer—great sights and museums, lively neighborhoods, an enticing array of eateries, and ample nightlife—you could easily linger for a week in Lisbon. And several sights are within easy day-tripping distance of Lisbon: Sintra, Évora, and Óbidos.

Historians will find much to study in Portugal: ancient Roman ruins (Évora), medieval monasteries (Batalha and Alcobaça), knight sights (Tomar), castles and palaces (Sintra is tops), and remnants from the country's Age of Discovery and Golden Age (in Belém and Cape Sagres). To witness a pilgrimage, visit Fátima when the pilgrims do (every 12th and 13th, May-Oct).

Art lovers are drawn to Lisbon's Gulbenkian Museum. Connoisseurs of port savor Porto, the Douro Valley's *quintas,*

Portugal's Best Two-Week Trip by Car

Day	Plan	Sleep
1	Arrive in Lisbon	Lisbon
2	Sightsee Lisbon	Lisbon
3	Lisbon	Lisbon
4	Optional side-trip to Sintra by train	Lisbon
5	Morning in Lisbon; in the afternoon, pick up car and drive to the Algarve (3 hours)	Salema
6	Beach day in Salema	Salema
7	Side-trip to Cape Sagres and more beach time	Salema
8	To Lagos (30 minutes), then Évora (3 hours)	Évora
9	Morning in Évora; afternoon to Nazaré via Óbidos (3 hours)	Nazaré
10	Nazaré	Nazaré
11	To Coimbra (2 hours) with possible stops in Alcobaça, Batalha, Fátima, or Tomar	Coimbra
12	Coimbra	Coimbra
13	To Douro Valley (2.5 hours)	Douro Valley
14	To Porto (2 hours), drop off car	Porto
15	Porto	Porto
16	Fly home	

For Drivers: Driving times are estimates and could be longer in bad traffic. If you plan to fly home from Lisbon, park your car while in Porto, then drive to the Lisbon airport (about 3 hours) and drop it there.

By Bus and Train: Using public transportation, modify the itinerary as follows: From Lisbon, take the bus to Salema (change in Lagos). Take the bus or train to Évora (with transfers). From Évora, bus to Nazaré (changing in Lisbon). Using Nazaré as your home base, see your choice of nearby sights (Alcobaça, Batalha, and Fátima; add an extra night to fit in everything), or skip the sights as it's less efficient without your own wheels. Or consider spending the night in far-flung Tomar before heading to Coimbra. From Nazaré, take the bus straight to Coimbra. From Coimbra, catch the train to Porto. Visit the Douro Valley on a day-long boat tour from Porto. Fly out of Porto or return to Lisbon by train for your flight out.

Douro

Douro

Porto

DOURO VALLEY

Atlantic Ocean

Douro

N

50 Kilometers
50 Miles

Coimbra

Batalha
Nazaré
Alcobaça

Fátima
Tomar

SPAIN

Óbidos

Sintra
LISBON

Évora

ALGARVE
Lagos
SALEMA

Cape Sagres

LEGEND
2 Number of Overnights
• Other Stops
▲▲▲ Must See
▲▲ Try Hard to See
▲ Worthwhile

and Lisbon. For a youthful university vibe, visit Coimbra. Beach baskers happily unroll their towels in Salema or Nazaré—some never want to leave. Photographers want to go everywhere.

Decide when to go.

Spring and fall offer the best combination of good weather, light crowds, long days, and plenty of tourist and cultural activities.

Summer months are the most crowded and expensive in the coastal areas. Beach towns (such as Nazaré or along the Algarve) are packed with vacationers in July and especially in August—when rates go sky-high and it can be tough to find a room. Those same towns are a delight in shoulder season (mid-May-June and Oct), when the weather is nearly as good and the crowds subside—but they can be dreary and pretty lifeless in the winter.

In the off-season (roughly Nov-March), expect shorter hours, more lunchtime breaks at sights, and fewer activities; confirm your sightseeing plans locally.

For weather specifics, see the climate chart in the appendix.

Connect the dots.

Link your destinations into a logical route. For a Portugal only trip, you'd likely fly into and out of Lisbon (although Porto has growing service from its international airport). For an Iberian trip, you could, say, fly into Barcelona and out of Lisbon. Begin your search for transatlantic flights at Kayak.com.

Decide if you'll travel by car or public transportation, or a combination. A car gives you the freedom to stop whenever you want, but is useless in big cities (pick up the car after visiting Lisbon). Portugal is compact and well-connected by good roads; you'll pay tolls to use the superhighways, but it's worth it for the time saved.

If relying on public transportation, buses are usually your best bet, though some train routes are useful, particularly the Lisbon-Coimbra-Porto line. With more time, everything is doable without a car.

To determine approximate travel times between destinations, study the driving map in the Practicalities chapter or check Google Maps. The durations of bus and train journeys are given in this book (in the "Connections" sections of each chapter); as for schedules, confirm bus departures locally and see Bahn.com for trains. For travel beyond Portugal, check budget intra-European flights at Skyscanner.com.

Write out a day-by-day itinerary.

Figure out how many destinations you can comfortably fit in your time frame. Don't overdo it—few travelers wish they'd hurried more. Allow enough days per stop (see estimates in "Portugal's Top Destinations," earlier). Minimize one-night

Ponte Luis I Bridge at sunset in Porto (opposite); Porto's elegantly tiled São Bento train station; rooms for rent in Salema

The adorable town of Óbidos; appreciating art in Lisbon's Gulbenkian Museum

stands. It can be worth taking an evening drive or bus ride to settle into a town for two consecutive nights—and gain a full uninterrupted day for sightseeing. Include sufficient time for transportation; major destinations are roughly two to three hours apart by car (a little longer by bus or train, especially when transfers are necessary).

Staying in a home base (like Lisbon) and taking day trips can be more time-efficient than changing locations and hotels.

Take sight closures into account. Avoid visiting a town on the one day a week its must-see sights are closed; for example, give Lisbon and Porto a miss on Monday (or plan activities other than museums).

Check if any holidays or festivals fall during your trip— these attract crowds and can close sights (for the latest, visit Portugal's tourist website, www.visitportugal.com). Note major sights where advance reservations are smart or a free Rick Steves audio tour is available.

Give yourself some slack. Every trip, and every traveler, needs downtime for doing laundry, picnic shopping, people-watching, and so on. Pace yourself. Assume you will return.

Trip Costs Per Person

Run a reality check on your dream trip. You'll have major transportation costs in addition to daily expenses.

Flight: A round-trip flight from the US to Lisbon costs about $900-1,500, depending on where you fly from and when.

Public Transportation: For a two-week trip, allow $300 for buses and second-class trains ($400 for first class).

Car Rental: Allow roughly $250 per week, not including tolls, gas, parking, and insurance.

AVERAGE DAILY EXPENSES PER PERSON

$160
Applies to cities, figure on less for towns

Lodging
Based on two people splitting the cost of a $150 double room
$75

Meals
$15 for lunch and $30 for dinner
$45

City Transit
Buses, Metro, and trams
$10

Sights and Entertainment
This daily average works for most people.
$30

Budget Tips

To cut your daily expenses, take advantage of the deals you'll find throughout Portugal and mentioned in this book.

Buses are often more flexible and affordable than trains, and sometimes the only choice on certain routes. It's economical to buy bus and train tickets as you go. Rail passes are a waste of money for a Portugal-only trip.

Some businesses—especially hotels and walking-tour companies—offer discounts to my readers (look for the RS% symbol in the listings in this book).

Reserve your rooms directly with the hotel. Some hotels offer a discount if you pay in cash and/or stay three or more nights (check online or ask).

Rooms can cost less outside of peak-season summer. In resort towns, consider *quartos* ▶▶▶

Rick Steves Portugal

▶▶▶ (a room in a private home) for a low-cost alternative to hotels. And even seniors can sleep cheap in hostels (most have private rooms) for about $30 per person. Or check Airbnb-type sites for deals.

It's no hardship to eat inexpensively in Portugal. You can get tasty, affordable meals at cafés, bars, bakeries, and takeout shops. Cultivate the art of picnicking in atmospheric settings.

When you splurge, choose an experience you'll always remember, such as a food-tasting tour or a fado concert. Minimize souvenir shopping; focus instead on collecting wonderful memories. ■

Trolley ride; ginjinha *tasting at a Lisbon bar; market scene in* Coimbra

BEFORE YOU GO

You'll have a smoother trip if you tackle a few things ahead of time. For more information on these topics, see the Practicalities chapter, and check RickSteves.com for helpful travel tips and talks.

Make sure your travel documents are valid. If your passport is due to expire within six months of your ticketed date of return, you need to renew it. Allow up to six weeks to renew or get a passport (www.travel.state.gov). You may also need to register with the European Travel Information and Authorization System (ETIAS).

Arrange your transportation. Book your international flights. Overall, Kayak.com is the best place to start searching for flights. Figure out your transportation options: If renting a car, reserve it before you go. (If relying on trains and buses, buy tickets in Portugal.) Drivers: Consider bringing an International Driving Permit (sold at AAA offices in the US, www.aaa.com) along with your license. If traveling beyond Portugal, book any cheap European flights you'll need. (You can wing it once you're there, but it may cost more.)

Book rooms well in advance, especially if your trip falls during peak season or any major holidays or festivals.

Reserve ahead for crowded Sintra sights. To save time in line, purchase tickets online for the Pena Palace, Moorish Castle, and National Palace a few days before your visit. It's also smart to reserve a timed-entry ticket for King João's Library—the highlight of the university in Coimbra.

Hire local guides in advance. Reserve ahead by email; popular guides can get booked up.

Consider travel insurance. Compare the cost of insurance to the cost of your potential loss. Check whether your existing insurance (health, homeowners, or renters) covers you and your possessions overseas.

Call your bank. Alert your bank that you'll be using your debit and credit cards in Europe. Ask about transaction fees and get the PIN number for your credit card. You don't need to bring euros for your trip; you can withdraw euros from cash machines in Europe.

Use your smartphone smartly. Sign up for an international service plan to reduce your costs, or rely on Wi-Fi in Europe instead. Download any apps you'll want on the road, such as maps, translators, transit schedules, and Rick Steves Audio Europe (see sidebar).

Pack light. You'll walk with your luggage more than you think. I travel for weeks with a single carry-on bag and a day pack. Use the packing checklist in the appendix as a guide.

Rick's Free Video Clips and Audio Tours

Travel smarter with these free, fun resources:

Rick Steves Classroom Europe, a powerful tool for teachers, is also useful for travelers. This video library contains over 400 short clips excerpted from my public television series. Enjoy these videos as you sort through options for your trip and to better understand what you'll see in Europe. Check it out at Classroom.RickSteves.com (just enter a topic to find everything I've filmed on a subject).

Rick Steves Audio Europe, a free app, makes it easy to download my audio tours and listen to them offline as you travel. For this book (look for the ∩), my "Lisbon City Walk" audio tour covers sights and neighborhoods in Lisbon. The app also offers interviews from my public radio show with experts from Europe and around the globe. Find it in your app store or at RickSteves.com/AudioEurope.

Travel Smart

If you have a positive attitude, equip yourself with good information (this book), and expect to travel smart, you will.

Read—and reread—this book. To have an "A" trip, be an "A" student. Note opening hours of sights, closed days, and any crowd-beating tips. Check the latest at RickSteves.com/update.

Be your own tour guide. As you travel, get up-to-date info on sights, reserve tickets and tours, reconfirm hotels and travel arrangements, and check transit connections. Visit local tourist information offices (TIs). Upon arrival in a new town, lay the groundwork for a smooth departure; confirm the road, bus, or train you'll take when you leave.

Outsmart thieves. Pickpockets abound in crowded places where tourists congregate (like Lisbon's trolley cars). Treat commotions as smokescreens for theft. Keep your cash, credit cards, and passport secure in a money belt tucked under your clothes; carry only a day's spending money in your front pocket or wallet. Don't set valuable items down on counters or café tabletops, where they can be quickly stolen or easily forgotten.

Minimize potential loss. Keep expensive gear to a minimum. Bring photocopies or take photos of important documents (passport and cards) to aid in replacement if they're lost or stolen. Back up photos and files frequently.

Beat the summer heat. If you wilt easily, choose a hotel with air-conditioning, start your day early, take a midday siesta at your hotel, and resume your sightseeing later. Churches offer a cool haven. Take frequent breaks.

Guard your time and energy. Taking a taxi can be a good value if it saves you a long wait for a cheap bus or an exhausting walk across town. To avoid long lines, follow my crowd-beating tips, such as making advance reservations, or sightseeing early or late.

Be flexible. Even if you have a well-planned itinerary, expect changes, strikes, closures, sore feet, bad weather, and so on. Your Plan B could turn out to be even better.

Attempt the language. Many Portuguese—especially in the tourist trade and in cities—speak English, but if you learn some Portuguese, even just a few phrases, you'll get more smiles and make more friends. Practice the survival phrases near the end of this book, and even better, bring a phrase book.

Connect with the culture. Interacting with locals carbonates your experience. Enjoy the friendliness of the Portuguese people. Ask questions; most locals are happy to point you in their idea of the right direction. Set up your own quest for the best seafood, fado bar, viewpoint, or custard tart. When an opportunity pops up, make it a habit to say "yes."

Portugal...here you come!

LISBON

Lisboa

Lisbon is ramshackle, trendy, and charming all at once—an endearing mix of now and then. Vintage trolleys shiver up and down its hills, bird-stained statues mark grand squares, taxis rattle and screech through cobbled lanes, and Art Nouveau cafés are filled equally with well-worn and well-dressed locals—nursing their coffees side-by-side. It's a city of proud ironwork balconies, multicolored tiles, and mosaic sidewalks; of bougainvillea and red-tiled roofs with antique TV antennas; and of foodie haunts and designer boutiques.

Lisbon, Portugal's capital, is the country's banking and manufacturing center. Residents call their city Lisboa (leezh-BOH-ah), which comes from the Phoenician *Alis Ubbo,* meaning "calm port." A port city on the yawning mouth of the Rio Tejo (REE-oo TAY-zhoo—the Tagus River), Lisbon welcomes large ships to its waters and state-of-the-art dry docks. And more recently, it has become a hugely popular stop with cruise ships.

Romans (2nd century BC) and Moors (8th century) were the earliest settlers in Lisbon, but the city's glory days were in the 15th and 16th centuries, when explorers such as Vasco da Gama opened new trade routes around Africa to India, making Lisbon one of Europe's richest cities. Portugal's Age of Discovery fueled rapid economic growth, which sparked the flamboyant art boom called the Manueline period—named for King Manuel I (r. 1495-1521).

On the morning of All Saints' Day in 1755, a tremendous offshore earthquake rocked Lisbon, followed by a devastating tsunami and days of fires. Chief Minister Marquês de Pombal rebuilt downtown Lisbon on a grid plan, with broad boulevards and generous squares. It's this "Pombaline"-era neighborhood where you'll spend

LISBON

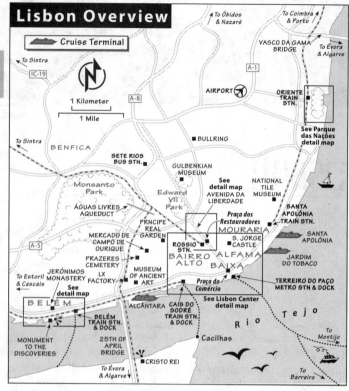

much of your time, though remnants of Lisbon's pre-earthquake charm survive in Belém, the Alfama, and the Bairro Alto district. The bulk of your sightseeing will likely be in these neighborhoods.

As the Paris of the Portuguese-speaking world, Lisbon (pop. 548,000 in the core) is the Old World capital of its former empire, which once had some 100 million people and stretched from Europe to Brazil, and Africa to China. Portugal remains on largely good terms with its former colonies—and immigrants from places such as Mozambique and Angola add diversity and flavor to the city; it's likely that you'll hear African music as much as Portuguese fado.

With its characteristic hills, trolleys, famous suspension bridge, and rolling fog, Lisbon has a San Francisco feel. Enjoy all that this world-class city has to offer: elegant outdoor cafés, exciting art, fun-to-browse shops, stunning vistas, delicious food, entertaining museums, and a salty sailors' quarter with a hill-capping castle.

PLANNING YOUR TIME

Lisbon merits at least three days, including a day for a side-trip to Sintra. If you have more time, there's plenty to do.

Day 1

Get oriented to Lisbon's three downtown neighborhoods (following my three self-guided walks): Alfama, Baixa, and Bairro Alto/Chiado. Start where the city did, at its castle (hop a taxi or Uber to get there at 9:00, before the crowds hit). After surveying the city from the highest viewpoint in town, walk downhill into the characteristic Alfama neighborhood and end at the Fado Museum. From there, zip over to the big main square (Praça do Comércio) to explore the Baixa, then ride up the Elevador da Glória funicular (or taxi) to begin the Bairro Alto and Chiado walk. Art lovers can then hop the Metro or a taxi to the Gulbenkian Museum (open until 18:00, closed Tue), while shoppers can browse the boutiques of the Chiado neighborhood and Príncipe Real. Consider dinner at a fado show in the Bairro Alto or the Alfama. For more evening options, see "Entertainment in Lisbon," later.

Day 2

Trolley to Belém and tour the monastery, tower, and National Coach Museum. Have lunch in Belém, then tour the Museum of Ancient Art on your way back to Lisbon.

Day 3

Side-trip to Sintra to tour the Pena Palace and explore the ruined Moorish castle.

More Time

With extra days, slow down and relax—spreading the "Day 1" activities over two days. Or use the time to explore and window-shop characteristic neighborhoods and nurse drinks bought from kiosks on relaxing squares. You could also head to the Parque das Nações or take a food tour.

Monday Options

Many top sights are closed on Monday, particularly in Belém. That'd be a good day to visit the Gulbenkian Museum, take my self-guided neighborhood walks, day-trip to Sintra, go on a guided walking tour (see "Tours in Lisbon," later), or head to Parque das Nações for a dose of modern Lisbon.

Orientation to Lisbon

LISBON: A VERBAL MAP

Greater Lisbon has close to three million people and intimidating sprawl. Most visitors spend virtually all their time in the old city

LISBON

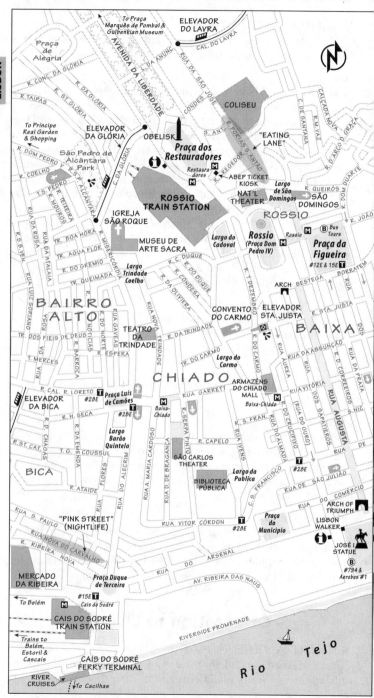

LISBON

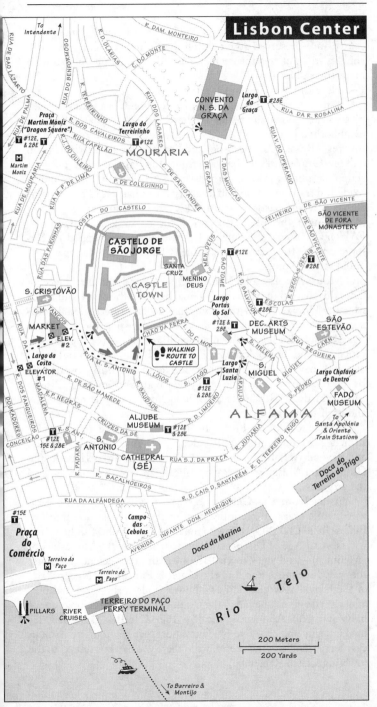

Lisbon Center

To Intendente

R. DAM. MONTEIRO

RUA DE SÃO LÁZARO

RUA DE PALMA

RUA DO OLARIAS

R. D. OLARIAS

C. DO MONTE

RUA DOS LAGARES

CONVENTO N. S. DA GRAÇA

Largo da Graça

#28E

RUA DA R. ROSALINA

R. TERREIRINHO

R. DOS CAVALEIROS

Praça Martim Moniz ("Dragon Square")

#12E & 28E

Martim Moniz

Largo do Terreirinho

#12E

R. DA J. DO OULEIRO

R. D. CAPELÃO

MOURARIA

C. DE GRAÇA

T. DAS MÓNICAS

RUAY. DO OPERARIO

DE SÃO VICENTE

C. DE SÃOVICENTE

SÃO VICENTE DE FORA MONASTERY

RUA M. P. DE LIMA

P. DE COLEGINHO

C. DE SANTO ANDRÉ

COSTA DO CASTELO

CASTELO DE SÃO JORGE

SANTA CRUZ

MEN DEUS

R. SÃO TOMÉ

#12E

DE SÃOVICENTE

S. CRISTÓVÃO

C.M. TANCOS

CASTLE TOWN

MENINO DEUS

Largo Portas do Sol

R. D. SALVADOR

ESCOLAS

#28E

RUA DAS FARINHAS

MARKET

ELEV. #2

Largo da Costa

ELEVATOR #1

RUA M. S. ANTONIO

CHÃO DA FEIRA

R. DO C. MOR

#12E & 28E

DEC. ARTS MUSEUM

ESCOLAS TEXAS

#28E

SÃO ESTEVÃO

WALKING ROUTE TO CASTLE

L. LOIOS

S. TIAGO

S. HELENA

S. MIGUEL

RUA REGUEIRA

RUA DOS FANGUEIROS

R. DE SÃO MAMEDE

R.P. NEGRAS

CRUZES DA SÉ

Largo Santa Luzia

#12E & 28E

S. MIGUEL

S. PEDRO

Largo Chafariz de Dentro

CONCEIÇÃO

R.S. ANT.

#12E 15E & 28E

R. SAUDADE

R. D. LIMOEIRO

R. ARAUJO

ALFAMA

FADO MUSEUM

S. ANTONIO

ALJUBE MUSEUM

#12E & 28E

R. PADARIA

CATHEDRAL (SÉ)

RUA S.J. DA PRAÇA

R. JUDIARIA

R. D. TERREIRO TRIGO

To Santa Apolónia & Oriente Train Stations

R. BACALHOEIROS

RUA S. J. DA PRAÇA

R. D. CAIS D. SANTARÉM

R. D. TERREIRO TRIGO

Doca do Terreiro do Trigo

#15E

Praça do Comércio

RUA DA ALFÂNDEGA

Campo das Cebolas

INFANTE DOM HENRIQUE

AVENIDA

Doca da Marina

Rio Tejo

Terreiro do Paço

Terreiro do Paço

PILLARS

RIVER CRUISES

TERREIRO DO PAÇO FERRY TERMINAL

200 Meters

200 Yards

To Barreiro & Montijo

center, a delightful series of parks, boulevards, and squares in a crusty, well-preserved architectural shell. But even on a brief visit, you'll also want to venture to Belém, the riverfront suburb with many top sights.

Here's an overview of the city's layout:

Baixa (Lower Town): Downtown Lisbon fills a valley flanked by two hills along the banks of the Rio Tejo. In that valley, the neighborhood called Baixa (BYE-shah) stretches from the main squares—Rossio (roh-SEE-oo) and Praça da Figueira (PRAH-sah dah fee-GAY-rah)—to the waterfront. The Baixa is a flat, pleasant shopping area of grid-patterned streets. As Lisbon's main cross-roads and transportation hub, touristy Baixa has lots of hotels, venerable cafés and pastry shops, and kitschy souvenir stands.

Alfama: The hill to the east of the Baixa is the Alfama (al-FAH-mah), a colorful tangle of medieval streets, topped by São Jorge Castle. The lower slopes of the Alfama are a spilled spaghetti of old sailors' homes.

Mouraria: The old Muslim Quarter and the birthplace of fado, this district (next to the Alfama, between the castle and Praça Martim Moniz) is now the center of Lisbon's international community and emerging as a fun and trendy place to explore.

Bairro Alto (High Town): The hill to the west of the Baixa is capped by the Bairro Alto (BYE-roh AHL-too), with a tight grid of steep, narrow, and characteristic lanes. Downhill toward the Baixa, the Bairro Alto fades into the trendy and inviting **Chiado** (shee-AH-doo), with linger-a-while squares, upmarket restaurants, and high-fashion stores.

Modern Lisbon: From the historic core, the modern city stretches north (sloping uphill) along wide Avenida da Liberdade and beyond (way beyond), where you find Edward VII Park, the Gulbenkian Museum, breezy botanical gardens, the bullring, and the airport.

Away from the Center: Along the riverfront are several worthwhile areas. Three miles west of the center is the suburb of **Belém** (beh-LAYNG), home to much of Lisbon's best sightseeing, with several Age of Discovery sights (particularly the Monastery of Jerónimos)—and you can visit the Museum of Ancient Art along the way. Five miles north of the center is **Parque das Nações,** site of the Expo '98 world's fair and now a modern shopping complex and riverfront promenade (the National Tile Museum is about halfway there). And across the Rio Tejo, **Cacilhas** (kah-SEE-la-hsh) is a tiny and characteristic little port that few tourists visit (an easy ferry ride from the center; from there you can bus or taxi to the towering Cristo Rei statue).

TOURIST INFORMATION

Lisbon has several tourist offices—all branded "ask me L¿sboa"— and additional information kiosks sprout around town during the busy summer months (www.visitlisboa.com). The main city TIs have the same hours (daily 9:00-20:00) and are located on **Praça dos Restauradores** at Palácio Foz (+351 213 463 314; national TI in same office; there's also a kiosk across the street) and on Praça do Comércio (two locations; +351 210 312 810). Another TI is at the airport (daily 7:00-24:00, +351 218 450 660).

Smaller TI kiosks are at the bottom of **Rossio**; across the street from the monastery in **Belém**; at **Parque das Nações**, at the riverfront side of the **Vasco da Gama mall;** and inside **Santa Apolónia train station** (end of track 3). At any TI, you can buy a LisboaCard (see next) and pick up the free city map and information-packed *Follow Me Lisboa* booklet (monthly, cultural and museum listings—also available at www.visitlisboa.com, "Publications" tab).

LisboaCard: This card covers all public transportation (including trains to Sintra and Cascais) and free entry to many museums (including the Museum of Ancient Art, National Tile Museum, National Coach Museum, Monastery of Jerónimos, and Belém Tower). It also provides discounts on river cruises, my two recommended city tours, and many museums (including sights at Sintra). You can buy the card at Lisbon's TIs (including the airport TI), but not at participating sights. If you plan to museum-hop, the card is a good value, particularly for a day in Belém, though it does not allow you to skip lines at busy monuments (like those in Belém). The card is unnecessary if you're a student or senior, for whom most sights are free or half-price. Carry the LisboaCard booklet with you—some discounts require coupons contained inside (€20/24 hours, €34/48 hours, €42/72 hours, kids 5-11 nearly half-price, includes excellent explanatory guidebook, www.visitlisboa.com). Remember that many sights are closed on Monday—it's best to buy the card when you can use it for consecutive days.

ARRIVAL IN LISBON

For complete information on arriving at or departing from Lisbon by plane, train, bus, and cruise ship, see "Lisbon Connections" at the end of this chapter.

By Plane: International and domestic flights arrive at Lisbon's Portela Airport. On arrival, check in at the handy TI—it's a smart place to buy your LisboaCard. Options for getting into town include taxis, Uber, Aerobus, or Metro (all described later).

By Train: Lisbon has four primary train stations: Santa Apolónia (Spain and most points north), Oriente (Algarve, Évora, Sintra, and fast trains to the north), Rossio (Sintra, Óbidos, and Naz-

LISBON

aré), and Cais do Sodré (coastal Belém, Estoril, and Cascais). For schedules, see www.cp.pt.

By Car: It makes absolutely no sense to drive in Lisbon. Dump your rental car at the airport and connect to your hotel by taxi or Uber (car return clearly marked; the airport is also a good place to pick up a car on your way out of town).

If you must drive and are entering Lisbon from the north, a series of boulevards takes you into the center. Navigate by following signs to *Centro, Avenida da República, Marquês de Pombal, Avenida da Liberdade, Praça dos Restauradores, Rossio,* and *Praça do Comércio.* If coming from the east over the Vasco da Gama Bridge and heading for the airport, just follow the signs. There are many safe underground pay **parking** lots in Lisbon (follow blue *P* signs; the most central is at Praça dos Restauradores), but they discourage longer stays by getting more expensive by the hour. Expect to pay over €20/day.

HELPFUL HINTS

Free Days and Monday Closures: The Gulbenkian Museum is free every Sunday after 14:00 (and one of the few museums open on Monday). Many major sights are closed on Monday, including Lisbon's Museum of Ancient Art, National Tile Museum, and Fado Museum, as well as Belém's Monastery of Jerónimos, Coach Museum, and Belém Tower.

Theft Alert: Lisbon has piles of people doing illegal business on the street. Enjoy the sightseeing, but wear your money belt and keep your pack zipped up. Pickpockets target tourists at popular sights and on trolleys, elevators, and funiculars. Some thieves pose as tourists by wearing cameras and toting maps. Be on guard whenever you're in a crush of people or jostled as you enter or leave a tram or bus. Beggars are often pickpockets. Teams of pickpockets create confusion and congestion.

Violence is very rare, and you'll see lots of police stationed throughout town. While the city is generally safe, if you're looking for trouble—especially after dark—you may find it.

Market Days: Tuesdays and Saturdays are flea- and food-market days in the Alfama's Campo de Santa Clara. On Sundays, the LX Factory zone, in the shadow of the 25th of April Bridge, hosts a lively farmers market (9:30-16:00; for location, see the "Lisbon Overview" map, earlier).

Pedestrian Warnings: Lisbon's unique black-and-white patterned tile pavement, while picturesque, can be very slippery. And trams can be quiet and sneak up on you if you're not paying attention. Even some of the tuk-tuks are "eco" (electric) and can zip up behind you silently.

Laundry: Centrally located **5àSec Lavandaria** can usually provide same-day service if you drop off early (Mon-Fri 8:00-20:00, Sat from 10:00, closed Sun, next to the bottom level of the Armazéns do Chiado mall and lower entry to the Baixa-Chiado Metro stop at Rua do Crucifixo 99, +351 213 479 599). **WashStation Baixa-Castelo** is a small self-service launderette just up from Praça da Figueira (daily 8:00-22:00, Rua da Madalena 231, mobile +351 919 772 701). For locations, see the "Lisbon Center Hotels" map on page 134.

Travel Agency: GeoStar is helpful for train tickets (Portugal only) and flights (Mon-Fri 9:00-18:30, closed Sat-Sun, Praça Duque da Terceira 1, near the Cais do Sodré station, +351 213 405 380).

Ticket Kiosk: The green **ABEP kiosk** at the bottom end of Praça dos Restauradores is a handy spot to buy a city transit pass, LisboaCard, and tickets to bullfights, soccer games, concerts, and other events (daily 9:00-20:00).

GETTING AROUND LISBON
By Public Transit

Lisbon is easy—even fun—to navigate by Metro, funicular, trolley, and bus. And one transit card covers them all.

Tickets

If you have a **LisboaCard** (see "Tourist Information," earlier), you can use it to ride Lisbon's public transit. Otherwise, buy a Viva Viagem card, which works on the Metro, funiculars, trolleys, buses, Santa Justa elevator, ferry to Cacilhas, and some short-distance trains (on some transit you can buy tickets from the driver, but that's more expensive). For transit information, see www.carris.pt.

Viva Viagem Card: Transit tickets are issued on the scannable, reloadable Viva Viagem card (€0.50 for the card itself, not shareable—each rider needs one). You can buy or reload the card at ticket windows or machines in Metro stations (touch "without a reusable card" for first-time users, or "with a reusable card" to top up; bright yellow machines accept only credit cards). Keep your Viva Viagem card handy—you'll need to place it on the magnetic pad when entering and leaving the system.

You can use the Viva Viagem in three ways:

A **single-ride ticket** costs €1.50 (good for one hour of travel within Zone 1). But if you're taking even a few rides, "zapping" is a much better deal (see later).

A **24-hour pass** costs €6.40 (this version does not cover trains). If taking five or more rides in a day, this is the best deal. If you're side-tripping to Sintra or Cascais, consider the €10.60 version, which includes trains to those towns (but not the bus at Sintra). Skip the €9.55 version of the 24-hour pass, which adds the ferry to Cacilhas (it's cheaper to buy that separately).

"Zapping" lets you preload the card with anywhere from €3 to €40 and lowers the per-ride cost to €1.35 for all forms of transit. Figure out how much you'll need and load it up (estimate conservatively—you can always top up later, but leftover credit is nonrefundable). Unlike the 24-hour pass, zapping can be used for trains to Sintra and Cascais.

Without Viva Viagem: Although it's possible to **pay the driver** as you board buses (€2), trolleys (€3—more than double the Viva Viagem price), funiculars (€3.80 for two trips), and the Santa Justa elevator (€5.30), only suckers do that. It's much cheaper if you get comfortable zapping with Viva Viagem.

Metro

Lisbon's simple, fast, and color-coded subway system is a delight to use (runs daily 6:30-1:00 in the morning). Though it's not nec-

essary for getting around the historic downtown, the Metro is handy for trips to or from Rossio (M: Rossio or Restauradores), Praça do Comércio (M: Terreiro do Paço), the Gulbenkian Museum (M: São Sebastião), the Chiado neighborhood (M: Baixa-Chiado), Parque das Nações and the Oriente train station (both at M: Oriente), Sete Rios bus and train stations (M: Jardim Zoológico), and the airport (M: Aeroporto). Metro stops are marked above ground with a red "M." *Saída* means "exit." You can find a Metro map at any Metro stop, on most city maps, and at www.metrolisboa.pt.

Sightseeing by Metro: To make your sightseeing commutes quicker and easier, link together sights on the same Metro line. For example, Praça do Comércio, Rossio, and the Gulbenkian Museum can be laced together by Metro faster than via taxi. You can even sightsee as you travel: All Metro stations have wonderful, museum-worthy tile panels. The blue line between Parque and Colégio Militar/Luz has some of the best art; with a 24-hour transit pass, you can hop on and off and explore as many stations as you like.

Buses and Trolleys

Buses and trolleys usually share the same stops and routes. Signs for bus stops list the bus number, while signs for trolley stops in-

clude an E (for *eléctrico*) before or after the route number. Though Lisbon's buses are fine, for fun and practical public transportation, ride the trolleys (and funiculars—see later).

Like San Francisco, Lisbon sees its classic trolleys as part of its heritage, and has kept a few in use: Trolleys #12E (circling the Alfama), #24E (to Campolide), and #28E (a scenic ride across the old town) use vintage cars; #15E (to Belém) uses a modern, air-conditioned version. Make sure you have a ticket or pass and that you validate your Viva Viagem card as you enter...or risk a big fine on the spot. Trolleys rattle by every 10 minutes or so (every 15-20 minutes after 19:00) and run until about 23:00. Most pickpocketing in Lisbon takes place on trolleys, so enjoy the ride, but keep an eye on your belongings.

While lines #28E and #12E seem made-to-order for tourist use, they are often unbearably crowded. If you can deal with the often-overwhelming crowds (see the tips, next), these trolleys can work as hop-on, hop-off do-it-yourself tours. For a stop-by-stop rundown, see "Touring Lisbon by Trolley" in the next section.

Crowd-Beating Tips: Lisbon's trolleys are an absolute joy...*if* you're sitting down and looking out the window with the wind in your face. But if you have to stand, you won't be able to see out the (low) windows, and you'll spend the jostling ride trying to steady yourself. At peak times, hordes of tourists wait at trolley stops (particularly at starting points) and pickpockets abound. To enjoy a trolley with fewer crowd frustrations, consider these strategies:

1. Rather than being determined to take a particular trolley at a particular time, keep an eye on trolleys as they roll by. If an empty trolley pulls up, hop on and take advantage of the open space.

2. Consider waking early and making a trolley ride your first experience of the day. Trolleys "open" before any museums, so if you arrive in the early morning you can beat the tourist crush, get a seat, and see the city wake up. Late departures (after dinner) also have fewer crowds.

3. Ride line #24E, which runs a less-touristy route and can be less crowded.

4. Take a private trolley tour (see "Tours in Lisbon," later).

5. If you'll be going to Porto, wait to enjoy a vintage trolley

LISBON

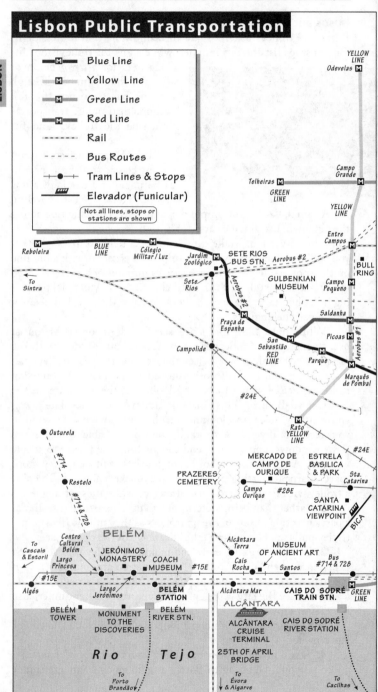

Lisbon Public Transportation

Legend:
- M Blue Line
- M Yellow Line
- M Green Line
- M Red Line
- Rail
- Bus Routes
- Tram Lines & Stops
- Elevador (Funicular)

Not all lines, stops or stations are shown

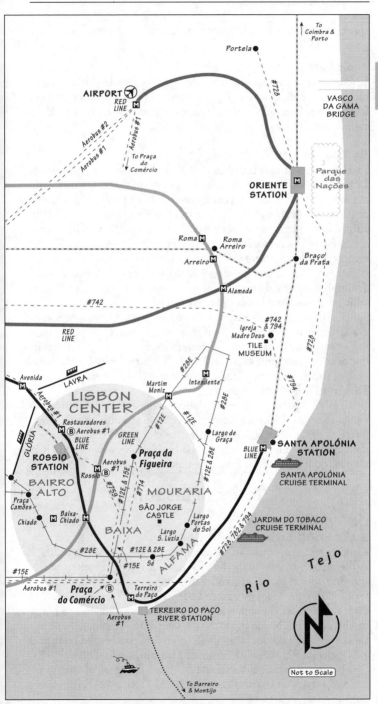

there: Porto's trolleys are just as memorable as Lisbon's and have no crowds.

Funiculars

Lisbon's funiculars include the Elevador da Glória (linking Avenida da Liberdade to the Bairro Alto) and the Elevador da Bica (rising from Rua de São Paulo, near the river, to the Bairro Alto). Funiculars depart about every 10 minutes.

By Taxi or Uber

Lisbon is a great **taxi** town. Especially if you're with a companion, Lisbon's cabs are a cheap time-saver; groups of three or four should taxi everywhere. Rides start at €4, and you can go anywhere in the center for around €6. Window decals clearly spell out all charges in English. Be sure your driver turns on the meter; it should start at about €4 and be set to *Tarifa 1* (Mon-Fri 6:00-21:00, including the airport) or *Tarifa 2* (same drop rate, a little more per kilometer; for nights, weekends, and holidays). If the meter reads *Tarifa 3, 4,* or *5,* simply ask the cabbie to change it, unless you're going to Belém, which is considered outside the city limits.

Cabs are generally easy to hail on the street (green light means available, lit number on the roof indicates it's taken). If you're having a hard time flagging one down, it's likely because you're standing near but not quite at a taxi stand. Ask a passerby for the location of the nearest taxi stand: *praça de taxi* (PRAH-sah duh taxi). They're all over the town center.

Lisbon is also an excellent **Uber** town. The ride-sharing app works here just like back home; it's at least as affordable as a taxi (often cheaper, except during "surge" pricing); and the drivers and their cars are generally of great quality. If you've never tried Uber abroad, do it here. Sit in front and talk!

Tours in Lisbon

ON WHEELS
▲▲Touring Lisbon by Trolley

Lisbon's trolleys—many of them vintage models from the 1920s—shake and shiver through the old parts of town, somehow safely weaving within inches of parked cars, climbing steep hills, and offering sightseers breezy views (rubberneck out the window and you die). You can use the following trolley lines as an inexpensive way to tour the city. As you board, swipe your Viva Viagem card or pay the driver, and take a seat (zapping tickets are good for an hour, and a 24-hour pass comes with unlimited hopping on and off).

Be aware that lines #28E and #12E are jam-packed with tourists and often come with ridiculous lines. Trolley #24E runs away

Lisbon's Best Viewpoints

The first three viewpoints are included in the self-guided walks described in this chapter:

- Miradouro de São Pedro de Alcântara (view terrace in Bairro Alto, at top of Elevador da Glória funicular; see the "Bairro Alto and Chiado Stroll," later)
- São Jorge Castle (on top of the Alfama; see photo above and the "Alfama Stroll and the Castle," later)
- Miradouro das Portas do Sol (south slope of Alfama; see the "Alfama Stroll and the Castle," later)
- Elevador de Santa Justa (in the Baixa, page 78)
- Cristo Rei (statue on hillside across the Rio Tejo, page 116)
- Edward VII Park (at north end of Avenida da Liberdade)
- Miradouro de Santa Catarina (near the top of the Elevador da Bica funicular)
- Miradouro da Graça and Miradouro da Senhora do Monte (same neighborhood overlooking the São Jorge Castle)

from the central tourist zone and can be less crowded. For tips on riding the trolley, including avoiding crowds, see "Getting Around Lisbon," earlier.

Trolley #28E

Trolley #28E is a San Francisco-style Lisbon joyride (runs about 5:45-22:30; after 21:15, service is limited to stops between Estrela and Graça). The following are notable stops from west to east:

Campo Ourique: The **Prazeres Cemetery,** at the western terminus of route #28E, is a vast park-like necropolis with good bridge views, dense with the mausoleums of leading Lisbon families and historic figures dating back to the 19th century (daily 9:00-17:00).

Igreja Sto. Condestável: The first stop after the cemetery is next to an angular modern church. Hiding just behind the church is the **Mercado de Campo de Ourique,** a 19th-century iron-and-glass market that's now a trendy food circus (see page 147).

Estrela: Two stops later, the trolley pulls up in front of another large church (on the right). The 18th-century, late Baroque **Estrela Basilica** has stairs winding up to the roof for a view both out and down into the church (€4, daily 10:00-18:00). Across the street is the gate into **Estrela Park,** a cozy neighborhood scene with exotic plants, a pond-side café, and a playground.

Assembleia da República: At the next stop, you'll see a garden poking up on the left behind a high wall (which hides the prime minister's residence). Next up is the huge, stately Assembly of the Republic building—home to Portugal's parliament. Soon after, the trolley enters a relatively narrow street at the edge of the Bairro Alto.

Santa Catarina: A couple of stops into the Bairro Alto, this area is enjoyable for a stroll through characteristic streets downhill to the **Miradouro de Santa Catarina,** a view terrace with inviting cafés and bars.

Calhariz-Bica: Keep an eye on the streets to your right. You'll spot the top of the **Elevador da Bica funicular,** which drops steeply through a rough-and-tumble neighborhood to the riverfront.

City-Center Stops: From here, the downtown stops come fast and furious—**Chiado** (at Chiado's main square, Lisbon's café meeting-place); **Baixa** (on Rua da Conceição between Augusta and Prata); **Sé** (the cathedral); **Miradouro das Portas do Sol** (the Alfama viewpoint); **Campo de Santa Clara** (flea market on Tue and Sat); and the pleasant and untouristy **Graça** district (with two excellent viewpoints, one at Graça Church and another nearby at Nossa Senhora do Monte). The route finishes at **Praça Martim Moniz.**

Trolley #12E

For a colorful, 20-minute loop around the castle and the Alfama, catch trolley #12E on **Praça da Figueira** (departs every few minutes from the stop at corner of square closest to castle; runs about 8:00-20:45, shorter hours on Sat-Sun). The driver can tell you when to get out for the **Miradouro das Portas do Sol viewpoint** near the castle (about three-quarters of the way up the hill), or you can stay on the trolley and be dropped back where you started. Here's what you'll see on this loop ride:

Leaving Praça da Figueira, you enter **Praça Martim Moniz**—named for a knight who died heroically while using his body as a doorjamb to leave the castle gate open, allowing his Christian Portuguese comrades to get in and capture Lisbon from the Moors in 1147. These days, this gathering point is nicknamed "Dragon

Square" for the modern sculpture erected in the middle by the local Chinese community to celebrate the Year of the Dragon.

At the next stop, on the right, is the picturesque **Centro Comercial da Mouraria,** a marketplace filled with products and aromas from around the world. The big, maroon-colored building capping the hill on the left was a Jesuit monastery until 1769, when the dictatorial Marquês de Pombal booted the pesky order out of Portugal and turned the building into the Hospital São Jose. Today, this is an immigrant neighborhood with lots of cheap import shops.

Turning right onto Rua de Cavaleiros, you climb through the atmospheric **Mouraria neighborhood** on a street so narrow that a single trolley track is all that fits. Notice how the colorful mix of neighbors who fill the trolley all seem to know each other. If the trolley's path is blocked and can't pass, lots of horn-honking and shouts from passengers ensue until your journey resumes. Look up the skinny side streets. Marvel at the creative parking and classic laundry scenes. This was the area given to the Moors after they were driven out of the castle and Alfama. Natives know it as the home of the legendary fado singer Maria Severa as well as modern-day singer Mariza. The majority of residents these days are immigrants from Asia, making this Lisbon's most visible melting pot.

At the crest of the hill—at the square called **Largo Rodrigues de Freitas**—you can get out to explore, eat at a cheap restaurant (see "Eating in Lisbon," later), or follow Rua de Santa Marinha to the Campo de Santa Clara flea market (Tue and Sat).

When you see the river, you're at **Largo das Portas do Sol** (Gates of the Sun), where you'll also see the remains of one of the seven old Moorish gates of Lisbon. The driver usually announces *"castelo"* (cahzh-TAY-loo) at this point. Hop out here if you want to visit the Museum and School of Portuguese Decorative Arts (see page 58), enjoy the most scenic cup of coffee in town, explore the **Alfama,** or tour the **castle.**

The trolley continues downhill. First you'll pass (on the right) the stout building called **Aljube**—a prison built on a site dating from Roman times that, more recently, housed political opponents of Portugal's fascist dictator Salazar (now housing a museum about that regime; see page 83). Just downhill is the fortress-like **Lisbon Cathedral** (on the left—see page 82). Finally you roll into the Baixa (grid-planned Pombaline city—get off at **Praça do Comércio** to take my self-guided Baixa walk). After a few blocks, you're back where you started—Praça da Figueira.

Trolley #24E
Although it doesn't go past many of my recommended sights, a 20-minute ride on line #24E can show you a nice slice of workaday Lisbon (runs about 7:00-20:00, shorter hours on Sat-Sun). Catch

the trolley at **Praça Luís de Camões** (just uphill from Chiado); ride past **Príncipe Real** and its beautiful park, prime shopping, and good restaurants; the enormous cistern at the end of the aqueduct; and the **Amoreiras** mall, ending in **Campolide**. Hop off and hop on again right away, or wander over to **Edward VII park** to stroll down the tree-lined Avenida da Liberdade to return to the city center.

Private Trolley Tours
Yellow Bus—the dominant local tour operator (see next)—operates two 1.5-hour hop-on, hop-off trolley tours that use the same tracks and stops as the public trolleys described above. Though pricier and less frequent than public trolleys, Yellow Bus trolley tours often have fewer crowds, come with recorded commentary, and allow you to hop on and off as often as you like for 24 hours. Both tours start at Praça do Comércio and run every 30 minutes (fewer off-season). There are two lines: Hills Tramcar Tour (€20, runs 9:30-19:00, 13 stops, red trolleys) and Belém Tramcar Tour (€15, runs 10:00-18:30, 9 stops, green trolleys).

Hop-On, Hop-Off Bus Tours
Various companies operate hop-on, hop-off bus tours around Lisbon. While uninspiring and not cheap—and Lisbon's sights are compact enough to easily see on your own—these tours can be handy and run daily year-round.

Yellow Bus (www.yellowbustours.com) and **Gray Line** (www.cityrama.pt) run multiple loops through town, targeting different sights; figure around €15 for 24 hours on one loop, or about €25 for 48-hour access to all loops. Each company also offers a dizzying array of combo- tickets (trolley tours, tuk-tuks, boat trips, Segway tours, museum discounts, and so on). Buses depart from Praça da Figueira (buy tickets from driver). When comparing your options, note that Yellow Bus tickets include some Lisbon city transit as well (public trolleys, buses, Elevador de Santa Justa, and funiculars, but not the Metro).

Tuk-Tuks
Goofy little tuk-tuks—Indian-style, three-wheel motorcycles—have invaded Lisbon. You'll see them parked in front of tourist landmarks all over town. They have no meter—negotiate with the driver for a tour or hire one for a point-to-point ride. Tuk-tuks are most practical as a way to tailor your own private tour (€45/hour, €30 if demand is slow and the driver owns his own rig). The key is finding a likeable driver with good language skills and a little charm. A ride comes with light guiding, can get you into little back

Ways to Get from the Baixa Up to the Bairro Alto and Chiado

- Ride the Elevador da Glória funicular (a few blocks north of Rossio on Avenida da Liberdade, opposite the Hard Rock Café), or hike alongside the tracks if the funicular isn't running.
- Walk up lots of stairs from Rossio (due west of the central column).
- Taxi or Uber to the Miradouro de São Pedro de Alcântara.
- Take the escalators at the Baixa-Chiado Metro stop. From outside the station on Rua do Crucifixo, you'll first ride down, then walk past the turnstiles for the Metro entrance, then ride back up, up, up.
- Catch trolley #28E from Rua da Conceição.
- Hike up Rua do Carmo from Rossio to Rua Garrett.
- Take the elevators inside the Armazéns mall (go through the low-profile doors at Rua do Crucifixo 89 or 113); ride to floor 5 and pop out at the bottom of Rua Garrett.
- Take the Elevador de Santa Justa, which goes right by the Convento do Carmo and Chiado (long lines at busy times—but if it's jammed, other options are nearby).

lanes, lets you hop on and off for quick visits and photo stops, and leaves you where you like.

BY BOAT

To get out on the Rio Tejo, take a sightseeing cruise or ride a public ferry. Either way, the main destination across the river is the port of Cacilhas.

Tourist Cruise: Yellow Boat—part of the big Yellow Bus tour company—offers a 1.5-hour loop that links Terreiro do Paço (near Praça do Comércio) to Belém. You can hop on and off, but there are just eight boats per day (€20/24 hours, discounts and combo-tickets with their bus tours and other offerings, May-Oct only, details at www.yellowbustours.com).

Public Ferry Ride to Cacilhas: For a quick, cheap trip across the river with great city and bridge views in the company of Lisbon commuters rather than tourists, hop the ferry to Cacilhas from the Cais do Sodré terminal. See page 114 for details.

ON FOOT

Two walking-tour companies—Lisbon Walker and Inside Lisbon—offer excellent, affordable tours led by young, top-notch guides with a passion for sharing insights about their hometown. Both have an easygoing style and small groups (generally 2-12 people); with either, you'll likely feel you've made a friend in your

Lisbon at a Glance

In Lisbon

▲▲▲**Alfama Stroll and the Castle** Tangled medieval streets topped by São Jorge Castle. See page 52.

▲▲▲**Baixa Stroll** The lower town—Lisbon's historic downtown—gridded with streets and dotted with major squares. See page 60.

▲▲▲**Bairro Alto and Chiado Stroll** The high town's views, churches, and Chiado fashion district. See page 72.

▲▲**Gulbenkian Museum** Lisbon's best museum, featuring an art collection spanning 5,000 years, from ancient Egypt to Impressionism to Art Nouveau. **Hours:** Wed-Mon 10:00-18:00, closed Tue. See page 86.

▲▲**Museum of Ancient Art** Portuguese paintings from the 15th- and 16th-century glory days. **Hours:** Tue-Sun 10:00-18:00, closed Mon. See page 91.

▲▲**Parque das Nações** Inviting waterfront park with a long promenade, modern mall, aquarium, and the Expo '98 fairgrounds. See page 112.

▲**Fado Museum** The story of Portuguese folk music. **Hours:** Tue-Sun 11:00-17:00, closed Mon. See page 60.

▲**São Roque Church and Museum** Fine 16th-century Jesuit church with false dome ceiling, chapel made of precious stones, and a less-interesting museum. **Hours:** Mon 14:00-18:00, Tue-Sun 9:00-19:00—until 18:00 in winter, Thu until 20:00. See page 74.

▲**Lisbon Cathedral** From the outside, an impressive Romanesque fortress of God; inside, not much. **Hours:** Tue-Sat 9:00-19:00, Sun-Mon until 17:00. See page 82.

▲**Aljube Museum of Resistance and Freedom** Exhibits documenting fascist António Salazar's rise to power, housed in a for-

guide. These tours can be time and money very well spent (both give my readers a discount).

Lisbon Walker

Standard tours include "Lisbon Revelation" (best 3-hour overview, with good coverage of Baixa and main squares, quick look at Bairro Alto, and trolley ride across town to Portas do Sol viewpoint); "Old Town" (2.5-hour walk through Alfama that examines the origins of

mer prison building. **Hours:** Tue-Sun 10:00-18:00, closed Mon. See page 83.

▲**Mouraria District** Historic Moorish quarter turned buzzing international zone with inviting eateries. See page 85.

▲**National Tile Museum** Tons of artistic tiles, including a panorama of preearthquake Lisbon. **Hours:** Tue-Sun 10:00-18:00, closed Mon. See page 113.

In Belém

▲▲▲**Monastery of Jerónimos** King Manuel's giant 16th-century, white limestone church and monastery, with remarkable cloister and the explorer Vasco da Gama's tomb. **Hours:** Tue-Sun 10:00-18:30, Oct-April until 17:30, closed Mon. See page 99.

▲▲**National Coach Museum** Dozens of carriages, from simple to opulent, displaying the evolution of coaches from 1600 on. **Hours:** Tue-Sun 10:00-17:00, closed Mon. See page 96.

▲**Casa Pastéis de Belém** Sprawling café and bakery where you can enjoy Lisbon's famous custard tarts where they were first created. **Hours:** Daily 8:00-23:00. See page 98.

▲**Maritime Museum** Salty selection of exhibits on the ships and navigational tools of the Age of Discovery. **Hours:** Daily 10:00-18:00, Oct-April until 17:00. See page 105.

▲**Monument to the Discoveries** Giant riverside monument honoring the explorers who brought Portugal great power and riches centuries ago. **Hours:** Daily 10:00-19:00; Oct-April Tue-Sun until 18:00, closed Mon. See page 106.

▲**Belém Tower** Consummate Manueline building with a worthwhile view up 120 steps. **Hours:** Tue-Sun 10:00-18:30, Oct-April until 17:30, closed Mon. See page 109.

Lisbon); and "Downtown" (2-3 hours, covers 1755 earthquake and rebirth of Lisbon). Each tour includes a shot of *ginjinha* or a tasty *pastel de nata*—two edible icons of Lisbon (€20/person, RS%—€15 with this book; tours run daily year-round—check schedule online; meet at northwest corner of Praça do Comércio near Rua do Arsenal, in front of the TI—see map on page 134, +351 218 861 840, www.lisbonwalker.com).

Inside Lisbon

Tours include the "Best of Lisbon Walk" (good 3-hour highlights tour of the main squares, Chiado, and Alfama; €18/person, €13 with this book; daily year-round at 10:00) and food and wine tours (see "Food Tours," later). Most tours meet at the statue of Dom Pedro IV in the center of Rossio and last three to four hours (reserve a day ahead via website or phone, mobile +351 968 412 612, www.insidelisbon.com). They also offer daily private tours and day trips by minivan (€75/person, RS%—€5 discount with this book or online with code "RICKLISBON") to Sintra/Cascais (8 hours) and Obidos/Fátima (9 hours). You can organize a private city tour with them, or use their helpful website as a resource for seeing Lisbon on your own.

Lisbon Chill-Out Free Walking Tours

Many companies offer "free" tours, but most are led by expats who memorize a script and are cluttered with cross-selling and promotions. In the end, you'll be hit up hard for a tip. If you're looking for a free tour, I'd choose Chill-Out. Your Chill-Out guide is a local who will share cultural insights as you walk through the Bairro Alto, across the Baixa, and into the Alfama. It's refreshing to get a hometown perspective, and they are upfront about "it's not really free—you tip what you like at the end." Three-hour walks start in the Bairro Alto at the statue on Praça Luís de Camões (look for the guide wearing the yellow travel bag) daily at 10:00 and 15:00 (www.lisbonfreetour.blogspot.pt).

FOOD TOURS

Guided food tours are trendy these days. Several companies offer three- to four-hour multistop tours that introduce you to lots of local food culture while filling your stomach at the same time. This is a quickly evolving scene, so it pays to do a little homework on the latest offerings. But I've enjoyed tours by several good outfits, listed below. In each case, the groups are small, the teaching is good, and—when you figure in the cost of the meal—the tours are a solid value.

Inside Lisbon offers three food-related itineraries (RS%—€5 discount with this book): Their "Food and Wine Walk" makes five to six short, tasty, and memorable stand-up stops (€45/person, 3 hours, Mon-Sat at 16:30). The "Sunset, Fado, and Tapas" walk includes an evening stroll and samples of local food and music (€65/person, 4 hours, departs at 19:00, 5/week in summer, 2/week in winter). And their "Lisbon Experience Walk" is a tour through the Mouraria neighborhood with some food stops mixed in, ending with a ferry to Cacilhas for seafood (€45/person, 4 hours, Mon-Sat at 10:30; www.insidelisbon.com).

Taste of Lisboa food tours, designed by Filipa Valete, connects you with a Lisboan guide and offers a fast-moving feast with lots of visits and lots of information. Their primary tour is the "Lisbon Roots, Food & Culture Walk" with seven stops (€70/person, 4 hours, Mon-Sat at 15:00 and 15:45, 2 to 12 per group, English only, sign up at www.tasteoflisboa.com). They offer several other cultural food experiences, all explained on their website.

Eat Drink Walk does a €85 "Tapas Downtown" walk (3-4 hours, 5-6 stops in the Baixa), as well as a €95 "Chiado Gourmet" walk (4-5 hours, www.eatdrinkwalk.pt). Both tours run Mon-Sat at 11:30 and are expertly led by Filomena or Duarte, both locals and pioneers in the food tour world of Lisbon.

LOCAL GUIDES

Hiring a private local guide in Lisbon can be a wonderful luxury: Your guide will meet you at your hotel and tailor a tour to your interests. Especially with a small group, this can be a fine value. Guides charge roughly the same rates (€125/half-day, €200/day; car and driver options are available).

Cristina Quental works with a trio of good local guides (€150/half-day, €240/day, mobile +351 919 922 480, www.lisbon4smile.com, anacristinaquental@hotmail.com).

Claudia da Costa, who appears on my Lisbon TV show, is also excellent (mobile +351 965 560 216, claudiadacosta@hotmail.com).

Cristina Duarte knows Lisbon well, also appears on my TV show, and leads private tours in Lisbon when not on the road leading Portugal tours for my company (mobile +351 919 316 242, www.lisbonbeyond.pt, acrismduarte@gmail.com).

Teresa Ferreira works in Lisbon and the surrounding area (mobile +351 966 139 564, www.borninlisbon.com, maria-te@live.com.pt).

Your Friend in Lisbon is a group of four guides who book private three-hour walks for €120 (price for one or two, more for larger groups, daily at 11:00 or 15:00, mobile +351 919 292 151, www.yourfriendinlisbon.com, alex@yourfriendinlisbon.com, run by Alex Almeida). They also have a minivan and driver (€400 for all-day, for up to six).

Neighborhood Walks in Lisbon

The essential Lisbon is easily and enjoyably covered in three ▲▲▲ self-guided walking tours through three downtown neighborhoods: Alfama, Baixa, and Bairro Alto/Chiado. You can do them as individual walks, or lace them together into a single tour (allow a minimum of five hours for all three, but could be done as a more leisurely all-day experience—or, for maximum lingering, spread it over two days). You can do the walks in any order, but starting with the Alfama gets you to the castle before the crowds hit, kicking things off with a grand city view from Lisbon's fortified birthplace. And you'll finish in the liveliest quarter for evening fun—the Bairro Alto/Chiado.

∩ My free Lisbon City Walk audio tour covers the same territory as the walks, from Praça do Comércio through the Baixa, and up through the highlights of the Bairro Alto (but not the Alfama or castle).

ALFAMA STROLL AND THE CASTLE

On this ▲▲▲ walk, you'll explore the Alfama, the colorful sailors' quarter that dates to the age of Visigoth occupation, from the sixth to eighth centuries AD. This was a bustling district during the Moorish period, and eventually became the home of Lisbon's fishermen and mariners (and of the poet Luís de Camões, who wrote, "Our lips meet easily, high across the narrow street"). The Alfama's tangled street plan, one of the few features of Lisbon to survive the 1755 earthquake, helps make the neighborhood a cobbled playground of Old World color. While much of the Alfama's grittiness has been cleaned up in recent years, it remains one of Europe's more photogenic neighborhoods.

When to Go: The best times to visit are during the busy midmorning market, or in the cooler late afternoon or early evening, when the streets teem with residents.

Getting There: This walk begins at the highest point in town, São Jorge Castle. Get to the castle gate by **taxi;** by **minibus #737** from Praça da Figueira; or by two free **elevator rides** up from the Baixa and then a short uphill walk. To find the elevators, head to Rua dos Fanqueiros and go through the easy-to-miss door at #178 (for location, see the map on page 61; you'll see faint, white lettering spelling out *elevador castelo* on the red rooftop—illuminated at night). Ride the elevator to the top floor and exit, angling left across the street and through the little square. Then head up Largo Chão do Loureiro, where you'll see the second elevator (*elevador castelo;* handy supermarket at bottom, view café and fine panoramic terrace at top). When exiting the second elevator, simply follow brown *Castelo de S. Jorge* signs up to the castle (right, then hooking left; about 8 minutes uphill).

❶ São Jorge Castle Gate and Fortified Castle Town

The formidable gate to the castle is part of a fortification that, these days, surrounds three things: the view terrace, the small town that stood within the walls, and the castle itself. The ticket office and

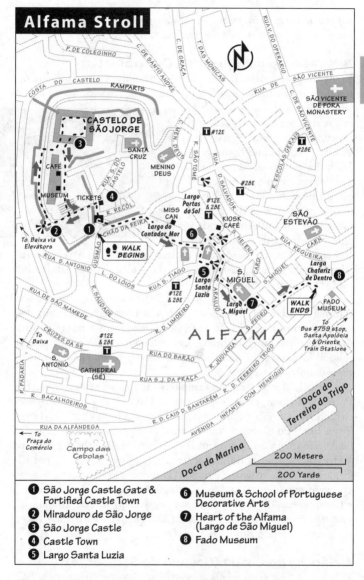

Alfama Stroll

- P. DE COLEGINHO
- COSTA DO CASTELO   RAMPARTS
- C. DE SANTO ANDRE
- C. DE GRAÇA
- T DAS MONICAS
- RUA V. DO OPERARIO
- RUA DE SÃO VICENTE
- C. DE SÃO VICENTE
- SÃO VICENTE DE FORA MONASTERY

- CASTELO DE SÃO JORGE
- ❸
- SANTA CRUZ
- MEN. DEUS
- R. SÃO TOMÉ
- T #12E
- T #28E
- R. ESCOLAS GERAIS
- CAFÉ
- RUA S. DO CASTELO
- MENINO DEUS
- MUSEUM
- TICKETS
- ❹
- R. RECOL.
- Largo Portas do Sol
- #12E & 28E
- T
- KIOSK CAFÉ
- R. D. SALVADOR
- T #28E
- SÃO ESTEVÃO
- MISS CAN
- ❷
- ❶
- CHÃO DA FEIRA
- GUSMÃO
- Largo do Contador Mor
- ❻
- R. S. HELENA
- RUA REGUEIRA
- To Baixa via Elevators
- WALK BEGINS
- RUA S. ANTONIO
- L. DO LÓIOS
- RUA S. TIAGO
- T #12E & 28E
- ❺
- Largo Santa Luzia
- S. MIGUEL
- CARD.
- S. MIGUEL
- S. PEDRO
- Largo Chafariz de Dentro
- ❽
- RUA DE SÃO MAMEDE
- R. SANDADE
- ARAUJO
- R. D. LIMOEIRO
- Largo S. Miguel
- ❼
- WALK ENDS
- FADO MUSEUM
- ALFAMA
- To Bus #759 stop, Santa Apolónia & Oriente Train Stations
- CRUZES DA SÉ
- To Baixa
- #12E & 28E
- T
- S. ANTONIO
- CATHEDRAL (SÉ)
- RUA DO BARÃO
- K. JUDIARIA
- R. D. TERREIRO TRIGO
- R. PADARIA
- R. BACALHOEIROS
- RUA S.J. DA PRAÇA
- Doca do Terreiro do Trigo
- RUA DA ALFÂNDEGA
- To Praça do Comércio
- Campo das Cebolas
- R. D. CAIS D. SANTAREM   R. D. INFANTE DOM HENRIQUE
- AVENIDA   INFANTE   DOM   HENRIQUE
- Doca da Marina
- 200 Meters
- 200 Yards

- ❶ São Jorge Castle Gate & Fortified Castle Town
- ❷ Miradouro de São Jorge
- ❸ São Jorge Castle
- ❹ Castle Town
- ❺ Largo Santa Luzia
- ❻ Museum & School of Portuguese Decorative Arts
- ❼ Heart of the Alfama (Largo de São Miguel)
- ❽ Fado Museum

the turnstile are situated so that those without a ticket are kept away from the view terrace and castle proper (castle entry-€8.50, daily 9:00-21:00, Nov-Feb until 18:00).

If money is tight, the castle and view are skippable—the castle is just stark, rebuilt ruins from the Salazar era, and while the hill-capping park has a commanding view, there are other fine views coming up...just jump ahead to stop #4 on this walk.

• *If you decide to go in, follow the cobbles uphill past the first lanes of old Lisbon to the yellow ticket office, and then into the...*

❷ Miradouro de São Jorge (Viewpoint)

Enjoy the grand view. The Rio Tejo is one of five main rivers in Portugal, four of which come from Spain. (Only the Mondego River, which passes through Coimbra, originates inside Portuguese territory, in the Serra de Estrela.) While Portugal and Spain generally have very good relations, a major sore point is the control of all this water. From here, you have a good view of the Golden Gate-like 25th of April Bridge, which leads south to the Cristo  Rei statue. Past the bridge, on a clear day, you can barely see the Monument to the Discoveries and the Belém Tower (under and past the bridge on north side).

Look up at the statue marking the center of this terrace. **Afonso Henriques,** a warlord with a strong personal army, was the founder of Portugal. In 1147, he besieged this former Moorish castle until the hungry, thirsty residents gave in. Every Portuguese schoolkid knows the story of this man—a Reconquista hero and their country's first king.

Stroll inland along the **ramparts** for a more extensive view of Pombal's Lisbon, described in a circa 1963, tiled panorama-chart (which lacks the big 25th of April Bridge—it was built in 1969). From Praça do Comércio on the water, the grid streets of the Baixa lead up to the tree-lined Avenida da Liberdade and the big Edward VII Park, on the far right. Locate city landmarks, such as the Elevador de Santa Justa (the Eiffel-style elevator in front of the ruined Convento do Carmo) and the sloping white roof of Rossio station.

• *Continue walking along the viewpoint, passing several old cannons. Just after going under the second arch (just before the café terrace), take a right into the mostly ruined courtyard of...*

❸ São Jorge Castle (Castelo de São Jorge)

While the first settlements here go back to the 7th century BC, this castle dates to the 11th century when Moors built it to house their army and provide a safe haven for their elites in times of siege. After Afonso Henriques took the castle in 1147, Portugal's royalty lived here for several centuries. The sloping walls—typical of castles from this period—were designed to withstand 14th-century cannonballs. In the 16th century, the kings moved to their palace on Praça do Comércio, and the castle became a military garrison.

Despite suffering major damage in the 1755 earthquake, the castle later served another stint

as a military garrison. In the 20th century, it became a national monument.

The strolling **peacocks** remind visitors that exotic birds like these came to Lisbon originally as trophies of the great 16th-century voyages and discoveries. (Today the jaded birds ignore the tourists and cry as if to remember some long-forgotten castle captives.)

Bear left to find the **inner castle**—the boxy, crenelated fort in the middle. There's little to see inside the empty shell, but it's fun to climb up the steep stone steps to scramble around the top of the ramparts and towers, with ever-changing views of Lisbon, the Alfama, and the castle itself. (Up top, you'll also find a thrillingly low-tech camera obscura, which is demonstrated twice hourly—times and languages posted.)

As you explore the castle's inner sanctum, imagine it lined with simple wooden huts. The imposing part of the castle is the exterior. The builders' strategy was to focus on making the castle appear so formidable that its very existence was enough to discourage any attack. If you know where to look, you can still see stones laid by ancient Romans, Visigoths, and Moors. The Portuguese made the most substantial contribution, with a wall reaching all the way to the river to withstand anticipated Spanish attacks.

When finished, head back out the inner castle gate, and continue straight ahead toward the castle's entrance. On your right, you'll pass the café, then the humble **museum.** This houses archaeological finds from the 7th century BC to the 18th century, with emphasis on the Moorish period in the 11th and 12th centuries. You'll also see 18th-century tiles from an age when Portugal was flush with money from the gold, diamonds, and sugarcane of its colony Brazil. While simple, the museum has nice displays and descriptions.

• *Leave the castle. Across the ramp from the castle entrance is a tidy little castle district, worth a wander for its peaceful lanes and a chance to enjoy the Manueline architecture.*

❹ Castle Town

Just outside the castle turnstile is the tiny neighborhood within the castle walls built to give Moorish elites refuge from sieges and, later, for Portuguese nobles to live close to their king. While it's

Pombal's Lisbon

In 1750, lazy King José I (r. 1750-1777) turned the government over to a minor noble, the Marquês de Pombal (1699-1782). Talented, ambitious, and handsome, Pombal was praised as a reformer, but reviled for his ruthless tactics. Having learned modern ways as the ambassador to Britain, he battled Church repression and promoted the democratic ideals of the Enlightenment, but enforced his policies with arrests, torture, and executions. He expelled the Jesuits to keep them from monopolizing the education system, put the bishop of Coimbra in prison, and broke off relations with the pope. When the earthquake of 1755 leveled the city, within a month Pombal had kicked off major rebuilding in much of today's historic downtown—featuring a grid plan for the world's first quake-proof buildings. In 1777, the king died, and the controversial Pombal was dismissed.

partly taken over by cute shops and cafés, if you wander up Rua de Santa Cruz do Castelo (to the left as you exit the castle) and stroll into its back lanes, you can enjoy a peaceful bit of Portugal's past. (Make a big clockwise loop back to where you entered—you can't get lost, as it's within the walls and there's only one way in or out.) Most of the houses date from the Middle Ages. Poking around, go on a cultural scavenger hunt. Look for: 1) clever, space-efficient, triangular contraptions for drying clothes (hint: see the glass bottle bottoms in the wall used to prop the sticks out when in use); 2) Benfica soccer team flag (that's the team favored by Lisbon's working class—a hint that the upper class no longer chooses to live here); 3) short doors that were tall enough for people back when these houses were built; and 4) noble family crests over doors—dating to when important families wanted to be close to the king.

When you're ready to leave, make your way back to where you started, and head down the ramp to return to the real world. On your way out, just before exiting the lower gate, notice the little statue in the niche on your right. This is the castle's namesake: **St. George** (São Jorge; pronounced "sow ZHOR-zh") hailed from Turkey and was known for fighting valiantly (he's often portrayed slaying a dragon). When the Christian noble Afonso Henriques called for help to eliminate the Moors from his newly founded country of Portugal, the Crusaders who helped him prayed to St. George...and won.

• *Exit the castle complex grounds through the large archway, follow the castle wall, then turn right down the second street, Travessa do Chão da Feira. Follow this striped lane downhill through* **Largo do Contador Mor**. *This small, car-clogged square has a Parisian ambience, some tour-*

LISBON

isty outdoor restaurants serving grilled sardines, and the inviting little **Miss Can** *shop and eatery—where traditional Portuguese canned fish gets a modern twist (for ideas on lunching here, see page 150).*

Exit the square at the bottom, continue downhill 50 yards farther, pass the trolley tracks, and jog right around the little church to reach a superb Alfama viewpoint at...

❺ Largo Santa Luzia

From this square (with a stop for trolleys #12E and #28E), admire the panoramic view from the small terrace, **Miradouro de Santa Luzia**, where old-timers play cards and Romeos strum their guitars amid lots of tiles.

In the distance to the left, the **Vasco da Gama Bridge** (opened in 1998) connects Lisbon with new, modern bedroom communities south of the river.

At your feet sprawls the Alfama neighborhood. We'll head that way soon, to explore its twisty lanes. Where the Alfama hits the river, notice the recently built embankment. It reclaimed 100 yards of land from the river to make a modern port, used these days to accommodate Lisbon's growing cruise ship industry.

On the wall of the church behind you, notice two 18th-century **tile panels.** The one on the left shows the preearthquake Praça do Comércio, with the royal palace (on the left). It was completely destroyed in the 1755 quake. The other tile (10 steps away, to the right) depicts the reconquest of Lisbon from the Moors by Afonso Henriques. You can see the Portuguese hero, Martim Moniz, who let himself be crushed in the castle door to hold it open for his comrades. Notice the panicky Moors inside realizing that their castle is about to be breeched by invading Crusaders. It was a bad day for the Moors. (A stairway here leads up to a tiny view terrace with a café.)

For an even better city view, hike back around the church and walk out to the seaside end of the **Miradouro das Portas do Sol** catwalk. The huge, frilly building dominating the ridge on the far left is the Monastery of São Vicente, constructed around 1600 by the Spanish king Philip II, who left his mark here with this tribute to St. Vincent. A few steps away, next to a statue of St. Vincent, is a kiosk café where you can enjoy perhaps the most scenic cup of coffee in town.

• *Across the street from the café, you'll find the...*

❻ Museum and School of Portuguese Decorative Arts

The Museum and School of Portuguese Decorative Arts (Museu Escola de Artes Decorativas Portuguesas) offers a stroll through

a richly decorated, aristocratic household. The palace, filled with 15th- to 18th-century fine art, offers the best chance for visitors to experience what a noble home looked like during Lisbon's glory days (€4, Wed-Mon 10:00-17:00, closed Tue, Largo das Portas do Sol 2, +351 218 814 640, www.fress.pt). Inside, a coach on the ground level is "Berlin style," with a state-of-the-art suspension system, on leather straps. The grand stairway leads upstairs past 18th-century glazed tiles (Chinese-style blue-and-white was in vogue) into a world of colonial riches. Portuguese aristocrats had a special taste for "Indo-Portuguese" decorative arts: objects of exotic woods such as teak or rosewood, and inlaid with shell or ivory, made along the sea routes of the age.

From here, it's downhill all the way. From Largo das Portas do Sol (the plaza with the statue of local patron St. Vincent, near

the kiosk café on the terrace), go down the looooong **stairs** (Rua Norberto de Araújo, between the church and the catwalk). A few steps down on the left, under the big arch, notice the public WCs and the fun, vivid **cartoon mural** illustrating Lisbon's history (if you know the key dates, you can enjoy it even without understanding Portuguese).

The massive eighth-century **fortified wall** (on the right of the staircase) once marked the boundary of Moorish Lisbon. Consider that the great stones on your right were stacked here over a thousand years ago. At the bottom of the wall, continue downhill, then turn left at the railing...and go down more stairs.

• *Explore downhill from here. The main thoroughfare, a concrete stepped lane called* ***Escadinhas de São Miguel***, *funnels you to the Alfama's main square.*

❼ Heart of the Alfama

This square, **Largo de São Miguel,** is the best place to observe a slice of Alfama life. When city leaders rebuilt the rest of Lisbon after the 1755 quake, this neighborhood was left out and consequently retains its tangled medieval streets.

If you've got the time, **explore the Alfama** from this central square. Its urban-jungle roads are squeezed into confusing alleys—

the labyrinthine street plan was designed to frustrate invaders. What was defensive then is atmospheric now. Bent houses comfort each other in their romantic shabbiness, and the air drips with laundry and the smell of clams. Get lost. Poke aimlessly, peek through windows, buy a fish. Locals hang plastic water bags from windows in the summer to keep away the flies. Favorite saints decorate doors to protect families. St. Peter, protector of fishermen, is big in the Alfama. Churches are generally closed, since they share a priest. As children have very little usable land for a good soccer game, this square doubles as the neighborhood playground.

The tiny balconies were limited to "one-and-a-half hands" in width. A strictly enforced health initiative was designed to keep the town open and well-ventilated. If you see carpets hanging out to dry, it means a laundry is nearby. Because few homes have their own, every neighborhood has a public laundry and bathroom. Until recently, in the early morning hours, the streets were busy with residents in pajamas, heading for these public baths. Today, many younger people are choosing to live elsewhere, lured by modern conveniences unavailable here, and old flats with older residents are under the watchful eye of real estate developers. Many long-term

residents have been evicted due to landlords claiming "necessary reforms," only to sell the entire building for development as tourist housing. In just one generation, the Alfama is feeling the pressure of gentrification.

Traditionally the neighborhood here was tightly knit, with families routinely sitting down to communal dinners in the streets. Feuds, friendships, and gossip were all intense. Historically, when a woman's husband died, she would wear black for the rest of her life—a tradition that's just about gone.

The Alfama hosts Lisbon's most popular outdoor party dedicated to St. Anthony (whose feast day is June 13, but the party goes on all month). Imagine tables set up everywhere, bands playing, bright plastic flowers strung across the squares, and all the grilled sardines *(sardinhas grelhadas)* you can eat. The rustic paintings of festive characters (with hints of Moorish style) remind locals of past parties, and strings and wires overhead await future festival dates when the neighborhood will again be festooned with colorful streamers.

While there are plenty of traditional festivals here, the most action on the Alfama calendar is the insane, annual mountain-bike street race from the castle to the sea (which you can see hurtle by in two minutes on YouTube; search "Lisboa downtown race").

Continue exploring downhill from here. Just below the square you'll see A Baiuca, a recommended amateur fado restaurant. Then, a few steps farther downhill, you'll hit the cobbled pedestrian lane, **Rua São Pedro.** This darkest of the Alfama's streets, in nearly perpetual shade, was the logical choice for the neighborhood's fish market. Modern hygiene requirements (which forbid outdoor stalls) killed the market, but it's still a characteristic lane to explore.

• *Turn left and follow Rua São Pedro out of the Alfama to the square called Largo do Chafariz de Dentro and, across the street, the...*

❽ Fado Museum

This ▲ museum tells the story of fado in English—with a great chance to hear these wailing fisherwomen's blues. Three levels of wall murals show three generations of local fado stars, and the audioguide lets you listen to the Billie Holidays of Portugal (€5, includes audioguide, Tue-Sun 11:00-17:00, closed Mon, Largo do Chafariz de Dentro, +351 218 823 470, www.museudofado.pt).

• *This walk is over. To get back downtown (or to Praça do Comércio, where the next walk starts), walk a block to the main waterfront drag and cruise-ship harbor (facing the museum, go left around it) where busy Avenida Infante Dom Henrique leads back to Praça do Comércio (to the right). While it's a 15-minute walk or quick taxi ride to Praça do Comércio, just to the left is a bus stop; hop on any bus for two stops, and you're there in moments. (Also, bus #759 goes on to Praça dos Restauradores.)*

BAIXA STROLL

This ▲▲▲ walk covers the highlights of Lisbon's historic downtown, the Baixa, which fills a flat valley between two hills. The district slopes gently from the waterfront up to Rossio, Praça dos Restauradores, Avenida da Liberdade, and the newer town. The walk starts at Praça do Comércio and ends at Praça dos Restauradores.

• *Start your walk at the statue of King José I in the center of* **Praça do**

LISBON

Baixa Stroll

To Elevador
do Lavra

COLISEU

200 Meters

200 Yards

ELEVADOR
DA GLÓRIA

OBELISK

Praça dos
Restauradores

WALK
ENDS

Restauradores

ABEP TICKET
KIOSK

NAT'L
THEATER

ROSSIO
TRAIN
STATION

CALÇADA
WORKER
MEMORIAL

Largo do
Cadoval

ROSSIO

Rossio
(Praça Dom
Pedro IV)

Rossio

Largo
de São
Domingos

SÃO
DOMINGOS

QUERIOZ

Praça
Martim
Moniz

Martim
Moniz

#12E
& 28E

Bus Tours

Rossio

Praça da
Figueira

#714

#12E
&15E

R. BORRATEM

SWEETS

R. C. DUQUE

R. DO DUQUE

R. DA OLIVEIRA

R.T. DEZEMBRO

ARCH

R. BESTEGA

R. DA
CONDESA

RUA NOVA
TRINIDADE

R. DA TRINDADE

CONVENTO
DO CARMO

Largo do
Carmo

TR. DO CARMO

ELEVADOR
STA. JUSTA

RUA SANTA
JUSTA

BAIXA

RUA DA ASSUNÇÃO

To
Alfama

ELEVADOR
UP TO
SÃO JORGE
CASTLE

CHIADO

To Bairro
Alto

RUA GARRETT

Baixa-
Chiado

R. SERPA PINTO

ARMAZÉNS
DO CHIADO
MALL

Baixa-Chiado

RUA IVENS

R. S. FRAN.

RUA DO CRUCIFIXO

RUA DO OURO

RUA AUREA

RUA DA VITORIA

(RUA DO OURO)

RUA DOS SAPATEIROS

RUA AUGUSTA

RUA DOS CORREEIROS

S. NICOLAU

To
Alfama

R. DO ALMADA

R. DE SÃO JULIÃO

#28E

"HIDDEN
CHURCH"

MUDE

MARTINHO DA
ARCADA CAFÉ

C. S. FRANCISCO

RUA DE SÃO JULIÃO

RUA DO COMÉRCIO

RUA DE
CONCEIÇÃO

Praça
do
Município

ARCH OF
TRIUMPH

LISBON
WALKER

Praça do
Comércio

#15E

Bus
Tours

WALK
BEGINS

WINE-TASTING
CENTER

Terreiro
do Paço

AV. RIBEIRA DAS NAUS

To Cais do Sodré
Station via Riverside
Promenade

PILLARS

Rio Tejo

1. Praça do Comércio
2. Lisbon's Riverfront
3. Rua do Comércio
4. Rua de São Julião
5. Church of St. Nicholas
6. Praça da Figueira
7. Church of São Domingos
8. Largo de São Domingos
9. Ginjinha Bars (2)
10. Rossio Square
11. Rossio Station
12. Praça dos Restauradores
13. To Avenida da Liberdade & Pombal Statue

Comércio. *Find a spot of shade in José's shadow (or take cover under the arcades) and read a bit about the Baixa's history.*

Background: After the disastrous 1755 earthquake, the Baixa district was rebuilt on a grid street plan. The uniform and utilitarian Pombaline architecture (named after the Marquês de Pombal, the chief minister who rebuilt the city—see sidebar, earlier) feels almost military. That's because it is. The Baixa was constructed by military engineers who had experience building garrison towns overseas. The new Lisbon featured the architecture of conquest—simple to assemble, economical, with all the pieces easy to ship. The 18th-century buildings you'd see in Mozambique and Brazil are interchangeable with those in Lisbon.

The buildings are all uniform, with the same number of floors and standard facades. They were designed to survive the next earthquake, with stone firewalls and wooden frameworks that had flexible crisscross beams. The priorities were to rebuild fast, cheap, and shake-proof.

If it had been left up to the people, who believed the earthquake was a punishment from God, they would have rebuilt their churches bigger and more impressive than ever. But Pombal was a practical military man with a budget, a timeline, and an awareness of his society's limits. Large churches didn't fit into the new, orderly grid. In those austere postearthquake days, Pombal got his way.

The Baixa has three squares—two preearthquake (Comércio and Rossio) and one added later (Figueira)—and three main streets: Prata (silver), Aurea (gold), and Augusta (relating the Portuguese king to a Roman emperor). The former maze of the Jewish quarter was eliminated, but the area has many streets named for the crafts and shops once found there.

The Baixa's pedestrian streets, inviting cafés, bustling shops, and elegant old storefronts give the district a certain charm. City-government subsidies make sure the old businesses stay around, but modern ones find a way to creep in. I find myself doing laps up and down Rua Augusta in a people-watching stupor. Its delightful ambience is perfect for strolling.

• *Now turn your attention to the square itself.*

❶ Praça do Comércio (Commerce Square)

At this riverfront square bordering the Baixa—along the gateway to Lisbon—ships used to dock and sell their goods. This was the site of Portugal's royal palace for 200 preearthquake years, but

after the 1755 earthquake/tsunami/fire, the jittery king fled to more stable Belém, never to return. These days, government ministries ring Praça do Comércio. It's also the departure point for city bus and tram tours, and boats that cruise along the Rio Tejo. The area opposite the harbor was conceived as a residential neighborhood for the upper class, but they chose the suburbs. Today, the square has two names ("Palace Square" and "Commerce Square") and little real life. Locals consider it just a big place to pass through.

The statue is **José I,** the king who gave control of the government to his chief minister, the Marquês de Pombal. Built 20 years after the quake, it shows the king on his horse, with Pombal (on the medallion), looking at their port. The king on horseback strikes a heroic pose, bravely riding through the ground covered in snakes (a contrast to his actual behavior after the earthquake, refusing to sleep in a stone building ever again). The snakes actually hide support mechanisms for the heavy statue. Triumph and Fame toot the king's arrival, while a horse represents Portugal's European power and an elephant asserts the country's dominance in Asia. In its glory days, this city was where east met west. The statue proved such a success that it jump-started sculptor Joaquim Machado de Castro's career (see more at his museum in Coimbra).

The big arch marking the inland side of the square is Lisbon's **Arch of Triumph** (with Vasco da Gama on the left and Pombal on the right). Disregarding his usual austerity, Pombal restored some of the city's Parisian-style grandeur at this central approach into downtown.

Facing the Arch of Triumph, get oriented to a few landmarks on the square (moving from left to right):

At 9 o'clock is the cozy **Wines of Portugal Tasting Room,** a nonprofit wine-appreciation venue. About two dozen local wines are offered; English descriptions are above each tap, and a helpful attendant is happy to explain things. To taste, you buy a chip card (€3 minimum and €1 deposit for the card), take a glass, and serve yourself samples of Portuguese wines of every variety: white, red, green *(vinho verde),* and a few ports (each €1 and up; focused flights of five wines can be reserved for €8-15; daily 11:00-19:00).

At 10 o'clock is the **TI.**

At 2 o'clock, under the arcade just right of the arch, is **Martinho da Arcada,** a fine option for a coffee, pastry, or snack (Praça do Comércio 8, at the corner of Rua da Prata). It was founded in

1782—when the wealthy would come here to savor early ice cream made with mountain snow, lemon, and spices. While it has a fancy restaurant, I'd enjoy just a coffee and pastry in its café bar. This place was one of poet Fernando Pessoa's old haunts (they display a few Pessoa artifacts, lots of old photos, and a shrine-like table that was his favorite). In the early 20th century, painters, writers, and dreamers shared revolutionary ideas here over coffee.

At 3 o'clock is the much-promoted **"Lisbon Story Center,"** a childish exhibit with no artifacts—you pay €8 to stand for an hour looking at animated history on computer screens. Nearby is another branch of the **TI** (in case the first one is too crowded).

And at 5 o'clock is the **Terreiro do Paço Metro stop** (see the red *M* on a post). Finally, look up to see the tree-covered home to São Jorge Castle from the previous walk.

• *Before moving on, use the crosswalk at the bottom of the big square for a quick look at...*

❷ Lisbon's Riverfront

An inviting balustrade and a pair of Pombaline pillars—Lisbon's gateway to the sea, an arrival and departure point for everyone from Philip II of Spain to dictator António de Oliveira Salazar—mark a little pier (called the Cais das Colunas) that offers a fine, water-level view of the Tejo riverscape. To your left is the busy Terreiro do Paço ferry terminal—one of many that connect commuters to the far side of the river. To your right are the 25th of April Bridge and Cristo Rei statue. Down here at water level, you can really see that the Tejo is a tidal river—the Atlantic is just around the bend (past the bridge). At low tide, the humble little rocky beach reveals worlds of sea life in rocky pools. Any tide poolers out today?

• *Now, head back up through the square, cross the busy street, pass under the big arch, and walk down Rua Augusta into the Baixa district. (Skip the chance to pay to go to the top of the arch—it affords only a mediocre view from its empty rooftop.)*

The first cross-street you meet is...

❸ Rua do Comércio

Look right to see the old **cathedral** with its Romanesque fortress-like crenellations (de-scribed later, under "Sights in Lisbon"). No-tice that many of the surrounding buildings are in the austere architectural style adopted immediately after the earthquake. Exterior decoration was adopted here in Lisbon only in the 19th century, after the Portuguese in colonial Brazil found that the tiles protected against humidity.

The characteristic black-and-white cobbled **sidewalk** *(calçada)* is uniquely Portuguese. These mosaic limestone and basalt cobbles were first cut and laid by 19th-century prison laborers, but maintaining them has since developed into a skilled craft. To this day patterns are chosen from acceptable designs made from large, wooden stencils. One benefit of these sidewalks is that they move and flow with the earth; even as tree roots spread or the ground shifts, the asphalt does not crack. But as the stones can be slippery and require skilled labor, the city government is talking about replacing them with modern pavement. Locals are crying out to keep the tradition.

Across the street, on the right, you'll pass the **MUDE**, Lisbon's museum of 20th-century design and fashion, occupying a former bank building (likely closed for renovation).

• *The next cross-street is...*

❹ Rua de São Julião

Churches blend into the postearthquake Baixa. There's one about 30 yards to the left down Rua de São Julião (hiding on right side

of street; look for the triangular pediment over door). Churches were rebuilt to be better incorporated into the no-nonsense grid plan of the Baixa. Look up for evidence of how downtown Lisbon's population is shrinking as more people move to the suburbs: The upper floors of many buildings are now mostly empty.

At the next block, **Rua da Conceição**, there's a stop for the handy trolley #28E. Ahead on the right (in the windows of the Millennium Bank) are Roman artifacts—a reminder that Lisbon's history goes way back.

• *Go two more blocks to the intersection with Rua da Vitoria. Turn right and walk two blocks to Rua da Prata, where you'll see the camouflaged...*

❺ Church of St. Nicholas (Igreja de São Nicolau)

Notice how a typical church facade faces the square, but on the

streetfront side, the entire exterior is covered with green tiles, as just another stretch of post-earthquake Baixa architecture. The church made extra income by leasing what is technically their property to the businesses on busy Rua da

Prata. Several of the fine, tiled buildings near this square have been refurbished. In fact, the one at the very top of the square hides a free elevator that takes you partway up to the castle atop the Alfama.

• *Head north down Rua da Prata toward the statue marking Praça da Figueira. At Rua de Santa Justa, look left for a good view of Elevador de Santa Justa before continuing straight to the square.*

❻ Praça da Figueira (Fig Tree Square)

This was the site of a huge hospital destroyed in the earthquake. With no money to replace the hospital, the space was left open until the late 1880s, when it was filled with a big iron-framed market (similar to Barcelona's La Boqueria). That structure was torn down decades ago, leaving the square you see today.

The big building on the left, with its upper floors long neglected, has been purchased in part by Spanish tennis star Rafael Nadal for a total of €62 million. It's an example of the neighborhood being reinvigorated—though likely at the expense of long-time tenants.

The nearby **Confeitaria Nacional** shop (on the corner of the square, 20 yards to your left) is a venerable palace of sweets little changed since the 19th century. In the window is a display of "*conventuel* sweets"—special nun-made treats often consisting of sugar and egg yolks. (Historically, the nuns, who used the egg whites to starch their laundry, had an abundance of yolks.) Consider a light lunch in the recommended upstairs dining room.

The square is a transportation hub, with stops for minibus #737 to the castle; old trolley #12E to the Alfama viewpoint; modern trolley #15E and bus #714 heading out to Belém; and hop-on, hop-off tour buses.

Walk to the far-left corner of the square, past skateboarders oblivious to its historical statue—Portugal's King João I on a horse. Continue straight out of the square on **Rua Dom Antão de Almada**. This lane has several characteristic shops. Pop into the classic cod shop (on the left at #1C—you'll smell it). Cod *(bacalhau)* is part of Portugal's heritage as a nation of seafaring explorers: Salted cod could keep for a year on a ship. Just soak in water to rinse out the salt and enjoy. The adjacent ham counter serves *pata negra (presunto ibérico)* from acorn-fed pigs—the very best. Many say the *alheira* sausage, made with bread, game, and garlic instead of pork, was a favorite among Lisbon's Jews back when they needed to fake being

Christians (during the forced conversions of the Inquisition era). In reality, the sausage was a way to preserve other types of meat for long winter months.

• *At the end of the lane stands a big church facing another square.*

❼ Church of São Domingos

A center of the Inquisition in the 1600s, this is now one of Lisbon's most active churches (daily 7:30-19:00). The evocative interior—

rebuilt from the ruins left by the 1755 earthquake—would continue to play an important role in local history due to its location so near Rossio. Two famous royal weddings were held here in the 1800s. But the current state of the church—with black soot on the walls and charred stonework at the altar—is due to

a raging fire in 1959. Closed for decades, São Domingos finally reopened to the public in the 1990s, with all its scars still visible. Tabloid photos of fire damage can be seen at the exit. Our Lady of Fátima is Portugal's most popular saint, and her chapel (in the left rear of the church) always has the most candles. Her statue is accompanied by two of the three children to whom she miraculously appeared (the third was still alive when this chapel was made and so is not shown in heaven with the saint).

• *Step into the square just beyond the church.*

❽ Largo de São Domingos

This area was just outside of the old town walls—long a place where people gathered to keep watering holes busy and enjoy bohemian

entertainment. Today the square is home to classic old bars (like the *ginjinha* bar described next) and a busy "eating lane," Rua das Portas de Santo Antão (kitty-corner from where you entered the square, to the right of the National Theater on the far side of the square).

A stone monument on the square remembers the Jewish massacre of 1506. Many Jews expelled from Spain in 1492 took refuge in Portugal. But when a drought ravaged the country, Lisbonites killed several thousand of them on this square.

The city's 16th-century slave market also took place here, but the square is now a meeting point for the city's African community—immigrants from former Portuguese colonies such as Angola, Mozambique, and Portuguese Guinea. They hang out, trade news from home, and watch the tourists go by.

With that unfortunate heritage, the city today calls itself the "City of Tolerance." You'll see that phrase—in the language of all the communities that now live peacefully together here—on a wall behind the benches. Just beyond this square is a square called Praça Martim Moniz, the springboard for the tangled and characteristic Mouraria district, the immigrant neighborhood between here and the castle (described later, under "Sights in Lisbon").

• *Look toward the big adjoining square to find the colorful little tavern serving a traditional berry brandy.*

❾ Liquid Sightseeing (*Ginjinha* Bars)

Ginjinha (zheen-ZHEEN-yah) is a favorite Lisbon drink. While nuns baked sweets, the monks took care of quenching thirsts with this sweet liquor, made from the *ginja* berry (like a sour cherry), sugar, and brandy. It's now sold for €1.40 a shot in funky old shops throughout downtown. Buy it with or without berries (*com elas* or *sem elas*—that's "with them" or "without them") and *gelada* (if you want it poured from a chilled bottle). In Portu-

gal, when people are impressed by the taste of something, they say, "*Sabe que nem ginjas*"—literally "It tastes like *ginja*," but meaning "finger-lickin' good."

The oldest *ginjinha* joint in town is a hole-in-the-wall at Largo de São Domingos 8. If you hang around the bar long enough, you'll see them refill the bottle from an enormous vat. (Another *ginjinha* bar, Ginjinha Sem Rival, serves the prized *Eduardinho* liqueur, considered the most authentic; it's just across the square, at the start of the restaurant row—Rua das Portas de Santo Antão—at #7.)

• *A big square is around the corner (fronting the National Theater). This is...*

❿ Rossio Square

Lisbon's historic center, Rossio, is still the city's bustling cultural heart. Given its elongated shape, historians know it was a Roman racetrack 2,000 years ago; these days, cars circle the loop instead of chariots. It's home to the colonnaded National Theater, American fast-food chains, and street vendors who can shine your shoes, lam-

The Lisbon Earthquake of 1755

At 9:40 on Sunday, November 1—All Saints' Day—an underwater earthquake estimated to be close to 9.0 in magnitude occurred off the southern Portuguese coast. Massive tremors  rumbled through Lisbon, punctuated by three main jolts. The quake came midway through Mass, when devout locals filled the churches. Minutes later, thousands lay dead under the rubble.

Along the waterfront, shaken survivors scrambled aboard boats to sail to safety. They were met by a 20-foot wall of water, the first wave of a tsunami that rushed up the Rio Tejo. The ravaging water capsized ships, swept people off the docks, crested over the seawall, and crashed 800 feet inland.

The tremors were felt throughout Europe—as far away as Finland. Imagine a disaster similar to 2004's Indian Ocean earthquake and tsunami, devastating Portugal's capital city.

Fires turned the city into an inferno. The flames blazed for five days, ravaging the downtown from the Bairro Alto across Rossio to the castle atop the Alfama.

Of Lisbon's 270,000 citizens, over 10,000 may have perished, and two-thirds of the city was leveled. The city's biggest buildings—its churches, designed to connect earth with heaven—had simply collapsed, crushing the faithful. Understandably, the quake shook conservative Portugal's moral and spiritual underpinnings. Had God punished Lisbon for the Inquisition killings carried out on nearby Praça do Comércio? To the people of the time, it must have felt like the Apocalypse.

King José I was so affected by the earthquake that he moved his entire court to an elaborate complex of tents in the foothills of Belém and resisted living indoors for the rest of his life. He left his energetic (and eventually dictatorial) second-in-command—his chief minister Marquês de Pombal—the task of rebuilding. For more on Pombal, see "Pombal's Lisbon," earlier.

inate your documents, and sell you cheap watches, autumn chestnuts, and lottery tickets. The column in the square's center honors Pedro IV—king of Portugal and emperor of Brazil. (Many maps refer to the square as Praça Dom Pedro IV, but residents always just call it Rossio, for the train station at one corner.)

The square once held a palace that functioned as the headquarters of the Inquisition. Damaged by the 1755 earthquake, it was demolished, and in an attempt to erase its memory, the National Theater was built in its place.

From here you can see the Elevador de Santa Justa and the ruined convent breaking the city skyline. Notice the fine stone patterns in the pavement—evoking waves encountered by the great explorers. (If you're prone to seasickness, don't look down as you cross the square.)

• *Crossing the square in front of the National Theater, you see...*

⓫ Rossio Station

The circa-1900 facade of Rossio station is Neo-Manueline. You can read the words *"Estação Central"* (central station) carved on its strik-

ing horseshoe arches. Find the empty niche where a statue of King Sebastian once stood in the center of two arches. Unfortunately, the statue fell and broke into many pieces in 2016 when a tourist climbed the facade to take a selfie (I'm not kidding). It has since been repaired but has yet to return...much like his legend. This romantic, dashing, and young soldier-king was lost in 1580 in an ill-fated crusade to Africa. As Sebastian left no direct heir, the crown ended up with Philip II of Spain, who became Philip I of Portugal. The Spanish king promised to give back the throne if Sebastian ever turned up—and ever since, the Portuguese have dreamed that Sebastian will return, restoring their national greatness. Even today, in a crisis, the Portuguese like to think that their Sebastian will save the day—he's the symbol of being ridiculously hopeful.

• *Just uphill from Rossio station is Praça dos Restauradores, at the bottom of Lisbon's long and grand Avenida da Liberdade. Between Rossio station and the square is Lisbon's oldest hotel, the **Avenida Palace.** Built as a terminus hotel at the same time as Rossio station, it has a fun interior, with an elegant yet inviting oasis of a bar/lounge—popular with WWII spies in the 20th century, and tourists needing a little break in the 21st century (nice after this walk).*

⓬ Praça dos Restauradores

This monumental square connects Rossio with Avenida da Liberdade. The obelisk at its centerpiece celebrates the restoration of

Lisbon's Kiosks

The kiosk—that's *quiosque* in Portuguese—is a standard feature of squares and viewpoints all over town. These little pavilions got their start in the 19th century selling snacks and drinks. But they fell out of favor, with some being converted to newsstands or lottery sales points. Now they're back, with outdoor cafés turning parks and squares into neighborhood hangouts and meeting points. Older kiosks have been restored, and new ones are being built all the time and can be quite trendy.

Portuguese independence from Spain in 1640 (without any help from the still-missing Sebastian mentioned earlier).

Looking uphill at the lower left corner of the square, find a statue remembering the generations of laborers who made the city's characteristic black-and-white *calçada* sidewalks. Lisboners love the patterns decorating their pavements throughout the town. Here, these bronze workers have made the symbol of the city: a ship, carrying the remains of St. Vincent, guarded by two ravens.

Overlooking the square is the 1930s Art Deco facade of the Eden Theater. About 100 yards farther up the boulevard (past a Metro station and TI, on the left) is the Elevador da Glória funicular that climbs to the Bairro Alto.

• *While this walk ends here, you can stroll up Avenida da Liberdade for a good look at another facet of this fine city. The next walk (Bairro Alto and Chiado Stroll) starts at the funicular just up the street on your left.*

⓭ Avenida da Liberdade

This tree-lined grand boulevard, running north from Rossio, connects the old town (where most of the sightseeing action is) with the newer upper town. Before the great earthquake, this was the city's royal promenade. After 1755, it was the grand boulevard of Pombal's new Lisbon—originally limited to the aristocracy. The present street, built in the 1880s and inspired by Paris' Champs-Elysées, is lined with hotels, high-fashion shopping, expensive office buildings...and eight lanes of traffic. The grand "rotunda"—as the roundabout formally known as Marquês de Pombal is called—tops off Avenida da Liberdade with a commanding **statue of Pombal**. Allegorical symbols of his impressive accomplishments decorate the statue. (An absent king and an iron-willed minister left in charge can do a lot in 27 years.) Beyond that lies the fine Edward VII Park. From the Rotunda (M: Marquês de Pombal), it's an enjoyable 20-minute downhill walk along the mile-long avenue back to the Baixa.

Whether strolling uphill or down, one of the joys of modern Lisbon is to simply walk this grand boulevard, dotted with monuments, statues, and food kiosks with inviting seating—perfect for enjoying a drink or snack.

BAIRRO ALTO AND CHIADO STROLL

The Old World-feeling Bairro Alto (High Town) and trendy Chiado perch just above the busy Baixa. This walk (rated ▲▲▲) connects dramatic viewpoints, leafy parks with inviting kiosk cafés, skinny streets lined with fado clubs, a dramatic church, an earthquake-toppled convent, Chiado's trendy dining and shopping scene, and a classic coffee house.

Getting There: Rise above the Baixa on the funicular called Elevador da Glória, located near the obelisk at Praça dos Restauradores (opposite the Hard Rock Café, €3.70 for two trips if you pay driver, €1.30 if zapping with Viva Viagem card, every 10 minutes); you can also hike up alongside the tracks.

• *Leaving the funicular on top, turn right (go 100 yards, up into a park) to enjoy the city view from the...*

❶ Miradouro de São Pedro de Alcântara (Viewpoint)

A tile map guides you through the view, which stretches from the twin towers of the cathedral (on far right, near the river), to the ramparts of the castle birthplace of Lisbon (capping the hill, on right), to another quaint, tree-topped viewpoint in Graça (directly across, end of trolley #28E), to the skyscraper towers of the new city in the distance (far left). Whenever you see a big old building in Lisbon, it's often a former convent or monastery.

With the dissolution of monastic religious orders in 1834, these buildings were nationalized and are now occupied by hospitals, museums, schools, or the military.

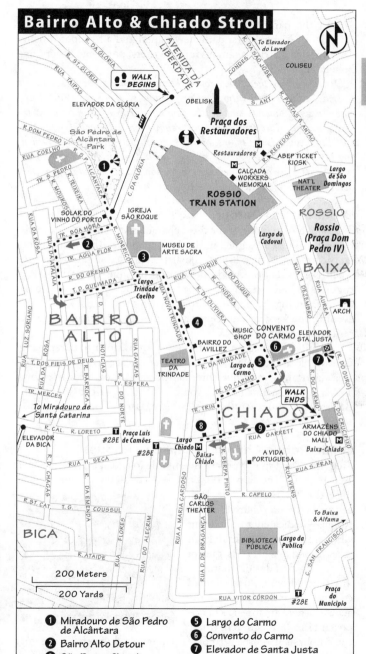

Bairro Alto & Chiado Stroll

1 Miradouro de São Pedro de Alcântara
2 Bairro Alto Detour
3 São Roque Church
4 Cervejaria da Trindade
5 Largo do Carmo
6 Convento do Carmo
7 Elevador de Santa Justa
8 Café A Brasileira
9 Rua Garrett

In the park, a bust honors a 19th-century local journalist (founder of Lisbon's first daily newspaper) and a barefooted delivery boy. This district is famous for its writers, poets, publishers, and bohemians.

• Directly across the street from where you got off the Elevador da Glória is **Solar do Vinho do Porto**, run by the Port Wine Institute—a good place to sample the famous fortified wine from northern Portugal (it's been closed for renovation but should reopen by the time you visit). If it's open, step inside—or consider returning later for a do-it-yourself tasting (for a description, see page 127).

Next, walk directly across from the top of the funicular for a short detour into the old grid-plan streets of the Bairro Alto.

❷ Bairro Alto Detour

The Bairro Alto is one of the most characteristic and appealing districts in Lisbon. Designed in the 16th century with a very modern (at the time) grid-plan layout, the district housed ship workers back when Portugal was a world power and its ships planted the Portuguese flag all around the globe. Today, the Bairro Alto is quiet in the morning, but buzzes with a thriving restaurant scene in the evening and a rowdy bar scene later—much to the chagrin of elder residents.

While it's fun to wander, follow this route for a good sampling: Go two blocks gently uphill on Travessa da Boa Hora, turn left on Rua da Atalaia, continue three blocks, and then head left down Travessa da Queimada until you cross the big street (leaving the Bairro Alto) and reach the small square, Largo Trindade Coelho.

• On Largo Trindade Coelho is the...

❸ São Roque Church (Igreja São Roque)

Step inside and sit in a pew in the middle to take it all in (free; Mon 14:00-18:00, Tue-Sun 9:00-19:00—until 18:00 in winter, Thu until 20:00). Built in the 16th century, the ▲ church of St. Roque—dedicated to the saint who protects the faithful from disease and plagues—is one of Portugal's first Jesuit churches. The painted-wood, false-domed ceiling is perfectly flat. The acoustics here are top-notch, important in a Jesuit church, where

the emphasis is on the sermon. The numbered panels on the floor were tombs, nameless because they were for lots of people. They're empty now—the practice was stopped in the 19th century when parishioners didn't want plague victims rotting under their feet.

Survey the rich side chapels. The highlight is the **Chapel of St. John the Baptist** (left side of church, gold and blue lapis lazuli columns). It looks like it came right out of the Vatican...because it did. Made in Rome from precious materials, the chapel was the site of one papal Mass before it was disassembled and shipped to Lisbon. Per square inch, it was the most-costly chapel ever constructed in Portugal. Notice the mosaic floor (with the spherical symbol of Portugal) and, on the walls, three intricate, beautiful mosaics—a Vatican specialty, designed to take the place of real paintings, which were vulnerable to damage from candle smoke and incense. Notice also the delicate "sliced marble" symmetry and imagine the labor involved in so artfully cutting that stone five centuries ago.

The chapel to the left of St. John the Baptist features a riot of babies. Individual chapels—each for a different noble family—seem to be in competition. Keep in mind that the tiles are considered as extravagant as the gold leaf and silver. To the left of the main altar, a glass case is filled with relics trying to grab your attention.

Between the Chapel of St. John the Baptist and the relics, find the **sacristy** where, along with huge chests of drawers for vestments, you can see a series of 17th-century paintings illustrating scenes from the life of St. Francis Xavier—one of the founders of the Jesuit order along with St. Ignatius of Loyola and Peter Faber (irregular hours, only open when staffed).

On your way out, you might pop a coin into a rack of fake candles and power a prayer.

The **São Roque Museum** (Museu de Arte Sacra) to the left as you leave the church, is more interesting than your typical small church museum (€2.50, same hours as the church). It's filled with perhaps the best-presented collection of 16th- and 17th-century church art in town, and it's well-described in English. The church and this art, rare survivors of the 1755 earthquake, illustrate the religious passion that accompanied Portugal's Age of Discovery, with themes including the mission of the Jesuits and their response to the Reformation; devotion to relics; and devotion to the Virgin.

• Back outside in the church square (WC underground), visit the statue of a friendly lottery-ticket salesman. Two lottery kiosks are nearby. Locals who buy into the Totoloto (which, like lotteries everywhere, is a form of taxation on gamblers that helps fund *social outreach programs) rub the statue's well-polished ticket for good luck.*

Continue (kitty-corner left across the square) downhill along Rua Nova da Trindade, following the tram tracks. At #20 (on the left), pop into...

❹ Cervejaria da Trindade

The famous "oldest beer hall in Lisbon" is worth a visit for a look at its 19th-century tiles. The beautifully tiled main room, once a dining hall for monks, still holds the pulpit from which the Bible was read as the monks ate. After monastic orders were abolished in 1834, the monastery became a brewery—you'll notice that while the oldest tiles have Christian themes, the later ones (from around 1860) are all about the beer. Among the Portuguese beers on tap are Sagres, the standard lager; Sagres Preta, a good dark beer (like a porter); and Bohemia, which is sweet, with more alcohol. At the bar in front you can get a snack and beer, while more expensive dining is in the back (see page 152).

• *Continue down the hill. You'll pass the recommended **Bairro do Avillez**—one of more than a dozen Lisbon eateries owned by celebrity chef José Avillez, who is helping to bring traditional recipes (like the ones at the cervejaria we just left) into the 21st century.*

Continue until the next intersection, where signs point left to the ruined Convento do Carmo. Follow the inside trolley tracks downhill and to the left. Just before you reach the square, notice (on the left) the well-stocked music shop—selling (among other instruments) the unique Portuguese guitars used to perform fado music.

You'll wind up in the leafy, inviting square called...

❺ Largo do Carmo

On this square decorated with an old fountain, lots of pigeons, and jacaranda trees from South America (with purple blossoms in June), police officers guard the headquarters of the National Guard. Famous among residents, this was the last refuge of the dictatorial Salazar regime. The Portuguese people won their freedom in 1974, in a peaceful uprising called the Carnation Revolution. The name came when revolutionaries  placed flowers in the guns of the soldiers, making it clear it was time for democracy here. For more history, see the sidebar.

• *On Largo do Carmo, check out the ruins of...*

The Carnation Revolution

António de Oliveira Salazar, who ruled Portugal from 1926 to 1968, was modern Europe's longest-ruling dictator (he died in 1970). Salazar's authoritarian regime, the Estado Novo, continued in power under Prime Minister Marcelo Caetano until 1974.

By the 1970s, fighting in Portugal's far-flung colonies over the previous decade had demoralized much of Salazar's military, and at home, there was a growing appetite for a modern democracy. On April 25, 1974, several prominent members of the military decided it was time to oust the government. Their withdrawal of government support spelled the end of the Salazar era. Five people died that April day, in a well-planned, relatively bloodless coup. Citizens spilled into the streets to cheer and put flowers in soldiers' rifle barrels, giving the event its name: the Carnation Revolution. Suddenly, people were free to speak aloud what they formerly could only whisper in private.

In the revolution's aftermath, the country struggled to get the hang of democratic practices. Its economy suffered as overseas colonies fell to nationalist uprisings, with some 800,000 immigrants taking advantage of democratic Portugal's attempt to make amends for colonial wars: immediate citizenship. For colonial overlords, life went from "shrimp day and night" to a sudden collapse of the empire; for their own safety, they fled back to Portugal. A good number of these "returnees" didn't fit into their newly democratic old country. Feeling like people without a homeland, many ultimately left Portugal (joining Salazar's henchmen, who took refuge in Brazil). Even those who stayed were generally pro-dictator and angry about the revolution, contributing to a polarization of modern Portuguese society that exists to this day.

In 1976, the Portuguese adopted a constitution that separated church and state. These changes helped to break down an almost medieval class system and established parliamentary law. Mario Soares, a former enemy of the Salazar regime, became the new prime minister, ruling as a stabilizing presence through much of the next two decades. Today, Portugal is enthusiastically democratic.

❻ Convento do Carmo

After the convent was destroyed by the 1755 earthquake, the Marquês de Pombal directed that the delicate Gothic arches of its church be left standing—supporting nothing but open sky—as a permanent reminder of that disastrous event. If you pay to enter, you'll see a fine memorial park in what was the nave, and (filling the former apse at the far end) a simple museum with Bronze Age and Roman artifacts, medieval royal sarcophagi, and a couple of Peruvian mummies—all explained in English (€4—cheapskates can do a deep knee-bend at the ticket desk, sneak a peek, and then crawl away; Mon-Sat 10:00-19:00, Oct-May until 18:00, closed Sun year-round).

• *Facing the convent, take the little lane that cuts around its right side. Head up the stairs next to the Bella Lisa Elevador restaurant to reach the gray, iron...*

❼ Elevador de Santa Justa

In 1902, an architect who had studied under Gustav Eiffel completed this 150-foot-tall iron elevator, connecting the lower and upper parts of town. The elevator's Neo-Gothic motifs are an attempt to match the ruined church near its top. It's free to peer through the railings from the entry-level ramp, but I'd spring for a ticket to climb the spiral stairs up to the top-floor lookout—with unobstructed views over the city (for details, see the sight listing on page 83).

Stroll around this celebration of the Industrial Age, enjoy the view, then retrace your steps to the square in front of the convent. (The nearby Leitaria Académica, a venerable little working-class eatery with tables spilling onto the delightful square, can be handy for a pricey snack or drink.)

• *Continue straight up through Largo do Carmo, walking a block slightly uphill on Travessa do Carmo. At the next square, take a left on Rua Serpa Pinto, walking downhill to Rua Garrett, where—in the little pedestrian zone 50 yards uphill on the right—you'll find a famous old café across from the Baixa-Chiado Metro stop.*

❽ Café A Brasileira

Slinky with Art Nouveau decor, this café is a 100-year-old institution for coffeehouse junkies. A Brasileira was originally a shop selling Brazilian products, a reminder that this has long been the city's shopping zone. Drop in for a *bica* (Lisbon slang for espresso) or a *pingado* (with a dollop of steamed milk; either costs €0.70 at the bar). A *pastel de nata* custard tart costs just €1.30—but the best place in downtown for one is just a short walk away (see "Exploring More of the Bairro Alto," later). WCs are down the stairs near the entrance.

The statue out front is of the poet

Fernando Pessoa, making him a perpetual regular at this café. He was the literary and creative soul of Lisbon in the 1920s and 1930s, when the country's avant-garde poets, writers, and painters would hang out here.

At the neighboring **Baixa-Chiado Metro stop,** a slick series of escalators whisks people effortlessly between Chiado Square and the Baixa. It's a free and fun way to survey a long, long line of Portuguese—but for now, we'll stay in the Chiado neighborhood. (If you'll be coming for fado in the evening—recommended places are nearby—consider getting here by zipping up the escalator.)

• *The Chiado district is popular for its shopping and theaters. Browse downhill on...*

❾ Rua Garrett

As you stroll, notice the mosaic sidewalks, ironwork balconies, and fine shops. The streetlamps you see are decorated with the symbol

of Lisbon: a ship, carrying the remains of St. Vincent, guarded by two ravens.

As you walk, peek into classy stores, such as the fabric lover's paradise **Paris em Lisboa**—imagine how this would have been the ultimate in *ooh là là* fashion in the 19th century (at #77, on the right). The next cross street, Rua Serpa Pinto, leads (in one block) to the **São Carlos Theater**—Lisbon's opera house. Celebrity chef José Avillez, whose eatery we passed earlier, and his culinary rivals have revitalized this sleepy quarter with several restaurants. (Avillez's Belcanto has often appeared high on the list of the "50 Best Restaurants in the World.") Between here and the theater is the recommended **Burel Mountain Originals,** selling traditional and modern Portuguese wool and flannel products (see "Shopping in Lisbon," later).

Continuing along Rua Garrett, at the next corner (after the church, at #73) is the venerable **Bertrand** bookstore—according to Guinness, the oldest bookstore in continuous operation (since 1732) with English books and a good guidebook selection. **A Vida Portuguesa**—my favorite shop for Portuguese gifts (quality textiles, soaps, home decor, sardines, wine, and so on) is at the end of the street behind the bookstore (Rua Anchieta 11).

Along the main drag, you'll start to see more and more international chains before Rua Garrett ends abruptly at the entrance of the big **Armazéns do Chiado mall.** This grand, six-floor shopping center connects Lisbon's lower and upper towns with a world of ways to spend money (including a handy food court on the sixth

Portugal's Greatest Poets

The Portuguese are justifiably proud of their two most famous poets, whose names, works, and memorials you may encounter in your travels.

Portugal's most important poet, **Luís de Camões** (1524-1580), was a Renaissance-age equivalent of ancient Greece's Homer. Camões' masterpiece, *The Lusiads (Os Lusíadas)*, tells the story of an explorer far from home. But instead of Odysseus, this epic poem describes the journey of Vasco da Gama, the man who found the route from Europe to India. Camões—who had sailed to Morocco to fight the Moors (where he lost an eye), to Goa (where he was imprisoned for debt), and to China (where he was shipwrecked)—was uniquely qualified to write about Portugal's pursuit of empire on the high seas. For more on Camões, see page 101.

Fernando Pessoa (1888-1935) used multiple personas in his poetry. He'd take on the voice of a simple countryman and express his love of nature in free verse. Or he'd write as an erudite scholar, sharing philosophical thoughts in a more formal style. By varying his voice, he was able to more easily explore different viewpoints and truths. While Pessoa loved the classics—reading Milton, Byron, Shelley, and Poe—he was a true 20th-century bohemian at heart.

Café A Brasileira, where he'd often meet with friends, has a statue of Pessoa outside. Today, fado musicians still remember Pessoa, paying homage to him by putting his poetry into the Portuguese version of the blues.

floor). For Italian-style gelato, locals like **Santini em Casa,** a few steps downhill to the left as you face the mall (at #9).

• *Our walk is over. Whether you leave the Bairro Alto or stay to explore, directions are below.*

Leaving the **Bairro Alto:** *To get from the mall to the Baixa—the lower town—take the elevator (press 1) down to the ground level. To get* *from the mall to the Metro, exit through the lowest floor of the mall, turn right, and walk 50 yards to the Baixa-Chiado Metro stop.*

Or, if you have time and interest, consider...

Exploring More of the Bairro Alto

A short walk from the mall gives you a more complete look at this high-altitude neighborhood and a scenic viewpoint. Backtrack (heading west) up Rua Garrett to the

square **Praça Luís de Camões,** where the great writer stands on a pillar, leaning on a sword—more warrior than poet.

Left of Camões, head uphill along Rua do Loreto. Just where the square and street meet, on the right at #2, notice the hubbub at the recommended **Manteigaria,** which serves downtown's best *pastel de nata* custard tart. Even if it's crowded, you'll typically get served quickly (cashiers come along the line to take your order). Pastry in hand, shimmy down the narrow hall inside, where you can stand at the counter and watch the pastry chefs in action—perpetually cutting cross-sections of delicate dough, pressing it into little tins, filling the pastries with gooey custard, and popping big trays into the oven (at 750 degrees Fahrenheit, to get just the right amount of caramelizing on top). Be sure to sprinkle your piping-hot pastry with powdered sugar and cinnamon.

Continue three more blocks on Rua do Loreto, passing the picturesque **Elevador da Bica funicular.** Then, one block farther,

turn left on Rua Marechal Saldanha to reach the **Miradouro de Santa Catarina,** a terrace—flanked by bars—that overlooks the city's harbor and river. This is a popular hangout for the dreadlocked granola crowd on a balmy evening. You'll see a monument to the Cape of Good Hope (a.k.a. the Cape of Torment) that personifies the cape as a monster. This mythic treatment was popularized by poet Camões' *The Lusiads,* which celebrated and nearly deified the great explorers of Portugal's Age of Discovery (such as Vasco da Gama, portrayed as Ulysses), who had to overcome such demons in their conquest of the sea.

Sights in Lisbon

CENTRAL LISBON

To get a full picture of the best of central Lisbon, take the three neighborhood walks (covering the Bairro Alto, Alfama, and Baixa; see earlier). Several central Lisbon sights are described in detail in those self-guided walks: São Jorge Castle, the Museum and School of Portuguese Decorative Arts, and the Fado Museum (in "Alfama Stroll and the Castle"), and the São Roque Church and Museum (in "Bairro Alto and Chiado Stroll").

▲Lisbon Cathedral (Sé de Lisboa)

The cathedral, just a few blocks east of Praça do Comércio, is not much on the inside, but its fortress-like exterior has been through as many refits as there are styles of architecture. The final remodel during the Salazar years turned the facade into a textbook example of the stark and powerful Romanesque "fortress of God." Twin, castle-like, crenellated towers solidly frame an impressive rose window.

Cost and Hours: Free, Tue-Sat 9:00-19:00, Sun-Mon until 17:00. You can pay extra to visit the cloister (€2.50) and treasury (€2.50), but I'd skip them unless you dig archaeology or fancy gold monstrances. It's on Largo da Sé, several blocks east of the Baixa—take Rua da Conceição east, which turns into Rua de Santo António da Sé. Trolleys #12E and #28E stop right out front, where the square is clogged with tuk-tuks offering tours around town.

Visiting the Church: Started in 1150, this was the first place of worship that Christians built after they retook Lisbon from the Moors. Located on the former site of a mosque, it made a powerful statement: The Reconquista was here to stay. The church is also the site of the 1195 baptism of St. Anthony—a favorite saint of Portugal (locals appeal to him for help in finding a parking spot, true love, and lost objects). Naturally for Portugal, tile panels around the baptismal font (in the back-left corner) portray St. Anthony preaching to the fish. Also, some of St. Vincent is buried here—legend has it that in the 12th century, his remains were brought to Lisbon on a ship guarded by two sacred black ravens, the symbol of the city. Take a stroll through the vast, dark interior—with rounded arches and a dim, windowless nave, it's quintessentially Romanesque. Near the altar, the darkness gives way to a slightly lighter Baroque zone. Here you can pay to enter the ambulatory and peaceful **cloister** (an archaeological work-in-progress—they're currently uncovering Roman ruins). The humble **treasury,** back near the entrance, is worth its fee only if you want to climb some stairs and see a silver box containing what's left of St. Vincent.

▲Aljube Museum of Resistance and Freedom (Museu do Aljube)

This museum is the best place to learn about Portugal's troubled mid-20th century. It fills a stern building called the Aljube (from a Moorish word meaning "waterless well"), immediately behind the cathedral. Once a Muslim prison, then a jail during the Inquisition (and on a site that dates back to Roman times), the Aljube later became the main political prison of Portugal's fascist regime under António Salazar. Today, it houses a modern, well-presented, three-floor exhibit detailing Salazar's rise to power, the creation of the Estado Novo, crimes against the Portuguese people, and the eventual end of the regime with the 1974 Carnation Revolution. Exhibits tell the story (in English) with photos and subtitled video clips, as well as some original documents and other artifacts. While often overshadowed by Franco in Spain and the communist regimes of eastern Europe, Salazar was hardly a Boy Scout—and this much-needed museum documents his abuses, filling a gap for those with an appetite for recent history.

Cost and Hours: €3, free Sun before 14:00, open Tue-Sun 10:00-18:00, closed Mon, Rua de Augusto Rosa 42, +351 218 172 400, www.museudoaljube.pt. The entrance is tucked under a tall staircase, on a little square with a stop for trolleys #12E and #28E, between the cathedral and the Alfama.

Elevador de Santa Justa (Santa Justa Elevator)

This 150-foot-tall iron tower, built in 1902, connects the flat Baixa district with the Bairro Alto/Chiado districts up above. One of the city's main landmarks, it offers a sweat-free connection to the upper town, as well as a fine city view up top. You can climb to the rooftop lookout alone (and skip the elevator ride) if you're already in the Bairro Alto/Chiado.

During busy times, the long line (which wraps up the stairs and around behind the elevator's base) moves slowly. If it's backed up, skip it or come back at a quieter time. Two much faster routes up to Chiado are nearby: the elevators inside Armazéns do Chiado mall, or the escalators inside the Baixa-Chiado Metro station (see the sidebar on page 47).

Cost and Hours: Elevator and rooftop view deck-€5.15 (round-trip tickets only), view deck only-€1.50; elevator covered—without the deck—by 24-hour Viva Viagem card, or €1.30 with

António Salazar

Q: What do you get when you cross a lawyer, an economist, and a dictator?

A: António Salazar, who was all three—a dictator who ruled Portugal through harsh laws and a strict budget that hurt the poor.

Shortly after a 1926 military coup "saved" Portugal's floundering democracy from itself, General Oscar Carmona appointed António de Oliveira Salazar (1889-1970) as finance minister. A former professor of economics and law at the University of Coimbra, Salazar balanced the budget and the interests of the country's often-warring factions. His skill and his reputation as a clean-living, fair-minded patriot earned him a promotion. In 1932, he became prime minister, and he set about creating his New State (Estado Novo).

For nearly four decades, Salazar ruled a stable but isolated nation by harmonizing the traditional power blocs of the ruling class—the military, big business, large landowners, and the Catholic Church. He enforced his Christian fascism with the backing of the military—and his secret police.

As a person, Salazar was respected, but not loved. The son of a farm manager, he originally studied to be a priest before going on to become a scholar and writer. He never married. Quiet, low-key, and unassuming, he attended church regularly and lived a nonmaterialistic existence. But when faced with opposition, he was ruthless, and his secret police became an object of fear and hatred.

Salazar steered Portugal through the turmoil of Spain's Civil War (1936-1939), remaining officially neutral while secretly supporting Franco's fascists. He detested Nazi Germany's "pagan" leaders, but respected Mussolini for reconciling with the pope. In World War II, Portugal was officially neutral, but was often friendly with longtime ally Britain and used as a base for espionage. After the war, Salazar's regime benefited greatly from the United States' Marshall Plan for economic recovery (which Spain missed out on during Franco's rule). The country joined NATO in 1949.

Salazar distracted his poor and isolated masses with a cynical credo: *"Fado, Fátima, and Futebol"* (the three "Fs"). Salazar was undone by two factors: the liberal 1960s and the unpopular, draining wars Portugal fought abroad to try to keep its colonial empire intact. When Salazar died in 1970, the regime that followed became increasingly less credible, leading to the liberating events of the Carnation Revolution in 1974 (see "The Carnation Revolution" sidebar, earlier).

zapping; departures every 10 minutes, daily 7:00-23:00, until 21:00 in winter.

▲Mouraria District

The Mouraria stretches steeply from Praça Martim Moniz up to the back side of São Jorge Castle. This historic tangled quarter was where Muslim Moors were banished after the Christian Reconquista of Lisbon in 1147. And 500 years later it is still the Muslim quarter—shared with other immigrant communities. Portugal's far-flung empire was given up in the last couple of generations; here in the old colonial capital you'll see people from Brazil, Goa, Mozambique, Angola, and many other former Portuguese outposts.

Visiting Mouraria: Young, edgy **Martim Moniz square** is the stage and living room of the roughly two dozen nationalities that call the Mouraria home: Many recent arrivals speak little or no Portuguese, and you'll even see stylized Arabic script in the Martim Moniz Metro station.

Two giant department stores, Centro Comercial Mouraria and Centro Comercial Martim Moniz—one Chinese owned and the other Indian owned—flank the square. Women in traditional colorful garments watch children dance while Goans play cricket. Meanwhile, in the "fusion market" on and around the square, entrepreneurs run small stalls with spicy and multiethnic foods. A long line of tourists wait to catch the #28E trolley, while unemployed people just hang out.

Near the trolley stop, an escalator carries people high into Mouraria. Beyond the escalator is the small **Chapel of Nossa Senhora da Saúde,** dedicated to Our Lady of Good Health, recalling an era when the Black Death killed millions; it's worth popping in to see its *azulejos* tiles (Rua da Mouraria 1). Look down at the unique *calçada* out front to find a full-scale outline of the chapel's facade by op art guru Eduardo Nery. This marks the start of the main street of the community: Rua da Mouraria.

At #90 on Rua da Mouraria, **Rua do Capelão** leads uphill into the back lanes of this world. Considered unsafe just a few years ago, it's now Lisbon's new happening spot.

The guitar monument at the intersection is a reminder that this is considered the birthplace of fado. Today, the lanes are decorated with black-and-white photos on walls (with English descriptions) marking homes of famous local fado musicians, noisy street art, and playgrounds just being fun.

There are plenty of inviting little eateries. For lunch, consider Zé da Mouraria (lunch only, Rua João Outeiro 24). It's an amazing scene. For a moveable feast, consider taking one of the popular Mouraria food tours (see "Tours in Lisbon," earlier).

The highest street, Rua das Farinhas, leads right to **Largo São**

Cristóvão. You could continue around toward the castle, past a former five-floor market, **Chão do Loureiro,** where each floor is a "gallery" filled with works by one of the country's top street artists (Calçada Marquês de Tancos 1). The top floor hides a café with a nice viewpoint. Or, from there, steps lead down past great street art to the edge of the Baixa (Rua da Madalena) and into the regular world once again.

NORTH LISBON

The main sight here is the Gulbenkian Museum, two miles north of the city center and just a few minutes' ride on the Metro blue line. A visit here can be combined with sightseeing in Belém, a quick taxi ride away.

▲▲Gulbenkian Museum (Museu Calouste Gulbenkian)

This is the best of Lisbon's 40 museums, and it's worth the trip for art lovers. This wide-ranging collection, with nothing Portuguese, spans 5,000 years of European, Egyptian, Islamic, and Asian art. It offers the most purely enjoyable museum-going experience in Iberia—it's both educational and just plain beautiful. The museum is cool, uncrowded, gorgeously lit, and easy to grasp, displaying only a few select and exquisite works from each epoch. Art Nouveau fans love the museum's stunning Lalique jewelry collection. Walk through five millennia of human history, appreciating our ancestors by seeing objects they treasured.

The museum is actually two museums—the main collection and the Gulbenkian Garden and Modern Collection (Coleção Moderna), a five-minute walk away through a delightful 18-acre lushly landscaped park. If walking from the main museum back to the Metro, the garden and Modern Collection are on the way (the museum's info desk has a handy map of the entire site).

Cost and Hours: €10, includes main branch and Modern Collection (located across park), free on Sun after 14:00; open Wed-Mon 10:00-18:00, closed Tue; Berna 45, +351 217 823 000, www.gulbenkian.pt.

Getting There: From downtown, hop a cab or take the Metro to the São Sebastião stop; leave the platform by following *Avenida de Aguiar (norte)* signs. Then, to leave the station, follow signs to *Avenida de Aguiar (nascente).* Once at street level, it's about a five-minute walk: Go a long block downhill on Avenida de Aguiar with the massive El Corte Inglés department store behind you. Just be-

LISBON

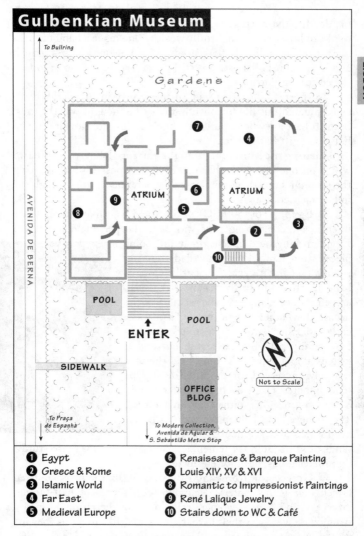

Gulbenkian Museum

To Bullring

Gardens

ATRIUM

ATRIUM

AVENIDA DE BERNA

POOL

ENTER

POOL

SIDEWALK

OFFICE BLDG.

Not to Scale

To Praça de Espanha

To Modern Collection, Avenida de Aguiar & S. Sebastião Metro Stop

1 Egypt
2 Greece & Rome
3 Islamic World
4 Far East
5 Medieval Europe

6 Renaissance & Baroque Painting
7 Louis XIV, XV & XVI
8 Romantic to Impressionist Paintings
9 René Lalique Jewelry
10 Stairs down to WC & Café

fore the roundabout, you'll see a small sign pointing right to the *fundação*—the museum entrance is up the stairs and straight ahead through this park, past a long concrete office building, about 100 yards away.

Cuisine Art: Cafeterias are in both museum buildings, though I like the one in the Modern Collection building much better.

Background: Calouste Gulbenkian (1869-1955), an Armenian oil tycoon, gave Portugal his art collection (or "harem," as he called it) in gratitude for the hospitable asylum granted him in Lisbon during World War II (where he lived from 1942 until his death). The Portuguese consider Gulbenkian an inspirational model of how to be thoughtfully wealthy: He made a habit of "tithing for art," spending 10 percent of his income on things of beauty, and his billion-dollar estate is still a vital arts foundation promoting culture in Portugal.

In short, Gulbenkian had all the money in the world, dedicated much of his life to collecting what he thought was the most beautiful art anywhere, built this fine building to show it off, and left it as a gift to posterity.

Visiting the Museum: From the entrance lobby, there are two wings on one floor: roughly pre-1500 and post-1500. Following the museum's mostly chronological layout, you'll pass through the following sections:

❶ **Egypt** (2500-500 BC): If this room feels like a tomb, that's intentional. Everything here was once the personal property of

Egyptian kings and queens, including some pieces from King Tut—who died thinking you *can* take it with you. Ancient Egyptians, believing that life really began after death, carved statues to preserve the memory of the deceased, whether it be the head of a pharaoh carved out of "harder-than-stone" obsidian or a family pet. The cat statue nurses her kittens atop a coffin that once held the cat's mummy, preserved for the afterlife. Egyptians honored cats—even giving them gold earrings (notice this statue's ears are pierced). They believed cats helped the goddess Bastet keep watch over the household. Now, thousands of years later, we remember the Egyptians for these sturdy, dignified statues, built for eternity.

❷ **Greece and Rome** (500 BC-AD 500): The black-and-red Greek vase (calyx-crater), decorated with scenes of half-human satyrs chasing human women, reminds us of the rational Greeks' struggle to overcome their barbarian, animal-like urges as they invented Western civilization. Alexander the Great (r. 336-323 BC, seen on a series of gold medallions filling a glass case) used war to spread Greek culture throughout the Mediterranean, creating a cultural empire that would soon be taken over by Roman emperors. Gulbenkian loved collecting coins: The first treasure he acquired was a coin, purchased at age 11.

A carved stone on the wall near the exit brings you even further back in time to Mesopotamia (modern Iraq) and the very roots of civilization. The Assyrian relief of Ashurnasirpal II (884-859 BC) evokes this distant culture, which invented writing. Note the inscription chiseled over the portrait.

❸ **Islamic World** (700-1500): The Muslims who lived in Portugal—as far west of Mecca as you could get back then—might have decorated their homes with furnishings from all over the Islamic world. Imagine a Moorish sultan, dressed in a shirt from Syria, sitting on a carpet from Persia in a courtyard with Moroccan tiles. By a bubbling fountain, he puffs on a hookah.

Glazed and painted ceramics are from 13th-century Syria—specifically from the region in and around Raqqa (in the news recently as the capital of ISIS).

The intricate patterns on the Eygptian gilded and enameled glass lamps from a 14th-century mosque (behind the partition on the left) are not only beautiful...they're actually Arabic quotes from the Quran, such as "Allah is the light of the world, shining like a flame in a glass lamp, as bright as a star." Explore this large and rich collection, and then head a few thousand miles east.

The carpets you'll see were a passion for Gulbenkian (his family was long in the carpet trading business). He considered a carpet a garden you can bring inside your home.

❹ **Far East** (1368-1644): For almost 300 years, the Ming dynasty ruled China, having reclaimed the country from Genghis Khan and his sons. When Portuguese traders reached the Orient, they brought back blue-and-white ceramics such as these. They became all the rage, inspiring the creation of both Portuguese tiles and Dutch Delftware. Writing utensils fill elaborately decorated boxes from Japan. Another type of box—a Japanese *bento*—was the ultimate picnic basket, perfect for an excursion to the Japanese countryside.

Crossing into the next wing, you enter the section on European art.

❺ **Medieval Europe** (500-1500): While China was thriving and inventing, Europe was stuck in a thousand-year medieval funk (with the exception of Muslim Arab-ruled Iberia). Most Europeans from the "Age of Faith" channeled their spirituality into objects of Christian devotion. A priest on a business trip could pack a portable, collapsible altarpiece in his backpack, travel to a remote village that had no church, and deliver a sermon illustrated by scenes carved in ivory. In monasteries, the monks with the best penmanship laboriously copied books (illuminated manuscripts) and decorated them with scenes from the text—and left wacky doodles in the margins. These books are virtual time capsules, preserving the knowledge of Greece and Rome until it could emerge again, a thousand years later, in the Renaissance.

❻ **Renaissance and Baroque Painting** (1500-1700): Around 1500, a cultural revolution was taking place—the birth of humanism. Painters saw God in the faces of ordinary people, whether in Domenico Ghirlandaio's fresh-faced maiden, Frans Hals' wrinkled old woman, or Rembrandt's portrait of an old man, whose crease-lined hands tell the story of his life. Also in this section are exquisite works by Van der Weyden, Van Dyck, and Rubens.

Propelled by the Italian-born Renaissance, Europe's focus shifted northward to the luxurious court of France, where a new secular culture was blossoming—as illustrated in sumptuous tapestries. The three-part series *Playing Children* (c. 1540) features Fishing, the Dance, and the Ball Game.

❼ Louis XIV, XV, XVI (1700-1800): This furniture, once owned by French kings (and Marie-Antoinette and Madame de Pompadour), is a royal home show. Anything heavy, ornate, and gilded (or that includes curved legs and animal-clawed feet) is from the time of Louis XIV. The Louis XV style is lighter and daintier, with Asian motifs, while furniture from the Louis XVI era is stripped-down, straight-legged, tapered, and more modern.

❽ Romantic to Impressionist Paintings (1700-2000): Europe ruled the world, and art became increasingly refined. Young British aristocrats (Thomas Gainsborough portrait) traveled Europe on the Grand Tour to see great sights like Venice. They would take home small, photo-realistic Venicescapes—such as an entire room of Guardi landscapes (c. 1780)—as souvenirs.

Follow the progression in styles from stormy Romanticism (J. M. W. Turner's tumultuous shipwreck) to Realism's breath-of-fresh-air simplicity (Manet's bubble-blower, Degas' portraits) to the glinting, shimmering Impressionism of Monet and Renoir. Statues by Rodin are Impressionism in stone.

❾ René Lalique Jewelry: Finish your visit with the stunning, sumptuous Art Nouveau glasswork and jewelry of French designer René Lalique (1860-1945). Fragile beauty like this, from the elegant turn-of-the-century belle époque, was about to be shattered by the turbulent 20th century. Art Nouveau borrowed forms from nature and valued the organic and artisanal over the mass-produced. Ordinary dragonflies, orchids, and

beetles become breathtaking when transformed into jewelry. Sarah Bernhardt wore Lalique—art you hang not on a wall, but on your body. The work of Lalique—just another of Gulbenkian's circle of friends—is a fitting finale to this museum of history and beauty.

Modern Collection and Garden: Stimulating if you like contemporary and abstract art, the Modern Collection's temporary exhibits offer a fun bit of whimsy if you have the energy and inclination. The classy modern building is set in a delightful garden—a favorite for locals enjoying a quiet or romantic moment—and often hosts classical music concerts in its auditoriums.

WEST LISBON

The Museum of Ancient Art, west of downtown, is halfway to Belém and can be combined with an excursion there.

▲▲Museum of Ancient Art (Museu Nacional de Arte Antiga)

Not "ancient" as in Roman and Greek—but "antique" as in Age of Discovery—this is Portugal's finest museum for artwork from the time when the Portuguese ruled the seas: the 15th and 16th centuries. (Most of these works were gathered from Lisbon's abbeys and convents after their dissolution in 1834.) You'll also find a rich collection of furniture, as well as paintings by renowned European masters such as Hieronymus Bosch, Jan van Eyck, and Raphael—all in a grand palace that's sleekly renovated and well-presented.

Cost and Hours: €6, Tue-Sun 10:00-18:00, closed Mon; good cafeteria with shaded garden seating overlooking the river, Rua das Janeles Verdes 9, +351 213 912 800, www.museudearteantiga.pt.

Getting There: It's about a mile west of downtown Lisbon. From Praça da Figueira, take trolley #15E to Cais Rocha, cross the street, and walk up a lot of steps. To stop right in front, take bus #714 from either Praça da Figueira or Praça do Comércio. Note that trolley #15E and bus #714 both continue to the sights in Belém; consider stopping here at the end of your Belém day.

Visiting the Museum: Here are some of the museum's highlights, starting on the top floor. From the ticket desk, turn right to find the elevator and press button 3.

Top Floor, Portuguese Painting and Sculpture: From the elevator, veer right through the atrium and find the big, red room at the far end. *The Panels of St. Vincent* are a multi-part altarpiece by the late-15th-century master Nuno Gonçalves. A gang of 60 real people—everyone from royalty to sailors and beggars—surrounds Lisbon's patron saint. Of

note is the only recognized portrait of Prince Henry the Navigator, responsible for setting Portugal on the path to exploration. Find him on the third panel—an elder gentleman dressed in black with a wide-brimmed hat, hands together almost in prayer. Other masterworks by Gonçalves, painted just before the Age of Discovery, hang behind the panels. Also of note is a small but lifelike portrait of King João I, with hands clasped in prayer, by an unknown artist. This is the very first painting ever of a Portuguese monarch, winner of the Batalha battle and founder of a new dynasty.

Explore the rest of the floor clockwise from the panels: Opposite the panels, find an exceptional portrait of the baby-faced King Sebastian—who died young when he led an incursion into Africa. The armor is typical of Iberia for the era, as is the royal jaw and pursed lips caused by inbreeding with many generations of Habsburgs from Spain. If you've visited the sights in Belém, you'll recognize the Monastery of Jerónimos before it was fully decorated (1657 painting by Felipe Lobo).

Before you head down the stairs (in the middle of the atrium) to the next floor, notice the statue of a pregnant Mary *(The Virgin of Expectation,* c. 1340-1350). This unusual theme was common in rural parts of Portugal (such as the Alentejo, the close-to-the-ground region in the southeast), where the Virgin's fertility was her most persuasive quality in recruiting local followers.

Middle Floor, Art from the Portuguese Discoveries: This floor collects items that Portuguese explorers brought home from their far-flung travels. Coming down the stairs, bear left, then right, to find the room with four large, enchanting Namban screen paintings *(Namban,* meaning "southern barbarians," the catch-all term the Japanese applied to all foreigners). These show the Portuguese from a 16th-century Japanese perspective—with long noses, dark complexions, and great skill at climbing rigging, like acrobats. The Portuguese, the first Europeans to make contact with Japan, gave the Japanese guns, Catholicism (Nagasaki was founded by Portuguese Jesuits), and a new deep-frying technique we now know as tempura.

Now exit right and do a counterclockwise circle around this floor, stocked with furniture, large vases, ivory carvings, fine china, and ceramics. Imagine how astonishing these treasures must have seemed when the early explorers returned with them. Facing the atrium are some beautiful tiles from Damascus—a gift from Calouste Gulbenkian (founder of the Gulbenkian Museum). After a lot of ceramics, eventually you reach a treasury of gold and silver items. Look for the freestanding glass case with a gorgeous golden monstrance, with its carrying case displayed just behind it—the bejeweled Rococo Communion-host holder was made for Lisbon's Bemposta Palace. Farther along is the smaller yet even more exquisite Monstrance of Belém, commissioned by Manuel I and made from East African tribute gold brought back by Vasco da Gama. Squint at the fine enamel creatures filling a tide pool on the base, the 12 apostles gathered around the glass case for the Communion wafer (the fancy top pops off), and the white dove hanging like a mobile under the all-powerful God bidding us peace on earth.

Heading back to the atrium, don't miss the small, dimly lit room (on the left) displaying an impressive jewelry collection, including pieces decorated with the red cross of the affluent Order of Christ, whose members helped plan and fund Portuguese explorations.

Back in the atrium, before continuing downstairs, stop to admire a 17th-century painting of Lisbon before the 1755 earthquake. Notice the royal palace on Praça do Comércio, the shipyards next to the royal palace (now a public park), and the ship-clogged Rio Tejo.

Ground Floor, European Paintings: Pass through the gift shop, veer left, and follow the one-way route through paintings from all over Europe. A few rooms in, note the larger-than-life paintings of the 12 apostles by the Spanish master Zurburán. Continue to the end of the hall, then loop back around to find the room with Bosch's *Temptations of St. Anthony* (a three-paneled altarpiece fantasy, c. 1500) and Albrecht Dürer's *St. Jerome*. St. Jerome—you'll see other portraits of him in this collection, always with a skull—is all-important to Lisbon as the primary figure behind the Monastery of Jerónimos in Belém. Finally, wander through the few remnants of the palace. Note the Pombal coat-of-arms that decorates the elaborate, Baroque doorway at the top of the staircase (find the star); the palace was originally purchased by the brother of the powerful Marquês de Pombal. Take a well-earned break at the museum cafeteria. Sit outside in the gardens, with wonderful river views, and watch all the boats go by.

BELÉM DISTRICT

About five miles west of downtown Lisbon, the Belém district is a stately pincushion of important sights from Portugal's Golden Age, when Vasco da Gama and company turned the country into Europe's wealthiest power. Belém was the sending-off point for voyages in the Age of Discovery. Before embarking, sailors would stay and pray at the Monastery of Jerónimos, and when they returned, the Belém Tower welcomed them home. The grand buildings of

LISBON

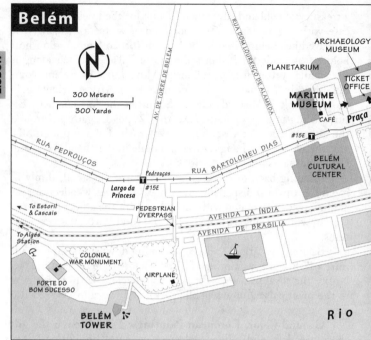

Belém survived the great 1755 earthquake, so this is the best place to experience the Manueline architectural style (for more on this style, see the sidebar on page 104). After the earthquake, safety-conscious (and rattled) royalty chose to live uphill from here—in tents rather than stone buildings. The modern-day president of Portugal calls Belém home.

To celebrate a double anniversary (800 years since the founding of Portugal and 300 years of independence from Spain), a grand exhibition was held here in 1940, resulting in fine parks, fountains, and monuments.

Getting to Belém: You have multiple options. By **taxi** or **Uber,** figure no more than about 20 minutes and €10 from downtown. **Buses** #714 and #728 serve Belém, and the coastal train line running from Lisbon's **Cais do Sodré station** gets you there in about 10 minutes.

When I have the time, I prefer riding the slower **trolley** #15E (30 minutes, catch at Praça da Figueira or Praça do Comércio). In Belém, the first trolley stop is at the National Coach Museum (stop is called simply "Belém"—you'll see the brown sign for *Museu dos Coches* just before the stop); the second stop (Belém-Jerónimos) is at the Monastery of Jerónimos (it's huge—you can't miss it); and another (Pedrouços) is two stops farther, at a little square two blocks inland from the Belém Tower.

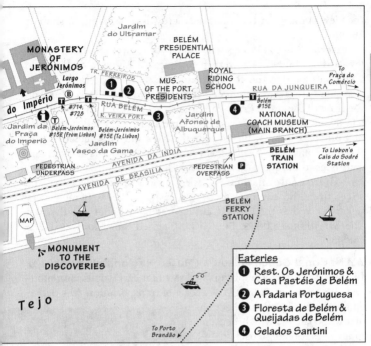

Eateries

❶ Rest. Os Jerónimos & Casa Pastéis de Belém

❷ A Padaria Portuguesa

❸ Floresta de Belém & Queijadas de Belém

❹ Gelados Santini

Planning Your Time: Nearly all of Belém's museums are closed on Monday (though the Monument to the Discoveries is open Mon May-Sept). Consider doing Belém's sights from east to west, in the order you'll reach them from the tram or train: the National Coach Museum, pastry and coffee break, Monastery of Jerónimos, Maritime Museum and/or lunch at its cafeteria (public access, museum entry not required), Monument to the Discoveries, and Belém Tower. If arriving by taxi, you could start at Belém Tower—the farthest point—and do the recommended lineup in reverse, ending at the National Coach Museum (which has easier public transit connections than the tower). Belém also has a cultural center, a children's museum, and a planetarium—not priorities for a quick visit. While walking between sights, be aware that train tracks to Cascais cut off access to the riverside from inland museums. Three pedestrian passes (an overpass at the Coach Museum, an underpass at the Monument to the Discoveries, and another overpass near Belém Tower) are the only ways to cross over. For recommended eateries in this area, see the sidebar in this section.

Crowd-Beating Tips: Belém's sights are often crowded in the morning. In peak season, there can be long lines at the Belém Tower and at the monastery. If there is a line at the tower, I simply wouldn't go in. There's almost nothing inside to see (though the view is nice). At the monastery, crowds usually diminish after 16:00.

Returning to Downtown: When you're through, hop on trolley #15E or bus #714 to return to Praça da Figueira or Praça do Comércio, or ride the coastal train back to Cais do Sodré. Note that there are two different end stops for the #15E listed clearly on the front of the tram: Praça da Figueira or Cais do Sodré; both take you to the city center. If you have time and energy left, you could hop off the trolley or bus to tour the Museum of Ancient Art on the way home. Bus #728 takes you to Santa Apolónia station, and continues to Parque das Nações and Oriente station.

Tourist Information: A little TI kiosk is directly across the street from the entrance to the monastery. They sell monastery tickets as well as the LisboaCard (sporadic hours but usually open Tue-Sat 10:00-13:00 & 14:00-18:00, closed Sun-Mon, +351 213 658 437).

▲▲National Coach Museum (Museu Nacional dos Coches)

In 1905, the last queen of Portugal saw that cars would soon obliterate horse-drawn carriages as a form of transportation. She decided to preserve her fine collection of royal coaches, which became today's National Coach Museum. The impressive collection is split between two buildings, each with its own ticket. The main branch—in a huge, blocky, concrete building closer to the river—has the bulk of the collection, with 70 dazzling coaches, all described in English.  The Royal Riding School, closer to the trolley tracks, is a historical space with a gorgeous interior but only about 10 coaches on display. If you want to really appreciate the coaches themselves, focus on the main branch. But to see regal spaces (which are rare in Lisbon), add on the Royal Riding School.

Cost and Hours: Main branch-€8, Royal Riding School-€4, €10 combo-ticket covers both, open Tue-Sun 10:00-17:00, closed Mon, +351 213 610 850, www.museudoscoches.pt.

Visiting the Main Branch: The museum is right across the street from the Belém tram stop (on one side) and the Belém train station (on the other). Find the ticket office under the building (opposite the museum entrance), then ride an elevator or take steps up to the collection, where you'll loop through two long rooms.

The first coach dates from around 1600. This crude and simple vehicle was once used by Philip II, king of Spain and Portugal, to shuttle between Madrid and Lisbon. Notice that the coach has no driver's seat—its drivers would actually ride the horses. You'll have to trust me on this, but if you lift up the cushion from the passengers' seat, you'll find a potty hole—also handy for road sickness. Imagine how slow and rough the ride would be with bad roads and a crude leather-strap suspension.

From here, walk through the historical collection, displayed chronologically. Study the evolution of suspension technology, made in the 15th century in the Hungarian town of Kocs (pronounced "coach"—hence the name). By the 17th century—when this collection begins—coaches had caught on in a big way in Portugal, which was an early adopter. Trace the improvements made through the next century, noticing that as the decoration increases, so does the comfort. A Portuguese coat of arms indicates that a carriage was part of the royal fleet. Ornamentation often includes a folk festival of exotic faces from Portugal's distant colonies.

In the middle of the hall shines the lumbering Oceans Coach, as ornate as it is long. At the stern, gold figures symbolize the Atlantic and Indian Oceans holding hands, a reminder of Portugal's mastery of the sea. The Oceans Coach is flanked by two equally stunning coaches with similar symbols of ocean exploration. These were part of a thematic convoy sent by King João V to Pope Clement XI in 1716.

Next you'll see a pair of carriages from the royal couple ruling Portugal when the 1755 earthquake struck. King José I rode in a sumptuously carved Baroque masterpiece while Queen Mariana Victoria opted for a more subdued ride. At the far end of the hall, peek inside the Table coach, which must have been a cozy place to hang out and wait for the exchange.

In the next room, you'll mainly see "Berlins"—a new coach type (pioneered in that city, in the late 17th century) that suspended the main compartment on thick leather straps to improve the ride. You'll see ecclesiastical coaches (suggesting the high status of clergy); single-horse chaise and cabriolet coaches (including some sleek, black leather, 19th-century, Sherlock Holmes-style ones); hunting vehicles; sedan chairs; scaled-down play carriages for kids who had everything; and mail coaches. You may see the "Landau of the Regicide"—the coach in which King Carlos I and his heir were shot and killed on February 1, 1908. You can still see the bullet holes. (This carriage is often out on loan.)

Royal Riding School: You'll find this regal building along the trolley tracks through Belém, kitty-corner from the main museum. The elegant old riding room with its dramatically painted ceiling is as remarkable as the carriages. Under that ceiling, you'll see a handful of fine specimens (but if you've already been to the main branch, this is a rerun). Firefighters will appreciate the second

Eating in Belém

You'll find snack bars at Belém Tower, a cafeteria at the Maritime Museum, and fun little restaurants along Rua de Belém, between the National Coach Museum and the monastery. Here are a few other eateries worth checking out:

$$ Restaurante Os Jerónimos: Popular for fresh fish, this is where hardworking Carlos treats his customers well and serves fine, affordable meals and a fish-of-the-day special (Sun-Fri 12:00-21:30, closed Sat, Rua de Belém 74, +351 213 638 423, next to renowned Casa Pastéis de Belém pastry café).

$ A Padaria Portuguesa: This respected chain bakery has fine fresh-baked bread, hearty sandwiches, and salads (daily 7:30-20:00, Rua de Belém 46).

$$ Restaurant Row Options: Many more fine places with outdoor seating are in the restaurant row beyond the McDonald's facing the park, including **Floresta de Belém,** the local favorite for their home-style Portuguese cooking, such as tasty grilled sardines and *feijoada* bean stew. They have minimal seating inside, but two cozy terraces outside (closed Sun dinner, all day Mon, and Sept; Praça Afonso de Albuquerque 1A, +351 213 636 307). Next door, **Queijadas de Belém** is a good bet for its salads, sardines, and outside seating (daily, Rua de Belém 1, +351 213 630 034).

Dessert: In addition to the original *pastel de Belém* place (**Casa Pastéis de Belém,** described below), **Gelados Santini**—a local favorite for gelato—is near the entrance to the National Coach Museum.

room, displaying a history of horse-drawn vehicles used to put out Lisbon blazes.

Nearby: Just past the Royal Riding School, on the landscaped hill behind the wall, is the stately, pink **Belém Palace**—the residence of Portugal's president. The palace interior is tourable only on Saturdays (€5, most tours in Portuguese), but if you're fascinated by Portuguese history, you can drop in anytime at the modern little **Museum of the Portuguese Presidents** (Museu da Presidència da Repùblica). It offers a little lesson on each of Portugal's democracy-era presidents (since 1910) and lots of state gifts (€2.50, Tue-Sun 10:00-18:00, closed Mon, look for entrance just west of Royal Riding School and palace gate).

▲Casa Pastéis de Belém

This café is the birthplace of the wonderful custard tart that's called *pastel de nata* throughout Portugal, but here it's dubbed *pastel de Belém*. You can explore this sprawling temple to Portugal's beloved custard tart like a museum, with a peek at the bakery in the rear.

Since 1837, residents have been coming to this café to get their tarts fresh. Its popularity stems mainly from the fact that their recipe is a closely guarded secret—supposedly only three people know the exact proportions of the ingredients. While the recipe is fine, my hunch is that their undeniable goodness is simply because the café cranks out 20,000 or so a day—you get them fresh and crunchy, literally hot out of the oven. (Take one back to your hotel and eat it tonight and it'll taste just like any other in town.) Sit down and enjoy one with a *café com leite*. Sprinkle on as much cinnamon and powdered sugar as you like.

Tarts are €1.10 whether you eat in or carry out. There are two separate lines for take-away; both move quickly (pay, then bring receipt to counter to claim your tart). If the lines are extremely long, table service inside the café may be faster (daily 8:00-23:00, Rua de Belém 84, +351 213 637 423).

▲▲▲Monastery of Jerónimos (Mosteiro dos Jerónimos)

This giant, white limestone church and monastery stretches for 300 impressive yards along the Belém waterfront. It was built over a hundred years and is basically a Gothic structure with Manueline ornamentation. King Manuel (who ruled from 1495) erected it as a "thank you" for the discoveries made by early Portuguese explorers (Vasco da Gama's tomb is inside). This is a "Pepper

Monument," financed in part with "pepper money," a 5 percent tax on spices brought back from India. Manuel built the church near the site of a humble chapel where sailors spent their last night ashore in prayer before embarking on frightening voyages.

Cost and Hours: Church-free, cloister-€10, €12 combo-ticket with Archaeology Museum; monastery open Tue-Sun 10:00-18:30, Oct-April until 17:30, closed Mon year-round; www.mosteirojeronimos.pt.

Getting In: Buy your monastery ticket at the Archaeology Museum (to the left of the monastery) or at the TI kiosk in the park across the street. Note that LisboaCard holders must get a voucher (from either the Archaeology Museum ticket office or the TI kiosk) before heading to the monastery. At the monastery, you'll see two lines. The fast-moving right queue is for the church (free to enter); the line on the left is for the cloister.

Background: As you circle around the complex, ponder the great history of this serene place. Monks often accompanied the

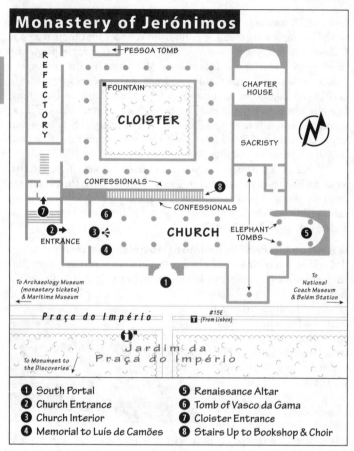

Monastery of Jerónimos

← PESSOA TOMB

REFECTORY

FOUNTAIN

CLOISTER

CHAPTER HOUSE

SACRISTY

CONFESSIONALS →

❽

❼

CONFESSIONALS

❻

❷ → ENTRANCE

❸ ◄

CHURCH

ELEPHANT TOMBS

❺

❹

To Archaeology Museum (monastery tickets) & Maritime Museum

❶

To National Coach Museum & Belém Station

Praça do Império

#15E
🚊 (From Lisbon)

Jardim da
Praça do Império

To Monument to
the Discoveries ↓

❶ South Portal
❷ Church Entrance
❸ Church Interior
❹ Memorial to Luís de Camões

❺ Renaissance Altar
❻ Tomb of Vasco da Gama
❼ Cloister Entrance
❽ Stairs Up to Bookshop & Choir

sailor-pirates on their trading/pillaging trips, hoping to convert the heathens to Christianity. Many expeditions were financed by the Order of Christ, a brotherhood of soldier-monks. The monks who inhabited this cloister were Hieronymites—followers of St. Jerome, hence the monastery name of Jerónimos. (You'll see several paintings of St. Jerome, living in a Holy Land desert in the fourth century, doing what he was best known for: translating the Bible into the Church's official Latin version.)

King Manuel, who did so much to promote exploration, was also the man who forcibly expelled all Jews from the country. (In 1497, the Spanish *Reyes Católicos*—Ferdinand and Isabel—allowed him to marry one of their daughters on the condition that he deport the Jews.) It was a time of extreme Christian faith. The sheer size of this religious complex is a testament to the religious motivation that—along with money—propelled the Age of Discovery.

LISBON

❯ Self-Guided Tour: Start outside the monastery:

❶ South Portal: The fancy portal, facing the street, is textbook Manueline. Henry the Navigator stands between the doors with the king's patron saint, St. Jerome (above on the left, with the lion). Henry (Manuel's uncle) built the original sailors' chapel on this site. This door is only used when Mass lets out or for Saturday weddings. (The electronic snapping sound you hear is designed to keep the pigeons away.)

• *To the left of the portal is the...*

❷ Church Entrance: As you approach the main entrance, the church is on your right and the cloister is straight ahead. Flanking the church door are kneeling statues of King Manuel I, the Fortunate (left of door, with St. Jerome), and his second Spanish wife, María (right, with John the Baptist).

❸ Church Interior: The Manueline style is on the cusp of the Renaissance. The space is more open than earlier medieval

churches. Slender, palm-tree-like columns don't break the interior space (as Gothic columns would), and the ceiling is all one height. Motifs from the sea hide in the decor. The sea brought Portugal 16th-century wealth and power, making this art possible. You'll see rope-like arches, ships, and monsters that evoke

the mystery of undiscovered lands. Artichokes, eaten for their vitamin C to fend off scurvy, recall the hardships sailors faced at sea. Thankfully, except for the stained glass (which is 20th century), the church survived the 1755 quake.

• *On your right as you face the altar is the...*

❹ Memorial to Luís de Camões: Camões (kah-MOISH, 1524-1580) is Portugal's Shakespeare and Casanova rolled into one, an adventurer and writer whose heroic poems, glorifying the nation's sailing exploits, capture the spirit of the Portuguese people. It was Camões who described Portugal as the place "where land ends and the sea begins."

After college at Coimbra, Camões was banished from the court (1546) for flirting with the noble lady Dona Caterina. He lost an eye soldiering in Morocco (he's always portrayed squinting), served jail time for brawling with a bureaucrat, and then caught a ship to India and China, surviving a shipwreck on the way. While serving as a colonial administrator in India, he plugged away at the epic poem that would become his masterpiece. Returning to Portugal, he published *The Lusiads* (*Os Lusíadas*, 1572), winning minor recognition and a small pension.

The long poem describes Vasco da Gama's first voyage to India in heroic terms, on the scale of Homer's *Odyssey*. *The Lusiads* begins:

> *Arms and the heroes, from Lisbon's shore,*
> *sailed through seas never dared before,*
> *with awesome courage, forging their way*
> *to the glorious kingdoms of the rising day.*

The poem goes on to recite many events in Portuguese history, from the time of the Lusiads (the original pre-Roman natives) onward. Even today, Camões' words are quoted by modern Portuguese politicians in search of a heroic sound bite. And Portugal's national holiday, June 10, is known as Camões Day, remembering the day in 1580 when the great poet died. The stone monument here—with literary rather than maritime motifs—is an empty tomb (his actual burial spot is unknown).

• *Now head up to the front of the church, and the...*

❺ **Renaissance Altar:** This is a rare, pre-1755 interior in Lisbon (except for the stained glass, which is from 1940). Here, under the 90-foot wide towering main vault, are buried the royals of 16th-century Portugal. In the niches surrounding the main altar, elephants—a Far Eastern symbol of power, more powerful and kingly than the lion—support two kings and two queens (King Manuel I is front-left). Like many Portuguese churches (such as the cathedrals in downtown Lisbon and Évora), this was renovated in Renaissance and Baroque times, resulting in an odd mix of dark, older naves and pretty pastel altars.

Skip the **sacristy** (entrance in the corner), a single-columned room wrapped in paintings on wood featuring scenes from the life of St. Jerome (not worth the admission fee). Instead, do an about-face and head up the aisle on the right, back toward the entrance (noticing more elephants in the transept). You'll pass **seven wooden confessional doors** (on your right). Notice the ornamental carving around the second one: a festival of faces from newly encountered corners of the world. Head back toward the entry.

• *Under a ceiling that's a veritable Boy Scout's Handbook of rope and knots is the...*

❻ **Tomb of Vasco da Gama:** On the night of July 7, 1497, in the small chapel that once stood here, da Gama (1460-1524) prayed for a safe voyage. The next day, he set sail from Belém with four ships (see the caravel carved in the middle of the tomb's side) and 150 men. He was armed with state-of-the-art maps and sailing technology, such as the carved armillary sphere (to the right of the caravel)— a globe surrounded by movable rings designed to determine the positions of the sun or other stars to help sailors track their location on earth. (Some say its diagonal slash is sym-

bolic of the unwritten pact and ambition of Spain and Portugal to split the world evenly, but it actually represents the zodiac—the path of the planets as they move across the heavens.)

Da Gama's mission? To confirm what earlier navigators had hypothesized—that the ocean recently discovered when Bartolomeu Dias rounded Africa's Cape of Good Hope was the same one seen by overland travelers to India. Hopefully, da Gama would find a direct sea route to the vast, untapped wealth of Asia. The symbols on the tomb show the icons of the period—the cross (symbolizing the religious military order of the soldier-monks who funded these voyages), the caravel (representing the method of travel), and Portugal's trading power around the globe (the result).

By Christmas, da Gama rounded the Cape of Good Hope. After battling hostile Arabs in Mozambique, he hired an Arab guide to pilot the ships to India, arriving on the southwest coast in Calicut (from which we get the word "calico") in May 1498. He traded for spices, networked with the locals for future outposts, battled belligerent chiefs, and then headed back home. Da Gama and his crew arrived home to Lisbon in September 1499 (after two years and two months on the seas) and were greeted with all-out Vasco-mania. The few spices he'd returned with (many were lost in transit) were worth a staggering fortune. Portugal's Golden Age was launched.

King Manuel dubbed da Gama "Admiral of the Sea of India" and sent him out again, this time to subdue the Indian people, establish more trade outposts, and again return home to wealth and honor. Da Gama died on Christmas Eve 1524, in India. His memory lives on due to the tribute of two men: Manuel, who built this large church, and Luís de Camões (honored opposite Vasco), who turned da Gama's history-making voyage into an epic poem.

Before leaving, enjoy the big picture from a 500-years-ago perspective. It's the full package for Portugal: the country's finest church containing the great poet, the great explorer, and the royal family.

• *Leave the church, turn right, show your monastery ticket, and enter the...*

Manueline Architecture, c. 1480-1580

Portugal's unique decorative style (from its peak of power under King Manuel I, the Fortunate, r. 1495-1521) reflects the wealth of the times and the many cultural influences of the Age of Discovery. It is more an ornamental than structural style, blending late Gothic features with Mudejar (Moorish) elements. Craftsmen applied it equally to buildings with pointed Gothic or rounded Renaissance arches; you'll see elaborate Manueline carved stonework particularly around windows and doors.

The Manueline aesthetic is ornate, elaborate, and intertwined, often featuring symbols from a family's coat of arms (shields with castles, crosses, lions, banners, and crowns) or motifs from the sea (rope-like columns or borders, knots, shells, coral, anchors, and nets). Manuel's personal symbol was the armillary sphere—a celestial globe—which was an indispensable navigational aid for sailors. You'll also see imports of the age, from opium poppies to exotic animals.

Architecture students will recognize elements from Gothic's elaborate tracery, the abstract designs of Moorish culture, similarities to Spain's intricate Plateresque style (which dates from the same time), and the elongated excesses of Italian Mannerism.

❼ **Cloister:** This restored cloister is the architectural highlight of Belém. The lacy arcade is Manueline; the simpler diamond and decorative rose frieze above the top floor is Renaissance. Study the carvings, especially the gargoyles above the lower set of arches. Among these functioning rainspouts, find a monkey, a kitten, and a cricket.

Heads of state are often received in the cloister with a warm welcome. This is also the site of many important treaty signings, such as Portugal's admittance to the European Union in 1986. Turn left and do a clockwise spin around this fine space.

In the first corner, a small lion-topped basin (where the monks washed up before meals) marks the entrance to the **refectory**, or dining hall—today an occasional concert venue—lined with fine 18th-century tiles. The tiles are considered textbook Rococo, which ignores the parameters set by the architecture (unlike Baroque, which works within the structure).

Down the next stretch of cloister, on the left, is the burial spot

LISBON

of Portugal's most revered modern poet, **Fernando Pessoa** (see sidebar on page 80).

Continuing around, the former **chapter house** contains an exhibit of the lengthy restoration process, as well as the tomb of Alexandre Herculano, a Romantic 19th-century historian and poet. Quotes from Herculano adorn his tomb: "Sleep? Only the cold cadaver that doesn't feel sleeps. The soul flies and wraps itself around the feet of the All-Powerful."

· *Continuing around the cloister, find the stairs and head up.*

❽ **Upstairs:** At the top of the stairs, on the left, step into the Upper Choir (above the main door)—peering down into the vast sanctuary, at the feet of a powerful crucifix.

Back out in the upper cloister, circle around to find a bookshop (and the exit). All the way around are great cloister views. At the far end of the cloister is an exhibition that juxtaposes the historical timeline of this monastery and Portugal with contemporaneous world events (but no real artifacts).

▲Maritime Museum (Museu de Marinha)

If you're interested in Portugal's historic ships and navigational tools, this museum, which fills the west wing of the Monastery of Jerónimos (listed above), is worth a look. It's refreshingly uncrowded, and sailors love it.

Cost and Hours: €6.50, daily 10:00-18:00, Oct-April until 17:00, ccm.marinha.pt. It's at the far end of the long monastery building, facing the planetarium; the museum entrance is to your right, and its good **$$** cafeteria (open to the public) is to your left.

Visiting the Museum: You'll enter past huge statues of great explorers, then follow the one-way route (with English explanations) through the sprawling collection, offering a well-presented recap of an age when Portugal ruled the waves. It's loaded with artifacts and reproductions: nautical paintings, model ships, cannons, uniforms, and maps illustrating Portuguese explorations. The exhibit takes you right up to the present day, covering not just explorers and military vessels but also the fishing industry.

LISBON

You'll see the reconstructed king's and queen's staterooms from aboard King Carlos I's royal yacht *Amélia*. Then you'll walk outside (under a connecting gallery) to reach a vast warehouse of actual boats—from rustic *rabelos* (see page 407) to yawls to ceremonial royal barges. The centerpiece is the massive barge of King João VI, with 38 oars pulled by some 80 oarsmen, and plush royal quarters at the stern.

▲Monument to the Discoveries (Padrão dos Descobrimentos)

In 1960, the city honored the 500th anniversary of the death of Prince Henry the Navigator by rebuilding this giant riverside monument, which had original-

ly been constructed for a 1940 world's fair. It takes the shape of a huge caravel ship, in full sail, with Henry at the helm and the great navigators, sailors, and explorers on board behind him. The elevator inside takes you up to the tiptop for a tingly vista—including a fine aerial view down over the mural in front.

Cost and Hours: €5; daily 10:00-19:00; Oct-April Tue-Sun until 18:00, closed Mon; +351 213 031 950, www.padraodosdescobrimentos.pt.

Visiting the Monument: To get here, find the pedestrian tunnel under the busy boulevard, then walk around the huge monument. The 170-foot concrete structure shows that exploring the world was a team effort. The men who braved the unknown stand on the pointed, raised prow of a caravel, about to be launched into the Rio Tejo.

Leading the charge is Prince Henry the Navigator (for more about him, see page 197), holding a model of a caravel and a map, followed by kneeling kings and soldiers who Christianized foreign lands with the sword. Behind Henry (on the west side, away from bridge), find the men who financed the voyages (King Manuel I, holding an armillary sphere, his personal symbol), those who glorified it in poems and paintings (like Luís de Camões, holding his famous poem *The Lusiads* on a scroll), and at the very end, the only woman, Philippa of Lancaster, Henry's British mother.

On the east side (closest to bridge—as you walk, notice the optical illusion of waves on the flat cobbled surface), Vasco da Gama stands with his eyes on the horizon and his hand on his sword. Magellan holds a circle, representing the round earth his ship circumnavigated, while in front of him, Pedro Cabral puts

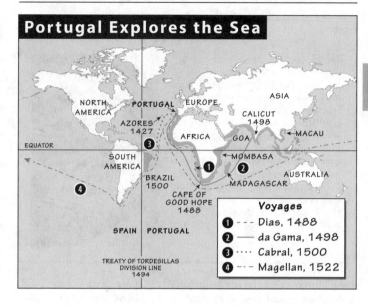

Portugal Explores the Sea

his hand to his heart, thankful to have (perhaps accidentally) arrived in Brazil. Various monks, navigators with maps, and crusaders with flags complete the crew. Check out the pillory, decorated with the Portuguese coat of arms and a cross, erected in each place "discovered" by the Portuguese—leaving no doubt as to which Europeans had arrived first.

In the **marble map in the pavement** (a gift from South Africa) in front of the Monument to the Discoveries, follow Portugal's explorers as they inched out into monster-infested waters at the edge of the world. From their tiny, isolated nation in Europe, the Portuguese first headed south to the coast of Morocco, conquering the Muslims of Ceuta in God's name (1415) and trying to gain control of North African trade routes. They braved the open Atlantic to the west and southwest, stumbling on the Madeiras (1420), which Prince Henry planted with vineyards, and the remote Azore Islands (Açores, 1427).

Meanwhile, the Portuguese slowly moved southward, hugging the African coast, each voyage building on the knowledge from previous expeditions. They cleared the biggest psychological hump when Gil Eanes sailed around Cape Bojador (western Sahara, 1434)—the border of the known world—and into the equatorial seas where it was thought that sea monsters lurked, no winds blew, and ships would be incinerated in the hot sun. Eanes survived, returning home with 200 enslaved Africans, the first of what would become a lucrative, abhorrent commodity. Two generations later, Bartolomeu Dias rounded the southern tip of Africa (Cabo da Boa Esperança,

Caravels

These easily maneuverable trading ships were fast, small (80 feet), and light (100 tons), with few guns and three triangular-shaped sails (called lateen-rigged sails) that could pivot quickly to catch the wind. They were ideal for sailing along coastlines. Many ocean-going caravels were also rigged with a square foresail for stability. (This photo shows the model held by Prince Henry on Belém's Monument to the Discoveries.) Columbus' *Niña* and *Pinta* were rerigged caravels.

1488), discovering the sea route to Asia that Vasco da Gama (1498) and others would exploit to establish trade and outposts in India, Indonesia, Japan, and China (Macao in 1557, on the south coast).

In 1500, Pedro Cabral (along with Dias and 1,200 men) took a wi-i-i-ide right turn on the way down the African coast, hoping to avoid windless seas, and landed on the tip of Brazil. The country proved to be an agricultural treasure for Portugal, which profited from sugar plantations worked by enslaved African. Two hundred years later, gold and gemstones were discovered in Brazil, jump-starting the Portuguese economy again.

In 1520, Portuguese Ferdinand Magellan, although employed by Spain, sailed west with five ships and 270 men, broke for R&R in Rio, stopped in Patagonia, and continued through the straits that were later named for him (tip of South America); along the way he suffered through mutinies, scurvy, and dinners of sawdust and ship rats before touching land in Guam. Magellan was killed in battle in the Philippines, but one remaining ship continued west and arrived back in Europe, having circumnavigated the globe after 30 months at sea.

By 1560, Portugal's global empire had peaked. Tiny-but-filthy-rich Portugal claimed (though they didn't actually occupy) the entire coastline of Africa, Arabia, India, the Philippines, and south China—a continuous stretch from Lisbon to Macao—plus Brazil. The Treaty of Tordesillas (1494) with Spain had already divvied up the colonial world between the two nations, split at 45 degrees west longitude (bisecting South America—and explaining why Brazil speaks Portuguese and the rest of the continent speaks Spanish) and 135 degrees east longitude (bisecting the Philippines and Australia).

LISBON

The Age of Discovery, 1400-1600

In 1560, you could sail from Lisbon to China without ever losing sight of land explored by Portugal. The riches of the world

poured into the tiny nation—spices from India and Java (black pepper, cinnamon); ivory, diamonds, and enslaved people from Africa; sugarcane, gold, and diamonds from Brazil; and, from everywhere, knowledge of new plants, animals, and customs. How did tiny Portugal pull this off?

First, its people were motivated by greed, hoping to break the Arab and Venetian monopoly on Eastern luxury goods (the price of pepper was jacked up 1,000 percent by the time it reached European dinner tables). They pioneered—and profited from—the transatlantic slave trade, supplying enslaved Africans to Portuguese and Spanish colonies (all told Portugal ships are estimated to have transported over 4 million slaves to the New World).

They were also driven by a crusading Christian spirit, a love of science, and a spirit of adventure. An entire 15th-century generation was obsessed with finding the legendary kingdom of the fabulously wealthy Christian named "Prester John," supposedly located in either India or Africa. (The legend may be based on a historical figure from around 1120 who visited the pope in Rome as "patriarch of India.")

Portugal also had certain natural advantages. Its Atlantic location led to a strong maritime tradition. A unified nation-state (one of Europe's first) financed and coordinated expeditions. And a core of technology-savvy men used and developed their expansive knowledge of navigational devices, astronomy, maps, shipbuilding, and languages.

But all that wealth was wasted on Portugal's ruling class, who neglected to reinvest it in the future. Easy money ruined the traditional economy and stunted industry, hurting the poor. Over the next four centuries, one by one, Portugal's colonies were lost to other European nations or to local revolutions. Today, only the islands of the Azores and Madeiras remain from the once-global empire.

▲Belém Tower (Torre de Belém)

Perhaps the purest Manueline building in Portugal (built 1515-1520), this white tower protected Lisbon's harbor. Today it celebrates the voyages that made Lisbon powerful, with carved stone representing ropes, Manuel's coat of arms, armillary spheres, and shields with the cross of the Order of Christ, charged with spreading the faith in new territories. There's often a very long line to get into this tower, but there's nothing inside worth waiting very long to see.

Cost and Hours: €6, Tue-Sun 10:00-18:30, Oct-April until 17:30, closed Mon; from the monument it's a pretty, 15-minute waterfront walk, but be ready to detour around the big yacht marina; +351 213 620 034, www.torrebelem.pt.

Visiting the Tower: This was the last sight sailors saw as they left their homeland, and the first as they returned, loaded with gold, spices, and social diseases. When the tower was built, the river went nearly to the walls of the monastery, and the tower was midriver. Its interior is pretty bare, but the views of the bridge, river, and Cristo Rei statue are nice (though I prefer the lookout from the Monument to the Discoveries, which has a better view of the monastery).

The floatplane on the grassy lawn is a monument to the first flight across the South Atlantic (Portugal to Brazil) in 1922. The original plane (which beat Charles Lindbergh's *Spirit of Saint Louis* across the North Atlantic by five years) is in Belém's Maritime Museum.

MODERN LISBON AT PARQUE DAS NAÇÕES

Lisbon celebrated the 500th anniversary of Vasco da Gama's voyage to India by hosting Expo '98 here at Parque das Nações. The theme was "The Ocean and the Seas," emphasizing the global importance of healthy, clean waters. And today, the city has thoughtfully repurposed the fairgrounds into a residential area with parks and a shopping mall. To get out of the quaint, Pombal-esque old town and enjoy a peek at some modern architecture, ride the Metro to Oriente station. From here, you can stroll through an airy shopping mall, explore the sprawling site of the 1998 world's fair, and promenade with locals along the Rio Tejo riverfront park. It's worth a visit any day but makes most sense on Monday (when most museums in town are closed). It's also particularly vibrant when people are out early on summer evenings and weekends.

• *Your visit begins when you step off the train, inside...*

Oriente Train Station (Gare do Oriente)

Oriente means "facing east." This impressive hub ties together trains (to the Algarve and Évora), the Metro, and buses under a swooping concrete roof designed by the Spanish architect Santiago Calatrava.

• *Walk across the street to the Vasco da Gama Mall and look back at Oriente station: It looks like a futuristic sun-bleached fish skeleton. Look left and right and feel the urban energy. Learning from the mistakes of Sevilla's 1992 Expo, Lisbon made sure that its massive investment and construction for its Expo would plant the seeds for a thriving new neighborhood long after the party was over. Now step into the...*

Vasco da Gama Mall

The inviting, soaring glass facade of Lisbon's top shopping mall—originally the grand entrance to Expo '98—was also designed by Calatrava (daily 9:00-24:00). Inside, its design is reminiscent of a luxury cruise ship's main hall. Notice the water cascading down the glass roof—a clever and eye-pleasing way to keep things cool and avoid any greenhouse effect. From the mall's entrance, climb the stairs to a small outdoor terrace for a good view of the train station. Look up at the two skyscraping luxury condo buildings. With fine transportation connections and modern office space, this area holds lots of promise, both for residences and businesses. Microsoft set up its Portuguese headquarters in this area, cell phone giant Vodafone has one of the coolest buildings here, and the Portuguese national court occupies contemporary new buildings nearby.

Now stroll through the upper level of the mall to the opposite end, where (just past a big food court) you can step out to another outdoor terrace. From here you can look toward the river and survey Parque das Nações—the grounds for Expo '98. Straight ahead are the flags lining the Grand Esplanade (described next). The striped oval dome to the left, once the Atlantic Pavilion (Pavilhão Atlântico), is now an 18,000-seat concert hall. The oil refinery tower far to the right marks the west end of the park and is a remnant of the industrial wasteland that was here before the fair.

• *Exiting the mall at the far end from the train station, you'll be smack-dab in the middle of...*

▲▲Parque das Nações

From the Vasco da Gama Mall, you're at the top of the Grand Esplanade (Rossio dos Olivais), lined by 155 flags—one for each country represented at Expo '98. The flags are arranged in alphabetical order, so the first ones are South Africa (Africa dul Sul), Albania, and Germany (Alemanha). In the middle you'll find the US (Estados Unidos), Spain (Espanha), and Estonia side by side.

At the far end of the line of flags you'll reach a basin (on your right) that predates the fair. Back before World War II, this was a watery "parking lot" (just 1.5 yards deep) for seaplanes. Across the basin to your right, the blocky building that resembles an aircraft carrier with a spiky rooftop is the Lisbon Oceanarium (described next)—the big hit of the fair and still the park's major attraction. From behind that the cable car (€4 one-way,  €6 round-trip, nothing special, daily 11:00-19:00) drifts east to the Vasco da Gama Tower, which marks that end of the park. Two miles away, built as part of the 1998 celebrations, is the Vasco da Gama Bridge. A delightful promenade (Caminho dos Pinheiros; "The Way of the Pine Trees") runs along the riverfront from the marina all the way to a park at the base of the Vasco da Gama Bridge.

Lisbon Oceanarium (Oceanário de Lisboa)

Europe's largest aquarium—housed in what looks like a drilling platform or a big, modern ship at sea—simulates four oceanic underwater and shoreline environments, from the Atlantic to the Pacific to the Indian to the Arctic. You'll circle around the upper level, seeing surface dwellers from each climate (such as otters, puffins, penguins, and other sea birds). Then you'll head downstairs and do another loop, this time seeing underwater creatures. The centerpiece—which you'll keep circling back to—is an enormous and mesmerizing central tank crammed full of fascinating fish big and small, including several sharks. Weekday-morning school groups are also happily on display.

Cost and Hours: €19, €10 for kids 4-12; €38.50 combo-ticket with 48-hour Gray Line hop-on, hop-off bus; daily 10:00-20:00, Nov-March until 19:00, last entry one hour before closing, +351 218 917 000, www.oceanario.pt.

Vasco da Gama Bridge (Ponte Vasco da Gama)

Europe's longest bridge (10.7 miles) was opened in 1998 to connect the Expo '98 grounds with the south side of the Rio Tejo, and to alleviate the traffic jams on Lisbon's only other bridge over the river, the 25th of April Bridge. The Vasco da Gama Bridge helped connect north and south Portugal, back when a freeway was a big deal in this late-to-develop European nation. Built low to the water, the bridge's towers and cables are meant to suggest the sails of a caravel ship.

EAST LISBON
▲National Tile Museum (Museu Nacional do Azulejo)

Filling the former Convento da Madre de Deus, the museum features piles of tiles, which, as you've probably noticed, are an art form in Portugal. The collection occupies a stun-
ning, tile-covered convent
that received donations
from buildings all over
Portugal after the dissolution of religious orders in
1834. They've showcased
the tiles as they would
have originally appeared

(note the diamond-shaped staircase tiles) and arranged the visit in chronological order. The presentation is low-tech to keep the focus on the beauty and diversity of this traditional handicraft. For aficionados, this is a handy one-stop survey. And the circa-1700 tile panorama of Lisbon (upstairs) is fascinating, letting you pick out landmarks that were toppled in the 1755 quake. Don't miss the cafeteria, covered in rescued tiles from a former smokehouse, appropriately painted with food-related themes.

Cost and Hours: €5; Tue-Sun 10:00-18:00, closed Mon; located about a mile east of Praça do Comércio—15 minutes on bus #794 from Praça do Comércio or bus #742 from near the Gulbenkian Museum (bus leaves around the corner from São Sebastião Metro station—along Rua Marquês de Fronteira), both buses stop right at museum entrance on Rua da Madre de Deus 4, +351 218 100 340, museudoazulejo.gov.pt.

SOUTH OF LISBON, ACROSS THE RIVER
Ferry Ride and Visit to Cacilhas

For an interesting and easy excursion to the small port town of Cacilhas (and a destination fish restaurant), catch the ferry from Lisbon for a 15-minute ride. The well-worn, graffiti-caked utility vessel is completely enclosed, serving thousands of daily commuters.

Getting There: The ferry leaves from the Cais do Sodré terminal (€1.25 each way, covered by public transit tickets/cards; at the ferry terminal, follow signs to *Cacilhas,* not *Montijo;* 4/hour, more during rush hours, less in evening, www.transtejo.pt). Plan on hitting or missing the rush-hour scene, depending on your taste. Upon arrival in Cacilhas, note when the next ferries return so you can plan your time smartly.

Visiting Cacilhas: The town's main street, **Rua Candido dos Reis,** is pedestrianized and charming, with lots of cute shops and eateries. The only "sight" in Cacilhas is the historic **Frigate *Don Fernando II and Gloria*** (Fragata *Dom Fernando II e Glória*), permanently moored at the dock. This was the last Portuguese ship to make the "Indian Run," which for three centuries connected Portugal with its colony in Goa. Launched in 1843 (and making its maiden voyage in 1845), in 33 years it sailed—defended by its 44 cannons—over 100,000 miles (the equivalent of five times around the world). It made its last trip in 1878, accidentally burned in 1963, and was rebuilt in 1997. Explore three decks for a taste of life on a 19th-century frigate. There's a guides' school nearby and you may find students standing by to give free tours as part of their training. The submarine drydocked adjacent was one of the Portugal navy's last subs (€4, Tue-Sun 10:00-18:00, Mon from 12:00, Oct-April daily until 17:00; buy booklet for English description, https://ccm.marinha.pt).

Eating in Cacilhas: **$$$ Restaurante Farol** is the best restaurant for eating fish—which is the reason most come to Cacilhas. The dining hall (no outside seating) is bright and airy with big view windows, an open kitchen, and an entire wall devoted to a blue-tile depiction of the spot and view in 1870 when this place opened (daily 12:00-23:00, 30 steps from the ferry terminal, on the right facing the river, +351 212 765 248).

Azulejos

During visits to neighboring Spain, King Manuel I not only acquired wives, but he also obtained
several thousand tiles to decorate
palaces throughout Portugal. Vibrant colors must have attracted
the king's attention, and some examples from his visits can still be
seen in the National Palace in Sintra. It wasn't long before Portuguese artists began producing
them for local clients, and the
tiles—called *azulejos* (ah-zoo-
LAY-zhoosh, from an Arab word
meaning "small polished stone")—
became synonymous with the
seafaring empire.

The biggest challenge for
early artisans was keeping colors
from running together during firing. A number of techniques
developed to solve this problem: *Alicatados* are mosaic pieces, cut after firing, to form intricate geometric patterns; *corda
seca* fills thick outlines of manganese oxide with different colors, like a children's coloring book; and *aresta* sculpts color
wells directly into the tile. The biggest breakthrough came
with the development of *majólica*, or *faiança*—the undecorat-
ed clay tile is baked first, then covered with an opaque glaze
that makes a canvas for the painted design, which is set by a
second firing.

Brazilians loved tilework, too, and after the return of the
Portuguese king to European shores, factories began producing tilework for the masses. But tilework began to fall out of
fashion by the early 20th century. Then Lisbon's 1959 Metro
system gave tile artists a new playground. While not originally
in the budget, artist Maria Keil could not bear to see the walls
vacant. Her original designs are still on display, and future artists continue to make the Metro an underground art museum.

Unfortunately, others have noticed the beauty (and prof-
itability) of historic tilework panels. Theft is common—often
for resale on the black market—and many of Lisbon's older
panels are at risk. In the past decade, local watch groups have
documented several hundred cases of missing panels and
helped recover several of them. And the law is changing to
help preserve Portugal's most visible art form; historic tiles
can now only be legally purchased via antique dealers. Please
don't purchase tilework at the Feira da Ladra flea market.

To go on your own *azulejo* scavenger hunt, check out
Endless Mile's tile guide to Lisbon that lists nearly 100 of the
city's best tile panels (www.endlessmile.com).

▲25th of April Bridge (Ponte 25 de Abril)

Imagine that before 1966, there was no way across the Rio Tejo except by ferry. This suspension bridge—1.5 miles long (3,280

feet between the towers—bears an uncanny resemblance to San Francisco's Golden Gate Bridge (it was built in 1966 by the same company that made its famous cousin—but notice the lower deck for train tracks). The foundations are sunk 260 feet below the surface into the riverbed, making it the world's deepest bridge. Originally named for the dictator Salazar, the bridge was renamed for the date of Portugal's 1974 revolution and liberation. For a generation, natives would show their political colors by choosing which name to use. While conservative Portuguese called it the "Salazar Bridge," liberals referred to it as the "25th of April Bridge" (just as Washington, DC's airport is still called "National" by some and "Reagan" by others).

Cristo Rei Statue (Christ the King)

A huge, 330-foot concrete statue of Christ (à la Rio de Janeiro, in the former Portuguese colony of Brazil) overlooks Lisbon from

across the Rio Tejo, stretching its arms wide to symbolically bless the city (or, as less reverent Portuguese say, "to dive into the river"). Lisbon's cardinal, inspired by a visit to Rio de Janeiro in 1936, wanted a replica built back home. Increased support came after an appeal was made to Our Lady of Fátima in 1940 to keep Portugal out of World War II. Portugal survived the war relatively unscathed, and funds were collected to build this statue in appreciation. After 10 years of construction, it opened to the public in 1959. It's now a sanctuary and pilgrimage site, and the chapel inside holds regular Sunday Mass.

The statue was designed to be seen from a distance, and there's little reason to go to the trouble of actually visiting it. If you do visit, an elevator will take you to the top for a panoramic view: From left to right, see Belém, the 25th of April Bridge, downtown Lisbon (Praça do Comércio and the green Alfama hilltop with the castle), and the long Vasco da Gama Bridge.

Cost and Hours: €5, daily 9:30-18:15, slightly later in summer, +351 212 751 000, www.cristorei.pt.

Getting There: To get to Cristo Rei, catch the ferry from downtown Lisbon to Cacilhas (described earlier in this section, under "Ferry Ride and Visit to Cacilhas"), then hop on the bus marked *101 Cristo Rei* (3/hour, exit ferry dock left into the maze of bus stops to find the #20 stop with the "101 Cristo Rei" schedule under the awning, 15-minute ride). Because of bridge tolls to enter Lisbon, taxis from the site are expensive. For drivers, the most efficient visit is a quick stop on your way to or from Évora or the Algarve.

WEST OF LISBON, ON THE COAST
Cascais

The seafront resort town of Cascais (kahsh-KAYSH), about 17 miles due west of Lisbon, provides a fun and quick escape from the big city of Lisbon. Before the rise of the Algarve, Cascais was the haunt of Portugal's rich and beautiful. Today it's an elegant and inviting escape from the city with pleasant beaches and a relaxing ambience.

Before the 20th century, aristocrats wanted to avoid the sun and exaggerate their lily-white skin—and a day at the beach made just no sense. But about 1900, the Portuguese queen Maria Pia (daughter of King Victor Emmanuel II of Italy) made Cascais her summer vacation getaway—and Portugal's high society followed. A train line made Cascais easily accessible from the city, and between the world wars, the area was developed as a kind of Portuguese answer to the French Riviera.

Getting There: Just hop the train at Lisbon's Cais do Sodré station (M: Cais do Sodré) and you're in Cascais in 40 minutes or less (3/hour, www.cp.pt).

Visiting Cascais: The Cascais station (the last stop on the Cais do Sodré line) faces the town center. From there, the main cobbled street, Rua Frederico Arouca, parallels the waterfront past shops and eateries to Largo Cidade Vitória, where you'll find a helpful TI kiosk (daily 9:00-18:00).

Cascais still has a fishing industry. Adjacent to the TI, you'll find the Serviços de Pescado, a wholesale fish market where most days at 17:00 visitors can witness the quick fish auction as local retailers snap up the day's catch. Just beyond is the main beach and a palm-lined promenade leading to an old fort. Deeper into town are several little museums; the Museu do Maris is best for the story of the town and its relationship with the sea (free, Tue-Sun 10:00-17:00, closed Mon, about 10 minutes from the center at Rua Júlio Pereira de Mello, www.cm-cascais.pt/museumar). Walk out for dramatic views at Boca do Inferno (a unique rock formation) to see what fishermen have to deal with.

Returning to Lisbon via Estoril: A paved seaside promenade leads from Cascais past several beaches to Estoril, its sister beach resort town (a half-hour stroll away). Of the several small sandy beaches, Praia da Conceição and Praia das Moitas conveniently have showers. If you have time and like seaside strolls, I'd recommend walking this strip and catching the train back to Lisbon from Estoril (all trains stop at both Estoril and Cascais).

Estoril is famous for its casino and many grand hotels. From the Lisbon-Cascais train you can look past the Estoril station and across the park at the modern casino. Ian Fleming hatched his first 007 story here in the early days of World War II, when Portugal was neutral and this area was a hotbed of spies. The Estoril casino where Fleming gambled must have been part of the inspiration for his first James Bond novel, *Casino Royale*. But Cascais rather than Estoril is clearly the most rewarding stop for today's traveler.

Shopping in Lisbon

Lisbon is a marvelous shopping city: creative, with a trendy vibe but also respectful of tradition—and it's affordable. My suggestions below focus on one-off shops that specialize in unique slices of Lisbon life. I've also included a few big malls for handy one-stop shopping.

WHAT TO BUY

The shops mentioned here are scattered around central Lisbon, but most are concentrated in the hip and artsy Chiado district.

Cork

Portugal is famous for its cork, a versatile material that can be put to hundreds of uses (see sidebar on page 255). Shops all over town show off practical and eye-pleasing items made of cork, from handbags to wallets to umbrellas. For fashionable, top-end products, head up to the flagship store of the internationally respected **Pelcor,** in the Príncipe Real shopping zone (Pátio do Tijolo 4, just off Rua Dom Pedro V, www.pelcor.pt). In the Bairro Alto, **Cork & Co** is a more affordable boutique with a wider array of products—including jewelry (closed Sun mornings, Rua das Salgadeiras 10, www.corkandcompany.pt).

Wine

If you're in the market to buy fine bottles of wine to enjoy in Portugal or to ship home, consider these two options. While touristy—and with somewhat inflated prices—both have helpful staff who can talk you through your options and arrange shipping. (They may suggest that you make your selection in the shop, then place your order on their website.) **Napoleão Wine Shop** has free samples of three unique Portuguese options: port, *vinho verde,* and *ginjinha* (daily, main branch at Rua Conceição 16 specializes in Portuguese wines, second branch across the street also has international booze; www.napoleao.eu). **Garrafeira Nacional** has a similar set-up in the Baixa (closed Sun, Rua da Conceição 20) and a user-friendly location open daily inside Mercado da Ribeira (www.garrafeiranacional.com).

Another place is **Wines of Portugal Tasting Room,** which sells regional favorites at affordable prices (many also available for tasting, Praça do Comércio, see details on page 63).

Azulejos (Colored Tiles)

Portugal's iconic colored tiles make vivid souvenirs—for use as trivets, wall hangings, or even (for the ambitious) a backsplash renovation project. It's easy to find affordable, basic, painted replicas of classic *azulejo* designs—many souvenir shops stock a small selection. For better-quality replica *azulejos,* try **Viúva Lamego** (closed Sat-Sun, Largo do Intendente 25), **Fábrica Sant'Anna** (closed Sun, in Chiado at Rua do Alecrim 95), or the more tourist-oriented **Loja dos Descobrimentos** (daily, below the cathedral at Rua dos Bacalhoeiros 12). If you're shopping for authentic antique tiles, try **d'Orey Azulejos** (closed Sun, in Chiado at Rua do Alecrim 68) or the cramped **Antiquário Solar** (a.k.a. Albuquerque e Sousa; closed Sat afternoon and all day Sun, in the Bairro Alto at Rua Dom Pedro V 68). Discontinued mid-20th-century industrial tiles (think solid colors but in bold relief) can be found at **Cortiço & Netos** (closed Sun, between Mouraria and the castle at Calçado de Santo André 66).

Conservas (Canned Fish)

Canned fish (collectively called *conservas*) is a Portuguese staple, are not the harsh, cured-in-salt sardines you might think of back home. This is quality fish in olive oil (sardines, cod, mackerel, and tuna are most common), often mixed with herbs, spices, or infused oils to impart extra flavor. Best of all, colorful packaging turns the cans into great souvenirs or gifts and makes window-shopping a delight. The best *conservas* place in town—near Mercado da Ribeira—is **Loja das Conservas,** with shelves upon shelves of attractively decorated cans from all over Portugal. This shop is operated by a local consortium, and prides itself on educating its customers

LISBON

1 To Pelcor
2 Cork & Co.
3 Napoleão Wine Shop
4 Garrafeira Nacional (2)
5 Wines of Portugal Tasting Room
6 To Viúva Lamego
7 Fábrica Sant'Anna
8 Loja dos Descobrimentos
9 d'Orey Azulejos
10 Antiquário Solar
11 Cortico & Netos
12 Loja das Conservas

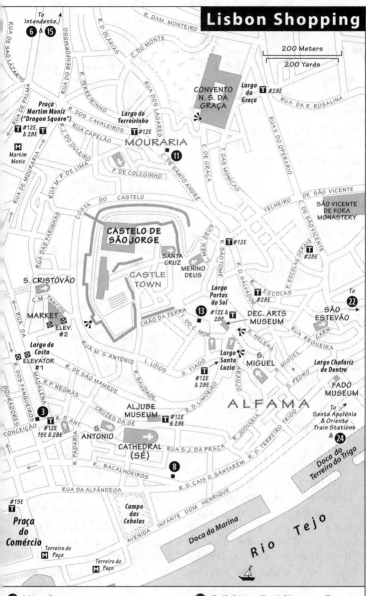

Lisbon Shopping

200 Meters
200 Yards

13 Miss Can
14 Conserveira da Trindade
15 A Vida Portuguesa (3)
16 Lisbon Shop (2)
17 Burel Mountain Originals
18 Luvaria Ulisses
19 Salão Musical de Lisboa

20 To Príncipe Real Shopping District
21 Mercado da Ribeira
22 To Feira da Ladra Flea Market
23 Armazéns do Chiado Mall
24 To Vasco da Gama Mall
25 To El Corte Inglés

(daily, Rua do Arsenal 130). In the upper part of the Alfama, just below the castle, **Miss Can** sells a small selection of their own production, with clever packaging and a little café where you can enjoy a light meal (see "Eating in Lisbon" later, daily, Largo do Contador Mor 19). And in Chiado, you'll find the upscale **Conserveira da Trindade,** with a carefully curated selection and the option to nibble right there (daily, Rua Nova da Trindade 11).

Other Quality Portuguese Souvenirs

A Vida Portuguesa is the best shop in town for a well-chosen selection of high-quality, artisanal Portuguese products—everything from stationery and toiletries to housewares and decorative objects to toys and jewelry (daily, Rua Anchieta 11, www.avidaportuguesa. com). They have two other locations: a bigger flagship store in the Intendente neighborhood (daily, Largo do Intendente 23), and a smaller location inside the Mercado do Ribeira.

If you're in a pinch for souvenirs, local TIs have a small but nicely stocked **"Lisbon Shop"** with some basic items emblazoned with Lisbon's trademarks—sardines, fado, or trolleys—as well as fado CDs, at prices typically better than elsewhere in the Baixa (daily, main branch in Praça do Comércio TI, smaller selection at the TI on Praça das Restauradores).

Woolens: The delightful **Burel Mountain Originals** boutique showcases fashionable items made from the heavy Portuguese wool called *burel.* This company took over an abandoned wool factory high in the mountains of northern Portugal and brought back skilled but out-of-work old-timers to revive a dormant industry. Today the factory churns out high-quality blankets, handbags, coats, shoes, and other products with a mix of traditional and contemporary style (daily, Rua Serpa Pinto 15B, www.burelfactory. com).

Leather Gloves: The Lisbon institution **Luvaria Ulisses** sells top-quality leather gloves *(luvas)* one pair at a time, with individual attention to help you find just the right style and fit. The shop is nestled into a tiny storefront just a few steps off Rossio. You squeeze into the shop, then the clerks squeeze your hands into the gloves: they'll nest your elbow on a dainty little pillow, squirt a puff of talcum powder into the glove, then massage your fingers in, one at a time (after a visit here, you'll better appreciate the expression "fits like a glove"). While popular with tourists from faraway lands (expect to wait at busy times), they're still cranking out quality gloves at decent prices (many pairs around €50-60, closed Sun, Rua do Carmo 87, www.luvariaulisses.com).

Musical Instruments: If you're captivated by fado and want to check out a Portuguese guitar, **Salão Musical de Lisboa** has a fine selection and a handy location, right on Largo do Carmo square (closed Sun, Rua da Oliveira ao Carmo 2, www.salaomusical.com).

WHERE TO SHOP
Consider a shopping spree in one of these areas.

Príncipe Real Shopping District
For cutting-edge fashion and design, and one of Lisbon's most appealing little green parks, head to the Príncipe Real Garden at the top of Chiado (about a five-minute walk, a speedy bus trip from the top of the Elevador da Glória funicular, or a stop on the #24E trolley route).

The anchor of this area is the **Embaixada** complex, across the street from the park. Young entrepreneurs have given a grand 19th-century Arabian-style townhouse a modern makeover and filled its two floors with goods from high-end local designers and vendors, attracting hipsters, well-dressed urbanites, and in-the-know tourists. You'll see fashion, home decor, kidswear, high-end tailors, art galleries, pop-up shops, and much more.

Climb the grand old staircase, on scuffed tiles and under peeling plaster ceilings, to feel the artful "ramshackle chic" vibe. In the atrium, the Less café has affordable light meals and a gin bar; there's also a little garden café out back (daily 12:00-20:00, Praça do Príncipe Real 26).

Just a few doors down (walking with the park on your left), at the smaller but similarly chic **REAL "Slow Retail" Concept Store,** creative local vendors display their wares in a clean, cool, industrial-mod, space. You'll see stacks of coffee-table books, creative housewares, summer dresses, burlap backpacks, colorful shoes and sandals, hipster toddler garb, and horn-rimmed sunglasses (Mon-Wed 10:30-20:00, Thu-Sat until 23:00, closed Sun, Praça do Príncipe Real 20).

A bit farther down are more fun shops, including **Corallo,** where Bettina and Niccolò make their own chocolates and roast their own coffee (closed Sun, Rua da Escola Politécnica 4), and the old-school **Príncipe Real Enxovais,** specializing in top-quality linens for the home (daily, Rua da Escola Politécnica 12). And in the opposite direction, a block up Rua Dom Pedro V back toward the heart of Chiado, is the **Pelcor** cork products flagship store (described earlier).

This is also a great part of town to get a bite; for details, see the Chiado listings in "Eating in Lisbon," later.

Markets

Mercado da Ribeira (a.k.a. Time Out Market) is a renovated market hall offering Lisbon's best one-stop shopping for culinary souvenirs (it's described in detail on page 146). In addition to bottles of wine, chocolates, canned fish, and other edible goodies, it has an outpost of Lisbon's best souvenir shop, A Vida Portuguesa. And, of course, it's also great for a meal. Most restaurant stalls are open daily from 12:00 to 24:00. On Sunday mornings, a

coin market jingles here. Note that the Loja das Conservas cannedfish shop is just down the street (described earlier).

On Tuesdays and Saturdays, the **Feira da Ladra flea market** attracts bargain hunters to Campo de Santa Clara in the Alfama (8:00-15:00, best in morning).

Shopping Malls and Department Stores

Lisbon has several malls and huge department stores (all open long hours daily). Most central is **Armazéns do Chiado,** with six modern floors—and handy elevators connecting the Baixa and Chiado (food court on the sixth floor, www.armazensdochiado.com). North of downtown, **Vasco da Gama Mall** fills the grand entryway to the Expo '98 site at the Oriente train/Metro station (described on page 111). And the Spanish megadepartment store, **El Corte Inglés,** has a huge branch at the top of Edward VII Park (near Gulbenkian Museum at Avenida António Augusto de Aguiar 31, M: São Sebastião).

Entertainment in Lisbon

NIGHTLIFE

The Baixa is quiet at night, with touristy al fresco restaurants and not much else. Head instead up to the Bairro Alto for fado halls, bars, and the Miradouro de São Pedro de Alcântara (view terrace), a pleasant place to hang out. Nearby Rua Diario de Noticias is lined with busy bars and fun crowds spilling onto the street.

Rua Nova do Carvalho (a.k.a. Pink Street)

This happening, crazy street is a short walk downhill from Chiado in the Cais do Sodré neighborhood (just behind Mercado da Ribeira). Rua Nova do Carvalho, otherwise known as "Pink Street,"

was once notorious as the sailors' red-light zone. Now the prostitutes are just painted onto the walls, and the made-over street is painted a bright pink. After the bars in other neighborhoods close, late-night revelers hike 10 minutes from Chiado down Rua do Alecrim to reach Pink Street. Surrounded by largely uninhabited Pombaline buildings, Pink Street's four bars are allowed to make noise—and they do—until very late into the night. Many of the nightspots here are rowdy, youthful dance halls with names like Tokyo, Musicbox, Viking, and Sabotage Rock Club, with a few striptease clubs mixed in. But the following places—lively earlier and accessible to a wider clientele—are my Pink Street picks.

Pensão Amor ("House of Love") is a velvety place for a cocktail. Wallpapered with sexy memories of the not-long-ago days when it was a brothel, it's a grungy tangle of corners to hang out in and enjoy a drink (or just stare at the graffiti), often against a backdrop of live jazz. It even has a sexy library if you feel like reading (no food, Rua Nova do Carvalho 38, also possible to enter from along the bridge at Rua do Alecrim 19, +351 213 143 399).

Sol e Pesca Bar, a nostalgic reminder of the sailor-and-fisherman heritage of this street, sells drinks and preserved food in tins. Just browse the shelves of classic tinned seafood—from pâté and sardines to caviar—and wash down your salty seafood tapas with a glass of wine amid the lures and nets (Rua Nova do Carvalho 44, +351 213 467 203).

Povo Lisboa is a trendy little bar serving delightful Portuguese tapas (from 18:00) and enlivening things with fado (Tue-Sun 20:30-23:00, closed Mon, no cover—just buy a drink, light food, Rua Nova do Carvalho 32, +351 213 473 403).

LX Factory

LX Factory is a typical riverside industrial zone gone hippie-chic. Passing through the factory gate (under the 25th of April Bridge), you'll find a youthful crowd sorting through a collection of restaurants, clubs, shops, and galleries. LX Factory

is lively each night and all day on weekends (www.lxfactory.com).

LISBON

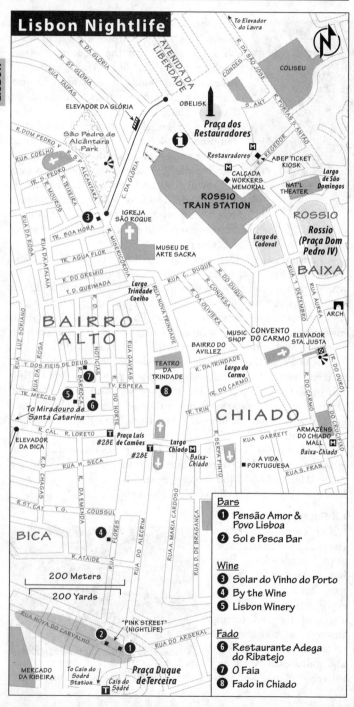

Serious Port Wine Tastings

Solar do Vinho do Porto, run by the Port Wine Institute, has perhaps the world's greatest selection of port—the famous fortified wine that takes its name from the city of Porto. If you're not headed to Porto, this is your best chance for serious exposure. The tasting room has been closed for renovation but should be reopen by the time you visit. The plush, air-conditioned, Old World living room is furnished with leather chairs (this is not a shorts-and-T-shirt kind of place). You can order from a selection of more than 150 different ports (€2-22/glass). Fans of port describe it as "a liquid symphony playing on the palate." Read the instructive, easy menu for a do-it-yourself education. Start white and sweet (cheapest), taste your way through spicy and ruby, and finish mellow and tawny. A *colheita* (single harvest) is particularly good. Appetizers *(aperitivos)* are listed in the menu with small photographs. Table service can be slow and disinterested when it's busy; to be served without a long wait, go to the bar (Mon-Fri 11:00-24:00, closed Sat-Sun, across from top of Elevador da Glória funicular at Rua São Pedro de Alcântara 45). For more on port, see page 380.

Evening Stroll

In the summer, you'll find lots of people out strolling. Here are four good places to join them: Rua Augusta through the heart of the Baixa district; along the seaside promenade near Belém Tower; along the fine riverfront promenade at Parque das Nações; and the river walk at Ribeira das Naus (from the water at Praça do Comércio to Cais do Sodré).

FADO MUSIC

Fado is the ▲▲ folk music of Lisbon's back streets. Since the mid-1800s, it's been the Lisbon blues—mournfully beautiful and haunting ballads about lost sailors, broken hearts, and bittersweet romance. While generally sad, fado can also be jaunty—in a nostalgic way—and captivating. An aging widow in a mourning shawl singing passionate fado can be as sexy as any performer.

While authentically traditional, most Lisbon fado bars cater to tourists these days. Don't expect to find a truly "local" scene. Even the seemingly homemade "fado tonight" *(fado esta noite)* signs are mostly for tourist shows. Still, if you choose well—and can find a convivial restaurant with relatively reasonable prices and fewer tour groups—it's a very memorable evening. (And be wary of your hotel's recommendations, which are often skewed by hefty kickbacks.)

The two main areas for fado in Lisbon are on either side of the Baixa: the Bairro Alto and the Alfama. Later, I've listed options in each neighborhood. To avoid disappointment, it's smart to reserve ahead.

Fado

Fado songs reflect Portugal's bittersweet relationship with the sea. Fado means "fate"—how fate deals with Portugal's adventurers...and the women they leave behind. These are songs of both sadness and hope, a bittersweet emotion called *saudade* (meaning yearning or nostalgia). The lyrics reflect the pining for a loved one across the water, hopes for a future reunion, remembrances of a rosy past or dreams of a better future, and

the yearning for what might have been if fate had not intervened. (Fado can also be bright and happy when the song is about the virtues of cities such as Lisbon or Coimbra, or of the warmth of a typical *casa portuguesa*.)

The songs are often in a minor key. The singer *(fadista)* is accompanied by a 12-string Portuguese *guitarra* (with a round body like a mandolin) or other stringed instruments unique to Portugal. Many singers crescendo into the first word of the verse, like a moan emerging from deep inside. Though the songs are often sad, the singers rarely overact—they plant themselves firmly and sing stoically in the face of fate.

A verse from a typical fado song goes:

> *O waves of the salty sea,*
> *where do you get your salt?*
> *From the tears shed by the women in black*
> *on the beaches of Portugal.*

Ways to See Fado: Your basic choices are a polished restaurant with a professional-quality staged show; or—my preference—a more rustic place with *fado vadio,* a kind of open-mic fado evening when suspiciously talented "amateurs" line up at the door of neighborhood dives for their chance to warble. Waiters—hired more for their vocal skills than hospitality—sometimes take a turn entertaining the crowd.

Most people combine fado with a late dinner. The music typically begins between 20:00 and 21:00; arrive a bit earlier to be seated and order. Night owls can have a cheaper dinner elsewhere, then show up for fado when the first round of diners is paying their bills (around 22:30 or 23:00). Both elegant, high-end places and holes-in-the-wall generally let nondiners in late for the cost of an overpriced drink and/or a €10-15 cover charge.

Prices for Fado: Prices for a fado performance vary greatly, but assume you won't leave any fado experience without spending at least €30 per person—and more like €50-60 per person for the fancier restaurants. Many places have a cover charge, others just expect you to buy a meal, and some enforce a €25-30 per person minimum. Remember, as throughout Portugal, appetizers, bread, or cheese that appear on your table aren't free—if you don't want these appetizers, it's safest to push them aside.

Fado in the Bairro Alto

In the Bairro Alto, wander around Rua Diario de Noticias and neighboring streets.

Restaurante Adega do Ribatejo is a homey and crowded good budget option: Just pay for your meal (main courses around €15) and drinks with no cover or required minimum (daily 11:00-24:00, dinner from 19:00, Rua Diario de Noticias 23, +351 213 468 343). After 22:30, you're welcome to just buy a drink and enjoy the music.

O Faia is a top-end fado experience, in a classy dining room under heavy, graceful arches. It's pricey (plan on €60/person for dinner and drinks), but the food and the fado are both professional and top-quality. If you come after dinner (23:00) for just drinks and music, there's a €25 minimum. Filled with an older, well-dressed, international clientele, it's a memorable evening (open Mon-Sat for dinner at 20:00, fado begins at 21:30, closed Sun, Rua da Barroca 54, +351 213 426 742, www.ofaia.com).

Concert Alternative: Fado in Chiado, a sterile 50-minute performance in a small modern theater, is for tourists who don't want to stay out late or mess with a restaurant. Sitting with other tourists and without food or drink, you'll enjoy four musicians: a man and a woman singing, a guitarist, and a man on the Portuguese guitar, which gives fado its balalaika charm (€19,  daily at 19:00 except Sun, conveniently located at Rua da Misericordia 14, on second floor of in Cine Theatro Gymnasio, mobile +351 961 717 778, www.fadoinchiado.com).

Trendier Alternative: In the hip Rua Nova do Carvalho (a.k.a. Pink Street) nightlife zone, just downhill from the Bairro Alto and Chiado toward the river, **Povo Lisboa** has fado most nights (see listing earlier, under "Nightlife").

LISBON

Fado in the Alfama

While often pretty lonely and dead after dark, the Alfama has several bars offering fado with their meals—just head uphill from the Fado Museum. Some bars are geared for tourists and tour groups, but others feel organic, spontaneous, and part of the neighborhood culture. While schedules at any particular place can be inconsistent, if you hike up Rua São Pedro de Alcântara to the Church of São Miguel, you'll hear the music wafting out from hole-in-the-wall eateries and be greeted by men hustling business for their fado restaurants. Generally, you simply pay for the meal and enjoy the music as included entertainment. If it's late and there's room, you can just buy a drink. For locations, see the "Alfama Restaurants" map, later.

A Baiuca, a tiny fun-loving restaurant, offers my favorite Alfama fado experience. A Baiuca—the name means a very rough tavern—packs people in and serves up spirited *fado vadio* (open mic for amateurs and waiters) with overpriced, basic food and lots of wine. As the English-speaking manager, Isabel, likes to say, "Fado needs wine." This intimate place has surround sound—as everyone seems to get into the music (€25 minimum—and be careful with the very pricey appetizers and bottles of wine that can push the bill much higher). If you come very late you can just buy a drink (music Thu-Mon 20:00-24:00, closed Tue-Wed, reservations smart, in the heart of the Alfama, just off Rua São Pedro up the hill from Fado Museum at Rua de São Miguel 20, +351 218 -867 284). When the door is closed, they're full, but you can peek at the action through the window around to the left.

Clube de Fado is much classier—one of the best places in town to hear quality fado. While expensive, there's not a bad seat in the house. Music plays nightly in this formal yet intimate setting. When busy, the musicians switch between two adjacent halls, giving waiters time to serve between sets, and diners get music about half the time (plan on €50/person for dinner with wine, plus €7.50 cover charge, meals from 20:00, dinner reservations required, music 21:30 until after midnight; after 23:00, pay just €10 cover plus cost of a drink; around corner from cathedral at Rua São João da Praça 94, +351 218 852 704, www.clube-de-fado.com).

Casa de Linhares, a block downhill from Clube de Fado, offers similar quality fado and an even nicer space, with dinner served under the stone vaults of a 16th-century palace (€15 cover for music, plan about €40/person for dinner, music nightly from 20:00, after 22:00 just cover plus drink purchase, Beco dos Armazéns Do Linho 2, +351 218 865 088, www.casadelinhares.com).

Concerts at the Fado Museum: At the base of the Alfama,

LISBON

the Fado Museum hosts occasional live, free concerts that let you focus on the music (check schedule at www.museudofado.pt). Taking in a show here, then having a budget dinner elsewhere, lets you enjoy Alfama fado on the cheap.

BULLFIGHTS, SOCCER, CONCERTS, AND MOVIES
Tickets to bullfights, concerts, and other events are sold at the green **ABEP kiosk** at the southern end of Praça dos Restauradores (daily 9:00-20:00).

▲Portuguese Bullfight
If you always felt sorry for the bull, this is Touro's Revenge: In a Portuguese bullfight, the matador is brutalized along with the bull.

Lisbon hosts only about a dozen fights a year, but if you're in town for one, it's an unforgettable experience.

In Act I, the horseman *(cavaleiro)* skillfully plants four beribboned barbs in the bull's back while trying to avoid the leather-padded horns. The horses are the short, stocky Lusitano breed, with excellent balance. In Act II, a colorfully clad eight-man suicide squad (called *forcados*) enters the ring and lines up single file facing the bull. With testosterone sloshing everywhere, the leader taunts the bull—slapping his knees and yelling, *"touro!"*—then braces himself for a collision that can be heard all the way up in the cheap seats. As he hangs onto the bull's head, his buddies pile on, trying to wrestle the bull to a standstill. Finally, one guy hangs on to *o touro*'s tail and "water-skis" behind him. (In Act III, the *ambulância* arrives.)

Unlike the Spanish *corrida de toros,* the bull is not killed in front of the crowd at the Portuguese *tourada*...but it is killed later. (Some brave bulls with only superficial wounds are spared to fight another day.) Spanish aficionados insist that Portuguese fights are actually crueler, since they humiliate the bull, rather than fight him as a fellow warrior. Animal-rights groups enliven the scene before each fight.

Fights are held at the **Campo Pequeno,** a spectacular, Moorish-domed brick structure that bears a resemblance to Madrid's bullring. The ring is small, so there are no bad seats. To sit nearly at ringside, try the cheapest *bancada* seats, on the generally half-empty and unmonitored main floor. Underneath the ring there's a shopping mall, and overhead there's a retractable roof for concerts. It hosts a variety of restaurants inside, including an Argentine steak restaurant. Maybe the beef served was in the ring earlier?

Cost and Hours: Tickets are always available at the door (€20-50); they're also sold at the ABEP kiosk on Praça dos Restauradores (10 percent surcharge). Fights are generally held from Easter through September, typically on Thursday evenings at 22:00; bullring is north of the Baixa in the Campo Pequeno district (M: Campo Pequeno); +351 217 932 143, www.campopequeno.com.

Important note: Half the fights are simply Spanish-type *corridas* without the killing. For the real slam-bam Portuguese-style fight, confirm that there will be *grupo de forcados* ("bull grabbers").

Soccer

Lisbon is home to two major league *futebol* teams, Benfica and Sporting CP, which means there are lots of games (1-2/week Aug-May, tickets €20 and up) and lots of team spirit. Benfica, with the red jerseys, plays at the 65,400-seat Stadium of Light, north of the city center (Estádio da Luz; M: Colégio Militar/Luz, www.slbenfica.pt). Sporting CP, with the green-and-white jerseys, plays at the 50,000-seat Estádio José Alvalade, which is also north of Lisbon's center (M: Campo Grande, www.sporting.pt). Tickets are generally available at the stadiums or at the ABEP kiosk on Praça dos Restauradores.

Concerts

The Gulbenkian Museum runs a classical concert season with about 180 events a year (www.gulbenkian.pt/musica). You can hear classical music by national and city orchestras at the cultural center in Belém (www.ccb.pt). Traditional Portuguese theater plays in the National Theater on Rossio, the fancy Teatro Nacional de São Carlos in Chiado, and in theaters along Rua das Portas de Santo Antão (the "eating lane"—described later, under "Eating in Lisbon") stretching north from Rossio. For popular music, these days you're more likely to find rock, jazz, Brazilian, and African music than traditional fado (which is more for tourists). The monthly *Agenda Cultural* provides the most up-to-date listing of world music, arts, and entertainment (free at TI, €0.50 at newsstands, online at www.agendalx.pt).

Movies

In Lisbon, unlike in Spain, films are shown in the original language with subtitles. (That's one reason the Portuguese speak better English than the Spanish.) Many of Lisbon's theaters are classy, complete with assigned seats, ushers, and intermissions. Check the newspaper or online to see what's playing. Modern options are in malls like Vasco da Gama (M: Oriente), El Corte Inglés (M: São

Sebastião), and at the Monumental complex in the ritzy Saldanha neighborhood (M: Saldanha).

Sleeping in Lisbon

Lisbon has a wide variety of accommodations. I've focused on a few categories: chic, international-style hotels offering a comfortable refuge at a high price; cheap, dingy, but affordable and safe old guesthouses (often up creaky old staircases in grimy buildings); boutique hotels offering a compromise between cost and comfort; and some famously classy hostels, which welcome travelers of all ages. For some travelers, short-term, Airbnb-type rentals can be a good alternative; search for places in my recommended hotel neighborhoods.

Lisbon has become increasingly popular, and rates have increased accordingly—especially on weekends (Thu-Sun), when many Brits and other Europeans fly in for brief urban vacations. Conventions can clog Lisbon at any time, and the busiest time is during the Festas de Lisboa (mainly the last three weeks of June) when parades, street parties, concerts, and fireworks draw crowds to the city.

I rank accommodations from $ budget to $$$$ splurge. To get the best deal, contact my family-run accommodations directly by phone or email. When you book direct, the owner avoids a commission and may be able to offer you a discount. Book well in advance for peak season or if your trip coincides with a major holiday or festival (see the appendix). For more information on reservations, short-term rentals, and more, see the "Sleeping" section in the Practicalities chapter.

THE BAIXA

Central as can be, the grid-planned, easy-to-navigate Baixa district bustles with shops, traffic, tourists, commuters, street musicians, pedestrian areas, and urban intensity. It's close to Rossio station, and the Aerobus to and from the airport cuts right through its middle. And it's handy to all of your sightseeing—wedged between the Alfama and the Bairro Alto/Chiado, with vintage trolleys zipping through every few minutes.

Upscale Hotels

$$$$ **Internacional Design Hotel** has 55 small, chic rooms centrally located at the southeast corner of Rossio. Each of its four floors has a different theme—pop, Zen, tribal, and urban. Having breakfast in their expansive restaurant overlooking Rossio is a fine way to start the day (air-con, elevator, underground pay parking nearby, Rua da Betesga 3, +351 213 240 990, www.idesignhotel. com, book@idesignhotel.com).

LISBON

Lisbon Center Hotels

OBELISK

S. ANT

To Praça Marquês de Pombal & Gulbenkian Museum

Praça dos Restauradores

R. DOM PEDRO V

RUA TAIPAS

São Pedro de Alcântara Park

R. COELHO

T.S. PEDRO

R. S.P. ALCANTARA

R. DA ROSA

R. MOUROS

R. TEIXEIRA

C. DA GLÓRIA

ELEVADOR DA GLÓRIA

Restauradores — Ⓜ

ABEP TICKET KIOSK

Ⓜ Restauradores

R. REGEDOR

❽

❷

ROSSIO TRAIN STATION

IGREJA SÃO ROQUE

R. MISERICÓRDIA

TR. BOA HORA

RUA DA ATALAIA

TR. AGUA FLOR

MUSEU DE ARTE SACRA

Largo do Cadova

R.5.B.VEN.

R. DO GREMIO

Largo Trindade Coelho

R. C. DUQUE

R. DO DUQUE

❿❼ ❶❷

TR. QUEIMADA

BAIRRO ALTO

RUA LUIZ SORIANO

R. DA ROSA

RUA DA

R.CONDESA

R. DA OLIVEIRA

❶❹

R. DO NORTE

RUA GAVEAS

❶❽

TEATRO DA TRINDADE

RUA NOVA TRINDADE

CONVENTO DO CARMO

❶❸

TR. DOS FIEIS DE DEUS

R. BARROCA

R. ESPERA

R. DA TRINDADE

Largo do Carmo

❶❻

T. MERCES

TR. DO CARMO

CHIADO

R. CAL. R. LORETO Ⓣ #28E

Praça Camões

RUA GARRETT

ELEVADOR DA BICA

❶❾

R.H. SECA

Ⓣ #28E

Ⓜ Baixa-Chiado

R. D. CHAGAS

R. DA EMENDA

❶❺

Ⓝ

Largo Barão Quintela

RUA D. DE BRAGANÇA

R. SERPA PINTO

RUA A. MARIA CARDOSO

R.ST. CAT.

T. G.

COUSSUL

RUA DO ALECRIM

R. CAPELO

SÃO CARLOS THEATER (OPERA)

BICA

R. ATAIDE

RUA FLORES

To Belém & ❷⓪

RUA

100 Meters

100 Yards

RUA S. PAULO

❶ Internacional Design Hotel
❷ Hotel Avenida Palace
❸ My Story Hotel Rossio
❹ My Story Hotel Tejo
❺ My Story Hotel Ouro
❻ Pensão Praça da Figueira
❼ Pensão Residencial Gerês

LISBON

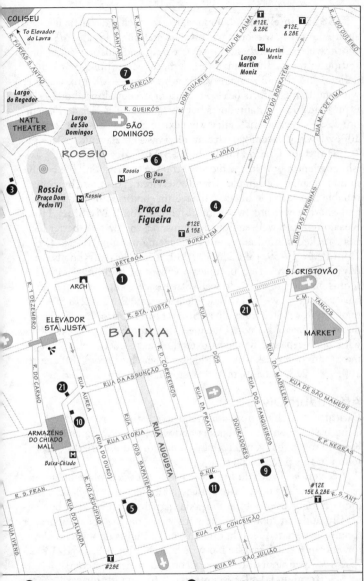

8 Lisbon Destination Hostel	**15** Casa do Barão
9 Home Lisbon Hostel	**16** Feeling Chiado 15
10 Living Lounge Hostel	**17** Zuza Guest House & Zuzabed & Breakfast
11 Lisbon Lounge Hostel	**18** Zuzabed Lisbon Suites
12 Casa Balthazar	**19** Chiado 44
13 Lisboa Carmo Hotel	**20** To Hotel As Janelas Verdes
14 Lisboa Pessoa Hotel	**21** Laundry (2)

$$$$ Hotel Avenida Palace, the most characteristic five-star splurge in town, was built with Rossio station in 1892 to greet big-shot travelers. Back then, trains were new, and Rossio was the only station in town. The lounges are sumptuous, dripping with chandeliers, and the 82 rooms—while a bit faded—still mix elegance with modern comforts (air-con, elevator, free parking, hotel's sign is on Praça dos Restauradores but entrance is at Rua 1 de Dezembro 123—down a small alleyway next to Starbucks, +351 213 218 100, www.hotelavenidapalace.pt, reservas@hotelavenidapalace.pt).

Boutique Chain Hotel: The **$$$ My Story** chain offers stylish, efficient rooms in the most central part of Lisbon. The combination of smart design plus friendly service makes these branches a reliable choice in the Baixa. All have air-conditioning and elevators and share a website (www.mystoryhotels.com). **My Story Hotel Rossio** rents 46 well-equipped, rooms in a couldn't-be-better location, tucked behind a strip of cafés facing bustling Rossio (Praça Dom Pedro IV 59, +351 213 400 380, rossio@mystoryhotels.com). **My Story Hotel Tejo** occupies two entire buildings with 135 rooms on the site of an old well. Street-side rooms on upper floors have a castle view (Rua Condes de Monsanto 2, +351 218 866 162, tejo@mystoryhotels.com). **My Story Hotel Ouro** has 51 rooms decorated in gold tones. Outside-facing rooms have great views, with double-paned windows over the busy streets below, but for maximum quiet, ask for an inside or upper-floor room (Rua Áurea 100, +351 213 400 340, ouro@mystoryhotels.com).

Affordable Dives

Basically a notch up from a hostel, these listings are worth considering if you're on a tight budget and want a handy Baixa location. Keep in mind that you get what you pay for—these are the best I've found in this price bracket.

$ Pensão Praça da Figueira is a backpacker place on a quiet back street with youth-hostel prices, a kitchen on every floor, a slick modern lobby overlooking Praça da Figueira, and 34 basic but colorfully updated rooms—some with views on the square (cheaper rooms have shared bath but no air-con, 2 flights up with no elevator, entrance is at Travessa Nova de São Domingos 9, +351 213 426 757, www.pensaopracadafigueira.com, reservas@ppf.com).

$ Residencial Florescente rents 67 straightforward rooms on the thriving, traffic-free "eating lane," a block off Praça dos Restauradores (air-con, elevator, Rua das Portas de Santo Antão 99—for location see "Lisbon's Avenida da Liberdade" map, later, +351 213 426 609, www.residencialflorescente.com, geral@residencialflorescente.com).

$ Pensão Residencial Gerês is a throwback, renting 20 well-worn, no-frills rooms with double-paned windows. The sweet

Nogueira family speaks some English (RS%, cheaper rooms with private bathroom down the hall, no breakfast, uphill a block off northeast corner of Rossio, Calçada do Garcia 6, +351 215 958 368, no website but book at www.booking.com, infogereslx@gmail.com).

Boutique Hostels in the Baixa

Among hostel aficionados, Lisbon is famous for having the best hostels anywhere. They welcome travelers of any age, come with an artistic flair, and, besides the usual dorm beds, have plenty of double rooms (except Home Lisbon Hostel). These come with extras like bike rental, movie nights, and cheap or "free" (tip-based) city tours and excursions out of town.

¢ **Lisbon Destination Hostel** feels designed for backpackers—young and old—who appreciate style, peace, and quiet. Located upstairs in the Rossio train station (literally next to the platforms), it provides a wonderful value and experience. The astroturfed lounge—with beanbag chairs and hammocks—sprawls beneath an Industrial Age glass canopy (many private rooms available, movie night in lounge, Largo do Duque de Cadaval 17, +351 213 466 457, www.destinationhostels.com, lisbon@destinationhostels.com).

¢ **Home Lisbon Hostel** is a little more rough and homey, with a loose camaraderie and friendly management. The hostel is dominated by its classic old wooden bar—an inviting place to socialize (7 private rooms—the rest are dorms, on the second floor at Rua de São Nicolau 13, near corner of Rua dos Fanqueiros, M: Baixa-Chiado, +351 218 885 312, www.homelisbonhostel.com, info@homelisbonhostel.com).

¢ **Living Lounge Hostel** is clean, modern, and centrally located near the Baixa-Chiado Metro stop. Each room is uniquely decorated (private rooms including singles, some rooms with aircon, Rua Crucifixo 116, second floor, +351 213 461 078, www.livingloungehostel.com, info@livingloungehostel.com).

¢ **Lisbon Lounge Hostel,** run by the same folks as the Living Lounge Hostel (above), is roughly midway between Praça da Figueira and Praça do Comércio (private rooms but no singles, Rua de São Nicolau 41, +351 213 462 061, www.lisbonloungehostel.com, info@lisbonloungehostel.com).

CHIADO

The Chiado district feels like Lisbon's uptown. For many, it's the best of all worlds: It's handy to the Baixa and Rossio area (just a few steps downhill), and to the artfully seedy Bairro Alto fado zone (just a few steps uphill), but it feels less touristy and congested than either. It's also a prime location for Lisbon's up-and-coming foodie restaurants and hipster shopping scene, making this a fun place simply to wander, graze, and window-shop. If I were buying an apartment in Lisbon, I'd look in Chiado. This area specializes in fresher, small, conscientiously-run boutique hotels—often upstairs in big buildings without elevators (expect lots of stairs).

$$$$ Casa Balthazar is an enticing splurge—an oasis-like private compound of stately old townhouses tucked amid characteristic, restaurant-lined stepped lanes just above Rossio, on the way up into the heart of Chiado. Classy and modern but still homey, each of its 17 rooms is different—some with views, terraces, and/or private whirlpool baths. There's an inviting little swimming pool, and breakfast is served in your room (air-con, Rua do Duque 26, mobile +351 917 085 568, www.casabalthazarlisbon.com, reservas@casabalthazarlisbon.com).

$$$$ Lisboa Carmo Hotel is bigger and has less personality than the others listed here, but it's in an appealing location: a few steps from charming Largo do Carmo. It has 48 sleek, straightforward, business-class rooms, not much in the way of public spaces, and the only elevator among my Chiado listings (air-con, elevator, Rua da Oliveira ao Carmo 1A, +351 213 264 710, carmo.luxhotels.pt, lisboa.carmo@luxhotels.pt). Their newer sister property, **$$$$ Lisboa Pessoa Hotel,** has similar rooms and a swimming pool just up the street in a neatly tiled building.

$$$ Casa do Barão is a delightful little refuge on a tame side-street just a block below the bustling Praça Luís de Camões in the heart of Chiado. Its 14 tidy, well-appointed, modern rooms share several fine common spaces, including a cozy library, winter-garden breakfast room, gravel patio, and tiny swimming pool. Complimentary coffee, tea, and snacks are available all day. At the lower end of this price range, it's a terrific value and a comfortable home base in Lisbon. As it's not staffed 24 hours a day, confirm your arrival details (air-con, Rua da Emenda 84, mobile +351 967 944 143, www.casadobarao.com, casasdobarao@gmail.com).

$$$ Feeling Chiado 15 is a fourth-floor walk-up with eight rooms high above the most appealing little leafy square, Largo do Carmo. Four of the rooms—at the cheaper end of this price range—look down over a residential patio; the pricier, "deluxe" rooms have views over Lisbon's rooftops and castle (most rooms have air-con, Largo do Carmo 15, +351 213 470 845, www.feelingchiado.com, feelingchiado@gmail.com).

Zuza, run by entrepreneurial Luis Zuzarte, has rooms in three different buildings around Chiado. The main branch, **$ Zuza Guest House,** has eight basic but neatly outfitted rooms with shared bathrooms in a creaky old building (no air-con, Rua do Duque 41). A few doors down, **$$ Zuzabed & Breakfast** has four rooms with bathrooms and castle views (air-con, Calçada do Duque 29). And a short walk away, up in the Bairro Alto, **$$$ Zuzabed Lisbon Suites** has seven classy rooms with vintage furnishings (Rua das

Gáveas 81). Let them know when you'll arrive: Morning check-in is likely at the Rua do Duque location; otherwise it'll be at the location you're sleeping at (contact for all: mobile +351 934 445 500, www.zuzabed.com, zuzabed@zuzabed.com).

$$ Chiado 44 is a simple place in a great location, just above Praça Luís de Camões. Its 11 small, basic, but comfortable rooms fill a historic building—expect plenty of stairs (air-con, Rua Horta Seca 44, mobile +351 918 352 901, www.chiado44.pt, info@chiado44.pt, Fabian).

ALONG AVENIDA DA LIBERDADE

Avenida da Liberdade is an upscale neighborhood facing a broad, tree-lined, very European-feeling boulevard. Most of my listings are a block or so off the main street. While it's a residential area, there are also lots of hotels—it's where many of Lisbon's tourists go to sleep. For this reason, it's a bit less characteristically "Lisbon" than some other neighborhoods...but for the sake of a quiet night's sleep, some consider that a good thing. These listings are a 10-minute walk or short Metro ride from the center. Most are near the Avenida Metro stop; Lisbon Dreams is closer to the Rato station.

High-End Chain Hotels

The **Hoteis Heritage Lisboa** chain has several branches, most near Avenida da Liberdade. These hotels distinguish themselves with classy public spaces and rooms, professional staff, and top-notch amenities (air-con, elevator, pay parking); guests are entitled to sightseeing deals—ask for details. Each hotel has its own style and personality, and all offer free port wine after 18:00 (www.heritage.pt).

$$$$ Hotel Britania maintains its 1940s Art Deco charm throughout its 33 spacious rooms, offering a clean and professional haven on a workaday street one block off Avenida da Liberdade. Three top-floor rooms are decorated in a luxurious Mod Deco style (Rua Rodrigues Sampaio 17, +351 213 155 016, britania.hotel@heritage.pt).

$$$$ Heritage Avenida Liberdade is the most contemporary, the only one actually on the leafy boulevard, and the closest to the center (a 5-minute walk from Rossio). Its stylish lobby/breakfast room is inviting, and the 42 rooms feel upscale-urban (Avenida da Liberdade 28, +351 213 404 040, avliberdade@heritage.pt).

$$$ Hotel Lisboa Plaza—a large, plush gem—mixes traditional style with bright-pastel classiness. Its 112 rooms are on a quiet street off busy Avenida da Liberdade, a block from the Avenida Metro station (Travessa do Salitre 7, +351 213 218 218, plaza@heritage.pt).

West of the Center: Another Hoteis Heritage branch is farther out, toward Belém. **$$$$ Hotel As Janelas Verdes** is next door to

LISBON

Lisbon's Avenida da Liberdade

Accommodations

1. Hotel Avenida Palace
2. Residencial Florescente
3. Hotel Britania
4. Heritage Avenida Liberdade
5. Hotel Lisboa Plaza
6. Hotel Alegria
7. Lisbon Dreams Guest House

Eateries

8. Pinóquio Restaurante
9. Bonjardim Restaurantes
10. Casa do Alentejo Restaurante & Bar
11. Restaurante Solar dos Presuntos
12. Cantinho São José
13. Cervejaria Ribadouro
14. Restaurante A Gina
15. Quermesse Restaurante
16. Esplanada do Príncipe Real
17. A Cevicheria
18. Pavilhão Chines

the Museum of Ancient Art, filling an 18th-century mansion with 29 cushy rooms and comfortably elegant public spaces. The third-floor library overlooks the river (Rua das Janeles Verdes 7, bus #714 stops nearby, +351 213 968 143, janelas.verdes@heritage.pt).

Other Avenida Liberdade Hotels

$$$ **Hotel Alegria** faces a quiet, inviting park in a peaceful neigh-

borhood 200 yards from the Avenida Metro station. Its bright, inviting public spaces and 30 comfortable, well-appointed rooms have hardwood floors varnished like a ship's deck (breakfast extra, air-con, elevator, Praça da Alegria 12, +351 213 220 670, www. hotelalegria.pt, info@hotelalegria.pt).

$ **Lisbon Dreams Guest House** has 18 fresh, relaxing, Ikea-style rooms, occupying three apartments and sharing seven bathrooms (shared kitchen and terraces; M: Marquês de Pombal, then take Rua Alexandre Herculano uphill and turn left on Rua Rodrigo da Fonesca, or M: Rato, take Rua Alexandre Herculano downhill, then right to reach Rua Rodrigo da Fonesca 29, +351 213 872 393, www.lisbondreams.com, reservations@lisbondreams.com).

Eating in Lisbon

Each district of the city comes with fun and characteristic restaurants. (Good eateries in Belém are described on page 98.) Ideally, have one dinner with a fado performance—several good options for music with your meal are listed in this section, with more fado options described earlier, under "Entertainment in Lisbon." Note that some smaller, family-run places take a few weeks off in the late summer or early fall—don't be surprised to find a handwritten *fechado para férias* (closed for vacation) sign taped to the window. For a great fish meal, combine a quick and fun ferry ride across the river to Cacilhas to dine at the grand **Restaurante Farol,** described on page 114.

Snack Bars: Quick, light meals are readily found in Lisbon's characteristic snack bars. On just about any street, you can belly up to a bar, observe, and order what looks good for a tasty, memorable, and inexpensive meal. You'll see lots of *pastel de bacalhau,* Lisbon's ubiquitous and delicious cod cake. Other good standbys are a *tosta* (panini filled with tuna or ham and cheese), a *prego* (steak sandwich) and a *bifana* (pork sandwich), each made with a secret sauce to give them character.

Food Tours in Lisbon: To simultaneously eat good food, learn about Portuguese cuisine, and meet a knowledgeable local guide, consider taking one of the food tours (described on page 50). These tours are informative, tasty, and a good value—filling you in while filling you up.

I rank eateries from $ budget to $$$$ splurge. For more advice on eating in Portugal, including ordering, tipping, and Portuguese cuisine and beverages, see the "Eating" section of the Practicalities chapter.

THE BAIXA AND NEARBY
On or near Rossio

The area around Rossio, with plenty of practical, inexpensive eateries, caters to busy locals commuting in and out by train. For locations, see the "Lisbon Center Restaurants" map on page 144.

$$$ Bastardo Restaurante—upstairs in the recommended Internacional Design Hotel—is a simple, solid, no-stress option for Portuguese cuisine with a modern twist overlooking the square. In a fun-loving way, they've bastardized traditional dishes. They also offer a classic Portuguese €15 lunch special. The space is fresh, bright, and accessible, like the menu. It can be smart to reserve (vegan options, daily 12:30-22:30, Rua da Betesga 3, facing Rossio, +351 213 240 993, http://restaurantebastardo.com).

$$ Confeitaria Nacional has been proudly satisfying sweet tooths for 180 years, and was once the favorite of Portuguese royalty. Stop in for a tasty pastry downstairs. Or, for a peaceful and inexpensive lunch, go upstairs, where you'll choose between a cheaper meal in the cafeteria or pay a little extra for service and Old World sophistication in the elegant dining room (Mon-Sat 8:00-20:00, pastry counter open Sun but upstairs may be closed, Praça da Figueira 18, +351 213 424 470).

$$ Café Nicola, founded in the 18th century as one of first coffee shops in town, was long a hangout of cultural elites. You'll find an Art Deco interior, formal waiters, and lots of locals eating its Nicola pepper steak. It's a sprawling, venerable café scene with classy seating inside and on the wide sidewalk facing Rossio's square (daily 8:00-24:00, Praça Dom Pedro IV 24, +351 213 460 579).

$ Casa Brasileira offers a characteristic budget snack or meal in a classic local scene. Fast lunch deals are served only at the bar (see blackboard at back for daily special); good, basic meals are served outside on sidewalk tables. Their *pastel de nata* (custard tart), made downstairs and in a second thriving kitchen next door, is as tasty as those that people line up for in Belém (daily 7:00-24:00, 100 yards from Rossio at Rua Augusta 265, +351 213 459 713).

$ Restaurante Beira-Gare is my choice for a quick, cheap meal immediately across the street from Rossio station. A classic greasy-spoon diner, it dishes out cod and vegetables prepared faster than a Big Mac and served with more energy than a soccer team. The house specialty is a pork sandwich *(bifana)*. Consider their soup-and-sandwich special; stand at the bar, grab a table, or sit outside for the pedestrian commotion (Mon-Sat 6:00-24:00, closed Sun, Rua 1 de Dezembro, +351 213 420 405). This is a great place for a quick cod cake *(pastel da bacalao)* at the bar.

Dive Bar with a View: Established in 1840 and run by Calheiros and Carmo, **$ A Tendinha do Rossio** is a classic *ginjinha* bar that also sells soups, sandwiches, and fishy snacks. While it's pretty dumpy, it's notable because it offers the only cheap tables on Rossio. Prices are dirt-cheap and the same whether you sit with the drunks at the bar, grab a tiny table inside, or serve yourself and sit outside overlooking Rossio (Mon-Sat 7:00-21:00, closed Sun, Praça Dom Pedro IV 6, +351 213 468 156).

Rua 1 de Dezembro: This street, which is active during the workday and dead after hours, is lined with cheap restaurants that make self-service speed a priority for busy office workers who eat here. Walk the street from Rossio station to the Elevador de Santa Justa to determine the prevailing menu of the day. Among your options is the handy self-service cafeteria at #97, **$$ Leão d'Ouro,** with an affordable lunch or dinner buffet featuring Brazilian grilled meats. It also has a fancy and more expensive sit-down restaurant next door (both daily 12:00-23:00).

There are two **grocery stores** on this street, both open long hours daily: the straightforward **Pingo Doce supermarket** (at #73, with very cheap 9-stool cafeteria), and the organic/health-food alternative across the street, **Celeiro,** which also has a self-service vegetarian lunch joint (called Tasquinha do Celeiro, at #53, Mon-Fri 8:00-18:00, closed Sat-Sun).

Lisbon's "Eating Lane" and Nearby

Just north of Rossio, Rua das Portas de Santo Antão is Lisbon's "eating lane"—a galaxy of eateries, many specializing in seafood (off the northeast corner of Rossio). While the waiters are pushy and it's all very touristy, the lane—lively with happy eaters—is enjoyable to browse. This is a fine spot to down a beer, snack on some snails, and watch people go by. For locations, see the "Lisbon's Avenida da Liberdade" map, on page 140.

$$$ Pinóquio Restaurante, a venerable seafood beer hall famous for its clams (€22 splittable portion), has a good local energy. You'll dine with a smart crowd at white-tableclothed tables yet with no pretense—the focus is on simple quality (daily 12:00-24:00, big portions, dine inside or outside facing the busy square, Praça dos Restauradores 79, +351 213 465 106).

$$ Bonjardim, a family-friendly diner on a small side street, is known for its tasty rotisserie chicken (pour on some spicy *piri-piri* sauce). Try their wonderful takes on *pastéis de bacalhau* (codfish fritters) or *esparregado* (spinach purée with garlic and olive oil), both Portuguese classics (daily 12:00-23:00, Travessa do Santo Antão 7 or 10, both branches run by same owner, one branch closes for a day off each week but the other takes up the slack, +351 213 427 424).

$$$ Casa do Alentejo Restaurante specializes in Alentejo

LISBON

Lisbon Center Restaurants

OBELISK

Praça dos Restauradores

To Praça Marquês de Pombal & Gulbenkian Mus

R. DOM PEDRO V

São Pedro de Alcântara Park

RUA TAIPAS

C. DA GLÓRIA

Restauradores

ABEP TICKET KIOSK

Restauradores

R. COELHO

R. S. P. ALCÂNTARA

R. TEIXEIRA

T.S. PEDRO

ELEVADOR DA GLÓRIA

RUA DA ROSA

R. MOUROS

ROSSIO TRAIN STATION

R.S.B. YEN

IGREJA SÃO ROQUE

7

TR. BOA HORA

MUSEU DE ARTE SACRA

Largo d Cadova

TR. AGUA FLOR

See Avenida da Liberdade detail map

R. DO GREMIO

R. MISERICÓRDIA

Largo Trindade Coelho

R. C. DUQUE

18 19

RUA DA ATALAIA

TR. QUEIMADA

29

R. DO DUQUE

R. CONDESA

R. DA OLIVEIRA

BAIRRO ALTO

RUA LUIZ SORIANO

RUA DA ROSA

R. NOTICIAS

R. DO NORTE

RUA GAYELAS

28 15

24

R. DA TRINDADE

CONVENT DO CARMO

TEATRO DA TRINDADE

Largo do Carmo

TR. DOS FIEIS DE DEUS

30

R. ESPERA

RUA NOVA TRINDADE

14

T. MERCES

RUA DA

R. BARROCA

31

TR. DO CARMO

CHIADO

22

R. CAL. R. LORETO

T #28E

RUA GARRETT

To 32

ELEVADOR DA BICA

R. H. SECA

Praça Camões

T #28E

Baixa-Chiado

R. D. CHAGAS

R. DA EMENDA

N

COUSSUL

Largo Barão Quintela

16

RUA DO LECRIM

RUA A. MARIA CARDOSO

RUA D. DE BRAGANÇA

25

R. SERPA PINTO

23

R. CAPELO

R. ST. CAT.

BICA

T. G.

20

SÃO CARLOS THEATER (OPERA)

BIBLIOTECA PUBLICA

17

R. ATAIDE

RUA FLORES

26

To Belém

100 Meters

100 Yards

27

RUA S. PAULO

RUA VITOR CÓRDON

13

LISBON

Baixa & Nearby
1. Bastardo Restaurante
2. Confeitaria Nacional
3. Café Nicola
4. Casa Brasileira
5. Restaurante Beira-Gare
6. A Tendinha do Rossio
7. Leão d'Ouro Rest./Buffet
8. Pingo Doce Supermarket
9. Celeiro Supermarket/Café
10. To Tentações de Goa
11. To Cervejaria Ramiro
12. Nova Pombalina

Chiado
13. Restaurante Vicente
14. Carmo Restaurante & Bar
15. Cervejaria da Trindade
16. Palácio Chiado
17. By the Wine
18. Café Buenos Aires & Solar do Duque
19. El Rei D'Frango
20. Café no Chiado
21. Armazéns do Chiado Mall
22. Manteigaria
23. Belcanto
24. Bairro do Avillez Taberna & Páteo
25. Café Lisboa
26. Cantinho do Avillez
27. Pizzaria Lisboa
28. Pitaria

Barrio Alto
29. Restaurante Bota Alta
30. A Primavera do Jerónimo
31. Lisbon Winery
32. To Mercado de Campo de Ourique
33. Martinho da Arcada Café Bar
34. Wines of Portugal Tasting Room

Lisbon's Gourmet Food-Circus Markets

The big news on Lisbon's eating scene is the transformation of traditional farmers markets into gourmet food circuses. These combine the stalls of traditional food-market vendors (selling produce, meat, fish, spices, etc.) with a food court filled with eateries run by locally respected chefs. If you love food—or even if you don't—these are fun to explore.

Mercado da Ribeira (a.k.a. Time Out Market)

Located at Cais do Sodré (between Chiado and the river), this is two markets in one: The bois-terous and venerable Ribeira market survives in one half of the Industrial Age, iron-and-glass market hall, while the other half has become a trendy food court curated by *Time Out* magazine, which has invit-ed a few dozen quality restau-rants to open outposts here. Eating here at long, noisy pic-nic tables is far from romantic,

but the quality and prices are great. The produce and fish market is open from 7:00 to 13:00 (closed Sun and no fish Mon), while the restaurants are open daily from 12:00 to 24:00. This place is no secret—to avoid a mob scene at dinnertime, arrive before 19:00.

Getting There: The Mercado da Ribeira (like many locals, I resist calling this venerable market by its new "Time Out" name) is across the street from the Cais do Sodré train station. It's con-veniently served by the Metro (Cais do Sodré stop) and tram #15E (on the way to/from Belém), and it's about a 10-minute walk from Praça do Comércio. If you're here for dinner, note that the crazy Pink Street—lined with clubs and bars—is just two blocks inland and lively late (described in "Entertainment in Lisbon," earlier). The entire neighborhood around the market is emerging as a live-ly and trendy food and bar scene.

Eating at Mercado da Ribeira: Entering the market from the main entrance (facing Cais do Sodré), the workaday market stalls are on your right, while the foodie festival is on your left. In

cuisine and fills an old, second-floor dining hall. The Moorish-looking building is a cultural and social center for transplants from the Alentejo, the traditional southern province of Portugal (and historically the poorest region in the country). While the food is mainly hearty and simple, come for the ambience. It's a good place to try regional specialties such as pork with clams, or the super-sweet, eggy almond dessert called *charcada*. The full-bodied Alentejo red wine is cheap and solid (lunch specials, Tue-

the food court, join the young, trendy, hungry, and thirsty crowd grazing among a wide variety of options. Assemble a sampling of local treats, and grab a seat at the big, shared tables in the middle. The north wall is a row of stalls run by big-name Lisbon chefs offering quality dishes at reasonable prices (enticing dinner plates for €10). And there are also branches of Honorato (a local "gourmet burger" chain), O Prego da Peixaria (fish and steak sandwiches), Sea Me (a Chiado institution for seafood—with their notorious "octopus hot dog"), Aloma (in the west outer aisle, for the best pastries), and Santini (the venerable Portuguese gelateria). Get wine and beer from separate stalls in the center. You may find affordable *percebes* (barnacles) at several seafood stalls. On the west side, an aisle just outside of the main hall is lined with wonderful seafood bars.

Restaurant and a View: Above the main entrance (south side) is a great viewpoint for a wide shot of the market din below, and the quality **$$$ Pap'Açôrda Restaurant,** a long-respected place for traditional Portuguese cuisine, with a top chef. They serve seasonal specials and a €20 three-course lunch special on weekdays (12:00-18:00) in a modern, spacious dining room with professional service and an inviting menu (daily Tue-Sun 12:00-24:00, closed Mon, +351 213 464 811).

Mercado de Campo de Ourique

A trendy marketplace fills this 19th-century iron-and-glass market. Compared to Mercado da Ribera, it's less crowded and more purely local. Produce stalls, fishmongers, and bakeries sell everything from pigs' ears to fragrant bunches of cilantro (most close in the evening). At lunch and dinner, local diners pick up meals from whichever counter appeals: pork, seafood, Japanese, wine, beer, coffee, meat, produce, artisanal gelato, and so on (most eateries open daily 10:00-23:00).

Getting There: It's a couple of miles west of Rossio. Take a taxi or Uber, or hop on trolley #28E and ride to the second-to-last stop (Igreja do Santo Condestável; market is behind the big church). Lisbon's most interesting cemetery is one stop farther, at the end of the trolley line.

Sun 12:00-15:00 & 19:00-22:00, Mon 19:00-22:00, slip into the closed-looking building at Rua das Portas de Santo Antão 58 and climb stairs to the right, +351 213 469 231). They host folk singing in the grand ballroom (often on Sat from 15:00) and ballroom dancing (on many Sun from 15:00 to 19:00), except in summer when it's too hot (mid-June–mid-Sept).

$ Casa do Alentejo Bar, in the same building, serves cheap bar food and wine, either in the sleek-and-trendy interior or out on the little patio (spicy meat dishes, hearty cheeses, other tapas; daily 12:00-23:00, to the right of the stairs, look for *taberna* sign on main floor).

$$$$ Restaurante Solar dos Presuntos keeps the theater crowd happily fed with meat and seafood specialties. Its upstairs is more elegant, while the downstairs—with a colorful, open kitchen—is higher energy. Photos of Lisbon's celebrities and politicians who eat here enliven the walls. This place can take advantage of its popularity and bulldoze tourists into spending a lot—order cautiously and know what you're paying for. Reservations are smart (big splittable portions, good wine list, see daily suggestions, Mon-Sat 12:00-15:30 & 19:00-23:00, closed Sun, at the top end of Rua das Portas de Santo Antão at #150, +351 213 424 253, www.solardospresuntos.com).

$ Cantinho São José is a wonderfully untouristy, cheap-and-cheery hole-in-the-wall a block beyond the main restaurant zone. Its extremely tight, tiled interior is jammed with tiny tables filled by big locals ordering hearty, splittable portions of Portuguese classics—for far less money than the tourist traps nearby (Sun-Fri 9:00-24:00, closed Sat, Rua São José 94, +351 213 427 866).

On or near Avenida da Liberdade

These spots are in a residential neighborhood, near my recommended accommodations (Avenida Metro stop). For locations, see the "Lisbon's Avenida da Liberdade" map on page 140.

$$$$ Cervejaria Ribadouro is a favorite splurge for locals for quality meat and shellfish (daily 12:00-24:00, Avenida da Liberdade 155 at intersection with Rua do Salitre, +351 213 549 411). Seafood prices are listed by weight—the waiter can help you determine the cost of a portion. For a fun, quick, €15 per-person meal, order a small draught beer *(uma imperial),* 100 grams (about a quarter pound) of *percebes* (barnacles), and *pão torrado com manteiga* (toasted bread with butter).

$$$ Restaurante A Gina, glowing like a mirage in a vacant lot that used to be a theater zone, is a good dinner option. Cloth bibs embroidered with Gina's name help you appreciate the tasty traditional Portuguese grilled meat and fish with abandon. Gina and her staff scramble to give this wonderful place a genuine friendliness; the son, Rui, speaks English. It's two minutes off of Avenida da Liberdade (directly behind recommended Hotel Lisboa Plaza—look for signs, RS%—free dessert port with this book, daily 12:00-15:00 & 18:00-24:00, reservations recommended, +351 213 420 296).

$$ Quermesse Restaurante is a fun, bright, and creative place serving Mediterranean dishes with plenty of cod and friendly service. Half the seating is in an old-school grocery store—when

---

Appetizers Aren't Free

Remember: In Portugal, there's no such thing as a free munch. Appetizers brought to your table before you order (such as olives, bread, and fancy pâtés) are not free. This is not a tourist gimmick—it's a Portuguese tradition, meant to curb your hunger while looking at the menu and waiting for your main dish to arrive. So if you don't want to pay for them, just push them aside after the waiter brings them. Don't eat any of it—not even one olive—or you'll be charged (only €1-2 for the simpler appetizers, but it can be annoying if you don't expect it).

---

reserving, request "in the store" (daily 12:00-15:00 & 19:00-24:00, Rua da Glória 85, +351 211 507 901).

Near Praça Martim Moniz

For locations, see the "Lisbon Center Restaurants" map on page 144.

$$ Tentações de Goa, run by Maria and her chef-owner husband from Goa, is a sweet hole-in-the-wall with authentic Goan cuisine and ambience. It's buried deep in a tangle of lanes in the Mouraria district, a block uphill from Praça da Figueira (Mon-Sat 12:00-15:00 & 19:00-22:00, closed Sun, from Poço do Borratém follow a lane uphill to Rua de São Pedro Mártir 23, +351 218 875 824).

$$$ Cervejaria Ramiro—an old-school restaurant serving well-respected seafood and steak, is hugely popular and becoming quite touristy. It's a good choice if you like bustle and happy energy with great seafood. Arrive early or late to avoid a very long line (Tue-Sun 12:00-24:00, closed Mon, a couple of blocks north of Praça Martim Moniz at Avenida Almirante Reis 1H, +351 218 851 024).

Below the Cathedral

These places are at the southeast corner of the Baixa, on the way to the Alfama.

$ Nova Pombalina is a busy little joint that serves quick sandwiches, soups, and exotic fresh-squeezed juices. It's famous among office workers for its suckling pig sandwich *(sandes de leitão)*. They have good *piri-piri* sauce on request. From Praça do Comércio, it's five blocks toward the castle, on the corner of Rua do Comércio and Rua da Madalena (Mon-Sat 8:00-19:00, closed Sun, Rua do Comércio 2, +351 218 874 360).

$$ Mesa Kreol offers a lively taste of Portugal's former overseas colonies—with cuisine from Cape Verde, Mozambique, Angola, and Brazil. Its interior is small, cozy, and nondescript, but the cuisine is a bold and flavorful change of pace. Manager Ju enjoys

LISBON

helping his guests navigate the menu, and there's often live music (Tue-Sun 19:00-24:00, closed Mon, Arco das Portas do Mar 29— see map on next page, mobile +351 910 629 690).

THE ALFAMA

Lunch on Largo do Contador Mor: This leafy and picturesque square, just under the castle, has a few interchangeable **$$** restaurants serving up decent plates of grilled sardines *(sardinhas grelhadas)*. But the real star of the square is **$ Miss Can,** an engaging, colorful, and stylish little shop that's injecting some contemporary class into the beloved Portuguese tradition of canned fish. Three young, hip Lisboners have returned to their roots (their families have been in the sardine biz for generations) to create fresh new packaging for a variety of canned sardines, mackerel, and cod. Peruse their shop, and pick a can or two to eat with bread, salad, and a drink at one of their inviting little café tables (daily 11:00-19:00, at #17, mobile +351 910 007 004, www.miss-can.com).

Near the Santa Luzia Viewpoint: $$$ Farol de Santa Luzia, which offers a nice seafood feast with a delicate and delightful dining area, is a favorite of mine for dinner at the top of the Alfama. A family-run place with a local clientele, it offers the Algarve *cataplana* style of cooking—simmered in a copper pot (€27 big *cataplana* of meat, fish, or shellfish for two; indoor seating only, Mon-Sat 17:30-23:00, closed Sun, Largo Santa Luzia 5, across from Santa Luzia viewpoint terrace, tiny sign, +351 218 863 884; Andre, Luis, and family).

Near Largo Rodrigues de Freitas: For more of an adventure with your meal, walk past Largo das Portas do Sol and follow the trolley tracks along Rua de São Tomé to a square called Largo Rodrigues de Freitas—if riding trolley #12E, it's the first stop over the big hill. On this square, **$$ Restaurante Frei Papinhas** is a classic, family-run, hole-in-the-wall where you can feast on fresh seafood with the neighborhood crowd. Dine inside, or at rickety tables across the street in a charming square—where you can watch the trolleys rattle by (daily 12:00-16:00 & 19:00-24:00, Rua de São Tome 13, +351 218 866 471).

Fado Deep in the Alfama: While the Bairro Alto is far livelier at night and has a better energy, the Alfama still has a unique charm. My favorite places for dinner with fado are described earlier, under "Entertainment in Lisbon."

CHIADO

This neighborhood has some of Lisbon's trendiest restaurants. If you don't mind paying a bit more to experience the city's burgeoning food scene, venture up into these inviting streets. Remember that the more traditional Bairro Alto neighborhood—covered in

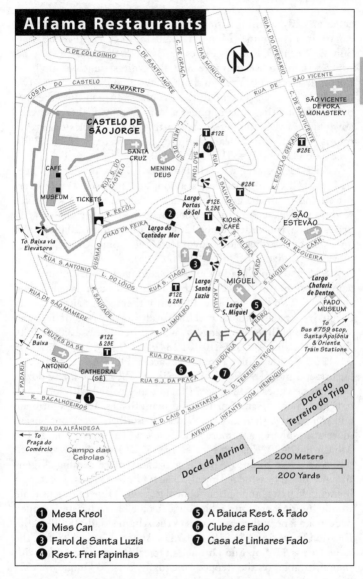

Alfama Restaurants

1 Mesa Kreol
2 Miss Can
3 Farol de Santa Luzia
4 Rest. Frei Papinhas

5 A Baiuca Rest. & Fado
6 Clube de Fado
7 Casa de Linhares Fado

the next section—is just a few minutes' walk away. For locations, see the "Lisbon Center Restaurants" map on page 144.

$$$ Restaurante Vicente, at the southern edge of Chiado, fills a former brick-arched coal warehouse with rustic-trendy decor and excellent Alentejo cuisine from Portugal's arid southern heartland. The hearty, delicious meals come with real history: Traditionally, coal cellars like this one came with a crow named "Vicente" to act as an early-warning system for polluted air—like the proverbial canary in a coal mine (Mon-Fri 12:30-15:30 & 19:30-24:00, Sat-Sun 19:30-24:00, Rua das Flores 6, +351 218-066-142).

$$ Carmo Restaurante and Bar offers delicious updated Portuguese cooking. You can share a few *petiscos* (Portuguese-style tapas), or get well-presented main courses. In good weather, sit out on the inviting square, under a leafy canopy. Otherwise, take advantage of the chic-but-homey setting, with a series of smaller rooms (weekday lunch deals, tempting desserts, daily 12:00-23:00, Largo do Carmo 11, +351 213 460 088).

$$$ Cervejaria da Trindade—a bright, boisterous, beer hall—is full of historic tiles, seafood, and tourists. While over-priced and in all the guidebooks, it's a historic landmark (see description on page 76). The seafood is charged by weight—clarify prices when you order (daily 12:00-24:00, liveliest 20:00-22:00, air-con, courtyard, a block down from São Roque Church at Rua Nova da Trindade 20C, +351 213 423 506).

$$$ Palácio Chiado took an abandoned, 18th-century private mansion and turned it into a luxurious but relaxed dining space with two bars and five differently themed restaurants, each occupying a palatial room. Feel like royalty as you ascend the grand staircase to chill with a hanging, winged lion (daily 12:00-24:00, Rua do Alecrim 70, +351 210 101 184).

$$$ By the Wine, a trendy yet accessible wine bar fills a cellar under a green-bottled vaulted ceiling. They serve a few dozen Portuguese wines by the glass, thoughtfully paired with local cold cuts and cheeses, small plates, and main dishes. It's less intimate and informative than Lisbon Winery (described later), but busier, more atmospheric, and more food-focused (Tue-Sun 12:00-24:00, Mon from 18:00, Rua das Flores 41, +351 213 420 319).

$$$ Café Buenos Aires is a friendly place serving Argentinian cuisine (lots of red meat), hearty dinner salads, vegetarian homemade pasta, and famous chocolate cake. Dine in the intimate woody interior, or at fun tables outside on a characteristic, stepped pedestrian lane with views across to the Alfama (daily 18:00-24:00, Rua do Duque 31, +351 213-420-739). Above this place and on the same lane is **$$ Solar do Duque,** a typical Portuguese eatery with romantic tables on the stepped lane (daily, Rua do Duque 67, +351 213 426 901).

$ El Rei D'Frango ("King of Chicken") is a local favorite for huge portions of affordable, stick-to-your-ribs grilled meat and fish specialties (but, strangely, not much chicken), served in an unpretentious little hole-in-the-wall. It's on the steep stepped lanes at the very bottom of Chiado, behind Rossio station (Mon-Sat 10:00-22:00, closed Sun, Calçada do Duque 5, +351 213 424 066).

$$$ Café no Chiado is a local favorite for its brief, accessible menu. Perched on an upper street overlooking the square in front of the São Carlos national theater, it has a casual-classy interior, and the outdoor tables—on a tiny square under red-and-black awnings—feel very European (daily 12:00-24:00, Largo do Picadeiro, +351 213 460 502).

Food Court Atop the Armazéns do Chiado Mall: The sixth-floor food court at this shopping center, between the Bairro Alto and the Baixa, hosts mostly fast-food and chain restaurants, but mixes in a few actual restaurants with castle views (daily 12:00-23:00, between Rua Garrett and Rua da Assunção; from the lower town, find the inconspicuous elevator at Rua do Crucifixo 89 or 113, next to the Baixa-Chiado Metro entrance). Among your many options are: **Loja das Sopas**, with hearty soups and cheap fixed-price meals; **Companhia das Sandes,** which offers up sandwiches and healthy, big-bowl pasta salads topped with tropical fruits; and **Restaurant Chimarrão,** serving Brazilian cuisine and an impressive *rodizio:* an all-you-can-eat buffet of salad, veggies, and endless beef, ham, pork, sausage, and chicken (€11 for weekday lunch, €13 for dinner and on weekends).

Heavenly Custard Tarts: $ Manteigaria is simply the best place in Lisbon's downtown for *pastel de nata*—everyone's favorite local pastry. They serve only this one treat, constantly churning out the lovable little €1 custard pies so you'll get them hot from the oven. While here, enjoy a look at the busy kitchen (daily until 24:00, Rua Loreto 2 just off Praça Luís de Camões).

José Avillez Restaurants in Chiado

One of Portugal's top celebrity chefs, José Avillez, has elevated and modernized Portuguese classics with international influences and techniques. He runs 16 restaurants and, judging by the energy in each and the local buzz, he's on a roll. While his **Belcanto** flagship restaurant boasts two Michelin stars (costly tasting menus, closed Sun-Mon, book well in advance, Largo de São Carlos 10, www.belcanto.pt), his other places are perfectly accessible. They have a common personality: trendy; high-energy; open kitchens; young, smart, English-speaking waitstaff; open daily (12:00-24:00); and, unless eating very early or very late, a reservation is smart. One call center works for all (+351 211 914 498) or book online (www.joseavillez.pt).

Bairro do Avillez Taberna and **Páteo** are two distinct and thriving places at the same address. **$$$ Taberna** is a casual place serving Portuguese classics as small plates and main courses. Its bar is a hit with well-dressed and mingling locals sharing plates family-style. **$$$$ Páteo,** in the back under a big skylight, is more formal and expensive, offering a full menu of fish and seafood, vegetarian dishes, and salads (Rua Nova da Trindade 18).

$$$ Café Lisboa is a romantic and elegant bistro with tasty modern Portuguese dishes and great seating both indoors and out (in front of the opera house at Largo de São Carlos 23).

$$$ Cantinho do Avillez has a casual vibe and a more international menu. Dining here, you'll feel like you're in on a Lisbon foodie secret (Rua dos Duques de Bragança 7).

$$$ Pizzaria Lisboa simply serves top-quality pizza in a dressy yet fun setting (Rua dos Duques de Bragança 5).

$ Pitaria, with a few stools at small tables, offers top-quality Middle-Eastern take-away and the best shawarma and falafel in town (Rua Nova da Trindade 11).

THE BAIRRO ALTO

For a characteristic meal in Old World surroundings, the Bairro Alto is hard to beat. For locations, see the "Lisbon Center Restaurants" map on page 144.

Fado with Dinner in Bairro Alto: For a most memorable dining experience with live fado music in the Bairro Alto, consider these two options: **Restaurante Adega do Ribatejo** (more casual, Rua Diario de Noticias 23), or **O Faia** (top-end splurge with quality food and fado, Rua da Barroca 54). Both are described earlier, under "Entertainment in Lisbon."

$$ Restaurante Bota Alta ("The High Boot") is a classic—if a bit touristy—little eatery with a timeless Portuguese ambience, tight seating, and reliably good food. Portions are big, and Paulo offers a fun dessert sampler plate. Reservations are smart (Mon-Sat 12:00-14:30 & 19:00-23:00, closed Sun, at corner of Travessa da Queimada and Rua da Atalaia, +351 213 427 959).

$$ A Primavera do Jerónimo is a quintessential Bairro Alto joint serving traditional home-style plates in a jam-packed, joyfully characteristic scene. Rafael and Helena love serving stuffed squid and Brás-style cod—whipped into a frittata with potatoes and onions (Mon-Sat opens at 19:30, closed off-season Sun; reserve, come early, or wait; at Travessa da Espera 38, a few steps below recommended fado place Canto do Camões, +351 213 420 477).

$$$ Lisbon Winery, a modern little wine bar, has a passion for the best wines, cheeses, and meats. With quality local ingredients, cork walls, and fado music playing, it's a perfect storm of Portuguese culture. Their expert staff knows Portuguese wines and ports and how to complement them with tasty foods. Tell your server your budget, and they'll work within it (Tue-Sun 15:00-23:00, closed Mon, Rua da Barroca 13, +351 218 260 132, www.lisbonwinery.com). They also do wine tastings (€65/person, typically starts at 15:30 or 17:30 and lasts 2 hours).

Príncipe Real Garden Eateries
(Jardim do Príncipe Real)

This delightful parklike square is just a five-minute hike up Rua Dom Pedro V above the top of the Elevador da Glória funicular and the Bairro Alto. While this area is a shopping mecca (see "Shopping in Lisbon," earlier), it also has a lovely array of eateries. For locations, see the "Lisbon's Avenida da Liberdade" map on page 140.

The park itself has an unforgettable cedar tree shaped into a canopy over shady benches and a *quiosque* that doubles as a trendy, youthful wine and beer hangout. Also below the tree's canopy is **$$$ Esplanada do Príncipe Real,** with delightful seating—either at outdoor tables under shady branches or in the glassed-in interior. Skip the pricey, forgettable food—I'd just order a drink and savor the ambience (+351 210 965 699).

$$$ A Cevicheria is the neighborhood's big foodie draw, where (under a giant stuffed octopus) Chef Kiko serves elegant Peruvian/Portuguese dishes—specializing in flavorfully marinated raw fish and seafood ceviche. This deservedly popular place takes no reservations; arrive early or expect to wait (daily 12:00-24:00, a block toward Bairro Alto from the square at Rua Dom Pedro V 129, +351 218 038 815).

$$ Pavilhão Chines ("Chinese Pavilion"), a few doors down, is an eccentric, smoky, private museum-like bar with room after room slathered with an enormous collection of esoteric treasures. Come here to settle into a club chair and sip a drink rather than to eat (daily from 18:00, Rua Dom Pedro V 89, billiards in back).

Lisbon Connections

BY PLANE

Lisbon's easy-to-manage Portela Airport is five miles northeast of downtown (code: LIS; for airport info, see www.aeroportolisboa.pt or call +351 218 413 700 or +351 800 201 201).

Getting Between the Airport and Downtown

Getting to and from the airport is a snap. Figure on 20 to 30 minutes by taxi, Uber, or bus (depending on traffic) or 30 to 40 minutes by Metro.

By Taxi or Uber: Taxis line up on the curb at the airport, but are notoriously aggressive in gouging arriving travelers. You're more likely to get a fair price—and skip any line—by going upstairs to the departures curb and hopping into a cab as it drops off its riders. Better yet, request a ride using Uber. Either way, a ride to or from town should cost €10-15 to the center. If taking a taxi, insist on using the meter—it should start at around €4 and be set to *Tarifa 1* (or *Tarifa 2* for nights, weekends, and holidays). There is no "airport fee" supplement, but there is a legitimate €1.60 fee for your luggage (not per bag).

To return to the airport from downtown, use Uber or hail a cab on the street. Skip the outrageously overpriced "taxi vouchers" sold by the airport TI—these are for rides outside the center and more than double your cost.

If heading for a town other than Lisbon, talk with cabbies about a set "off-the-meter" fare. I recently negotiated a fast and efficient ride from the airport directly to Nazaré by taxi for around €100.

By Bus: While dirt-cheap public buses leave from the airport curb, they are not intended for people with luggage. The Aerobus shuttle is faster and nearly as cheap (€4, 3/hour, runs 8:00-21:00, departs outside arrival level at bus stop marked "Aerobus #1," www.aerobus.pt). Be sure to use Aerobus #1, which heads to the city center, with stops at Marquês de Pombal, Avenida da Liberdade, Restauradores, Rossio, Praça do Comércio, and Cais do Sodré. Route #2 avoids the downtown and ends in the financial district, but makes a handy stop at the bus station at Sete Rios if you plan to go elsewhere immediately (see "By Bus," later). Aerobus tickets are sold at the airport TI or at the bus stop for the same price, or you can buy them online in advance at a discount. (But for three passengers, a taxi or Uber is likely cheaper than this bus.)

By Metro: The Metro gets you into town affordably (for the price of a single transit ticket) and avoids traffic. But to reach central Lisbon, you'll have to change from the airport's suburb-focused red line to the green line (at Alameda)—it's time-consuming (figure 30-40 minutes total) and inconvenient if you're packing heavy. To find the Metro, exit the airport arrivals hall and turn right to find the Aeroporto stop. Before boarding, buy a reloadable Viva Viagem card and your choice of ticket (zapping, single-ride, or all-day) at the ticket machine (see details under "Getting Around Lisbon" on page 37).

BY TRAIN

All of Lisbon's train stations are connected to the Metro system, making departures and arrivals a breeze. For train info, call +351 808 208 208, visit www.cp.pt, or check Germany's excellent all-Europe website, www.bahn.com.

Santa Apolónia station covers international trains and nearly all of Portugal. Located just east of the Alfama, it has ATMs, a morning-only TI, baggage storage, a Pingo Doce supermarket, and good Metro and bus connections to the town center. A taxi or Uber from Santa Apolónia to any of my recommended hotels costs roughly €8. Bus #728, #759, #782, and #794 go to or near Praça do

Comércio, and bus #759 continues to Rossio and Praça dos Restauradores. To get to the bus stop from the station, look for the Metro sign, walk past the escalators to exit the station, and go right along busy Avenida Infante Dom Henrique to the bus stop.

Most trains using Santa Apolónia also stop at **Oriente** station, farther from the center, near Parque das Nações (M: Oriente; for more on this architecturally interesting station, see page 111).

Rossio station, which is in the town center and an easy walk from most recommended hotels, handles the most convenient trains to Sintra (direct, 2/hour, 40 minutes, buy tickets from machines at track level on second floor). It also has trains to Óbidos and Nazaré (but since both destinations require multiple transfers, the bus is a better option). The all-Portugal ticket office on the ground floor (next to Starbucks) sells long-distance and international train tickets (Mon-Fri 8:00-14:30 & 15:30-20:00, closed Sat-Sun, cash only).

Cais do Sodré station, near the waterfront just west of Praça do Comércio (M: Cais do Sodré), is the terminus for a short regional line that runs along the coast from Lisbon, making stops at Belém (10 minutes), Estoril (30 minutes), and Cascais (40 minutes).

Train Connections

Note: Most trains leaving from Santa Apolónia pass through Oriente station a few minutes later.

From Lisbon by Train to: Madrid (likely 1/day, "Lusitânia" night train, 11 hours, departs from Santa Apolónia station, arrives at Madrid's Chamartín station), **Évora** (4/day, 1.5 hours, departs Oriente), **Lagos** (3/day, 4 hours, departs Oriente, transfer in Tunes), **Tavira** (4/day, 4.5 hours, departs Oriente, change at Faro), **Coimbra** (almost hourly, 2 hours, departs Santa Apolónia),

Nazaré/Valado (5/day, 3-4 hours, transfer in Caldas da Rainha or Coimbra-B; bus is better—see next page), **Óbidos** (3/day, 2.5 hours, departs Santa Apolónia; also 7/day, 2.5 hours, transfer in Melecas or Cacém, departs Rossio), **Porto** (hourly, 3 hours, departs Oriente), **Sintra** (Mon-Fri 2/hour, Sat-Sun hourly, 40 minutes, departs Rossio; 6/hour, 45 minutes, departs Oriente).

To Salema: To reach Salema, you'll first need to get to **Lagos,** which is about 4 hours from Lisbon by train (see above) or bus (see next). Trains from Lisbon to the Algarve leave from Oriente station on the Lisboa-Faro line. At Tunes, a transfer to a local train takes you as far as Lagos. From there, it's a cheap bus ride or a pricier taxi ride to Salema (see page 217 details).

BY BUS

Lisbon's efficient Sete Rios bus station is in the modern part of the city, three miles inland. It has ATMs, schedules, and two side-by-side information offices—one for buses within Portugal, the other for international routes (Rede Expressos, which sells tickets for routes—including to Spain—even if operated by other companies like Alsa). While it's possible to buy bus tickets up to a week in advance, you can almost always buy a ticket just a few minutes before departure. The EVA company covers the south of Portugal (www.eva-bus.com), while Rede Nacional de Expressos does the rest of the country (www.rede-expressos.pt; bus info for both companies—toll +351 707 223 344).

The bus station is across the street from the large Sete Rios train station, which sits above the Jardim Zoológico Metro stop. To get from the bus station to downtown Lisbon, it's a €6 taxi or Uber ride or a short Metro trip on the blue line (from bus station, walk down stairs and across to enter the Sete Rios train station, then follow signs for *Metro: Jardim Zoológico*).

From Lisbon by Bus to: Coimbra (hourly, 2.5 hours), **Nazaré** (6/day, 2 hours), **Fátima** (1-2/hour, 1.5 hours), **Batalha** (5/day, 2 hours), **Alcobaça** (7/day, 2 hours, some transfer in Caldas da Rainha), **Óbidos** (hourly, 1 hour, departs from near Campo Grande Metro stop), **Porto** (best via Rede Expressos, at least hourly, 3 hours), **Évora** (almost hourly, 1.5 hours), **Lagos** (hourly direct, 4 hours, easier than train, must book ahead, get details at TI), **Tavira** (5/day direct, 4 hours), **Madrid** (2-3/day, 9 hours, overnight option, www.avanzabus.com), **Sevilla** (4/day, 7 hours, overnight option, may be fewer off-season, run by Alsa, www.alsa.es).

BY CRUISE SHIP

Most cruise ships dock at one of three terminals: Jardim do Tabaco (immediately below the Alfama), Santa Apolónia (near the train station of the same name, just beyond the Alfama), or Alcântara (about two miles west of downtown, between the center and Belém).

The taxis that wait here are notoriously dishonest. You may be better off using Uber, walking a block or two away from the terminal and hailing a passing cab on the street (not at a taxi stand), or riding a cruise-line shuttle service to Praça da Figueira. Hop-on, hop-off bus tours, which conveniently link up major sights—stop at the cruise terminals (see "Tours in Lisbon" earlier in this chapter).

From **Alcântara,** you can hop on trolley #15E (use pedestrian underpass to reach trolley stop) or bus #728—either way, it's about a 15-minute ride. (Both of these also go—in the opposite direction—to the sights in Belém.)

Jardim do Tobaco and **Santa Apolónia** are close enough to walk to the Baixa (15-20 minutes)—just cross busy Avenida Infante Dom Henrique and walk along a row of houses with the river on your left) until you reach Praça do Comércio. Or you can take bus #728 from near either terminal to Praça do Comércio.

LISBON

SINTRA

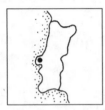

For centuries, Portugal's aristocracy considered Sintra (SEEN-trah)—just 15 miles northwest of Lisbon—the perfect place to escape from city life. Now tourists do, too. Sintra is a mix of natural and man-made beauty: fantasy castles set amid exotic tropical plants, lush green valleys, and craggy hilltops with hazy views of the Atlantic and Lisbon. This was the summer getaway of Portugal's kings. Those with money and a desire to be close to royalty built their palaces amid luxuriant gardens in the same neighborhood. Lord Byron called this bundle of royal fancies and aristocratic dreams a "glorious Eden," and even though it's mobbed with tourists today, it's still magnificent.

With extra time, explore the rugged and picturesque westernmost tip of Portugal at Cabo da Roca.

PLANNING YOUR TIME

Sintra makes a great day trip from Lisbon. Here you can romp along the ruined ramparts of a deserted Moorish castle, and climb through the Versailles of Portugal—the Pena Palace—on a neighboring hilltop.

It's such an ideal side-trip, in fact, that Sintra can be mobbed (especially July through Sept). Saturdays and Sundays are popular with Portuguese, while foreign tourists clog the town on Mondays (when many Lisbon museums are closed, but all major Sintra sights are open). Crowds are a bit lighter on Tuesdays through Fridays. Sintra's complicated landscape—with lots of hills and one-way roads between the big sights—adds to the challenge. A trip here requires patience and a flexible schedule. For the most stress-free visit possible, consider this good one-day plan:

Near Lisbon

To Coimbra & Porto

A-8   A-9   A-1

N-9   Sintra   N-9

Cabo da Roca

N-247   IC-19

Guincho Beach   N-9

N-247   A-5   Belém

Cascais   Estoril

PARQUE DAS NAÇÕES

Lisbon   Oriente ❷

Rossio ❸   Santa Apolónia ❶

Cais do Sodré ❹

Rio Tejo

VASCO DA GAMA BRIDGE

A-12

25TH OF APRIL BRIDGE   Cacilhas

CRISTO REI MON.   Barreiro

Costa da Caparica

Pinhal Novo   To Évora

A-2   A-6

To Algarve (by expressway)

Atlantic Ocean

Setúbal   IC-1

To Algarve (by scenic coastal route)

N-379

Portinho da Arrábida

Cabo Espichel

5 Km / 5 Miles

Major Train Stations
❶ Santa Apolónia
❷ Oriente
❸ Rossio
❹ Cais do Sodré

Leave Lisbon around 8:30 to arrive in Sintra by 9:15 (most major sights open between 9:30 and 9:45—if you arrive much later, you'll be hopelessly mired in crowds all day). Pick up a map at the TI in Sintra's train station and catch bus #434 in front of the station to Pena Palace. Visit the palace, walk down to the Moorish Castle ruins, scramble over its ramparts, then hike about 45 minutes back down to town via Vila Sassetti (or take bus #434). Have lunch (unless you already had a picnic, or lunched at the Pena Palace's café), explore the town, and—if you're not exhausted yet—visit the National Palace (in town) or the Quinta da Regaleira (a 10-minute walk). Finally, catch the train back to Lisbon in time for dinner. This general plan also works well for drivers, who ideally should leave their car in Lisbon (or park upon arrival in Sintra) and use public transportation to get between the sights.

Spending the night in Sintra lets you get an early start or visit the sights later in the day (the Moorish Castle is even better at closing time, with the sun low in the sky)—and lets you savor the small town after dark, when it's quieter. Drivers in particular could consider overnighting in Sintra on the way to or from Lisbon.

GETTING TO SINTRA

Catch the **train** to Sintra from Lisbon's central Rossio station (direct, Mon-Fri 2/hour, Sat-Sun hourly, 40 minutes; also 6/hour

SINTRA

from the less central Oriente station, 45 minutes). The trip is covered by the LisboaCard or the €10 version of Lisbon's all-day transit pass; if "zapping" with a Viva Viagem card, it's €1.90 each way (see page 37). Note that none of these passes work on local buses once you're in Sintra.

To avoid early-morning lines at the station in Lisbon, buy or charge up your card the night before (otherwise, buy it when you get to Rossio station—using the ticket machines or windows upstairs, at track level). During your ride, take in the views of the 18th-century aqueduct (on the left) and the workaday Lisbon suburbs. Relax...Sintra is at the end of the line.

Sintra is far easier by train than by **car** from Lisbon. Consider waiting until after you visit Sintra to pick up your rental car. If you do drive to Sintra, see "Route Tips" at the end of this chapter for advice.

Orientation to Sintra

Sintra is small. The town itself sprawls at the foot of a hill, an easy 10-minute walk (or quick bus ride) from the train station. The National Palace, with its unmistakable pair of cone-shaped chimneys, is in the center of the town, a block from the TI, and the Quinta da Regaleira is a 10-minute walk away. The other two main sights—Pena Palace and the Moorish Castle—hover on the hilltop above (you can see the castle's serrated wall on the

hilltop). Most people take the bus up, but avid hikers enjoy the walk (figure an hour steeply uphill; see "Hiking Between Sintra and the Castles," later.)

TOURIST INFORMATION

Sintra has two TIs: a small one in the train station (daily 9:00-13:00 & 14:00-18:00, +351 211 932 545) and a larger one a block off the main square in the Museu Regional building (daily 9:00-18:00, Aug until 19:00, +351 219 231 157, www.visitlisboa.com). Pick up a free map with information on sights and a local Scotturb bus schedule. Hikers can download walking routes from the park administration website (www.parquesdesintra.pt).

ARRIVAL IN SINTRA

By Train: Upon arrival, stop at the TI in the station to get a map. To **bus** to the town center, hop on Scotturb #434 (exit the station to the right, buy €6.90 all-day ticket from street vendors or from the driver, schedules posted at stop; for more bus info, see "Getting Around Sintra," later). The bus stops in town first (near the National Palace) before heading up to the Moorish

SINTRA

Castle and Pena Palace, then loops back down to the station and town.

You can also reach the town center easily on **foot** (exit the station and go left, then turn left when you hit the turreted town hall)—it's about a 10-minute walk along a mostly level road along the lip of a ravine. Along the way you'll see modern "art" and hippies selling handmade trinkets.

By Car: See "Route Tips" at the end of this chapter for tips including where to park.

HELPFUL HINTS

Festivals: The lively Festival de Sintra music and dance festival runs from late May to early July (www.festivaldesintra.pt).

Money: You'll find a few ATMs near the train station, another inside the main TI, and one on Rua das Padarias, just up the hill from the recommended Casa Piriquita.

WC: There's a free WC near the small, central parking lot where horse carriages wait (Calçada do Pelourinho).

Bring a Picnic: To save a few euros, consider bringing a picnic from Lisbon—restaurants here can be pricey, though there is a very basic grocery store (see "Eating in Sintra," later).

Local Guide: Cristina Quental works mainly in Lisbon, but lives near Sintra and can meet you at the station (€150/half-day, €240/day; mobile +351 919 922 480, anacristinaquental@ hotmail.com).

GETTING AROUND SINTRA

All forms of transportation use the same very congested, single-lane, one-way road that loops up the hill and passes the main monuments. That means that no way is faster than any other—maybe just a bit more comfortable. Note that the town center may be closed to traffic on busy weekends—confirm your stop with the driver.

By Bus: The best choice for most is Scotturb bus **#434,** which loops together all the important stops—the train station, the town center, the Moorish Castle ruins, and the Pena Palace—before

SINTRA

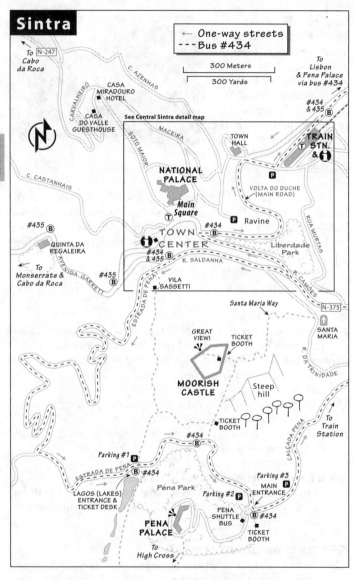

Sintra

← One-way streets
--- Bus #434

300 Meters
300 Yards

To N-247
Cabo
da Roca

C. AZENHAS

CARVALHEIRO

CASA
MIRADOURO
HOTEL

CASA
DO VALLE
GUESTHOUSE

C. CASTANHAIS

SOTO MAIOR

MACEIRA

See Central Sintra detail map

TOWN
HALL

To
Lisbon
& Pena Palace
via bus #434

#434
& 435 B

TRAIN
STN.
T &

NATIONAL
PALACE

Main
Square T

TOWN
CENTER i

VOLTA DO DUCHE
(MAIN ROAD)

P

Ravine

#434

P

RUA MUITAS

#435 B

QUINTA DA
REGALEIRA

To
Monserrate &
Cabo da Roca

AVENIDA GARRETT

#435 B

#434
& 435 B

R. SALDANHA

VILA
SASSETTI

ESTRADA DE PENA

Liberdade
Park

R. CAMOES

Santa Maria Way

N-375

SANTA
MARIA

R. DA TRINIDADE

GREAT
VIEW!

TICKET
BOOTH

MOORISH
CASTLE

Steep
hill

TICKET
BOOTH

CALÇADA PENA

To
Train
Station

#434

Parking #1 P

B #434

ESTRADA DE PENA

Pena Park

Parking #2 P

Parking #3

MAIN
ENTRANCE

P

LAGOS (LAKES)
ENTRANCE &
TICKET DESK

PENA
PALACE

PENA
SHUTTLE
BUS

B #434

TICKET
BOOTH

To
High Cross

heading back to town and the train station (4/hour—subject to traffic; €6.90 hop-on, hop-off ticket good all day; buy from driver or street vendors at train station; first bus departs train station at 9:15; last bus leaves station at 19:50; entire circuit takes 30 minutes without traffic).

A different bus, **#435,** goes from the train station to Quinta da Regaleira and the Monserrate gardens (3/hour, single-ride ticket priced by distance—about €2.50; €5 hop-on, hop-off ticket good all day; not covered by bus #434 ticket).

Crowd-Beating Tips: Busy days bring very long lines at popular bus stops, and buses crammed with people. If there's a long line at the train station bus stop, consider walking into town and catching the bus near the National Palace instead. When returning to town from the Pena Palace, consider walking about 10 minutes (mostly downhill) back along the road to the Moorish Castle bus stop, where there's usually no line. Scotturb's information office across from the train station is most crowded during morning hours.

By Tuk-Tuk: Noisy, bouncy, but fun tuk-tuks charge €5/person for a breezy ride from town or the station to the Moorish Castle, Pena Palace, or Quinta da Regaleira (you can also book tuk-tuks for a "guided tour" loop).

By Taxi: Figure €10 from the center up to any one of the sights.

By Carriage: Clip-clop horse carriages cost about €30 for 25 minutes. They can take you anywhere; you'll likely see them waiting on the little square near the bus stop just in front of the National Palace.

Sights in Sintra

Ticket Tips: For the Pena Palace, Moorish Castle, and National Palace, it's smart and simple to buy **single tickets online** a few days in advance at www.parquesdesintra.pt. Buying online will only save you about 5 percent, but it does save you a long, frustrating wait (usually 30 minutes or more) at ticket counters or ticket machines. **Combo-tickets** for these three sights offer similar cost savings but are not sold online. Unless you're going to all three sights, and didn't buy single tickets in advance, the combo deal is not worthwhile.

The **LisboaCard** gets you discounted entry at the Pena Palace, Moorish Castle, National Palace, and the Monserrate gardens (about 5 percent, only valid onsite). Be sure to bring the LisboaCard booklet, which contains coupons required for some of the discounts.

The Quinta da Regaleira is run by a private organization, so is not a part of any palace or castle combo-ticket.

ON THE HILL ABOVE SINTRA

These sights cap the hill high above Sintra—connected by bus #434. If walking between them, figure 10 minutes between the Pena Palace main entrance and the Moorish Castle, and another 10 minutes to the Pena Palace's lower "Lakes/Lagos" entrance. Be

SINTRA

careful walking along the congested road, with its narrow shoulder and ankle-twisting cobbles.

▲▲Pena Palace (Palácio de Pena)

This magical hilltop palace sits high above Sintra, above the Moorish Castle ruins. In the 19th century, Portugal had a very romantic prince, the German-born Prince Ferdinand. A contemporary and cousin of Bavaria's "Mad" King Ludwig (of Disneyesque Neuschwanstein Castle fame), Ferdinand was also a cousin of England's Prince Albert (Queen Victoria's husband). Flamboyant Ferdinand hired a German architect to build a fantasy castle,  mixing elements of German and Portuguese style. He ended up with a crazy Neo-fortified casserole of Gothic towers, Renaissance domes, Moorish minarets, Manueline carvings, Disneyland playfulness, and an *azulejo* (tile) toilet for his wife.

Cost and Hours: Palace and gardens-€14, shuttle bus-€3 round-trip; May-mid-Sept palace open daily 9:30-18:30, gardens 9:00-19:00, shorter hours off-season; audioguide-€3, +351 219 105 340, www.parquesdesintra.pt.

Getting In: There are two entrances to the castle grounds: the lower "Lakes/Lagos" entrance (at the bottom of the park, across from the first parking lot you come to), and the main entrance (just below the castle itself). It's a 20-minute walk between these two (you'll pass the Moorish Castle ticket booth between them). While the lower entrance is less crowded, it's best to use the main entrance if possible, since it's closer to the castle.

At the main entrance, purchase your ticket at the small hut next to the gate (if there's a long line, look for ticket machines just downhill—toward the Moorish Castle).

To avoid the 10-minute uphill climb from the entrance to the palace (and enjoy a lift back down later), you could catch the green shuttle bus, which departs from straight ahead as you enter (buy with your palace ticket—or inside gift shop—but *not* from driver, departs about every 10 minutes). Lines for the shuttle bus can be longer than ticket lines. Before buying your palace ticket, take a look inside the main gate to see how many people are waiting in line for the shuttle, then decide if you want to add the shuttle ticket to your palace entry.

Be sure to pick up the *Parques e Palácios* map, with a helpful illustration of the castle on one side and a circular, 1.5-hour walking route of the park on the other.

Eating: The palace has an inexpensive **$** view café and a pricier **$$** restaurant. If you brought your lunch with you, enjoy it in the picnic-perfect gardens either before or after your visit—with views fit for a king.

◐ Self-Guided Tour: The palace, built in the mid- to late-1800s, is so well-preserved that it feels as if it's the day after the royal family fled Portugal in 1910 (during a popular revolt that eventually made way for today's modern republic). This gives the place an intimacy rarely seen in palaces.

SINTRA

• *After you hop off the green shuttle bus, hike up the ramp and go through the Moorish archway with alligator decor. Cross the drawbridge that doesn't draw and join a slack-jawed world of tourists frozen in deep knee-bends with their cameras cocked.*

Palace Interior: Show your ticket again to enter the palace itself. Inside, at the base of the stairs, you'll see a bust of King Ferdinand II, who built this castle from 1840 until his death in 1885. Though German, he was a romantic proponent of his adopted culture and did much to preserve Portugal's architectural and artistic heritage.

• *Next you'll pop out into the...*

Courtyard: The palace was built on the site of a 16th-century monastery; the courtyard was the former location of the cloister. In spite of its plushness, the palace retains the monkish coziness of several small rooms gathered in two levels around the cloister.

Like its big brother in Belém, the monastery housed followers of St. Jerome, the hermit monk. Like their namesake, the monks wanted to be isolated, and this was about as isolated as you could be around here 500 years ago. The spot was also a popular pilgrimage destination for its statue of "Our Lady of the Feathers" (*pena* means feather—hence the palace's name). In 1498 King Manuel was up here enjoying the view when he spied Vasco da Gama sailing up the river, returning safely from his great voyage. To celebrate and give thanks, the king turned what was a humble wooden monastery into a fine stone palace.

• *From here, follow the one-way route counterclockwise around the courtyard, dipping into a variety of rooms. These are especially worthy of attention.*

Dining Room and Pantry: Stuck into a cozy corner, the monastery's original refectory was decked out with the royal family's finest tableware and ceiling tiles.

Atelier (Workshop) of King Carlos I: King Carlos was a talented artist and a great patron of the arts. He often found refuge in painting—specifically in the latest style, Art Nouveau. Unfinished paintings and sketches eerily predict the king's unfinished rule.

King's Bedroom and Bathroom: The king enjoyed cutting-edge comforts, including a shower/tub imported from England, and even a telephone to listen to the opera when he couldn't face the Lisbon commute. The bedroom is decorated in classic Romantic style—dark, heavy, and crowded with knickknacks.

• *Now head upstairs (gripping the funky dragon-like handrail). Circling around the courtyard, you'll enter the wing called the Piano Nobile ("noble floor"). Go through a few daintily decorated rooms that belonged to ladies-in-waiting, and then enter the...*

Queen's Bedroom and Dressing Room: Study the melancholy photos of Queen Amelia (Amélie of Orléans), King Carlos, and their family in this room. The early 1900s were a rocky time for Portugal's royal family. The king and his eldest son were assassinated in 1908. His youngest son, Manuel II, became king until he, his mother the queen, and other members of the royal family fled Portugal during the 1910 revolution.

As you shuffle through the palace, you'll see state-of-the-art conveniences—such as the first flush toilets and hot shower in Portugal, and even a telephone room. The whole place is lovingly cluttered, typical of the Victorian horror of empty spaces.

• *At the end of this floor, step out onto the...*

Queen's Terrace: Enjoy a sweeping view from Lisbon to the mouth of the Rio Tejo. Find the Cristo Rei statue and the 25th of April Bridge. The statue on the distant ridge honors the palace's architect.

• *Heading back inside, you'll pass through some smaller rooms, then enter...*

The New Wing: This spacious addition to the original series of rooms around the cloister includes the apartments of the last king, the smoking room (with a tiled ceiling), and the fantastically furnished Great Hall.

On your way down the spiral staircase, take a detour to see the **Stag Room**—with well-antlered walls and a dramatic dome supported by a stout, palm-tree-like column. From here, you'll head down to see the abundant kitchen.

Just after, a view café conveniently welcomes us peasants. While many people take this as a sign to leave, we haven't yet seen some of the most scenic parts of the castle.

• *From the café, turn left and walk alongside the palace, then duck through one of the two huge, ornamental gateways on your left (the second one has a scowling Triton overhead). You'll emerge into the...*

Inner Patio: Take the stairs up to the pointed dome covered in green and white tiles (in front of the tallest red tower). This was the royal family's sumptuous private **chapel,** decorated in a variety of styles. The structure is Manueline, reminiscent of the Monastery of Jerónimos in Belém.

• *Heading back down into the patio, don't miss the little door under the chapel marked...*

The Wall Walk: If you aren't afraid of heights, follow this for a rampart ramble with great views—of the onion-domed balustrade, of the palace itself, and of the surrounding countryside—including the Moorish Castle on an adjacent hilltop. When the entire circuit is open, you'll circle all the way around the outside of the palace, and wind up back at the entrance. Otherwise, walk back the way you came.

• *From here, you can return directly to the main entrance (walk 10 minutes or catch the green shuttle bus), or detour for a self-guided tour of the park.*

Pena Palace Park: The lush, captivating, and sprawling palace grounds—rated ▲—are dotted with romantic surprises and provide a refreshing break from Sintra's crowds. Several landmarks within the park are signposted near the shuttle bus stop. Highlights include the High Cross (highest point around, with commanding views), chapels, a temple, giant sequoia trees, and exotic plants. To walk through the park after you tour the palace, take a 40-minute stroll downhill (following the map that came with your palace entry)—past greenhouses, pavilions, and a series of five manmade lakes—to the lower park gate, at the Lakes/Lagos entry, where you'll find a bus stop and the Estrada de Pena loop road. From here, it's a ten-minute hike uphill to the Moorish Castle, or a 20-minute hike back to the Pena Palace's main entrance.

▲Moorish Castle (Castelo dos Mouros)

Sintra's thousand-year-old ruins of a Moorish castle are lost in an enchanted forest and alive with winds of the past. They're a castle lover's dream come true, and a great place for a picnic with a panoramic Atlantic view. Though built by the Moors, the castle was taken by Christian forces in 1147. It's one of the most classically perfect castles you'll find anywhere, with two hills  capped by hardy forts, connected by a crenellated wall walkway. (It's so idealized because it was significantly restored in the 19th century.)

SINTRA

Cost and Hours: €8, daily 9:00-18:30, +351 219 237 300, www.parquesdesintra.pt.

Getting In: From the main ticket booth (just uphill from the bus stop) to the castle entrance, it's an atmospheric 10-minute up-and-down stroll through a forested canyon, passing a few small exhibits and information plaques. If the main ticket booth is crowded, bypass it and simply continue to the castle itself, where there's another ticket booth that rarely has a wait. Either way, be sure to pick up the well-illustrated map, which has lots of insightful information.

Visiting the Castle: You'll enter the castle in a terraced area with a cafeteria, shop, and WCs, all sitting on top of a cistern. The castle walls and towers climb hills on either side of you. Do a hardy counterclockwise hike, conquering the lower one first, then heading up to the higher one. (Or, if you're tired, just walk up the central staircase to enjoy a breathtaking view.)

For the full experience, from where you entered, go right and take the stony stairs up to the keep. From the top tower, you can see how the wall twists and turns—following the contours of the land—as it connects over to the taller hilltop tower. Follow the crenellated path, with delirious views over Sintra down below and as far as the Atlantic. You'll go down, then back up the other side, ascending higher and higher to the top of the Royal Tower. From the summit, you enjoy great views across to Pena Palace, perched on its adjacent hilltop. From this pinnacle, you can gingerly descend to the cafeteria and entrance—having conquered the castle.

Hiking Between Sintra and the Castles

It's a steep one-hour hike from town up to the Moorish Castle and Pena Palace—challenging even for hardy hikers. But hiking back down to town after your hilltop visits (rather than cramming into an overstuffed bus) is an appealing 45-minute possibility for those with strong knees. Be sure to equip yourself with the TI's invaluable *Pedestrian Route* map—and get their advice—before you set out (maps may also be available at Moorish Castle or Pena Palace ticket offices).

The best route is to take a terraced path directly below the Moorish Castle, which leads past the **Vila Sassetti.** You'll find the trailhead at the end of the parking lot directly across from the Lakes/Lagos lower entrance of the Pena Palace grounds, and you'll also find a trail connecting to it near the Moorish Castle main ticket booth (near the bus stop). From here, the trail curls around the bottom of the Moorish Castle's rocky perch, then enters the grounds of the Vila Sassetti (open daily 10:00-18:00, until 17:00 off-season). Designed by theater set decorator Luigi Manini (who also did the Quinta da Regaleira, described later), the Vila Sassetti looks like an old Roman house with a terra cotta roof. You'll hike down to the villa itself, then traipse through its lower gardens into Sintra. (If the Villa is closed, you can also drop down—on steep steps—to footpaths that run through the woods above the main road.)

Yet another option is to walk down on the **"Santa Maria Way,"** which forks off in the opposite direction from the Moorish Castle entrance. However, this trail is mostly through thick woods and less scenic.

IN TOWN

These sights are all within easy walking distance of the town center.

▲National Palace (Palácio Nacional)

While the palace dates back to Moorish times, most of what you'll see is from the 15th-century reign of King João I, with later Manueline architectural ornamentation from the 16th century. This oldest surviving royal palace in Portugal is still used for official receptions. Having housed royalty for 500 years (until 1910), it's fragrant with history.

Cost and Hours: €10, daily 9:30-18:30, audioguide-€3; look for white, double-coned building in town center—a 10-minute walk from the train station; +351 219 237 300, www.parquesdesintra.pt.

Tours: Free English tours depart the entrance at 14:30. The audioguide is informative, but as dry as an Alentejo summer.

➋ Self-Guided Tour: The palace is a one-way romp with little information provided. If touring on your own, read the brief descriptions in each room, and tune into the following notable parts of the palace.

• *Show your ticket, then head upstairs into the...*

Swan Room: This first room is the palace's banquet room. A king's daughter—who loved swans—married into a royal house in Belgium. The king missed the princess so much that he decorated the ceiling with her favorite animal.

Central Patio: This was a fortified medieval palace, so rather than having fancy gardens outside, it has a stay-awhile courtyard within its protective walls. Notice the unique chimneys. They provide powerful suction that removes the smoke from the kitchen and also creates a marvelous open-domed feeling (as you'll see at the end of your tour).

SINTRA

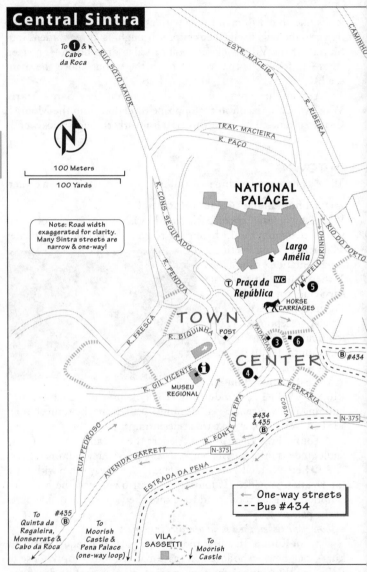

Central Sintra

To ① & Cabo da Roca

RUA SOTO MAIOR

ESTR. MACEIRA

CAMINHO

R. RIBEIRA

TRAV. MACEIRA

R. PAÇO

100 Meters

100 Yards

Note: Road width exaggerated for clarity. Many Sintra streets are narrow & one-way!

R. CONS. SEGURADO

R. PENDOA

R. FRESCA

NATIONAL PALACE

Largo Amélia

RIO DO PORTO

CAÇ. PELOURINHO

Ⓣ *Praça da República* WC Ⓕ

HORSE CARRIAGES

TOWN

R. BIQUINHA POST

R. GIL VICENTE Ⓘ

MUSEU REGIONAL

PADARIAS

❸ ❻

CENTER

❹

Ⓑ #434

R. FERRARIA

COSTA

N-375

RUA PEDROSO

#434 & 435 Ⓑ

R. FONTE DA PIPA

AVENIDA GARRETT

N-375

ESTRADA DA PENA

To #435 Ⓑ Quinta da Regaleira, Monserrate & Cabo da Roca

To Moorish Castle & Pena Palace (one-way loop)

VILA SASSETTI

To Moorish Castle

← One-way streets
--- Bus #434

Magpie Room: The queen caught King João I being a little too friendly with a lady-in-waiting. Frustrated by his court—abuzz with gossip—João had this ceiling painted with magpies. But to defend his honor, he illustrated each magpie quoting the king's slogan—*Por bem*, "For good." The 15th-century Moorish tiles are from Spain, brought in before the development of the famous, ubiquitous Portuguese tiles, and are considered some of the finest Moorish-Spanish tiles in all of Iberia.

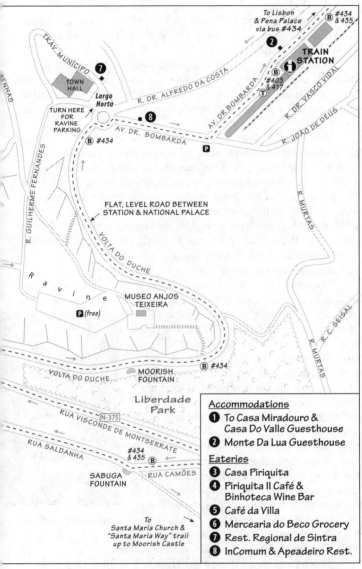

To Lisbon
& Pena Palace
via bus #434

Accommodations

1 To Casa Miradouro &
Casa Do Valle Guesthouse

2 Monte Da Lua Guesthouse

Eateries

3 Casa Piriquita

4 Piriquita II Café &
Binhoteca Wine Bar

5 Café da Villa

6 Mercearia do Beco Grocery

7 Rest. Regional de Sintra

8 InComum & Apeadeiro Rest.

Bedchamber of King Sebastian (Dom Sebastião): The king portrayed on the wall (to the right of where you enter) is King Sebastian, a gung-ho, medieval-type monarch who went to battle in Africa, following the Moors even after they were chased out of Europe. He disappeared in 1578 at age 24 (although he was almost certainly killed in Morocco, "Sebastianists" awaited his mythical return into the 19th century). With the king missing, Portugal was left in unstable times with only Sebastian's great uncle (King Henrique) as heir. The new king died within two years, and the throne passed to his great uncle, King Philip II of Spain, leading to 60 years of Spanish rule (1580-1640).

Note the ebony, silver, and painted copper headboard of the Italian Renaissance bed. The tiles in this room are considered the first Portuguese tiles—from the time of Manuel I. The corn-on-the-cob motif topping the tilework is a reminder of American discoveries.

More Main-Floor Rooms: From here, you'll walk through the **Julius Caesar Room,** with a Flemish tapestry of the Roman general-turned-ruler; the **Goddess Diana Courtyard;** and up the stairs to the **Galleon Room,** whose ceiling is painted with ships flying the flags of the great nautical powers of the day. Step out onto the balcony for views of a forested hillside scattered with the villas of aristocrats—and capped by the serrated wall of the Moorish Castle. Then, head up the stairs to walk through some smaller, simpler apartments with a few original furnishings.

• *Finally, you step into the glorious...*

Blazons Hall (a.k.a. Coat of Arms Room): The most striking room in the palace—under a golden dome and slathered in blue tiles—honors Portugal's loyal nobility. Study the richly decorated ceiling. The king's coat of arms at the top is surrounded by the coats of arms of his children; below that is a ring of stags; and just below, "supporting" the king are the coats of arms of Portugal's noble families. The Latin phrase circling the room reads, "Honoring all the noble families who've been loyal to the king." The 18th-century tiles hang from the walls like tapestries and show more stag hunting scenes. Enjoy the view: a garden-like countryside dotted with mansions of nobility who clamored to be near their king, the hill-capping castle, and the wide-open Atlantic. You're in the westernmost room of the westernmost palace on the European continent.

• *Continue through the upper halls, peeking into the...*

Bedchamber and Prison of Alfonso VI: This king suffered from a fever as a child that left him mentally unstable. After he became king, he was removed by his wife and his brother—who became King Pedro II, locked him in this room for the rest of his life, and married his queen.

Yet More Rooms: As you continue, you'll pass through the **Chinese Room** (with an exquisite ivory-and-bone model of a Chinese pagoda). Downstairs, you can step out onto a private balcony and peer down into the **Palatine Chapel,** with a Mudejar wood-carved ceiling. Then you'll pass through a room of coffers (literal treasure chests) and head downstairs to the **Arab Room**—decorated with Moorish tiles, and with a little fountain in the middle; this was the preferred bedroom of João I. From here, you'll walk through a fancy **guest room** and into the **kitchen.** With all the latest in cooking technology, the palace chef could roast an entire cow on the spit, keep the king's plates warm in the iron dish warmer (with drawers below for the charcoal), and get really dizzy by looking up and spinning around three times.

On your way out, as you step back into the big entry hall, be sure to detour left into the **Manueline Room,** with carved-stone ropes over the doors and a grand chandelier, and a handy WC in the corner. You'll walk back through the Central Patio (peek into the blue-tiled **Grotto of the Baths** in the corner) and head for the exit. On your way out, watch for the easy-to-miss door on the right that lets you explore the manicured, terraced **gardens** surrounding the palace. Sit with a carved lion and enjoy views from one palace to another.

SOUTHWEST OF THE CENTER

These two sights line up on a road southwest of central Sintra. You can walk to Quinta da Regaleira, but Monserrate is quite a bit farther. Bus #435 stops at each one (see details earlier, under "Getting Around Sintra"), or you can take a tuk-tuk or taxi.

▲▲Quinta da Regaleira

This Neo-Everything (Manueline/Gothic/Renaissance) 1912 mansion and garden has mystical and Masonic twists. It was de-

signed by Italian opera-set designer Luigi Manini for a wealthy but disgruntled monarchist two years after the royal family was deposed. While the mansion—prickly with spires—is striking from the outside, its interior is nothing compared to the Pena Palace or National Palace. But the grounds are an utter delight to wander, with fanciful follies, secret underground passages, and lush landscaping. Many travelers (especially younger ones) find romping around these grounds more enjoyable than shuffling around the crowded interiors of the more famous palaces. Ask a local to pronounce "Regaleira" for you, and just try to repeat it.

Cost and Hours: €10, daily 10:00-18:30, closes earlier off-season, last entry one hour before closing, 10-minute walk from downtown Sintra, café, +351 219 106 650, www.regaleira.pt.

SINTRA

Tours: Excellent two-hour English tours fill up, so book ahead online or by phone (€15, includes entry, about hourly April-Sept, fewer off-season). The tour focuses on the garden, and can be longish unless you're into quirky Masonic esoterica.

Visiting the Quinta: As you enter, be sure to pick up the superb illustrated map of both the house and the gardens.

The **mansion** itself is striking—as it was designed to be. (In fact, that was its sole purpose.) You'll enter through the finest space, the Hunting Room, with an outrageously carved fireplace. From here you can explore three floors, filled mostly with well-presented exhibits on the design and construction of the place, and biographical sketches of the aristocrat and the architect who brought it to life. At the top floor, find the tight spiral stone staircase up to the view terrace.

The real highlight is the playful **gardens,** which stretch uphill from the mansion. Work your way up, past the elaborate private chapel, then to higher and higher crenellated viewpoints. Follow *Waterfall* signs to reach a refreshing artificial canyon with ponds and a cascade. Stepping stones lead across the main pond to the grottos that hide beneath, giving you a unique perspective. From the top of the waterfall, continue up to the "Portal of the Guardians"; inside, secret tunnels lead to the dramatic, spiral-staircase-wrapped well—burrowed 90 feet down into the hillside, and, like the rest of Quinta da Regaleira, more about showing off than about being functional. From here, more tunnels lead to other parts of the property; use your map to explore to your heart's content.

Monserrate

About 2.5 miles outside of Sintra—on the road past the Quinta da Regaleira—are the wonderful gardens of Monserrate. If you like tropical plants and exotic landscaping, a visit is time well-spent, though many find that the gardens at Pena Palace or the Quinta da Regaleira are just as good as these more famous grounds.

Cost and Hours: €8, palace open daily 9:30-18:30, park 9:00-19:00, +351 219 237 300, www.parquesdesintra.pt.

WEST OF SINTRA, ON THE COAST
Cabo da Roca

Wind-beaten, tourist-infested Cabo da Roca (KAH-boo dah ROH-kah) is the westernmost point in Europe, perhaps the inspiration for the Portuguese poet Luís de Camões' line, *"Onde a terra se acaba e o mar começa"* ("Where land ends and the sea begins"). It has a little shop, a café, and a tiny TI that sells an expensive "proof of being here" certificate. Take a photo instead. Nearby, on the road south to Cascais, you'll pass a good beach for wind, waves, sand, and the chance to be the last person in Europe to see the sun set. For a remote beach, drive to Praia Adraga (north of Cabo da Roca).

Sleeping in Sintra

Sintra works well as an overnight—allowing you to beat the crowds by tackling the sights early or late, and have the charming town to yourself after hours. To reach the first two places, head into town, turn right to pass in front of the National Palace, then continue steeply downhill on the road past Hotel Tivoli; they face each other at the very bottom of the street (free street parking, steep 10-minute hike back up to the town center). The final listing—cheaper and handier for train travelers—is directly across the street from the train station.

$$$ Casa Miradouro is a beautifully restored mansion from 1893, now run by Belgian expat Charlotte Lambregts. The creaky old house feels like a homey, upscale British B&B, with eight spacious, stylish rooms, an elegant lounge, castle and sea views, and a wonderful garden (good breakfast extra, Rua Sotto Major 55, mobile +351 914 292 203, www.casa-miradouro.com, mail@casa-miradouro.com).

$$$ Casa Do Valle Guesthouse offers 11 comfortable, modern rooms on several levels in a peaceful hillside location. They have a lovely garden and large deck with valley and castle views, a swimming pool, and a shared kitchen (extra for continental breakfast in your room, reception open until 18:30, behind Casa Miradouro at Rua da Paderna 5, +351 219 244 699, www.casadovalle.com, info@casadovalle.com).

$ Monte Da Lua Guesthouse has seven clean, simple rooms with shiny hardwood floors; some rooms face the train station, while others face a quieter ravine in the back (cheaper rooms with shared bath, no breakfast, Avenida Dr. Miguel Bombarda 51, +351 210 129 659, montedalua51@gmail.com).

Eating in Sintra

These listings are in the town of Sintra. To eat at the hilltop sights, there are cafés at both Pena Palace and the Moorish Palace, or you can pack a picnic.

SINTRA

LIGHT MEALS

Most of these (except Café da Villa) are on or near Rua das Padarias, the touristy little cobbled lane across the street from the National Palace. The sit-down restaurants in this zone are very pricey and touristy, but these are handy for a light, quick meal.

$ Casa Piriquita bills itself as "the" *antiga fabrica de queijadas*—historic maker of tiny, tasty tarts with a cheesy filling. It's good for a sweet and a coffee or a simple lunch, such as toasted sandwiches. Take a seat in the café (up a few steps) to avoid groups who rush in for pastries to go, or do battle and grab a half-dozen for about €5 (Tue-Thu 8:30-22:00, closed Wed, Rua das Padarias 1, +351 219 230 626).

$ Piriquita II, sister to Casa Piriquita, is a block farther up the lane and may have less commotion. It has a more extensive menu and a view terrace (Wed-Mon 8:30-20:00, closed Tue, Rua das Padarias 18, +351 219 230 626).

$$ Binhoteca, a welcoming little *enoteca,* provides wine lovers with an astonishing array of Portuguese wines and ports available by the glass (starting at €5), along with tasty meat-and-cheese plates, sandwiches, and salads. The knowledgeable staff is happy to explain what you're enjoying. It's a fun experience, but prices can add up (daily 10:00-19:00—and often later, Rua das Padarias 16, +351 219 230 444).

$$ Café da Villa, a favorite of bus drivers and tour guides, offers generous portions of homemade-style soups and salads in a homey pub-like setting. It's good for a quiet, inexpensive lunch, with a variety of fixed-price meal options (daily 12:00-24:00, facing the little bus-stop square in front of the National Palace at Calçada do Pelourinho 2, +351 219 241 174).

Groceries: Mercearia do Beco, just a few steps off Rua das Padarias, is a basic grocery store where you can assemble a picnic (daily 9:00-20:00, Rua Arco do Teixeira 17).

DINING

While there are plenty of tourist eateries in Sintra's old center, for a serious meal I'd head a couple of blocks away to the station area.

$$ Restaurante Regional de Sintra, which feeds locals and tourists very well, is my favorite place for dinner in Sintra. Gentle Paulo speaks English and serves huge, splittable portions (Tue-Thu 12:00-16:00 & 19:00-22:30, closed Wed, tucked to the right of the turreted town hall at Travessa do Municipio 2, +351 219 234 444).

$$$ InComum is working hard to bring a modern sensibility to traditional Portuguese cooking. The owners, who lived in Switzerland, pride themselves on serving Portuguese-inspired dishes with updated, international flair. The minimalist dining room is especially popular at lunchtime, when the weekday lunch special offers an affordable taste of their cooking (Sun-Fri 12:00-24:00, Sat from 16:30, Rua Dr. Alfredo Coasta 22, +351 219 243 719).

$$ Apeadeiro Restaurante, named for the platform along the track at the train station just a block away, is a quality eatery serving good food at good prices. Their daily specials can be split, allowing two to eat affordably (Fri-Wed 11:30-23:00, closed Thu, Avenida Dr. Miguel Bombarda 3, +351 219 231 804).

Sintra Connections

From Sintra by Train and Bus to: Lisbon (Mon-Fri 2 trains/hour to Rossio station, Sat-Sun hourly, 40 minutes; 6 trains/hour to Oriente station, 45 minutes), **Cascais** (bus #403 via Cabo da Roca, 45-60 minutes, 1-2/hour; express bus #417, 30 minutes, hourly; both buses fewer on weekends, catch either one at the Sintra train station).

ROUTE TIPS
Sintra Day Trip from Lisbon by Car

Cars are the curse of Sintra—all traffic, from cars to buses to tuk-tuks, has to nudge through town on a two-lane road, and parking is difficult (especially up at the hilltop castles).

If you insist on taking a car to Sintra, take the IC-19/A-37 freeway out of Lisbon (allow 30 minutes, not counting traffic delays). When you arrive in Sintra, follow *Centro Histórico* signs. It's smartest to simply **park your car** and use bus #434 to get around. The road into town (Volta do Duche) has some pay-and-display parking (4-hour maximum). And there's free parking on the road just behind the train station.

If you anticipate crowds, park in the (relatively) large lot down in the ravine between the train station and the TI. As you come into town, watch for the colorful, turreted Town Hall building on your right; take the tiny lane immediately after that building (the *no entry* signs are just for campers) and head down to the lot next to the Museu Anjos Teixeira. Climb up the stairs next to the museum, and you're on the main road into town.

It's tempting to drive up the **Moorish Castle** and **Pena Palace,** but be warned that parking up top is very limited (often jammed by about 10:00). The road makes a very long, one-way loop with no backtracking, so if you don't find a space you'll have to complete the loop and return back to the center. But if you want to take your chances, here's the plan: Head up the road with every other car and bus in town. You'll twist up, up, up on a dozen switchbacks. Approaching the sights, there are three marked parking lots (one by the lower Lakes/Lagos entrance to Pena Palace; another just before the main entrance to Pena Palace—this is probably your most convenient choice, if it has space; and a third one, just past the main entrance to Pena Palace). Monitors along the road suggest which lots might have space, and which are *completo*. All along the congested, cobbled road are a few well-marked roadside spaces. It's best to park as soon as you find something—anything—and then walk the rest of the way to connect the sights.

It's possible to make a **70-mile circular trip** and drive to all the destinations near Lisbon within a day (Lisbon–Belém–Sintra–Cabo da Roca–Cascais–Lisbon), but traffic congestion around Sintra, especially on weekends and during rush hour, can slow you down.

Loop Trip by Public Transportation

If you're bent on seeing sights west of Lisbon—Sintra, Cabo da Roca, and Cascais)—in a single long day, it can be done using public transportation. Start at the Sintra train station and buy a day pass good for all routes of the Scotturb **bus** (€15.10). Use the pass to take bus #434 to Sintra's sights, then go to Cabo da Roca on bus #403. When you're ready, catch the next bus #403 for the jaunt to Cascais and a seafood dinner on the waterfront (for more on Cascais, see page 117). To head from Sintra straight to Cascais—without the Cabo da Roca detour—take the faster bus #417.

From Cascais, returning to Lisbon is a snap—just buy a one-way **train** ticket to Lisbon at the train station (or use your Zapping card). You'll get off at the last stop on the line (Cais de Sodré Station), a five-minute walk from Praça do Comércio in downtown Lisbon. Or, to return to Sintra, hop on bus #417.

THE ALGARVE

Salema • Cape Sagres • Lagos • Tavira

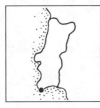

The Algarve—Portugal's warm and dry south coast, stretching for some 100 miles—was once known as Europe's last uncharted tourist frontier. Today's Algarve is far from undiscovered—and in some places can be miserably crowded and overdeveloped—but it still holds some gems ideal for a relaxing beach break.

You won't be the first one seeking the sun here. When the Moors ruled Portugal, they chose not to live in the rainy north, but here—where warm, sandy beaches framed by jagged rocks give way to rolling green hills dotted with orchards. They called this land Al-Gharb Al-Andalus ("to the west of Andalucía") and made it the westernmost fringe of the huge Islamic world at the time. Today, perceptive visitors notice echoes of Muslim culture all along the Algarve: groves of almond and orange trees, white-domed buildings with blue trim, traditional *azulejos* (tiles), and pointy chimneys—reflecting the region's minaret heritage.

Choose your home base carefully. If you go to the places featured in tour brochures (the middle stretch, roughly between Faro and Lagos), you'll find it much like Spain's Costa del Sol: paved, packed, and pretty stressful. Two worthwhile, midsize resort towns offer a better experience: In the west is Lagos, an urban resort with a vibrant old town, a youthful surfing buzz, and dramatically scenic beaches. And in the east—amid lagoon estuaries, just this side of Spain—is pleasant Tavira, a whitewashed town with a real soul, a fun-to-explore cobbled townscape, and boats to an island-beach getaway.

But even Lagos and Tavira are secondary to this region's best destination: the laid-back beach village of Salema. For some rig-

ALGARVE

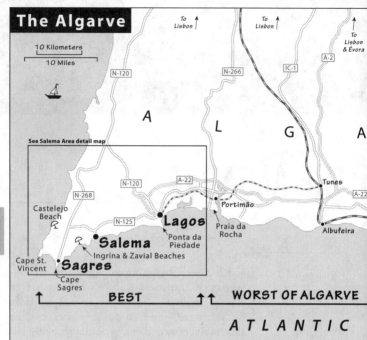

orous rest and intensive relaxation, make Salema your Algarve hideaway. Here the tourists and the fishermen sport the same stubble. It's just you, a beach with weathered fishing boats, no must-see attractions, and a few other globetrotting experts in lethargy. Nearby is Cape Sagres, Europe's "Land's End" and home of the scant remains of Henry the Navigator's famous

navigation school. But unless you're out for the extra credit, you could just stick around sleepy Salema...work on a tan and see how slow your pulse can get. If not now, when? If not you, who?

PLANNING YOUR TIME

The Algarve is your vacation from your vacation. How much time does it deserve? It depends upon how much time you have, and how much time you need to recharge your solar batteries. On a two-week trip of Portugal, I'd give it three nights and two days. After a full day of sightseeing in Lisbon (or Sevilla, if you're arriving from Spain—each is just three hours away by car), I'd push it by driving to Salema around dinnertime to gain an entirely free

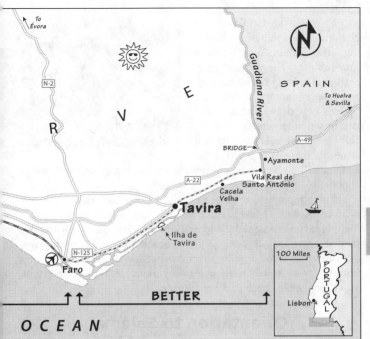

beach day. With two full days, I'd spend one enjoying side trips to Cape Sagres and Lagos, and another just lingering in Salema. The only other Algarve stop to consider is Tavira, farther to the east and most logical on the way to or from Spain. (If you're visiting in winter, Tavira—which is lively year-round—makes a better stop than tiny Salema, which hibernates in the off-season.)

GETTING AROUND THE ALGARVE

Trains and buses connect the main towns along the south coast (skimpy service on weekends and off-season). Buses take you west from Lagos, where trains don't go. The freeway crossing the Algarve from Lagos to the Spanish border (and on to Sevilla, Spain) makes driving quick and easy. (See "Route Tips for Drivers," at the end of this chapter.)

Salema

One bit of old Algarve magic still glitters quietly in the sun: Salema. Fronting a fine sandy beach, it's at the end of a small road just off the main drag between the big city of Lagos and the rugged southwest tip of Europe, Cape Sagres.

Salema (sah-LAY-mah) is changing but remains charming. The fishermen are fading into the past, the younger generation is moving to the big city, and the economy is evolving. Salema now draws visitors from nearby gated resorts and golfing clubs seeking local character and atmospheric restaurants. Yet Salema is still a place that will reward you with a great beach-town experience.

This simple fishing village has three beachside streets, a dozen or so restaurants, a few hotels and bars, time-share condos up the road, a paved promenade, and endless summer sun. Most important, it has a long, broad, gorgeous beach—luxurious with powder-fine sand, framed off by steep vivid-yellow cliffs, and relatively untrampled by rowdy tourists. For my money, it may be the most purely enjoyable beach in all of Europe.

Orientation to Salema

Tiny Salema meets the water at the parking-lot square called Largo da Liberdade. Most of my recommended accommodations and restaurants are within a few minutes' walk of here; a few are a steep but scenic walk above town.

TOURIST INFORMATION

Salema lacks a real TI, but people in its bars, restaurants, and pensions have heard all the questions and are happy to provide answers. Isabel (with Vibeltaxis), Romeu (at the Salema Market), and Daniel (look for his kayak rental shop where the road hits the beach) speak English and good sources of advice. TIs in nearby Sagres or Lagos can also offer some info on Salema.

ARRIVAL IN SALEMA

By Train and Bus: To get to Salema, you'll arrive first at Lagos, the western Algarve's transportation hub (with the closest train and bus stations; see "Lagos Connections," later in this chapter). From there, buses go every hour or two between Lagos and Sagres—Salema is about halfway between the two (7/day, 30-minute ride, last bus departs Lagos at 20:30, fewer buses on weekends, schedules at www.algarvebus.info and www.eva-bus.com).

About half the buses conveniently go right into the village of Salema (these are usually marked *Salema Village*). Confirm with the

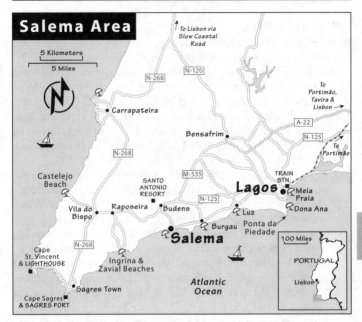

driver by asking: "*Você vai à praia de Salema?*" (voh-say vie ah pry-ah deh sah-LAY-muh).

The rest of the buses—marked with a cross ("X") in the schedule—stop at the top of the road, a 20-minute downhill walk into town. If you're on one of these buses, it's better to stay on and get off at the next stop, Figueira. From there you can backtrack 20 yards, then follow the sign for *Salema*. It's the same distance as the first downhill walk, but there's a sidewalk, so it's safer and easier.

By Car: From the A-22 freeway that parallels the coast, take the Lagos exit (marked *Lagos/Vila do Bispo/Sagres*), then follow *Sagres/Vila do Bispo* signs. The Salema turnoff (marked with just one small white sign) is at the roundabout after Budens and before Figueira. In Salema, parking is free just about everywhere. There are several handy spots on the main square, steps above the beach, and a larger overflow gravel lot over the little bridge on the inland side of town.

To stop in Lagos before continuing to Salema, take the exit marked *Lagos/Vila do Bispo/Sagres*, but follow signs to *Lagos centro*. When ready to continue to Salema, leave Lagos on Avenida dos Descobrimentos, and follow signs to *Sagres/Vila do Bispo*.

By Taxi: A cab from Lagos to Salema takes 20 minutes and costs about €30 (metered—but ask for an estimate first).

HELPFUL HINTS

Money: Many places here appreciate cash—stock up before you arrive. If you need to withdraw cash in Salema, there's an Orange ATM to the right of The Way Tours office on the town square. Avoid the privately run Euronet machines scattered around town—they have rip-off rates.

Laundry: Vilalaia Laundry, located up the hill at the Salema Beach Club, offers next-day wash-and-dry service (€8.50, no self-service, Mon-Fri 9:00-17:30, Sat 9:00-13:00, closed Sun, next to the Salema Market, mobile +351 915 229 993).

WCs: You'll find free public WCs in the little, white municipal building at the top of the main square/parking lot. The fountain in front of the building is a reminder of the old days. When water to the village was cut off, this was always running.

Taxi: Your hotel can arrange a taxi, but I'd rather work directly with a local family-owned company called **Vibeltaxis.** Run by Isabel Vitorino and her sons, their taxis have room for four to eight passengers. Rates vary with the number of people—try to split the cost (about €30 to Lagos; €70 for a two-hour guided tour of Cape Sagres; €400 to Sevilla, Évora, or Lisbon). Reserve in advance by phone, text, or email (mobile +351 919 385 139 or +351 919 422 061, www.vibeltaxis.com, info@vibeltaxis.com). Isabel and her sons all speak English and are happy to answer your questions about the area. A former tour guide, Isabel can also help organize transfers and tours.

The Way Tours: Entrepreneurial Daniel runs a little tourist activities desk in the town center. He rents kayaks, paddleboards, bikes, and sports gear; he also sells bike tours and is an agent for outdoor activity companies at nearby resorts. Daniel speaks English and is a great source of information. I'd just drop by to talk with him and review your options (mobile +351 916 457 684, www.facebook.com/TheWayToursAlgarve).

Sights in Salema

Salema has a split personality: The whitewashed Old Town is for locals, and the other half was built for tourists. Both groups pursue a policy of peaceful coexistence. Tourists laze in the sun, while locals grab the shade. You'll hardly see the snowbirds in the fancy gated community at the top of the hill.

It's a small town where everyone seems connected in one way or another. (As the saying goes, "When you kick one person, everyone limps.") A good percentage of the population has the surname Duarte, and people have nicknames like Cucumber Ze and Bread Roll Paulo. Several local men married visiting German women back in the 1980s, demonstrating the town's knack for making tourists feel welcome.

Fishing Scene

Salema is still a fishing village—but just barely. There are six or eight working boats, but it's a far cry from the days—just a generation ago—when the town's main drag, Rua dos Pescadores, was, as its name suggests, literally the street of the fishermen. (Locals now buy their fish from a fish truck that pulls into town tooting its horn each morning.) While the fishermen's hut no longer hosts a fish auction, you'll still see a few buckets of fish and old-timers enjoying its shade on rickety old plastic chairs, in front of the community-subsidized tractor they use to pull the boats ashore in the winter. (In the days before tractors, boat-hauling was a 10-person communal heave-ho.) In the calm of the summer, boats are left out on buoys. Oblivious to tourists, the old salts mend their nets and reminisce about the good ol' days when life was "only fish and hunger." To get permission before taking their photo, ask *"uma foto, por favor?"* (oo-mah foh-too poor fah-vor).

At night you'll see evenly spaced lights bobbing on the horizon: these are fishing boats out in search of squid, sardines, and the main catch—octopi. The pottery jars stacked everywhere are traps; owners take care to keep them clean because octopi prefer smooth, barnacle-free pots. Unwritten tradition allocates different chunks of undersea territory to each Salema family. The traps are tied about 15 feet apart in long lines and dropped offshore. Octopi, thinking these jars would make a cozy place to set an ambush, climb in and get ambushed themselves. (Octopi also take refuge in pots during a storm.) When the fishermen hoist them in, the octopi hang on—unaware they've made their final mistake. The fishermen mace them out of their pots with a squirt of bleach. The octopi flop angrily into the boat, bound for the market and—who knows—maybe onto your dinner plate.

Beach Scene

Sunbathers enjoy the beach May through early October. Knowing their tourist-based economy sits on a foundation of sand, locals hope and pray that the sand returns after

ALGARVE

Accommodations
1 Casa Praiamar
2 Pensión Maré
3 Hotel Residencial Salema
4 Filhas do Mar
5 Romantik Villa B&B
6 Villa M6

SALEMA BEACH CLUB

RUA 28 DE JANEIRO →

To Figueira Town (Bus stop) & Figueira Beach

"CONDO TOWN"

Eateries & Nightlife
7 Boia Bar & Restaurant
8 Atlântico
9 Mira Mar
10 Casa Pizza
11 Restaurante O Lourenço
12 Agua Na Boca
13 Café Pastelaria Solmar
14 Bar Central
15 Atabua Bar
16 Aventura Bar
17 Salema Market & Laundry
18 Mini-Market San Jose

Cliffs

Beach

To "End of the Earth"

being washed away each winter (some winters leave the beach just a pile of rocks).

A walk along the length of the beach, tracing the edge of the wet sand from the rocks in the west to the rocks in the east, is a peaceful experience. Doing it early or late is a fine way to start or finish your day.

Locals claim the ocean is safe for swimming—and in summer a lifeguard is often on duty (marked by signs)—but the water is rarely really warm. The flag indicates the swimming conditions: Green is good, yellow means the current merits extra caution, and

red means no swimming. You can rent beach items just below Atlântico restaurant (1 or 2 lounge chairs with umbrella, drink service, Wi-Fi, and showers-€12/day), or in front of Boia Bar (2 lounge chairs and bamboo sunshade-€10/day).

On the west end of the beach, at low tide, you may be able to climb over the rocks past tiny tide pools to secluded Figueira Beach. (But be aware of when the tide comes in, or your route back will have to be over land.) While the old days of black-clad widows chasing topless Nordic women off the beach are gone, topless bathing is still considered somewhat risqué: Northern European sun worshippers do so with discretion, sometimes tucking in at the end of the beach among the rocks.

To complement your beach time with a little workout, use the outdoor gym-with-a-view at the east end of town. (The big shot who built the mansion above it ignored local regulations but gave the town this gym as a consolation quid pro quo.)

Showers for Rick Steves Readers: Oddly, Salema (which survives on its beach-loving visitors) does not provide a public shower. My friends at the Atlântico restaurant have come to the rescue: If you show this book, even if you're not paying to use their beach lounges, you can use their shower for free (inside, just off the beach, immediately under the restaurant).

Hiking

From Salema, several beautiful hikes go along the beach and through the countryside out to neighboring villages such as Figueira. For routes, ask at your hotel.

Near Salema

The whole peninsula (west of Lagos) has been declared a natural park, and further development close to the beach is forbidden. But the village of Salema is becoming less and less ramshackle as it's gradually bought up by northern Europeans for vacation or retirement homes. Salema will live with past mistakes, such as the huge hotel in the town center that pulled some mysterious strings to go two stories over code. Up the street is a sprawling community of condos and Club Med-type vacationers who rarely leave their air-conditioned bars and swimming pools.

Across the highway and two miles inland is a big golf resort, **Santo Antonio at Parque da Floresta,** where several well-known European soccer players have snapped up holiday homes. Visitors can pay a daily rate to use the spa, gym, outdoor pool, golf course, and tennis courts (spa +351 282 690 086, www.saresorts.com; golf +351 282 690 054, parquedaflorestagolfclub.com).

Sleeping in Salema

Salema has a limited number of hotels; you'll feel the pinch in the busy summer months of July through mid-September (August is horribly packed). Prices jump in July and especially in August. Many Salema accommodations lack air-conditioning—locals insist they don't need it, thanks to stiff, cooling Atlantic winds that blow through most evenings. Salema is partially closed down in winter, when just a couple of restaurants stay open.

IN OR NEAR THE TOWN CENTER

$$$ Casa Praiamar—in a newer building just above the main square, with a pool and Astroturf—feels fresh and slick by Salema standards. It rents 10 modern rooms, most with kitchens and half with sea views and balconies (RS%, air-con, family rooms, no breakfast, mobile +351 962 619 037, www.casapraiamarsalema. com, casapraiamar@gmail.com).

$$ Pensión Maré, a blue-and-white building overlooking the village along the main road into town, is the best hotel value in Salema. It's managed by friendly Daniela, who offers six comfortable rooms, three fully equipped apartments, and an inviting breakfast terrace in a tidy paradise (RS%, air-con in some rooms, laundry service, +351 282 695 165, www.the-mare.com, daniela@the-mare. com).

$$ Hotel Residencial Salema rents basic, comfortable rooms handy to the beach. Their 32 rooms have air-conditioning, balconies, and partial views (RS%, elevator, Wi-Fi in lobby, usually closed Nov-Easter, +351 282 695 328, www.hotelsalema.com, info@hotelsalema.com, Andrea).

$$ Filhas do Mar, run by Dutch transplant Peter, has four big, multiroom apartments and two studios in a modern building tucked at the back end of town. While the location is more practical than romantic, this is a decent option if the others are full (air-con, some rooms have modest views, no breakfast, +351 282 695 943, www.filhasdomar.com).

$ *Quartos:* For economy, the experience, and an opportunity to practice your Portuguese, you can stay in a *quarto* (private room for rent). If you're brave, show up without a reservation and ask around for a room—these typically can't be reserved ahead. (Romeu at the Salema Market is a good person to ask; mobile +351 917 379 088, romeusalema@gmail.com). Most options line the main residential street, Rua dos Pescadores. For general info on staying at a *quarto*, see the "Sleeping" section in the Practicalities chapter.

ABOVE TOWN

These two places perch on the bluff overlooking town. Plan on a steep 10- to 15-minute walk up. To get here by foot, head up from the beach past Restaurante O Lourenço, take a right just after the *Salema Beach Club* sign, and carry on steeply uphill (with the white condos on your left). When you reach a fork at the big, rounded, white wall (and *Villa Oceanis* sign), bear left to find Romantik Villa or right to find Villa M6.

One-way streets take drivers on a slightly different route: Take the first left past Restaurante O Lourenço, and loop around past the parking lot over the beach; then, when you get back to the main road at the stop sign, turn right (back downhill) for a few yards, then take the first left. From there, follow the directions earlier.

$$$ Romantik Villa B&B is a chic, artsy house on top of the hill with one room, two apartments, a beautiful garden, and a swimming pool. Conscientiously run (with an eco-focus) by warm French couple Olivier and Geraldine, it's a tastefully decorated, serene, seaview retreat. This is a great option for those who don't mind the steep walk up from town (rooms include breakfast and daily cleaning; apartments have a 3-night minimum, kitchens, and breakfast and cleaning for an extra charge; self-service laundry, mobile +351 967 059 806, www.romantikvilla.com, romantikvilla@sapo.pt).

$$ Villa M6 is a simpler, no-frills alternative just around the corner. Heiwi (from Germany) rents four rooms, and there's a fine swimming-pool terrace with sea views (cheaper rooms with shared bath, some rooms with view, kitchen, +351 282 698 684, www. algarve-salema.de).

Eating in Salema

Eat fresh seafood here. The local specialty is *cataplana*—fish, tomatoes, potatoes, onions, and whatever else is available—cooked a long time in a traditional copper pot (somewhere between a pressure cooker and a steamer). Costing around €25, a single *cataplana* is enough food for two. Also look for grilled golden bream *(dourada grelhada)* and giant prawns *(camarões)*. For wine, try *vinho verde* (a refreshing young white wine).

For such a small town, Salema seems to specialize in good restaurants. You have fun choices: foodie, yacht club, fisherman's family, Italian, or German beach bum. Dinner with a view is tempting here; Boia Bar, Atlântico, and Casa Pizza all have modern glass fronts so you can be both comfortable and seaside in cold weather. The Mira Mar is right on the beach and can be chilly at dinnertime (they have blankets). For a memorable last course at any of these places, consider taking your dessert drink or coffee to the beach for some stardust with your surf.

$$ Boia Bar and Restaurant, at the base of the Rua dos Pescadores residential street, has a classy beachfront setting, noteworthy service by a friendly gang, and a knack for doing fish and shellfish just right, always with free seconds on vegetables (daily 9:00-24:00, +351 282 695 382, Anibal, Rui, and Carla).

$$$ Atlântico—big, busy, and right on the beach—has long dominated the Salema scene and comes with a fun energy. It's known for tasty fish (see the daily board), friendly service, and a wonderful beachside terrace (daily 12:00-22:00, +351 282 695 142, Cristiano and his sister Sandra run the place).

$$$ Mira Mar, easily accessed from the beach promenade, has outdoor tables on a covered patio facing the water. Dieter (a German who adopted Salema as his hometown decades ago) offers a creative rotating menu for those venturing away from seafood. He serves hearty salads for lunch and always has a vegetarian option (Sun-Fri 12:30-15:30 & 18:30-22:00, closed Sat, cash only, no reservations—arrive early to nab a table).

$$ Casa Pizza, across the street from the Boia Bar, isn't on the beach, but its upper deck has a great view. They serve a variety of tasty pizzas, salads, and fresh fish, as well as meat and pasta dishes (Wed-Mon 12:00-22:30, closed Mon, Rua dos Pescadores 100, +351 282 697 968; Stelios, Mariana, and George).

$$$ Restaurante O Lourenço, a block up the hill, has no beach view (choose between the classic old school dining room or the vine-covered terrace across the street), but offers good-value meals and is popular with both locals and tourists for its freshest of fish. This is truly a family-run, fisherman's restaurant: Father Paulo fishes, mother Aldina cooks, and son João serves. A fish dinner for two here will cost around €40 (Mon-Sat 12:00-22:00, closed Sun, cash only, +351 282 698 622).

$$$$ Agua Na Boca ("Mouth Watering") is sophisticated, romantic, and the closest thing to a gourmet restaurant in town. Run by Paulo and his wife-and-chef Irene, they serve upmarket local cuisine complemented by an extensive wine list. It's popular, especially with the fancy golf-club crowd, so reserve ahead. Dishes are innovative—more than the standard grilled fish—and their special plates are huge and splittable. For about €50 you can enjoy a three-course meal for two people (April-Sept daily from 18:00, Oct-May closed Sun, on Rua dos Pescadores 82, +351 282 695 651).

Picnics on the Beach

Two minimarkets have everything you need for a beach picnic in Salema or at the harbor in Cape Sagres. Look for fresh fruit, veggies, bread, sheep's cheese, sausage, and vinho verde. The **Salema Market** is up the hill at the Salema Beach Club (daily 8:30-19:00, sometimes later in summer, Nov-April closes 13:00-15:00, Romeu). **Mini-Market San Jose** is on the strip facing Hotel Residencial Salema (Mon-Sat 8:30-18:00, closed Sun). Two pizzerias (including Casa Pizza, mentioned earlier) do a thriving to-go business serving pizzas in a box for easy export.

Breakfast in Salema

Quartos and some hotels don't serve breakfast. To save money, go shopping and put your room's kitchenette to work by making your own. Or consider Salema's two good breakfast options—both on the main square:

$$ Boia Bar and Restaurant, listed earlier also serves a hearty €8 breakfast all day. They have a big menu of breakfast items and plenty of tables with glorious ocean views (see details, earlier).

$ Café Pastelaria Solmar, where locals go to start their day with a cigarette, is the only place for an early breakfast—serving toasties (grilled ham-and-cheese sandwiches), juice, coffee, and pastries from 7:00. It's less pretty—designed for people who need no ocean view—but it's a good basic hangout all day (on the strip facing Hotel Residencial Salema).

Nightlife in Salema

Salema has three late-night bars, one on the main square and the other two side-by-side on the main street. Each has a different vibe and all are worth a visit to sample local drinks. *Armarguinha* (ar-mar-GWEEN-yah) is a sweet, likeable almond liqueur. *Licor beirão* (LIK-kor bay-ROW, rhymes with "cow") is Portuguese amaretto, a "double distillation of diverse plants and aromatic seeds in accordance with a secret old formula." *Caipirinha* (kay-peer-EEN-yah), tasty and powerful, is made of fermented Brazilian sugarcane with lime, sugar, and crushed ice. And *moscatel* is the local sweet dessert wine.

Bar Central is Salema's "lounge bar" with spacious lizard-friendly seating inside and out, an international vibe, and plenty of cocktails and wines.

Atabua Bar is a gin bar but also serves a popular sangria set to mellow music. It feels a bit younger and more local, and has been run by Guilherme (William) since 1984 (open from 17:00).

Aventura Bar, the place for "curious cocktails," offers an intimate, laid-back atmosphere for sipping drinks whipped up by Karl and Zoe, an English couple who prefer the Eagles to hip-hop (from 18:00).

DIY Beach Bar: I enjoy capping my dinner by taking a drink from any beachside restaurant and grabbing a bench on the promenade or a place on the beach to peacefully ponder the moon and the waves.

Cape Sagres

In the days before Columbus, when the world was presumed to be flat, this rugged southwestern tip of Portugal was the spot closest to the edge of the Earth. Prince Henry the Navigator, determined to broaden Europe's horizons and spread Catholicism, founded his navigators' school here and sent sailors ever farther into the unknown. Shipwrecked and frustrated explorers were carefully debriefed as they washed ashore.

ALGARVE

Today, Cape Sagres (KAH-peh SAH-gresh) is popular among two sets of travelers: Those who want photographic evidence that they've been to the "end of Europe" (before retreating to the comfort of their concrete resorts); and a young, international crowd drawn by the strong surf, who settle into humble guesthouses in the town of Sagres and keep its many bars hopping. While the Henry the Navigator sights are worth a quick visit, and some of the surrounding sea cliffs are dramatic, the town itself is scrappy, humble, and visually underwhelming. It smells like sea spray, surfer B.O., and sweet wafts of marijuana...making it nirvana for some, and a hold-your-nose pass-through for others.

Orientation to Cape Sagres

Portugal's end of the road is two distinct capes. **Cape Sagres,** with its old fort and Henry the Navigator lore, is the more historic cape of the two. Windy **Cape St. Vincent** is actually the most southwestern tip. At either cape, look for daredevil windsurfers and fishermen casting from the cliffs.

Lashed tightly to the windswept landscape is the salty **town of Sagres,** above a harbor of fishing boats. Sagres (pop. 1,900)—which really does feel like the last town in Europe—is basically a scruffy main street (Avenida Comandante Matoso) with plenty of places to eat and sleep. The main square is a broad expanse called Jardim de Sagres, with the TI, a statue of Henry the Navigator wearing a rakish hat, and bus stops. The square—and the town—sits on a bluff above the shoreline, with cliffs on the horizon in all directions. At one end of town is Cape Sagres, and at the other is a hardworking fishing port with an auction (Docapesca, described later) and a few leisure boats. Running underneath the town is a fine crescent beach, with a good beachside restaurant.

Arrival in Sagres: If arriving by **bus,** hop off at the main square, near the TI. **Drivers** pass through tacky low-rise concrete sprawl before reaching the roundabout at the start of town. Here you have three choices: right for Cape St. Vincent; straight to Cape Sagres and the fortress *(fortaleza);* or left onto the main drag, which passes the main square (with free street parking), then goes through the middle of town before ending at the twisty road down to the port.

Tourist Information: The TI is on the main street (hours flex with demand, generally Mon-Fri 9:30-13:00 & 14:00-17:30, closed Sat-Sun, +351 282 624 873).

Getting Around: Without your own transportation, a trip with **Tuk Tuk Sagres** makes sense here where distances are long and shade trees are sparse. One- or two-hour tours connect all recommended sites and three beaches. They also offer a romantic sunset trip (€12-30, at TI when buses arrive, mobile +351 914 011 230, www.tuktuksagres.com).

Sights in Cape Sagres

Tourism here is all about surfing. When the surf's up, things are busy and there's a hip and youthful vibe. In low season, it feels pretty dead.

Docapesca
Sagres harbor hosts the biggest fish auction west of Lagos (which is actually saying very little, Mon-Fri at 7:30 and 15:00). Snack Bar A Sereia is perched above the auction, and from its big windows you can watch the fishy action as restaurateurs fill the two-dozen chairs above the conveyor belt and bid against each other for the best fish.

▲Cape Sagres Fort (Fortaleza de Sagres) and Navigators' School
The former "end of the world" is a craggy, windswept, wedge-shaped point that juts into the Atlantic (a short drive or 15-minute walk from Sagres; follow brown signs for *fortaleza*). In 1420, Prince Henry the Navigator used his order's funds to establish a school here for navigators. It was devastated by the 1755 earthquake (which also destroyed Lisbon), the center of which was 50 miles offshore from here. Today, little remains of Henry's school, except the site of buildings replaced by a few more modern structures. An 18th-century fortress, built on the school's original battlements and whitewashed in the 20th century, dominates the entrance to the point.

Prince Henry the Navigator (1394-1460)

No swashbuckling sailor, Infante Dom Henrique (as the Portuguese call him) was a quiet scholar, an organizer, a religious man, and the brains behind Portugal's daring sea voyages. The middle child of King João I of Portugal and Queen Philippa of England, he was one of what was dubbed "The Marvelous Generation" *(Ínclita Geração)* that drove the Age of Discovery. While his brothers and nephews became Portugal's kings, he worked behind the scenes.

At age 21, he planned the logistics for the large-scale ship invasion of the Muslim city of Ceuta (1415) on the north coast of Morocco, taking the city and winning knightly honors. Awed by the wealth of the city—a terminus of the caravan route—and intrigued by the high-quality maps he found there, Henry decided to organize expeditions to explore the Muslim world. He hoped to spread Christianity, contain Islam, tap Muslim wealth, and find Prester John's legendary Christian kingdom, said to exist somewhere in Africa or Asia.

As head of the Order of Christ—a powerful brotherhood of soldier-monks based in Tomar—Henry used their money to found a maritime school at Sagres. While Henry stayed home to update maps, debrief returning sailors, order supplies, and sign paychecks, brave seamen traveled off under Henry's strict orders not to return until they'd explored what was known as the "Sea of Darkness."

They discovered the Madeira Islands (1420), which Henry planted with vineyards, and the Azores (1427), which Henry colonized. But the next expeditions returned empty-handed, having run into a barrier—both a psychological and physical one. Cape Bojador (at the southwest corner of modern Morocco), with its reefs and currents, was seen as the end of the world. Beyond that, sea serpents roamed, while the hot equatorial sun melted ships, made the sea boil, and turned white men black.

Henry ordered scared, superstitious sailors to press on. After 14 unsuccessful voyages, Gil Eanes' crew returned (1437), unharmed, with new knowledge that was added to corporate Portugal's map library.

Henry gained a reputation as an intelligent, devout, celibate monk. In later years, he spent less time at court in Lisbon and more in desolate Sagres, where he died in 1460. (He's buried in Batalha; see page 272.) Henry died before finding a sea route to Asia and just before his voyages really started paying off commercially. A generation later, Vasco da Gama would sail to India, kicking off Portugal's Golden Age.

ALGARVE

ALGARVE

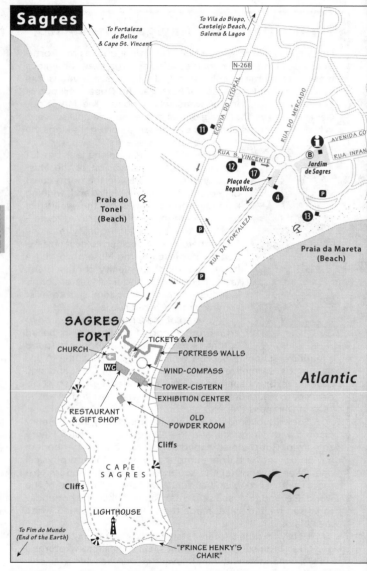

Sagres

To Fortaleza de Belixe & Cape St. Vincent

To Vila do Bispo, Castelejo Beach, Salema & Lagos

N-268

RUA DO MERCADO

AVENIDA CO

RUA INFANT

RUA S. VICENTE

11

ESTRADA DO LITORAL

12

17

Plaça de Republica

Jardim de Sagres

4

P

13

Praia do Tonel (Beach)

RUA DA FORTALEZA

P

P

Praia da Mareta (Beach)

SAGRES FORT

CHURCH

WC

TICKETS & ATM

FORTRESS WALLS

WIND-COMPASS

TOWER-CISTERN

EXHIBITION CENTER

OLD POWDER ROOM

RESTAURANT & GIFT SHOP

Atlantic

Cliffs

CAPE SAGRES

Cliffs

LIGHTHOUSE

To Fim do Mundo (End of the Earth)

"PRINCE HENRY'S CHAIR"

Cost and Hours: €3, daily 9:30-20:00, Oct-April until 17:30, +351 282 620 140. Parking is free.

Visiting the Fort: After entering through the 18th-century battlements, turn back and look above the entry arch. Find the carved **stone plaque** that honors Henry. The ship in the plaque is a caravel, one of the small, light craft that was constantly being reinvented by Sagres' shipbuilding grad students. The astrolabe, a

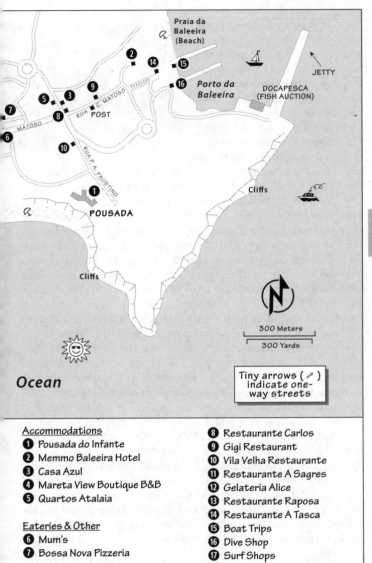

ALGARVE

<u>Accommodations</u>
1 Pousada do Infante
2 Memmo Baleeira Hotel
3 Casa Azul
4 Mareta View Boutique B&B
5 Quartos Atalaia

<u>Eateries & Other</u>
6 Mum's
7 Bossa Nova Pizzeria

8 Restaurante Carlos
9 Gigi Restaurant
10 Vila Velha Restaurante
11 Restaurante A Sagres
12 Gelateria Alice
13 Restaurante Raposa
14 Restaurante A Tasca
15 Boat Trips
16 Dive Shop
17 Surf Shops

compact instrument that uses the stars for navigation, emphasizes Henry's role in the exploration process.

Head a few more steps into the complex and look right. The stone column capped with a **cross** honors Henry, who died here in 1460 (erected on the 500th anniversary of his death). The top is a replica of the stone used by Portugal's great mariners to claim new territory.

Poke around...though there's little to actually see here. Sagres' most impressive sight—a circle on the ground, 100 feet across and outlined by round pebbles—is a mystery. Some think it was a large **wind-compass** *(rosa-dos-ventos)*. A flag flying from the center could immediately announce the wind's direction. Others speculate it's a large sun-dial. A pole in the center point-

ing toward the North Star (at a 37-degree angle, Sagres' latitude) would cast a shadow on the dial showing the time of day.

The row of buildings beyond the wind-compass is where Henry's **school** once was. Today these modern buildings house the shop, cafeteria, and a planned exhibition (though a long-delayed renovation means any or all of these may be closed for your visit). At the far-left end, the **tower-cistern** is part of the original dorms. You can climb it for the view. At the far-right end, the small, whitewashed **Church of Our Lady of Grace** (with St. Vincent and St. Francis flanking its humble altar) replaced Henry's church. The **windbreak wall** dates from Henry's time, but is largely rebuilt.

For a better view of the complex, climb up the ramps to the **rooftop of the fortress.** Look out to sea and consider the epic history of this strategic location: The Sagres school taught map-making, shipbuilding, sailing, astronomy, and mathematics (for navigating), plus botany, zoology, anthropology, languages, and salesmanship for mingling with the locals. The school welcomed Italians, Scandinavians, and Germans, and included Christians, Muslims, and Jews. Captured Africans gave guest lectures. (The next 15 generations of Africans passing through Portugal were not so lucky, being sold into slavery by the tens of thousands.)

Besides being a school, Sagres was Mission Control for the explorers. Returning sailors brought spices, gold, diamonds, silk, and ivory, plus new animals, plants, peoples, customs, communicable diseases, and knowledge of the routes that were added to the maps. Henry ordered every sailor to keep a travel journal that could be studied.

Shipbuilding was a big industry in the Algarve in the 15th and 16th centuries. And it was here that ship designs were analyzed and tweaked, resulting in the square-sailed, oceangoing caravels that replaced earlier, less-nimble coast-hugging ships.

It's said that Ferdinand Magellan (circumnavigator), Vasco da Gama (found sea route to India), Pedro Cabral (discovered Brazil), and Bartolomeu Dias (Africa-rounder) all studied at Sagres (after Henry's time, though). In May of 1476, the young Italian Christopher Columbus washed ashore here after being shipwrecked by pirates. He went on to study and sail with the Portuguese (and marry a Portuguese woman) before beginning his American voyage. When Portugal denied Columbus' request to sail west, Spain accepted. The rest is history.

Beyond the buildings, the granite **point** itself is windswept, eroded, and largely barren, except for hardy, coarse vegetation admired by botanists. This is a popular stop for birds on their migration south (and a popular stop for bird-watchers, too). Walk on level paths around the edge of the bluff (a 40-minute round-trip walk), where locals cast lines and tourists squint into the wind. You'll get great seascape views of Cape St. Vincent, with its modern lighthouse on the site of an old convent (described next). At the far end of the Sagres bluff are a naval radio station, a natural cave, and a promontory called "Prince Henry's Chair."

Sit on the point and gaze across the "Sea of Darkness," where monsters roam. Long before Henry's time, Romans dubbed it Promontorium Sacrum—Sacred ("Sagres") Promontory. Pilgrims who came to visit this awe-inducing place were prohibited from spending the night here—it was for the gods alone.

In Portugal's seafaring lore, capes, promontories, and land's ends are metaphors for the edge of the old, and the start of the unknown voyage. Sagres is the greatest of these.

Cape St. Vincent (Cabo São Vincente)

About a 10-minute drive past Cape Sagres, this spit of land is the actual southwestern tip of Europe. It has a desolate lighthouse that marks what was thought of even in prehistoric times as "the end of the world." Today it's an impossibly tacky tourist trap, with a parking lot jammed with salt-of-the-earth merchants selling seaworthy sweaters and a stand boasting the *"Letzte Bratwurst vor Amerika"* (last hot dog before America).

The cape's tip is marked by the **St. Vincent Lighthouse.** Stepping through the gate of the complex (Tue-Sun 10:00-18:00, until 17:00 Oct-March, closed Mon), on your right you'll see the entrance to a humble little museum, which is worth a few minutes and the modest admission. Its exhibits focus on ship technology, ancient legends, celestial navigation, the evolution of Portuguese lighthouses, and the history of this lighthouse in particular. In 1846, you could see the light of the oil lamp from six miles away. Now the beam is one of the strongest in Europe, said to reach 60 miles.

To visit the **lantern,** wait for a while at the door marked *Privado Staff Only* (directly across from the museum's gift shop)—the lighthouse keeper may eventually show up to take you on a free little tour. He's formally scheduled to lead tours on Wednesdays from 14:00-17:00 but seems happy to do it at other times, too (for a tip). The "tour" is a 20-minute romp (with broken English) around the lighthouse, climbing steep stairs and briefly sharing the tranquility enjoyed by the couple of families who live here maintaining the now-automatic beacon. (If it's quiet and you want to make sure that a tour is possible, ask at the little gift shop downstairs, near the WCs). Also in the courtyard are a salty café and wild views of the often stormy coastline and the adjacent, jagged cliffs.

Just off the road—about a half-mile before the lighthouse—you'll see **Fortaleza de Belixe,** the eroded remains of a 16th-century castle hanging precariously on a bluff over the sea. It was used as a kind of headquarters by the English pirate "sir" Francis Drake. Drake, who pillaged with the queen's blessing, waited here for his Mediterranean-bound victims.

ALGARVE

Beaches

In the town of Sagres itself, **Mareta Beach** (Praia da Mareta), just below the town center, has rental gear and showers in the summer and the fun little recommended Raposo Restaurante.

Drivers can visit many beaches tucked away on the drive **between Salema and Cape Sagres.** Most of them require a short walk after you stop along N-125. In some cases, you leave your car on access roads or cross private property to reach the beach—make sure no valuables are visible in your vehicle and be considerate as you walk. Furnas beach is fully accessible by car. You can access Ingrina and Zavial beaches by turning south in the village of Raposeira. Many beaches have bars (the one at Ingrina beach is famous for its spicy garlic prawns—*camarão piri-piri*).

The best secluded beach in the region is **Castelejo Beach** (Praia do Castelejo), north of Cape Sagres (from the town of Vila do Bispo, drive west to the ocean, following the signs for 15 minutes). If you have a car and didn't grow up in Fiji, this really is worth the drive. Overlooking the deserted beach is **$$$ Castelejo Restaurante,** which specializes in octopus dishes, *percebes* (barnacles), and *cataplana,* the hearty seafood  stew (daily 12:00-22:00, 7.5 miles from Salema at Praia do Castelejo, +351 282 639 777). While beaches between Salema and Sagres offer more of a seaside landscape, beaches north of São Vicente are more rugged and wild because they're exposed to ocean wind and weather. If there's no sand in Castelejo when you visit, blame it on nature and enjoy the rock formations instead.

For a resort beach, consider **Luz** (the first town west of Lagos), which feels like a Portuguese Riviera playground with a fine promenade and all the trappings of a beach-vacation destination.

Activities

There's no shortage of options for beach fun in Sagres. Several outfitters (renting surfboards, organizing excursions, and so on) line the streets of town, particularly at the end near the TI. Down at the port, you'll find boat excursions and the diving school.

Boat Trips: Two competitive outfits with storefronts at the port sell tourist boat excursions into the waters near Sagres. Popular options include a dolphin-watching cruise (€35/1.5 hours), a seabird-watching tour (€45/2.5 hours—they toss in chum so you can observe the spectacle), a straightforward sightseeing cruise to Cape St. Vincent and back (€20/1.5 hours), fishing trips, and more. Comparison-shop at **Cape Cruiser** (mobile +351 919 751 175, www.capecruiser.org) and **Mar Ilimitado** (mobile +351 916 832 625, www.marilimitado.com).

Diving: At the port, **Divers Cape Sagres** is a diving school offering dive classes and excursions (mobile +351 965 559 073, www.diverscape.com).

Surfing: Near the entrance to town (between the two main roundabouts, on Rua São Vincente), two companies offer surfing gear and lessons: **Sagres Natura Sport** (+351 282 624 072, www.sagresnatura.com) and **Pure Surf Camps** (www.puresurfcamps.com).

Sleeping in Sagres

$$$$ Pousada do Infante, with 51 rooms on a bluff overlooking the sea, provides a touch of elegance in Sagres. Like other *pousadas* (historic inns), it's staid, stuffy, and a bit dated—but worth it for the magnificent setting. At breakfast, you can sip coffee and enjoy the buffet while gazing out to sea (air-con, elevator, +351 282 620 240, www.pousadas.pt, recepcao.infante@pousadas.pt).

$$$ Memmo Baleeira Hotel, with views over the port of Sagres, is your big hotel option—a 144-room resort that caters to groups. While a bit faded, it remains chic and minimalist, with pure white bedrooms—most with sea views (air-con, elevator, beautiful swimming pool terrace, +351 282 624 212, www.memmohotels.com, baleeira@memmohotels.com).

$$$ Casa Azul—youthful and cheery—feels like an upgraded old guesthouse on an urban street, with 11 vivid rooms (each a different color, nearly all with a small private balcony) and four apartments (air-con, just up the street next to the Spar supermarket, Rua Dom Sebastião, +351 282 624 856, www.casaazulsagres.com).

$$ Mareta View Boutique B&B, a delightful and stylish refuge on a quieter back street, is perched on a bluff at the edge of town. Its 18 modern rooms have access to a fine garden and a seaview hot tub (air-con, Beco D. Henrique, +351 282 620 000, www.maretaview.com, reservations@sagresholidays.com). Its sister hotel, Mareta Beach (a block closer to town), is bigger, less tranquil, and less appealing.

$ Quartos Atalaia, run by English-speaking Jorge, is your budget option—with seven basic rooms and four huge apartments on a workaday corner in the center of town (family rooms, no breakfast, across the street from Caza Azul—see earlier, +351 282 624 681, mobile +351 911 046 068, apart.atalaia@gmail.com).

Eating in Sagres

ON OR NEAR THE MAIN DRAG

Sagres feels designed to feed visitors, with lots of inviting little eateries along its main drag, Avenida Comandante Matoso.

$$$ Mum's has a hip retro vibe and a mix of traditional Portuguese and international comfort food (Wed-Mon 18:00-24:00, closed Tue, mobile +351 968 210 411).

$$ Bossa Nova Pizzeria serves tasty pizzas, pastas, salads, and vegetarian dishes in a converted stable (daily 18:00-24:00, closed Sun off-season, tucked down a little pedestrian lane behind the row of bars that includes Paü de Pita and Dromadário, +351 282 624 219).

$$ Restaurante Carlos offers good Portuguese standards—such as a stellar *cataplana*—for reasonable prices and with friendly service (Wed-Mon 12:00-23:00, closed Tue, Avenida Comandante Matoso, +351 262 624 228).

$$ Gigi Restaurant is a big modern place with happy eaters spilling out onto a covered terrace. They have a passion for traditional Portuguese dishes and fish (Thu-Tue 12:00-15:00 & 19:00-22:30, closed Wed, Avenida Comandante Matoso, +351 282 624 316).

$$$$ Vila Velha Restaurante, the pricey top-end option in town, offers wonderful meals—especially their rabbit stew (Tue-Sun 18:30-22:00, closed Mon, reservations smart, a block above the main drag on Rua Patrão Antonio Faustino—on the way up to the *pousada,* +351 282 624 788, www.vilavelha-sagres.com).

$$$ Restaurante A Sagres, owned by João Pedro with his wife Paula running the kitchen, has a homey, nautical feel and dishes up everything fresh from the market. Buttery clams and seafood stew are local favorites (Thu-Tue 13:00-23:00, closed Wed, near the roundabout heading into town on Ecovia do Litoral, +351 282 624 171).

Ice Cream: Look for interesting flavors at **Gelateria Alice,** with a small selection of freshly made, top-quality gelato on the little street between the two roundabouts at the start of town (Rua São Vincente).

WITH A VIEW
$$$ Restaurante Raposo ("Fox") is right on the pristine, sandy, and picturesque Mareta Beach. It's a fun spot for snacks (try *percebes*—barnacles), drinks, or a serious meal, inside or outside on a terrace. Have a dip in the sea right after your meal (meals served daily 12:00-21:00, closed Wed, +351 282 624 168).

$$$ Restaurante A Tasca, known for good seafood, has dressy indoor seating with an open kitchen and a huge, sunny terrace overlooking the harbor. It sits like a yacht club at the far (port) end of town (Thu-Tue 8:00-24:00, closed Wed, Porto da Baleeira, +351 282 624 177).

Cape Sagres Connections

From Salema, Sagres is a 20-minute drive or a 30-minute bus trip (runs every 1-2 hours, stop is at the edge of town—near the big park and TI, just after the roundabout with the giant anchor). A handful of buses continue to the Cape St. Vincent (Cabo São Vincente). You can check bus times online at www.eva-bus.com or www.algarvebus.info.

A taxi ride from Salema to Sagres costs about €30 (see "Helpful Hints" in Salema, earlier in this chapter).

Lagos

With a beach-party old town and a jet-ski marina, Lagos (LAH-goosh) is as enjoyable as a city resort can be. This major town on the west end of the Algarve was the region's capital in the 13th and 14th centuries. The first great Portuguese maritime expeditions embarked from here, and the first African slave market in Europe was held here. Today, with nothing of earth-shaking importance to see or do, it's just a purely enjoyable little bit of urban Algarve.

In some ways, big-city Lagos is the yin to sleepy Salema's yang. While

Salema is far more relaxing, even sedate, Lagos attracts a younger and rowdier crowd. The big draw here is Lagos' stunning beaches, which are framed by jagged sandstone-colored sea stacks that poke up, like serrated teeth, from the aquamarine deep. While little Salema's streets are lined with take-your-time fish restaurants and napping cats, Lagos is jammed with funky cafés, hard-partying bars and nightclubs, and sales kiosks hawking all manner of boat, kayak, scuba diving, and other excursions.

Lagos is a whitewashed jumble of pedestrian streets, bars, hippie craft shops, outdoor restaurants, mod fountains and sculptures, and sunburned tourists. Except for a stroll among the rocks on the beach, there are no major sights—though to get your bearings, the town walk (described later) makes for a delightful morning or afternoon. Search out the sea-creature designs laid in the pavement—some of them will probably be on your plate at dinner.

Orientation to Lagos

Most visitors to Lagos (pop. 27,000) focus on the **old town.** Defined by its medieval walls, old Lagos stretches between the main square (Praça Gil Eanes) and the fort. Across the Benasfrim River and just upstream are a colorful marina, excursion boats, and the train station.

The **beaches** with the exotic rock formations begin just past the fort, with easy access on foot via boardwalks and higher trails, or by local buses, taxis, and a tourist train. While the Praia da Batata, next to the old fort, is walkable from the center and perfectly good for a short visit, serious beachgoers may want to head farther out along the point to the south of the old town. This road is lined with scenic beaches (Dona Ana is best), culminating at the Ponta da Piedade viewpoint.

TOURIST INFORMATION

The TI, which covers the entire Algarve, is in the former City Hall on the south side of Praça Gil Eanes (daily 9:30-17:30, shorter hours and closed Sun off-season, +351 282 763 031, www.visitalgarve.pt).

ARRIVAL IN LAGOS

By Train or Bus: The train and bus stations are a five-minute walk apart, separated by the marina and a ramped pedestrian bridge over a river. Neither station has baggage storage.

By Car: From the A-22 freeway, exit at Lagos and follow signs to *centro*. On your way into town, the road forks: turn left (white *centro* signs) to the town center, or carry on straight (brown *praia* signs) for the farther-flung scenic beaches (each is individually signposted).

In town, the most convenient free parking lot is just outside the old city wall off Rua Infante de Sagres. More central (and still affordable) is the large underground parking garage on Avenida dos Descobrimentos, near Praça do Infante Dom Henrique. Another pay lot is near the marina. For a short visit, you can pay-and-display anywhere along the harborfront promenade.

HELPFUL HINTS

Car Rental: English-speaking Nuno at **Lagorent Rent-a-Car** can set you up with four wheels for around €45 a day (3-day minimum, daily, Avenida dos Descobrimentos 43, +351 282 762 467, www.lagorent.com, info@lagorent.com).

Local Guide: Good licensed guide **Carla Andrez de Sousa** lives and works in Lagos (€100/family or group for a two-hour private town tour, longer tours available, mobile +351 964 670 661, carlasousa64@gmail.com).

Lagos Town Walk

While the actual sights of Lagos are humble, the town itself has an endearing charm that is best experienced by strolling. This simple self-guided walk, worth ▲▲, takes about an hour (allow more time if you enter the sights along the way) and covers the essence of the city. It starts on the main square, cuts straight up the main street to the town museum, and then down to the site of the slave market and harborfront, where you can walk the promenade and/or hike the exotic beaches.

Praça Gil Eanes

This city's inviting cobbled pedestrian streets seem to converge in this square around the playful statue of King Sebastian (Sebastião). The big, yellow building housing the TI is the former City Hall. The local hippie community provides street music, and the cafés are tempting. While Lagos was a regional power from 1578 to 1756—in fact, the capital of the Algarve—today

it feels like the capital of sun-starved tourists.

ALGARVE

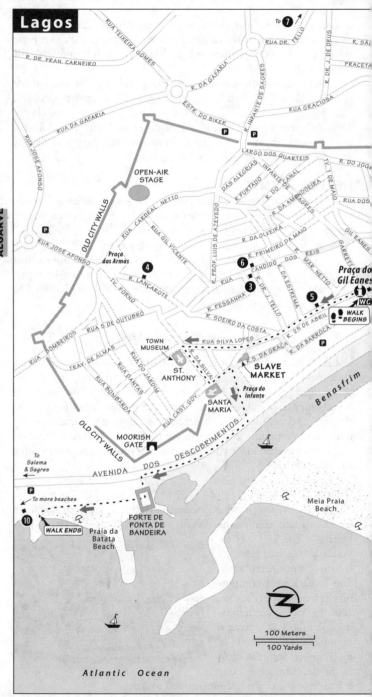

Lagos

To **7**

OPEN-AIR STAGE

Praça das Armas

4

6

3

5

Praça do Gil Eanes

WC

WALK BEGINS

TOWN MUSEUM

ST. ANTHONY

SANTA MARIA

SLAVE MARKET

Praça do Infante

Benasfrim

OLD CITY WALLS

MOORISH GATE

AVENIDA DOS DESCOBRIMENTOS

To Salema & Sagres

To more beaches

10

WALK ENDS

Praia da Batata Beach

FORTE DE PONTA DE BANDEIRA

Meia Praia Beach

100 Meters

100 Yards

Atlantic Ocean

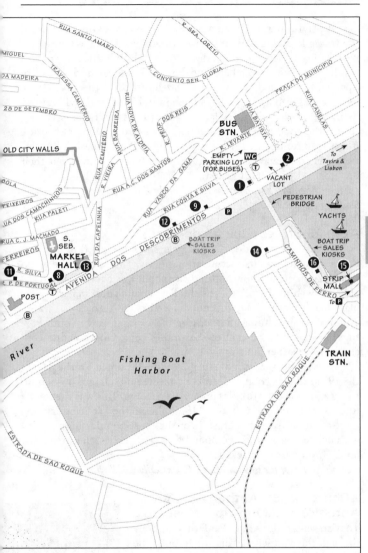

Accommodations

1. Lagos Avenida Hotel
2. Hotel Marina Rio
3. Hotel Riomar
4. Youth Hostel

Eateries & Other

5. Restaurante Dom Sebastião
6. Restaurante dos Artistas
7. Restaurante Calhou
8. Casa do Pasto do Zé
9. Adega da Marina
10. Café do Mar Restaurante Bar
11. Taquelim Gonçalves House of Regional Sweets
12. Supermarket
13. Mare Restaurant Bar
14. Bom Dia Boat Trips
15. Seafaris Boat Trips
16. Blue Fleet Kayaking

A playful statue commemorates the romantic **King Sebastian,** the young Portuguese ruler who ventured into Africa to Christianize "the Dark Continent"...and was killed. With his death, Spanish royalty came to power here and Portugal entered into a kind of Spanish-dominated Dark Age (1580-1640). And the Portuguese have never given up hope that somehow, their lost king will return. Sebastian is symbolic of ridiculous hopefulness. When he returns, so will the good times. This statue is particularly poignant because it was inaugurated in 1973, the year before the Carnation Revolution—when the people of Portugal were hungry to toss out their dictator and win their freedom.

• *From the square, head down Lagos' main drag. It's behind Sebastian, leading to the left.*

April 25 Street (Rua 25 de Abril)

Forca Portugal, a patriotic soccer gear shop, is a good example of how Portugal takes its soccer very seriously. Throughout the world when people (who know nothing else about this country) say Ronaldo, they think Portugal (he's the Portuguese superstar who now plays for the Italian club Juventus as well as for his national team). The next shop features another icon of Portugal: cork. South Portugal produces 50 percent of the world's cork. Good quality cork can be like leather but softer.

This marks the start of April 25 Street—named for the date of the 1974 military coup. Follow the street through Lagos' restaurant row. Enjoy the colorful tiles on building fronts. This was the town's finest street, and home to its noble families in the 19th century. The crest of the hill marks the start of the most popular night spots, with boisterous bars and popular discos (after hours, the streets just uphill from here are packed).

• *Stroll the street for several blocks. Eventually you'll run into the...*

▲Church of St. Anthony (Santo António) and Municipal Museum

Tourists enter the Church of St. Anthony through the Municipal Museum (around the right side). Lagos' humble little **museum,** while old-school, has some fascinating exhibits with good English descriptions (may be closed for renovation in 2021—check ahead; otherwise €1.50, Tue-Sun 10:00-12:30 & 14:00-17:30, closed Mon).

If the museum's open, look for ancient Roman mosaics, amphorae, and busts, models of traditional boats, octopus jugs, and other fishing gear. The chimneys, so characteristic of those you see all over the Algarve, are nicknamed "chimneys of the new Christians." According to tour guides, while Muslim Moors forced to convert in the 13th century became nominal Christians, they worshipped privately under chimneys like these, which were inspired by and reminiscent of the minarets of their destroyed mosques.

The **Church of St. Anthony** was first constructed in the 16th century, then rebuilt in the decades following the 1755 earthquake that devastated so much of Portugal (and led to Lagos' decline). Considered one of the finest Baroque/Rococo churches in Portugal, it's dedicated to the patron saint of the military. The altar (from 1719, before the big 1755 earthquake) is the oldest surviving artifact from the original church and is shiny with Brazilian gold leaf. Paintings show the miracles of St. Anthony (each described in English); the ceiling is a festival of 3-D; and the exuberant cupids are all very expressive.

• *Work your way downhill to a big square facing the harbor. Facing that square is the next church,* **Santa Maria.** *After being rebuilt many times, it's more modern and vibrant.*

Across the square, with the low-profile, double-arched arcade, is the...

▲Slave Market Museum (Mercado de Escravos)

This modern museum, located on the site of the original Lagos slave market, documents the tragic history of slavery in the region, which began at this very spot in 1444. Although information is scant, this museum takes an important first step in addressing the most reprehensible aspect of the Portuguese Age of Discovery.

Cost and Hours: €1.50, Tue-Sun 10:00-12:30 & 14:00-17:30, closed Mon, +351 282 762 301.

Visiting the Museum: Displays include 15th-century coins, African ceramics and beads, and a skeleton—one of several sadly found in a nearby rubbish dump. In the small portico outside, chained slaves were paraded around to be bid on. From 1444 until the mid-1700s, over 100,000 individual people were sold into slavery under these arches. In the early days of Portuguese exploration, the king made a rule that ships needed to bring back dirt, plants, and people from "discovered" lands. Upon arrival here, enslaved people were quarantined for 40 days. Those who survived were cleaned up and sold, adding to Portugal's wealth at a terrible cost.

Under the ceiling are navigational charts showing the slave-trade routes.

The exhibit continues around the corner uphill, where staff check your ticket and give you a tablet to use with a few interactive displays.

• *The square between the slave market and Santa Maria Church is...*

Praça do Infante Dom Henrique

This square honors its namesake, **Henry the Navigator,** with a statue (erected along with the city's fine harborfront promenade in 1960 to celebrate the 500th anniversary of his death; he died just down the coast in Sagres in 1460).

Portugal's Age of Discovery started in 1415 in Lagos under Prince Henry (before he earned his nickname "the Navigator"). Up to 400 ships would depart on huge royal-sponsored expeditions from this port. The glory days of Lagos lasted through the 1400s, but by 1500 the action shifted to Lisbon. The slave trade enriched the city in the 15th and 16th centuries. Later, Lagos was a tuna-fishing center and the military capital of the Algarve. But the 1755 earthquake/tsunami devastated the city, spelling the end of its importance.

• *From the square, turn right and walk between the church and the water along the old city walls toward the striking fortress on the harbor. The **walls** of Lagos, measuring nearly two miles, are the longest in the Algarve. Pause at the fortified **Moorish gate**, with its stout twin crenelated towers. The first wall here dates from the ninth century—another indication of the strategic importance of Lagos even before the Reconquista. Across the street is the...*

Fort Ponta da Bandeira

Fort Ponta da Bandeira, while cute today, was a state-of-the-art defense back in the 17th century, built to protect the city against pirates and Spaniards. Notice how, with the advent of cannon fire, castles became low and stout. Today it offers the visitor only stony ramparts and harbor views (€2, Tue-Sun 10:00-12:30 & 14:00-17:30, closed Mon).

• *Continue walking beyond the fort, passing the Lagos Nautical Club (which rents canoes and kayaks), a public WC, and a boardwalk across the sand leading to...*

Praia da Batata

"Potato Beach" is the most accessible of Lagos' many fine beaches, and a popular student hangout. At low tide, you can enjoy a fascinating beach walk through exotic rocks and tunnels for nearly a mile. (But be careful, as the tide can come in quickly.) At high tide, a stepped and paved path takes you along the beach but higher up, with fine views of remote, photogenic little beaches with striking rock formations.

• *From Praia da Batata, stairs lead up to the street. Up to the left, crowning the bluff, is the recommended **Café do Mar**, with wonderful outdoor tables overlooking the harbor and sea.*

Activities in Lagos

Lagos Market Hall

The slick and modern market hall faces the harbor as if waiting for the fishermen to unload their catch (as they do almost daily at 8:00 and 11:00; hall open Mon-Sat 9:00-13:00, closed Sun). The Algarve's third-biggest fish market welcomes visitors to peruse an impressive array of fish, all netted within a few miles of town. Upstairs are fresh fruits and vegetables, dried figs, and nuts. You'll also see fun, gifty local products like spicy homemade *piri-piri* sauce and "flower of salt" from Tavira's renowned salt beds. Snails *(caracois)*, which come out after rain, are sold by merchants, but their prices are generally undercut by street vendors. If you climb to the rooftop you'll find the **Mare Restaurant Bar** (fun menu, not cheap but tasty, daily until 23:00).

▲Lagos' Promenade

This pedestrian avenue stretches about a mile from the fort to the marina. It's a joy to stroll along the black-and-white patterned cobbles (Portugal's unique *calçada* stonework), with views of palm trees and busy little boats, the occasional sailboat heading out to sea, a soundtrack of gulls and hustlers of various sea activities, and the smell of "the perfume of the Atlantic."

Coastal Boat Tours

All over town, you'll be hustled to take a sightseeing cruise. There's plenty of creativity and competition among the 15 or so companies in town, giving you lots of options. Old fishermen ("who know the nickname of each rock along the coast") sit at anchor on board, while salespeople on the promenade hawk their services. Everyone offers the same basic excursions at the same price: nearby grotto tours (€20), dolphin watching (€40), and half-day cruises (€55). Specialized trips such as kayak tours, RIB (high-speed rigid inflatable boat) tours, snorkeling, fishing, and more are also available.

To comparison-shop, you'll find the highest concentration of vendors (and sales pitches) in two places: along the promenade, and lining the marina between the pedestrian bridge and the pink-and-white strip mall. It's actually enjoyable to stroll over the bridge and around the marina to consider your options. Some pleasant cafés are in the mall—sip a *sumo de laranja* (fresh orange juice) while observing the comings-and-goings of the yachts. Tours are similar and prices are not negotiable, so choose your excursion after careful comparison shopping.

Bom Dia has been offering trips since 1980 and is one of the more respected companies in Lagos (+351 282 087 587, www.bomdia-boattrips.com). **Seafaris** also has a stellar reputation (+351 282 798 727, www.seafaris.net). **BlueFleet** offers kayaking with small groups and good customer care (mobile +351 911 963 309, www.bluefleet.pt).

▲▲Scenic Beaches and Viewpoints

The beaches near Lagos are famed for their dramatic scenery. The soft, sandstone was carved out and artfully shaped by centuries of pounding surf, creating steep stratified cliffs and stunning formations just offshore.

Praia da Batata is the easiest choice—giving you a taste of this scenery close to the center, just beyond the fort in the heart of town (described at the end of the "Lagos Town Walk," earlier). While smaller and often more crowded, Batata—a few minutes' walk from the town center—is the handiest for nondrivers.

Praia Dona Ana, a few minutes' drive south of town, offers the best combination of scenery (jagged sea stacks) and services (rentable chairs and umbrellas, and a basic restaurant). While it feels (relatively) secluded once you're there, it's tucked below a sprawling resort area with high-rise hotels. From the big free parking lot (pay WC), a wooden staircase takes you down to the beach. In the summer, parking is very tight as the beach is packed. But the handy bus connection (and tourist train) makes getting there easy.

Praia do Camilo, the next beach along the coastal road, is less busy and less developed—BYO blankets, chairs, and umbrellas. While there are no services on the beach, the restaurant by the parking high above has a shower.

Ponta da Piedade Viewpoint: If you take the beach road to its far end, you'll reach a dusty parking lot at a lighthouse with a tacky café. This popular spot offers no beach but great views down on the dramatic rock formations offshore. Wander (carefully) around

the top of the bluff to discover various perspectives
on those postcard vistas,
which are far more dra-
matic than the "end of
Europe" views from Cape
St. Vincent near Sagres.
Stairs lead down closer to
water level, and "grotto
cruise" boat trips offer an
even more intimate look at the formations.

Getting to the Beaches: From Lagos, drivers follow brown
praias signs, then track individual beaches (turnoffs individually labeled). Nondrivers can hop on the **bus.** Local line #2 departs hourly from along the old town's riverfront embankment (stops are in
front of the fish market, at the post office just toward the river from
the TI, and just below Henry the Navigator Square) and stops near
several beaches (€1.20, buy ticket on board, runs hourly). The **tourist train** departs from near the old town and loops to the beaches.

Sleeping in Lagos

Lagos is enjoyable for a resort its size, but it feels very touristy and
can be rowdy with young partiers after hours. If that's not your
scene—or if you prefer a mellow village experience with even easier
beach access (but fewer big-city amenities)—remember that Salema is a short drive, taxi, or bus ride away. My heart lies in Salema,
but for some travelers Lagos can be a good choice.

$$$$ Lagos Avenida Hotel sits just across from Hotel Marina Rio, on the main avenue and facing the marina. As the new-
est and most modern hotel in town, its 46 rooms are worth the
splurge if you want chic accomodations—a rarity in Lagos (air-con,
elevator, rooftop pool/bar with marina views, Avenida dos Descobrimentos 53, +351 282 780 090, www.sonelhotels.com, avenida@
sonelhotels.com).

$$$ Hotel Marina Rio is big, slick, and comfortable, and also
faces the marina and the busy main street immediately in front of
the bus station. Its 36 modern rooms have all the amenities. Pricier
marina views come with noise; somewhat quieter rooms face the
bus station in the back. All rooms have twin beds (air-con, elevator,
small heated rooftop pool and sun terrace, Avenida dos Descobri-
mentos, +351 282 780 830, www.marinario.com, marinario@net.
vodafone.pt).

$ Hotel Riomar, popular with tour groups, is a dreary, aging,
and cheap budget option offering 42 dimly lit rooms in a blocky,
1960s-feeling building. Front-facing rooms come with little bal-

conies but bar noise, while the courtyard-facing rooms are quieter (family rooms, air-con, elevator, Rua Candido dos Reis 83, +351 282 770 130, www.hotelriomarlagos.com, hotelriomar@sapo.pt).

The ¢ **youth hostel** is well-run and nicely located, a couple of blocks above the main drag and near a busy nightlife zone. It offers some budget-priced private rooms and a sunny interior courtyard (Rua Lançarote de Freitas 50, +351 282 761 970, www. pousadasjuventude.pt, lagos@movijovem.pt).

Eating in Lagos

You'll find a variety of lively choices for dinner branching out in all directions from Praça Gil Eanes—especially along Rua 25 de Abril. Most offer a similar sampling of grilled fish with plenty of vegetables, but other options range from Italian to Indian. Home-style cooking is likely better closer to the market.

$$$ Restaurante Dom Sebastião feels like a venerable establishment hiding in a tangle of tourist joints. With quality cuisine and a huge wine cellar, it's busy with expats and tourists. Antonio runs his restaurant in a hands-on way, with thoughtful touches. While the people-watching is great from the outside tables, I like the energy in the more-dressy interior. Portions are big and split-able. When shared (OK if the second person buys a small dish—soup, salad, etc.), the €19 *cataplana* becomes a great value (daily 12:00-22:00, reservations smart, Rua 25 de Abril 20, +351 282 780 480, www.restaurantedonsebastiao.com).

$$$ Restaurante dos Artistas offers a refreshing, plant-filled oasis from the crowds with elegantly presented international dishes and professional service. As one of the fancier places to dine in Lagos, reservations are smart (Mon-Sat 12:00-14:00 & 18:30-22:00, closed Sun, Rua Cândido dos Reis 68, +351 282 760 659, www.artistasrestaurant.com).

$$ Restaurante Calhou is a warm, family-style tavern tucked into a residential neighborhood just outside the city walls. Popular with locals and tourists alike, both meat and fish dishes come from the kitchen with care (Tue-Fri 12:00-15:00 & 18:00-23:00, Sat-Sun dinner only, closed Mon, Rua Dr. António Guerreiro Telo 10, +351 282 769 237).

$$ Casa do Pasto do Zé is a very traditional, family-run diner facing the harbor next to the market. It's just right if you want to feel like a temporary local and write a poem (daily 12:00-22:00, Rua Portas de Portugal 65, +351 282 762 038).

$$ Adega da Marina is a sprawling, simple eatery buzzing with energy and soccer scarves overhead. Fish is always super fresh but be aware it's priced by the kilo. Snails in season (*caracois*, May-

Sept) are a popular starter (daily 12:00-24:00, Avenida dos Desco-brimentos 35, near Intermarché supermarket, +351 282 764 284).

$$ Café do Mar Restaurante Bar is perched on a bluff over-looking the sea and the city, just above the first of the exotic beach-es. It's at the end of my town walk and is good for a drink or a bite. Along with cocktails, there are affordable sandwiches, salads, and omelets. They serve a burgers-and-salads beach menu (last order at 18:00) during the day and then switch to a more serious and ex-pensive menu for the evening. Choose between great outdoor tables or the fresh, stylish interior (daily, kitchen open 10:00-24:00, just above and beyond the fortress overlooking Praia da Batata, +351 282 788 006).

Dessert: A local favorite since 1935, **Taquelim Gonçalves House of Regional Sweets** has fresh-baked pastries, ice cream, and coffee. It offers a fine vantage point for enjoying the scene on the square. Their almond torta and marzipan are hits (long hours daily, Rua da Porta de Portugal 27, +351 282 762 882).

Picnics: Find a wide selection at **Intermarché** supermarket (daily 8:00-21:00, until 22:00 in summer, on the waterfront op-posite the marina).

Lagos Connections

From Lagos by Train and Bus to: Lisbon (3 trains/day, 4 hours, transfer in Tunes or Faro; hourly direct buses, 4 hours), **Évora** (2 trains/day, 5 hours, transfer in Pinhal Novo and Tunes; 4 buses/day direct July-mid-Sept, otherwise transfer in Albufeira—confirm with driver, 5 hours), **Tavira** (8 trains/day, 4.5 hours, some change in Faro but others simply have a long wait there—ask conductor; 6 buses/day, 4 hours, transfer in Faro). Confirm times locally. Train info: +351 808 208 208, www.cp.pt. Bus info: +351 289 899 760 or +351 282 762 944, www.eva-bus.com or www.algarvebus.info.

From Lagos to Salema: Take a bus (7/day, every 1-2 hours, fewer on weekends, 30 minutes) or a taxi (€30, 20 minutes). In Lagos, to get from the train station to the bus station, exit the sta-tion toward the pink-and-white shopping mall. Turn left just be-fore the mall and follow the pleasant pedestrian promenade along the marina, then cross the pedestrian drawbridge. Once across the bridge, jog right to find the bus station. Before heading to Salema, pick up return bus schedules and train schedules for your next des-tination.

Connecting Lagos and Sevilla, Spain, by Bus: There are four buses per day in each direction during summer, and two per day off-season (about 5.5 hours from Lagos bus station to Sevilla's Plaza de Armas bus station). Ask the TI or a local travel agency for the latest bus schedule, or check www.algarvebus.info or www.eva-bus.com. In summer (May-Oct), it's important to book your ticket a day or two in advance. Note that Spanish time is one hour ahead of Portuguese time, so the time you arrive in Lagos is about 4.5 hours after you depart Sevilla, and the time you arrive in Sevilla is about 6.5 hours after departing Lagos. This bus also stops in Tavira en route—a pleasant town and a nice midway point.

Tavira

Straddling a river, with a lively park, chatty locals, and boats that share its waterfront center, Tavira (tah-VEE-rah) is a low-rise, easygoing alternative—and a refreshing break—from the more aggressive Algarve resorts. That's because Tavira is a real, living town. Whitewashed, red-roofed, and cobbled, it feels close to Morocco...because it is. More than a glitzy beach town, Tavira is a mini-Évora, with real culture that runs deeper than its beaches.

Because Tavira has good connections by bus and train (it's on the trans-Algarve train line, with frequent departures both east and west), the town is more accessible than Salema. If you're driving from Sevilla to Salema, it's the perfect midway stop on the four-hour trip (just 2 miles off the freeway). You can also get to Tavira by bus from Sevilla.

You'll see many churches and fine bits of Renaissance architecture sprinkled throughout the town. These clues are evidence that 500 years ago, Tavira was the largest town on the Algarve (with 1,500 dwellings according to a 1530 census) and an important base for Portuguese adventurers in Africa. The silting up of its harbor, a plague in 1645, the 1755 earthquake, and the shifting away of its once-lucrative tuna industry left Tavira in a long decline. Today, the town has a wistful charm and lives off its tourists.

Orientation to Tavira

Tavira (pop. 26,000) straddles the Rio Gilão two miles from the Atlantic. Everything of sightseeing and transportation importance is on the south bank. A clump of historic sights—the ruined castle and main church—fills its tiny fortified hill and tangled Moorish lanes. But today, the action is outside the old fortifications along the riverside Praça da República square and the adjacent, shaded, bench-filled park (with the old market hall at the park's far end). Just beyond that is the boat to Tavira's beach island.

Tavira's old pedestrian-only Roman Bridge leads from Praça da República to the more local-feeling north bank (with most of the evening and restaurant action). With the exception of a fun, fascinating camera obscura show, the town's sights are pretty dull.

TOURIST INFORMATION

The TI is on the main square, Praça da República, right across from City Hall. It offers a helpful town brochure (daily 9:30-17:30, Praça da República 5, +351 281 322 511).

ARRIVAL IN TAVIRA

By Train: The train station is a 15-minute walk from the town center. To get there, leave the station via the roundabout and follow the signpost to *centro* (center). Follow this road downhill to the river and Praça da República (or take a cab from the station for around €4).

By Bus: The riverside bus station is three blocks from the town center; simply follow the river into town.

By Car: Drivers can park on the street in much of the old town. It's pay-and-display for up to two hours (€0.40/hour, Mon-Fri 9:00-19:00, Sat until 14:00, Sun free, look for *zona pago* signs, pay at blue boxes marked *caixa*, change required). Free parking is available farther from the center, including some large lots at the western end of town (just beyond the bus station) and in the east (go past the old market hall and look for free lots on either side of the big car bridge).

HELPFUL HINTS

Bike Rental: For a great selection of electric and road bikes, check with **Abilio Bikes,** which also runs bike tours (basic bike-€8/day, "comfort bike" with fancy suspension-€12/day; open Mon-Sat 9:00-13:00 & 15:00-19:00, closed Sun; Rua João Vaz Corte Real 23A, +351 281 323 467, www.abiliobikes. com). Rental prices include helmet, lock, biking map, and emergency kit. They can give you lots of tips on nature, bird-watching, and bike-friendly towns nearby.

Taxi: A taxi stand is across the Roman Bridge on Praça Dr. António Padinha; another is in the town center, near the old cinema.

Shopping Tips: The strip facing the river behind the old market hall is lined with enticing shops. The **Soares Wine Shop** has a good selection of port wine and other Portuguese drinks (Mon-Sat 10:00-22:00, until 19:00 off-season, closed Sun year-round, facing market hall at Rua José Pires Padinha 66).

ALGARVE

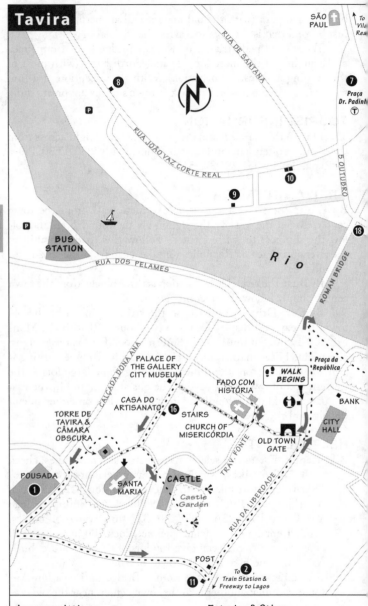

Tavira

SÃO PAUL
To Vila Rea

RUA DE SANTANA

8

P

7
Praça
Dr. Padinh

RUA JOÃO VAZ CORTE REAL

10

9

5 OUTUBRO

P

BUS
STATION

18

RUA DOS PELAMES

Rio

ROMAN BRIDGE

CALÇADA DONA ANA

PALACE OF
THE GALLERY
CITY MUSEUM

Praça da
República

WALK
BEGINS

FADO COM
HISTÓRIA

CASA DO
ARTISANATO

BANK

16

STAIRS

TORRE DE
TAVIRA &
CÂMARA
OBSCURA

CHURCH OF
MISERICÓRDIA

TRAV. FONTE

OLD TOWN
GATE

CITY
HALL

POUSADA

SANTA
MARIA

CASTLE

Castle
Garden

1

RUA DA LIBERDADE

POST

To 2
Train Station &
Freeway to Lagos

11

Accommodations

1. Convento da Graça Pousada
2. To Tavira House Hotel
3. Residencial Marés & Launderette
4. Hotel Princesa do Gilão
5. Residencial Lagôas

Eateries & Other

6. Aquasul Restaurante
7. Praça António Padinha Eateries
8. D'gusta Restaurant
9. Beira Rio Restaurante & Black Anchor Irish Pub

ALGARVE

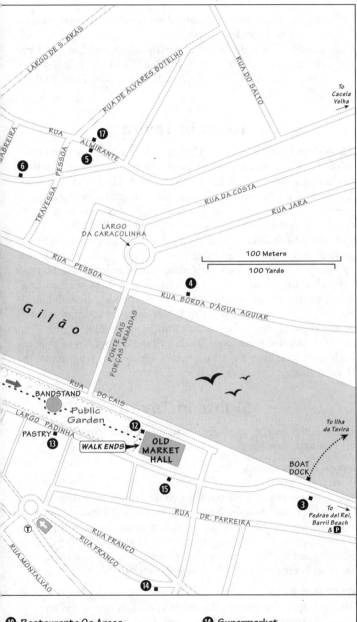

10 Restaurante Os Arcos & Abilio Bikes

11 Restaurante O Castelo

12 Gilão Restaurant

13 Pasteleria Ramos

14 Supermarket

15 Soares Wine Shop

16 Casa do Artisanato Shop

17 Tavira Walking Tours

18 Tourist Train

And the **Casa do Artisanato shop** (in the old town) offers a way to buy direct from artisans.

Launderette: The well-designed, totally automated **Lava & Leve self-service** laundry comes with free Wi-Fi (daily 7:00-24:00, across from the ferry to the beach at Rua José Pires Padinha 168).

Tours in Tavira

Tavira Walking Tours, run by Filipe, offers private one-hour town walks for €25 (contact them to book the time you like). On their "Farms and Watermills Country Walk," you ride a van to the starting point for a five-mile, 3.5-hour, guided rural experience (€25/person). They also offer Tuk Tuk tours and other creative activities (Rua Almirante Cândido dos Reis 43, +351 913 352 830).

The **Abilio Bikes** rental shop offers various guided and non-guided "bike hikes." The most popular is a four-hour excursion to Cacela Velha and back. It's about an hour-long ride nonstop through a mix of park and towns, half on bike lanes, with an English-speaking guide (12 km each way, €30/person, 2-person minimum). For €60 you can book this tour in advance and they may sell more people to join it. For contact info, see page 219.

The **tourist train** does an hour-long loop tour of Tavira's highlights (one loop-€4, all-day ticket-€6, departs from across the Roman Bridge, details at TI, www.delgaturis.com).

Sights in Tavira

I've linked the sights in a logical walking order starting near the TI on Praça da República.

Praça da República
Tavira gets good use out of its main square. The arena built into the square is popular for open-air concerts and gatherings during Tavira's various festivals. Notice the stern WWI monument with the wrapped bundle of sticks—a fascist symbol—held high. This was erected in 1968, during the rule of Portugal's fascist dictator Salazar. Facing the square is the TI and, next door, a small museum with artifacts from the Moorish period.

Old Town Gate
This unimpressive gate (to the left of the TI) is one of the few sections left from Tavira's medieval wall. Check out the gate's crown and spheres—meant to remind visitors that they are in the kingdom of Portugal—and the holes for bars that once locked the door. Tavira was long a strategic town worth fortifying. For centuries a Moorish port with an imposing castle, it was reconquered from the

Moors in 1242 and granted city status by King Manuel in the 16th century.

• *At the top of the lane, above the gate, stands a church.*

Church of Misericórdia

Tavira has 21 churches, but only a couple of active priests. Many of its churches—including this one—are open primarily as tourist attractions. Dating from 1541, this church's Renaissance facade is considered the finest in the Algarve. Inside, you'll see a multitude of blue-and-white tile panels that illustrate how to lead a good Christian life and an over-the-top, gold-plated altar. Throughout the year, the church transforms into a beautiful concert venue. Ask the attendant if any performances are scheduled during your visit. You can climb the belltower for a view.

Cost and Hours: €2, enter on the left side, generally Mon-Sat 9:00-12:30 & 14:00-17:30, closed Sun.

• *Around the right side of the gate is...*

Fado com História

This humble but endearing fado show, in a tasteful little theater, is the brainchild of local *fadistas* who grew tired of performing for unappreciative crowds in local restaurants. Their goal is to share the history and beauty of fado with tourists, with a little explanation (in English) before each song. Three times a day, they show an insightful 10-minute film about the history of fado, then perform for about 20 minutes (two guitarists and a singer). While the fado shows in Lisbon and Coimbra may be of better quality, this is worth considering if it's your only chance to sample Portugal's most beloved musical form.

Cost and Hours: €8; schedule posted at door—usually Mon-Sat at 12:45, 15:15, and 17:15; closed Sun and Aug, Rua Damião de Brito Vasconcelos 4, mobile +351 968 774 613, Virgilio).

• *Crossing back in front of the church, head up the stepped lane on its left side. At the top of the stairs is the...*

Palace of the Gallery City Museum

This 17th-century Baroque palace is the biggest private mansion in town and houses an exhibition center, open to the public, with rotating themes: contemporary art or Tavira's maritime history. Even if you don't go into the museum itself, pop inside the door to see some Phoenician ritual pits, visible through glass covers on the foyer floor (€2, Tue-Sat 9:15-16:30, closed Sun-Mon).

• *From the palace, continue climbing uphill. On the left at #11 is **Casa do Artesanato,** a cooperative shop where local artisans and producers show off and sell their work. Hike farther up to the big Church of Santa Maria. Before visiting there, look to your left, where you can go through a door in what's left of the castle. Detour here if you'd like to visit.*

Castle Garden

The base of the castle wall is supposedly Neolithic, while later inhabitants added their own layers—the Phoenicians in the eighth century BC, the Moors in the eighth century AD (as they pushed the Christians north), and the Portuguese in the 13th century (as they pushed the Moors south). The castle grounds are now a fragrant garden.

Cost and Hours: Free, Mon-Fri 8:00-17:00, Sat-Sun from 10:00, daily until 19:00 in July-Sept.

Visiting the Garden: Climb the stubby tower at the far end for a fine city view. Overlooking the city, notice Tavira's unique "treasury" rooftops—a little roof for each room of a building. Tour guides have two explanations for this: The small roofs were inspired by visions brought home from Asia by local explorers. Or they are the result of this region having a shortage of big trees and therefore using small timbers for beams. (Portugal has long been short on timbers, naming its major colony "Brazil," the Portuguese word for a very valuable type of wood—apparently the colonists were particularly excited about that raw material.) Or, perhaps it just helps with the ventilation.

Gaze to the right and see tower-wall remnants sprouting up between houses. In the distance, along with the open Atlantic, you'll see salt flats and two red-brick chimneys marking old tuna processing plants. Salt (evaporated from the sea in big shallow pools) and tuna were the town's main industries in the 19th century.

• *Now backtrack to visit the church that dominates the square out front. You'll find the small tourist entrance on the right side, as you face the church.*

Church of Santa Maria

Once a mosque, this church was transformed in the 13th century. Buy a ticket and head inside to enjoy relatively crude but lovingly made art that shows a knack for faking 3-D scenes on 2-D painted surfaces. On the left side of the nave are two inset chapels. One—with blue and yellow tiles—is the only part of the church to survive the 1755 earthquake. The other chapel has fine pink columns. The "marble" is actually painted wood, since there was no marble in the Algarve and no money to bring it from the Alentejo. Immediately to the right of the main altar, notice the little row of seven red crosses on the right side of the apse (inaccessible to the public). These mark the remains of seven near-legendary Reconquista heroes who were ambushed and killed by Moorish forces during a truce—inspiring the Portuguese forces to take up arms and conquer Tavira. Your church ticket also includes a small museum and the bell tower.

Cost and Hours: €2.50, Mon-Fri 10:00-13:00 & 14:00-17:00, Sat 10:00-13:00, closed Sun (English Mass at 11:00).

• *Next to the church, you can't miss the tall, white water tower, which has an interesting new use.*

▲Camera Obscura in the Tavira Tower (Torre de Tavira and Câmara Obscura)

This 1931 water tower has been converted into an elevator-accessible viewpoint, with a darkroom designed to accommodate an early

optical device called a camera obscura. This centuries-old technology uses nothing more than a pinhole of light, mirrors, and a well-calibrated lens (from 1899) to project a huge, live image of the town onto a circular canvas. Clive, the British owner, narrates an entertaining and informative 15-minute, 360-degree view of Tavira—a delightful orientation to the entire town, from the comfort of a cool dark room. With his levers and pulleys, Clive masterfully zooms in and out on live images of people walking across the Roman Bridge or boats plying the river. It's not "rain or shine"—without the sun, there's no image.

Cost and Hours: €3.50, July-Sept Mon-Fri 10:00-17:00, Sat-Sun until 13:00, closed Sat-Sun off-season.

From the *Pousada* Back to the Main Square

Just beyond the camera obscura is the recommended convent-turned-*pousada* (Convento da Graça), built upon what was the Jewish Quarter until the Jews were expelled. Go downhill on the cobbled lane directly in front of the *pousada*.

Notice the big white church facade with the painted banner. The Emblem of St. James shows the saint killing Muslims with his sword raised high. Below that is the blue-and-gold scallop shell sign indicating that this is the pilgrim's trail to Santiago. (Tavira is actually the starting point of Portugal's Eastern Camino de Santiago.)

The lane dead-ends on Rua da Liberdade—Tavira's main street. It's named for the liberty people won in 1974 with their "Carnation Revolution" (when they ended the Salazar regime). The festival of sporty color a few doors to the left is a football (soccer) team store, a reminder of how powerful elites use sports as a kind of opiate to placate unhappy masses. Like Roman emperors were sure to give their people "bread and circuses," the dictator Salazar was careful to give his people what he called "the three Fs": Fado, Football, and Fátima.

• Follow Rua da Liberdade back to the main square and TI, where we started this walk. Continue to the pedestrian bridge.

Roman Bridge

The "Roman Bridge" may not actually be Roman, but at least it was here when the Moors came. And it's seen some action. A memorial plaque (on the right at the start of the bridge) recalls the 1383 battle when Portugal stopped a Castilian incursion on this bridge. The current structure is from 1657, with parts rebuilt after it was knocked over in a 1989 flood. Since it was replaced, it's been a pedestrians-only option for crossing between the two parts of town.

• But don't cross the bridge. Alongside the south side of the river, an inviting park stretches along the riverbank.

Riverside Park and Old Market Hall

This is where old folks gossip and children play. Walk past the bandstand to the old market hall. In the 1990s, this was a noisy, colorful fish and produce market. Today, the hall has gift shops, cafés, and eateries with riverside seating.

Beyond the market hall are a few fishing boats. Fishermen have mostly moved to larger ports nearby. For a sticky local sweet (perhaps an almond cake) perfect with a *galão* (milky coffee), you could drop by Pasteleria Ramos—a traditional pastry shop facing the park.

Sights near Tavira

▲Tavira's Beach Island (Ilha de Tavira)

A hit with visitors, Ilha de Tavira is an almost treeless, six-mile-long sandbar with a campground, several restaurants, and a sprawling beach. It's an enjoyable boat trip even if you just go round-trip without getting off.

Getting There: In summer, it's easiest to hop on a **shuttle boat** for the 20-minute ride (€2 round-trip, June-Sept about hourly 9:30-19:00, timetable at TI, departs from dock just past the old market hall). **Water taxis** are generally standing by to make the trip in less time for more money (about €15). A third option—also year-round—is to take the **Quatro Aguas ferry.** It's a longer riverside stroll: Keep going past the market hall and first boat dock, then take the series of causeways past the salt pans and fish farms (about a mile all together, no shade) out to Quatro Aguas. From here, a five-minute ferry ride shuttles sunbathers to the beach island (€1.50 one-way, daily 8:30-20:00, runs constantly year-round with demand).

If you're not up for the walk, you can get to Quatro Aguas by car, bus, taxi, bike, or on the cheesy tourist train.

More Beach Options

Barril Beach, a fine beach resort worth ▲, is about three miles from Tavira. Walk, rent a bike, or take a city bus to Pedras del Rei, and then catch the little train (usually runs year-round), or walk 10 minutes through Ria Formosa Natural Park to the beach.

Santa Luzia, just a few minutes' drive out of Tavira, is an adorable little fishing town with a line of seafood joints facing its long harbor and a ferry to its beach (€2). Nicknamed "the octopus town" for its wonderful seafood, it's a lazy and inviting place.

Island Beach Hike: For a nice long walk on the sand, take the ferry to Ilha de Tavira and stroll six kilometers or so along the treeless sandbar. Enjoy the Atlantic surf and breeze on the way to the more built-up Barril Beach, and walk from there to Santa Luzia. Get details at the TI.

Cacela Velha

This tiny village lies through the orange groves about eight miles east of Tavira (half-mile off the main road and the bus route). It's the most popular destination for those renting bikes in Tavira (see "Helpful Hints," earlier). Cacela Velha sits happily ignored on a hill with its fort, church, one restaurant, a few *quartos* and apartments, and a beach with the open sea just over the sandbar a short row across its lagoon.

Cacela Velha's lone restaurant—**$$ Casa De Igreja**—serves sausages *(chouricos)* and cheese *(queijo)* specialties fried at your table, along with local oysters and *vinho verde* (daily July-Sept, March-June weekends only, closed Oct-Feb, +351 281 952 126, Patricio speaks English). If you're driving, swing by, if only to enjoy the coastal view and to imagine how nice the Algarve would be if people like you and I had never discovered it.

Sleeping in Tavira

In Tavira, prices usually shoot up in August.

$$$$ Convento da Graça is a *pousada* (government-sponsored historic inn) with 36 elegantly appointed rooms inside a renovated Augustine convent. The cloister is perfect for relaxing, and there's even a pool if you can't tear yourself away to go to the beach. It's at the top of the Old Town, near the castle ruins and camera obscura, a five-minute walk above the main square (air-con, eleva-

ALGARVE

tor, Rua D. Paio Peres Correia, +351 210 407 680, www.pousadas.
pt, recepcao.conventograca@pestana.com).

$$$ Tavira House is a classy nine-room boutique B&B filling a
lovingly renovated army officer's house from 1860. Manager Chris-
tophe has given the place a Moroccan flair, with splashes of bright
color—especially on the inviting roof terrace. It's out of the busy
central area, but just a five-minute walk away (air-con, Rua Miguel
Bombardo 47, +351 281 370 307, http://tavirahouseportugal.com).

$$ Residencial Marés, on the busy side of the river amid all
the strolling and café ambience, is an endearing throwback. Dated
but well-maintained, with a dark-wood-and-earth-tone-tile ambience, it has 24 good rooms, a friendly reception, and an inviting
rooftop terrace with lounge chairs. Some rooms have balconies
overlooking the river, but also come with a little noise from cafés
immediately below (air-con, Rua José Pires Padinha 134/140—just
beyond old market hall, +351 281 325 815, www.residencialmares.
com, mail@residencialmares.com, Paulo and Dulce).

$$ Hotel Princesa do Gilão overlooks the river across from
the town center and rents 24 simple and modern rooms. Choose
between riverfront or quiet rooms on the back with a terrace (fam-
ily rooms, air-con, elevator, Rua Borda de Agua de Aguiar 10, cross
Roman Bridge and turn right along river, +351 281 325 171, www.
hotelprincesadogilao.com, geral@hprincesadogilao.com).

$ Residencial Lagôas is homey, colorful, and a block off the
river. Friendly Claudia and Miquel offer 17 rooms, a communal
refrigerator, and a rooftop patio with a view made for wine and
candles (RS%, cash only, most rooms with air-con, cheaper rooms
with shared bath, no breakfast, lots of stairs, Rua Almirante Can-
dido dos Reis 24, +351 281 328 243, al.lagoas@hotmail.com).

Eating in Tavira

Tavira is filled with reasonable restaurants. Most places on the
south bank are more touristy; several lively places face the river-
bank just beyond the old market hall. Your best bets lie just across
the river and inland a couple of blocks. It's fun to walk around and
scout out your options; while the ones I recommend are a good
start, the choices are ample and locals love to give tips.

ACROSS THE RIVER (NORTH BANK)

$$ Aquasul—mod, bright, cheery, on a back lane, and open only
for dinner—serves a modern fusion of Italian, Mediterranean,
and international dishes, including nightly vegetarian specials,
good pizzas out of the wood oven, and tasty homemade desserts.
The vibe is happy and it's understandably popular—reservations
are smart (Tue-Sat 18:30-22:30, closed Sun-Mon, tucked down

an easy-to-miss paved lane at Rua Dr. A. S. Carvalho 13, +351 281 325 166). If Aquasul is full or doesn't do it for you, check out several other appealing places spilling out onto the same street; **$$ O Tonel** is popular (at #6-8).

Praça António Padinha is a pleasant square ringed by small restaurants and *petiscos* (tapas) bars.

$$$ D'gusta Restaurant is the local favorite serving creative *petiscos* (3 family-style plates will fill 2 diners) and famous desserts. The bustle of the kitchen adds to a fun energy, the clientele is smart, and every plate is tempting. Run by what feels like a gang of friends, there's no pretense here, just good food and good service in a plain building facing a parking lot. Order with a spirit of adventure (Tue-Sun 19:00-24:00, closed Mon, Rua João Vaz Corte Real 80, +351 281 326 089, reservations smart).

ON THE RIVER

For dining along the river, these popular **$$** places offer good value (if not top cuisine). To reach them, cross the Roman Bridge, turn left, go through the tunnel, and look for tables on the waterfront.

Beira Rio is Irish-owned, with a menu that's an odd mix of international pub-grub standards and lots of local fish (daily 12:00-23:00, Rua Borda d'Agua da Asseca 46, +351 281 323 165). Next door, **Black Anchor Irish Pub** is clearly "Tavira's happiest place at night," where you're likely to find singing and live music along with your beer and a river view.

A bit closer to the Roman Bridge, **Restaurante Os Arcos** is the lowbrow option, with cheap and tasty grilled fish served at rustic little riverside tables—or in a non-descript old dining hall (Mon-Sat 12:00-15:00 & 19:00-22:00, closed Sun, Rua João Vaz Corte Real 15, mobile +351 963 583 527).

IN CENTRAL TAVIRA (SOUTH BANK)

$$ Restaurante O Castelo, with rustic seating inside and tables outside on a pleasant square, has a fun menu and is a popular place for steaks. There's often live guitar music and singing (dinner daily from 19:00, Avenida da Liberdade 72, mobile +351 915 087 614).

$$ Gilão Restaurant is a good basic standby in the riverside marketplace for fish, *cataplanas,* and Mediterranean cuisine. They have seating inside and on the square (nightly, +351 281 322 050).

$ Pasteleria Ramos is a diner with simple meals *(petiscos)*, breakfasts, and great sweets. Near the market end of the park opposite a green kiosk, they make their own sweet almond cakes—perfect with a *galão* (milky coffee) at an outdoor table (long hours daily).

Supermarket: Centrally located **Minipreço** has all the groceries you'll need for a good picnic. It's a few blocks inland from the market hall (daily 9:00-21:00, Rua D. Marcelino Franco 40).

Tavira Connections

From Tavira by Train and Bus to: Lisbon (4 trains/day, 4.5 hours, transfer in Faro, arrive at Oriente; 5 direct buses/day, 4 hours), **Lagos** (8 trains/day, 4.5 hours, some change in Faro while others simply have a long wait there—ask conductor; 6 buses/day, 4 hours, change in Faro), **Sevilla** (4 buses/day in summer, 2/day in winter, 3 hours, check TI or bus station to verify schedules, buy ticket a day or two in advance May-Oct, note that Spain is an hour ahead when calculating arrival times). Luggage storage is not available. Train info: +351 808 208 208, www.cp.pt. Bus info: +351 281 322 546, www.eva-bus.com or www.algarvebus.info.

ROUTE TIPS FOR DRIVERS

Lisbon to the Algarve (185 miles, 3.5 hours): A modern freeway, light traffic, and the glory of waking up on the Algarve make doing this drive in the evening after a full day in Lisbon a good option.

Following the blue *Sul Ponte* signs from central Lisbon, drive south over Lisbon's 25th of April Bridge. A short detour just over the bridge takes you to the giant concrete statue of Cristo Rei (Christ the King). Then stay on the A-2 expressway as it heads east toward Alentejo, then bends south toward the Algarve. You'll pass through cork groves, and finally—about 1.5 hours after leaving Lisbon—you'll run into the A-22 expressway (which runs east-west, parallel to the coast). At the A-22 junction, you can choose to head west to Lagos (and beyond it, Salema and Sagres) or east to Tavira and, eventually, Spain (signed for *Espanha*).

If heading to Salema, stay on A-22 to the Lagos/Vila do Bispo exit, and follow signs to *Vila do Bispo* and *Sagres*. Pay close attention to spot the turnoff for Salema before Vila do Bispo.

Algarve (Lagos) to Sevilla, Spain (175 miles, 3 hours): It's a 1.5-hour drive east from Salema to Tavira, with some hills crowned by rotting windmills and others by mobile-phone towers. From Lagos, hit the freeway (A-22, direction: Lisboa/Faro, then Espanha) to Tavira. Leaving Tavira, follow the signs to *Espanha*. You'll cross the bridge into Spain (where it's one hour later) and glide effortlessly (1.5 hours on the A-49 freeway) into Sevilla.

Be aware that there's an electronic tolling system on the A-22 highway from Lagos to the Spanish border. Just pop in a credit card—your receipt explains that you've opened an account that will be billed every time you pass a toll station on the highway in Portugal. (For details, see the "Driving" section of the Practicalities chapter.)

ÉVORA

Deep in the heart of Portugal, in the sizzling, arid plains of the southern province of Alentejo, historic Évora (EH-voh-rah) has been a cultural oasis for 2,000 years. With an untouched provincial atmosphere, a fascinating whitewashed old town, museums, a cathedral, a chapel of bones, and even a Roman temple, Évora (pop. 57,000) stands proudly in a vast sea of cork groves and olive trees.

From Romans to Moors to Portuguese kings, this little town has a big history. Évora was once a Roman town (second century BC to fourth century AD), important because of its wealth of wheat and silver, as well as its location on a trade route to Rome. You'll still see Roman sights, including several fragments of an aqueduct and the towering columns of a temple. But most of Évora's Roman past is buried under the cityscape of today (often uncovered by accident when plumbing work needs to be done in basements).

The Moors ruled Évora from the 8th to the 12th century. Around the year 1000, Muslim nobles divided the caliphate into small city-states (like Lisbon), with Évora as this region's capital. And during its glory years (15th-16th century), Évora was favored by Portuguese kings, often serving as the home of King João III (1502-1557, Manuel I's son who presided over Portugal's peak of power...and its first decline).

Évora—a traditional, conservative city with a small-town feel—reopened its historic university about 40 years ago. You'll see plenty of black-caped students here, along with lots of retirees, but comparatively few 30- to 40-year olds. There's not much to keep graduates around, and this generation gap gives the town an intriguing mix of old and new—strong traditions underlie its youthful bustle.

PLANNING YOUR TIME

With easy bus and train connections to Lisbon (buses almost hourly, four trains a day; both take 1.5 hours), Évora makes a decent day trip from Portugal's capital city. Better yet, spend the night—ideally en route to or from the Algarve. Along the way, drivers can explore dusty droves of olive groves, scruffy seas of peeled cork trees, and some dramatic prehistoric monuments.

A day in Évora is enough to fully experience the town. Follow my self-guided walk in this chapter, have a quick lunch, see the remaining sights (cathedral, Chapel of Bones, university), and enjoy a leisurely, top-notch dinner. Late in the evening, stroll the back streets and ponder life, like the old-timers of Évora seem to do so expertly.

Orientation to Évora

Évora's Old Town, contained within a medieval wall, is surrounded by the sprawling newer part of town. The walled center (where you'll spend virtually all your time) is large and quite hilly—it takes about 20 minutes to cross from one end of town to the other, on cobbled streets that are anything but straight. The major sights—the Roman Temple and the cathedral—crowd together at the Old Town's highest point. A subtle yet still-powerful charm is contained within the medieval walls. Find it by losing yourself in the quiet lanes of Évora's far corners.

TOURIST INFORMATION

Pick up a free map at the TI on the main square at Praça do Giraldo 73 (daily 9:00-19:00, shorter hours off-season, +351 266 777 071, www.cm-evora.pt/en).

ARRIVAL IN ÉVORA

By Bus: The bus station is west of the center, on Avenida de São Sebastião. To reach the town center, take a short taxi ride (€5) or a 10-minute walk (exit station right, continue straight all the way into town, past the cemetery wall and through the city gates at the halfway point).

By Train: The train station is south of the center, on Avenida Dr. Barahona. To get to the center, take a taxi (€7), or walk a long 25 minutes up Avenida Dr. Barahona, continuing straight on Rua da República after you enter the city walls.

By Car: Drivers will find Évora's Old Town frustrating because of its tiny one-way streets. Park in one of the big, free parking lots that circle the town just outside the walls (see the "Évora" map, later, for locations). The green-and-white Trevo shuttle bus (see below) serves the parking lots and gets you near most hotels, or—if you're packing light—you can walk (though some streets can be steeper than maps suggest).

HELPFUL HINTS

Taxis: Cabs wait on the main square (€4 minimum for 2.5 miles—4 kilometers—likely the farthest you'd go in compact Évora).

Shuttle Bus: Blue line on the streets mark the route of the green-and-white Trevo shuttle bus that circles through town, offering tourists easy transport to and from the parking lots outside the walls. Hop on for a city joyride (€1); they stop for anyone who waves.

Tours in Évora

Walking Tour

A group of local guides offers excellent two-hour city walks every morning, departing from the TI at 10:00 (€15, 2-person minimum, call ahead to confirm tour will run, mobile +351 963 702 392, info@alentejoguides.com). The tour hits the sights described in this chapter, but it's also a great opportunity to connect with a local and enliven your visit. They are happy to schedule tours at other times (€95, 2-person minimum).

Bus Tours

In Town: Évora City Tour runs a small, red bus that makes an hourly loop around town with a recorded narration for €7.50.

Nearby Sights: A bus tour is a good option for seeing the prehistoric sights near Évora, since getting there by public transport is nearly impossible. **Ebora Megalithica Guided Tours** runs an interesting three-hour minivan tour led by archaeologist Mário to Cromeleque dos Almendres, the standing stone of Menhir dos Almendres, and the Zambujeiro burial mound (€25, Mon-Sat at 10:00 and 14:30, no tours Sun, 7-person maximum, reserve a day ahead, mobile +351 964 808 337, www.eboramegalithica.com).

RSI offers several half-day bus and minivan tours into the surrounding countryside. Their "Megalithic Circuit Tour" visits the main prehistoric sights, including Cromeleque dos Almendres (departs daily at 9:30 and 14:30 from Praça do Giraldo, €30/half-day, 2-person minimum, discounts for larger groups, reserve a day ahead, +351 266 747 871, www.rsi-viagens.com).

Local Guides

Mélanie Wolfram loves to walk visitors informally around Évora at a relaxed pace—hence her company's name, Vagar ("to wander").

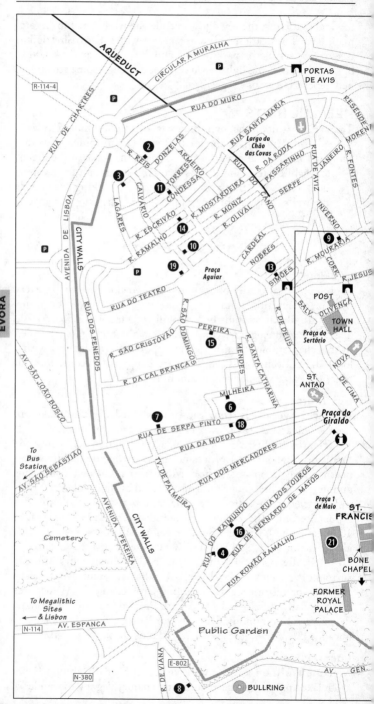

ÉVORA

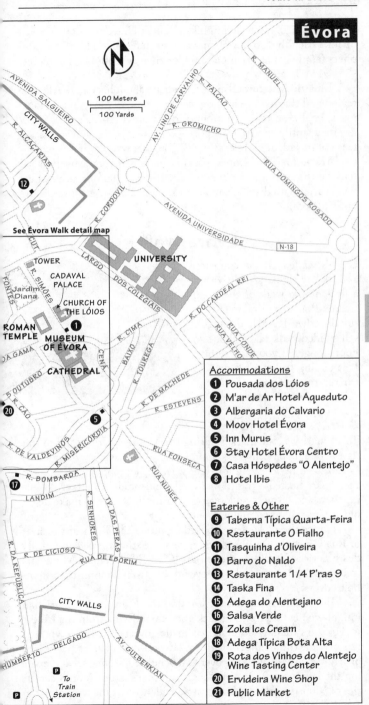

Évora

100 Meters
100 Yards

See Évora Walk detail map

ÉVORA

Accommodations
1 Pousada dos Lóios
2 M'ar de Ar Hotel Aqueduto
3 Albergaria do Calvario
4 Moov Hotel Évora
5 Inn Murus
6 Stay Hotel Évora Centro
7 Casa Hóspedes "O Alentejo"
8 Hotel Ibis

Eateries & Other
9 Taberna Típica Quarta-Feira
10 Restaurante O Fialho
11 Tasquinha d'Oliveira
12 Barro do Naldo
13 Restaurante 1/4 P'ras 9
14 Taska Fina
15 Adega do Alentejano
16 Salsa Verde
17 Zoka Ice Cream
18 Adega Típica Bota Alta
19 Rota dos Vinhos do Alentejo
   Wine Tasting Center
20 Ervideira Wine Shop
21 Public Market

Whether you're interested in history and architecture or you're just up for a friendly stroll, Mélanie makes you feel like a local. She also offers family game-oriented tours for all ages (€60/4 hours, mobile +351 914 032 561, www.vagarwalkingtours.com).

Libânio Murteira Reis is passionate about his native Alentejo region and sharing it with others. He organizes town and regional tours; he'll even take you around in his car (€150/half-day, €270/day for a family up to 4, transport—when required—and admission fees not included, mobile +351 917 236 025, www.evora-mm.pt).

Maria José Pires does walking tours of Évora as well as car tours of the surrounding area (€95/half-day, €180/day, price of car tours varies with distance, mobile +351 917 232 147, m-jose-pires@hotmail.com).

Évora Walk

Évora's walled city is compact, and its key sights are all within a five-minute walk of the main square, Praça do Giraldo (PRA-suh doo zhee-RAHL-doo). This self-guided walk takes about an hour (longer if you visit sights). If it's going to be a hot day, go early in the morning.

• *Start at Évora's main square.*

❶ Praça do Giraldo

This square was the market during the Moorish period, and to this day, it remains a center of commerce and conviviality for country folk who come to Évora for their weekly shopping. Until recently, the square hosted a traditional cattle-and-produce market. While ranchers and farmers no longer gather in the square to make deals, old-timers still gravitate here out of habit.

Notice the *C.M. Évora* board (opposite the TI, near the start of Rua Cinco de Outubro), where people gather to see community death notices. You'll see the initials "C.M.E."—Câmara Municipal (municipality) de Évora—all over town, from lampposts to manhole covers.

The square is named for Giraldo the Fearless, the Christian knight who led a surprise attack and retook Évora from the Moors in 1165. As thanks, Giraldo was made governor of the town, and he's become the symbol of the city. (Évora's coat of arms is a knight on a horse, usually walking over two beheaded Moors; see it crowning the lampposts.) On this square, all that's left of several centuries of Moorish rule is their artistry, evidenced by the wrought-iron

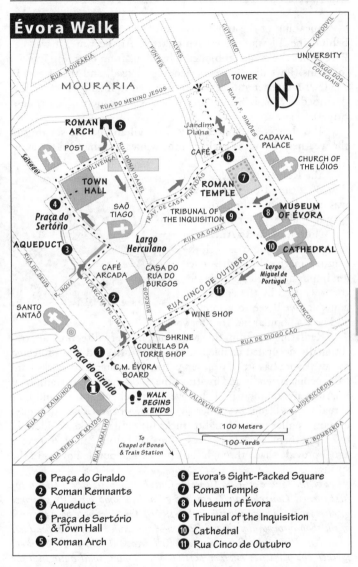

Évora Walk

MOURARIA

RUA MOURARIA

RUA DO MENINO JESUS

ROMAN ARCH ⑤

POST

Salvador

TOWN HALL

④ Praça do Sertório

SAÕ TIAGO

AQUEDUCT ③

R. NOVA

CAFÉ ARCADA

② CASA DO RUA DO BURGOS

SANTO ANTAÕ

① Praça do Giraldo

C.M. ÉVORA BOARD

WALK BEGINS & ENDS

To Chapel of Bones & Train Station

UNIVERSITY

LARGO DOS COLEGIAIS

TOWER

Jardim Diana

CAFÉ ⑥

ROMAN TEMPLE ⑦

CADAVAL PALACE

CHURCH OF THE LÓIOS

TRIBUNAL OF THE INQUISITION ⑨

⑧ MUSEUM OF ÉVORA

Largo Herculano

RUA DA GAMA

⑩ CATHEDRAL

Largo Miguel de Portugal

RUA CINCO DE OUTUBRO ⑪

WINE SHOP

SHRINE

COURELAS DA TORRE SHOP

RUA DE DIOGO CÃO

RUA DE VALPEDEVINOS

RUA MISERICÓRDIA

RUA BOMBARDA

100 Meters

100 Yards

ÉVORA

① Praça do Giraldo
② Roman Remnants
③ Aqueduct
④ Praça de Sertório & Town Hall
⑤ Roman Arch

⑥ Evora's Sight-Packed Square
⑦ Roman Temple
⑧ Museum of Évora
⑨ Tribunal of the Inquisition
⑩ Cathedral
⑪ Rua Cinco de Outubro

balconies of the buildings that ring the square. You'll also spot the occasional, distinctive Mudejar "keyhole" window throughout the town.

King João III lived in Évora off and on for 30 years. The TI is inside the **palace** where the king's guests used to stay, but others weren't treated as royally. A fervent proponent of the Inquisition, João was king when its first victims were burned as heretics on this square in 1543.

Speaking of the Inquisition, until the 16th century, the area behind the TI was the **Jewish quarter.** At the time, it was believed that the Bible prohibited Christians from charging interest for loans. Jews did the moneylending instead, and the streets in the Jewish quarter still bear names related to finance, such as Rua da Moeda (Money Street) and Rua dos Mercadores (Merchants' Street).

The characteristic **arcades** you see all around the square suit the weather, providing shelter in the winter and shade in the summer.

The Roman triumphal arch that once stood on this square was demolished in the 16th century to make way for the looming **Church of Santo Antão.** In front of the church is a 16th-century marble fountain—once an important water source for the town (fed by the end of the aqueduct we'll see in a minute) and now a popular hangout for young and old.

Radiating out from this town hub, in every direction, are traditionally decorated cobbled streets—centuries old and protected by law. Évora has strictly preserved the old center, and works hard to be people-friendly and inviting. The colors you see are traditional in Alentejo: Yellow trim is believed to repel evil spirits, and blue actually does keep away flies. Monster garbage cans hide under elegant smaller ones; at night, trucks lift entire hunks of sidewalk to empty them. Jacaranda trees—imported from Brazil 200 years ago—provide shade through the summer and purple flowers in the spring.

• *Leave the square on Rua Cinco de Outubro (opposite the TI). On the first corner,* **Courelas da Torre** *is a good little shop for gifty gourmet goodies from the region (daily 10:30–19:30). Outside, note how the back of the shop incorporates the old Roman-Arab wall. From here, head left (past Mr. Pickwick's Restaurante) on Alcárcova de Cima. A few steps farther on, you'll see another portion of a Roman wall built into the buildings on your right.*

❷ Roman Remnants

Looking through a series of modern windows, you see more of the Roman wall, which used to surround what is now the inner core of the town. Through the last window, look down to see the red paint of a Roman villa's dining room built over by the wall. Behind the counter of the inviting pastry shop on the right is another exposed stretch of Roman wall. If you look at your town map, you'll notice

Alentejo Region

Southeastern Portugal is very sunny and very dry. The rolling plains of the Alentejo (ah-len-TAY-zhoo) are dotted with large orchards and estates, Stone Age monoliths, Roman aqueducts, Moorish-looking whitewashed villages, and thick-walled, medieval Christian castles.

During the Christian reconquest of the country, Alentejo was the war zone. When Christian conquerors defeated the Muslims, they turned over huge tracts of recaptured land to the care of soldier-monks. These recipients came from various religious-military orders, including the Knights Templar and the Order of Christ (which Prince Henry the Navigator once headed). Évora was governed by the nearby House of Avis, which produced the kings of Portugal's Age of Discovery.

Despite its royal past, the Alentejo (the land "beyond the River Tejo") is the unpretentious terrain of farmers. Irrigated since Roman and Moorish times, the region is a major producer of wheat, cattle, wine...and trees. You'll see cork oak trees (green leaves, knotted trunks, red underbark of recently harvested trunks), other types of oak (native, once used to build explorers' caravels), olive (dusty green-silver leaves, major export crop), and eucalyptus (tall, cough drop-smelling trees imported from Australia, grown for pulp).

Today, the Alentejo region is known for being extraordinarily traditional, and it is even considered backward by snooty Lisboans. The people of Alentejo don't mind being the butt of jokes. My friend from Évora said it was the mark of a people's character to be able to laugh at themselves. He asked me, "How can you tell a worker is done for the day in Alentejo?" I didn't know. He said, "When he takes his hands out of his pockets." He continued more philosophically: "In your land, time is money. Here in Alentejo, time is time. We take things slow and enjoy ourselves." I'm impressed when a region that others are inclined to insult has a strong local pride.

ÉVORA

how the Roman wall, which surrounded the ancient city, left its footprint in the circle of streets defining the city core. The bulk of the wall that currently encircles Évora is from the 14th century, with a more modern stretch from Portugal's 17th-century fight for independence from Spain.

• *Walk straight. Cross the street (Rua Nova) and stop at the...*

❸ Aqueduct

This blunt granite-columned end of the town's aqueduct is a relic from the 16th century. The Portuguese have such a fondness for their aqueduct reservoirs that they give them a special name—*Mãe d'Água* (Mother of Water). Notice the abnormally high sidewalk just beyond the columns—it's the aqueduct channel. (On the outskirts of town, the channel sets higher, supported by stone pillars that kept the water flowing downhill.)

• *Turn left and keep walking along the aqueduct to the next square.*

❹ Praça de Sertório and Town Hall

Until recently, this square was congested with parked cars—but it's now a good example of how the town has become pedestrian-friendly. The tallest white building on the square is the Town Hall. They love visitors, so step inside. The lobby is often used to show off local projects the mayor wants to promote. In the corner on the right is a view of a Roman bath that was uncovered during a building repair.

Exiting the Town Hall, turn right. Look up to see a church and convent (one of about 20 in town—but this one is now a post office). Notice how the buildings are built right into a Roman tower (once part of the Roman wall you saw earlier). The grilled windows at the top of the tower enabled the cloistered sisters to enjoy looking at the busy town without being seen. Smile.

• *Take a right turn and walk under the arcades past the post office (signed CTT) and take the first left, on Rua de Dona Isabel. You'll immediately see a...*

❺ Roman Arch

This arch, the Porta de Dona Isabel, was once a main gate in the Roman wall. Below are some of the original Roman pavement stones, large and irregular in size and placement.

Beyond the arch is a neighborhood called **Mouraria** ("district of the Moors"). After Giraldo the Fearless retook Évora, the Moors were still allowed to live in the area, but on the other side of this gate, beyond the city walls. They were safe here for centuries...until the Inquisition expelled them in about 1500.

• *Don't go under that arch. Instead, head uphill behind you one block and then left further uphill on the stony little Travessa das Casas Pintadas, which leads to...*

ÉVORA

❻ Évora's Sight-Packed Square

Here, at the town's high point (1,000 feet above sea level), you'll see many of Évora's main landmarks. There's the **Roman Temple,** and the palace and the private chapel of the powerful local Cadaval clan (**Palacio Cadaval,** on the left side of the square—not worth the entry fee). Just beyond the Cadaval chapel is the recommended **Pousada dos Lóios,** once a 15th-century monastery but now a luxurious hotel with small rooms (blame the monks). At the far end of the square (not visible from here, but we'll go there soon) are the **Museum of Évora** and the headquarters of the Inquisition.

The fine little park facing the Roman Temple is the **Jardim Diana,** named when the temple was (mistakenly) thought to be dedicated to Roman goddess Diana. And facing the temple is a delightful little café, the **Jardim Diana Quiosque,** serving drinks and snacks in the shade.

• *With the temple behind you, head to the **viewpoint** at the edge of the park to enjoy a commanding view. You're standing upon what was the medieval wall. Find the tower to your right and look straight down. The higgledy-piggledy town stretching before you was the old Moorish Quarter (the Mouraria). In the Alentejo distance you can see vineyards and (at 10:00) the old aqueduct.*

Back on the square are the stirring ruins of the...

❼ Roman Temple

Imagine this spot 2,000 years ago: a fine colon-naded square with reflecting ponds on three sides of a grand temple dedicated to Rome's emperors. Little is left today, beyond the 14 Corinthian columns and marble capitals (locally sourced from the Alentejo region). This temple was part of the Roman forum and the main square back in the first century AD. Today the town's open-air concerts and events are staged here against an evocative ancient temple backdrop. It's beautifully floodlit at night.

• *Continue past the Roman Temple. Straight ahead, you'll see the...*

❽ Museum of Évora

This ▲ museum stands where the Roman forum once sprawled. Housed in the old archbishop's palace since 1929, the museum covers the city's history beginning with prehistoric times. An excavated section of the forum is in the museum's courtyard, surrounded by a delightful mix of Roman finds, medieval statuary, and 16th-century Portuguese, Flemish, Italian, and Spanish paintings. The highlights are 13 cathedral altar panels painted with exquisite detail (from Belgium, c. 1500). The museum also contains megalithic artifacts, including some found near Évora at the tomb known as the Anta Grande do Zambujeiro. The included audioguide does an earnest job taking the obscure works of art seriously and describing them well.

Cost and Hours: €3, Tue-Sun May-Sept 10:00-18:00, Oct-April 9:30-17:30, closed Mon year-round, Largo Conde de Vila Flor, +351 266 702 604, www.museudevora.pt.

• *Across the square from the museum is a white building with the top windows trimmed in yellow. This was the...*

❾ Tribunal of the Inquisition

This building stands as a reminder of Évora's notorious past as a tribunal site during Portugal's Inquisition—a dark and violent period that holds lessons worth learning even today. This was the first of four such headquarters of fear and hatred in Portugal. Here, thousands of innocent people, many of them Jews, were tried by a tyranny of the majority and found guilty of crimes against faith. Punishment could be anything from whipping, imprisonment, banishment, slave labor, or, for the most unlucky, death by burning on the main square.

More recently, the structure has been converted into the Fórum Fundação Eugenio de Almeida—a contemporary art museum, with exhibits that change every four months. Art lovers can see what's on and decide whether it's worth the cost of entry.

• *Directly across the square from the former Inquisition building, set on its own little leafy square, is the cathedral. (Note that Évora's historic university building is just a few blocks away and, while not on this walk, makes a convenient detour from this point. See the listing under "Sights in Évora," later.)*

❿ Évora Cathedral (Sé de Évora)

Portugal has three archbishops, and one resides here in Évora. This important cathedral of Santa Maria de Évora, worth ▲ and built in the late 12th century, is a

transitional mix of Romanesque and Gothic styles. As happened throughout Iberia, this church was built upon a mosque after the Reconquista succeeded here. That mosque was built upon a Christian Visigothic chapel, proving that religious and military tit-for-tat is nothing new.

Cost: There's a dizzying variety of tickets, combining the cathedral interior, the cloisters, the Museum of Sacred Art (called treasury/*tesouro*), and the viewpoint (called both terrace/*terraço* and tower/*torre*). Choose what you like; a ticket for the whole shebang is €4.50.

Hours: Daily 9:00-17:00, last entry to Museum of Sacred Art one hour before closing. There's a WC in the cloister.

Visiting the Cathedral: Inside the **cathedral,** in a sumptuous Baroque chapel midway down the nave on the left, is a 15th-century painted marble statue of a pregnant Mary. It's thought that the first priests, hoping to make converts out of Celtic pagans who worshipped mother goddesses, felt they'd have more success if they kept the focus on fertility. Throughout Alentejo, there's a deeply felt affinity for this ready-to-produce-a-savior Mary. Loved ones of mothers giving birth pray to her for blessings during difficult deliveries. Across the aisle, a more realistic Renaissance Gabriel, added a century later, comes to tell Mary her baby won't be just any child.

ÉVORA

The 16th-century pipe organ still works. Step up close to the high altar to view the ornately decorated chapel filling the apse. The royal box (high on the right, covered in gold leaf) looks down on the space, which is decorated almost entirely with colored marble. Only the muscular, crucified Jesus is not marble—he's carved in wood, yet matches the marble all around.

The **Museum of Sacred Art** (Museu de Arte Sacra) is to the right of the main altar. Signage is sparse, but make your way through the chapel reproduction at the entrance, go past the elevator, then turn right. You'll enter a long series of rooms displaying ornaments and artifacts used in the cathedral over the centuries. The highlight (at the end) is a sparkling reliquary heavily laden with more than a thousand gems—diamonds, rubies, emeralds, and sapphires—and supposedly containing pieces of the True Cross (in a cross shape). Backtrack and go up a flight of steps to floor 2 to find an intricate 14th-century, French-made, puzzle-like ivory statue of Mary *(Virgem do Paraiso)*. Her "insides" open up to reveal scenes of her life. A photo below shows Mary folded up and ready to travel. Not much else of interest is on this floor except perhaps Our Lady of Good Death—*Nossa Senhora da Boa Morte*—displayed toward the chapel.

Return to the church (scan your ticket again to leave the museum). The entrance to the Gothic **cloister** is past the ticket booth to the left. The cloister's openness and orange trees make it a cool haven, even on the hottest of Alentejo afternoons. Carvings of the four evangelists decorate the corners. Near where you enter, a tight spiral stairway leads to the "roof," with close-up views of the cathedral's fortress-like crenellations and grand views of the Alentejo plains. This "fortress of God" design was typical of the Portuguese Romanesque style. Notice the small relief (carved in the wall to the right as you face the church) showing the local Christian hero Giraldo the Fearless with two severed Muslim heads. Back on ground level, a simple chapel niche (opposite the cloister entry) has a child-sized statue of another pregnant Virgin Mary (midway up wall on left).

For the best views of the surrounding plains, return to the ticket booth and climb even more stairs to reach the church's rooftop terrace. Get up close to the church bells and the cathedral's fine lantern tower. Baroque flaming vases provide an interesting foreground to the rolling hills.

• *Head downhill on the little street opposite the cathedral's entrance. You're walking on...*

⓫ Rua Cinco de Outubro

This shopping street, which has served this same purpose since Roman times, connects Évora's main sights with its main square. Its name celebrates October 5, 1910, when Portugal shook off royal rule and became a republic. The street is lined with products of the Alentejo region: cork (even used to make postcards), tile, leather, ironwork, and Arraiolos rugs (handmade with a distinctive weave, in the nearby town of the same name).

For a chance to taste Alentejo wines, stop in at the **Ervideira Wine Shop** at #56. It sits in the old family home of the Count of Ervideira—look for the shrine remnants holding some of the oldest bottles from their nearby winery. They make crisp whites (even from the red tempranillo grape), earthy reds from a secret family recipe, rosés, and the occasional sparkling wine (€2.50 tasting fee for 3 wines, daily 11:00-19:00). If you like what you taste and want to try more local wines—by a wider variety of producers—visit the Rota dos Vinhos wine-tasting center, described under "Sights in Évora," later.

As you stumble down the shopping street, look left and up (at #28) to see a blue **shrine** protruding from the wall of a building. The town built it as thanks to God for sparing it from the 1755 earthquake that devastated much of Lisbon. The entire region is chock full of marble, which helped absorb much of the shockwave.

Ahead of you is the main square. The Chapel of Bones and town market are just a few blocks away on your left. But first, stop by the venerable **Café Arcada,** under the arcade to the right (just right of the church). With its Salazar-dictatorship ambience (and service), it's considered the best pastry shop in town. It serves good coffee and the local specialty: fresh, sweet cheese tarts (*queijada*, kay-ZHAH-duh, pay at the register, no table service).

Sights in Évora

NEAR THE ROMAN TEMPLE

Church of the Lóios and Cadaval Palace (Palacio Cadaval)

This is the palace and lavish mausoleum chapel of the noble Cadavals, who are still a big-time family—which is why they charge a stiff entry price. If you're on a budget, it's skippable, but if you appreciate beautiful and serene churches, the impressive gold altarpiece is worth seeing.

Cost and Hours: €7, covers the church and the palace, daily 10:00-18:00, on the square facing the Roman Temple, mobile +351 967 979 763, www.palaciocadaval. com.

Visiting the Church and Palace: Directly in front of the *pousada* (next to the Roman Temple), stairs lead down into the **church.** You'll walk upon Cadaval tombstones throughout your visit; taped chants and liturgical music add to the ambience. Look for the two small trapdoors in the floor that flank the aisle, midway up the church. The one on the right opens up to a deep, dark well (the palace and its church sit upon the remains of a Moorish castle—this was its cistern); the one on the left reveals an ossuary stacked with bones, supposedly belonging to former monks. The noble box (middle of the church, high above the pews) is a reminder that the aristocratic family didn't worship with commoners below. The tilework around the altar is from the 17th century—mere decoration with traditional yellow patterns. Along the nave, the tiles are 18th-century, with scenes illuminating Bible stories. The popularity of these tiles (inspired by the blue-and-white Delft tiles of the Netherlands) coincided with the flourishing of tapestries in France and Belgium that had the same teaching purpose.

The grilled windows allowed the Cadaval family to worship without being seen. The room to the right of the altar contains religious art, including a cleverly painted Crucifixion and rare Muslim tilework.

Your ticket includes—whether you want it or not—a walk through the **Cadaval Palace.** Next to the church entrance, you'll pop into the inviting family courtyard (now filled by a restaurant they operate), and follow signs upstairs and around the courtyard to the palace interior. The rooms are filled with old furniture, portraits, handwritten documents, and other historic icons. All told, it ranks pretty low on a European scale and is skippable unless you have time to kill.

AT THE SOUTHERN END OF THE OLD TOWN

These sights are within a few steps of each other, about a five-minute walk south of the main square, on Praça 1 de Maio.

▲▲Church of St. Francis and the Chapel of Bones (Igreja de São Francisco/Capela dos Ossos)

The Franciscan order arrived in Évora in 1224. In the 14th century, they built this Gothic church and a convent surrounding a fine cloister. The church and its Chapel of Bones are worth the stroll to the southern edge of the old town. The main attraction is the macabre chapel, with the skulls and bones of 5,000 monks tightly cemented to the walls, with barely a gap in sight.

Cost and Hours: Church-free, Chapel of Bones-€4, daily 9:00-18:30, Oct-May until 17:00.

Visiting the Church and Chapel: Imagine the **church** in its original, pure style—simple, as St. Francis would have wanted it. It's wide, with just a single nave lined by chapels. In the 18th century, it became popular for wealthy families to buy fancy chapels, resulting in today's gold-leaf hodgepodge. The huge Baroque chapel to the left of the altar is dedicated to St. Francis and Claire—his partner in Christ-like simplicity. You'll see them both flanking the altar, surrounded by anything but poverty. The chapel is slathered in gold leaf from Brazil. The fine 18th-century tiles tell stories of St. Francis' life.

The entrance to the **bone chapel** (Capela dos Ossos) is outside, to the right of the church entrance. After buying your ticket, head

to the right to find the macabre chapel. The message above the door translates: "We bones in here wait for yours to join us." Inside, bones line the walls, and a chorus of skulls stares blankly from walls and arches. They were unearthed from various Évora churchyards. This was the work of three monks who were concerned about society's values at the time. They thought this would provide Évora, a town noted for its wealth in the early 1600s, with a helpful place to meditate on the transience of material things in the undeniable presence of death. The bones of the three Franciscan monks who founded the church in the 13th century are in the small white coffin by the altar (at the far end of the bone chapel).

Your ticket also includes a few sights **upstairs** (entrance back near the ticket desk): a low-impact museum of ecclesiastical art, and a worthwhile collection of nativity scenes filling two corridors, separated by a view terrace. St. Francis famously "invented" the manger scene as a tool to teach the Christmas story. This exhibit displays just a fraction of the 2,600 pieces donated by a local collector who really, really liked nativity scenes. More than half are from Portugal, but those are joined by examples from around the world.

▲Public Market (Mercado Público)

Across the square in front of the Church of St. Francis is a modernized yet still charming farmers market. The more fragrant fish section is a free-standing section out back. It's busiest in the morning and on Saturday (Tue-Sun 7:00-18:00, generally closed Mon though a few rogue stands might be open). Wander around. It's a great slice-of-life look at this community. People  are proud of their produce. *"Posso provar?"* (POH-soo proo-VAHR) means "Can I try a little?" *Provar* some cheese and stock up for a picnic (perhaps in the adjacent gardens). There are also several good little eateries in the market and nearby.

▲Public Gardens (Jardim Público)

Take a refreshing break in the town's public gardens (main entrance across from market, at the bottom of Praça 1 de Maio). Just inside the gate, Vasco da Gama looks on with excitement as he discovers a little kiosk café nearby selling sandwiches, freshly baked goodies, and drinks. For a quick little lunch, try an *empada de galinha* (tiny chicken pastry) and perhaps a *queijada* (sweet cheese tart—a local favorite). The gardens, bigger than they look, contain an overly restored hunk of the 16th-century Royal Palace (right of the entry gate). Behind the palace, look over the white concrete balustrade to see a kids' playground and playfields. Life goes on—make no bones about it.

NORTHEAST OF THE ROMAN TEMPLE

From Évora's Roman Temple and cathedral, the university is about a five-minute walk.

ÉVORA

▲University of Évora (Universidade de Évora)

While far less monumental or interesting than Coimbra's (see page 321), Évora's historic university building is worth exploring—especially during the school year, when it offers a chance to rub elbows with students filling its blue-tiled galleries.

Cost and Hours: €3, Mon-Sat 9:30-18:00, closed Sun; Largo dos Colegiais 2, +351 266 740 800, www.uevora.pt.

Background: First known as the College of the Holy Spirit, this institution was established as a Jesuit university in 1559 by Henrique, brother of King João III and the cathedral's first archbishop (1512-1580). Henrique later became king himself after his great-nephew Sebastian (Sebastião, who had succeeded João III) died in a disastrous attempt to chase the Moors out of North Africa. Because Henrique was a cardinal—and therefore chaste—he left no direct descendants when he died only two years later. Portugal's throne passed to Sebastian's uncle, King Philip II of Spain, beginning 60 years of Spanish rule—and the start of Évora's decline.

Two hundred years after the founding of the Jesuit university, Marquês de Pombal (see sidebar, page 56), the powerful minister of King José I, decided that the Jesuits had become too rich, too political, and—as the sole teachers of society—too closed to modern thinking. He abolished the Jesuit society in 1759, confiscated their wealth, and closed the university. Another 200 years later, in 1979, it reopened, but this time as a secular university. Injecting 7,000 students into this town of 57,000 people (with about 10,000 inside the walls) brought Évora a new vitality—and discos. Unlike an American-style centralized campus, the colleges are scattered throughout the town. But this building is its historic core, and the closest thing to a student union building.

Visiting the University: The university's main entrance is the old courtyard on the ground level (downhill from the original Jesuit chapel—facing the grassy quad-like square). Enter the inner courtyard. Attractive blue-and-white tiles (one of the biggest and best-preserved collections south of Lisbon) ring the walls of the courtyard as well as the classrooms lining the courtyard arcades. Explore. If class is not in session, they usually leave the door open for curious tourists to peek in. The tiles within classrooms portray the subject originally taught in each room. Notice the now-ignored pulpits. (Originally, Jesuit priests were the teachers, and information coming from a pulpit was not to be questioned.)

Enter the **ceremonial room** directly across the courtyard from the entrance. Major university events are held here under the watchful eyes of Cardinal Henrique (the painting to the left) and young King Sebastian (to the right).

Sala 114, to the right of this room, gives you a great look at more tiles. In the 16th century, this was a classroom for students of astronomy—note the spheres and navigational instruments mingled with cupids and pastoral scenes. Imagine the class back then. Having few books, if any, the students (males only) took notes as the professor taught in Latin from the lectern in the back.

To find the university's **cafeteria,** follow the passage to the right of Sala 114, which connects to a smaller courtyard. The cafeteria (marked *bar*) is in the far-right corner. In the alcove just outside, notice the big marble washbasin. The cafeteria thrives with students and offers anyone super-cheap meals (Mon-Fri 8:30-18:00, closed Sat-Sun, WC).

NORTHWEST OF THE MAIN SQUARE

This sight sits on Praça Joaquim António de Aguiar, a five-minute walk northwest of the main square.

▲Rota dos Vinhos do Alentejo Wine Tasting Center

This modern promotional center for wine offers tastings of four to six local wines, bottles of which are available for purchase (most are €5-20). Familiarize yourself with little-known Portuguese grape varietals *(castas)*. Wines change weekly and are posted on the front door. Large info-panels in English hold perfume sprays that capture the essence of each varietal. Try to identify the various scents—it's more difficult than you think. The staff can give you details about the Alentejo wine route and schedule visits to nearby cellars.

Cost and Hours: €3, Mon 14:00-19:00, Tue-Fri 11:00-19:00, Sat 10:00-13:00, closed Sun, Praça Joaquim António de Aguiar 20, +351 266 746 498.

MEGALITHIC SITES NEAR ÉVORA

This region has been a historic crossroads for millennia—the three river basins that intersect here provided a rich, fertile area for prehistoric people to thrive. Human civilization's long presence here on the plains of Alentejo is marked by megalithic sites—some of the most important such stony configurations in the Iberian Peninsula—dating from 5,500-3,000 BC.

Near Évora, you'll find menhirs (solitary standing stones, near Nossa Senhora de Guadalupe and elsewhere), cromlechs (monolith circles, at Cromeleque dos Almendres), and dolmens (stone slabs such as the rock tombs of Anta Grande do Zambujeiro, near Val-

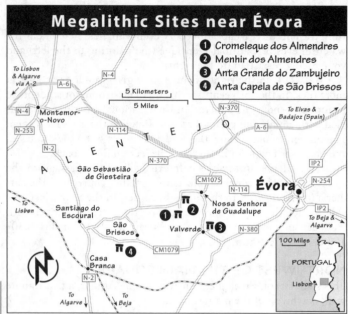

Megalithic Sites near Évora

1 Cromeleque dos Almendres
2 Menhir dos Almendres
3 Anta Grande do Zambujeiro
4 Anta Capela de São Brissos

verde; and Anta Capela de São Brissos—which was later Christianized, capped with a terra cotta roof, and painted white and blue). The most interesting to visit are Cromeleque dos Almendres and the Anta Grande do Zambujeiro, described next. Both of these sights are immersed in classic Alentejo scenery: cork-tree groves and a dusty, parched terrain.

Depending on how much you want to see, you can do a 15- to 45-mile loop from Évora by **bus tour** or hire a **guide** with a car (see "Tours in Évora," earlier), or **rent a car** to do the loop on your own (Évora's TI has a list of rental-car agencies and a map of the sites).

▲Cromeleque dos Almendres

This Portuguese Stonehenge, dating from about 5500 BC, stands in the midst of cork trees down a dirt road.

Getting There: It's five miles (20 minutes) west of Évora, down a dirt road that begins in the village of Nossa Senhora de Guadalupe (just south of where N-114 highway meets A-6 expressway). In the village, look for the brown *Almendres* signposts that lead you down a well-tended dirt road through cork trees. It's a bit over a mile to the menhir, then another mile-plus to the cromlech.

Visiting the Stones: Heading down the road, first you'll pass the pullout for the less-interesting sight, a lone 10-foot **menhir**—it's about a five-minute walk along a rutted dirt path from the parking pullout. This menhir lines up with the cromlech at sunrise on the summer solstice.

For a more dramatic site, continue to where the road ends, park, and walk a couple of dusty minutes to the **cromlech** (*cromeleque*, meaning "enclosure")—95 rounded granite stones erected in the shape of an oval. It's the largest mega-lithic monument in Ibe-

ria and one of the oldest in Europe, some 2,000 years older than Stonehenge. Discovered in the 1960s, it was carefully re-erected in its current position. Look closely at the stones; some have raised carvings, barely visible, of circles and shapes resembling a shep-herd's hook.

Some believe that Stone Age sun-worshippers gathered at this pagan sanctuary in search of harmony between the "micro" environment on earth and the "macro" environment of the entire cosmos. The stones functioned as a celestial calendar, with the far ends of the ellipse lining up with the rising and setting sun on each solstice. A posted description (in English) at the site tells more. Stop and comfort a peeled cork tree, or pet the sheep that are often grazing nearby.

▲Anta Grande do Zambujeiro

This large megalithic dolmen, a burial tomb, is one of the tallest of its kind and dates to 4,000-3,000 BC.

Getting There: The dolmen is located just outside the town of Valverde, a 20-minute drive southwest of Évora on N-380, and just a few minutes' drive from Nossa Senhora de Guadalupe. In Valverde, carefully track the brown *Zambujeiro* signs, which lead through a little industrial zone, then along a poorly maintained dirt road. Drive until the road ends, park, walk over the footbridge, and stroll a few more minutes to the dolmen (easy to see thanks to its modern roof).

Visiting the Dolmen: When it was discovered in 1964, the tomb was completely covered by a large mound of dirt. Excava-tion left the structure exposed to the elements, and although now protected by a roofed enclosure, it's believed the tomb will eventu-ally collapse. Walk up behind the dolmen and look into the bare interior, which once contained one of the largest artifact caches ever found in Iberia. Weapons, ceramics, gold and ivory jewelry, as well as 30 male skeletons had all been buried here over several generations (some of these items are now on display at the Museum of Évora). Off to the side you can see the original capstone, which was blasted off with dynamite during excavation.

Entertainment in Évora

Bullfighting
Évora's bullring (Arena d'Évora, just outside the southern city wall) has been turned into a multipurpose pavilion, and routinely draws crowds as a concert venue. While bullfights are still held here, they're rare (about four per year), in contrast to nearby towns that advertise fights on Saturday and Sunday throughout the summer (details at TI). Female bullfighters are on the program now, perhaps to give a tired sport a little kick.

Fado Music Dinner Show
Although fado is not as popular here as it is in Lisbon or Coimbra, the **Adega Típica Bota Alta** restaurant has live fado music on Friday and Saturday evenings from about 22:00 until the wee hours. Esperança runs "her house" with a loving passion for the art of fado. Arrive no later than 20:30 to finish your meal in the charming eight-table eatery before the music starts at 22:00. If they're full (or you'd rather just see the show without dinner), you can generally slip in after dinner for just a drink (€10 minimum, Rua de Serpa Pinto 93, mobile +351 968 655 166).

Sleeping in Évora

$$$$ Pousada dos Lóios, formerly a 15th-century monastery, is now a luxury hotel renting 36 well-appointed cells. While the rooms are tiny, this hotel sprawls with fine (if somewhat faded) public spaces, courtyards, and a swimming pool in a peaceful garden (air-con, free parking, Convento dos Lóios, across from Roman Temple, +351 266 730 070, www.pousadas.pt, recepcao.loios@pousadas.pt.

$$$$ M'ar de Ar Hotel Aqueduto is the place if you want a modern, spa-like splurge inside the city walls, with the old Roman aqueduct literally running through its back garden. The hotel has 64 rooms, a spa, an outdoor swimming pool, generous grounds, sleek modern style, and a whiff of snobbery in this otherwise unpretentious town (air-con, elevator, free parking, Rua Cândido dos Reis 72, +351 266 740 700, www.mardearhotels.com).

$$$ Albergaria do Calvario is a stylish 22-room hotel on the site of a 16th-century olive mill. Friendly Peter and Nina will take very good care of you. When you reserve a three-night stay directly and mention this book, they'll throw in one load of free laundry service—and may offer an upgrade (confirmed on arrival) to their best available room (air-con, elevator, free private parking, excellent organic breakfast, just inside the old town walls at the Porta

Nova entrance, Travessa dos Lagares 3, +351 266 745 930, www.
adcevora.com, hotel@adcevora.com).

$ Moov Hotel Évora is a great value: a minimalist oasis offer-
ing 80 small, professional, crisp rooms in a residential part of the
walled city. The building incorporates part of the facade of Évora's
first bullring, and the decor is equestrian-inspired. An interior patio
with a reflecting pool is relaxing even on the hottest of afternoons
(breakfast extra, elevator, secure pay garage, Rua do Raimundo 99,
+351 266 240 340, www.hotelmoov.com, evora@hotelmoov.com).

$ Inn Murus is a family-friendly guest house with a classic
tiled staircase, 11 fresh rooms with modern flair, and a shared terrace and kitchen (cheaper rooms with shared bath, family rooms,
breakfast extra, air-con, Rua de São Manços 10, mobile +351 935
804 609, https://innmurus.webnode.pt, innmurus@gmail.com).

$ Stay Hotel Évora Centro, renting 46 comfortable rooms
on a quiet side street, is solid, professional, and tour-friendly. It
has a sterile business-class vibe, but comes with a good location
and price (breakfast extra, air-con, elevator, free parking, Travessa
da Milheira 19, +351 266 704 141, www.hotelsantaclaravidigueira.
com, evora@stayhotels.pt).

$ Casa Hóspedes "O Alentejo" feels like a time warp: an old
noble house renting 22 well-worn but thoroughly cared-for rooms,
a homey TV salon, and endearing attention to quaint detail (family
rooms, no breakfast, air-con, Rua de Serpa Pinto 74, +351 266 702
903, residencial.oalentejo@gmail.com, charismatic Rosa speaks
very little English).

$ Hotel Ibis, a cheap chain hotel, has 87 identical Motel
6-type rooms that are a 15-minute walk from the center, just outside the city walls. Simple to find and offering easy parking, it's a
cinch for drivers—but staying here is like eating at McDonald's
in Paris (family deals, breakfast extra, air-con, elevator, parking,
Rua de Viana 18, +351 266 760 700, https://ibis.accorhotels.com,
h1708@accor.com).

Eating in Évora

You'll notice I list an unusual number of splurges in this otherwise budget-priced town. That's because the Alentejo region has
its own proud cuisine—rustic and hearty, with lots of pork and
robust wines. (Think of it as the Tuscany of Portugal.) You can
sleep and sightsee cheap here, but consider dining royally. Local
dishes to look for include *arroz de tamboril,* a rice and seafood stew,
and *açorda de marisco,* a soup with clams, shrimp, and bread spiced
with Alentejo herbs like cilantro. Don't order *vinho verde* or port
here—Alentejo produces some of Portugal's best wines, which are

both full-bodied and fruity. A good local *vinho licoroso* (sweet dessert wine) is Mouchão.

These places can be pretty aggressive at pushing the pricey little appetizers. Nibble if you like, but remember that you'll pay. Otherwise, let them be.

Finer Dining

$$$ Taberna Típica Quarta-Feira is a rustic 14-table tavern, festooned with patriotic Portuguese decor, where Zé Dias and his family proudly cook and serve. Don't expect to order from a menu—they usually serve just the food they felt like cooking that day. Sit down and enjoy the "Trust Zé Special"—he'll bring out the works, offering fun samples of whatever's in season, including his house wine (there's no wine list...just one decent house wine), fine desserts, dessert wine, and coffee. This is no place for vegetarians (Mon 12:30-15:00, Tue-Sat 12:30-15:00 & 19:30-22:00, closed Sun, hidden on a narrow street just north of Rua da Mouraria at Rua do Inverno 16, +351 266 707 530).

$$$$ Restaurante O Fialho is expensive and enjoyably (almost comically) pretentious, with bowtied waiters serving Alentejo cuisine to Bogart-like locals. Enjoy the photos of VIP diners on the wall, or ask for a look at the photo album showing O Fialho's great moments since it opened in 1948. For decades, this was virtually the only fine restaurant in town, and it arguably still offers Évora's best food. Go all-local with your waiter's recommendations. Reservations are generally necessary—they serve 90 people in four seatings: 12:30, 15:00, 19:30, and 22:00 (closed Mon, Travessa das Mascarenhas 16, +351 266 703 079, www.restaurantefialho.com).

$$$$ Tasquinha d'Oliveira is where Manuel (who was a cook for years at O Fialho) and his wife, Carolina, offer an intimate dining experience with all the quality of his mentor's restaurant, but less pretense. In a tiny, 14-seat abode of cooking love, they work with a respect for Alentejo cuisine and heritage (main dishes are easily splitable, Mon-Sat 12:30-15:00 & 19:30-22:00, closed Sun, reservations smart, Rua Cândido dos Reis 45, +351 266 744 841).

$$$ Barro do Naldo has a playful and unique format: There's no menu and no choice. For €20 you get "a trio of trios": three courses of three small selections—all a creative take on traditions by chef Reginaldo Branco. You'll eat in a spacious, modern setting that feels like a ceramic workshop. The chef is hands-on and the cod and pork cheeks are understandably popular (Fri-Wed 12:00-15:30 & 19:00-22:30, closed Thu, Rua das Alcaçarias 1, mobile +351 967 776 461).

Simpler Eating

$$$ Restaurante ¼ P'ras 9 ("Quarter to Nine") has a big, rus-

Versatile Cork

The cork extracted from the bottle of wine you're having with dinner is very local. The Alentejo region is known for its cork. (The wine you're drinking is likely local, too—the Alentejo produces lots of wine as well.) Besides bottle-stoppers, cork is used for many things, from bulletin boards to floor tiles, and from car-engine gaskets to the center of a base-ball. Cork is a remarkable substance—spongy and pliable but resistant to water.

Cork comes from the bark of the cork oak *(Quercus suber)*, a 30-foot tree with a sprawling canopy and knotty trunk that grows well in dry heat and sandy soil. After 25 years, a tree is mature enough for harvest. The outer bark is stripped from the trunk, leaving a "wound" of red-colored "blushing" inner bark. It takes nine years for the bark to grow back, and then it's harvested again. A cork tree keeps producing for more than 100 years. After harvesting, the bark is boiled to soften it up, then flattened. Machines cut the cork into desired shapes or punch out bottle stoppers.

Portugal produces half the world's supply of cork (with Spain and North African countries making much of the rest). These days, many wine stoppers are made from plastic, which could become a threat to cork production. So far the business remains strong, thanks to cork's insulating and acoustical applications, but some fear that if cork eventually loses its economic value, the survival of the forests—and the special ecosystem they support—will be at risk.

tic dining room with an open kitchen that steams up with local families and tourists chowing down on traditional Alentejo cooking (Thu-Mon 12:30-15:00 & 19:30-22:00, Tue 12:30-15:00 only, closed Wed, some outdoor seating, Rua Pedro Simões 9A, near exposed kink in aqueduct off Rua do Menino Jesus, +351 266 706 774).

$$ Taska Fina is a classic little mom-and-pop eatery with a tight dining room, red-and-white tablecloths, bullfighting decor, and a little punch of modern style. The owners are friendly, the Alentejo classics are delicious, and the price is reasonable—attracting a local crowd along with the tourists (Mon-Sat from 11:30 and 19:00, closed Sun, Rua do Apóstolo 10, +351 266 707 070).

$$ Adega do Alentejano is like an aboveground wine cellar. Locals choose from affordable traditional dishes, including tasty pork options. The proudly Alentejano menu is scrawled on paper tablecloths and chalkboards. Ask to watch them pour your *jarro* of house wine from the large earthenware vats at the back (Mon-Sat 12:00-15:00 & 19:00-22:00, closed Sun, Rua Gabriel Victor do Monte Pereira 21A, +351 266 744 447).

$$ Salsa Verde is an excellent self-service vegetarian place for a light, inexpensive lunch or dinner. They serve up flavorful salads and meatless versions of Alentejo classics in a crisp, clean, modern setting (Mon-Fri 11:00-15:30 & 18:00-21:30, Sat 11:00-15:30 only, closed Sun, Rua do Raimundo 93, +351 266 743 210).

Ice Cream: Zoka, a local favorite for ice cream, has tables on a quiet, inviting square just 100 yards off the main square (daily 9:00-22:00, off Largo de S. Vicente, Rua Miguel Bombarda 14, +351 266 703 133).

Évora Connections

From Évora by Bus to: Lisbon (almost hourly, 1.5 hours), **Lagos** (4/day direct in July-mid-Sept, otherwise transfer in Albufeira—confirm with driver, 5 hours), **Coimbra** (3/day direct, 4.5 hours; otherwise almost hourly with transfer in Lisbon, 4.5 hours), **Madrid** (in summer daily at 11:15 and 23:15, 7 hours, off-season only the night bus is available, book a day ahead at the bus station—Eurolines/Intersul office, second floor). Portugal bus info (no English spoken): +351 217 524 524.

From Évora by Train to: Lisbon (4/day, 1.5 hours, arrives at Lisbon's Oriente station), **Coimbra** (3/day direct, 4.5 hours, more options with change in Lisbon), **Lagos** (2/day, 5 hours, change in Pinhal Novo and Tunes). Check with TI or online at www.cp.pt for schedules.

NAZARÉ & CENTRAL PORTUGAL

Nazaré • Batalha • Fátima • Tomar • Alcobaça • Óbidos

Nazaré (nah-zah-RAY), an Atlantic-coast fishing town turned resort, is both black-shawl traditional and beach-friendly. The beach town is just the start of the region called "Centro Portugal." Several worthy sights are within easy day-trip distance: Drop by Batalha to see its monastery, the patriotic pride and architectural joy of Portugal. If the spirit moves you, the pilgrimage site at Fátima is nearby. Alcobaça has Portugal's largest church (and saddest romance). Portugal's incredibly (almost artificially) cute walled town of Óbidos is just down the road. And Tomar delivers workaday charm under a castle filled with Knights Templar mystique. (The most interesting city in central Portugal, Coimbra, is covered in its own chapter.)

PLANNING YOUR TIME

While the far north of Portugal has considerable charm, those with limited time can enjoy maximum travel thrills here—in its "Midwest." This area is an ideal stop if you're interested in a small, resort-town side trip north from Lisbon, or if you're coming

in from Salamanca or Madrid, Spain. Expect crowds in July and August, particularly on weekends. Pilgrims flock to Fátima on the 13th of every month between May and October, so expect multitudes then.

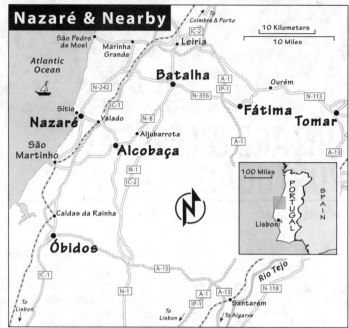

NAZARÉ & CENTRAL PORTUGAL

On a two-week trip through Portugal, Nazaré merits a day. Another day's worth of sightseeing is in Alcobaça, Batalha, and Fátima (which I'd prioritize in that order). Tomar is also worth a day. Óbidos is a light palate-cleanser, if you can squeeze it in on the way to or from Lisbon.

Day-Tripping from Nazaré by Bus: If you're traveling by bus, you can see both Alcobaça and Batalha in one day (but not on Sunday, when bus service is sparse). Alcobaça is easy to visit on the way to or from Batalha (and both are connected by bus with Óbidos). Ask at the bus station or TI for schedule information, and be flexible. Tomar and Fátima have few connections and are farthest away. Without a car, Fátima is not worth the trouble for most, but if you're heading by bus to Coimbra, you can go via Fátima. Tomar has the fewest connections of all, but there is extra service from July to September that connects all these dots twice a day. A taxi from Nazaré to Alcobaça costs a little more than €15; agree on the price before leaving town.

Nazaré

Nazaré is an ideal place for a summertime Portuguese beach break (especially if you're not making the trip south to the Algarve). It falls somewhere between a real-life, narrow-laned fishing village and a busy resort with a beach littered with frolicking families. You'll be greeted by the energetic applause of the surf, widows with rooms to rent, and big plates of *percebes* (barnacles). Relax in the Portuguese sun in a land of eucalyptus and pine trees, ladies in petticoats, and men who stow cigarettes and fishhooks in their stocking caps.

It seems that most of the town's 15,000 inhabitants are in the tourist trade, but it's not at all hard to find pockets of vivid and authentic culture. Somehow Nazaré traditions survive, and the townspeople go about their old-school ways. Stroll through the market for some ideal people-watching. Wander the back streets for a fine look at Portuguese family-in-the-street life. Laundry  flaps in the wind, kids play soccer, and fish sizzle over tiny curbside hibachis. Squadrons of sun-dried and salted fish are crucified on nets pulled tightly around wooden frames and left under the midday sun. Off-season Nazaré is almost empty of tourists—inexpensive, colorful, and relaxed, with enough salty fishing-village atmosphere to make you pucker.

Nazaré doesn't have any real "sights." The beach, tasty seafood, and the funicular ride up to the Sítio headland (for a great coastal view) are the bright lights of my lazy Nazaré memories.

Plan some beach time here. Sharing a bottle of chilled *vinho verde* on the beach at sundown is a good way to wrap up the day.

Orientation to Nazaré

Nazaré is simple: super-skinny streets with three- to five-story apartment blocks stretching away from an extra-long and extra-wide beach. Rua Sub-Vila cuts through all those narrow streets midway through town and has a lot of local vibe. The beach sweeps between the new harbor in the south and the cliffs on the north, which are capped by the old town of Sítio (SEE-tee-oo).

To get your bearings, survey the town from anywhere along the main beachfront drag, Avenida da República. Scan the cliffs.

Nazaré Fashions: Seven Petticoats and Black-Clad Widows

Nazaré is famous for its women who wear skirts with seven petticoats (one for each day, or for the seven colors of the rainbow, or...make up your own legend). While this is partially just a creation for the tourists, there is some element of truth to the tradition. In the old days, women would sit on the beach waiting for their fishermen to sail home. To keep warm in the face of a cold sea wind while staying modestly covered, they'd wear several petticoats so they could fold layers over their heads, backs, and legs. Even today, older and more traditional women wear short skirts made bulky by several—but not seven—petticoats. The ensemble is completed with loudly patterned stockings and house slippers, an apron  (hand-embroidered by the wearer), a small woolen cape, a head scarf—handy when the wind whips up— and flamboyant jewelry, including chunky gold earrings (often passed down from generation to generation).

You'll see some women wearing black, a sign of mourning. Traditionally, if your spouse died, you wore black for the rest of your life. While this tradition is still observed, mourning just ain't what it used to be—in the last generation, widows began remarrying.

The funicular climbs to Sítio, which boasts breathtaking views over the entire town and its beach. Just below those cliffs, notice the road kinking inland, marked by the yellow balconies of Ribamar Hotel. This street marks the main square, Praça Sousa Oliveira (with ATMs). Many of my recommended hotels and restaurants are near this square.

TOURIST INFORMATION

The TI is next to the entrance to the market hall, a long block off the beach (daily July-Aug 9:00-20:00, May-June and Sept 9:30-13:00 & 14:30-19:00, Oct-April 9:30-13:00 & 14:30-18:00, Avenida Vieira Guimarães, +351 262 561 194, www.centerofportugal.com).

ARRIVAL IN NAZARÉ

The town lacks an official **bus** station, but buses arrive along Avenida do Município, a few blocks up from the beach. **Drivers** can pay to park along the beachfront in street-side spots, or in the big

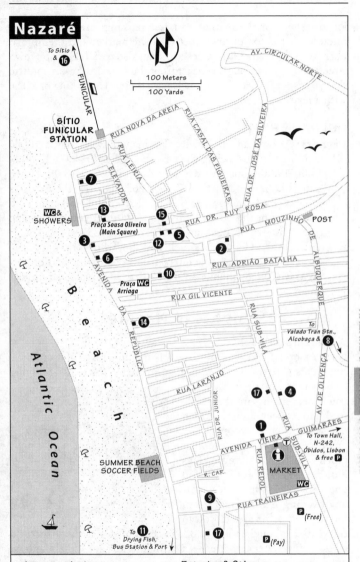

Map labels: Nazaré; To Sítio & 16; FUNICULAR; AV. CIRCULAR NORTE; SÍTIO FUNICULAR STATION; RUA NOVA DA AREIA; RUA LEIRIA; ELEVADOR; RUA CASAL DAS FIGUEIRAS; RUA DR. JOSÉ DA SILVEIRA; WC & SHOWERS; Praça Sousa Oliveira (Main Square); RUA DR. RUY ROSA; RUA MOUZINHO DE ALBUQUERQUE; POST; RUA ADRIÃO BATALHA; Praça Arriaga WC; RUA GIL VICENTE; RUA SUB-VILA; To Valado Train Stn., Alcobaça & 8; AVENIDA DA REPÚBLICA; RUA LARANJO; RUA DR. JUNIOR; AV. DE OLIVENÇA; Atlantic Ocean; Beach; SUMMER BEACH SOCCER FIELDS; R. CAR.; AVENIDA VIEIRA GUIMARÃES; RUA REDOL; RUA SUB-VILA; To Town Hall, N-242, Óbidos, Lisbon & free P; MARKET; i; T; WC; RUA TRAINEIRAS; P (Free); P (Pay); To 11, Drying Fish, Bus Station & Port

100 Meters / 100 Yards

Accommodations
1. Hotel Praia
2. Hotel Magic
3. Hotel/Rest. Mar Bravo
4. Hotel Âncora Mar
5. Hotel Maré
6. Ribamar Hotel-Restaurant
7. Hotel A Cubata
8. To Quinta das Rosas

Eateries & Other
9. Taberna d'Adélia
10. Restaurante A Tasquinha
11. To Wine Taverna "do 8 ó 80"
12. Tosca Gastrobar
13. Restaurante O Casalinho
14. Cervejaria Galé
15. Mr. Pizza
16. To Restaurante O Luís & Sitiado
17. Laundry (2)

lot just south of the market. For free parking, use the unmonitored lot at the top of town (between the market and the library, near Avenida Vieira Guimarães); you can also park for free on town streets that aren't along the beachfront, but check signs to confirm that your spot is legal. Most hotels have their own parking or a deal with a nearby garage.

HELPFUL HINTS

Laundry: At **Lavanderia Nazaré,** Fátima will wash, dry, and fold your laundry for pickup the next day (Mon-Fri 9:00-13:00 & 15:00-19:00—open all day July-Aug, Sat 9:00-13:00, closed Sun, Rua Branco Martins 17, +351 262 552 761). There's also a **self-service launderette** a half-block from the market and TI, just up from the beach (daily 7:30-22:00, attendants around from 9:30-17:30, Rua Sub-Vila 50, mobile +351 914 755 365).

Regional Guide: Helpful **Manuela Rainho,** who works out of Alcobaça, can assist anyone interested in seeing this part of Portugal (€170/day, mobile +351 968 076 302, manuelarainho@gmail.com).

Sights in Nazaré

▲▲Nazaré's Beach

Nazaré's broad and generous beach is the domain of the summertime tents *(barracas)*—a tradition in Portugal. The tents are run as a cooperative by the old women you'll see sitting in the shade ready to collect around €10 a day. The beach is groomed and guarded, and in the evening, piped music is played. Flags indicate danger level: red (no one allowed in the water), yellow (wading is safe), and green (no problem). The area closest to

the cliffs has rougher surf and is marked off for surfers. There's a world of fun water activities—jet skiing, stand-up paddleboarding, dolphin-seeking boat rides, and more. You'll see sales and rental shacks around the beach, or drop by the TI for details on your options.

If you see a mass of children parading through town to the beach, they're likely from a huge dorm, where poorer kids from inland areas are put up for a summer break. Plentiful modern benches along the boardwalk allow tourists and locals to sit and listen to the waves. In summer months, soccer areas (pro and not-so-pro) are set up where the busy Avenida Vieira Guimarães meets the boardwalk.

Boats used to line the beach in summer and fill the squares in winter, but they moved to a big, purpose-built harbor just south of town a few decades ago.

If you stroll south along the promenade toward the harbor, you'll come to a few restored **traditional boats** (each with different functions, English descriptions) in the sand, with high prows to cut through the surf. Try to imagine the beach littered with boats like these, with old men mending their nets. Oxen (and later, tractors) hauled the boats out each day. Across the street

is the town's Cultural Center—located in the former fish market—with interesting exhibits that explain Nazaré's fishing heritage and exactly how to dry all those fish (free, Mon-Fri 9:30-13:00 & 14:00-17:30, Sat-Sun 15:00-18:00).

Near the boats is a **mackerel crucifixion zone**—where ladies still sun-dry their mackerel, sardines, and other goodies from the sea. (They may try to sell them to you, but the fish need to be cooked again before eating.) Preparing and selling fish is the lot of Nazaré women married to fishermen. Stroll to people-watch. Traditions survive even among younger women.

The buildings beyond this point are new. While it may seem that most locals are older than most of the buildings, the town is a Portuguese Coney Island—thriving with young people who flock here for fun-in-the-sun on the beach.

Head back into town. Just under the bluff (near the funicular to Sítio) is the oldest square in Nazaré, **Praça Sousa Oliveira.** This main square is lined with the oldest buildings in the lower town.

▲Market (Mercado Municipal)

Filling a rusting old industrial hall with slices upon slices of Nazaré life, the town market sits just one long block up from the busy beach (daily 8:00-13:00 except closed Mon Oct-May; at the intersection of Rua Sub-Vila and Avenida Vieira Guimarães, in the green building near a taxi stand). While you'll see traditionally clad locals scattered around town, the market is one-stop shopping for people-watching (and, if you like, assembling a picnic). Most of the main floor has produce, with dried fruits and nuts, butchers, and bakers off to the left. Up a few stairs in the back is the fragrant fish market.

For another slice of local life, on the main street in front of the market (and near the bus station), look for petticoat-wearing women holding *quartos* signs—advertising rooms in private homes. They line the street coming into town, hit up tourists on the beachfront promenade, and meet each bus as it pulls into the station. You may enjoy dropping by for the commotion as the grannies fight over the tourists.

Flea Market: A flea market often pops up alongside the public library, except in August (9:00-13:00, longer hours Sat-Sun).

IN SÍTIO

Sitting quietly atop its cliff, the Sítio neighborhood used to be a totally separate village. Its people don't fish; they farm. But in 1912 the entire area had grown so much that Sítio merged with a neighboring village (Perderneira) and the beach folks (Praia) to make Nazaré. Take the funicular up to the top for a spectacular view and the exquisitely decorated village church.

Getting There: The handy Sítio **funicular** was originally built in 1889—the same year as the Eiffel Tower—by the same disciple of Eiffel who built the much-loved Elevador de Santa Justa in Lisbon. The equipment and stations, however, have been modernized. To get to the lift, follow signs to *ascensor;* it goes every 15 minutes (€1.50 one-way, €2.90 round-trip, June-Sept 7:30-24:00, Oct-May until 20:30, WCs at each station). Off-season, buses replace funicular service after 20:30, but run only about twice hourly. If dining in Sítio off-season, check bus times at the funicular station before you eat (funicular round-trip ticket valid for bus ride down). Notice the monitor above the turnstile at the top: It shows video clips of Nazaré's monster wintertime waves being conquered by daredevil surfers.

Upon arrival at the top, exit straight ahead, walk downhill, and turn left to reach the main square and the promontory.

Walking Down: If the funicular stops running or you'd like to descend with even more views, walk up the steps behind the funicular station to another viewpoint at Rua do Horizonte. A series of wide, cobblestone steps zigzag down the cliffside, ending at the upper part of town. Follow the road, now paved, through an upscale residential neighborhood until reaching Rua Dr. Ruy Rosa. Turn right and you'll be almost at the main square, Praça Sousa Oliveira. The walk takes less than 15 minutes.

Sítio's Main Square

Historic Sítio gathers around its dominant square. The bandstand marking the center of the square is a reminder that this is the main venue for the town's busy festival schedule. In the summer, smoke rises from the many outdoor grills, and the savory fragrance entices you to sit down for a plate of sardines.

• *At the top of the square, check out the...*

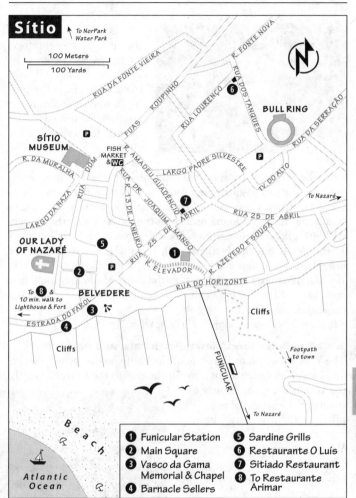

Map labels:
Sítio ↑ To NorPark Water Park

100 Meters / 100 Yards

RUA DA FONTE VIEIRA
R. FONTE NOVA
RUA DOS TANGUES
RUA LOURENÇO
ROUPINHO
FUAS
RUA DA SERRAÇÃO
BULL RING
SÍTIO MUSEUM
R. DA MURALHA
FISH MARKET & WC
RUA DOM
LARGO PADRE SILVESTRE
R. AMADEU GUADENCIO
TV. DO ALTO
RUA DR. 13 DE JANEIRO
RUA DR. JOAQUIM MANSO
25 DE ABRIL
To Nazaré →
RUA 25 DE ABRIL
LARGO DA NAZA
OUR LADY OF NAZARÉ
RUA R. AZEVEDO E SOUSA
R. ELEVADOR
RUA DO HORIZONTE
BELVEDERE
To ⑧ & 10 min. walk to Lighthouse & Fort
ESTRADA DO FAROL
Cliffs
Cliffs
Footpath to town
FUNICULAR
To Nazaré
B e a c h
Atlantic Ocean
To Nazaré

① Funicular Station
② Main Square
③ Vasco da Gama Memorial & Chapel
④ Barnacle Sellers
⑤ Sardine Grills
⑥ Restaurante O Luís
⑦ Sitiado Restaurant
⑧ To Restaurante Arimar

NAZARÉ & CENTRAL PORTUGAL

▲Church of Our Lady of Nazaré

The neighborhood's main church, built in the late 16th century and proudly restored by small local donations, contains what was the most important religious discovery in Portugal until the Miracle of Fátima. The faithful circulate behind the main altar and then go up to venerate the Black Madonna, brought here by the last Visigothic king in AD 714 before invading Muslims took over the entire Iberian peninsula. Supposedly the image originally came from Jesus' hometown of Nazareth (hence the name of this town: Nazaré). The Madonna, hidden in nearby rocks throughout the Muslim Moorish rule, was rediscovered after 468 years of being hidden...by a miracle.

On the left side of the nave at the entrance, a large painting shows the story you'll find all over town: Dom Fuas Roupinho, a nobleman from the area, was hunting deer and became so absorbed in the chase that he didn't realize he was about to go over a cliff. The Virgin Mary appeared suddenly and stopped him, saving his life. The unfortunate deer didn't see Mary in time. As locals came to venerate the spot where the noble's life was saved, they found the Black Madonna hidden in the rocks. Today the church, with its gilded Baroque-Neoclassical interior and 17th-century Delft tiles (from the Netherlands), is popular for weddings and other family religious occasions (which is why it has lots of flowers). If you'd like to pay your respects to the Black Madonna, you'll first have to pay €1 to the left of the altar (daily April-Sept 9:00-19:00, off-season until 18:00).

• *In front of the church, admire the view from...*

▲▲▲The Belvedere: Views, Petticoats, and Barnacles

The Vast View: From the edge of the bluff you can survey Nazaré and its golden beach stretching all the way to the town harbor. In the distance are the mostly un-inhabited Berlenga Islands. The pillar on the belvedere ("beautiful view") is a stone memorial for Vasco da Gama, erected in 1497 after he stopped here before leaving Europe for India. The tiny chapel next to the monument sits on the spot where the Black Madonna hid in the rocks

for 400 years, as if waiting for the Moors to leave and for the Christians to return.

Seven-Petticoat Fisherwomen: Several women (mostly from the same family, but competitive nevertheless) camp out here in their over-the-top traditional fashions, selling munchies, barnacles, and Nazaré knickknacks.

Barnacles: This is a fine opportunity to buy *percebes*—boiled, addictively tasty, and ready-to-eat barnacles (€3 for 100 grams, that's the size of their tiny wooden box). If you've yet to try them, this is the cheapest and best way to enjoy one of my favorite treats anywhere in Portugal. Grab the barnacles one at a time, hold the hard shell or beak, gently break off the leathery neck where it meets the shell and slide it away revealing the long slinky neck (which is what you eat; merchants have a finger bowl for rinsing).

The Lighthouse and Monster Waves

From the belvedere, it's a 10-minute walk to the end of the road at the **Farol lighthouse,** where you can enjoy panoramic views of the north beach *(praia norte).* In the winter, this bluff will be filled with gawking spectators witnessing one of the great surfing spectacles of our planet: little watercraft towing adrenaline-junkie, world-class surfers out to catch 80-foot waves. Surfers around the world regard Nazaré as the home of the ultimate thrill. (For a peek at the action, search "Nazaré surfing" on YouTube.)

• If you cross back over the square, then head up the street past the church, soon you'll reach the...

Sítio Museum
(Museu Dr. Joaquim Manso—Museu da Nazaré)

Dedicated to Dr. Joaquim Manso, this museum is the only place in Nazaré where you can see artifacts of the colorful traditional fishing culture—boats, rustic tools, costumes, historic photos, miniature models of Nazaré's distinctive boats, and so on (but without a word of English).

Cost and Hours: Free, Tue-Sun 10:00-12:30 & 14:00-18:00, slightly shorter hours Oct-June, closed Mon year-round, one block inland from Sítio's main square, Rua Dom Fuas Roupinho, +351 262 562 801, http://mdjm-nazare.blogspot.com.

Activities in Sítio

Sítio stages Portuguese-style **bullfights** on Saturday nights in summer (typically mid-July-Aug, get schedule at TI, tickets at kiosk in Praça Sousa Oliveira). Sítio's NorPark is a family-friendly **water park** with a pool, slides, and hot tub (open only mid-June-mid-Sept, get details at TI, free shuttle bus if you call ahead, +351 262 562 282).

Restaurante Arimar, on the left along the way to the lighthouse, is a good place to **take in the sunset** with drinks or dinner (avoid windy days). For more dining suggestions, see "Eating in Nazaré," later.

Sleeping in Nazaré

You should have no problem finding a room, except in August, when the crowds, temperatures, and prices are all at their highest (particularly during the Nazaré Beach Party in mid-Aug). Anywhere you stay in Nazaré, lower your expectations—this is a ragtag beach town, not a glitzy resort. And count on noise—from passing

NAZARÉ & CENTRAL PORTUGAL

cars, from karaoke-belting revelers, and from your neighbors (since most buildings in town are cheaply constructed, with thin walls and doors). Bring earplugs and be on vacation.

Prices vary wildly with the season. The price ranges in my listings are based on the cost of a standard double room with no view in medium-high season (approximately June-mid-July and Sept). Expect to pay about 50 percent more from mid-July through mid-August, and much less off-season. For locations, see the "Nazaré" map, earlier.

$$$ Hotel Praia feels big and muscular, filling two buildings across from the market hall. It's along the main road into town and an easy walk from the beachfront. Its 80 rooms are spacious, if a bit well-worn, with a bright and beachy color scheme. It comes with a rooftop terrace with a pool and its own attached parking garage—free for those who book direct (air-con, elevator, Avenida Vieira Guimarães 39, +351 262 569 200, www.hotelpraia.com, geral@hotelpraia.com).

$$ Hotel Magic, the most stylish choice near Nazaré's beach, is a short walk up from the main square. It has 19 sleek, white, minimalist, well-equipped rooms with splashes of color, as well as an inviting ground-floor lounge with old movie posters. For those more swayed by contemporary chic than Old World kitsch, this "art hotel" is the place to stay (air-con, elevator, Rua Mouzinho de Albuquerque 58, +351 262 569 040, www.hotelmagic.pt, info@hotelmagic.pt).

$$ Hotel Mar Bravo is on the main square and the waterfront. Its 16 comfy rooms are modern, bright, fresh—and they come with balconies, nearly all of them with views (RS%, double-paned windows, air-con, elevator, view breakfast room, recommended restaurant serves good seafood with a sea view, Praça Sousa Oliveira 71-A, +351 262 569 160, www.marbravo.com, info@marbravo.com, owner Fátima). Parking for the Mar Bravo is several blocks away, at Hotel Praia on Avenida Vieira Guimarães.

$$ Hotel Âncora Mar is a big, modern, almost institutional place, with 27 spacious, bright, and functional rooms and a generous roof terrace with a pool. It's on a quiet street a block from the market hall, and a relatively short walk from the beach (air-con, elevator, limited free parking, Rua Sub-Vila 49, +351 262 569 010, www.ancoramar.com, info@ancoramar.com).

$$ Hotel Maré, just off the main square, is a big, modern, American-style hotel with 43 straightforward rooms (all with balconies), some tour groups, and a rooftop terrace (family deals, double-paned windows, air-con, elevator, pay parking 500 yards away, Rua Mouzinho de Albuquerque 10, +351 262 550 180, www.hotelmare.pt, geral@hotelmare.pt).

$$ Ribamar Hotel-Restaurant, at the lower end of this price range, has a rare Old World atmosphere and 25 small rooms with dark wood. While it feels like a throwback (no air-con, no elevator), you're paying for the prime waterfront location. To spot the hotel from along the beach, just look for its yellow balconies (four rooms have balconies, good attached restaurant downstairs, pay parking; Rua Gomes Freire 9, +351 262 551 158, www.ribamarnazare.com, reservas@ribmarnazare.com).

$$ Hotel A Cubata, a last resort on the waterfront on the north end, has 20 small, nondescript rooms above a noisy bar. To save money and sleep better, forgo a private balcony and take a back room (Avenida da República 6, +351 262 569 150, www. hotelcubata.com, geral@hotelcubata.com).

$ *Quartos:* Private rooms for rent—called *quartos*—are a Nazaré specialty, but most can't be booked in advance. If you're willing to travel without reservations, you can just show up and ask around to find a cheap but modern, comfortable room. Sometimes *quartos* hosts find you first—if you stand around near the bus station with your luggage, you may be approached by a petticoat-clad local with a *quartos* sign. For more on this option, see the "Sleeping" section in the Practicalities chapter.

A TRANQUIL *QUINTA* OVERLOOKING NAZARÉ

$$ Quinta das Rosas, perched high above the congestion and chaos of Nazaré (but still just a few minutes' drive away), is a restful retreat thoughtfully run by a Portuguese-Canadian mother-and-daughter team—Anna Maria and Anna. It's a working farm with resident chickens and fine views over Nazaré and its beach. The five rooms are comfortable and country-classy (most with balconies, some with views), the breakfast includes farm-fresh eggs and Algarve-fresh OJ, and your hosts are generous with travel advice (Caminho Real, Pederneira, +351 262 562 706, www. quintadasrosas.com, reservations@quintadarosas.com). Driving up out of Nazaré, head toward the marina, then drive through the village of Pederneira, following signs for *Miramar Hotel* (the *quinta* is just before the hotel—watch for the gate on the right). They also have three family-friendly apartments with kitchens—called **$$ Seashell Apartments**—in a well-soundproofed building right along the beach in Nazaré.

Eating in Nazaré

Nazaré is a fishing town, so don't order *hamburguesas*. Fresh seafood is tasty all over town, more expensive (but plenty affordable) along the waterfront, and cheaper farther inland.

In this fishing village, even the snacks come from the sea. *Percebes* are boiled barnacles; in season they're sold as munchies in bars

NAZARÉ & CENTRAL PORTUGAL

and on the street (described earlier). Sardines are yummy any time of year but amazing when in season—May to September, but best in July and August.

Try Portugal's light, young wine, *vinho verde,* which pairs well with shellfish. *Amêndoa amarga* is the local amaretto. For a tasty pastry, try a *pastel de feijão* (fay-ZHOW) from any café. This small tart with a puff-pastry shell has a filling similar to pecan pie, but made of white beans.

Unless otherwise noted, for locations see the "Nazaré" map, earlier.

$$$ **Taberna d'Adélia** is a family-run *restaurante típico* popular with Portuguese visitors for its honest service, fresh fish, and unpretentious jovial ambience. Marco and his family pride themselves on respecting the customer (daily 12:00-15:30 & 19:00-22:30, reservations smart in summer, one block off the beach at Rua das Traineiras 12, +351 262 552 134).

$$ **Restaurante A Tasquinha** dishes up authentic Portuguese cuisine with a cozy blue-and-white-tile, picnic-bench ambience. Friendly, hardworking Carlos, his son Carlos II, and family serve their fish with the best bread in town and a special sauce that's good on just about everything. This is a fine place for *cataplana* (Tue-Sun 12:15-15:15 & 19:15-22:15, closed Mon, Rua Adrião Batalha 54, +351 262 551 945). Any traveler with this book gets a free glass of port wine for dessert (just ask).

$$$ **Wine Taverna "do 8 ó 80"**—with a stylish, modern, wine-and-tapas-bar setting—defies Nazaré's fishing heritage with a menu heavy on beef and pork dishes. The main attraction is the wine list: With hundreds of bottles of wine on-site and lots available by the glass, it's a short course in Portuguese enology. Sidewalk tables let you watch the tide roll in (Wed-Mon 12:00-23:00, closed Tue, a 5-minute walk along the beachfront south of the colorful boats at Edifício Atlântico, Loja 8, +351 262 560 490).

$$$ **Tosca Gastrobar** is a foodie option just above the main square. The mod, appealing menu (with both seafood and land food) combines Portuguese and international flavors with artful presentation. This is great for people who need a break from sardines and pork (Fri-Tue 12:00-24:00, Thu 19:00-24:00, closed Wed, Rua Mouzinho de Albuquerque 4, +351 262 562 261).

Main Square with a Beach View: Competitive, pricey restaurants ring the main square. These two offer decent value: $$$ **Mar Bravo**'s friendly staff serves fresh seafood at on-square tables overlooking the beach. Their dining room is inviting and modern (RS%—10 percent with this book, no outside seating, daily 12:00-23:00, inside hotel of same name, Praça Sousa Oliveira 71-A, +351 262 569 160). $$$ **Restaurante O Casalinho** has good outdoor seating, plain decor, and a solid reputation (daily 12:00-23:00, Praça Sousa Oliveira 7, +351 262 551 328).

Along the Waterfront: If you just want a nice meal with a view of the sea, there's a strip of fine eateries along the beach with lots of great options. **$ Cervejaria Galé** (Avenida da República 30), run by António Brígido Afonso, is the last fisherman's dive on the strip with lots of shellfish and salty options to go with your beer.

Public Market for a Picnic: To experience the colorful market, buy a picnic there and enjoy it on the beach (see description earlier, under "Sights in Nazaré," market open daily 8:00-13:00, closed Mon Oct-May, a long block up from the beach on Avenida Vieira Guimarães). Other to-go and picnic options can be found in any number of mini markets along Rua Sub-Vila. And **Mr. Pizza** (top of main square, across from Hotel Maré) has pies to go for a pizza party on the beach.

In Sítio
Remember that off-season, the funicular stops running at 20:30—before settling in for dinner, check the schedule for the bus back down to Nazaré. For locations, see the "Sítio" map, earlier.

$$ Restaurante O Luís serves excellent seafood and regional cuisine to an enthusiastic crowd in a cheery, air-conditioned atmosphere. While few tourists go here, the friendly white-coated waiters make you feel welcome. This place is worth the funicular ride if you want to eat well (Fri-Wed 12:00-24:00, closed Thu, reserve on weekends, Rua Dos Tanques 7, +351 262 551 826, David speaks English).

$$ Sitiado, just off the main square, is a bit trendier but retains a respect for tradition, with delicious *petiscos* (Portuguese tapas, designed to share family-style) served on earthenware plates in a casual bar setting. As it's both good and very small, reservations are smart (Wed-Mon 12:00-15:00 & 19:00-23:00, closed Tue, Rua Amadeu Guadêncio 2, +351 262 087 512, run by Wilson).

Nazaré Connections

BY BUS
Nazaré has no real bus station, but there is a ticket office in a small portable building behind the library on Avenida do Município, a few blocks inland from the Cultural Center and beach. Buses merely stop along the avenue. Service is reduced on weekends (especially Sun), so verify schedules beforehand online or at the TI. Two bus companies serve Nazaré: Rede Expressos, which covers most of Portugal (+351 707 223 344, www.rede-expressos.pt) and

RodoTejo, which focuses on central Portugal (+351 262 767 676, www.rodotejo.pt). To know your options, check both sites.

If you're heading to Lisbon, buses are faster and more direct than trains. You will arrive at Lisbon's Sete Rios bus station, a Metro (or taxi) ride away from the center.

Nazaré by Bus to: Alcobaça (stopping at Valado, about every half-hour, 20 minutes), **Batalha** (5/day, 1 hour), **Óbidos** (4/day, 1 hour, *Rápida* service is direct, most transfer in Caldas da Rainha), **Fátima** (4/day, 1.5 hours), **Tomar** (3/day, 2 hours), **Coimbra** (5/day, 2 hours, some via Leiria), **Lisbon** (6/day, 2 hours). Buses are scarce on Sunday.

BY TRAIN

The nearest train station is at Valado dos Frades (3 miles toward Alcobaça, connected by semiregular buses and reasonable, easy-to-share €8-10 taxis). The train to Lisbon requires a bus or taxi ride from Nazaré to the station in Valado, then several transfers—not worth the hassle. To avoid this train-station headache, consider using intercity buses instead of trains.

From Nazaré/Valado by Train to: Coimbra (3/day direct, 2 hours, bus is easier), **Lisbon** (5/day, 3-4 hours, involves transfers in Caldas da Rainha, Cacém, or Coimbra-B; bus is better). Train info: +351 808 208 208.

Batalha

The town of Batalha (bah-TAHL-yah) is worth a stop only to see its great Monastery of Santa Maria (also known as the Monastery of Batalha), considered Portugal's finest architectural achievement. It celebrates a dramatic medieval battlefield victory (hence the town's name, "Battle").

On August 14, 1385, two armies faced off on the rolling plains here to decide Portugal's future—independence or rule by foreign kings? Self-proclaimed King João I of Portugal ordered his 6,500 men to block the road to Lisbon. The Castilian king, with 31,000 soldiers and 16 modern cannons, ordered his men to hold their fire. But when the Portuguese knights dismounted from their horses to form a defensive line, some hotheaded Castilians—enraged by such a display of unsportsmanlike conduct by supposedly chivalrous knights—attacked.

Shoop! From the side came 400 arrows from English archers fighting for Portugal. The confused Castilians sounded the retreat, and the Portuguese chased them, literally, all the way back to Castile. A mere hour (and several hundred deaths) after it began, the

Battle of Aljubarrota was won. King João I claimed the Portuguese crown, and thanked the Virgin Mary with a new church and monastery.

Tourist Information: The TI is behind the monastery by the unfinished chapels (daily 10:00-13:00 & 14:00-18:00, Praça Mouzinho de Albuquerque, +351 244 765 180, www.visitcentrodeportugal.com.pt). Batalha's market is Monday morning (200 yards behind monastery).

Arrival in Batalha: If you take the **bus** to Batalha, you'll be dropped off a block behind the monastery, near an Intermarché supermarket. There's no official luggage storage, but you can leave luggage at the TI if you ask nicely. If you're **driving,** follow the signs to *Batalha*. Once in town, you'll loop around the back end of the huge monastery complex (the Unfinished Chapels), then park in the big, free lot behind the church.

Monastery of Santa Maria

This ▲▲▲ monastery, the symbol of Portugal's national pride, was built by King João I after winning the Battle of Aljubarrota. Construction stretched over two centuries (1388-1533), but the result was an original take on Gothic style and Manueline decoration. Today, a highway runs directly in front of the monastery, which is now behind a sound-deadening concrete wall covered with plants.

ORIENTATION TO THE MONASTERY

Cost: Church-free; worthwhile Founders' Chapel, Unfinished Chapels, and cloisters-€6, includes audioguide (usually free first Sun of every month); combo-ticket with Monastery of Santa Maria in Alcobaça and the Convent of Christ in Tomar-€15.

Hours: Daily 9:00-18:00, Oct-March until 17:00.

Information: +351 244 765 497, www.mosteirobatalha.gov.pt.

Changing of the Guard: See it at the top of each hour in the Chapter Room.

❂ SELF-GUIDED TOUR

• *Start by surveying the...*

❶ **Exterior:** The Church of Our Lady of Victory is a fancy Flamboyant Gothic (pointed-arch) structure decorated with lacy tracery—stained-glass windows, gargoyles, railings, and pinnacles representing the flickering flames of the Holy Spirit. (Inside, we'll see even more elaborate Manueline-style ornamentation, added toward the end of its construction.) The church's limestone has mellowed over time into a warm, rosy, golden color.

The equestrian statue outside the church is of **Nuno Álvares Pereira,** who commanded the Portuguese in the battle and masterminded the victory over Castile.

Before entering the church, study the **carvings** on the main entrance (much restored after serious damage in the 1755 earthquake). Notice the six lanes of heavenly traffic in the archway over the entrance: inside track—angels with their modesty wings; second track—the angel band with different instruments, including a hillbilly washboard; third—evangelists (those holding scrolls are from the Old Testament, those hold-

ing books are from the New Testament); fourth—Biblical kings and secular kings (those with globes in their hands); fifth—doctors of the Church with symbols of their martyrdom; and the express lane—female saints. Overseeing all this traffic is Jesus with the four evangelists in the tympanum. And the 12 apostles provide a foundation for it all. The statues are 19th-century copies of 14th-century originals. At the top of the pointed arch are two small coats of arms: Portugal's on the right and the House of Lancaster's on the left (a reminder of the marriage of João I and Philippa that cemented centuries of friendship between Portugal and England).

• *Enter the church.*

❷ **Church Interior:** The tall pillars leading your eye up to the "praying hands" of pointed arches, the warm light from stained-glass windows, the air of sober simplicity—this is classic Gothic, from Europe's Age of Faith. The church's lack of ornamentation reflects the vision of the project's first architect, Afonso Domingues (worked 1388-1402). Compared with Alcobaça's monastery (described later), this interior is dimmer and feels more somber, though the stained glass more dramatically colors the floors and columns (only the glass around the altar is original).

• *Buy a ticket for the cloisters and chapels (at the ticket counter on your immediate left as you enter). You'll need it to enter the rest of the sights described here. The first chapel on the right—directly across from the ticket desk—is the...*

❸ **Founders' Chapel** (Capela do Fundador): Center-stage is the double sarcophagus (that's English-style) of King João I and his English queen, Philippa. The tomb statues lie together on

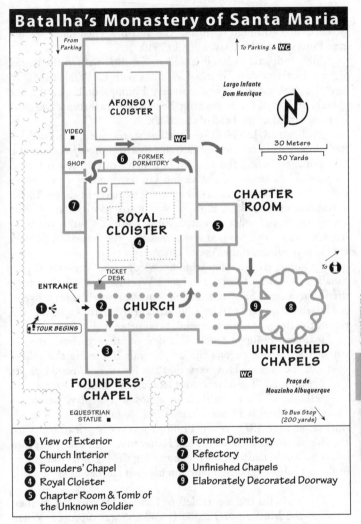

Batalha's Monastery of Santa Maria

From Parking

To Parking & WC

Largo Infante Dom Henrique

N

30 Meters

30 Yards

AFONSO V CLOISTER

VIDEO

WC

SHOP

6 FORMER DORMITORY

7

CHAPTER ROOM

ROYAL CLOISTER

4

5

TICKET DESK

ENTRANCE

1

TOUR BEGINS

2 CHURCH

3

9 **8**

UNFINISHED CHAPELS

WC

FOUNDERS' CHAPEL

Praça de Mouzinho Albuquerque

EQUESTRIAN STATUE

To Bus Stop (200 yards)

To ⓘ

1 View of Exterior	**6** Former Dormitory
2 Church Interior	**7** Refectory
3 Founders' Chapel	**8** Unfinished Chapels
4 Royal Cloister	**9** Elaborately Decorated Doorway
5 Chapter Room & Tomb of the Unknown Soldier	

their backs, holding hands for eternity. This husband-and-wife team ushered in Portugal's two centuries of greatness.

João I (born 1357, ruled 1385-1433), the bastard son of King Pedro I (see the "Pedro and Inês" sidebar later in this chapter), repelled the Castilian invaders, claimed the throne, consolidated his power by confiscating enemies' land to reward his friends, gave Lisbon's craftsmen a voice in government, and launched Portugal's expansion overseas. His five-decade reign greatly benefited Portugal. João's motto, *"Por bem"* ("For good"), is carved on his tomb. He established the House of Avis (see the coat of arms carved in the

NAZARÉ & CENTRAL PORTUGAL

tomb) that would rule Portugal through the Golden Age. João's descendants—through both the Avis and Bragança lines—would rule Portugal until the last king, in 1910.

João, indebted to English soldiers for their help in the battle, signed the friendship Treaty of Windsor with England (1386). To seal the deal, he was asked to marry Philippa of Lancaster, the granddaughter of England's king. You can see their respective coats of arms carved at the head of the tomb.

Philippa (c. 1360-1415)—intelligent, educated, and moral— had already been rejected in marriage by two kings. João was also reluctant, reminding the English of his vow of celibacy as Grand Master of the Order of the Cross. He retreated to a monastery (with his mistress) before finally agreeing to marry Philippa (1387). Exceeding expectations, Philippa won João's admiration by overseeing domestic policy, boosting trade with England, reconciling Christians and Jews, and spearheading the invasion of Ceuta (1415) that launched the Age of Discovery.

At home, she used her wide knowledge (she was trained personally by Geoffrey Chaucer and John Wycliffe) to inspire her children to greatness. She banished João's mistress to a distant convent, but raised his bastard children almost as her own, thus sparking the rise of the Bragança line that would compete for the throne.

João and Philippa produced a slew of talented sons, some of whom rest in tombs along the nearby wall. These are the golden youth of the Age of Discovery that the Portuguese poet Luís de Camões dubbed "The Marvelous Generation" *(Ínclita Geração)*.

"Henrique" (in niche directly opposite the entry, wearing a church for a hat) is Prince Henry the Navigator (1394-1460, see sidebar on page 197). When Philippa was on her deathbed with the plague, she summoned her son Henry to her side and made him swear he would dedicate his life to finding the legendary kingdom of Prester John—sending Henry on his own journey to explore the unknown.

Fernando (in the corner, left of Henry), Henry's kid brother, attacked the Muslims at Tangier (1437) and was captured. When his family refused to pay the ransom (which would have meant returning the city of Ceuta), he died in captivity. Son Pedro (tomb on far right), a voracious traveler and student of history, ruled Portugal as regent while his six-year-old nephew Afonso grew to manhood (Afonso's father, Duarte—João and Philippa's eldest—died of the plague after ruling for only five years).

The Founders' Chapel is a square room with an octagonal dome. Gaze up (like João and Philippa) at the ceiling, an eight-pointed star of crisscrossing pointed arches—a masterpiece of the Flamboyant Gothic style—that glow with light from stained glass. The central keystone (with João's coat of arms) holds all the arches-within-arch-

es in place. Remember this finished chapel—a lantern roof atop tombs in an octagonal space—when you visit the Unfinished Chapels later. Notice that some of the tracery in the arches still have their original red-and-green paint job.

· *Go back into the main part of the church, cross the nave, and bear right to find the entrance to the adjoining...*

❹ **Royal Cloister** (Claustro Real): Architecturally, this open courtyard exemplifies Batalha's essence: Gothic construction from about 1400 (the pointed arches surrounding the courtyard) filled

in with Manueline decoration from about 1500. The tracery in the arches features the cross of the Order of Christ (headed at one time by Prince Henry the Navigator) and armillary spheres—skeletal "globes" that showed what was then considered the center of the universe: planet Earth. The tracery is supported by delicate columns with shells, pearls, and coils of rope, plus artichokes and lotus flowers from the recently explored Orient.

Stop here and picture Dominican monks in white robes, blue capes, and tonsured haircuts (shaved crown) meditating as they slowly circled this garden courtyard.

· *Circle the courtyard counterclockwise, dipping into the...*

❺ **Chapter Room:** The self-supporting star-vaulted ceiling spans 60 feet, an engineering tour-de-force by Master Huguet, a Frenchman who became chief architect in 1402. Huguet brought Flamboyant Gothic decoration to the church's sober style. The ceiling was considered so dangerous to build (it collapsed twice) that only prisoners condemned to death were allowed to work on it. (Today, unknowing tourists are allowed to wander under it.) The architect who helped Huguet come up with the strong-enough, interlocking, spider-web design for this vast vault supposedly silenced skeptics by personally spending the night in this room. (It even survived the 1755 earthquake.) He's remembered with a little portrait figurine supporting the column in the far-right corner of the room. Besides this ceiling, Huguet designed the Founders' Chapel and the initial work on the Unfinished Chapels.

Portugal's **Tomb of the Unknown Soldier** sits under a mutilated crucifix called *Christ of the Trenches,* which accompanied Por-

Portugal's House of Avis and Its Coat of Arms

Seen on monuments at Belém, Batalha, Sagres, and even on the modern Portuguese flag, the Avis coat of arms is a symbol of the glorious Age of Discovery, when Portugal was ruled by kings of the Avis family.

In the center of the shield are five smaller shields arranged in the form of a cross. (One theory says that, after several generations of battle, the family shield—passed down from father to son—got beaten up, and the cross ripped apart into five pieces, held there by nails—the dots on the coat of arms.) Around the border are castles, representing Muslim cities conquered by Portugal's Christian kings. (Some versions have fleurs-de-lis and personal emblems of successive kings.)

Some Important House of Avis Kings

João I (r. 1385-1433): The bastard son of Pedro I, he protected Portugal from a Castilian takeover and launched overseas expansion.

Manuel I (r. 1495-1521): Ruler when all the overseas expansion began to pay off financially. He built the Monastery of Jerónimos at Belém, decorated in the ornamental style that bears his name (see architecture sidebar on page 104).

João III (r. 1521-1557): Ruler during Portugal's peak of power... and at the beginning of its decline.

Sebastian (r. 1557-1578): Because he died in battle without an heir, the nation had to rewind the family tree, ending up with a Spanish king, Philip II.

tuguese soldiers into battle on the western front of World War I. The three small soldiers under the flame—which burns Portuguese olive oil—are dressed to represent the three most valiant chapters in Portuguese military history: fighting Moors in the 12th century, Spaniards in the 14th century, and Germans in the 20th century. At the top of each hour, soldiers goose-step into the room to clear a path for a modest changing of the guard ceremony.

• *Leaving the Chapter Room, turn right and enter the* ❻ *former dormitory through the archway. Occasionally this space holds a history exhibit. Continue around the cloister to the big fountain in the corner. The monks would stop to wash their hands at the washbasin before stepping into the adjoining refectory (dining hall) for a meal.*

❼ The **refectory** contains a gift shop and a collection of all the offerings from various countries to the Portuguese unknown soldier. Of particular interest is a photograph taken in the WWI trenches of the mutilated crucifix (to right as you enter on the wall; the crucifix itself is the one displayed in the Chapter Room you just visited).

• *To leave the gift shop, look for an arch on the left that leads to the Alfonso V Cloister, where there's a video about Portugal (there's also a WC at the exit). Once outside, head right to the...*

❽ **Unfinished Chapels** (Capelas Imperfeitas): The grand-yet-unfinished room behind the main altar was intended as an octago-

nal room with seven niches for tombs, topped with a rotunda ceiling (similar to the Founders' Chapel). But only the walls, support pillars for the ceiling, and a double tomb were completed.

King Duarte and his wife, Leonor, lie hand-in-hand on their backs, watching the clouds pass by, blissfully unaware of the work left undone. Duarte (1391-1438), the oldest of João and Philippa's sons, was the golden boy of the charmed family. He wrote a how-to book on courtly manners. When, at age 42, he became king (1433), he called a *cortes* (parliament) to enact much needed legal reforms. He financed and encouraged his brother Prince Henry's initial overseas explorations. And he began work on these chapels, hoping to make a glorious family burial place. But Duarte died young of the plague, leaving behind an unfinished chapel, a stunned nation, and his six-year-old son, Afonso, as the new king.

Leonor became the regent while Afonso grew up, but she proved unpopular as a ruler, being both Spanish and female. Duarte's brother Pedro then ruled as regent before being banished by rivals.

In 1509, Duarte's grandson, King Manuel I, added the elaborately decorated ❾ **doorway** (by Mateus Fernandes), a masterpiece of the Manueline style. The series of ever larger arches that frame the door are carved in stone so detailed that they look like stucco. See carved coils of rope with knots, some snails along the bottom, artichokes (used to fend off scurvy), corn (from American discoveries), and Indian-inspired motifs (from the land of pepper). Manuel's tomb was destined to be in this section, but he abandoned the chapel after Vasco da Gama's triumphant return from India, channeling Portugal's money and energy instead to building a monument to the Age of Discovery launched by the Avis family—the

NAZARÉ & CENTRAL PORTUGAL

Jerónimos Monastery in Belém (where both Manuel and da Gama were ultimately buried).

Sleeping in Batalha

If you spend the night, don't count on nightlife—this town shuts down early.

$$ Hotel Villa Batalha is a big, American-style hotel offering 93 modern rooms with high-class comfort, complete with an in-house spa and swimming pool (air-con, elevator, Rua D. Duarte I 248, +351 244 240 400, www.hotelvillabatalha.pt, geral@hotelvillabatalha.pt). It's unromantically situated amid distant parking lots: With the monastery behind you, walk left on Rua Dona Filippa de Lencastre, continue straight through the roundabout, and you'll see the hotel.

Batalha Connections

From Batalha by Bus to: Nazaré (5/day, 1 hour), **Alcobaça** (3/day, 30 minutes), **Fátima** (2/day—or 4/day in summer, 1 hour), **Tomar** (2/day, 1 hour), **Coimbra** (3/day, 2 hours, transfer in Leiria), **Porto** (6/day, 3 hours), and **Lisbon** (5/day, 2 hours). Expect fewer buses on weekends (www.rodotejo.pt or www.rede-expressos.pt). Buy bus tickets for long trips at Café Frazão, across the street from the Batalha bus stop. For short rides (an hour or so and less), buy tickets from the driver.

By Car: Batalha is an easy 10-mile drive from Fátima.

Fátima

On May 13, 1917, three children were tending sheep when the sky lit up and a woman—Mary, the mother of Christ, "a lady brighter than the sun"—appeared standing in an oak tree (where a small, modern chapel is now located). In the midst of bloody World War I, and with the rise of an atheistic regime in Russia, she brought a message that peace was coming. The war raged on, so on the 13th day of each of the next five months, Mary dropped in again to call for peace and to give three messages. Word spread, bringing many curious pilgrims. The three kids—Lúcia, Francisco, and Jacinta—were grilled mercilessly by authorities trying to debunk their preposterous visions and were even briefly imprisoned. But the children remained convinced of what they'd seen.

Finally, on October 13, 70,000 people assembled near the oak tree. They were drenched in a rainstorm when suddenly, the sun

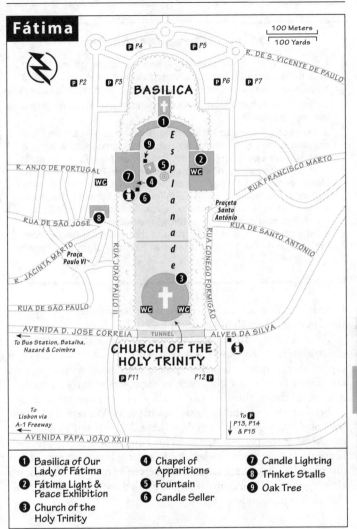

Fátima

BASILICA

Esplanade

Praçeta Santo António

Praça Paulo VI

R. DE S. VICENTE DE PAULO
R. ANJO DE PORTUGAL
RUA FRANCISCO MARTO
RUA DE SANTO ANTÓNIO
R. JACINTA MARTO
RUA DE SÃO JOSÉ
RUA DE SÃO PAULO
RUA JOÃO PAULO II
RUA CONEGO FORMIGÃO
AVENIDA D. JOSE CORREIA
ALVES DA SILVA
TUNNEL

To Bus Station, Batalha, Nazaré & Coimbra

CHURCH OF THE HOLY TRINITY

P11   P12

To Lisbon via A-1 Freeway

To P13, P14 & P15

AVENIDA PAPA JOÃO XXIII

100 Meters
100 Yards

1 Basilica of Our Lady of Fátima
2 Fátima Light & Peace Exhibition
3 Church of the Holy Trinity
4 Chapel of Apparitions
5 Fountain
6 Candle Seller
7 Candle Lighting
8 Trinket Stalls
9 Oak Tree

NAZARÉ & CENTRAL PORTUGAL

came out, grew blindingly bright, danced around the sky (writing "God's fiery signature"), then plunged to the earth—spreading fragrant flower petals everywhere. When the crowd came to its senses, the sun was shining and the rain had dried.

In 1930, the Vatican recognized the Virgin of Fátima as legit. And today, thousands of believers gather here to rejoice in this modern miracle. Many walk from as far away as Lisbon. Depending on the time of year you visit, you may see scores of pilgrims with reflective vests walking along the smaller highways. Fátima,

Mary's Three Messages

1. Peace is coming. World War I is ending. (Later, during World War II, the dictator Salazar justified keeping Portugal neutral by saying it was in accordance with Mary's wishes for peace.)

2. Russia will reject God and communism will rise, bringing a second great war.

3. Someone will try to kill a bishop dressed in white. This third message was kept a secret for decades, supposedly lying in a sealed envelope in the Vatican. In 1981, on May 13—the year's first pilgrimage day of Fátima—Pope John Paul II was shot. Upon recovering, he became convinced that he was the "bishop" of the prophecy. In the Jubilee Year of 2000, the pope visited Fátima, met with the surviving visionary, beatified the two who had died, and publicly revealed this long-hidden third secret. And one of the bullets that hit John Paul is now in the crown of the Virgin's statue at Fátima's Light and Peace Exhibition.

Lourdes (in France), and Međugorje (in Bosnia-Herzegovina) are the three big Mary sights in Europe.

For Roman Catholic visitors, the Fátima experience is a religious highlight. For non-Catholics, whether Christian or not, it can be easy to approach such a place of pilgrimage with a negative attitude. I believe our challenge as travelers—whether visiting a mosque in Cairo, the venerated tomb of a saint in Rome, a temple in Sri Lanka, a shrine in Japan, a chapel in Wittenberg, or the wall of a long-destroyed temple in Jerusalem—is not to judge but to marvel at the deep-seated need for humans to get close to their heavenly maker. Since I've learned to respect how centuries of tradition and heritage have taken that quest in so many directions, my visits to places like Fátima have been filled, no longer with cynicism, but with wonder.

Orientation to Fátima

The pilgrim-friendly, modern Fátima (FAH-tee-mah) is a huge complex, with two big churches bookending a vast esplanade, adjacent to a practical commercial center. Wandering through the religious and commercial zones, you see the 21st-century equivalent of a medieval pilgrimage center: lots of beds, cheap eateries, fields of picnic tables and parking lots, and countless religious souvenir stands—all ready for the mobs of people who inundate the place on the 13th day of each month from May through October. Any other day, it's just big and empty.

At the start of the commercial zone, browse through the

horseshoe-shaped mall of stalls selling religious trinkets—wax body parts, serene statuettes of Mary, rosaries (which pilgrims get blessed after attending Mass here), and so on.

Arrival in Fátima: From the **bus** station, follow the main road to the right, and in about five minutes you'll hit the back of the big, circular Church of the Holy Trinity (at the bottom of the esplanade). **Drivers** come to a big roundabout, where exits are marked for individual, numbered parking lots. All parking is free; a green *GRATIS* on the directional signs means they have spaces available. The handiest lots are P3, P4, P5, and P6, which cluster just behind the basilica; others are farther out (see the "Fátima" map, earlier).

Tourist Information: The **town TI** is in a glassy modern kiosk behind the Church of the Holy Trinity (daily 9:00-13:00 & 14:00-17:00, Avenida José Alves Correia da Silva 213, +351 249 531 139, www.visitcentrodeportugal.com.pt). For information on the religious sites and the schedule of today's services, check in at the **shrine TI** at the western side of the esplanade, near the candles (daily 9:00-18:30, slightly shorter hours off-season, +351 249 539 600, www.fatima.pt).

Sights in Fátima

Esplanade

The huge assembly ground facing the basilica is impressive even without the fanfare of a festival day. The fountain in the middle provides holy water for pilgrims to take home. You'll see the information center; the oak tree and Chapel of the Apparitions marking the spot where Mary appeared; a place for lighting and leaving candles (with an inferno below where the wax melts into a trench

and flows into a vat to be resurrected as new candles—the shrine TI is right near here); and a long, smooth route on the pavement for pilgrims to approach the chapel on their knees.

A variety of tacky and overpriced for-profit "museums"—each within a couple of blocks of the esplanade—compete for your euros by trying to re-create the story of the visions. The steep admission fees (not one dime of which go to a good cause) make these perhaps the worst sightseeing values in Portugal.

Basilica of Our Lady of Fátima

The towering Neoclassical basilica (1928-1953) has a 200-foot spire with a golden crown and crystal cross-shaped beacon on top.

NAZARÉ & CENTRAL PORTUGAL

The facade features Mary of the Rosary, flanked by mosaics in the porticoes of the 14 Stations of the Cross (under the statues of the four Portuguese saints). Built into the grand staircase is a covered stage with an open-air altar, cathedra (bishop's chair), and pulpit—all awaiting the next 13th of the month,

when the masses will enjoy an outdoor Mass.

Cost and Hours: Free, daily 7:00-21:00.

Visiting the Basilica: Inside, giant letters arc across the ceiling above the altar, offering up a request for Mary in Latin, "Queen of the Holy Rosary of Fátima, pray for us." A huge painting depicting the vision is flanked by chapels dedicated to the Stations of the Cross and the tombs of the children who saw the vision. Two of the three died in the flu epidemic that swept the world shortly after the visions. Francisco's tomb (died 1919) is to the right of the altar. Jacinta (died 1920) and Lúcia rest in a chapel to the left of the altar. Lúcia (the only one with whom Mary actually conversed) passed away at the age of 97 in 2005. She lived as a Carmelite nun near Coimbra for most of her life.

The basilica is busy with many Masses throughout each day. During a visit by Pope Francis in May 2017—on the 100th anniversary of the first apparition—he made the two younger children, Francisco and Jacinta, saints. Lúcia will likely be named a saint soon.

Nearby: Filling a basement of a hall to the right of the basilica (as you face it) is the **Fátima Light and Peace Exhibition,** a serious exhibit sponsored by the Church to enhance your visit (free, daily 9:00-12:00 & 14:30-17:30). An inexpensive booklet explains the context of the exhibit (in English). The 15-minute movie, while not in English, is still worth watching. Explore several rooms of cases filled with gifts given to Our Lady of Fátima. It's here that you can see the crown of the Virgin that now holds one of the bullets that hit St. John Paul II when he was pope. The sisters who run the exhibit are sweet and helpful.

Church of the Holy Trinity (Igreja da Santíssima Trindade)

Construction of this grand church began in 2004 with its foundation stone, a fragment from St. Peter's actual tomb in the Vatican, given by Pope John Paul II. Completed in late 2007, the church can hold 9,000 devotees, 10 times the capacity of the older basilica. The striking architecture and decoration is intentionally multinational—the architect was Greek; the large orange iron crucifix in front is German; the dazzling, golden mosaic mural inside (the left side depicts Mary with the three children she visited and all the people who witnessed her in the last apparition in October 1917) is Slovenian; and the crucifix at the altar (with the strik-

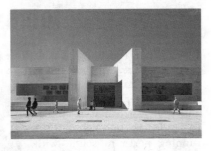

ingly different Jesus) is Irish. The church is circular, symbolizing the world. Each of its 12 doors is named for an apostle. Outside, statues of two popes kneel facing the esplanade (Paul VI, who was here on the 50th anniversary in 1967, and John Paul II, who had a special place in his heart for Fátima and visited three times). The long, smooth approach for pilgrims making their way to the Chapel of Apparitions on their knees starts here, with a pilgrims' prayer posted.

Cost and Hours: Free, daily 9:00-19:00.

Chapel of Apparitions
This marks the spot where Mary appeared to the three children (located outside the church, next to the big old oak tree, beneath a canopy). Services take place all day long in a variety of languages; check the posted schedule for English.

Pilgrimage
On the 13th of each month from May through October, and on August 19 (another day the children reported seeing Mary), up to 100,000 pilgrims come to Fátima. Some shuffle on their knees, traversing the mega-huge, park-lined esplanade (which is more than 160,000 square feet) leading to the church. Torch-lit processions occur on two nights (usually the 12th and 13th). In 2017, on the 100th anniversary of the miracle, half a million pilgrims—including Pope Francis—gathered here.

Fátima Connections

From Fátima by Bus to: Batalha (2/day—or 4/day in summer, 1 hour), **Alcobaça** (3/day, 1 hour, more frequent with transfer in Batalha), **Coimbra** (hourly, 1 hour), **Nazaré** (4/day, 1.5 hours), **Tomar** (6/day, 1 hour) and **Lisbon** (hourly, 1.5-2.5 hours, depending on route); service drops on Sunday. Note that the stop closest to the basilica is listed on bus schedules as Cova de Iria, *not* Fátima. Baggage storage is available at the bus station (€2.50/day).

Tomar

Lush, green Tomar is a quaint little town set under a fortified complex of great historic and artistic importance. Just a 30-minute drive east of Fátima, the town is remarkably untouristed and well worth a stop. Tomar is divided by the Nabão River running north to south, with its sights and pedestrian streets on the west bank (the east bank is modern and less interesting). The São João Baptista church, Town Hall, and several cafés  crowd around the main square, Praça da República. A steep walk uphill from there leads to a medieval masterpiece looking out over Tomar: the Castle of the Knights Templar and Convent of Christ (Convento de Cristo).

Tourist Information: The helpful TI occupies a quaint former residence, just across from the Mata Nacional dos Sete Montes Park entrance (daily 9:30-18:00, Oct-March 10:00-17:00, Avenida Dr. Cândido Madureira, +351 249 329 823, www.centerofportugal.com, turismo@cm-tomar.pt).

Arrival in Tomar: From the **bus** or **train** station (they're next to each other), it's a 10-minute walk to the city center. Head right down the wide Avenida Combatentes da Grande Guerra until you reach busy Rua Torres Pinheiro. Take a left and continue straight through the roundabout (with a bridge to the right), until you reach the foot of a second bridge. The pedestrian section of town is just to your left. Taxi stands outside both stations and are handy for day-trippers heading straight to the castle. **Drivers** coming from Fátima will hop on IC-9. Follow signs for *Tomar* and enter town via Rua de Leiria. Parking is located on the east bank of the Nabão River along Rua Santa Iria.

Sights in Tomar

Tomar Town

While there was a settlement here in Roman times, Tomar's importance started in the 12th century with the construction of the castle that still caps its hill. With 20,000 residents now in the old town, it's a place with lots of local ambience.

Stroll its riverside. The tiny Nabão River is all Tomar's—it starts nearby and flows just a few miles before emptying into the Tagus River outside of town. In mid-river look for a peaceful island

NAZARÉ & CENTRAL PORTUGAL

with a pleasant park and a rebuilt medieval waterwheel, showing off what must have been impressive technology in its day.

The old bridge, Ponte Velha, faces Rua Serpa Pinto which leads directly through the old grid center to the heart of town, Praça da República. This grid plan is a reminder that Tomar was a garrison town built to support the castle of the Knights Templar and their Christian mission.

Praça da República is one of those main squares where you just want to nurse a drink at a café and enjoy the relaxed tempo of local

life. Children on bikes test their training wheels, pigeons strut as if they own the place, old timers shake their heads at today's fashions, and tuk-tuk drivers hustle business (negotiating short town tours for a few euros). There are plenty of inviting spots to grab a bite or a drink. The classic old **Café Paraíso** (at Rua Serpa Pinto 127) is a time warp, retaining the humble vibe of Salazar days.

A statue of Gualdim Pais (1118-1195) overlooks the scene. The Grand Master of the Knights Templar and founder of the city, he put Tomar on the map, building the castle on the hilltop with architectural skills and techniques picked up in the Holy Land Crusades.

A large Spanish Jewish community lived in Tomar after Spain drove many of its Jews out of their country—and before Portugal decided to expel its Jews as well (1496)—adding to the city's economic and ethnic vitality. Today, you can visit the oldest synagogue in Portugal (15th century) a couple blocks off the main square at Rua Dr. Jacinto.

Castle of the Knights Templar and Convent of Christ

Towering above Tomar is its castle with an Oz-like circular church (or "oratory") built 800 years ago by the Knights Templar. The church (modeled after the Dome of the Rock and the Church of the Holy Sepulchre in Jerusalem) is where knights would go, often on horseback, to be blessed before battle as they defended Portugal against the Moors, protected pilgrims heading for the Holy Land, or just empowered Portugal in the Age of Discovery.

NAZARÉ & CENTRAL PORTUGAL

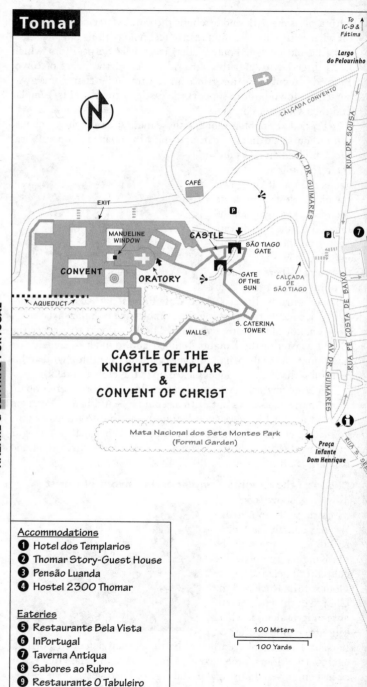

Tomar

To IC-9 & Fátima

Largo do Pelourinho

CALÇADA CONVENTO

AV. DR. GUIMARÃES

RUA DR. SOUSA

CAFÉ

EXIT

MANUELINE WINDOW

CASTLE

SÃO TIAGO GATE

CONVENT

ORATORY

GATE OF THE SUN

CALÇADA DE SÃO TIAGO

RUA PÉ COSTA DE BAIXO

AQUEDUCT

WALLS

S. CATERINA TOWER

AV. DR. GUIMARÃES

RUA S. SE...

CASTLE OF THE KNIGHTS TEMPLAR & CONVENT OF CHRIST

Mata Nacional dos Sete Montes Park (Formal Garden)

Praça Infante Dom Henrique

100 Meters

100 Yards

Accommodations
1. Hotel dos Templarios
2. Thomar Story-Guest House
3. Pensão Luanda
4. Hostel 2300 Thomar

Eateries
5. Restaurante Bela Vista
6. InPortugal
7. Taverna Antiqua
8. Sabores ao Rubro
9. Restaurante O Tabuleiro

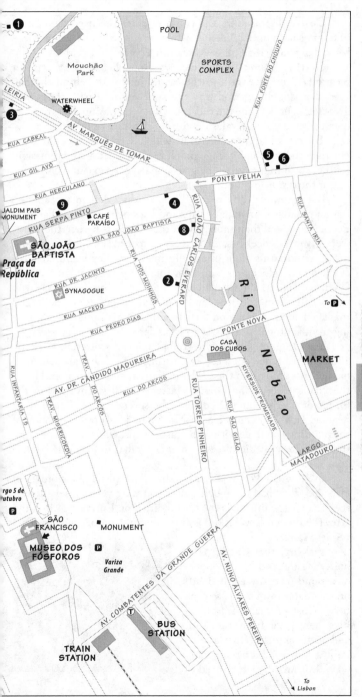

1

POOL

SPORTS
COMPLEX

RUA FONTE DO CHOUPO

Mouchão
Park

WATERWHEEL

LEIRIA

3

RUA CABRAL

AV. MARQUÊS DE TOMAR

RUA GIL AVÔ

5 **6**

PONTE VELHA

RUA HERCULANO

RUA SANTA IRIA

4

RUA JOÃO CARLOS EVERARD

JALDIM PAIS
MONUMENT

9

RUA SERPA PINTO

CAFÉ
PARAÍSO

8

SÃO JOÃO
BAPTISTA

RUA SÃO JOÃO BAPTISTA

Praça da
República

RUA DOS MOINHOS

RUA DR. JACINTO

2

Rio Nabão

SYNAGOGUE

RUA MACEDO

To **P**

RUA PEDRO DIAS

PONTE NOVA

RUA INFANTARIA 15

TRAV. DO ARCOS

AV. DR. CÂNDIDO MADUREIRA

RUA DO ARCOS

CASA
DOS CUBOS

MARKET

TRAV. MISERICÓRDIA

RUA TORRES PINHEIRO

RUA SÃO GILÃO

RIVERSIDE PROMENADE

LARGO
MATADOURO

rgo 5 de
utubro

P

SÃO
FRANCISCO

MONUMENT

MUSEO DOS
FÓSFOROS

P

Variza
Grande

AV. COMBATENTES DA GRANDE GUERRA

AV. NUNO ALVARES PEREIRA

T

BUS
STATION

TRAIN
STATION

To
Lisbon

Cost and Hours: €6, €15 combo-ticket also covers Monastery of Santa Maria in Batalha and Monastery of Santa Maria in Alcobaça; daily 9:00-18:30, Oct-May until 17:30.

Getting There: From Praça da República, it's a steep but pleasant 10-minute walk to the castle. Just walk behind the São João Baptista church and find the stairs up to a path that offers great views back to the town as you wind your way up. Day-trippers on a targeted visit can take a taxi from the train or bus station.

Tours: A helpful audioguide, which describes stops throughout the otherwise confusing complex, is included with admission. (If they're all in use, go to the gift shop near the exit and check the box at the drop-off point.)

Background: The Knights Templar was a rich organization—both a popular Christian charity and Europe's first great bankers. People deposited their money with the Templars here in the West, were given a "check" (safer than cash to travel with), and could make withdrawals along their pilgrimage as they ventured East. If they died, which was common, the Templars kept their estate. (When banking, always read the fine print.) The Templars—you could call them the first multinational corporation—built and managed about a thousand forts to aid Christian pilgrims stretching from Portugal all the way to Jerusalem.

The Order of the Knights Templar was dissolved in the early 1300s in Europe, but here in Portugal the order just changed names, morphing into the Order of Christ, and carried on. Henry the Navigator was the Grand Master—the first governor of the Order of Christ—and lived here for several years. Later, King Manuel I (who became Grand Master in 1484) ordered much of the building you'll see within the castle walls. Under his leadership, the stout early medieval castle was decorated in exquisite Manueline style.

In 1834 the Portuguese king dissolved all religious orders in Portugal (they had too much power and were very conservative—seen as an impediment to the liberal direction Europe was heading after the French Revolution) and this became property of the Portuguese state.

Visiting the Castle: The husky castle and the wonderous round (actually eight-sided) oratory dates from the 12th century. Most of the other buildings here date from the 15th and 16th centuries. The knights built a four-mile long aqueduct with 180 arches, which snakes

through the countryside leading to Tomar, to bring water to this castle and convent. The fine tile work is generally 17th century.

Standing in the oratory, imagine it in the 12th century—without the big entrance of today. There was one small entry/exit facing Jerusalem (the door with the window today). This was inspired by churches in Jerusalem where the order had its mother church. The original castle and oratory were built when such impressive architecture was new in Europe—inspired by stone work and architecture seen by the Crusaders in the Holy Land. The oratory was designed so even horses (important in the Knights Templar success on the battlefield) could be ridden in and blessed. Later, with the building projects of Manuel I, a big conventional church was added, and the oratory's wall was cut open to connect (with the grand triumphal arch you walk through today) the church and the circular oratory.

The Convent of Christ complex built around the oratory (which you are free to explore) is mostly 16th-century construction. You'll see various cloisters, a grand dormitory (with 40 cells), the refectory (dining hall), and jaw-dropping Manueline dressing on the older architecture.

NAZARÉ & CENTRAL PORTUGAL

Museo dos Fósforos

This quirky museum makes for a worthwhile stop if you've got time to kill. Housed in one section of the former São Francisco convent, the museum boasts a collection of 80,000 matchboxes on display—organized into 127 countries. Donated by a local resident in 1980, the collection keeps growing. Walk through arched doorways to the very last room, dedicated to

Portuguese matchboxes; the oldest is from the 1820s (free, Tue-Sun 10:00-13:00 & 15:00-18:00, closed Mon, Avenida General Bernardo Faria, +351 249 329 814).

Sleeping in Tomar

$$$ Hotel dos Templarios, located just north of the pedestrian zone, is Tomar's top hotel. This behemoth sports two pools and 171 spacious rooms—consider this an affordable splurge as mass tourism hasn't yet hit Tomar (air-con, elevator, free parking, Largo Cândido dos Reis 1, +351 249 310 100, www.hoteldostemplarios. com, geral@hoteldostemplarios.pt).

$ Thomar Story-Guest House has 12 rooms, each with clever local themes and different color schemes. Its crisp, modern design comes with minimal street noise at the edge of the pedestrian zone (air-con, Rua João Carlos Everard 53, +351 249 327 268, www. thomarstory.pt, thomarstory@gmail.com).

$ Pensão Luanda feels like a visit to grandma's house, with traditional decor, a nearby park, and friendly owners Mario and Vera. Its 12 rooms aren't fancy but very clean and comfortable (air-con, Avenida Marquês de Tomar 15, +351 249 323 200, www. residencialuanda.com, pensaoluanda@gmail.com).

¢ Hostel 2300 Thomar is smack dab on the main pedestrian street, with four double rooms and five dorm rooms. Portuguese motifs run through this budget option (air-con, common kitchen, Rua Serpa Pinto 43, mobile +351 927 444 144, www. hostel2300thomar.com, geral@hostel2300thomar.com).

Eating in Tomar

Since Tomar is inland, pork and beef are staples on any menu here. All over town you'll see loaves of bread stacked into a very tall "crown," decorated with flowers—women carry these trays on their heads in a festival every four years, incorporating pagan and harvest rituals into Catholicism (the next *Festa dos Tabuleiros* is in late July 2023). Expect some very good bread with your meal.

$$ Restaurante Bela Vista certainly has a "beautiful view" as its name suggests, with a romantic, lilac-covered terrace just across the riverbank. Traditional Portuguese fare is the specialty with an emphasis on grilled meat. Sip a glass of local Ribatejo wine or try a Portuguese craft beer (Wed-Sun 12:00-15:00 & 19:00-21:30, closed Mon-Tue, Rua Marquês de Pombal 77, +351 249 312 870).

$$ InPortugal bills itself as a modern *tasca* (tavern) with fresh and creative takes on Portuguese standards. Known for interesting *petiscos* (tapas), like wild boar croquettes and stewed mushrooms, it's easy to assemble a meal one dish at a time (Thu-Tue 12:00-15:30 & 17:30-24:00, closed Wed, Rua Marquês de Pombal 54, mobile +351 927 641 324).

$$ Taverna Antiqua has cozy terrace seating ideal for an afternoon drink, but return at night for a unique experience: dining completely by candlelight. Guests are placed at long communal tables with lots of candles, in a setting that plays on Tomar's medieval history. Don't expect a gourmet meal, but it's a fun way to end the day, especially after a visit to the Convent of Christ (Tue-Sun 12:00-23:00, closed Mon, Praça da República 23, +351 249 311 236).

$ Sabores ao Rubro is popular with locals who want a family-friendly place and good value. Hand-written daily specials are posted at the entrance, and the jovial spirit inside makes for a fun experience. Everything tastes like a Portuguese mom is in the kitchen (Wed-Mon 12:00-15:00 & 19:00-22:00, closed Tue, Rua João Carlos Everard 91, mobile +351 969 579 755).

$ Restaurante O Tabuleiro has a family-owned-yet-modern vibe and serves a wide variety of meat dishes. Half portions *(meia dose)* are reasonably priced. Try for a streetside table to enjoy the small-town vibe (Mon-Sat 8:00-24:00, closed Sun, Rua Serpa Pinto 140, +351 249 312 771).

Tomar Connections

From Tomar by Bus to: Lisbon (4/day, 2 hours), **Nazaré** (2/day, 2 hours), **Batalha** (2/day, 1 hour), **Fátima** (6/day, 1 hour), and **Coimbra** (2/day, 1 direct, 2 hours). On weekends, buy tickets directly from the driver since the bus station ticket counter is closed. A special summer bus service (July-Sept) adds two more departures per day from Tomar to Fátima, Batalha, Alcobaça, and Nazaré.

From Tomar by Train to: Lisbon (hourly, 2 hours), **Coimbra** (almost hourly, 2-3 hours) and **Porto** (almost hourly, 4 hours).

Alcobaça

This pleasant little town is famous for its monastery, one of the most interesting in Portugal. For its small-town atmosphere, I find Alcobaça (ahl-koh-BAH-sah) a better stop than Batalha if you have to choose.

Tourist Information: The TI is in the shopping district, between the monastery and the market (daily 9:00-12:30 & 14:00-17:30, Rua 16 de Outubro 9, +351 262 582 377, www.centerofportugal.com).

Arrival in Alcobaça: If you arrive by **bus,** it's a five-minute walk to the town center and monastery. Exit right from the station (on Avenida Manuel da Silva Carolino), walk a half-block uphill (car parking lot visible in distance), take the first right, and continue straight (on Rua Dom Pedro V). Hang a left just after passing a small plaza, and you are in the main square.

If you're arriving by **car,** follow the *Mosteiro* signs. For free parking, use the lot just uphill from the bus station (*estação rodoviárioi* signs). But it's easiest to simply park on the streets in front of the monastery, where the parking is cheap.

Sweets: Across from the entrance to the monastery, **Pastelaria Alcôa** wins awards for their traditional convent pastries, including the best *pastel de nata* in all of Portugal. See if you like it better than the famous version in Belém or buy a mixed box *(caixa)* to sample several (daily 8:00-19:30, Praça 25 de Abril 44, +351 262 597 474).

Sights in Alcobaça

▲▲Monastery of Santa Maria (Mosteiro de Santa Maria)

This Cistercian abbey church, despite its mainly Baroque facade, represents the finest Gothic building in Portugal. It's also the country's largest church, and a clean and bright break from the heavier Iberian norm. Afonso Henriques began construction in 1178 after taking the nearby town of Santarém from the Moors.

The first Cistercian monks arrived in 1228 and proceeded to make this one of the most powerful abbeys of the Cistercian Order and a cultural center of 13th-century Portugal. This simple abbey was designed to be filled with hard work, prayer, and total silence. With finely preserved old dormitories and dining halls, it's the easiest place in Portugal to really envision the life monastic.

Cost and Hours: Church and tombs-free; cloisters-€6; combo-ticket with Monastery of Santa Maria in Batalha and the Convent of Christ in Tomar-€15; daily April-Sept 9:00-19:00, Oct-March until 18:00, +351 262 505 128, www.mosteiroalcobaca.gov.pt.

⊖ Self-Guided Tour: As you view the **❶ church exterior** from the expansive square facing it, you can sense its former importance. The wings stretching to the right and left from the facade housed monks and pilgrims. As was generally the case, the monastery was an industrial engine (making ceramics and other products), and by the 16th century a town had grown around the abbey. When the abbey was dissolved in 1834, the town declined, too.

Stepping inside, you find a suitably grand yet austere house of prayer—just straight Gothic lines. The only decor is organic (such as leafy capitals).

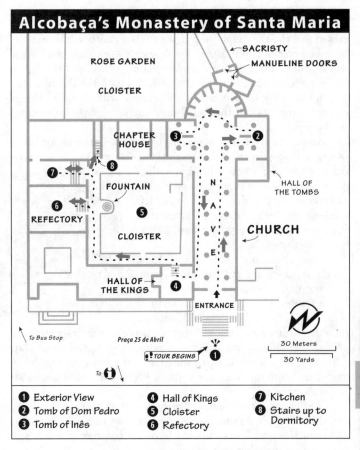

Alcobaça's Monastery of Santa Maria

ROSE GARDEN

CLOISTER

SACRISTY

MANUELINE DOORS

CHAPTER HOUSE

❸

❷

❼

❽

FOUNTAIN

HALL OF THE TOMBS

N A V E

❻

❺

REFECTORY

CLOISTER

CHURCH

HALL OF THE KINGS

❹

ENTRANCE

To Bus Stop

Praça 25 de Abril

⛨ TOUR BEGINS ❶

To 🛈

30 Meters

30 Yards

❶ Exterior View
❷ Tomb of Dom Pedro
❸ Tomb of Inês
❹ Hall of Kings
❺ Cloister
❻ Refectory
❼ Kitchen
❽ Stairs up to Dormitory

NAZARÉ & CENTRAL PORTUGAL

• *The long and narrow central nave leads to a pair of finely carved tombs that flank the main altar.*

❷ Tombs of Dom Pedro and ❸ Inês: These 1360 Gothic

tombs belong to Portugal's most tragic romantic couple, Dom Pedro (King Pedro I, 1320-1367, on the right) and Dona Inês de Castro (c. 1323-1355, on the left). They rest feet-to-feet in each transept, so that on Judgment Day they'll rise and immediately see one another again. Pedro, heir to the Portuguese throne, was hopelessly in love with the Spanish aristocrat Inês (see sidebar, page 297).

Start with **Pedro's** (on the right) and examine the exquisite carvings. Like religious alarm clocks, the attending angels are poised to wake the couple on Judgment Day. Pedro will lie here (as inscribed on the tomb) *"Até ao fim do mundo"*—until the end of the world, when he and Inês are reunited. The "Wheel of Life" below Pedro's finely combed head features the king on the throne at the top and the king in his tomb at the bottom, with the good things in life on the left and the bad things (including Inês' beheading) on the right.

Scenes from the life of St. Bartholomew—famous for being skinned alive (Pedro's patron saint, reflecting his life of sacrifice)—circle the tomb. The martyrdom of St. Bartholomew is depicted on a relief directly below the king's head on his left side—along with the creepy aftermath. Pedro's tomb is supported by lions, a symbol of royalty.

Now check out the tomb of **Inês,** which is supported by the lowly scum who murdered her...one holding a monkey, a symbol of evil. Inês' tomb features vivid scenes from the life of Christ, and the relief at her feet features Heaven up above, the dragon mouth of Hell (see photo), and jack-in-the-box coffins on Judgment Day. Although Napoleon's troops vandalized the tombs (that's why so many heads are missing), the story of Pedro and Inês endures *até ao fim do mundo.*

Stroll through the ambulatory (behind the altar) to the sacristy entrance. The two **Manueline doors,** courtesy of King Manuel I, add a touch of grandeur (think of Lisbon's Monastery of Jerónimos) to the rather plain but elegant church.

• *Return toward the entrance, show your ticket, and find the doorway next to the ticket desk to enter the...*

❹ **Hall of Kings:** This hall features terra-cotta ceramic statues of most of Portugal's kings. The last king portrayed is Joseph (above

the exit door), who ruled when the earthquake hit in 1755. Since then there has been no money for fancy statues. The next empty pedestal (to the left of Joseph) is wider than the rest—in anticipation of the reign of Portugal's first queen, Mary I, and her big fancy dress. The walls feature 18th-century tiles telling the story of the 12th-century conquest of the Moors and the building

Pedro and Inês

Twenty-year-old Prince Pedro met 17-year-old Inês, a Galician

noblewoman, at his wedding to Inês' cousin Constance. The politically motivated marriage was arranged by Pedro's father, the king. Pedro dutifully fathered his son, the future king Fernando, with Constance in Lisbon, while seeing Inês on the side in Coimbra. When Constance died, Pedro settled in with Inês. Concerned about Spanish influence, Pe-

dro's father, Afonso IV, forbade their marriage. You guessed it—they were married secretly, and the couple had four children. When King Afonso, fearing rivals to his ("legitimate") grandson's kingship, had Inês murdered, Prince Pedro went ballistic. He staged an armed uprising (1355) against his father, only settled after much bloodshed.

Once he was crowned King Pedro I the Just (1357), the much-embellished legend begins. Pedro summoned his enemies, exhumed Inês' body, dressed it in a bridal gown, and put it on the throne, making the murderers kneel and kiss its putrid rotting hand. (The legend continues...) Pedro then executed Inês' two murderers—personally—by ripping out their hearts, eating them, and washing them down, it is said, with a fine *vinho verde*. Now that's *amor*.

of the monastery (each with Latin supertitles and Portuguese subtitles). In the last scene (two scenes left of exit door), the first king lays the monastery's first stone.

The biggest sculpture—in its own niche, facing the entrance—features a fantastical image of Afonso Henriques, first king of Portugal and founder of this monastery, being crowned by Pope Innocent III and St. Bernard.

• *From here, steps lead to the...*

❺ Cloister: Cistercian monks built the abbey in 40 years, starting in 1178. They inhabited it until 1834 (when the Portuguese king disbanded all monasteries). The monks spent most of their lives in silence and were allowed to speak only when given permission by the abbot. To enjoy this cloister like the monks did: Meditate, pray, exercise, and connect with nature. As you multitask, circle clockwise until you reach the fountain—where the monks washed up before eating.

• *Traditionally, in any cloister, the fountain marks the entry to the...*

❻ Refectory (Dining Hall): Imagine this hall filled with monks eating in silence as one reads from the Bible atop the "Readers' Pulpit." Food was prepared next door.

• *Continue around the cloister and into the next room, the...*

❼ Kitchen: The 18th-century kitchen's giant three-part oven could roast seven oxen simultaneously. Survey the place: big sinks, wonderful hard surfaces, serious venting (look up the chimney). The industrious monks rerouted part of the Alcoa River to bring in running water. This kitchen fed huge numbers: The population of monks averaged about 450, and peasants who worked the church-owned land were rewarded with meals made here.

• *Head back out into the cloister, turn left, and take the stairs up to the bare...*

❽ Dormitory: Enjoy the beautiful austerity of the clean Gothic vaulting and pillars. In the hall where the monks slept, you can peer down on the transept of the church where Inês and Pedro lie buried. On this floor, there is also a terrace overlooking the adjacent cloister, with a garden. Monasteries generally had a medicinal herb garden (they were early leaders in herbal medicine) and grew their own produce.

• *Exit back through the church (where you entered).*

▲Mercado Municipal

An Old World version of Safeway is housed happily here under huge steel-and-fiberglass arches. Inside the covered market, black-clad dried-apple-faced women choose fish, uncaged and feisty chickens, ducks, and rabbits from their respective death rows. Wander among figs, melons, bushels of grain, and nuts (Mon-Sat 9:00-13:00, closed Sun, best on Mon and Sat). Imagine having a lifelong relationship with the person who

grows your produce. Women from Nazaré—with their distinctive dress—sell fish in a separate room. The market is a five-minute walk from the TI (just down the block from the bus station); ask a local, *"Mercado municipal?"* Also, a flea market happens Mondays by the Alcoa River.

Alcobaça Connections

From Alcobaça by Bus to: Lisbon (7/day, 2 hours, some transfer in Caldas da Rainha), **Nazaré** (2/hour, 20 minutes, stops at Valado), **Batalha** (3/day, 30 minutes), **Fátima** (3/day, 1 hour, more frequent with transfer in Batalha), **Óbidos** (5/day, 2 hours), **Coimbra** (2/day, 1.5 hours). Bus frequency drops on weekends, especially Sunday. A taxi to the Nazaré/Valado train station costs about €10; to Nazaré, a little over €15. Bus info: +351 808 200 370.

Óbidos

Postcard-perfect Óbidos (OH-bee-doosh) sits atop a hill, its 14th-century wall (45 feet tall) corralling a bouquet of narrow lanes and flower-bedecked whitewashed houses. Its name, dating from ancient Roman times, means—appropriately enough—"walled town." The 16th-century aqueduct connecting it like an umbilical cord to a nearby spring is a reminder of the town's importance during Portugal's boom century. Óbidos—now protected by the government from modern development—is ideal for photographers who want to make Portugal look as pretty as possible.

Founded by Celts (c. 300 BC), then ruled by Romans, Visigoths, and Moors, Óbidos was known as Portugal's "wedding city." In 1282, when King Dinis brought his bride Isabel here, she liked the town so much he gave it to her. (Whatta guy.) Later kings carried on the tradition—the perfect gift for a king to give to a queen who has everything. (Beats a toaster.) Today,  this medieval walled town is popular for lowly commoners' weddings. Preserved in its entirety as a national monument since 1951, it survives on tourism. And in 2015, it was named a "City of Literature"—you'll notice a book theme around town, and Óbidos is very proud of its annual literary festival.

Óbidos may well be Portugal's prettiest little town—but it's also one of its most touristy...and least authentic. For this reason, a quick visit outside of peak times is ideal. Every summer morning at 9:30, the tour groups flush into town (in August, it's absolutely packed). Ideally, arrive late one day and leave early the next, enjoying the town as you would a beautiful painted tile.

Tourist Information: The TI is at Óbidos' main pay parking lot, just outside the main gate (daily May-Sept 9:30-19:30, shorter hours off-season, +351 262 959 231, www.centerofportugal.com).

Arrival in Óbidos: There's no official place to store luggage in town, so it's smart to travel light.

If you arrive at the **train** station, you're faced with a 20-minute uphill hike into town. The **bus** drops you off much closer, right outside the main gate (upon arrival, go up the steps and through the archway on the right). If leaving by train, you can catch a taxi to the station in the lot outside the main gate (about €10).

If you arrive by car, don't drive into tiny, cobbled Óbidos. Ample tourist parking is provided just outside the main gate. The closest lot—right outside the main gate, near all the tour buses, the TI, and a public WC—is pay-and-display. The huge lot across the street (lined by the 16th-century aqueduct) is usually free, but they may charge during busy times or special events. If you're staying inside the town walls and want to park near your hotel, be sure to get details beforehand. Some hotels inside the walls have one or two spots, but it's generally easier to park outside the walls.

Óbidos Walk

There's not much to see in Óbidos—the main attraction is the town itself—but this walk covers it. In about 30 minutes, it goes from one end of town (the main gate) to the other (castle-turned-*pousada*).

• *From the parking lot or bus stop, enter Óbidos' 14th-century wall through the...*

Main Gate: Inside the gate, pause to gaze up at the scenes related to the town's history—depicting centuries of battles and religion in blue-and-white tiles. Tiles like these covered the entire face of the walls here until the 1755 quake shook them down.

Step into the town, and like Dorothy entering a medieval Oz, you're confronted by two wonderful cobbled lanes. The top lane is the town's main drag, littered with tourists shopping and leading straight through Óbidos to its castle (ahead, you can see its square tower, where this walk finishes). We'll start out on the quieter, restaurant-lined lower street. But first, let's get an aerial view over town.

• *From where you walked through the gate, you'll see steep stairs on your left. Hike up for a view from atop the...*

Town Wall: Enjoy the panoramas of the city and surrounding countryside from the 45-foot-high walls. This is one of several ac-

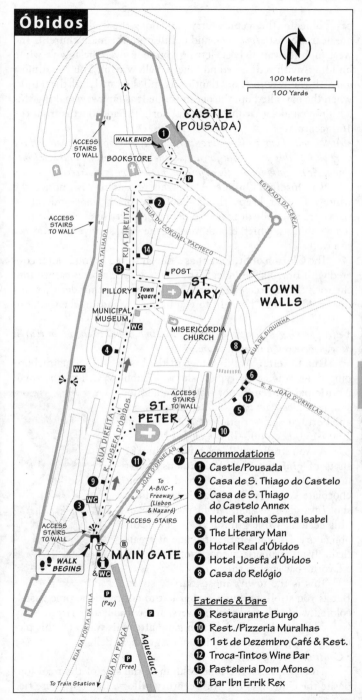

Óbidos

100 Meters
100 Yards

CASTLE (POUSADA)

ACCESS STAIRS TO WALL

WALK ENDS ❶

BOOKSTORE

ESTRADA DA CERCA

ACCESS STAIRS TO WALL

❷

RUA DO CORONEL PACHECO

RUA DIREITA

❶❹

❶❸

POST

PILLORY

Town Square

ST. MARY

TOWN WALLS

MUNICIPAL MUSEUM

WC

MISERICÓRDIA CHURCH

RUA DA TALHADA

RUA DE BIQUINHA

❽

❹

WC

❻

❶❷

R. S. JOÃO D'ORNELAS

ST. PETER

ACCESS STAIRS TO WALL

❺

❶⓪

RUA DIREITA

R. JOSEFA D'ÓBIDOS

❶❶

❼

To A-8/IC-1 Freeway (Lisbon & Nazaré)

❾

WC

R. S. JOÃO D'ORNELAS

❸

ACCESS STAIRS

ACCESS STAIRS TO WALL

WALK BEGINS

ⓣ

MAIN GATE

ⓘ & WC

ⓑ

RUA DA PORTA DA VILA

P (Pay)

P

RUA DA PRAÇA

Aqueduct

P (Free)

To Train Station ↓

Accommodations
❶ Castle/Pousada
❷ Casa de S. Thiago do Castelo
❸ Casa de S. Thiago do Castelo Annex
❹ Hotel Rainha Santa Isabel
❺ The Literary Man
❻ Hotel Real d'Óbidos
❼ Hotel Josefa d'Óbidos
❽ Casa do Relógio

Eateries & Bars
❾ Restaurante Burgo
❶⓪ Rest./Pizzeria Muralhas
❶❶ 1st de Dezembro Café & Rest.
❶❷ Troca-Tintos Wine Bar
❶❸ Pasteleria Dom Afonso
❶❹ Bar Ibn Errik Rex

cess points for the scenic sentry path along the wall (other options are near the castle/*pousada,* and uphill from the main church). The west (uphill) wall is best, letting you look over the town's white buildings with red roofs and blue or yellow trim. You can almost gaze all the way to the Atlantic, six miles away. Until the 1100s, when the bay silted up, the ocean was half as far away, making this a hilltop citadel guarding a natural port. The aqueduct is from the 16th century.

• *At the end of our walk, you can stroll along the top of the walls all the way back to this point. But for now, descend the staircase and head into town. At the fork, follow the right/downhill of the two streets...*

Rua Josefa d'Óbidos: Along this restaurant row, notice the whitewash that keeps things cool; the bright blue-and-yellow trims, traditionally designed to define property lines; and the potted geraniums, which bloom most of the year, survive the summer sun well.

The **Church of St. Peter** has a fine, restored Baroque altar covered with Brazilian gold leaf. The Maltese-type crosses carved into the rock throughout the church are a constant reminder that this fine building was "brought to you by your friends in the Order of Christ."

• *After peeking in, exit the church and climb uphill to the main tourist drag, where you'll turn right on...*

Rua Direita: Walking toward the castle on this main shopping drag, you'll pass typical shops, a public WC, and the small **Municipal Museum,** not worth the admission fee unless you enjoy stairs, religious art, and Portuguese descriptions (€1.50, Tue-Sun 10:00-13:00 & 14:00-18:00, closed Mon).

As you stroll, you'll see stands selling €1 shots of *ginjinha*—Óbidos' famous cherry liqueur. The tiny shots are served in edible chocolate cups (you'll pay a bit more for a shot in a glass, which can fit more booze). This custom, while gimmicky, is practically obligatory. (If you'd rather try one at a particularly atmospheric indoor spot, I've listed a favorite bar later in this walk.)

This is the town's most touristy street. But as you stroll, peek up to your left to notice a lonesome pastel-colored world, draped with flowers, and without a tourist in sight. Consider returning to the main gate (after this walk) on this picturesque upper lane, which is a photographer's delight.

• *Continue on and enter the...*

Town Square: The lone column at the side of the road (opposite the church) is the 16th-century **pillory.** Bad boys were tied to this to endure whatever punishment was deemed appropriate. Studying it closely, you'll notice it's capped by Queen Leonor's crown. On the side facing the castle, the carved hanging shrimp net represents how fishermen found the body of 16-year-old Afonso, son of Manuel I and Leonor, in the Tejo River after a tragic and mysterious death. The net eventually became part of the queen's coat of arms. The huge pots you see beneath the tile-roofed porch overlooking the square on the left were once in the central market and held olive oil instead of flowers.

· *At the bottom of the square, enter the...*

Church of St. Mary of Óbidos: Grab a seat on a front pew, surrounded by classic 17th-century tiles. Notice the fine painted-wood ceiling over each of the three naves. To the left of the altar is a niche with a delicate Portuguese Renaissance tomb, featuring a pietà carved out of local limestone. To the right of the altar are three paintings, including *The Mystical Marriage of St. Catherine,* all by Óbidos' most famous artist, the nun Josefa d'Óbidos (1634-1684).

To peek into another church, exit left and head a few steps down (behind the terrace bar). Look for Our Lady of Mercy sculpted in blue and white ceramic above the entrance. The **Misericórdia church** was built as part of the queen's charity institution, hence the royal coat-of-arms painted on the ceiling. It's lined with 16th-century "carpet tiles." To the right of the altar you can see one of the "religious floats" and a cross that's carried through town during Holy Week festivities.

· *Return to the main shopping drag and turn right for the...*

Final Stretch to the Castle: On the left, pop into the **Pastelaria Dom Afonso** (#113). This welcoming little coffee bar, dominated by a big old grape press, serves good pastries and sandwiches. Try the local version of *pastel de nata,* with chocolate or with the sour-cherry-like berries that go into *ginjinha* (open daily 8:00-19:00).

A few steps farther down the street, **Bar Ibn Errik Rex** (#100, on the right) is the most characteristic indoor spot to sip *ginjinha.* Bruno will take good care of you, with a backdrop of his dad's extensive collection of old liquor bottles. Rather than serve the liqueur in a chocolate cup, he'll give you a more generous (and pricey) pour in a shot glass for €3 (Wed-Mon 11:00-24:00, closed Tue most of the year).

The main drag ends at a big, white church—but it's not a church anymore. Step inside to find a huge and inviting **bookstore,** with giant shelves filling the nave and apse, and a good selection of books in English. This deconsecrated church was repurposed after Óbidos was named a "City of Literature" (daily 10:00-19:00).

· *Facing the big, white church/bookstore, you have a couple of choices:*

Stairs on the left lead up to the top of the town wall. But for now, instead turn right and follow pousada *signs. You'll pass the* pousada's *sweet little garden (an inviting spot for a coffee or drink), then continue up the curving stairs to the left and a view terrace (with a telescope) just in front of the former castle.*

Castle/*Pousada:* Óbidos' onetime castle is now a fancy **$$$$** hotel with nine rooms (+351 210 407 630, www.pousadas.pt). Looking out over these grand views, consider this history: On January 11, 1148, Afonso Henriques (Portugal's first king) led a two-pronged attack to liberate Óbidos from the Moors. Afonso attacked the main gate at the other end of town (where tourists enter), while the Moorish ruler huddled here in his castle. Meanwhile, a band of Afonso's men, disguised as cherry trees, snuck up the steep hillside behind the castle. The doomed Moor ignored his daughter when she turned from the window and asked him, "Daddy, do trees walk?"

After savoring the view, go back down toward the top of Rua Direita and enter the archway to your right. Walk uphill for a minute until you see the town wall. Turn around for a spectacular view of the castle—it's yours for the taking...even if you don't have a cherry-tree costume.

• *You can return to your starting point three ways: hiking along the upper town wall, exploring photogenic side lanes, or shopping and drinking your way back down the main drag.*

Sleeping in Óbidos

To enjoy Óbidos without tourists, spend the night. There are reasonable values in this overpriced toy of a town. In the first three weeks in August, prices spike up well above those indicted by these price ranges.

INSIDE THE OLD WALLS

$$ Casa de S. Thiago do Castelo, a fancy and characteristic little guesthouse at the base of the *pousada*/castle, rents eight elegantly appointed rooms around a chirpy *Better Homes and Tiles* patio. Lower levels offer three different, welcoming salons to relax in, including one with a classy billiards table (free parking, Largo de S. Thiago, +351 262 959 587, www.casas-sthiago.com, reservas@casas-sthiago.com, Alice speaks English). They also have an annex near the main gate, where they book overflow guests in six rooms (without breakfast or parking) at busy times.

$ Hotel Rainha Santa Isabel is an old-school hotel marked by flags on the main drag in the center of the old town. It has 20 traditional, musty rooms and a big lounge with comfy leather chairs (air-con, elevator, Wi-Fi in public areas only, minimal breakfast, some street noise, Rua Direita 63, +351 262 959 323, www.obidoshotel.com, arsio@mail.telepac.pt). If you're driving, call first to let them know you're approaching, stop long enough to drop your bags and get a parking permit, and drive on to the town square to park. If no one's at the front desk, the staff at the Doce Rainha café next door can help.

JUST BELOW THE OLD WALLS

While still in a cute cobbled zone, these accommodations sit just below the actual walls—so they have easier car access and fewer tourist throngs. All have free, public street parking nearby.

$$ The Literary Man was built as a convent, but now it celebrates Óbidos' proud literary status. Its 30 rooms come in two types: classic, old-fashioned tiled rooms, and sleek new postmodern rooms with concrete and warm wood. The public spaces—including a funky and delightful breakfast room/bar with books stacked under stout vaults—have books, books, everywhere. Dinner at the **$$** restaurant comes with showmanship flair (air-con, Rua Dom João d'Ornelas, +351 262 959 217, www.theliteraryman. pt, bookme@theliteraryman.pt).

$$ Hotel Real d'Óbidos takes guests back to medieval times with suits of armor, tapestries, and staff dressed in period costume. Don't worry; the tasteful rooms have modern conveniences, and there is a small swimming pool. Ask the front desk if you need help figuring out how to work your key, large enough to open any castle gate (air-con, Rua Dom João d'Ornelas, +351 262 955 090, www. hotelrealdobidos.com, reservas@hotelrealdobidos.com).

$ Hotel Josefa d'Óbidos, located just outside the town walls, is a great value, with 30 well-appointed, modern rooms and a sense of style rare in this price range (air-con, Rua Dom João d'Ornelas, +351 262 955 010, www.josefadobidoshotel.com, geral@ josefadobidoshotel.pt). The attached **$$$** restaurant serves nice fish and meat dishes, and offers vegetarian options.

$ Casa do Relógio is a rustic eight-room place at the downhill end of town, just outside the wall. It's friendly and easygoing, providing no-stress parking and great comfort for the price. English-speaking Sara offers a big sun terrace and happily does her guests' laundry for no extra charge (RS%, cash only, Rua Porta do Vale 2, +351 262 959 282, www.casadorelogio.com, info@casadorelogio. com).

Eating in Óbidos

Óbidos is tough on the average tourist's food budget. Consider a picnic or one of the many cafés that offer cheap, basic meals.

$$$ Restaurante Burgo, just inside the main gate on the

NAZARÉ & CENTRAL PORTUGAL

lower road, is a lively place with good seating in the small, stony dining room, or out on the cobbled street (daily 12:00-15:30 & 18:00-22:30, good ice cream, Rua Josefa d'Óbidos 11).

$$ Restaurante/Pizzaria Muralhas serves traditional Portuguese and Italian cuisine outside the city wall. Dine indoors, or on the back patio (Fri-Tue 12:00-15:00 & 19:00-22:00, closed Wed-Thu, Rua Dom João d'Ornelas 6, +351 262 958 550).

$$ 1st de Dezembro Café & Restaurante, tucked on a little square next to the Church of St. Peter, serves inexpensive pizza, salads, and omelets (Mon-Sat 8:00-24:00, closed Sun, Largo de San Pedro, +351 262 959 298).

$$ Troca-Tintos is a good spot for a glass of wine and light meal of *petiscos* (Portuguese tapas) in an intimate atmosphere. Try to sit at one of the outdoor tables (Mon-Sat 18:00 until late, closed Sun, Rua Dom João d'Ornelas, next to recommended Literary Man, mobile +351 966 928 689). They have fado weekly—reserve in advance (Mon 20:30-23:30, €5 plus your food).

Óbidos Connections

By Bus from Óbidos to: Nazaré (4 buses/day, 1 hour, *Rápida* service is direct, most transfer in Caldas da Rainha), **Alcobaça** (5/day, 2 hours). Far fewer buses run on weekends; be sure to check schedules at the TI.

By Bus or Train to Lisbon: The bus (hourly, 1 hour, www.rodotejo.pt) is a much better option than the train (7/day to Lisbon Rossio, 2.5 hours, transfer in Cacém or Mira Sintra-Melecas; also 3/day to Lisbon Oriente, 2.5 hours, transfer in Sete Rios).

By Car to Lisbon: From Óbidos, the tollway zips you directly into Lisbon in about an hour.

COIMBRA

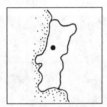

The college town of Coimbra—just two to three hours north of Lisbon by train, bus, or car—is Portugal's Oxford, and the country's easiest-to-enjoy city.

The earthquake that devastated Lisbon in 1755 spared Coimbra. The town's "earthquake" came much later, in the form of the 20th-century dictator Salazar—who demolished much of the old center for his bombastic building projects.

Today, Coimbra (pop. 144,000) is home to the country's oldest and most prestigious university (founded 1290). When school is in session, the town bustles with the spirited exuberance of youth—although many students go home on Friday, so weekend nights aren't as crazy as you might expect. (Over the summer holidays, it's almost sleepy.) During the school year, you'll see bands of black-caped students hanging out, rushing to class, or gathered in little clusters on the street singing traditional songs—to each other as much as for tourists. Coimbra's fado music also has its own special character: Here, it's performed by college-age men rather than women (as in Lisbon).

Any time of year, Coimbra's inviting Arab-flavored old town—a maze of people, narrow streets, and tiny *tascas* (restaurants with just a few tables)—awaits exploration. And its main drag—with glassy marbled stone underfoot, old-timey shops and bakeries winking their neon signs, and more locals than tourists—is a delight to simply wander. But for serious sightseeing, look no further than the historic university, capping the hill above town and offering a busy slate of cultural attractions. By the time you leave town, you'll know why graduating students sing, *"Coimbra tem mais encanto na hora da despedida*" (Coimbra is most enchanting at the moment you say goodbye).

PLANNING YOUR TIME

On a two-week swing through Portugal, give Coimbra two nights and a full day. If you plan to visit King João's Library, be sure to book a ticket in advance. You could spend the whole day simply following my self-guided walk and dipping into the various sights as you reach them, then wind down the afternoon and evening by strolling and exploring the town, enjoying a good meal, and taking in some fado (the Fado ao Centro show is an ideal introduction).

Orientation to Coimbra

Coimbra is a mini-Lisbon, with everything good about urban Portugal minus the intensity of a big metropolis. Skip Coimbra's modern center and stick to the charming old town.

From Largo da Portagem, the main square by the river, everything is within a short (if occasionally steep) walk. Plenty of budget rooms are within several blocks of the train station. The best views are from Coimbra's low and high points: looking up from the far end of Santa Clara Bridge (Ponte de Santa Clara) and looking down from the observation deck of the old university.

Coimbra's old town—a maze of timeworn shops, houses, and stairways—has two parts: the lower (Baixa) and the upper (Alta). The dividing line is the main pedestrian street, named Visconde da Luz at one end and Rua de Ferreira Borges at the other. It runs from the Praça 8 de Maio to the Mondego River.

To get from this main pedestrian thoroughfare to the university, follow the streets that wind their way up the hillside. These little lanes meander like the alleyways of a Moroccan medina up to the city's highest point, the old university. To save yourself some steep uphill climbing, use Coimbra's elevator/funicular, take a taxi, or ride the little electric minibus (see "Getting Around Coimbra," later).

TOURIST INFORMATION

The TI is a few steps off Largo da Portagem (daily, generally 9:00-17:00, entrance on Avenida Emídio Navarro—facing the bridge, +351 239 488 120, www.turismodocentro.pt). Ask for bus schedules here if needed.

ARRIVAL IN COIMBRA
By Train
There are two Coimbra train stations, Coimbra-B (Estação Velha, north of the center) and Coimbra-A (Estação Nova, more central; often written as just "Coimbra," without the A). Think B for "big": Nearly all major trains—such as those to and from Lisbon or Porto—stop only at Coimbra-B (some local trains stop at both). Any ticket to or from Coimbra includes a shuttle train that connects Coimbra-B with the more conveniently located Coimbra-A (5 minutes, 4/hour). To find a train to get you from B to A, check the electronic schedule boards or ask any station employee, *"Para Coimbra-A* (ah)*?"* Taxis wait across the tracks from Coimbra-B (figure about €5 to Coimbra-A or your hotel). Neither station has baggage storage.

Upon arrival at Coimbra-A, you're within a 10-minute walk of most lower-town (Baixa) landmarks. Several recommended hotels are right outside the station.

By Bus
The bus station, on Avenida Fernão de Magalhães (+351 239 855 270), has ATMs and baggage storage (closed Sat-Sun). The station is a quick taxi ride or 15-minute walk from the center; exit the bus station to the right, and follow the busy street into town. There's no need to make a special trip to the station to check schedules or buy tickets for your onward journey (both can be done online at www. rede-expressos.pt, and the TI can print timetables upon request). If you're walking *to* the station to catch a bus to leave Coimbra, take Avenida Fernão de Magalhães almost to its intersection with Cabral, and look to the left—the Neptuno café is by the station's subtle entrance.

By Car
From Lisbon, it's an easy two-hour straight shot on the slick *auto-estrada* A-1 (toll road). You'll pass convenient exits for Fátima and the Roman ruins of Conímbriga along the way. Leave the freeway on the easy-to-miss first Coimbra exit (Coimbra Sul), then follow the *Centro* signs. After 2.5 miles, you'll cross the Mondego River. Take Avenida Fernão de Magalhães directly into town. Most recommended hotels are near the Coimbra-A train station and the Santa Clara Bridge. If you arrive from northern Portugal or central Spain, follow signs for *Centro/Largo da Portagem.*

A large lot on the south bank of the river offers parking (but it's not guarded overnight—park at your own risk). In town, you'll find several big, convenient, clearly marked pay garages. The largest is centrally located in the lower old town under the government

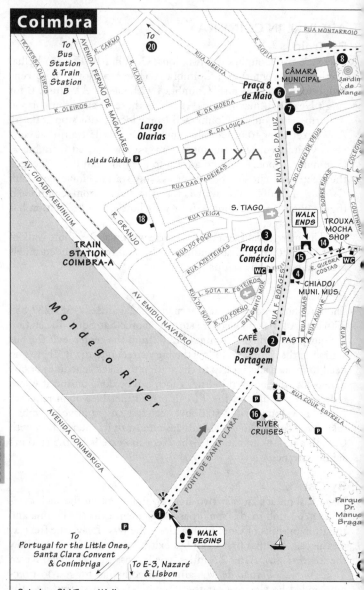

Coimbra

To Bus Station & Train Station B

To 20

TRAVESSA OLEIROS

R. CARMO

AVENIDA FERNÃO DE MAGALHÃES

R. OLÃO

R. OLEIROS

RUA DIREITA

RUA MONTARROIO

RUA SOFIA

CÂMARA MUNICIPAL

Jardim de Manga 8

Praça 8 de Maio 6

7

R. DA MOEDA

RUA VISC. DA LUZ

R. DO CORPO DE DEUS

AV. CIDADE AEMINIUM

Largo Olarias

Loja da Cidadão P

B A I X A

RUA DAS PADEIRAS

5

R. DA LOUÇA

R. SOBRE RIBAS

R. COUTINH

R. COLÉG

TRAIN STATION COIMBRA-A

R. GRANJO

18

RUA VEIGA

S. TIAGO

WALK ENDS

TROUXA MOCHA SHOP

14

RUA DO POÇO

RUA AZEITEIRAS

3

Praça do Comércio

15

WC

R. QUEBRA COSTAS

AV. EMIDIO NAVARRO

WC

L. SOTA R. ESTEIROS

RUA DA SOTA B. DO FORNO

SARGENTO MOR

RUA F. BORGES

4

CHIADO/ MUNI. MUS.

RUA TOMÁS

RUA AGUIAR

RUA ILHA

M o n d e g o   R i v e r

CAFÉ

2

PASTRY

Largo da Portagem

AVENIDA CONIMBRIGA

P

i

RUA COUR. ESTRELA

P

16

RIVER CRUISES

P

PONTE DE SANTA CLARA

1

Parque Dr. Manue Braga

WALK BEGINS

To Portugal for the Little Ones, Santa Clara Convent & Conímbriga

To E-3, Nazaré & Lisbon

Coimbra Old Town Walk

1 Santa Clara Bridge
2 Largo da Portagem
3 Praça do Comércio
4 Chiado Building/ Municipal Museum
5 Bragas Men's Store

6 Church of Santa Cruz
7 Café Santa Cruz
8 Jardim da Manga
9 Mercado Municipal
10 Elevador do Mercado

COIMBRA

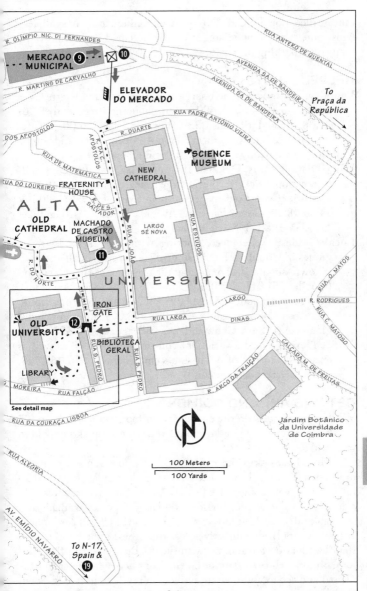

COIMBRA

⑪ Machado de Castro Museum/
Cryptoporticus
⑫ Iron Gate to Old University
⑬ Café Sé Velha
⑭ Fado ao Centro
⑮ Arco de Almedina

Other
⑯ River Cruises
⑰ To Kayak Tours
⑱ InterVisa Travel Agency (Bus Tickets)
⑲ To Pedro & Inês Bridge
⑳ To Launderette

office called Loja da Cidadão (on Avenida Fernão de Magalhães). Most hotels can provide advice on the best parking options, and many offer parking in city lots (about €5/day).

HELPFUL HINTS

Laundry: A modern, self-service **Lavamais** launderette is a 10-minute walk north of the main shopping street (daily 8:00-22:00, Rua Mário Pais 22, mobile +351 914 376 001). Cafés within two nearby grocery stores—Continente and Pingo Doce—are handy for passing the time.

Long-Distance Bus Tickets: The **InterVisa travel agency** sells international tickets. They charge a small commission, but it's worth it if you need in-person help (Mon-Fri 9:30-13:00 & 14:30-18:30, closed Sat-Sun, Avenida Fernão da Magalhães 11, +351 239 823 873).

Local Guides: I've enjoyed working with several good private guides in Coimbra. Each can give you a private half-day tour in town (about €100) or around the region: **Cristina Carvalho** (mobile +351 917 200 180, ccfb64@hotmail.com), **Maria Jose Fernandes** (mobile +351 934 093 542, mariajf76@gmail.com), and **Rosa Lopez** (mobile +351 966 103 277, mrosatoscano@gmail.com). **Sara Cruz** and her colleagues at **Go! Leisure & Heritage** lead a variety of cultural town walks, as well as excursions to out-of-town sights (mobile +351 910 163 118, www.gowalksportugal.com).

GETTING AROUND COIMBRA

While most visitors do the entire city on foot, **taxis** are cheap (€5 for a short ride) and a good option if you've been up and down too many hills.

Most **buses** skip the old town, but a few run through the university. You can buy a ticket for €1.60 per ride; or pay €0.50 for a rechargeable Viagem ConVIDA card for cheaper fares (€1/ride; better-value 3-ride, 10-ride, and one-day passes available and shareable; all are sold at kiosks or the Loja SMTUC offices—one is at Santa Clara Bridge directly across from the TI and another is at the Elevador do Mercado, www.smtuc.pt). Bus passes are also valid for Coimbra's **elevator/funicular** that runs between Mercado Municipal and the top of town (described on my "Coimbra Old Town Walk," later), and for the electric minibus that shuttles between the lower and upper town (described next).

This cute little Blue Line electric **minibus** (nicknamed *pantufinhas*, or "grandma's slipper") is silent and easy, designed to get grandmas—and anyone else—up and down the steep hills of the old town. It makes a continuous 20-minute loop through the lower old town (Baixa) and around the upper old town (Alta), passing through Largo da Portagem, down the pedestrian shopping lane to Praça 8 de Maio, past the market and elevator/funicular, then circling up to the cathedral (the bus' high point) before returning down to Largo da Portagem. There are just three regular stops—but you can wave down the bus anywhere you like, and the driver will let you off wherever you ask (€1.60, pay driver or use Viagem ConVIDA card). The loop route makes for a fun joyride.

Coimbra Old Town Walk

Coimbra is fun on foot, especially along its straight (formerly Roman) pedestrian-only main drag. This self-guided tour takes about an hour—but if you visit every sight en route (including the university), it could fill the better part of a day.

• *Start your walk at the far end of the...*

❶ Santa Clara Bridge (Ponte de Santa Clara)

This bridge has been an important link across the Mondego River since Roman times. For centuries, it had a tollgate *(portagem)*. The far end of the bridge offers a fine Coimbra view.

Until recently, Coimbra planned to redevelop its long-neglected riverside, but a flood washed away those dreams. Today it's a simple park (on the right) leading to the pedestrian bridge named for Dom Pedro and Dona Inês (Portugal's Romeo and Juliet—see page 297).

• *At the end of the Santa Clara Bridge on the Coimbra side is the parklike square called...*

❷ Largo da Portagem

In the center of the main square is a statue of the prime minister who, in 1834, shut down the city's convents and monasteries, earning him the nickname "friar killer." As elsewhere in Europe, Portugal's monasteries were the leading landowner in society and extremely powerful. They were seen as antiprogress and antimodernity, blocking the reforms that were sweeping Europe in the age of Napoleon and after the French Revolution. States or monarchs, wanting to run with the Industrial Revolution and new ideas—and wanting the Church's land—"dissolved" the monasteries, opening the way to the march of modernity in Europe.

Much of the old center is ornamented with fin-de-siècle

COIMBRA

Coimbra in History

1064 Coimbra is taken from the Moors.

1139 Portugal's first king, Afonso Henriques, makes Coimbra his capital.

1211 Portugal's first parliament of nobles *(cortes)* convenes at Coimbra.

1256 Lisbon replaces Coimbra as Portugal's capital.

1308 The university (founded in Lisbon in 1290 under King Dinis, r. 1279-1325) moves to Coimbra.

1537 The university, after another short stint in Lisbon, resettles permanently in Coimbra under Jesuit administration.

1810 Napoleon's French troops sack Coimbra, then England's duke of Wellington drives them out.

1928 António Salazar, professor of political economy at Coimbra, becomes minister of finance and eventually dictator of Portugal.

architecture (circa 1900) from a boom period; on the left side of the square, notice the fancy pink bank building and the exterior of Hotel Astória behind it.

This square is a great place for coffee or a pastry. The best goodies are at **Pastelaria Briosa,** at the start of the main drag; enjoy their creative window displays. The shop's name, meaning "pure, proud, respectable," is the nickname for the people of Coimbra (and their football team): Go Briosa! Another popular place is **Café Montanha,** with a big brass palm tree inside and delightful seating on the square. The town's two special treats are *pastel de Santa Clara* (pastry made with almonds and marmalade) and *pastel de Tentúgal* (rolls of puff pastry filled with sweet custard and dusted with powdered sugar).

• *Stroll down the delightfully pedestrianized Rua de Ferreira Borges. After about 200 yards, take the stairs (on your left, under the gigantic graffiti portrait of what looks like Sigmund Freud) leading to a terrace overlooking the square below (pay public WCs—sanitários—are in the stairwell).*

❸ Praça do Comércio

This pleasant square is, literally, the place of commerce. It was originally just outside the city walls—a kind of medieval duty-free zone where merchants could trade tax-free. The streets branching off the square were named for the type of product traditionally made or traded there (such as Rua das Azeiteiras, named for olive oil pro-

COIMBRA

ducers). Two churches bookending the square are a reminder that religious orders also set up just outside the city walls. Beyond Praça do Comércio stretches the rough end of town.

Look at your map. The circular street pattern outlines the wall used by Romans, Visigoths, Moors, and Christians to protect Coimbra. Historically, only the rich could afford to live within the protective city walls of the Alta, or high town.

This square, the district beyond it, and the street you have been strolling along are all undergoing a sad change. Malls are pulling businesses to the suburbs. And a rising tide of tourism is changing the character of this venerable downtown. While there are plenty of shops selling cork souvenirs, there's less and less here for locals.

• *Return to the pedestrian street.*

Rua de Ferreira Borges to the Church

Across the way, notice the balconied building trimmed with lacy ironwork. This innovative iron structure, which opened as the ❹ **Chiado** department store in 1909, was big news in town when it was built. (Today it's the Municipal Museum, with textiles and artwork; see "More Sights in Coimbra," later.)

Next door is **Casa da Sorte,** a lottery shop—these are much loved in Portugal. Step inside and feel the energy of gamblers unwittingly letting the state take their money to fund social programs. What's the total for the Euromilhões (European-wide "euro millions" lottery)? You may see circles of friends huddling here who've invested collectively in a gambling partnership. (If you like to send postcards, this shop is a convenient place to buy stamps.)

At the corner (on your right), steps lead up through an ancient arched gateway—**Arco de Almedina**—into the old city and to the old cathedral and university. Later, after visiting the university, we'll finish this walk by going downhill through this arch.

A block farther along the pedestrian drag, stop at the picturesque corner (where the building comes to a triangular corner). The steep road to your right climbs into Coimbra's historic former Jewish quarter.

Stick with the main drag and check out the newsstands, where the daily papers have mostly sport news fixated on football (meaning soccer). The ❺ **Bragas men's store** (near the end of the street, on the right at #35), with hats and ties, is one of a shrinking number of old-time shops left on this street.

• *The pedestrian street ends at Praça 8 de Maio, with the...*

❻ Church of Santa Cruz (Mosteiro de Santa Cruz)

Enjoy this church's grand facade. While almost invisible, wires on the statuary are electrified to keep pigeons from dumping their cor-

rosive loads on the tender limestone. Go inside; it's the most
active religious spot in town.

Cost and Hours: Church-
free, sacristy-€3; Mon-Sat 9:00-
17:00 except closed Sat 12:00-
14:00, Sun 16:00-17:30; limited
access during Mass.

Visiting the Church: The
musty church is lavishly deco-
rated with 18th-century tiles that tell the stories of the discovery of
the Holy Cross (by Roman Emperor Constantine's mother, Saint
Helena, on the left) and the life of St. Augustine (on the right; the
church is of the Augustinian order).

Head up the nave, pausing at the side altar on the left (under
the organ with horizontal trumpets). Here you see St. Anthony
of Padua—known locally as St. Anthony of Lisbon (his birthplace)—dressed as an Augustinian monk. He studied in Coimbra
as a young monk in the 13th century. Just beyond the chapel, the
exquisitely carved pulpit is considered one of the finest pieces of
Renaissance work in Portugal.

• *From the sacristy (entrance to right of main altar), you can reach the
treasures of the church, get a close up look at some historic tombs, and
pass through the impressive chapter room into the Manueline Cloister
of Silence.*

Sacristy: The first room is the actual sacristy, with "carpet
tiles" blanketing the walls and huge banks of drawers for priests'
vestments.

Treasury: The room to the right has relics, including the skull
of St. Teotonio, the first Portuguese saint. (St. Teotonio's tomb is
in the chapter room, described later.)

Tombs: Head behind the high altar for a close-up look at
two fine 16th-century tombs. On the left lies the first Portuguese
king, Afonso "The Conqueror" Henriques (1109-1185). Afonso reclaimed most of Portugal from the Moors, declared himself king,
got the pope to approve the title, and settled down in his chosen
capital—Coimbra. His wife Mafalda of Savoy (1125-1157) gave
birth to young Sancho, who later became king. Sancho I (1154-
1211, tomb on right) was known as "The Populator." He saw the
destruction that war had brought to the country, and set about rebuilding and repopulating, inviting northern European Crusaders
(such as the Knights Templar) to occupy southern Portugal and
giving trade privileges to border towns to strengthen his country's
economy.

These tombs are carved in the richly ornamented Manueline
style. In the 16th century, while headed on a pilgrimage to San-

tiago de Compostela, King Manuel I dropped by this church and was underwhelmed by the two kings' original tombs. He commissioned these beautifully carved replacements—much more fitting for royalty. Study the intimate faces. Notice how the kings seem only to be resting. (To make themselves more comfortable, they've "hung" their helmets and arm guards just behind them.)

Chapter Room and Cloister: In the **chapter room**, note the painting of the Augustinian monks. Imagining you are a fellow monk, step outside into the **Cloister of Silence,** with its fine Manueline arches and late-18th-century tiled scenes of Christ teaching the beatitudes. Walk pensively clockwise, hands folded, pondering worshipfully each parable from Matthew and Luke

as a meditative monk would have in this space 200 years ago. Feel the tranquility. Notice that you are walking upon the tombs of the very monks who took this same stroll so long ago—and who chose to be buried so humbly. You're in the city center, but here, in the Cloister of Silence, about the only sound is the gurgle of the fountain. From here, stairs lead to the sanctuary and choir.

• *Exit the church into the main square. Once called the Square of Samson, it was renamed Praça 8 de Maio to mark May 8, 1833—the date when French Revolutionary ideas arrived in Portugal (a little behind the European trends, as usual for this country) and the state asserted its secular power over the Church. People (and pigeons) survey the scene from the terrace of the recommended...*

COIMBRA

❼ Café Santa Cruz

This coffeehouse was originally built as a church. It was abandoned with the dissolution of the monasteries in the 1830s, when the government took possession of many grand religious buildings and their surrounding land. As a café, this was the 19th-century haunt of the town's intellectuals. The altar is now used for lectures, poetry readings, small concerts, and art exhibits (the women's restroom is in a former confessional). They offer free fado performances many nights at 18:00 and 22:00.

• *Continue past the church and the City Hall (Câmara Municipal). At the noisy street, turn right, and go a block to find a park with a fountain.*

❽ Jardim da Manga (Garden of the Sleeve)

In the early 1500s this Renaissance garden decorated the cloister of the Santa Cruz monastery. It symbolizes the source of life in the middle of paradise (the garden) with four flowing rivers (the fountain) bringing life in all directions (the four cardinal points). Supposedly King João III drew his design for the fountain on his sleeve—hence the name. The cheap, handy, and recommended self-service restaurant Jardim da Manga is just behind the fountain.

• *Keep going uphill along the busy Rua Olímpio Nicolau di Fernandes past the blocky former post office to the...*

❾ Mercado Municipal

This modern covered market is fun to explore and great for gathering picnic supplies (Mon-Sat 8:00-14:00, closed Sun, busiest Tue and Fri). It's clean and hygienic, but maintains the colorful appeal of an old farmers market. See the "salt of the earth" in the faces of the women selling produce (their men are off in the fields...or in the bars—a.k.a. their beloved "little chapels"). These ladies aren't shy about trying to sell their goods, even to tourists.

For about the cheapest meal in town, pop into the Bar do Mercado Requinte at the end of the ground floor (menu posted on wall, €7 meals for two, public WC around the corner). In the bar's sit-down area, check out the photos of the old market on the wall. Then go upstairs for bread, more meat, and veggies. Follow your nose through the glass doors at the far end, with all the fresh fish and dried cod. The Portuguese are the world's  biggest cod eaters, but because cod is no longer found in nearby waters, the local favorite is imported from Norway. To the Portuguese, cod *(bacalhau)* tastes much better after having been dried, salted, and reconstituted than fresh. This section housed the original market—you can recognize the wrought-iron work from the photos you've just seen on the ground floor at the bar.

• *Swim through the fish hall and head outside at the far end, where you'll find the sleek city elevator/funicular.*

❿ Elevador do Mercado to the University

A combination elevator/funicular ride whisks you up the long, steep hill, offering commanding views of Coimbra en route (€1.60/trip, €1 with Viagem ConVIDA card, buy tickets from adjacent office or pay the attendant; Mon-Sat 7:30-21:00, Sun from 10:00).

You'll start in an elevator, then stop midway to transfer to a funicular. At the top, jog right, then head straight uphill (on Rua da Couraça Apóstolos) toward the university buildings at the top of the hill. Fifty yards up this lane, at the first intersection, you'll find a fraternity house called Real República Corsários das Ilhas ("Royal Commune of the Island Pirates"). Notice the faded skull-and-crossbones graffiti on the wall, linking McDonald's and the G8 (group of the eight most powerful countries). Look around for other graffiti. These small university frat houses, called *repúblicas*, are communes that traditionally housed about a dozen students from the same region or provincial town. These days, *repúblicas* also gather according to passion or personal philosophy (feminists, nonconformists, internationalists, etc.). While some are highly cultured, the rowdier ones are often decorated with plunder from their pranks—stolen traffic signs and so on—giving rise to the local saying, "At night, many things happen in Coimbra."

• *Continue walking. Across the street and uphill, you'll see the New Cathedral and some stark university buildings. Behind the cathedral is the* **Science Museum** *(you may want to detour and visit it first; it's included in the university ticket and they may be able to book your library reservation).*

On the right, you'll pass the ❶ **Machado de Castro Museum** *(visit on your way back downhill at the end of this walk; they also have a handy lunch buffet; described on page 329).*

Soon you pop out into the big, fascist-style university square (Praça da Porta Férrea). The **Iron Gate** *entry to the old university is on your right.*

❷ University

Explore the university (described later, under "Sights in Coimbra"), and then continue this town walk.

• *When you're finished, leave the university: Pass back out through the Iron Gate, turn left down the stairs, and, if you like, visit the Machado de Castro Museum. Then follow the steep lanes toward the old cathedral and into the old town. (If you've visited the Roman substructure inside the museum, seeing these stout walls and steep slope helps you understand the need for a sturdy foundation to support a sprawling and level market square, or forum.) Farther down, look through the metal grates on your right to see the old Roman street and remains of ancient houses.*

Downhill Streets Through the Upper Town

As you wander, notice the dark and abandoned buildings—many are victims of rent control (no profit for landlords resulting in no investment in the real estate) or inheritance squabbles where the actual ownership is in question so the building sits idle. If you notice white-paper squares and diamonds in the windows, these indicate that there's a student room available for rent.

Continuing on, you'll come to the **old cathedral** (Sé Velha, described later, under "Sights in Coimbra"). The colorful little ❸ **Café Sé Velha,** below the cathedral and tiled with traditional

Coimbran scenes, is a good place to sit and watch people climb up and down. From here, a very faded blue line on the cobbles marks the route of the electric minibus: If you happen to see the yellow minibus, hop on for the loop.

Take the steep stairway leading down (past the public WCs). This delightful quarter comes to musical life summer evenings with outdoor jazz. Next, you reach the **Rua Quebra Costas,** the "Street of Broken Ribs." At one time, this lane had no steps, and literally *was* the street of broken ribs. During a strong rain, this becomes a river. The lane's many tourist and gift shops show off the fine local blue-and-white ceramic work called *faiança*.

Descending farther, you emerge into a little square ringed by enticing al fresco cafés and funky shops catering to a mix of tour-

ists and students. On your left, the **Trouxa Mocha** shop has appealing clothes (leather shoes, wool sweaters) and accessories with modern style, but rooted in Portuguese tradition. Just below that shop, notice the statue of **Tricana** (the term given for a local woman in traditional folk dress) resting after a trip to the well. She represents the usual target of fado love songs—and student Romeos. Local men from the lower town had a tough time competing for the Tricana of Coimbra with all the rich and witty students... not to mention the talented singers. Across the street from Tricana is the recommended ⓮ **Fado ao Centro,** my favorite place in town for getting a concise and appealing taste of Coimbra's unique take on this Portuguese musical form—consider making a reservation now for a performance (see "Entertainment in Coimbra," later, for details).

• *Rua Quebra Costas ends at...*

⓯ Arco de Almedina

This is the double set of arches (named "Gate to the Medina" in Arabic by the Moors) we saw earlier from the pedestrian street Rua de Ferreira Borges. Part of the old town wall, the arches act as a double gate with a 90-degree kink in the middle for easier defense. Pause at the gift shop between the gates to enjoy the lilting, nostalgic sound of fado and the 12-string Portuguese guitar. That's sweet. But don't linger too long because—

look up: In times of attack, soldiers used those two square holes in the ceiling to pour down boiling oil, turning attacking Moors into fritters. The holes are rudely nicknamed *mata-cães* (dog killers).

A few steps farther down, before the second gate, admire from all sides the monument to fado. Featuring the Coimbra-style Portuguese guitar, draped both with the cape of the male student and the shawl of the woman, this bronze statue celebrates how fado connected the all-male-at-the-time university world with the women of the town. Locals say a good musician plays his guitar with art and passion, as if loving a woman.

• *Passing under the second arch, you're back on the pedestrian street near where this walk began.*

Sights in Coimbra

UNIVERSITY OF COIMBRA (UNIVERSIDADE DE COIMBRA)

This venerable centuries-old university, founded in 1290 and worth ▲▲, was modeled after Bologna's university (Europe's first, founded in 1139). It occu-

pies a stately three-winged former royal palace (from when Coimbra was Portugal's capital), beautifully situated overlooking the city. At first, law, medicine, grammar, and logic were taught. Then, with the rise of seafaring in Portugal, astronomy and geometry were added. While Lisbon's university is much larger, Coimbra's university (with 25,000 students) is still the country's most respected. For visitors, the university marks the top of the old town.

While most of it is mid-20th-century sprawl, the old core of the university (*velha universidade*—the palace section, with its Iron Gate, courtyard, fancy ceremonial halls, chapel, and library) makes for an interesting visit. It's free to see the gate, courtyard, and a few halls, but you'll need a ticket for the other sights, along with a timed entry for the best part—King João's Library.

Cost: €12.50, €7 without library (mainly intended for those who arrive without advance library reservations), both tickets include nearby Science Museum, €2 extra for tower climb (I'd skip it).

Hours: Daily 9:00-19:30 (ticket office opens at 8:45), Nov-March Mon-Fri 9:30-13:00 & 14:00-17:00, Sat-Sun 10:00-16:00.

Information: +351 239 242 745, www.uc.pt/turismo.

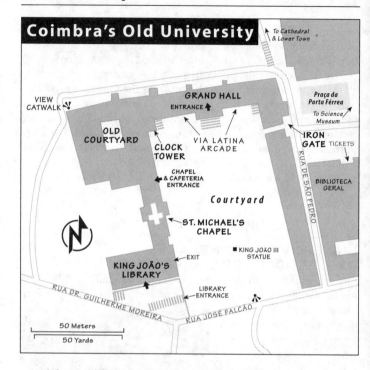

Coimbra's Old University

To Cathedral & Lower Town

VIEW CATWALK

OLD COURTYARD

GRAND HALL
ENTRANCE

Praça da Porta Férrea

To Science Museum

VIA LATINA ARCADE

CLOCK TOWER

IRON GATE TICKETS

RUA DE SÃO PEDRO

BIBLIOTECA GERAL

CHAPEL & CAFETERIA ENTRANCE

Courtyard

N

ST. MICHAEL'S CHAPEL

KING JOÃO III STATUE

EXIT

KING JOÃO'S LIBRARY

LIBRARY ENTRANCE

RUA DR. GUILHERME MOREIRA

RUA JOSÉ FALCÃO

50 Meters

50 Yards

Advance Tickets: King João's Library, the complex's highlight, is accessible only via a timed-entry ticket. To be sure you get in to this popular sight, book a time in advance on their website, https://visit.uc.pt/en/space-list/joanina. Tickets are also sold inside the Biblioteca Geral (the large building to the left as you approach the Iron Gate), and at the Science Museum. If you don't have an advance ticket, arrive by 10:00 or try buying your ticket at the Science Museum, where there's often no ticket-buying line—however, you won't get in to the library if it's already booked up.

Getting There: To reach the university, you could take my "Coimbra Old Town Walk" (described earlier), using the elevator/funicular from the Mercado Municipal to reach the top of the hill. Or take a taxi to the Iron Gate (on Praça da Porta Férrea), see the university, and then sightsee Coimbra on a downhill walk. For directions to the Science Museum from the Iron Gate, see page 328.

Planning Your Visit: The self-guided tour of the university takes less than an hour. Plan your visit around your timed-entry to King João's Library. The university can be seen in any order, but go to the Science Museum either first or last—it's farthest from the library (about a 10-minute walk) and also takes about an hour to see.

Tours: The €3 audioguide provides 1.5 hours of info.

◯ Self-Guided Tour

• *Begin your visit just outside the entrance to the old campus, at the...*

Iron Gate (Porta Férrea)

Before entering the old campus, stand with your back to the Iron Gate and look across the stark, modern square at the fascist architecture of the new university. In the 1940s, in what's considered one of the worst cultural crimes in Portuguese history, the dictator António Salazar tore down half of Coimbra's old town to build these university halls. The grandiose ceremonial approach to the university, bombastic and utilitarian to fit fascist taste, is flanked by the faculties of letters, medicine, science, and a new library (with the ticket office). The law school is behind you, inside the old campus.

Salazar, proud that Portugal was the last European power to hang onto its colonial empire, wanted a fittingly monumental university here. After all, Salazar—along with virtually everyone of political influence in Portugal—had been educated at Coimbra, where he studied law and then became an economics professor. If these bold buildings are reminiscent of Mussolini's E.U.R. in Rome, perhaps it's because they were built in part by Italian architects hired by Portugal's "little Mussolini."

OK, now turn and walk through the Iron Gate, noticing the bits of graduation robe in the grill, the remains of robes ripped by loved ones on that happy day. Traditionally, freshmen—proudly wearing their black capes for the first time—pass through the Iron Gate to enroll. Also traditionally, they had to pass through an Iron Gate gauntlet of butt kicks from upperclassmen to get out.

University Courtyard

The university's most important sights all face this square: the Grand Hall (up the grand stairway on the right), St. Michael's Chapel (straight ahead, through the door, then to the left), and King João's Library (across the square, farthest door on left, flanked by columns, timed entry required).

The statue in the square is of **King João III** (1502-1557). While the university was established in 1290, it went back and forth between Lisbon and Coimbra (back then, university students were adults, privileged, and a pain to have in your town). In 1537, João III finally established the school permanently in Coimbra. Standing like a good humanist (posing hand on hip, much like we're used to seeing his contemporary, England's King Henry VIII), João modernized Portugal's education system in the Renaissance style. But, unlike Henry, who broke the local power of the Church, João (grandson of the ultra-Catholic Queen Isabel of Spain) empowered the Church. He let the Jesuits—the guardians of orthodoxy—run this university, which became the center of Portugal's Inquisition.

COIMBRA

The black capes famously worn by local students originated with the capes worn by Jesuits and clergy during this period. Like the uniforms of students at American Catholic schools, standardized clothing removes the focus on power-dressing and equalizes people of all classes. To this day, standards of modesty prevail, keeping class divisions at a minimum among the students, and between students and professors. (Students, when wearing their gowns, are not allowed to show off by wearing gold.)

Survey the square with your back to the gate. The dreaded sound of the clock tower's bell—named the "baby goat" for its nagging—calls students to class. On several occasions, the clapper has been stolen. (No bell...no class. No class...big party.) A larger bell (the "big goat") rings only on important, formal occasions.

The arcaded passageway (on the right, up the stairs) between the Iron Gate and the clock tower is called Via Latina, from the days when only Latin was spoken in this part of the university.

• Now visit each of the university's sights, beginning with the...

Grand Hall (Sala dos Capelos)

From the middle of the Via Latina, climb the tiled stairway. Follow the route through an ornate room, then trudge around a narrow hallway, where you can peek out from little balconies into the Grand Hall—the site of the university's major academic ceremonies, such as oral exams and graduations. This regally red room was originally the throne room of the royal palace. Today, the rector's green chair sits high like a throne in front. Students defend their Ph.D. thesis here, sitting all alone at a small table before a jury of professors. During ceremonies, students in their formal attire fill

the benches, and teachers sit along the perimeter as gloomy portraits of Portuguese kings watch from above.

The fine, old, painted ceiling features "Indo-Portuguese" themes, reminding Portugal's next generation of leaders of the global reach of their nation. There is no clapping during these formal rituals, but a brass band (on the wooden platform in the back) punctuates the ceremonies with solemn music.

Continue past the end of the Grand Hall, to an ornately decorated

The Burning of Ribbons

Europe's third-oldest university has long-standing traditions to match. If you're lucky enough to be in Coimbra at the end of the academic year (early to mid-May), you'll witness a big party.

The "Burning of Ribbons" *(Queima das Fitas)* began in the 1850s, when a group of students who passed their final fourth-year exams gathered outside the Iron Gate and marched together to the lower town. They burned their ribbons (which were used to bind and carry their books) in a small fire, representing their passage from student life to professional life. Eventually, that simple event evolved into the biggest academic festival of the year, complete with floats and parades.

Students entering their last year of studies as well as recent graduates *(finalistas)* participate in the party these days, but of course the graduates get the most attention. Women wear simple white shirts with black skirts and black stockings. Men dress more formally in a long black suit, university cape, wide sash with various badges, top hat, and cane.

Different accent colors, proudly displayed on the top hats and canes, represent the different academic departments, indicating which degree the student earned (yellow for medicine, red for law, blue for science, and so on). For good luck after graduation, men take their canes and tap other students' top hats three times. (The taps can get out of control, and lots of students end up losing the tops of their hats.)

Much drinking accompanies this rite of passage. Ribbon-burning parties are also celebrated in Porto, and to a lesser extent in Lisbon. Join the fun, and offer an appropriately colored flower to a new graduate. You may be invited to the party.

former royal stateroom (where, until recently, students took their oral exams as portraits of past university rectors looked on). The ceiling has medallions representing the old faculties. (Identify them: medicine, canon law, civil law, and theology.)

• *Just past this room, a door leads to a narrow observation gallery offering the best views of Coimbra. If the door is closed, open it (it's locked in bad weather).*

View Catwalk (Varanda)

From the viewpoint, scan the old town from right to left. Remember, before Salazar's extension of the university, this old town completely surrounded the university. The Baroque facade breaking the horizon is the "new" cathedral—from the 16th century. Below that, with the fine arcade and modern café terrace, is the Machado de Castro Museum, housed in the former bishop's palace and located atop a Roman site (all described later). And below that, like an armadillo, sits the old cathedral with its tiled cupola.

Gaily painted yellow-and-blue windows mark *república* frat houses. If you visit during late October or November, you might see a student festival: Parades of rowdy students in funny costumes, draped in signs, dragging tin cans—these are all part of the traditional initiation rites marking the beginning of the school year. May provides the biggest spectacle, when new students receive—and graduating students burn—the small colored ribbons of their chosen major (see sidebar). Look beyond the houses to the Mondego River, the longest river that flows entirely in Portugal.

Over the bridge, beyond the university's sports facilities, stretches the restored 17th-century Santa Clara Convent—at 590 feet, the longest building in Coimbra. It's better known as the place where Inês (of Pedro and Inês fame) was murdered (for more on their tragic love story, see the sidebar on page 297).

• *From here stairs lead down to the original heart of the university—an arcaded courtyard with a gathering of old classrooms.*

Old University Courtyard

The university was not purpose built. It inhabited the 15th century royal palace and incorporated existing palace rooms into the plan according to the needs of the school in about 1600: The throne room became the Grand Hall, the prison became the prison, the guard room became the guard room, and this courtyard ringed by royal quarters became the heart of the school surrounded by the earliest classrooms.

Imagine this courtyard in 1600, with its fine Renaissance columns and the buzz of its students. Then observe the scene today. It's still the haunt of law students—taking a cigarette break, checking their phones, some working on the side as museum guards. Walk around. Peek into a classroom if possible. Inside, look high up in the corner of any room for a small balcony. This was used by the rector to spy down on professors. Anyone not sticking to the orthodoxy on the hot button issues of the day (climate change, civil liberties, corporate regulations, and women's rights issues of the 17th century) would spend some time in the university prison.

• *Stairs lead down to St. Michael's Chapel and the student cafeteria. If you end up back on the square, the chapel is behind a 16th-century facade (enter through door to the right of facade)—once inside, knock on the door on the left marked* capela.

St. Michael's Chapel (Capela de São Miguel)

The architecture of the church interior is Manueline—notice the golden "rope" trimming the arch before the altar. The chapel was begun in 1517, but much of the decor is from a later time. The altar is 17th-century Mannerist, with steps unique to Portugal (and her South American colonies); based on Jacob's Ladder, they symbolize the steps the faithful take on their journey to heaven. The carpet-style tiles covering the walls date from the 17th century and kept the chapel cool in the summer. Find the sleepy Adam and Eve, fully clothed, flanking the top of the arch—simple beauty from about 1600. The 2,100-pipe, 18th-century German-built organ is notable for its horizontal "trumpet" pipes. Found only in Iberia, these help the organist perform the allegorical fight between good and evil—with the horizontal pipes trumpeting the arrival of the good guys. The box seats for the royal family are high above the musicians' loft in the rear. Students and alums enjoy the privilege of having their weddings here.

Student Cafeteria

In the corridor just outside the chapel, you'll find WCs, the official university gift shop, and a cheap student-filled café (follow signs to *bar*). Visitors are perfectly welcome to eat here. During busy lunch times, every seat gets taken, people share tables, and you may find yourself sitting with law students and their professors.

• *Back out on the square, as you face the statue of King João, you'll see his descendant's library poking out into the courtyard, at the end, on the right.*

▲King João's Library (Biblioteca Joanina)

In this elegant building, one of Europe's best surviving Baroque libraries displays 40,000 books in 18th-century splendor. Visitors gather below (follow the arrows around and down a set of stairs). At each appointed time, 60 visitors are let in. Each visit is 20 minutes: 10 minutes for the academic prison (a few dreary rooms for those breaking the rules of the sternly-run school) and a  floor of overflow book stacks under stout arches (not much to see), followed by 10 minutes in the library itself. Don't delay entering the library when the door into this 300-year-old temple of thought finally opens for you.

Inside, at the "high altar," stands the library's founder, the ab-

COIMBRA

solute monarch King João V (1698-1750), who considered France's King Louis XIV an inspiration (and they have similar hairstyles).

The reading tables, inlaid with exotic South American woods (and ornamented with silver ink wells), and the precious wood shelves (with clever hideaway staircases) are reminders that Portugal's wealth was great—and imported (mostly from Brazil). Built Baroque, the interior is all wood. Even the "marble" on the arches of triumph that divide the library into rooms is painted wood. (Real marble would add to the humidity.) The small doors with glass windows lead to professors' tiny studies with big windows to read by. The resident bats—who live in the building, but not the library itself—are well cared for and appreciated. They eat insects, providing a chemical-free way of protecting the books, and alert the guard to changing weather with their "eee-eee" cry.

Look for the trompe l'oeil Baroque tricks on the painted ceiling. Gold leaf (from Brazil) is everywhere, and the Chinese themes are pleasantly reminiscent of Portugal's once vast empire. The books, each dating from before 1755, are in Latin, Greek, and Hebrew. Imagine being a student in Coimbra centuries ago, when this temple of learning stored the world's knowledge like a vast filing cabinet (and consider how readily accessible the world of information is to our age). The zealous doorkeeper  opens the big front door sparingly to keep out humidity and only long enough to let you sneak quickly out.

• *The final university sight is about a 10-minute walk away. Exit the courtyard through the Iron Gate, walk to the end of the fascist-style square. After two blocks, at the rear of the big statue in the street, turn left and walk a couple of blocks along Rua Estudos. After the towering haunted hall of learning, you come to the last academic building on your right—marked* Laboratório Chimico. *It houses the...*

▲Science Museum (Museu da Ciência)

This old-school museum provides a peek into a grand, Old World lecture hall with elegant wood details (across from entry hall) and half a dozen venerable rooms filled with old science gear. English descriptions are good and attendants in the rooms are there to help answer your questions. The Cabinet of Physics (with dusty cases) displays 18th- and 19th-century models, and the Gallery of Zoology (with six rooms of stuffed animals and skeletons) includes a 65-foot-long whale skeleton and a herd of African ungulates, arranged by size. Many of these specimens date back 300 years or more, emphasizing the university's rich academic heritage.

Cost and Hours: €5, covered by both university tickets, daily 10:00-19:00, Largo Marquês de Pombal, +351 239 854 350, www. museudaciencia.org. If you didn't get your King João's Library timed-entry ticket online in advance, you could try coming here to buy it (if slots are still available) with shorter ticket-buying lines than at the university.

MORE SIGHTS IN COIMBRA
▲▲Machado de Castro Museum and Cryptoporticus of Aeminium

Housed in an elegant old bishop's palace, the huge Machado de Castro Museum (Museu Nacional Machado de Castro) has two

parts: the vast, barren understructure (Criptoportico de Aeminium) of the ancient Roman forum upon which the palace was built; and a fine collection of art through the ages, particularly strong on sculpture (including 14th- to 16th-century statues taken from dissolved monasteries). To save needless climbing, visit this sight before or after the old university (since both are at roughly the same altitude).

Cost and Hours: €6 for museum and Roman site, €3 for just the Roman site, free first Sun of every month, Wed-Sun 10:00-18:00, Tue from 14:00, closed Mon, audioguide-€1.50, Largo Dr. José Rodrigues, +351 239 853 070, www.museumachadocastro.pt.

Eating: At the entry level, you'll find Loggia, a recommended restaurant on a terrace with a fine old-town view).

Visiting the Museum: Follow the one-way route through several levels of the sprawling museum. Attendants will keep you on track. Everything is described in English.

Begin by descending to the **Roman ruins.** Aeminium was the Roman city that became Coimbra. Two thousand years ago, its two main streets crossed here, marking the forum. Because the city was built on a slope, a vast understructure was required to provide a level place for the town square (like a modern "daylight basement")—and that "cryptoporticus" is what survives today. Walking through the vast two-level maze of the stout, vaulted galleries, evocative and beautifully lit, will leave you marveling at what you can do with slave labor.

Back up on the main level, you're routed through the exten-

COIMBRA

sive, chronologically displayed **art collection,** starting with Roman and Romanesque fragments—a 2,000-year-old rubble layer-cake of Coimbra's past—and on to the museum's strongest collection: statues from the 14th, 15th, and 16th centuries. Many of these are refugees from the dissolution of the monasteries (in the 1830s, following Portugal's Civil War). The highlight is a powerfully realistic 14th-century *Cristo Negro*—an evocative, spindly armed, crucified Jesus—carved in wood. Until a decade ago, when this statue was cleaned (and the candle soot was removed), it was considered to be a portrait of a black Christ. If this dramatic statue has an impact on you today, imagine its power in the 14th century. Gothic lasted here long after the Renaissance hit Italy and France.

Just beyond that is the stately Renaissance Treasurer's Chapel, moved here from a now-gone 16th-century monastery. Viewing this, consider how Coimbra with its university was Portugal's center of humanism and the Renaissance. Coimbra helped lead the country into the modern age.

There's much more to see, but (unless you have a special interest) it's mostly skippable. As you explore, note how aspects of Moorish culture and design were absorbed into the Christian culture that threw them out. Downstairs on floor -1, you'll find terra cotta sculpture, and on floor -2, 17th-century Portuguese sculpture. From there, an elevator zips you up to floor 1: northern European statues and paintings (a reminder of this country's wealth in its Golden Age heyday), Portuguese paintings, precious metals (including some fine gold and silver sculptures), ceramics and tiles, and religious vestments. The finale is the treasury of Queen St. Isabel, who donated some of her finest possessions to Coimbra's Santa Clara Monastery.

▲Old Cathedral (Sé Velha)

Same old story for the Iberian Peninsula: Christians build a church on a pre-Christian holy spot (Visigoths in sixth century), Moors destroy the church and build a mosque (eighth century), then Christians push out the Moors (1064), tear down their mosque, and build another church (consecrated in 1184).

If this structure reminds you of Lisbon's cathedral, it should. As in Lisbon, this was essentially a church-fortress, built in the middle of the Reconquista and designed by the same French architect. Notice the crenellations along the roof of this Romanesque church; the Moors, though booted out, were still considered a risk.

Cost and Hours: Church and cloisters-€2.50, Mon-Sat 10:00-18:00, Sun generally 11:00-17:00.

Visiting the Cathedral: Before entering, stand back and study the **west portal** (the main entrance, facing downhill). Notice how Moorish-style columns are decorated by neo-Byzantine capitals, but there are no Christian motifs. It is an unbreakable facade—fortified and practical, complete with arrow slits.

The **north portal** (around the left side) was added later, in Renaissance times. Made of soft limestone, it was cheap and easy to carve but hasn't weathered very well.

Study the stone blocks of the main structure, set up in the 12th century. You can see mason's marks and even some Arabic writing (on a block six rows up by the north portal), indicating that the conquered Moors worked within Christian society.

Now enter the **interior.** At the start of the nave, the giant holy-water font shells are a 19th-century gift from Indonesia. The walls are lined with some of the oldest tiles in the country—imported in the 16th century from Sevilla, Spain.

Head up the right aisle. At the altar just before the transept is a murky **painting of Queen Isabel** (St. Elizabeth) with a skirt full of roses. This 13th-century Hungarian princess—with family ties to Portugal—is a local favorite with a sweet legend. Against the wishes of the king, she always gave bread to the poor. One day, when he came home early from a trip, she was busy doling out bread from her skirt. She pulled the material up to hide the bread. When the king asked her what was inside (suspecting bread for the poor), the queen—unable to lie—lowered the material and, miraculously, the bread had turned to roses. For her astonishing kindness, she was canonized as a saint in 1625.

At the front of the church, the **three altars** are each worth a look. The main altar, a fine example of the late Flamboyant Gothic style, was made by Flemish artists (circa 1500). The 16th-century chapel to the right contains one of the best Renaissance altars in the country. The apostles all look to Jesus as he talks, while musical angels flank the holy host. Notice how the Renaissance passion for balance and proportion trumped fact—the composition had room for only 10 apostles. To the left of the main altar, the Chapel of St. Peter shows Peter being crucified upside down.

The peaceful **cloister** (entrance near back of church, near the ticket desk) is the oldest Gothic cloister in Portugal. Well maintained with an inviting lawn, the courtyard offers a fine, framed view of the cathedral's dome. A tomb from 1064 in the cloister (middle of far side) belongs to Coimbra's first Christian post-Reconquista governor.

Chiado Building/Municipal Museum
(Edifício Chiado/Museu Municipal)

Originally the site of Coimbra's first Chiado department store (a chain common throughout Portugal in the early 20th century), this refurbished building is notable for its construction—it was one of the first structures in Portugal to be built around an iron framework, like the then-revolutionary American skyscrapers. It now houses an eclectic assortment of artworks and textiles donated by local collector José Telo de Morais.

Cost and Hours: €2, Tue-Fri 10:00-18:00, Sat-Sun 10:00-13:00 & 14:00-18:00, closed Mon, Rue Ferreira Borges 85, +351 239 857 525.

Visiting the Museum: Take the elevator up to the top floor and walk your way down, noticing the exposed iron beams. The third floor has ceramics, drawings, and a collection of silverware. The second floor has 17th- and 18th-century furniture as well as religious paintings and objects. The first floor holds oil and pastel paintings from the 19th and early 20th centuries. The ground floor houses a free temporary exhibit, and the small (and also free) Galeria Almedina, which highlights emerging student artists.

Parque Dr. Manuel Braga

Coimbra's pleasant riverside park sprawls upstream from the Santa Clara Bridge to the Pedro and Inês Bridge. While recent flooding blocked attempts to enliven this area with cafés and businesses, it's still pleasant to walk through the park, over the pedestrian bridge, and back to town with views from the far side of the river.

River Cruise

To take advantage of Coimbra's Mondego River, try a cruise: Basófias boats float up and down the river on a 50-minute joyride (€6.50, April-Sept Tue-Sun, a few departures each afternoon—ask at dock across from TI, no cruises Mon, no narration, mobile +351 969 830 664, www.odabarca.com). Or you could just take a nap in the park—just as exciting...and free.

Portugal for the Little Ones (Portugal dos Pequenitos)

Across the Santa Clara Bridge is a children's (or tourists') look at the great buildings and monuments of Portugal and its former empire in miniature, scattered through a park a couple of blocks south of town. The first section displays typical building types and artifacts from each of Portugal's former colonies (still part of the empire when this park was built). The next section merges bits and pieces of the most famous buildings in Portugal according to region—made mostly of stone. Wanting to boost national pride, Salazar commissioned architect Cassiano Branco to build these mini-replicas in 1940. If you've been through some of Portugal already, it's fun to try to identify the buildings you've already seen. The final section recreates different regional styles of houses, mixed in with statues of famous historical figures. Some buildings contain modern toys (building blocks and tiny cars) for kids of all ages to play with.

Cost and Hours: €10, €6 for kids 3-13, free for kids under 3, daily June-mid-Sept 9:00-20:00, mid-Sept-Feb 10:00-17:00, March-May until 19:00, Rossio de Santa Clara, +351 239 801 170, www.portugaldospequenitos.pt.

NEAR COIMBRA
▲Conímbriga Roman Ruins (Conímbriga Ruínas)

Portugal's best Roman sight is impressive...unless you've been to Rome. What remains of the Roman city of Conímbriga is divided

in two, in part because its inhabitants tore down buildings to erect a quick defensive wall against an expected barbarian attack. You'll see what's left of homes, shops, and baths from the second and third centuries AD (some remnants are even older),

amazingly detailed mosaic floors, and peaceful gardens. Informative exhibits tell the city's history with excavated artifacts at the on-site museum.

Cost and Hours: €4.50, covers ruins and museum, daily 10:00-19:00, ruins close at 17:30 in winter, last entry 45 minutes before closing, www.conimbriga.pt.

Getting There: The ruins are nine miles southwest of Coimbra, just outside the town of Condeixa-a-Nova on the road to Lisbon. **Buses** leave for the ruins across from Coimbra-A train station (€2.45; Mon-Fri at 9:00, 9:30, 12:30, and 15:00; Sat at 9:30, 12:30, and 15:30; Sun at 9:30, 12:30, and 15:00; on the river side, look for the *Joalto* or *Transdev* sign, 30-minute trip). Return buses leave from Conímbriga's parking lot (Mon-Fri at 12:55, 16:25, and 17:55; Sat at 13:25 and 18:25; Sun at 13:55 and 18:25). Confirm the destination by asking, *"Vai para Conímbriga?"* Avoid the frequent buses to Condeixa (twice hourly) that stop a mile short of the ruins. Figure about €20 one-way for a **taxi** from Coimbra.

Drivers find that Conímbriga fits well on a trip between Coimbra and points south; the Conímbriga freeway exit is clearly marked from the A-1. To get there from the town center, cross the Santa Clara Bridge and go uphill, following signs to *Condeixa*.

Continue straight through town, and you will see brown signs guiding you to the ruins.

Eating: The museum's café is a fine spot to have lunch before catching the return bus to Coimbra. Or bring a picnic lunch—there's a good picnic area between the museum and the ruins.

Visiting Conímbriga: Allow at least an hour to tour the site and museum. I prefer to visit the museum first and then see the ruins, but you may want to do it in the other order in summer, when the ruins can be blazing hot in the afternoon.

Purchase tickets at a counter located between the museum building and the ruins, and have a quick look at the scale **model** at the end of the ticket counter that shows the discoveries from decades of excavation. Next, head to the delightful **museum,** stepping into the patio first, designed to re-create a typical Roman house. Keep the layout of this space in mind when you visit the ruins to bring them to life.

Now check out the **artifacts** inside. The room to the left of the museum gift shop shows objects from daily life in Conímbriga. You'll see coins, dinnerware, plumbing, and even grooming utensils (find the spoon-shaped ear cleaners)—all with good English descriptions. The opposite room contains a dazzling miniature replica of the forum, along with fine mosaics, statues, and a few tombstones. The best mosaic is of the mythological, bull-headed Minotaur—follow the maze from the center until you are safely out.

Head back outside and walk past the ticket counter to reach the ruins. Explore the remnants of the **old town** first, and save the mansion—under the protective modern roofing—for the grand finale. You'll first see remains of different houses and shopping arcades, most with wonderful mosaics intact. Note how the columns are made of preformed wedges. When you're a long way from Rome, imitation marble does the trick.

Dominating the site is a stout **wall,** which locals hastily built for their own protection...and it shows. Once the Roman Empire retreated from this area, invaders from northern Europe went on the offensive (beginning around AD 465). A Christian Germanic tribe—the Sueves, sometimes called the Suebi—conquered the city. Follow the wall to find a large public bath complex, then skirt the wall to see an early Christian basilica, with part of its structure incorporated into the defensive wall. Further out are the theater and what little remains of the forum.

Head back to the main entrance and the opening in the wall. Just to the left, you'll see a reconstructed arch of an aqueduct. Finish your visit at the most important find (under a protective roof): The **House of the Fountains** (Casa dos Repuxos) is an entire dwelling, with most of its rooms and mosaics intact. Check out the cheap fountain show, which may seem lazy, but it's one of the few houses outside of Rome with this 2,000-year-old touch of elegance. Continue on the catwalks and look down to enjoy the stories told in the mosaics. Simple portraits, horses, and numerous hunting scenes illustrate the daily routine in this town during Roman times.

Entertainment in Coimbra

▲▲Fado Music

Portugal's unique, mournful traditional music—fado—is generally performed by women. But in Coimbra, young men sing fado. The best performers are probably at Fado ao Centro or àCapella. But you may get to enjoy an impromptu concert on the streets: Roving bands of male students—similar to the *tuna* bands in Spain's Salamanca—serenade around town for tips and the admirers' hearts.

Fado ao Centro is an all-male ensemble of current and former Coimbra university students who sing fado in the unique local style. The 50-minute shows, held in a cute little 50-seat hall, end with a glass of port and a little Q&A with the musicians (€10, daily at 18:00, occasionally also at 19:00). This is a nice alternative to late-night shows, but can be popular with tour groups; reservations are smart in summer. Call or drop in to reserve a seat (just uphill from the Arco de Almedina on Rua Quebra Costas 7, +351 239 837 060, www.fadoaocentro.com). Money raised here supports musicians and promotes local culture.

Fado Hilário is a tiny taverna offering nightly fado performances in a delightfully intimate venue (€10 cover includes one drink, daily at 18:45, Rua Joaquim António de Aguiar 110, mobile +351 911 505 770). The show includes a short English explanation between each song.

Café Santa Cruz offers free 45-minute fado performances most nights at 18:00 and 22:00 (no tickets, just drop in and buy a drink, April-Oct). While this is a bargain, the other venues listed here are more serious and worth the euros to experience the intensity of the genre.

àCapella, on the hill above the Church of Santa Cruz, offers an intimate fado nightclub experience. The chapel has been turned into a temple for Coimbra-style traditional music, and it's fado almost every night all year long (musicians perform from 21:30 to about 23:00). Come for the music, the cool scene, the slick background videos adding context to each song, and the snacks and drinks (€5 minimum purchase/person, reservations wise; at the triangular corner midway down the main drag, climb the steep Rua do Corpo de Deus 100 yards until you see the old chapel on your left; +351 239 833 985, www.acapella.com.pt). Dinner is best elsewhere; go here for the music.

Bar Diligência has showcased fado since 1972 in a very informal way—locals join in with performers and sing along as well (guitar and voice). The cave-like setting feels like a neighborhood hangout, and owners Jorge and Patricia make everyone feel at home. A wide selection of *petiscos* (Portuguese tapas) make it easy to put a meal together during the show. Along with the occasional sing-along, up-and-coming groups often play here. If the music moves you, jump right in (no cover, kitchen opens at 20:00, shows Mon-Sat 23:00 until late, closed Sun; from Praça 8 de Maio, take Rua Sofia to your second left—Bar Diligência is 2 blocks up on your right at Rua Nova 30; +351 239 827 667).

More Fado: The mayor organizes Thursday street concerts that feature fado music through the summer. And Restaurante O Trovador offers fado with its dinner service on summer weekends (Largo Sé Velha 15, +351 239 825 475, www.restaurantetrovador. com).

Kayaks and Adventure Sports

Kayaking: O Pioneiro do Mondego buses you from Coimbra to Penacova (15 miles away), where you can kayak four hours down the Mondego River back into Coimbra (€24.50, +351 239 478 385, www.opioneirodomondego.com, Kristien and Jonas speak English). Most people stop to swim or picnic on the way back, so it often turns into an all-day journey. For the first 12.5 miles, you'll go easily with the flow, but you'll get your exercise paddling the remaining stretch. To avoid the workout (and the more boring part of the Mondego River), ask to be picked up 2.5 miles before Coimbra, at Portela do Mondego, where the river's current slows down.

Adventure Sports: Located in the nearby town of Foz da Figueira, **Capitão Dureza** specializes in at-your-own-risk activities: rappelling, rafting, mountain biking, hiking, and canyoning (pickup and drop-off in Coimbra, +351 239 476 701, mobile +351 918 315 337, www.capitaodureza.com).

Sleeping in Coimbra

Coimbra's hotels are cheap...in every sense. Don't expect luxury here. These are basic, thin-walled, well-worn hotels where nighttime noise is par for the course. Most of these listings are just outside the central Coimbra-A station, within a few minutes' walk of the main drag, Santa Clara Bridge, and most recommended restaurants and sights in the lower town.

$$$ Hotel Tivoli Coimbra, a classy, Houston-esque skyscraper, is Coimbra's closest thing to contemporary luxury while still at a reasonable price. It rents 100 spacious (if faded) rooms with all the modern amenities, a 10-minute walk from Coimbra-A and the core (air-con, elevator, pay parking, Rua João Machado 4, +351 239 858 300, www.tivolicoimbra.com, htcoimbra@tivolihotels.com).

$$ Hotel Astória gives you the experience of staying in the city's finest (but desperately faded) old hotel with Coimbra's first Art Deco lounges. This venerable time warp, with 62 rooms, is overdue for a thorough renovation. In the meantime, it offers historical charm at reasonable prices. Rooms with river views cost the same, but come with some street noise. I prefer the quieter city-view rooms at the back (RS%, air-con, elevator, public parking opposite hotel, central as can be at Avenida Emídio Navarro 21, +351 239 853 020, www.astoria-coimbra.pt, astoria@almeidahotels.com).

$ Hotel Vitória is a well-located hotel renting 21 modern rooms over a good restaurant, between Coimbra-A and the main drag. Some rooms have uphill views to the university. In terms of value, quality, and location, this is the most appealing option in town (air-con, elevator, a block from Coimbra-A at Rua da Sota 9, +351 239 824 049, www.hotelvitoria.pt, reservas@hotelvitoria.pt).

$ Hotel Bragança's brown-on-brown lobby leads to 83 clean if outmoded rooms with modern bathrooms. The wood paneling and furniture transport you to the 1950s (RS%, family rooms, air-con, elevator, free parking in tiny lot at entrance if space available, Largo das Ameias 10 next to Station A, +351 239 822 171, www.hotel-braganca.com, geral@hotel-braganca.com).

$ Ibis Hotel, a modern high-rise, has 110 orderly little rooms that come with all the comforts. Well located near the riverside Parque Dr. Manuel Braga, this impersonal but reliable chain hotel is three blocks past the Santa Clara Bridge and the old town (breakfast extra, air-con, elevator, easy pay parking, Avenida Emídio Navarro 70, +351 239 852 130, https://ibis.accorhotels.com, h1672@accor.com).

$ RiverSuites offers 25 rooms just across the Santa Clara Bridge, overlooking the Santa Clara Convent. The five-minute walk from the hotel across the bridge comes with fine views of

COIMBRA

Coimbra Hotels & Restaurants

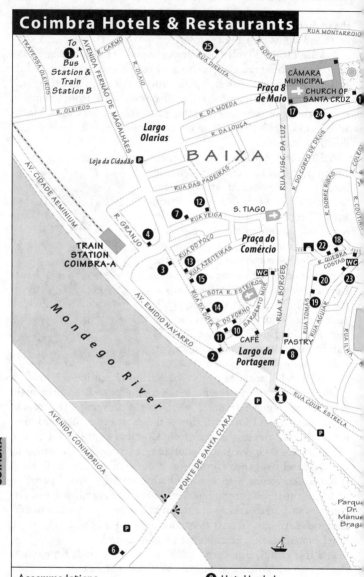

COIMBRA

Accommodations
1 To Hotel Tivoli Coimbra
2 Hotel Astória
3 Hotel Vitória
4 Hotel Bragança
5 Ibis Hotel
6 RiverSuites & Dona Taska
7 Hotel Domus
8 Hotel Larbelo
9 Serenata Hostel

Eateries & Entertainment
10 Restaurante Zé Manel dos Oss
11 O Bizarro
12 Adega Paço do Conde
13 Restaurante Solar do Bacalhau

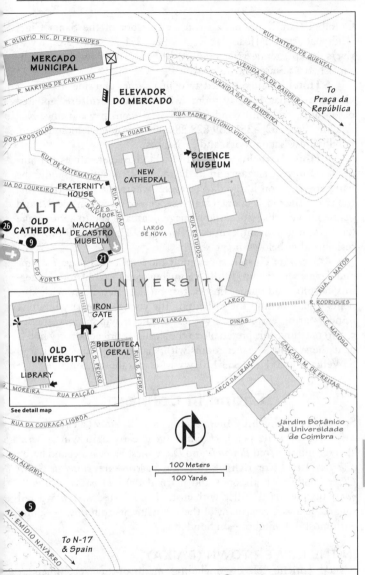

MERCADO MUNICIPAL

R. OLÍMPIO NIC. DI FERNANDES

RUA ANTERO DE QUENTAL

R. MARTINS DE CARVALHO

AVENIDA SÁ DE BANDEIRA

AVENIDA SÁ DE BANDEIRA

To Praça da República

ELEVADOR DO MERCADO

RUA PADRE ANTÓNIO VIEIRA

DOS APÓSTOLOS

R. DUARTE

RUA DE MATEMÁTICA

SCIENCE MUSEUM

UA DO LOUREIRO

FRATERNITY HOUSE

NEW CATHEDRAL

ALTA

R. DE S. SALVADOR

RUA S. JOÃO

OLD CATHEDRAL

26

MACHADO DE CASTRO MUSEUM

9

LARGO SÉ NOVA

RUA ESTUDOS

R. DO NORTE

21

U N I V E R S I T Y

LARGO

RUA O. MATOS

R. RODRIGUES

IRON GATE

DINAS

RUA C. MATOSO

OLD UNIVERSITY

RUA LARGA

CALÇADA M. DE FREITAS

BIBLIOTECA GERAL

RUA S. PEDRO

LIBRARY

RUA S. PEDRO

MOREIRA

RUA FALCÃO

R. ARCO DA TRAIÇÃO

See detail map

RUA DA COURAÇA LISBOA

Jardim Botânico da Universidade de Coimbra

RUA ALEGRIA

100 Meters

100 Yards

5

AV. EMÍDIO NAVARRO

To N-17 & Spain

COIMBRA

14 Tartufo Italian Restaurant & Pizzeria	**21** Loggia Restaurante
15 Calado e Calado Restaurante	**22** Fado ao Centro
16 Restaurante Jardim da Manga	**23** Fado Hilário
17 Café Santa Cruz	**24** àCapella
18 Tapas nas Costas	**25** Bar Diligência
19 Fangas Mercearia Bar	**26** Restaurante O Trovador
20 Fangas Maior	

Coimbra (family rooms, air-con, at the foot of the Santa Clara Bridge at Avenida João das Regras 82, +351 239 440 582, www. riversuites.pt, geral@riversuites.pt). They also offer two large, well-furnished **$$$** apartments nearby.

$ Hotel Domus, tucked away in a corner of a side street near Coimbra-A, has 15 cozy rooms with antique furniture, updated bathrooms, and thin windows (RS%, air-con, pay parking, Rua Adelino Veiga 62, +351 239 828 584, www.residencialdomus.com, hoteldomus@sapo.pt, Sra. and Sr. Santos).

¢ Hotel Larbelo, with Old World character, mixes frumpiness and former elegance in its 17 rooms. Its location couldn't be handier—right on Largo da Portagem, where the main street hits the river. The old-fashioned staircase, classic reception rooms, and gentle non-English-speaking management take you to another age (no breakfast, air-con, Largo da Portagem 33, +351 239 829 092, residencial.larbelo@sapo.pt.

¢ Serenata Hostel, appealingly modern, offers private rooms and dorms with views. It fills a gorgeously restored historic maternity hospital and music conservatory on the often-noisy-with-students square behind the cathedral. The young-at-heart who don't mind wearing earplugs (or request a quieter windowless interior room) may find this preferable to the similarly priced, dreary hotels near the station (cheaper rooms with shared bath, air-con, Largo Sé Velha 21, +351 239 853 130, www.serenatahostel.com).

Eating in Coimbra

Specialties of this hilly Beira region include *leitão* (suckling pig), *cabrito* (baby male goat), *chanfana* (goat cooked in wine), *Serra* cheese, and rich, red *Bairrada* and *Dão* wines. For a sweet and herby *digestivo*, try Licor Beirão. The local pastries are *pastel de Santa Clara* (made with almonds and marmalade) and *pastel de Tentúgal* (flaky puff pastry filled with custard and dusted with powdered sugar). Be aware that many of these restaurants shut down—along with most of Coimbra—on Sunday.

IN THE LOWER TOWN (BAIXA)

Several enticing places—including many of my recommendations—are buried in the tight lanes between Hotel Astória and the main walking street. These first six listings are within a couple blocks of each other.

$$ Restaurante Zé Manel dos Ossos is tiny, rustic, and authentic. Judging from the walls—caked with notes from happy eaters—and the line of smart eaters waiting hungrily in the alley, this place is a favorite. They serve a dozen good, typical Coimbran dishes. (The *ossos*—meaty bones of goat or wild pork cooked with veggies, mushrooms, and beans—are all popular here.) To order, I'd trust Mario, who speaks a lee-tle English (Mon-Sat 12:30-15:00 & 19:30-22:00, closed Sun and off-season; no reservations—arrive early or wait, as the line moves very slowly; Beco do Forno 12, +351 239 823 790).

$$ O Bizarro is a small, family-run, checkered-tablecloth hole-in-the-wall where Rafael and his mother serve up tasty Portuguese food at a good price. *Chanfana* (goat simmered in wine) is the house specialty. Mom takes the goat home to marinate overnight... it slides off the bone (great lunch special, lunch served Mon-Sat 12:00-15:00, dinner Mon-Thu 19:00-22:00, Rua Sargento Mor 44).

$ Adega Paço do Conde—humble but popular—knows how to grill, and Coimbra's students love it. Choose your seafood or meat selection from the display case as you enter. They'll pop it right on the grill and then bring it to your table. Students, travelers, families, and pigeons like this homey place that just seems right (big, splittable plates, Mon-Sat 11:30-15:00 & 19:00-22:00, closed Sun, Rua Paço do Conde 1—on the small square called Largo Paço do Conde, +351 239 825 605, Alfredo).

$$ Restaurante Solar do Bacalhau serves good Portuguese standards focusing on (what else?) cod and grilled meats, plus Italian favorites in a huge, contemporary, stony-chic dining room that feels fancier than its prices. It's big, busy, and bright, and is deservedly popular with locals and tour groups alike (daily 12:00-15:00 & 19:00-24:00, Rua da Sota 12, +351 239 098 990).

$$ Tartufo Italian Restaurant & Pizzeria seems to have more eating energy than the rest of the town combined. The fun space with a bustling and open kitchen, and a busy pasta-making table in the center, is great for anyone needing a break from Portuguese cooking (daily 12:00-14:00, Rua da Sota 34, +351 239 820 546).

$$ Calado e Calado Restaurante is a big, plain diner with a laser focus on one thing: traditional Portuguese cuisine. It's sunny, spacious, and happy, with a great €7.50 lunch deal and enticing €10 dinner plates (Sun-Fri 12:00-15:00 & 19:00-22:00, closed Sat, next to recommended Restaurante Solar do Bacalhau at Rua da Sota 14, +351 239 827 348).

$$ Restaurante Jardim da Manga is handy for a quick, cheap, self-service meal with locals. Sit indoors or outdoors next to a cool and peaceful fountain. It's family-friendly and cheap enough to be a popular choice for children's birthday parties. Just slide a tray down the counter and point to what you like (Sun-Fri 12:00-15:00 & 19:00-22:00, closed Sat, in the Jardim da Manga garden behind Church of Santa Cruz, +351 239 829 156).

$$ Dona Taska sits across the river with tables spilling out onto the busy sidewalk. Portuguese standards form part of the menu, but their specialty is Spanish cuisine. For a break from fish, try the "broken eggs" served with jamón over fried potatoes, or a sizzling grilled steak (Tue-Sun 12:00-15:00 & 19:00-24:00, closed Mon, call for reservations on weekends, Avenida João das Regras 86, +351 918 888 878).

$ Café Santa Cruz, next to the Church of Santa Cruz and filling one of its former buildings, is Old World elegant, but totally unpretentious. It has good, cheap coffee, simple toasted sandwiches, Wi-Fi, and outdoor tables offering great people-watching over Praça 8 de Maio. Their signature pastry *cruzios* (€1, named for the church's friars) are inspired by nun-baked sweets (Mon-Sat 7:00-24:00, Sun 8:00-20:00 in summer, closed Sun off-season, Victor). The café hosts free live fado most nights in season (see "Entertainment in Coimbra," earlier).

IN THE UPPER TOWN (ALTA)
These restaurants sit on the slopes above the main drag.

$$ Tapas nas Costas invites you in with its stylish, modern ambience, friendly service, and an interesting mix of Portuguese classics and traditional Spanish favorites. Portions are splittable so order a couple to start, then ask for more if you're still hungry (Tue-Sat 12:00-15:00 & 19:00-23:00, Sun lunch only, closed Mon, Rua do Quebra Costas 19, +351 239 157 425).

$$$ Fangas Mercearia Bar, my Coimbra favorite, is an intimate five-table wine bar where English-speaking Luisa serves delightful *petiscos* (Portuguese tapas) matched by a nice selection of quality Portuguese wines by the glass (3 or 4 tapas will fill 2 people, or try a sampler plate; daily 12:30-16:00 & 19:00-24:00, Rua Fernandes Tomás 45, reserve ahead, +351 934 093 636). A few steps away, their sister location, **Fangas Maior,** has the same menu and philosophy, but a bit less coziness—you're more likely to get a table here, and that's just fine (same hours and phone number, Rua Fernandes Tomás 29).

$$$ Loggia Restaurante is a dressy place at the Machado de Castro Museum with seating inside or outside on the view terrace overlooking the old town. It's a convenient stop while sightseeing, as it's next to the university, and there's a good-value €9.50 weekday lunch buffet available 12:30-14:30 (€11.50 on weekends). If you don't mind the long hike, it's also a romantic and classy option for dinner—at higher prices than you'll pay in town, but still reasonable (Tue and Sun open 10:00-18:00 for lunch, Wed-Sat open 10:00-22:30 with dinner from 19:30, closed Mon, +351 239 853 076).

COIMBRA

Coimbra Connections

If you're traveling by train, remember that Coimbra has two stations—A and B—but any ticket covers the five-minute shuttle train between stations (see page 309 for details).

From Coimbra by Bus to: Alcobaça (2/day, 1.5 hours), **Batalha** (3/day, 2 hours, transfer in Leiria), **Fátima** (hourly, 1 hour), **Nazaré** (5/day, 2 hours, some with transfer in Leiria), **Lisbon** (hourly, 2.5 hours), **Évora** (3/day direct, 4.5 hours; otherwise almost hourly with transfer in Lisbon, 4.5 hours), **Porto** (almost hourly, 1.5 hours). Bus info: +351 239 855 270, www.rede-expressos.pt. Frequency drops on weekends, especially Sunday.

By Train to: Nazaré/Valado (3/day direct, 2 hours; the bus is a better option—see above—because Nazaré/Valado train station is 3 miles outside Nazaré), **Porto** (hourly, 1 hour on Alfa Pendular line or Intercidades service, 2 hours on regional line; most long-distance trains end at Porto's noncentral Campanhã station but include a transfer to the more central São Bento station), **Lisbon** (almost hourly on Alfa Pendular or Intercidades service, 2 hours; regional service equally frequent but takes 4 hours; for Lisbon center, get off at Santa Apolónia Station; for Lisbon airport, hop off at Oriente station and take the Metro to airport; all Coimbra/Porto trains stop at both Lisbon stations, 7 minutes apart). Train info: +351 808 208 208, www.cp.pt.

To Salamanca, Spain: The best option is the Alsa **bus** (1-2/day, departs daily at 9:45 with connection at Albergaria; some days a faster, direct bus departs at 10:00 or 10:30; all arrive by 17:30 in Salamanca on Spain time—add one hour from Portugal). To guarantee a place, book a couple of days in advance (www.alsa.com). You can also confirm schedules and buy your bus ticket in person at the friendly InterVisa travel agency, near Coimbra-A station (see "Helpful Hints," at the beginning of this chapter) more easily than at Coimbra's bus station (Alsa office, +351 904 422 242, some English spoken).

I'd avoid taking the **train** to Salamanca because of its inconvenient early-morning arrival time: One train per day on the Sud-Expresso line departs Coimbra at 23:30 and drops you in Salamanca at 4:53 (4.5 hours).

COIMBRA

PORTO

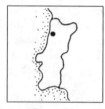

Porto (POR-too)—the capital of the north and Portugal's second city—is fiercely proud of what distinguishes it from its rival, Lisbon. Yes, Porto's a bit less polished. But block for block, it may be even more full of gritty, Old World charm. In many ways, a visit to Portugal isn't complete without experiencing Porto.

Spared by the 1755 earthquake that toppled Lisbon, Porto is appealingly well-preserved. Houses with red-tiled roofs tumble down the hills to the riverbank, prickly church towers dot the skyline, mosaic-patterned stones line streets, and flat-bottomed boats called *rabelos* ply the lazy river.

Internationally, the city is synonymous with the port wine that ages on its riverbanks. But the Portuguese think of Porto as a hardworking engine of industry, with an endearing warts-and-all character. It's a solid city—it seems made entirely of granite—with equally solid people. The town's two most famous foods—tripe stew and a beloved quadruple-decker, sauce-drenched, gut-bomb of a sandwich—say it all: This place is unpretentious. Locals claim they're working too hard to worry about being pretty. As an oft-repeated saying goes, "Coimbra studies, Braga prays, Lisbon parties...and Porto works."

Not long ago, Porto was a somewhat depressed industrial city, but it has enjoyed a cultural renaissance over the past decade. European Union money has poured in, funding upgrades to the public transportation system and historical sites. Meanwhile, tourism has taken off in a big way (thanks largely to cheap flights to Porto's international airport attracting weekend vacationers from Britain and the Continent). Locals are rising to the occasion, filling the characteristic streets with trendy eateries and boutiques.

Fun-to-visit Porto offers two high-impact sightseeing thrills: the postcard-perfect ambience of the riverfront Ribeira district, and the opportunity to learn more about (and taste) the port wine that ages across the river in Vila Nova de Gaia. (Aficionados of port—or of dramatic scenery—can use Porto as a springboard for visiting the Douro Valley, where grapes grow on dramatic stone terraces; see next chapter.) But you'll discover that Porto also features many unexpected treats: sumptuous Baroque churches and civic buildings, a bustling market hall, atmospheric lanes of glorious tiled houses, a variety of good restaurants and appealing boutiques, and quirky but worthwhile museums.

Porto's weather is always changing, blown in and out by the steady ocean breeze. You're likely to get sun and rain at the same time—causing the locals to exclaim, "A widow's going to remarry."

PLANNING YOUR TIME

Porto offers one very busy day's worth of sightseeing—or better yet, two relaxed days. Start your day in the market area (when it's most thriving). Then head to the main boulevard, Avenida dos Aliados, and follow my self-guided Porto Walk through the rest of town. If time allows, the activities most worth considering along the way are climbing Clérigos Tower for a visual orientation, touring the Stock Exchange Palace, and visiting the glorious São Francisco Church and its spooky crypt. My walk ends on the Ribeira. You can continue another 15 scenic minutes across the bridge to the opposite riverbank to do some port wine tastings in Vila Nova de Gaia. Have dinner in the Ribeira (for touristy bustle) or up in the city center (for more interesting local eateries).

With a second day, slow down. Taste more port, visit the cathedral, cruise the river, ride a vintage trolley, and visit the Serralves Museum, the Art Deco mansion, or the plush park. Or just head to the Atlantic beaches at Foz to mellow out.

The only sight in town that requires a reserved, timed entry is the Stock Exchange Palace tour. It's not available online, so call ahead or drop by to get your spot. You also may be able to book through the TI.

If you're renting a car for your trip and driving directly from Coimbra to Porto (skipping the Douro Valley), think again. You don't need a car in either town and the 1.5-hour train ride is a delight.

Orientation to Porto

Porto (pop. 238,000, with a metro area sprawling to 1.7 million) blankets the hilly north bank of the Douro River, near where the river meets the Atlantic Ocean. The tourist's Porto is fairly compact

but hilly—and therefore tricky to navigate. Even though maps can
be deceptive (given the variable
terrain), get a good one and use
it. Comfortable walking shoes
are a must. And don't hesitate
to grab a taxi or Uber whenever
you need a quick connection.
Uber in particular is cheap, hon-
est, fast, and will save you lots of
climbing.

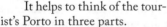

It helps to think of the tourist's Porto in three parts.

Ribeira (ree-BAY-rah): Down along the river, the Ribeira
neighborhood has narrow streets and oodles of atmosphere. Praça
do Infante Dom Henrique (Henry the Navigator Square), two
blocks above the Ribeira, hosts two intriguing sights: the Stock
Exchange Palace and São Francisco Church.

City Center: Ramshackle old townhouses scramble steeply
uphill toward the second part of town, the modern city center,
which hovers above the Ribeira and surrounds the broad boulevard
called Avenida dos Aliados (Avenue of the Allies). This area is the
urban business center of Porto, packed with office buildings and
shoppers, and peppered with hotels and enticing restaurants. You'll
also find a smattering of squares, monuments, and sights (including

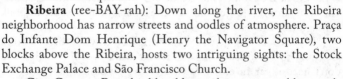

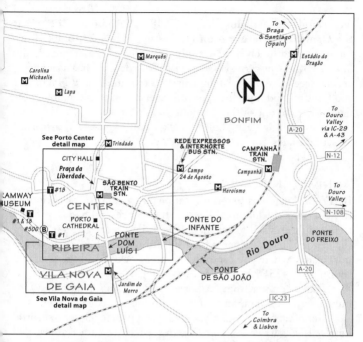

the market hall and cathedral). Clérigos Tower stands as the city's most recognizable landmark.

Vila Nova de Gaia: Across the river shine the signs of Porto's main tourist attraction, the port wine cellars *(caves do vinho do porto)* in Vila Nova de Gaia—technically a separate town.

The Douro is spanned by six bridges (two steel, four concrete). The only one you're likely to cross is the monstrous steel **Ponte Dom Luís I** bridge (cars use lower level, Metro trains run along upper level; pedestrians can use either level).

Visitors venturing farther out find Porto to be a city of contrasts. Its outskirts boast bright, spacious, and prim residential neighborhoods, such as the areas surrounding the Boavista Rotunda and the Serralves Museum and park. The upscale Atlantic beach neighborhood, Foz, is a nice escape from the congested center and a great place to watch the sun set.

TOURIST INFORMATION

Porto's TIs share a website: www.visitporto.travel. The two main TIs are in the **city center** across from City Hall (at the top of Avenida dos Aliados, Rua Clube dos Fenianos 25), and in the crenellated tower just below **cathedral square** (both open daily 9:00-20:00, until 19:00 off-season, +351 222 081 833). You'll also find TI kiosks in highly trafficked areas: on the **Ribeira** waterfront (May-Oct daily 10:30-19:00) and near the Imperial McDonald's on **Avenida dos Aliados** (daily 9:30-18:30). Additional TIs are at the **Campanhã train station** (June-Aug daily 9:30-18:00, closes for an hour at lunch break—timing varies) and the **airport** (daily 8:00-23:30, at the arrivals level). **Vila Nova de Gaia** has its own TI, as well (see page 377). Many *tourist service* and *tourist info* offices you'll see around town are for-profit agencies in disguise; for an official TI, go to one of the locations mentioned here.

The TI near City Hall sells the useful Andante transit card (described later, under "Getting Around Porto"). Skip the Porto Card sold by all TIs (it's rarely worth it).

ARRIVAL IN PORTO

By Train: Porto has two train stations. Regional trains, including those serving the Douro Valley, use the very central **São Bento** station (a sight in itself for its magnificent tiles; see page 364). Facing the exit in the left corner is the helpful Loja da Mobilidade **transport office,** where you can purchase train tickets and the Andante transit card (+351 226 158 158, www.stcp.pt).

Trains coming from farther away, including Lisbon and Coimbra, arrive at **Campanhã station**, on the east edge of town.

Get off at São Bento if your train stops there (closer to central hotels). If you arrive at Campanhã instead, hop on any train labeled *São Bento* to get downtown (trains leave every few minutes). The five-minute ride is included in your ticket.

By Bus: As each of Porto's many bus companies operates its own garage, there's no central bus station. All the bus garages are more or less in the city center. The main ones are **Rede Expressos** (to Lisbon and Coimbra; Campo 24 de Agosto 125, Metro: 24 de Agosto, +351 707 223 344, www.rede-expressos.pt); **Rodonorte** (to points north; Rua Ateneu Comercial do Porto 19, +351 222 005 637, www.rodonorte.pt); and **Internorte** (to Spain, including Madrid; Campo 24 de Agosto 123, +351 707 200 512, www.internorte.pt). The Spanish bus company **Autna** runs buses to Vigo, Spain (with connections to Santiago), that leave from in front of the Imperial McDonald's on Avenida dos Aliados (www.autna.com).

By Car: Central Porto is a headache by car—the streets are confusing and congested, and parking is very expensive (over €30/day). Try to pick up your rental on your way out of town (or drop it off on the way in); otherwise, just stow it at your hotel. Approaching from Lisbon and Coimbra on the A-1 expressway, pay a toll and follow signs for *Ponte da Arrábida*. After crossing the bridge, take the first right and follow *centro* signs (or the little bull's-eyes) into downtown.

By Plane: See "Porto Connections" at the end of this chapter.

HELPFUL HINTS

Thieves and Scams: Children work the streets begging, scamming, and picking pockets. In São Bento train station, keep one eye on the tiles and the other on your belongings. Porto cabbies are not above ripping off tourists—count your change carefully.

Closed Day: Most Porto museums are closed on Monday. Many traditional shops close early on Saturday and all day Sunday (but trendy or tourist-oriented stores stay open on weekends).

Festivals: Porto's big holiday is São João Day (for St. John the Baptist) on June 24. Festivities start the night of June 23 with partying and fireworks at Ponte Dom Luís I bridge, and continue on the 24th with a *rabelo* regatta.

Laundry: A small **full-service** laundry hides almost underground at the west end of the Ribeira district (between São Francisco Church and the river at the top of Rua da Reboleira, unpredictable hours, +351 222 084 621). The **self-service** Lavanderia do Infante is just a couple of blocks uphill (daily 8:30-22:00, Rua do Comércio do Porto 43, mobile +351 968 902 713).

Best Views: There are fine views all along the Ribeira riverfront embankment, but they're even better from across the river in Vila Nova de Gaia (looking back toward Porto)—especially from the cable car or Porto Cruz's rooftop bar. You can also enjoy the views from the top of Clérigos Tower, from the terrace next to the cathedral, from the funicular, or from the picnic-friendly public gardens next to Mosteiro da Serra do Pilar (the monastery across the river, just above the big steel Ponte Dom Luís I bridge).

Oporto or Porto? The British—who've traded with the city for centuries—refer to the city as "Oporto" due to an old language misunderstanding. "O porto" in Portuguese means "the port," exactly where Brits placed their interests. Although various guidebooks and postcards call it this, locals never do. And while we're on the topic, Vila Nova de Gaia is simply called "Gaia" (GUY-uh) by locals.

Lisbon vs. Porto: Lisbon and Porto are proud rivals. Lisboners, known as *alfacinhas* or "little lettuces," drink an imperial (as a small glass is called) of Sagres beer while rooting for Benfica (the working-class soccer team) or Sporting (the upper-class rival). Meanwhile, the people of Porto, known as "tripe eaters," drink a *fino* (small glass) of Super Bock beer while rooting for FC Porto. Differences extend to coffee breaks, too. When it's time for a shot of espresso, Lisboners ask for a *bica* while in Porto they request a *cimbalino*.

PORTO

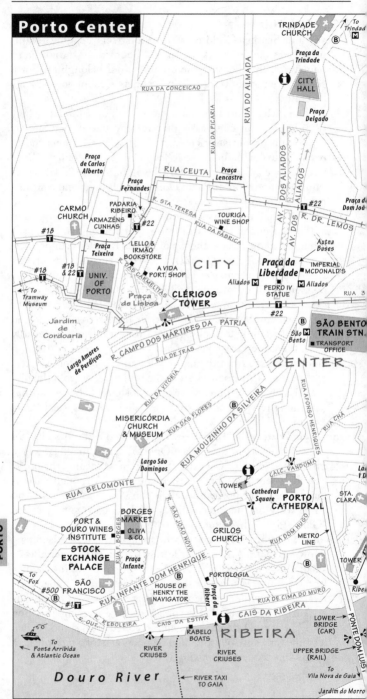

Porto Center

TRINDADE CHURCH
To Trindad M

Praça da Trindade

RUA DO ALMADA

RUA DA CONCEICAO

RUA DA PICARIA

CITY HALL

Praça Delgado

Praça de Carlos Alberto

RUA CEUTA

Praça Lencastre

Praça Fernandes

R. STA. TERESA

AV. DOS ALIADOS

Praça da Dom João

CARMO CHURCH

Padaria Ribeiro

#22

TOURIGA WINE SHOP

R. DR. LEMOS

#18

ARMAZÉNS CUNHAS

LELLO & IRMÃO BOOKSTORE

RUA DA FABRICA

Autna Buses

Praça Teixeira

A VIDA PORT. SHOP

CITY

Praça da Liberdade

IMPERIAL McDONALD'S

#18 & 22

#18

UNIV. OF PORTO

DAS CARMELITAS

Aliados M

PEDRO IV STATUE

M Aliados

To Tramway Museum

Praça de Lisboa

CLÉRIGOS TOWER

RUA 3

Jardim de Cordoaria

R. CAMPO DOS MÁRTIRES DA PÁTRIA

#22

SÃO BENTO TRAIN STN.

São Bento M

Largo Amores de Perdicao

RUA DE TRÁS

TRANSPORT OFFICE

CENTER

RUA DA VITÓRIA

MISERICÓRDIA CHURCH & MUSEUM

RUA DAS FLORES

RUA MOUZINHO DA SILVEIRA

RUA AFONSO HENRIQUES

RUA CHÃ

Largo São Domingos

La 1 D

RUA BELOMONTE

CALC. VANDOMA

TOWER

Cathedral Square

PORTO CATHEDRAL

STA. CLARA

PORT & DOURO WINES INSTITUTE

BORGES MARKET

OLIVA & CO.

R. SÃO JOÃO NOVO

GRILOS CHURCH

RUA DOM HUGO

METRO LINE

STOCK EXCHANGE PALACE

Praça Infante

TOWER

To Foz

#500

SÃO FRANCISCO

RUA INFANTE DOM HENRIQUE

PORTOLOGIA

Praça da Ribeira

Ribe

#1

HOUSE OF HENRY THE NAVIGATOR

RUA DE CIMA DO MURO

R. OUT.

R. REBOLEIRA

CAIS DA ESTIVA

CAIS DA RIBEIRA

RIBEIRA

LOWER BRIDGE (CAR)

PONTE DOM LUIS

To Ponte Arrabida & Atlantic Ocean

RABELO BOATS

RIVER CRIUSES

RIVER CRIUSES

UPPER BRIDGE (RAIL)

To Vila Nova de Gaia

Douro River

RIVER TAXI TO GAIA

Jardim do Morro

PORTO

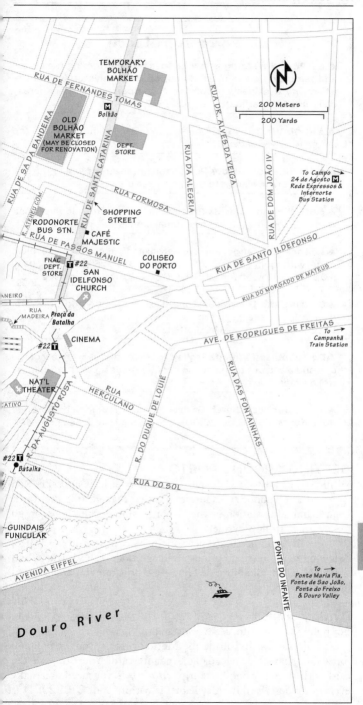

RUA DE FERNANDES TOMAS

TEMPORARY
BOLHÃO
MARKET

RUA DR. ALVES DA VEIGA

N

200 Meters

200 Yards

Bolhão

OLD
BOLHÃO
MARKET
(MAY BE CLOSED
FOR RENOVATION)

DEPT.
STORE

RUA DE SÁ DA BANDEIRA

RUA DE SANTA CATARINA

RUA DA ALEGRIA

RUA DE DOM JOÃO IV

To Campo
24 de Agosto M,
Rede Expressos &
Internorte
Bus Station

RUA FORMOSA

R. ATENEU COM.

SHOPPING
STREET

RODONORTE
BUS STN.

CAFÉ
MAJESTIC

RUA DE PASSOS MANUEL

COLISEO
DO PORTO

RUA DE SANTO ILDEFONSO

RUA DO MORGADO DE MATEUS

FNAC
DEPT.
STORE

#22

SAN
IDELFONSO
CHURCH

ANEIRO

RUA
MADEIRA

Praça da
Batalha

CINEMA

#22

AVE. DE RODRIGUES DE FREITAS

To
Campanhã
Train Station

NAT'L
THEATER

RUA
HERCULANO

R. DO DUQUE DE LOULE

RUA DAS FONTAINHAS

CATIVO

R. DA AUGUSTO ROSA

#22

Batalha

RUA DO SOL

GUINDAIS
FUNICULAR

PONTE DO INFANTE

PORTO

AVENIDA EIFFEL

To
Ponte Maria Pia,
Ponte de Sao João,
Ponte do Freixo
& Douro Valley

Douro River

Porto at a Glance

▲▲▲Port Wine Lodges in Vila Nova de Gaia Touring the cellars and sampling Porto's most famous product is this city's top tourist activity, especially for connoisseurs. **Hours:** Vary, but generally daily, last tours at 18:00. See page 377.

▲▲Porto Walk Two-part self-guided walk linking the city's top landmarks. See page 357.

▲▲Avenida dos Aliados Porto's top urban street, where the city goes to work in elaborate buildings. See page 357.

▲▲Strolling the Cais da Ribeira Porto's picturesque riverfront, with arcades and colorful traditional homes. See page 368.

▲▲Stock Exchange Palace Astonishing monument to civic pride, with room after sumptuous room. **Hours:** By tour only, daily 9:00-18:30, Nov-March 9:00-13:00 & 14:00-17:30. See page 375.

▲Cruising the Douro Lazy one-hour cruises up and down the river, offering the city's top views. **Hours:** Generally daily 10:00-18:30 in summer (until 17:00 off-season). See page 357.

▲Do-It-Yourself Vintage Trolley Tour Wonderful overview of the city and a trip out to the ocean park beach using all three vintage trolley lines. See page 355.

▲São Francisco Church Gothic church dripping with Baroque gold. **Hours:** Daily 9:00-20:00, Oct-Feb until 17:30. See page 376.

GETTING AROUND PORTO

While steep, Porto is walkable. On a short visit, it's possible you won't take any public transportation (other than getting into town from Campanhã station or the airport)—unless you choose to go for a vintage trolley joyride.

The city's public-transit network includes buses and the Metro. A few more interesting options—vintage trolleys, a funicular, and the cable car in Vila Nova de Gaia—are privately run and covered by separate tickets.

By City Transit

For public-transit info, see www.stcp.pt.

Andante Card: To ride the Metro or buses, you'll pay €0.60 for a non-shareable, reloadable Andante card. You can load the card with as many one-hour trips *(títulos)*, as you need. Virtually everything described in this chapter is within Zone 2 (€1.20).

▲**Clérigos Church and Tower** Porto's towering landmark, with a 225-step climb to sweeping views over the urban sprawl. **Hours:** Daily 9:00-19:00. See page 372.

▲**São Bento Train Station** Entry hall decorated with impressive *azulejo* (tile) murals. See page 364.

▲**Porto Cathedral** Huge church overlooking the town, with fine *azulejo*-decorated cloister and otherwise dull interior. **Hours:** Daily 9:00-12:30 & 14:30-19:00, until 18:00 in winter, cloister closed Sun morning year-round. See page 372.

▲**Rua de Santa Catarina** Main shopping drag, with Art Nouveau and Art Deco landmarks. See page 371.

▲**Misericórdia Church and Museum** Church connected to a former hospital, now home to a fine exhibit showing the good works and treasures of Porto's all-powerful charity. **Hours:** Daily 10:00-18:30, off-season until 17:30. See page 366.

▲**Bolhão Market** Lively produce and meat market may be in a temporary home but is still worth visiting. **Hours:** Mon-Sat 8:00-20:00, closed Sun. See page 371.

▲**Serralves Foundation Contemporary Art Museum and Park** Sprawling park with impressive museum, Art Deco mansion, and relaxing grounds. **Hours:** Mon-Fri 10:00-19:00, Sat-Sun until 20:00, closes one hour earlier Oct-March. See page 383.

The card is sold at ticket machines (English-speaking attendants are often available to answer questions), the TI near City Hall (but not at other TIs), the Loja da Mobilidade transport office in São Bento station, and at some bus, Metro, and train ticket offices. To use the card, pass it over the scanner's grey circle on the Metro or bus.

Buses: Buses #900, #901, and #906 go from São Bento station to the port wine lodges in Vila Nova de Gaia, across the river; bus #500 runs from the Ribeira to Foz; and bus #203 goes from the beach in Foz to the Serralves Museum. Service is generally speedy, but avoid buses during rush hour, when traffic slows to a crawl. Without an Andante card, you can pay the driver €1.95 for a ticket.

Metro: Five Metro lines run east-west along the same tracks in the city center (blue A, red B, green C, purple E, and orange F). One Metro line runs north-south (yellow D) and connects São Bento station to Vila Nova de Gaia across the river. All Metro lines

PORTO

converge at the Trindade stop, one block behind City Hall and Avenida dos Aliados. The purple E line connects the airport to the center and Campanhã station. To ride the Metro, you must have an Andante card. If you transfer Metro lines, you must swipe your card again.

By Vintage Trolley

Porto has three interconnecting trolley lines that seem made for tourists: #1, #18, and #22. These restored trolleys—privately run and just a little more expensive than a bus or Metro ride—are used primarily by tourists for the simple joy of rambling through this scenic old town. They are both fun and practical (€3.50/trip, €6 for two same-day trips, €10 two-day pass, not covered by Andante card, 2/hour, daily 9:00-20:00, www.portotramcitytour.pt).

While Lisbon's trolleys are overwhelmed with tourists and pickpockets, Porto's are easy, safe, and rarely crowded. For a fun, DIY trolley tour, see the "Porto Vintage Trolley Joyride" sidebar.

Trolley #1 shudders along the Douro River from the Ribeira, past the Tramway Museum to the Jardim do Passeio Alegre, a 10-minute walk to the Foz district and the Atlantic Ocean.

Trolley #18 begins at Carmo Church and wobbles down past views of Vila Nova de Gaia to the Tramway Museum.

Trolley #22 makes a loop through the city center, beginning and ending at Carmo Church and clattering past Avenida dos Aliados, São Bento Praça da Batalha, and the funicular (for the route, see the "Porto Center" map, earlier).

By Funicular

A handy funicular (Funicular dos Guindais) connects the Ribeira district (at the base of the Ponte Dom Luís I bridge) to the top of the steep hill above (at the remains of the city wall, down the Rua de Augusto Rosa from Praça da Batalha, near the midway stop for trolley #22). This is the only public-transit option for saving yourself the steep hike between the Ribeira and the city center (€2.50, not covered by Andante card, every 10 minutes, daily 8:00-22:00 plus summer weekends until 24:00, Nov-April daily until 20:00).

By Cable Car

The overpriced Teleférico de Gaia cable car soars above Vila Nova de Gaia, connecting the riverfront with the Jardim do Morro, just under the Mosteiro da Serra do Pilar monastery and at the foot of the upper part of the Ponte Dom Luís I bridge. The five-minute ride offers a unique view and is handy for connecting the upper and lower parts of Vila Nova de Gaia (€6 one-way, €9 round-trip, daily 10:00-20:00, until 18:00 off-season, www.gaiacablecar.com).

Porto Vintage Trolley Joyride

Consider this grand Porto trolley joyride, worth ▲, that takes you on all three vintage lines (#1, #18, and #22) for a good overview of the city. **Praça de Parada Leitao** near the Carmo

Church is the starting point for trolleys #18 and #22, which both leave at :15 and :45 past the hour and do a 30-minute loop. Buy a €10 two-day pass from the driver so you can hop off and on as you like.

Start with **trolley #22** to cover the downtown area (Avenida dos Aliados, Praça da Batalha, and the beginning of Rua de Santa Catarina shopping street). Depending on traffic, you may make it back to Carmo Church in time to switch immediately to #18. (Each line runs on a strict schedule; they don't wait for another trolley to arrive.) If you miss #18 and have a half-hour wait, consider getting a quick coffee on the terrace at the neighboring (and recommended) Café Piolho d'Ouro.

Next, jump on **trolley #18,** which takes you to the Tramway Museum (see page 382). Before entering the museum, check the trolley schedule to see when the #1 will pass by (it runs every 20 minutes). If you have a wait after your museum visit, grab some quick refreshment (or a picnic lunch) inside the Continente supermarket next door. Finally, hop on **trolley #1** to get to Jardim do Passeio Alegre park at the ocean in Foz, where you can enjoy the park and the scenery. When you've gotten enough of the Atlantic, ride #1 all the way back to its opposite terminus, the Ribeira district.

By River Taxi

Douro River Taxi runs a shuttle service between the Ribeira and Vila Nova de Gaia. The ride takes less than ten minutes—a quick and easy way to get across the river to your port wine tastings (€3, departures every 15 minutes, daily 10:00-19:00, https://dourorivertaxi.com/en/home-en).

By Taxi

Taxis are a good option in this hilly city. Most rides are fairly short and cost only around €5. For rides within the city limits, the meter should be on "T1" during the day (€2 drop charge) and "T2" at night (21:00-6:00, €2.50 drop charge). Each kilometer costs about €0.40. A luggage surcharge of €1.60 is legit (per ride, not per

PORTO

piece). It's easy to find taxi stands—you'll pay €1 more to call one (try Invicta, +351 225 076 400).

By Uber
If you like Uber at home, you'll love it here. Cars are clean, drivers speak English and are happy to chat, rates are about half the taxi rate, and you can generally get a car in three minutes. I like to sit in the front seat and interview my driver about life in Portugal (but that's just me).

Tours in Porto

ON WHEELS
Hop-On, Hop-Off Bus Tours: Steep Porto with its spread-out sights is a good city for these bus tours. Three different companies with different colored buses—red, blue, and yellow—do loops through town, connecting the city center, the Ribeira, Vila Nova de Gaia, and the Foz suburb. All have open-top buses, headphone commentary, and run twice per hour, and all offer bus-plus-river cruise combo-tickets. The companies are essentially interchangeable, but the blue bus is slightly cheaper (€10/1 day rather than €13/1 day).

Tourist Train: For a cheaper (and more humiliating) option, the "Magic Tour" tourist train does a loop around the town center and includes a stop at a port wine lodge across the river (€9, 2/hour, 1.25 hours, leaves from in front of cathedral).

Tuk-Tuks: You'll see these little three-wheeled, three-seater taxis parked at touristy sights around town, especially in front of Clérigos Tower. Guided tours cost €15-60, depending on length, and rates can be soft. While a tuk-tuk ride can be noisy, smelly, and jostling, it can work well for a sweat-free tour around this very vertical city.

ON FOOT
A good local guide or tour can be well worth the expense.

Maria Jose Aleixo (mobile +351 969 468 347, aleixo19@ sapo.pt) and **Margarida Falcao** (mobile +351 913 499 382, margaridafalcao.gio@gmail.com) are two excellent, English-speaking local guides who charge €110 per group for a half-day walk tailored to your interests.

The City Tailors Tours are led by Ricardo Brochado, who truly loves his work. He tailors half-day Porto experiences for groups of one to six for €85 per person (cheaper for larger groups, children free). This rate includes snacks, drinks, and a light meal along the way (mobile +351 917 574 983, www.thecitytailors.com).

Taste Porto Food Tours is run with gusto by tour guide André, who has a contagious enthusiasm for good food and embracing life Portuguese-style. André and his team take groups (2-10 people) on a two-mile walk with six tasty stops. It's fun, educational, relaxed, and delicious. Two 3.5-hour tours run Monday through Saturday: "Downtown" (€65, at 10:45 and 16:00, 6 stops) and "Vintage" (€70, at 10:00 and 16:15, 6 stops plus a port wine stop). Book and pay in advance online (mobile +351 920 503 302, www.tasteporto.com).

BY BOAT
The city's well-promoted **"Six Bridges" river cruises,** worth ▲, leave from the waterfront in the Ribeira district (generally around €15, daily 10:00-18:30 in the summer and until 17:00 off-season, 50 minutes, multi-lingual narration). For a longer cruise, consider a **day trip along the Douro,** with a boat ride to Peso da Régua or Pinhão and return trip by train, plus breakfast and/or lunch on board (figure €60-85 to Peso da Régua, €75-100 to Pinhão, price depends on what's included, www.rotadodouro.pt; for details, see the next chapter).

Porto Walk

This two-part self-guided walk, worth ▲▲, links Porto's top landmarks. The first part is a brief, uphill-downhill loop through the city center, connecting the main square with some relatively untouristed back streets and the city's main landmark (Clérigos Tower). The second part begins at the São Bento train station and angles downhill to Porto's finest interiors (Stock Exchange Palace and São Francisco Church) before ending in its characteristic waterfront zone, the Ribeira. Doing the entire walk gives you a great overview of the city's charms and takes about two hours (one hour per part)—assuming you don't stop to enter sights along the way.

Porto is decentralized, with important sights scattered on many levels. I'll point out additional landmarks that you could detour to, if you have the time and interest.

UPPER PORTO—THE CITY CENTER
• *Begin at the equestrian statue that marks the bottom end of Porto's main square/boulevard...*

❶ Avenida dos Aliados (Avenue of the Allies)
Worth ▲▲, this is the main urban drag of Porto, where Portugal's hardworking second city goes to work. Porto—often invaded, never conquered—is known as *cidade invicta,* the "Invincible City." It's also called "The Granite City"—both for its stone-built cityscape and its sturdy, stubborn people (who like to say they have granite in their DNA). Rounding out the defiant symbolism is the

PORTO

Porto Walk

UPPER PORTO
1. Avenida dos Aliados
2. Rua da Fábrica
3. Praça Guilherme Gomes Fernandes
4. Praça de Gomes Teixeira & Praça de Parada Leitao
5. Lello & Irmão Bookstore
6. Praça de Lisboa Park
7. Clérigos Church & Tower

LOWER PORTO
8. São Bento Train Station
9. Rua das Flores
10. Misericórdia Church & Museum
11. Henry the Navigator Square
12. The Ribeira
13. Praça da Ribeira

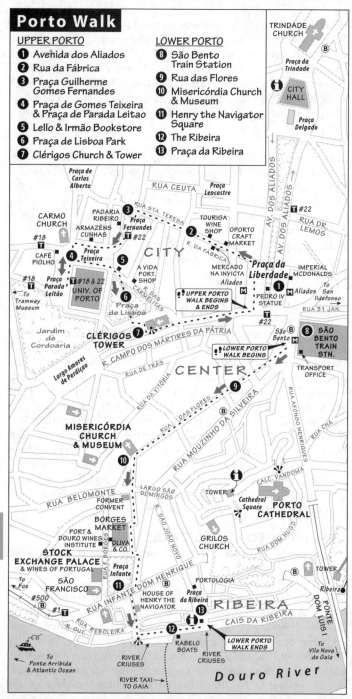

PORTO

dragon—the mascot of the locally beloved soccer team, FC Porto.

Avenida dos Aliados is named for the alliance created when Portugal joined the winning side during World War I. The wide boulevard, lined with elaborate examples

of various architectural eras (mostly Art Nouveau and Art Deco) was inspired by early 20th-century Paris and is also reminiscent of Prague's Wenceslas Square. The twin bank towers flanking the street midway up were designed by Portuguese architect Marques da Silva (c. 1920). And crowning the square is the huge City Hall (Câmara Municipal), built in 1957, with a balcony where VIPs are presented.

This esplanade is where locals gather for good times and bad times. Recently, 600,000 people celebrated here when Porto won the 2018 national football championship.

Praça da Liberdade (Liberty Square) marks the bottom of the avenue. The statue honors King Pedro IV (1798-1834), a hero in the 1832 Civil War, who advocated for a limited constitutional monarchy in Portugal (while maintaining his title as Emperor of Brazil). King Pedro prevailed...and he's holding the constitution to prove it. A true "peoples' king," he left his heart to the people of Porto—literally. (It's buried in a local church.)

The square is a strong statement for a secular and modern Portugal: It's topped not by a church, but by the City Hall (which blocks the view of Trindade Church—the namesake of the nearby station where all of Porto's Metro lines converge). Throughout Porto, after the king dissolved the monasteries and confiscated church property in the 1830s, large tracts of land that had been the domain of the church became the domain of the people. Then, in the 1920s and 1930s (especially with the coming of the dictator António Salazar), Portugal demonstrated its national pride by razing many characteristic medieval quarters to modernize the country, building bigger squares and bigger buildings (as here). While this feels like a celebration of art, it's the old financial center of Porto and these buildings are all about commerce.

"The Imperial McDonald's" is directly to the right of King Pedro, hiding behind the trees. Filling what was once the Imperial Café, this is one of the fanciest McDonald's in Europe. Check it out, and ponder the battle of cultural elegance against global economic efficiency. Portugal is the only country where McDonald's

PORTO

serves soup. It's a very soupy culture—even McDonald's had to include it to gain locals' acceptance.

Now stand at the very bottom of the square, along the busy street. Notice that nothing is level in Porto. Looking uphill, you'll see the blue-tiled Church of San Ildefonso, and just downhill is São Bento station. This walk connects key landmarks, with a little uphill walking (at the start), then lots of downhill walking.

• *Next, head one short block up Avenida dos Aliados, to the over-the-top bank tower on the left side of the square (labeled* Unic—indeed it is). *Angle up the little street just in front of that building (Rua do Dr. Artur de Magalhães Basto). After one short block, continue up the same street, now called…*

❷ Rua da Fábrica

This street—named for the tobacco factories that once helped power local industry in this town—is one of many appealing shopping lanes in downtown Porto. The city has been transformed in recent years. Not long ago, streets like this were neglected and deserted. And while they may still be (artfully) seedy, like the derelict place on the left, life is fast returning—with clever boutiques and tempting eateries opening all the time. Pop into a few such shops as you climb to the top of this street.

Oporto Craft Market (at Rua do Almada #125, on the first corner on the right), offers high-quality, locally handcrafted items: leather shoes, jewelry, cork products, sardines, and more.

At **Mercado na Invicta** (at #15 on the left), every table holds the work of a different artisan. Creative enterprises like these were born out of the economic crisis.

Touriga Wine Shop (at #32) offers tastings and shelves stocked with local wines (see page 392).

• *As you hike two steep blocks further, notice the fine tiled facades. Keep going up Rua da Fábrica, huffing your way up three more short but steep blocks. You'll pop out at a cute little triangular square called…*

❸ Praça Guilherme Gomes Fernandes

Firefighters take note: The square's namesake—honored by a statue in the middle—led the fire brigade that contained an 1888 blaze, which otherwise might have devastated the city.

Guilherme is eyeing the main reason to linger on this cozy square: the recommended **Padaria Ribeiro** pastry shop, a local favorite. Step inside and take your pick from the extensive sweet and savory offerings. You can either order something to go or have them bring it out to you on the square. You've finished the uphill portion of this walk—now's the time for a little pastry break with the bustle of Porto passing by.

• *With the pastry shop at your back, turn right and follow the trolley tracks around the corner to the right. You'll quickly emerge into a grand square.*

❹ Praça de Gomes Teixeira and Praça de Parada Leitao

The centerpiece of **Praça de Gomes Teixeira** is the Fountain of Lions, and behind that is the main building of the **University of Porto.** U. Porto is a fairly young school (founded 1911), but the second-biggest in Portugal, with about 30,000 students who give this city—and this neighborhood (one of three main campuses)—a special energy. The square is named for its first rector and beloved math prof.

At the top of the square (facing the university), the **Armazéns Cunhas** department store demonstrates the sleek Art Deco style

that took hold in Porto in the early 20th century—sprucing up a city of granite and *azulejos*. This neon facade, though now faded, might look more at home in Hollywood or Miami Beach. The peacock at the top trumpets the new fashions of the age, and neon announces *novidades—vendemos mais barato* ("new fashions—we sell cheaper!").

Just past the end of the square, you can't miss the brilliant blue *azulejos* on the side of **Carmo Church,** depicting the founding of the Carmelite Order. Circling around to the front, you'll see this is two fine Rococo churches in one: On the right, Carmo Church; on the left, the Carmelite church, with a huge white convent that once housed an order of Carmelite friars. (Like other convents and monasteries, it was nationalized in 1834 and today serves as the headquarters of Portugal's national guard.) These two churches were divided by what they like to call the "world's narrowest house"—with the green gate and door. The house served as a secret meeting place for order members during wartime and as a temporary shelter (for people such as doctors who worked in the order's hospital, artists who worked in the church, and the sacristan).

Stretching downhill from the church is the delightful cobbled square called **Praça de Parada Leitao** and the venerable (and recommended) **Café Piolho d'Ouro,** beloved by the local "bats." Over the years in Porto, students with their black capes and habit of coming out in flocks after dark earned the nickname, and this café is bat central. If you wander inside, you'll see plaques on the walls celebrating decades of graduating classes.

Lately this entire neighborhood has become a lively zone of student cafés, bars, and hangouts. If you're looking for some action after dinner, this neighborhood would be the top local recommendation.

In front of the café, notice the **trolley stop** for two of Porto's three historic lines. As in Lisbon, rickety trolleys have long been

a part of Porto's history, and the city is committed to bringing them back as an integral part of the public-transit system. In 1872 (40 years after being invented in the US), the first trolleys in Iberia began operating in Porto, pulled by horses and oxen. Dubbed *americanos* based on their origin, the trolley network was electrified in 1904. Essential for connecting suburbs with the city center, more than 100 trolley lines were still in use by the 1970s. However, buses and cars—the by-products of modern prosperity—almost eliminated this important part of the city's heritage.

Today, a few lines survive as vintage trips appealing mainly to tourists, although some locals of an older generation use them as public transport. From here, trolley #18 rattles to the Tramway Museum down to the river, while trolley #22 does a very handy loop through the town center. (For a fun, do-it-yourself tour, follow my "Porto Vintage Trolley Joyride"—see the sidebar, earlier. You'll leave from this point.)

• *Walk back to the big square with the university building on your right. An elevated park sits just ahead. On the left side of the downhill street that runs along the park, you'll see...*

❺ Lello & Irmão Bookstore

Built in 1906, the shop boasts a lacy exterior and a fancy Art Nouveau interior. It looks like wood, but it's mostly made of painted plaster with gold leaf. J. K. Rowling, who worked in Porto for a year, was reportedly inspired by this Harry Potter-esque shop. And sure enough, the interior feels like something you'd see on Diagon Alley.

The Harry Potter connection—which was attracting 2,000 Potterheads a day to ogle the interior—became too much for this fragile, little bookshop to handle. So now visitors must buy a voucher to enter. (Warning: Lines can be ridiculous and, while it's charming, there's really not a lot to see inside.) Once inside, follow the quaint tracks to the book trolley. Climb the sagging staircase to find the old cash register and admire the stained-glass ceiling and the slinky hanging lights.

Cost and Hours: €5-can be applied toward any book purchase (good selection of books in English by leading Portuguese authors), daily 10:00-19:30, Rua das Carmelitas 144. Buy tickets and check your bag at #166, four doors uphill, then join the queue at the bookstore's front door.

• *The cross street just downhill from the bookstore is Galeria de Paris, lined with characteristic shops and bars. On this corner is a branch of* **A Vida Portuguesa,** *the Lisbon-based shop for quality, authentic local souvenirs (Rua Galeria de Paris 20). Across the street, just uphill from the bookstore, is some brilliant city planning at...*

❻ Praça de Lisboa Park

This innovative solution shows what smart urban planners can do to camouflage an ugly concrete parking garage in the historic heart of a city: build a park on top of it. The most direct way to our next stop—the church tower—is through the modern concrete mall, which tunnels past shops and cafés under the middle of the park. But I'd rather head up the stairs (just to the right of the mall) to walk across the park itself—a green respite dotted with inviting olive trees in the heart of a congested city. Up top, a hip bar called Base serves drinks, which you can enjoy at picnic tables or under one of the 50 gnarled olive trees. This is a great spot for a drink after dark.

• *Make your way across the park—either down below or up top—to reach the can't-miss-it...*

❼ Clérigos Church and Tower (Igreja e Torre dos Clérigos)

This church, which consumed three decades of Nicolau Nasoni's life (1731-1763), shows the ambitious architect's flair for theatrics and is worth ▲. He fit the structure into its hilltop location, putting the tower at the back on the highest ground, dramatically reinforcing its height. Nasoni worked in stages: first the church, then the hospital and the Chapter House (meeting room for priests and monks). He topped it all off with the outsized tower. You can go

Nicolau Nasoni (1691-1773)

In the 1720s—a boom time in Porto—the Italian Nasoni found work as a painter here. His swirling, colorful paintings wowed Porto, and Nasoni got plenty of work. He married a Portuguese woman, had five kids, and made Porto his home. Soon, he was employed as an architect, hiring skilled local artisans to turn granite, wood, and poured plaster into his trademark cherubs, garlands, and cumulus clouds. Even stark medieval churches had their facades topped with Baroque towers and their interiors paneled and spackled in billowy gilded designs. Prolific to the max, Nasoni redid Porto in the Baroque style (much as Bernini did in Rome), creating palaces and churches throughout the area. His tour de force was the hill-topping Clérigos Church, where he was later buried.

inside the church for free or pay to climb the tower (see listing later, under "Sights in Porto").

• *Take the atmospheric, traffic-free, trolley-track-lined lane to the right of the tower—an urban canyon of azulejos and funky shops. Heading downhill, you'll find yourself back where you started—at the Avenida dos Aliados. This time, keep going straight, one more block. You'll run right into São Bento train station.*

The second of our walk begins just inside the station. But if you'd like to explore one more part of Porto's city center—the traditional market hall, bustling shopping street (Rua Santa Caterina), and azulejo-slathered church on Praça da Batalha—you can hike up the hill just to the left of the station (toward the pretty church you see perched on the hill). All of these are described later.

LOWER PORTO—GRAND INTERIORS AND RIBEIRA WATERFRONT

• *Begin inside the main entry hall of Porto's stately...*

❽ São Bento Train Station (Estação São Bento)

The station, worth ▲, has a main entry hall that features some of Portugal's finest *azulejos*—vivid, decorative hand-painted tiles that show historical and folk scenes from the Douro region. Originally a Benedictine convent, the land and building were nationalized and used to provide an ideal welcome for trains when they arrived in the 1870s. The distinctive tiles tell the story of Porto in a romanticized way, typical of that age. The trackside tiles celebrate the traditional economy, such as the transport of port wine.

Tiles: As you face the tracks, the large, blue, upper tiles on the left show medieval battles back when Spain and Portugal were at war. Victorious in their Reconquista over the Moors, the Portuguese had to settle on their borders with neighboring Castilla.

Tiles on the opposite wall (far right when facing the tracks) show a pivotal event from Porto's past: the 1387 wedding of Portugal's King João I and the English princess Philippa, which established the Portuguese-English alliance—the oldest in Europe.

Notice also the cathedral as it looked in the 14th century and the fine portrait of Philippa on her horse. She's not happy with the arranged political marriage or her king's concubine—the brightly lit woman behind him. But things eventually work out. Philippa left the king and went home to her native England. João then realized he loved her and begged her to return. She did so, and they had nine children, who went on to be instrumental in starting the Golden Age of Portugal. Below is their most famous son, Prince Henry the Navigator, shown conquering Ceuta for Portugal in 1415. While humble Ceuta was just a small chip of Morocco (across from Gibraltar), it marked an important first step in the creation of a soon-to-be vast Portuguese empire.

The multicolored tiles near the top show different modes of transportation, evolving from Roman chariots (next to the big clock), and progressing counterclockwise 360 degrees to the arrival of the first train (left corner above Philippa).

Notice the words *Douro* and *Minho* overhead. These are the major rivers in this part of Portugal, and the key regions linked by these trains (basically the north of the country). All this art seems old, but it's really Portuguese revival art from the period just after World War I, celebrating the country's heritage.

Nearby: Before continuing downhill to the Ribeira, stand in front of the station's entrance to get oriented. Consider a detour to Porto's **cathedral** and its viewpoint square. With the station to your back, you can see the cathedral's serrated roofline on the ridge to the left—about a 10-minute walk away. Just beyond the cathedral is the upper level of the Luís I Bridge, which crosses scenically over the Douro to **Villa Nova de Gaia** and its port wine lodges. Buses to Vila Nova de Gaia leave across the street from the station's entrance (the stop closest to the Metro entrance, buses #900, #901, or #906).

• *To continue our walk downhill to the Ribeira waterfront, cross the street, turn left, then take the right street at the fork. This puts you on a delightful, mostly pedestrianized lane connecting the town center with the riverbank.*

PORTO

❾ Rua das Flores

This traffic-free street is lined with iron railings, vivid *azulejos*, outdoor café tables, and enticing shops selling jewelry, antiques, chocolates, and other temptations. A decade ago, this was a deserted no-man's-land; today, it's a touristy main drag—and a great example of how Porto is blossoming. And yet, some funky graffiti (a Porto specialty) and ragtag housefronts still survive, as a reminder that Porto is a work in progress. Enjoy this strip for a few blocks downhill.

At #213, notice the flowers on the facade celebrating the street's name. The protected sign, *Ourivesaria*, recalls a jewelry shop—one of many that have long lined the street. This was the end of the Jewish quarter and right up until 1496 was lined with silver, gold, and jewelry shops. That's the year King Manuel I ordered all Jews to convert to Christianity—or be expelled. Beginning in 1497, the remaining Jews were forced to convert. Many became Christians in name but not in practice (as the secret synagogues found under these buildings attest). Meanwhile, the gold and silver shops stayed open and their heritage survives to this day. The ornate wrought-iron balconies were a way for wealthy aristocratic families to boast their status.

At #222, look down the narrow street and up at the four-story cat. Fun and surreal street art is an endearing dimension of Porto. While the city is constantly fighting graffiti (the wolf is favorite tag of anti-government gangs), Porto gives fine art students opportunities to show their talent by decorating sections of streets and walls. You'll notice the little electric boxes all along this street are painted with city-related themes by art students.

• *Eventually you'll reach some modern art spewing from a facade on the right. Symbolic of Christ's blood connecting heaven and earth, this marks the...*

❿ Misericórdia Church and Museum

Porto's Santa Casa da Misericórdia (Holy House of our Lady of Mercy) is a powerful church-run organization dedicated to helping people with both their physical and spiritual needs. Since the 16th century it's been the city's United Way and Gates Foundation rolled into one. The organization remains a huge and important landowner in Porto, operating hospitals, schools, and other social services.

This building was once a hospital. Today it's an impressive little museum housing lots of artifacts (including early medical implements), paintings of leading benefactors of old, and treasures donated over the years, all well-described in English. Upon entering, head to the fourth floor and work your way back down, finishing in the dazzling, Mannerist-style church ornamented with fine *azulejos*. It was designed by Nicolau Nasoni, the prolific Baroque architect who left his mark all over the city (see sidebar earlier).

Cost and Hours: €5, daily 10:00-18:30, off-season until 17:30, Rua das Flores 15, +351 220 906 960, www.mmipo.pt.

• *Rua das Flores ends at a former Dominican convent overlooking Largo de São Domingos. The big granite building is now filled with creative startups (part of a government-subsidized "incubator" program for entrepreneurs).*

Continue straight across the busy, cobbled street and head down Rua do Dr. Sousa Viterbo. Soon, on your right, you'll pass the big, red Borges Market—now a popular nightclub. Just past the market, you'll emerge at the top of...

❶ Henry the Navigator Square (Praça do Infante Dom Henrique)

Arguably the most important Portuguese person of all time—who put his country on the (figurative) map by putting many mysterious, faraway lands on the (literal) map—hailed from Porto. In this **statue,** Henry the Navigator is pointing toward the sea. For more on Henry, see the sidebar on page 197.

The **Stock Exchange Palace** (Palácio da Bolsa) dominates this square. This is the palatial home of the Commercial Association of Porto. Commerce came to define Porto as royalty defined Lisbon and religion defined Braga. The association even had its own system of courts and a representative to the king. In 1832, the monastery of the São Francisco Church next door burned down, and the queen offered the property to the Commercial Association. They seized the opportunity to show off, crafting a building that would demonstrate the considerable skill of Porto's tradesmen. The interior—which you can visit only with a 45-minute guided tour (see listing later, under "Sights in Porto")—is a proud showcase of decorative prowess. Finely carved granite, inlaid-wood floors, plaster painted to resemble carved wood, and other details adorn everything from the glorious glass-roofed atrium to the exactingly detailed Arabian Hall. Drop in now to see when the next tour is available (this walk ends nearby).

São Francisco Church is just to the left of the Stock Exchange Palace. This has the finest church interior in town, and its adjacent crypt is stacked with anonymously numbered tombs holding the remains of past parishioners (see listing later, under "Sights in Porto"; enter around the left side).

After you've admired the impressive buildings, consider a couple of options for **port wine and olive oil tasting** around the square. If you don't have a tour ticket for the Stock Exchange Palace, you can get into it and see its main courtyard by requesting to see the **Wines of Portugal Tasting Room** inside the Stock Exchange building. A much better port experience is in the stately **Port and Douro Wines Institute** across from the red market hall on Rua Ferreira Borges. (Both of these port stops are described later in the sidebar on page 392.) If you're more in the mood for olive oil, get a little tasting at the fine **Oliva & Co. shop** across the street from the institute.

• *To continue our walk, head down the little street directly downhill from Henry the Navigator (Rua Alfândega—the aptly named "Customs Street"). On the left, you'll see the **House of Henry the Navigator**, where the great explorer is believed to have been born (the house has no Henry artifacts, and is not worth a visit for most.) From Henry's pad it's just a few more steps downhill to...*

⓬ The Ribeira, Porto's Romantic Riverfront

The riverfront Ribeira (ree-BAY-rah, meaning "riverbank") district is the city's most scenic and touristy quarter, with its highest concentration of restaurants and postcard racks. Narrow, higgledy-piggledy homes face the busy Douro River. Head down to the riverbank and do the same, scanning the horizon from left to right.

The **Ponte Dom Luís I bridge** rises 150 feet above the river on your far left. In the 1880s, Teofilo Seyrig, a protégé of Gustave Eiffel, stretched this wrought-iron contraption across the 500-foot-wide Douro. The Eiffel Tower-sized bridge is growing fragile, so starting in 2022 this Porto landmark will be open only to trams and pedestrians, and a new bridge for cars will be built further upstream. (Eiffel himself designed a bridge in Porto, the **Ponte Dona Maria Pia,** a bit upstream—barely visible from here.)

Vila Nova de Gaia (or just "Gaia") is the port wine lodge district directly across the river. If you followed the Douro 60 miles upriver—beyond those bridges—you'd reach a wonderland of hand-built stone terraces where grapes enjoy a hardy existence. Port wine is harvested and stomped there, then floated downriver to age here. Until recently, the wine could be legally called "port" only if it aged in Gaia—though recent deregulation now permits vintners to age their port where it's grown. You'll see the proud signs of 18 different company names marking their lodges here—each one inviting you in for a sample. (For more on the port-tasting scene in Gaia, see page 377.)

Look to your right and see how the river bends as it heads out toward the open Atlantic. To get out of the congested urban center, consider side-tripping out to the pleasant beach community of Foz, where the Douro meets the sea (see the "Sights Away from the Center" section, later).

Now turn around and face the **skinny houses along the embankment** (signed *Cais da Estiva*). Before tourism, the Ribeira was a working port. The city wall fortified Porto from the river, and (until the 20th-century embankment was built) the water came right up to the arches—many of which were loading zones for merchants. Imagine the busy harbor scene before the promenade was reclaimed from the river: cargo-laden riverboats lashed to the embankment, off-loading their wine and produce into 14th-century cellars (still visible). Today the old arcades lining the Ribeira promenade are jammed with hole-in-the-wall restaurants and souvenir shops. Behind the arcades are skinny, colorful houses draped with drying laundry fluttering like flags, while the locals who fly them stand gossiping on their little balconies. The contrast of bright tourism and vivid untouched neighborhoods within 30 yards of each other is amazing.

• *From Cais da Estiva and with the river on your right, go for a stroll along the embankment known as the **Cais da Ribeira**, worth ▲▲.*

As you walk, notice the various interchangeable companies along this embankment selling scenic **"Six Bridges" cruises** on the Douro, which take you past landmarks not visible from here (including Eiffel's majestic steel Ponte Dona Maria Pia). If you're interested, comparison-shop as you stroll.

Soon you'll reach some distinctive boats—called *rabelos*—moored along the embankment. These were once the only way to transport wine from the Douro Valley vineyards downriver to Porto. These boats have flat bottoms, big square sails, and very large rudders to help them navigate the rough, twisty course of the river (for more about these boats, see page 407).

• *After about a block, you'll pop out at the bottom of the neighborhood's main square...*

⓭ Praça da Ribeira

This vibrant, ragtag space was long the city's front door. In the mid-18th century, city leaders attempted to clear it out and make a vast

wasteland like Lisbon's Praça do Comércio. But the proud people of Porto (who, remember, have granite in their DNA) asserted themselves— as they like to do—and that construction project was stopped. Today, this square is a thriving place of the people.

Stand on the riverfront and look inland: On the right is a classic line of Porto houses that survive (sometimes with old ladies looking out at the crowd from their windows). Check out the artwork in the square: the cube fountain and the statue of St. John the

Baptist with his rough cloak, who overlooks the happy scene from above. For yet another wine-tasting opportunity, just a few steps above the square on Rua de São João (on the right, at #28) is the recommended **Portologia wine bar.**

• *Our Porto orientation walk is over. There's a lot more of the Ribeira to see—just walk with the river on your right, following the rabelos. Or venture into the maze of distinctive, tiny lanes that climb up the hill from the water.*

*At the end of the embankment is the towering bridge; its lower level takes you efficiently to **Vila Nova de Gaia** for some port tasting. Or save your feet and make a little cruise out of the crossing by catching the Douro River river taxi that shuttles back and forth.*

*Or, to head back up to the **cathedral area or Porto's shopping neighborhood,** ride the funicular—it departs from this side of the river, just past the bridge.*

Sights in Porto

Many of Porto's top sights are connected by my self-guided walk, earlier.

PORTO'S SHOPPING NEIGHBORHOOD

Porto's bustling, local-feeling shopping district is a wonderful place to people-watch. Most of the action occurs along Rua de Santa Catarina, which runs roughly parallel to Avenida dos Aliados a few blocks east. Begin at Praça da Batalha (just up Rua 31 de Janeiro from São Bento station) and follow this route to the modern market hall (the original building is currently under restoration).

Praça da Batalha (Battle Square)

This square has a fine tiled church (San Ildefonso), the 19th-century National Theater (originally the Opera House), and the impressive (but closed) Art Deco Cinema Batalha. The church's *azulejo* tiles, reminiscent of Delft blue-and-white ceramics, were all the rage in Baroque Portugal. But these tiles, depicting scenes from the life of the church's patron saint, aren't Baroque. Like the tiles at the train station, they were fit-ted into the walls of the church during the early 1930s, an era that celebrated Portuguese heritage.

This square, while a bit seedy, has benches where old-timers hang out. If you'd like a classic little hot dog with the local gang,

PORTO

drop by the recommended **Cervejaria Gazela** (just to the right of the National Theater).

• *At the north end of the square, branching off to the left of the blue-tiled church, is...*

▲Rua de Santa Catarina

Porto's main shopping street is busy and (mostly) traffic-free by day, and quiet by night. A stroll along here gives you a sense of today's Porto—as well as yester-day's.

Peek into the vener-able Art Nouveau **Café Majestic,** the circa-1900 hangout for the local intel-ligentsia (a block down on your right). It's extremely touristy...understandably. (While I wouldn't eat a se-rious meal here, it's nice for breakfast or for a late-night dessert of its famous *rabanadas*—a special French toast with an unforgettable syrup.) Kitty-corner from Café Majestic is the **FNAC** department store—handy for whatever you might need.

The Rua de Santa Catarina sidewalk is a good example of *calçada portuguesa,* Portugal's unique limestone and basalt mosaic work. It's handmade and high-maintenance...but apparently worth the effort and expense to locals. Notice all the shoe stores. Along with wine, textile and shoe factories power northern Portugal's in-dustry. (My Eccos are made right here.)

At #326, a modern **department store** hides behind an out-landish art installation covering the entire facade. The top floor is a food court designed to look like an old-time harborfront—a kitschy but popular place for pensioners to hang out. Across the street is a bakery that cranks out beloved *pastel de nata* custard pies.

• *Keep walking up Rua de Santa Catarina until you hit Rua de Fernandes Tomas. The historic **Bolhão Market**, a block to the left, may be closed for renovation. If so, head to the right on Rua de Fernandes Tomas a block to the...*

▲Temporary Bolhão Market

In a modern department store basement, the temporary replace-ment for Porto's famed Bolhão market is still lots of fun to visit. Taking the escalator down, you'll pass photos of the women mer-chants who are the heart and soul of the market. At the bottom, on the right, a statuette of Virgin of the Immaculate Conception is strewn with necklaces and jewelry as thanks for the steady com-merce (and to help this community of merchants get through this difficult interim period). Fun little eateries and market stalls spread out from there, complete with lots of samples (Mon-Sat 8:00-20:00, closed Sun).

IN THE CITY CENTER

▲Clérigos Church and Tower (Igreja e Torre dos Clérigos)

This oval-shaped church with a disproportionately tall tower is one of the best known masterworks of Baroque architect Nicolau Nasoni. There are free, 30-minute organ concerts here daily at noon, preceded by the carillon ringing from the tower.

Cost and Hours: Church-free, tower and exhibits-€5, daily 9:00-19:00, Rua São Filipe de Nery, +351 222 001 729. You can also climb the tower after dark (€5, daily in season 19:00-23:00).

Visiting the Church and Tower: The **church facade** displays Nasoni's characteristic frills, garlands, and exuberant cornices. Notice how Nasoni built the tower in six sections, each one more elaborate than the last, topped with a round dome and spiked with pinnacles.

The **interior** is an oval-shaped Baroque nave built out of granite and pink marble, but covered with ornate carvings (c. 1725). Look for the high altar—a wedding-cake structure with Mary on top—and thought to be the tomb of Nasoni, who asked to be buried here. Statues of the eight patron saints of Portugal circle the nave.

The main attraction is climbing 225 steps to the top of the 250-foot **tower**—one of Porto's icons. (On busy days, you may have to kill time waiting for your turn on the upper stairs—ask before you buy your ticket.) On the way up, you'll peek into the assembly rooms, walk along upper galleries offering views into the church interior from above, and check out the "Christus Collection," with depictions of Jesus from all over Portugal and around the world (many brought home by Portuguese explorers). Reaching the top, you get a close-up look at the carillon and commanding views of the city with its jumble of tightly packed red roofs.

▲Porto Cathedral (Sé do Porto)

This hulking, fortress-like, 12th-century Romanesque cathedral, while graced with fine granite stonework typical of northern Portugal and lavish 18th-century Baroque altars, feels gloomy and stark inside. But its history is palpable. Henry the Navigator was baptized here, and it was the scene of many royal weddings (including that of Henry's parents, João I and Philippa).

Cost and Hours: Cathedral-free, cloister and sacristy-€3; open daily in summer 9:00-12:30 & 14:30-19:00, until 18:00 in winter; cloister closed Sun mornings year-round; Terreiro da Sé, +351 222 059 028.

Visiting the Cathedral: The **main altarpiece** sums up the exuberance of Porto in the 1720s, when the city was booming, the local bishop was tem-

porarily away in Lisbon, and Italian Baroque was sweeping through town. On the side walls flanking the altar are faded faux-architecture paintings by Nicolau Nasoni, the Italian who came to Porto to paint the cathedral's sacristy and soon became the city's most influential architect (see sidebar on page 364).

Look at the chapel just left of the high altar. Inside is a dreamy, carved-and-painted limestone statue of the **Lady of Vendôme,** brought to Porto in the 14th century by monks from France. It originally stood at one of the fortified gates of the city and remains close to the hearts of the townsfolk.

Just left of the Lady of Vendôme is the **Silver Altar of the Holy Sacrament** (c. 1700)—made with 1,500 pounds of silver. When French troops under Napoleon pillaged Porto, the church guards plastered over the altar to hide it.

The **cloister** and its adjacent rooms are worth the time and entrance fee. The cloister's walls are decorated with elaborate *azulejos*

(tiles) illustrating the amorous poetry of the Bible's "Song of Songs." (The €0.30 pamphlet is skimpy, but the €5 English guidebook explains it all, including the text that inspired the *azulejos*.) Entering, turn right and go for a counterclockwise stroll. The adjacent **Chapel of St. Vincent,** with 17th-century painted carvings of Bible scenes, has a trapdoor into a crypt, where centuries of bishops' bones were ultimately tossed. Up the Nasoni staircase, the richly ornamented **chapter room** is where the bishop and his gang met in the 17th century to wield their religious and secular power. Note the holy figures depicted on the ceiling and the fine city views from the windows. There's also a typical **treasury,** with vestments and monstrances.

PORTO

Cathedral Square

From the cathedral's small square—until the 1920s a congested medieval quarter—you'll get a great view of the old town. The Baroque spiral pillory (20th-century copy) is a reminder of the harsh justice once doled out here. Dominating the square (and the skyline of Porto) is the massive **Bishop's Palace,** still the home of the bishop and his offices; the immensity of this 18th-century building reflects the bishop's past power. The crenellated tower just down the stairs from the cathedral square houses a TI.

Facing the cathedral, walk around to the left to the statue of **Vímara Peres,** a Christian warrior who reconquered this region from the Moors in 868. (It was lost again within two generations, and remained under Muslim control until the final reconquest in about 1100.) Step into the portico on the side of the cathedral to admire the original 18th-century blue tiles.

From the **viewpoint banister** to the left of Vímara Peres, survey the city and find the church with the blue facade in the middle ground. São Bento station is just to its right, and the green copper dome and steeple of the City Hall breaks the skyline above it. Below you spreads the seedy district called Sé (meaning "cathedral," it refers to the *Se*at of the Catholic Church). This neighborhood, the oldest in town, was famously run-down and depopulating. Things are changing, as the government is encouraging people to move in by offering economic incentives. The streets beyond the medieval gate—once a ratatouille of drug users and prostitutes, but now touristy—twist their way down into the Ribeira district.

Hidden Church and City Wall

A segment of the restored city wall is visible near the top of the funicular. To get there, walk past the top of the Ponte Dom Luís I bridge (behind the cathedral) and up Rua de Saraiva de Carvalho to the leafy square called Largo Primeiro de Dezembro. Through the arched doorway hides the **Santa Clara Church**—think of this as a free version of São Francisco Church (see listing later), with an equally impressive, if musty, Baroque interior decorated with carved wood and lots of gold leaf (Mon-Fri 10:00-12:30 & 14:30-17:00, Sat 10:00-12:30, closed Sun, may be closed for renovation).

Walk back to the main street, then take a right to find a small portion of the **former city wall.** The funicular that departs for the Ribeira riverfront is just across the street (**Funicular dos Guindais,** station below ground).

JUST ABOVE THE RIBEIRA, ON HENRY THE NAVIGATOR SQUARE

These sights are on or near Praça do Infante Dom Henrique, a steep block uphill from the Ribeira district.

▲▲Stock Exchange Palace (Palácio da Bolsa)

This bold building is neither a stock exchange nor a palace, but the headquarters of the Commercial Association of Porto (Associa-

ção Comercial do Porto). Built over the course of 70 years, it's a breathtaking monument to civic and commercial pride, with some of the most lavishly decorated rooms in Portugal. The building—with its finely-carved granite rooms—celebrates Porto's renowned work ethic and dedication to international trade.

For more on the history of the building, see "Porto Walk," earlier.

Cost and Tours: The interior can only be visited on a 45-minute guided tour (€11). Tours leave every 30 minutes in various languages (with only about six a day in English). To avoid the wait, call to ask when the next English tour departs—or, if you're nearby, drop in and check the screens in the lobby. It's smart to pay for and reserve a spot on an English-language tour in person (while tickets are sold online, you can't reserve a tour time).

Hours: Daily 9:00-18:30, Nov-March 9:00-13:00 & 14:00-17:30, these are last tour times.

Information: Located in big building marked *Associação Comercial do Porto* on Rua Ferreira Borges, +351 223 399 013, www.palaciodabolsa.com. Note that the building still houses the offices of the Chamber of Commerce, and often closes when rented out for events.

Visiting the Stock Exchange: You'll tour several rooms, big and small. You'll begin in the dramatic main hall—decorated

with the coats of arms of 20 international trading partners—then climb the grand staircase to tour a variety of fine rooms. The place is rife with symbolism and intricate, time-consuming craftsmanship: the complex patterned floors, carefully pieced together with Brazilian and African wood (from Portugal's colonies); an incredibly detailed inlaid table, created over three years using wood scraps from those same floors; and a room that looks like it's made of finely carved woodwork and bronze—until you realize it's all painted plaster and gold leaf.

The knock-your-socks-off finale is the sumptuous Arabian

PORTO

Hall. This grand space—inspired by Granada's Alhambra and 18 years in the making—was painstakingly decorated in the Moorish style with wood, plaster, and gold leaf.

Nearby: Before exiting (or while awaiting your tour), consider a break in the **Wines of Portugal Tasting Room,** in this same building (just inside the turnstiles) and described on page 392.

▲São Francisco Church

This is Porto's only church in the Gothic style—complete with a rose window, stair-step buttresses, and a statue of St. Francis of Assisi on the front. Today, a visit comes in two parts: the extravagantly decorated church and its jam-packed catacombs.

Cost and Hours: €6, daily 9:00-20:00, Oct-Feb until 17:30, guidebooklet-€1, Rua do Infante Dom Henrique.

Visiting the Church: Buy your ticket at the office across from the church entrance. Although the church was ravaged by Napoleon and by the Portuguese during their 19th-century civil war, the interior remains stunning, with lavish chestnut carvings slathered in gold leaf. Wander down the main aisle like a bewildered 18th-century peasant. The first big, ornate altar on the right shows how Franciscans weren't always warmly received—at the top they are being cruelly tortured and crucified by Japanese (portrayed with Arabic features), and at the bottom they are being beheaded by Moors. Still, in the center, St. Francis encourages his followers on. A few steps forward and to the left, find the extremely fertile Tree of Jesse (1718), which is a very literal interpretation of the family tree of Jesus, resting upon a sleeping Jesse. Below that, Mary lies in a boat as Our Lady of Good Voyage, a patron saint of navigators. Note the wooden boards on the floor—once graves of parishioners. These graves are now empty, but you can see the bones in the crypt.

To get there, cross back over to the ticket desk. You'll walk through a smaller chapel and a modest museum, then head down the steps to the church's crypt—its walls and floors neatly lined with tombs. The remains of former parishioners eventually end up in an inglorious bone heap or ossuary. Peer down through the trapdoor near #32 (look for signs to the *ossário*) to see their final refuge.

House of Henry the Navigator (Casa do Infante)

Six hundred years ago, Porto's favorite son was supposedly born in this granite mansion (once the largest house in town, and later the main customs house and even minted coins for the city). Modern exhibits offer a look at Henry and the explorations he promoted, but there are few actual artifacts. You'll see a model of city in Henry's day, a few bits of broken pottery, and wonder "Where's the beef?". Still, if you're in a seafaring mood, it's a good reminder of all the new ground (well, water) that Portuguese explorers covered over the centuries.

Cost and Hours: €2.20, Tue-Sun 9:30-13:00 & 14:00-17:30, closed Mon, Rua da Alfândega 10, +351 222 060 423.

PORT WINE LODGES IN VILA NOVA DE GAIA

Just across the river from Porto, the town of Vila Nova de Gaia—or just Gaia (GUY-yuh)—is where much of the world's port wine comes to mature. Port  wine grapes are grown, and a young port is produced, about 60 miles upstream in the Douro Valley. Then, after sitting for the winter in silos, the wine is shipped downstream to Vila Nova de Gaia, to age for years in lodges on this cool, north-facing riverbank. Over a dozen companies run these lodges, holding down the port fort and offering tours and tastings. There are also several independent tasting rooms. For wine connoisseurs, touring a port wine lodge *(cave do vinho do porto)* and sampling the product is a ▲▲▲ attraction; for those with a casual interest, dropping into one or two is fun, educational, and worth ▲.

Gaia is technically a separate town from Porto, even though it's just across the river and feels like part of the city. Venturing here is well worth the trip. But if you're very tight on time, consider just dropping into one of the wine tastings on the Porto side of the river (see page 392).

Getting There: From the city center, take bus #900, #901, or #906 to get to the waterfront, with a stop at Cálem lodge, where you can then walk along the river. Buses #901 or #906 then continue uphill to Taylor's wine lodge (every 30 minutes, stop across from São Bento station near the Metro entrance). From the Ribeira district, walk (or catch a cab or Uber) across the Ponte Dom Luís I bridge or take a river taxi (see page 355).

Services: Vila Nova de Gaia operates its own handy **TI** with information about the lodges (daily 10:00-18:00, longer hours in summer, on the riverbank at Avenida Diogo Leite 135, +351 223 758 288, www.cm-gaia.pt). Drinks-with-a-view options are available all along the waterfront. A pricey **cable car** links the riverfront with the hilltop Jardim do Morro, at the foot of the Ponte Dom Luís I bridge (see page 354).

PORTO

▲▲▲Tours and Tastings

Port tasting is a subjective business, and no single lodge is necessarily the best. If you're a port enthusiast, you probably already have a favorite (or can quickly decide on one, with a little enjoyable research). Although more serious European visitors choose one lodge to visit, American tourists are known to hop between three or four in a single day...before stumbling back to their hotels.

Visiting a Port Wine Lodge: At any lodge, the procedure is similar. Individual travelers simply show up and ask for a tour; if it's busy, they may assign you a time. Pass any wait time by browsing the small on-site museum or watching a video, or simply get started on the tasting. A standard tour/tasting costs €12 and takes about 30 minutes. Tours generally come with a walk through the warehouse (with wooden barrels and vats);

a 5- to 10-minute video produced by that label giving you a quick peek at their process and the scenic Douro Valley; sometimes a small museum; and, finally, two or three tastings. Tours at fancier lodges (like Taylor's) take longer and cost more. At any lodge, serious students may opt for more involved tours, offering tastings of finer wines (generally €20, with smaller groups, 5 tastings, book in advance if possible). Before you go (or while you're waiting for your tour), you can read about the "Port Wine Crash Course" (page 380), "Brits on the Douro" (page 403), and "Growing—and Stomping—Grapes in the Douro Valley" (page 402).

Sandeman, the most high-profile company, is the Budweiser of port. They were the first port producer to create a logo, which you'll see everywhere: a mysterious man wearing a black cloak (representing a Portuguese student's cape) and a rakish *Shadow* hat (worn by Spanish horse-riders, symbolizing the sherry that Sandeman makes in Jerez). Sandeman provides the most corporate, mainstream, accessible experience for firsttimers—with a short walk led by a caped guide, a 10-minute video, and two tastings. It's also the most crowded, often giving times for you to return or sending you to their sister manufacturers. It's exciting to think that the entire Portuguese production of Sandeman Port ages right in this building (€14 basic visit, €23 for 1.5-hour tour with 5 tastes; daily 10:00-20:00, Nov-Feb until 18:00; faces its own little square with tables and bar service along the riverfront at Largo Miguel Bombarda 3, +351 223 740 533, www.sandeman.com).

Cálem, the first place you see after crossing the bridge, offers a fine tour wandering among its huge oak casks (€14 includes 2 sam-

Vila Nova de Gaia

RIBEIRA DISTRICT

To Porto Center

PONTE LUÍS I
UPPER LEVEL

D o u r o   R i v e r

RIVER TAXI
LOWER LEVEL

SERRA DO PILAR MONASTERY

Largo Miguel Bombarda

BOAT TRIPS & RIVER TAXI

Cable Car

Largo Cruz

AVENIDA RAMOS PINTO
RUA 7 PASS

Jardim do Morro

To 10

R. REI RAMIRO

RUA DR. A GRANJO

R. SERRA PINTO

R. AZENHAS

R. RAMADA ALTA

R. LEO. DE FREITAS

R. BARÃO

R. FERN.

R. COSTA SANTOS

R. DO CHOUPELO

RUA PILAR

AV. D. LEITE

RUA GENERAL TORRES

R. CANDIDO DOS REIS

AVENIDA DA REPUBLICA

R. LUIS CAMÕES

RUA JAU

General Torres

Port Wine Lodges & Shops
1 Sandeman
2 Cálem
3 Taylor's & Restaurante Barão Fladgate
4 Ferreira
5 Kopke Shop
6 Quinta de Santa Eufêmia
7 Vasques de Carvalho

Eateries
8 Adega e Presuntaria Transmontana Restaurante
9 Ar de Rio Restaurante
10 To Vinum Restaurant-Wine Bar
11 Porto Cruz Rooftop Bar

ples, 25-minute tours in English depart about every hour, May-Oct daily 10:00-19:00, off-season fewer tours and closes at 18:00, mobile +351 916 113 451, www.calem.pt). They also offer 45-minute fado shows that include a port tasting (€21, Tue-Sun at 18:30, at 18:00 in winter, none on Mon)—a handy and entertaining alternative if you show up just after most of the lodges have closed.

Taylor's—near the top of the hill—is a good choice for more discriminating tastes. It's classy and more time-consuming than the options down on the riverbank, and comes with stunning views back on Porto. You'll follow a one-hour audioguide through the sprawling complex, including modern museum exhibits, and end with two tastings—which you can enjoy with grand views (€15, daily 12:00-20:00, high up but worth the hike at Rua do Choupelo 250, +351 223 772 973, www.taylor.pt). Their splurge restaurant, **$$$$ Barão Fladgate,** offers stunning lunchtime views along with an opportunity to recharge for more tastings. Many consider it among the best dining spots in Porto (reservations smart, daily

PORTO

Port Wine Crash Course

Port is a medium-sweet wine (around 20 percent alcohol), usually taken as a *digestif* after dinner. The wine is fortified at a ratio of about 4:1 with *aguardente*, a grappa-like brandy distilled from the same grapes. The brandy is introduced before fermentation is complete—and kills the remaining yeast—which leaves more sugar in the port (standard wines ferment for 10-12 days; port for only 2-3 days). After the brandy is added, the wine ages for at least two years.

For most people, "port" means a tawny port aged 10-20 years—the most common type. But there's a whole spectrum of port, using more than 40 varieties of grapes. The two broad categories are wood ports (aged in wooden barrels or vats) and vintage ports (aged in bottles). Here's a rundown:

Tawny, the wood port with a leathery color, is the most typical version. It's older, lighter, mellower, and more complex than L.B.V. (described later). It's aged in smaller barrels, maximizing exposure to wood and giving it a nuttier flavor. Tawny port stays in the barrel for 10, 20, 30, or 40 years. But to enhance the complexity of the flavor, any tawny is actually a blend of several vintages (for example, a "30-year-old tawny" is predominantly 30 years old, but also has components that are 10 or 20 years old). Once blended, the various ports "marry" in the bottle for about eight months.

Inexpensive **ruby port** ages in oak vats for only three years, and then it's bottled. It's deep red, fruity, and has a strong, fiery taste of grape and pepper.

Vintage port—the most expensive—is a ruby that comes from a single harvest. Only wine from the very best vintages is

12:30-15:00 & 19:00-22:00, +351 223 772 951, www.baraofladgate. com).

Ferreira's lodge comes with classical music "to help age the wine." It's an interesting tour and shows off some fine museum artifacts (€14 includes 2 tastings, daily 10:00-12:30 & 14:00-18:00, look for big sign at the end of the riverfront promenade at Avenida Ramos Pinto 70, +351 223 746 107).

Wine Shops: Several producers have tasting rooms separate from their lodges. **Kopke** is recognized as one of the best in the business because they were first. Unfortunately, their lodge doesn't receive visitors, but their shop along the waterfront allows

selected (typically two or three per decade; 2011 was a great year, and 2000 was one of the best ever). After two years of aging in wooden casks, potential vintage port must be tested by the authorities. If they reject it, the wine stays in the casks longer to become L.B.V. (see next). If they give it the go-ahead, it's bottled and aged another 10-30 years (or more). Sediment is common, so bottles must be decanted. And if a bottle is really old, the cork may deteriorate—so the top of the bottle is heated up with a pair of red-hot tongs, then cold water is poured over it to break it off cleanly.

Late Bottle Vintage (L.B.V.) was invented after World War II, when British wine lovers couldn't afford true vintage port. L.B.V. is a blend of wines from a single year, which age together in huge wooden vats for four to six years. The size of the vats means less exposure to wood, which makes it age more quickly, but without losing its fruitiness and color. It's bottled after five years (later than a vintage port, which ages for only two years—hence the name). This more-affordable alternative saved the port wine industry.

You'll also see **white** ports, which are young, robust, and typically consumed before dinner as an *aperitif*. Most are dry (similar to Spain's *fino* sherries); for a sweet version, look for *lágrima* on the label. Aging the white ports has become trendy and produces a darker wine with some characteristics of a tawny. More recently, some vintners have experimented with **rosé** ports. And **Douro table wines** are becoming a popular and respected secondary business for many producers.

Port's stodgy image makes it unpopular among young Portuguese. Lodges have not escaped the multinational conglomerate game, but new owners often retain the brand name to keep loyal customers even as they market aggressively to attract new ones. For some, port is an acquired taste—but it's one worth cultivating. As I always say, "Any port in a storm..."

people to experience—one delightful sip at a time—what they've been doing well since 1638. The staff offers concise explanations and some fine ports by the glass in an elegant, upstairs tasting room far from the crowds outside (€3-7/glass, flights start at €25—decide and pay before going upstairs, daily 10:00-19:00, Nov-April until 18:00, next to Cálem at Avenida Diogo Leite 312, mobile +351 915 848 484).

Quinta de Santa Eufêmia has a large, open tasting room situated on a back street just behind the riverfront. Fourth-generation Carvalho siblings make innovative wines such as a 20-year white port and showcase the success of a non-corporate winery (€5-13 tastings, daily 10:00-19:00, take a left before Ramos Pinto to Santa Marinha 77, mobile +351 927 691 345, www.qtastaeufemia.com).

Vasques de Carvalho may be the new kid on the block, but their wines are anything but. The family—different Carvalhos than at Quinta de Santa Eufêmia—began making port in 1880. In the 1970s, the matriarch increased production, and son António has now entered the very competitive market with a bang. Their intimate and stylish tasting venue has four different areas (flights starting at €15 or taste by the glass, daily 10:00-19:00, Rua de Santa Marinha 19, +351 223 710 445, www.vasquesdecarvalho.com).

SIGHTS AWAY FROM THE CENTER
Tramway Museum (Museu do Carro Eléctrico)

This clever museum-in-a-warehouse displays beautifully restored examples of trolleys from different eras, including 1950s buses and a brand-new hydrogen-powered city bus. You can climb aboard many for a fun, Rice-A-Roni-style experience...just ding the bell.

Cost and Hours: €8, discount with all-day trolley pass, Mon 14:00-18:00, Tue-Sun 10:00-18:00, Alameda Basílio Teles 51, +351 226 158 185, www.museudocarroelectrico.pt.

Getting There: The most atmospheric way to arrive at the museum is via trolley #1 or #18. You can include a museum visit as you rattle around the city on my "Porto Vintage Trolley Joyride" (see the sidebar on page 355). Sit on restored leather seats and see a little of workaday Porto, plus some river views from up above.

Foz

Foz do Douro (or simply "Foz") is one of Porto's trendiest, greenest, wealthiest, and most relaxing quarters, situated where the river meets the Atlantic. There's no real destination in Foz; simply wander through the park (Jardim do Passeio Alegre, with miniature golf, a fancy old WC pavilion, and a nondescript café), ponder the sea, and smell the seaweed. Walk out to either of the lighthouses to watch fishermen mending their nets and see where the Douro River ends. If you have the time and good weather, take a boardwalk stroll to the Praia dos Ingleses beach and its fancy pergola. With more time, walk all the way to the Castelo do Queijo fortress... no, it isn't made of cheese. But the rugged rock formations apparently look like cheese  to some people. Foz is a relaxing break from the busy downtown area, and sunset can be romantic on warm days.

Getting There: The vintage trolley (line #1) scenically rattles its way from the Ribeira district along the Douro River and to the Jardim do Passeio Alegre, a 10-minute walk to the center of the Foz district. From the trolley stop, you can stroll at leisure or catch bus #500 for an Atlantic coast ride. Alternately, bypass the trolley by taking bus #500 from the Ribeira all the way to Foz (catch trolley or bus in front of São Francisco Church, departures roughly every 20 minutes, fewer after 19:00, 20-minute trip).

Nearby: You can combine a trip to Foz with a visit to the Serralves Museum. From Foz, either catch bus #203—it runs near the beach on Rua de Dui—or take a taxi or Uber.

▲Serralves Foundation Contemporary Art Museum and Park (Fundação de Serralves)

Porto's contemporary art museum, surrounding park, and unique Art Deco mansion are an enjoyable half-day excursion for art lovers—and worthwhile for anyone looking to relax in a lush green space.

Cost and Hours: €5 for park and villa, €10 to add the museum; Mon-Fri 10:00-19:00, Sat-Sun until 20:00; closes one hour earlier Oct-March; +351 226 156 500, www.serralves.pt.

Eating: The museum's **$$** restaurant serves a lunch buffet, and coffee and snacks are available until park closing time.

Getting There: The complex is about 1.5 miles west of the city center in a wealthy residential neighborhood at Rua Dom João de Castro 210, just south of the busy Avenida da Boavista. From the center, you can reach it most easily via taxi, Uber, or on a hop-on, hop-off bus tour. Public bus service isn't great, but you can take bus #203 to the Serralves stop (less convenient from downtown—the most central place to catch it is at the big Boavista Rotunda near Casa da Música).

Background: The Serralves Foundation was formed in 1989 with two goals: the advancement of contemporary art and the appreciation of landscape and environment as an artistic concept. These goals, symbolized by the giant, red, hand shovel near the front gate, drive the layout of the complex: a gigantic contemporary art facility on the edge of a carefully planned park. The whole thing is based around the Art Deco villa of a count who lived here in the 1930s.

Visiting the Museum and Park: The **museum** presents temporary exhibits by Portuguese and global artists. The enormous, blocky U-shaped building was designed by prominent Portuguese architect Álvaro Siza, who was greatly inspired by the existing mansion.

The **park** around the museum has been designed very carefully to compartmentalize each section; when you're in one part of the grounds, you can't see the rest. This is a very peaceful, romantic place to wander. Hiding in here somewhere are a pleasant rose garden, a tea house overlooking a former tennis court, a lake, a small farm with animals, a gardening school, and Casa de Serralves itself.

The **villa** (Casa de Serralves) is, for many, the most interesting part of the whole experience: a huge pink Art Deco mansion that looks like the home of an Old Hollywood star. On two sides, long manicured hedges and fountains stretch to the horizon. Look for the private chapel in back—also pink Art Deco. You can usually go inside the villa to check out the cavernous interior. Ponder how the design of this place is reflected in the museum. The best part is upstairs: the mirrored, pink-marbled bathroom, dramatically overlooking the grounds.

House of Music (Casa da Música)

This landmark 1,200-seat concert hall opened in 2005. The angular, white concrete building with rippling glass windows was designed by the firm of Dutch architect Rem Koolhaas (OMA), which also built Seattle's Central Library. Contemporary-architecture fans will find it at the big Boavista Rotunda northwest of the city center (Metro: Casa da Música). Guided tours take you through the interior, or you can attend an affordable concert of anything from world music to classical to jazz to fado.

Cost and Hours: One-hour tours focused on the concert hall's unique architecture run daily in English at 11:00 and 16:00 (€10, info/reservation +351 220 120 210, www.casadamusica.com).

Nightlife in Porto

The best after-dinner fun in Porto is to prowl the streets between the Clérigos Tower and the University of Porto, which are lively with student bars and often feature live music. Another good option is the street scene along Rua de Cândido dos Reis (one block from the Lello & Irmão bookstore). Pick one of the bars here to try the latest cocktail invention, a "Porto Tonic": one part white port and two parts tonic water.

Fado—a blues-like Portuguese music popular with tourists—is not really a Porto thing, but if you really want to hear it, try the recommended **Café-Restaurante Guarany** (free fado Wed, Thu, and Sat from 21:30-23:00, Avenida dos Aliados 85, +351 223 321 272). The **House of Music** (described earlier) offers classical, jazz, fado, and more, as does the centrally located **Coliseu do Porto** theater (Passos Manuel 137, uphill around the corner from Café Majestic, +351 223 294 940, www.coliseu.pt).

Sleeping in Porto

You'll pay more to be in the scenic, atmospheric, and very touristy Ribeira district; or you can save a bit (and be closer to more interesting restaurants and local life) by sleeping higher on the hill, in the city center. The Stock Exchange Palace area offers a nice mix. You'll almost always have to climb a few stairs to get to the elevator, if they have one.

SPLURGES IN THE RIBEIRA

$$$$ Guest House Douro is nestled right in the heart of the Ribeira bustle, overseen by owners Carmen and João, who are generous with local advice. It has eight small but cozy and tastefully decorated rooms with all the modern comforts (including much-needed soundproofing), and the generous breakfast is a great way to start your day (air-con, elevator, curfew—1:00 in the morning, closed Jan-Feb, near House of Henry the Navigator at Rua Fonte Taurina 99, +351 222 015 135, www.guesthousedouro.com, guesthousedouro@sapo.pt).

$$$$ 1872 River House is a classy B&B at the far end of the Ribeira embankment. It fills old river houses with industrial-mod finishes, eight compact, stone-walled rooms (half facing the river), and gorgeous shared public spaces, including a cozy river-view lounge (Rua do Infante Dom Henrique 133, +351 222 039 033, www.1872riverhouse.com).

$$$$ Pestana Porto Hotel is a stylish, overpriced, and slightly snobby top-end place, filling several colorful old townhouse buildings right along the embankment and main square with 109 plush rooms (air-con, elevator, Praça de Ribeira 1, +351 223 402 300, www.pestana.com, pestana.porto@pestana.com).

$$$$ Carrís Hoteles Porto Ribeira sits on the back side of the Ribeira, occupying four conjoined former warehouses. Its 159 business-like rooms offer all the basic comforts plus double-paned glass to keep out street noise. Large lounges with exposed stone let you see the history of these buildings (air-con, elevator, Rua do Infante Dom Henrique 1, +351 220 965 786, www.carrishoteles.com).

NEAR THE STOCK EXCHANGE PALACE

$$$$ A.S. 1829 Hotel is a splurge that owns a wonderfully central location, overlooking the base of thriving Rua das Flores, a long and steep block above the Stock Exchange Palace. The public spaces and 41 rooms are decorated with both a sense of style and respect for tradition—such as the vintage stationery store at the reception (air-con, Largo de São Domingos 45, +351 223 402 740, www.as1829hotel.pt).

PORTO

Porto Hotels & Restaurants

TRINDADE CHURCH

Praça da Trindade

CITY HALL

Praça Delgado

RUA DA CONCEIÇÃO

200 Meters
200 Yards

RUA DO ALMADA

RUA DA PICARIA

AV. DOS ALIADOS

Praça de Carlos Alberto

18

14

Praça Lencastre

RUA CEUTA

32 Praça Fernandes

R. STA. TERESA

13

37

30

R. DR. LEMOS

CARMO CHURCH

16

17 #22

RUA DA FÁBRICA

26

15

Autna Buses

IMPERIAL MCDONALD'S

#18 **20**

Praça Teixeira

LELLO & IRMÃO BOOKSTORE

CITY

Praça da Liberdade

#18 **20**

#18 & 22

UNIV. OF PORTO

RUA DAS CARMELITAS

CLÉRIGOS TOWER

Aliados M

PEDRO IV STATUE

M Aliados

RUA

Jardim de Cordoaria

Praça de Lisboa

R. CAMPO DOS MÁRTIRES DA PÁTRIA

#22

SÃO BENTO TRAIN ST.

São Bento M

TRANSPORT OFFICE

Largo Amores de Perdição

RUA DE TRÁS

CENTER

RUA DA VITORIA

27

RUA AFONSO HENRIQUES

RUA CHÃ

MISERICÓRDIA CHURCH & MUSEUM

RUA DAS FLORES

RUA MOUZINHO DA SILVEIRA

Largo São Domingos

28

5

RUA BELMONTE

TOWER

CALC. VANDOMA

Cathedral Square

PORTO CATHEDRAL

STA. CLARA

7

25

29

BORGES MARKET

OLIVA & CO.

R. DE S. JOÃO NOVO

6

GRILOS CHURCH

RUA DOM HUGO

METRO LINE

38

39

STOCK EXCHANGE PALACE

R. DE F. BORGES

Praça Infante

35

SÃO FRANCISCO

RUA INFANTE DOM HENRIQUE

36

TOWER

(B)

#500

(B)

#1

39

R. REBOLEIRA

31

HOUSE OF HENRY THE NAVIGATOR

4

Praça da Ribeira

3

RUA DE CIMA DO MURO

PONTE DOM

To Foz

2

R. OUT.

CAIS DA ESTIVA

1

33

CAIS DA RIBEIRA

LOWER BRIDGE (CAR)

To Ponte Arrábida & Atlantic Ocean

34

RIVER CRUISES

RABELO BOATS

RIBEIRA

UPPER BRIDGE (RAIL)

RIVER CRUISES

To Vila Nova de Gaia

RIVER TAXI TO GAIA

Douro River

Jardim do Mor

PORTO

Accommodations

1. Guest House Douro
2. 1872 River House
3. Pestana Porto Hotel
4. Carrís Hoteles Porto Ribeira
5. A.S. 1829 Hotel
6. InPátio Guest House
7. Hotel da Bolsa
8. NH Collection Porto Batalha
9. Quality Inn Praça da Batalha
10. Mercure Porto Centro Hotel
11. Moov Hotel Porto Centro
12. Pensão Residencial Belo Sonho
13. Hotel Infante Sagres
14. Hotel Pão de Açúcar
15. Pensão Grande Oceano
16. Duas Nações Guest House

Eateries

17. Padaria Ribeiro
18. Taberna Taxca
19. Cervejaria Gazela
20. Café Piolho d'Ouro
21. Café Santiago F
22. Restaurante Abadia
23. Confeitaria-Restaurante do Bolhão
24. Taberna Santo António
25. Prova Wine Food & Pleasure
26. Ö Tascö
27. Vegetariano Restaurante daTerra
28. Cantinho do Avillez
29. Mistu
30. DROOP Food & Wine; Café-Restaurante Guarany
31. Restaurante A Grade & Restaurante Adega São Nicolau
32. Solar Moinho de Vento
33. Muro dos Bacalhoeiros
34. Wine Quay Bar

Wine Tasting & Other

35. Wines of Portugal Tasting Room
36. Portologia
37. Touriga Wine Shop
38. Port & Douro Wines Institute
39. Laundry (2)

PORTO

$$$ InPátio Guest House, tucked down a tiny alley just above the Ribeira scene, provides a quiet, secluded oasis of comfort away from the crowds. Five beautiful, sleek, well-priced rooms with modern interiors and unique bathrooms hide inside a renovated 19th-century building. Fernando and Olga make you feel very welcome (air-con, luggage elevator, Pátio de São Salvador 22, mobile +351 934 323 448, www.inpatio.pt, info@inpatio.pt).

$$ Hotel da Bolsa, a few blocks above the Ribeira scene, is a straightforward business hotel, with a great location and 36 fine but aging rooms—some with views (air-con, elevator, Rua Ferreira Borges 101, +351 222 026 768, www.hoteldabolsa.com, reservas@hoteldabolsa.com).

IN THE CITY CENTER
On and near Praça da Batalha

This appealing location—on a borderline-seedy square capped by the beautiful *azulejo*-covered Church of San Ildefonso—is close to Porto's market and shopping zone, and just uphill from São Bento station, the cathedral, the bridge to Villa Nova de Gaia, and the funicular down to the Ribeira.

$$$$ NH Collection Porto Batalha has converted an elegant old post office into a sleek and inviting top-end hotel. It has an open-concept lobby, 107 well-equipped rooms, and a subtle but clever postal theme (air-con, elevator, Praça da Batalha 62, +351 227 660 600, www.nh-hotels.com, nhcollectionportobatalha@nh-hotels.com). Two other (less elegant) business-class hotels share the same square, and are worth considering if you can score a deal: **$$$ Quality Inn Praça da Batalha** (at #128, +351 223 392 300, www.choicehotelseurope.com) and **$$$ Mercure Porto Centro Hotel** (at #116, +351 222 043 300, www.mercure.com).

$ Moov Hotel Porto Centro has 125 sleek, modern rooms occupying a remodeled movie theater. Black-and-white photos of movie stars decorate the walls in tribute to its former life. It's temptingly affordable and nice for the price, with no frills and a handy location (family rooms, breakfast extra, air-con, elevator, parking, quiet back patio, Praça da Batalha 32, +351 220 407 000, www.hotelmoov.com, porto@hotelmoov.com).

¢ Pensão Residencial Belo Sonho is a well-maintained, family-run (no English spoken) budget throwback, just around the corner from Praça da Batalha. Its 15 rooms are an excellent value if you don't mind the language barrier (noisy on Fri and Sat nights, no breakfast, Rua Passos Manuel 186, +351 222 003 389).

West of Avenida dos Aliados

These choices are on the steep streets just west of Avenida dos Aliados, mixed among some tempting eateries.

$$$$ Hotel Infante Sagres showcases Portugal's luxurious, mid-20th-century style with an elegant stained-glass-lined staircase and proper breakfast room. Recently updated rooms spoil guests, and warm service complements on-site amenities such as a wading pool, sundeck, and the Vogue café-bar (air-con, elevator, Praça D. Filipa de Lencastre 62, +351 220 133 115, www.infantesagres.com).

$$$ Hotel Pão de Açúcar treats guests to a vintage experience. A stunning spiral staircase and fun retro decor (bumper cars, anyone?) make its public spaces and large rooms fun and friendly. The terrace has great views of the City Hall clock tower (air-con, elevator, Rua do Almada 262, +351 222 002 425, http://www.paodeacucarhotel.pt).

$ Pensão Grande Oceano, a good value in a central location, is a steep walk-up with shiplap floors. It has 15 clean, basic rooms on four floors—all but two have private baths and air-con (family rooms, no breakfast, no elevator, Rua da Fábrica 45, +351 222 038 770, www.grandeoceano.net, geral@pensaograndeoceano.com).

¢ Duas Nações Guest House is a well-run backpacker place with 16 simple but colorful rooms—as comfy as such a cheap place can be. It overlooks a square straight up Rua da Fábrica, a few blocks from Avenida dos Aliados. The "two nations" are Portugal and Brazil, still friends after all these years (private rooms available, cash only—or prepay on Booking.com, breakfast extra, Praça Guilherme Gomes Fernandes 59, +351 222 081 616, www.duasnacoes.com.pt, duasnacoes@sapo.pt). They also rent several apartments—all recently remodeled with small kitchens, washing machines, air-con, and double-paned windows.

Eating in Porto

Porto is famous for its tripe. Legend has it that when Porto's favorite son, Prince Henry the Navigator, set out for his explora-tions, the city slaughtered all of its mature livestock to send along with his crew—keeping only the guts for themselves. Por-to's cooks then devised many ingenious ways of preparing innards. The tradition stuck, and to this day, people from Porto are known as *tripeiros*. These days, tripe plays a subtler role. You'll most typically see it prepared "Porto-style" *(tripas à moda do Porto):*

barely present in a thick stew, with beans, sausage, chicken, and scant vegetables.

For something easier to stomach, try a *bifana*—shredded pork cooked slowly in spicy sauce on a bun. And locals love their soup, especially *caldo verde*—a tasty broth thickened with potatoes and thinly chopped kale.

For a quick meal, locals slog through a monster patty-melt called a *francesinha* ("little French girl"). The standard *francesinha* wedges pork cutlets, sliced sausages, and gooey Swiss cheese between two (or more) thick slices of dense bread. The whole thing is grilled and topped with melted cheese and an optional fried egg, then finally drenched with a slightly spicy beer-based sauce. This gut bomb easily feeds two (some places charge a euro to split).

Super Bock is the local favorite beer, available almost everywhere on tap.

Food Tours: To maximize your eating experience, consider **Taste Porto Food and Wine Tours** (see "Tours in Porto" near the beginning of this chapter).

IN THE CITY CENTER
Bars, Cafés, and Basic Eateries in the City Center

Good, cheap restaurants are scattered all around the city center. You'll see hand-written menus with €1 soups and €5 plates. Remember that most coffee and pastry shops do double duty as lunch spots, so wander around and see what people are having.

$ Padaria Ribeiro is a bright, happy bakery handy for a breakfast, light lunch, or snack. They serve savory and sweet pastries, sandwiches, and popular cookies. Mini almond tarts are a good choice, but chocolate lovers can get their fix with a *brigadeiro:* butter, condensed milk, and chocolate rolled into a gooey ball and covered with chocolate sprinkles. You can get your treat to go, or order inside and have them bring it to you at the small seating area or at a table on the square (Mon-Sat 7:00-20:00, closed Sun, Praça Guilherme Gomes Fernandes 21, +351 222 005 067).

$ Taberna Taxca is a concrete man cave offering up beer, soup, and sandwiches. The menu is cheap and extremely basic. They serve two soups (great *caldo verde* and the much heavier *papas*—made with shredded pork, gravy, and cumin) and sandwiches that celebrate simplicity: smoked ham with fried egg, meat from black crockpots of cooked pork *(rojão)*, or spicy shredded pork *(bifana)*. I like to sit under the hanging hams at the bar to enjoy the scene. They serve a few salads, kept secret in the lower window. While you're safe ordering a salad, if you order water, they'll ring the cowbell of shame—try it (Mon-Sat 12:00-24:00, closed Sun, Rua da Picaria 26, +351 222 011 807).

$ Cervejaria Gazela, a gritty little hole-in-the-wall just off

Praça da Batalha, is beloved among locals for its "little hot dogs" or *Cachorro Especial*. Sit down at the bar, order one and a beer, and watch the staff lovingly lay the sausage and cheese on the fresh buns and then grill these little snacks just right (Mon-Fri 12:00-22:30, Sat until 17:00, closed Sun, facing National Theater just to the right at #3, +351 222 054 869).

$ Café Piolho d'Ouro is a venerable student diner/café/bar with fun seating both inside and out on a big square. Plaques lining the walls celebrate decades of graduating classes (Mon-Sat 7:00-16:00, closed Sun, Praça de Parada Leitao 41, +351 222 003 749).

$ Café Santiago F is just a basic diner, long and skinny with a classic bar, that famously serves what many consider Porto's best signature sandwich, the hearty *francesinha*. While its tables are often full, the bar has a great energy. The sandwiches easily feed two—they charge €1 for an extra plate. Go a little early to avoid the lines (Mon-Sat 12:00-23:00, closed Sun, Rua Passos Manuel 198, another location just up the street at #226, +351 222 055 797).

Restaurants in the City Center

$$ Restaurante Abadia is a big, bright, old-school place with two floors of customers dining on large splittable portions of straightforward Portuguese cuisine. It's a touristy place with no stress, spacious seating, and formal waiters. Popular dishes are grilled cod, wild boar, Porto-style tripe (split a half portion with your partner), and a sizzling hibachi of roasted chicken and potatoes (Mon-Sat 12:00-15:00 & 18:30-23:00, closed Sun, head one block east of Sá da Badeira to side street Rua do Ateneu Comercial do Porto 22, +351 222 008 757).

$ Confeitaria-Restaurante do Bolhão has been pleasing local shoppers since 1896—and feels like it. This bustling bakery/brasserie offers enticing takeout items in front and an inviting old-time dining hall in the rear (the more elegant basement is less lively and soulful). You'll find cheap lunch deals, daily specials, fresh-baked goods, omelets, and fish. And don't miss the fun selection of mini pastries, just waiting to be experienced (Mon-Sat 7:00-20:00, closed Sun, facing the old Bolhão market hall entrance at Rua Formosa 339, +351 223 395 220).

$$ Taberna Santo António is a convivial, hole-in-the-wall place—the quintessence of a family-run, neighborhood favorite. There's a tight dining room and a few prime seats at the bar where eaters choose from six traditional stews, marvel at the homemade desserts, and joke with the waitstaff (Tue-Sun 12:00-15:00 & 19:00-22:00, Rua das Virtudes 32, +351 222 055 306).

$$$ Prova Wine Food & Pleasure is a lounge-y little wine bar with a relaxing jazz ambience. It's the passion of sommelier Diogo, who speaks English and enjoys coaching visitors through

Wine Tastings in Porto

In addition to the port wine lodges across the river in Vila Nova de Gaia, various wine bars and shops in Porto specialize in introducing you to port and other Portuguese wines (for locations, see the map on page 386). Port tasting can be costly; fortunately, couples are welcome to split a single top-quality flight.

Wines of Portugal Tasting Room, inside the Stock Exchange Palace, is a sister organization of the tasting venue in Lisbon's Praça do Comércio. If you don't have a ticket to the Stock Exchange, ask the guard to let you into the tasting room—you'll get to see the palace's grand courtyard on your way in. Inside, buy a rechargeable chip card and help yourself to as many wines as you like (€3 minimum, pours start at €1.50, Mon-Sat 11:00-19:00, closed Sun).

Portologia, a few steps uphill from Praça da Ribeira, serves flights of port wines from scores of open bottles, highlighting smaller producers (rather than the big, corporate outfits across the river). The menu explains how tastings can be either "horizontal," showcasing different types of port wines or producers, or "vertical," sampling different ages of wines by the same producer (€10-17/3 wines, €25-30/6 wines, €35/8 wines—price depends on quality, daily 11:00-24:00, Rua de São João 28, +351 222 011 050). They also offer small sharable plates—both savory and sweet.

Touriga Wine Shop, in the city center and less touristy, is well-stocked with local wines—mostly from north Portugal. David is happy to talk you through your tastings. Most try three ports for €5, €8, or €20 (priced by quality). I'd go for the most expensive option and share it (Mon-Sat 10:00-13:00 & 14:30-20:00, closed Sun, Rua da Fábrica 32, +351 225 108 435).

The Port and Douro Wines Institute, where industry regulations and standards are managed, welcomes the public to six historic rooms. Here's a chance to see the laboratories and tasting rooms that guarantee fine wine year after year. The €5 audioguide finishes with a tasting. This is a good spot to sample a vast array of ports (Mon-Fri 10:00-19:00, closed Sat-Sun, just uphill from Stock Exchange Palace at Rua Ferreira Borges 27, +351 222 071 699).

his list of Portuguese wines (including ports) and then matching it with his selection of fine meats and cheeses (Wed-Mon 17:00-24:00, closed Tue, near the Stock Exchange Palace at Rua Ferreira Borges 86, mobile +351 916 499 121).

$$ Ö Tascö serves traditional Portuguese food with a youthful spirit in a trendy space. The menu mixes old and new, featuring *petiscos*—small plates designed to be eaten family-style. The smart-aleck waiters have a fun shtick (daily 12:00-23:00, Rua do Almada 151, +351 222 010 763).

$ Vegetariano Restaurante daTerra, *the* place for a meatless meal, is sleek and modern with a self-serve all-you-can-eat buffet of tasty dishes. Charging €7.50 for lunch and €10 for dinner, it's a great value. While you can go back for seconds, you'll pay extra for drinks and dessert (daily 8:30-23:00, Rua Mouzinho do Silveira 249, +351 223 199 257).

Fancier Dining in the City Center

$$$ Cantinho do Avillez, a colorful, upscale-casual space, is the Porto outpost of Lisbon-based celebrity chef José Avillez (see page 153). The enticing menu focuses on modern Portuguese cooking: traditional dishes with an international twist inspired by the chef's travels. If tables are full, it's fun to eat at the bar (reservations a must, weekday lunch specials, daily 12:00-15:00 & 19:00-24:00, Rua de Mouzinho da Silveira 166, +351 223 227 879, www.cantinhodoavillez.pt).

$$$ Mistu is a mod, dressy place with high ceilings, sexy art, and a smart clientele. The name refers to mixing cultures—fusion with a Portuguese base. The menu is divided between cold and hot plates designed to share (three plates fill two people). While the upper level is quieter, I much prefer the lower level and would reserve a table there (daily 19:30-22:30, lunch service on weekends 13:00-15:30, Rua do Comércio do Porto 161, mobile +351 926 682 620).

$$$ DROOP Food & Wine, classy, minimalist, and contemporary, fills a small room with tight tables. Like other new foodie places, it serves gourmet *tapiscos* that mix Portuguese and international cuisines. The pricey plates are beautifully presented (Tue-Sun 16:00-23:00, closed Mon, next to the recommended Café-Restaurante Guarany at Rua Elísio de Melo 29, +351 222 033 113).

$$$ Café-Restaurante Guarany is a dressy and sprawling café facing Porto's main boulevard. It feels like it must have been *the* place to see and be seen back in 1933 when it opened. It's been the musicians' coffee shop for generations and is now popular with tourists. You'll enjoy Art Deco elegance with a Brazilian flair (read the brochure for the story of the murals) and crisp-yet-friendly service. They also have seating out on Avenida dos Aliados (good meat and fish plates, daily specials, daily 9:00-24:00, Avenida dos Aliados 85, +351 223 321 272, www.cafeguarany.com). There's no extra charge for the live music starting at 21:30—some nights fado, other nights piano.

ON THE RIBEIRA RIVERFRONT

Dining options in the Ribeira are touristy, with predictable tourist-trap quality and prices accompanying the fine views and fun scene. Strolling along the waterfront and following your nose is a good option. You can also try wandering the back lanes, trading river views for lower prices and local color. The seafood's fresh, except on Mondays (since fishermen don't go out on Sundays).

$$ Restaurante A Grade is a small mom-and-pop restaurant on a delightful alley just off the Ribeira. Ferreira serves while wife Helena cooks good, home-style Portuguese food. The baked octopus is a favorite among regulars (big, splittable portions of seafood and meat dishes; Mon-Sat 12:00-16:00 & 18:30-22:30, closed Sun, Rua de São Nicolau 9, +351 223 321 130, reservations smart for dinner).

$$ Restaurante Adega São Nicolau, just above Restaurante A Grade, is homey, small, and sparkling, with a few outside tables and a tight interior under a shiplap vault. While touristy, this spot is great for tasty, traditional cuisine with lots of fish (Mon-Sat 12:00-23:00, closed Sun, Rua São Nicolau 1, +351 222 008 232).

$$$ Solar Moinho de Vento, on a small plaza just above Praça Guilherme Gomes Fernandes, offers proper-but-friendly service and Portuguese cuisine in a tile-covered, white-tablecloth dining room upstairs. Their version of *Bacalhau à Brás*, a salted cod dish, draws raves, as does the tender octopus rice (Mon-Sat 12:00-15:30 & 19:00-22:00, Sun 12:00-15:30, Rua de Sá Noronha 81, +351 222 051 158, www.solarmoinhodevento.com).

Muro dos Bacalhoeiros is a narrow lane over the harbor with a handful of **$$** restaurants, each with a single line of little tables outside capturing the riverfront scene. I wouldn't eat inside here—pick a place where you can sit out and enjoy the view.

$$$ Wine Quay Bar is all about *vinho*, paired with high-quality *petiscos* (plates of Portuguese cured meats, cheeses, olives, and other munchies; no cooked dishes). While they have inside seating, I'd come here for a spot at their bannister facing the river (Mon-Sat 16:00-23:00, closed Sun, Muro dos Bacalhoeiros 111).

IN VILA NOVA DE GAIA

Eating across the river in Vila Nova de Gaia, just a 10-minute scenic stroll over the bridge from the Ribeira, is a fine option. It's basically as touristy as the Ribeira, so don't expect great quality or values—except at the port wine lodges themselves—but the views over to Porto are marvelous. The last port lodges finish their tasting tours at 19:00, so working a dinner here into your sightseeing schedule is easy. Gaia rolls up the sidewalks early, so don't expect much activity after dinner. For locations see the "Vila Nova de Gaia" map, earlier.

PORTO

$$$ Adega e Presuntaria Transmontana serves up quality Portuguese fish and meat plates as well as *petiscos*—Portuguese tapas. Their tapa sampler (listed on the menu as "Mixed of Titbits") stuffs two to four people for €34. And for an education in the sweet treats of Portugal, enjoy their all-you-can-eat dessert buffet (daily 12:00-24:00, Avenida Diogo Leite 80, +351 223 758 380).

$$$ Ar de Rio Restaurante, where modern design meets traditional Portuguese cuisine, is located in a park right on the river. Their €10 *francesinha* (a local super-grilled meaty sandwich that makes a triple cheeseburger seem like health food) is considered one of the best in town. You can eat inside or out on the deck (daily 12:00-24:00, modern steel-and-glass "box" along the embankment at Avenida Diogo Leite 5, +351 223 701 797). Consider a drink from their bar while enjoying a lounge chair on the riverbank here.

$$$$ Vinum Restaurant-Wine Bar delivers on their mission statement: to marry their port wines with locally sourced products. Located within the cellar of the Graham's port wine lodge (past the end of the Gaia boardwalk), their elegant, white-tablecloth dining room sits alongside barrels of aging port. They also have terrace view seating...a worthy splurge (daily 12:30-23:00, Rua do Agro 141, +351 220 930 417, www.vinumatgrahams.com, reservations smart).

Scenic Drinks: Porto Cruz has a delightful rooftop bar with a great view over both the bustle of the Gaia embankment and Porto across the river (lunches and light snacks, Tue-Sat 10:00-23:30, Sun until 19:00, closed Mon and in bad weather, just past Sandeman at Largo Miguel Bombarda 23).

Picnic Perfect: The Vila Nova de Gaia mayor is determined to make his city (which is actually bigger than Porto) visitor-friendly. A sign of that is the inviting waterfront, welcoming picnickers with picnic tables, grass, rockery, piers, and the best views in town. A higher option is the park at Jardim do Morro at the top of the cable car and the upper level of the Dom Luís I bridge. Grab snacks at a local supermarket, then snack and watch the sunset fall over Porto.

Porto Connections

BY PLANE

Porto's small and speedy Francisco Sá Carneiro airport is 11 miles north of downtown (airport code: OPO, +351 229 432 400, www. aeroportoporto.pt). It's an international airport with connections beyond Iberia.

Getting Between the Airport and Downtown: Connecting the city center and the airport is easy. Figure €20-25 and 30-40 minutes by taxi or Uber. Or hop on the Metro with an Andante card to get to multiple stops in the city center (€2, 3/hour, 40 minutes, zone 4).

BY TRAIN

Regional trains use the more central São Bento station; long-distance trains use Campanhã station on the east edge of town. The two stations are connected by frequent commuter trains (see "Arrival in Porto" on page 348). All trains leaving São Bento also stop at Campanhã (the next station). Some trains only depart from Campanhã station, so check the schedule carefully.

From Porto's São Bento Train Station to: Peso da Régua (3/day direct, 2 hours; many more with change in Caide, 2-2.5 hours), **Pinhão** (5/day, 2.5-3 hours, direct at 9:00, others transfer at Campanhã station or Peso da Régua).

From Campanhã Train Station: Fast Alfa Pendular and Intercidades trains (both require reservation, buy at station) go to **Coimbra** (hourly, 1 hour on Alfa Pendular line or Intercidades service) and **Lisbon** (hourly, 3 hours). Note that Alfa Pendular and Intercidades trains are similarly speedy, but Alfa trains cost more.

To reach **Santiago de Compostela, Spain,** it's faster to go by bus (see below), but you can also take a train (1/day, 5 hours, departs around 8:15, change in Vigo).

BY BUS

Remember, each bus company has its own station; there's no single bus terminus except a few that share a garage on Campo 24 de Agosto (for addresses and telephone numbers, see "Arrival in Porto" on page 348). Various companies compete on the same route (for example, three companies go to Lisbon). Ask at the TI about the handiest bus for your itinerary. Don't bother trying to get to the Douro Valley (Peso da Régua or Pinhão) by bus; it takes twice as long as the train.

From Porto by Bus to: Coimbra (operated by Rede Expressos, Rodonorte, and others; best is Rede Expressos—almost hourly, 1.5 hours), **Lisbon** (best via Rede Expressos, at least hourly, 3 hours), **Santiago de Compostela, Spain** (ALSA buses leave from bus terminal on Rua do Capitão Henrique Galvão near Casa da Música Metro station, daily at 12:45, 4 hours, additional runs in summer, Spanish tel. +34 902 422 242, www.alsa.es).

PORTO

DOURO VALLEY

Vale do Douro

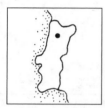

The scenic Douro Valley—the birthplace of port wine—is a vine-draped land of ever-changing terrain sculpted by centuries of hardy farmers. The Douro River's steep, craggy, twisting canyons have been laboriously terraced to make a horizontal home for grape vines and olive and almond trees. Unlike the Rhine, the Loire, and other great European rivers, the Douro (DOH-roo) was never a strategic military location. So, rather than fortresses and palaces, you'll see farms, villages...and endless tidy rows of rock terraces, which took no less work—and are no less impressive—than those castles and châteaux. Locals brag, "God made the earth, but mankind made the Douro."

The Douro River begins as a trickle in Spain (where it's called the Duero), runs west for 550 miles (350 miles of which are in Portugal), and spills into the Atlantic at Porto. The name means "river of gold"—perhaps because of the way the sun shines on the water, or the golden-brown silt it carries after a heavy rain.

In the 17th century, British traders developed a taste for the wines from the Douro region during a trade war with France. "Op-port-unity" knocked in 1756, when the Marquês de Pombal demarcated the region—establishing it as the only place that port wine could be produced. To this day, port remains the valley's top industry and top tourist draw. The 50-mile stretch on either side of Pinhão is home to some 4,000 vintners and scores of *quintas*— vineyards that produce port (and, increasingly, also table wine and olive oil). While many *quintas* are private, others offer tours and tastings, and some have accommodations as well.

The Douro hillsides change colors throughout the year, from dusty brown in winter, to scrubby green in summer, to glowing red

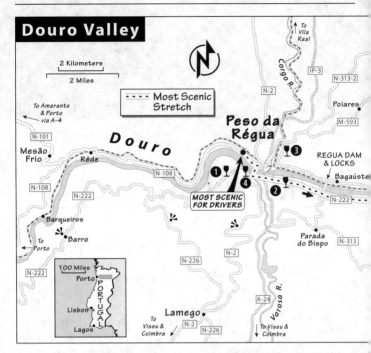

Douro Valley

2 Kilometers

2 Miles

···· Most Scenic Stretch

To Amarante & Porto via A-4

N-101

Mesão Frio

Douro

Rêde

N-108

N-108

N-222

Barqueiros

Barro

To Porto

N-222

100 Miles

Porto

PORTUGAL

Lisbon

Lagos

Peso da Régua

N-108

MOST SCENIC FOR DRIVERS

To Vila Real

Corgo R.

IP-3

N-2

N-313-2

Poiares

M-593

REGUA DAM & LOCKS

Bagaúste

N-222

Parada do Bispo

N-313

Lamego

To Viseu & Coimbra

N-2

N-226

N-226

N-2

A-24

Varosa R.

To Viseu & Coimbra

and gold in fall. The 5,000-foot-high Serra do Marão mountain range guards the region, pro-tecting it from the ocean air and creating a microclimate perfect for growing grapes. The tem-perature varies from snowy in the winter to arid and 100°F in the summer. Much of the Dou-ro's dramatic ambience changed in the 1970s, when a series of dams were built for hydroelec-tric power, taming the formerly raging river into the gentle giant seen today.

Although the scenery and the wines are sublime, the towns along the Douro (Peso da Régua and Pinhão) are fairly dull. If you've got wheels, consider staying at one of the many *quintas* that offer accommodations—ranging from simple rooms on fam-ily farms to modern country estates with jaw-dropping views. To many, the Douro Valley may feel low-energy and underwhelming (especially outside of September's harvest time), but some find its charm relaxing.

DOURO VALLEY

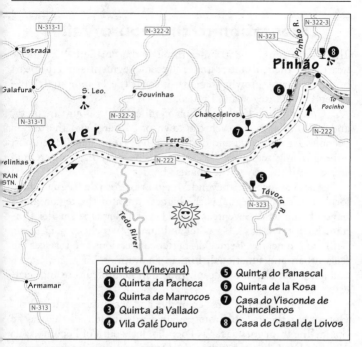

Quintas (Vineyard)
1. Quinta da Pacheca
2. Quinta de Marrocos
3. Quinta da Vallado
4. Vila Galé Douro
5. Quinta do Panascal
6. Quinta de la Rosa
7. Casa do Visconde de Chanceleiros
8. Casa de Casal de Loivos

PLANNING YOUR TIME

This area merits a full day and an overnight along the river. While the valley is pretty, Porto is more interesting—and, unless you're a port aficionado, more worth your limited vacation time. Note that the valley is packed during the grape harvest (mid-Sept-early Oct).

Drivers should make a beeline for the heart of the valley and explore at will. Without a car, you're limited as to where you can stay and which *quintas* you can tour, but you still have enough options to make the trip worthwhile. Using taxis, your choices multiply. With plenty of time and a desire to really slow down, take the meandering boat cruise from Porto to Peso da Régua and tour the museum (no lockers at the train station, but you can leave your bag at the museum desk, a 10-minute walk away—pack light). In the evening, take the train to Pinhão and settle in for the night. In the morning, hike to Quinta de la Rosa for the 11:30 tour and tasting, or take a taxi to wander through the vineyards at Quinta do Panascal. When you've had enough of the wine and rugged scenery, hop the train back to Porto (2.5 hours).

For just a glimpse, you can see the Douro as a day trip from Porto on your own (about 2 hours by car or 2 hours by train each way) or with a package tour (see "Getting Around the Douro Valley," later).

Orientation to the Douro Valley

The Douro runs for 350 miles through the northern Portuguese heartland. The most interesting and scenic segment—and the heart of the port wine-growing region—is easily the 17-mile stretch between Peso da Régua and Pinhão.

Coming from **Porto,** the first 55 miles of the Douro are pretty and lush. When you reach the town of **Mesão Frio,** the terrain becomes far more arid and dramatic. The prized, demarcated port wine-growing region of the Douro technically begins here and stretches all the way to the Spanish border.

About seven miles beyond Mesão Frio, **Peso da Régua** (which locals call simply Régua) is the biggest town of the region and a handy home base. Seventeen miles beyond Régua is smaller **Pinhão.** Each town has a big hotel and one or two cheap *residencials,* with *quintas* nearby. Régua has better connections and services but feels urban and functional; Pinhão enjoys more of a small-town ambience and feels more deeply rooted in Douro culture and scenery.

I've described the most enjoyable and accessible stretch of the Douro, but there's much more—vineyards stretch all the way to Spain. The train goes as far as Pocinho. Just south of Pocinho, Vila Nova de Foz Côa sits between the Douro and a fine archaeological park with cave paintings.

GETTING AROUND THE DOURO VALLEY

By Boat: Lazy cruise boats float up and down the Douro between Porto, Régua, and Pinhão. (The feisty Douro was tamed in the

1970s by a series of five dams with locks, including the highest one in Europe, the Barragem do Carrapatelo—which inches boats up and down, like a giant elevator, over 140 feet.)

The boat trip takes about seven hours from Porto to the heart of the Douro, and comes with lunch and passage through

two locks (longer trips include a third lock between Régua and Pinhão). If you've got the time and don't have a car, this is a slow but scenic way to enjoy the Douro Valley.

Boats generally run daily from March through November (no boats Dec-Feb). Most travelers take a train or bus back to Porto from Régua on the same day as part of a package deal. But if you want to spend the night on the Douro, it's easy to catch a train back on your own (or buy a two-day package, which includes lodging). Seniors should ask about discounts, especially on weekdays.

Several companies based in Porto run cruises up the Douro— from all-day side-trips to multiday cruises—including **Douro**

Azul (+351 223 402 500, www. douroazul.com) and **Rota do Douro** (+351 223 759 042, www.rotadodouro.pt). **Tremdouro** has shorter, daily cruises departing from Régua (see the "Peso da Régua" section, later).

By Train: From Porto, regional trains head to **Régua** (every 2 hours direct from Campanhã station, free connection from São Bento station, 2 hours); half of these trains continue on to **Pinhão** (2.5 hours total). On Saturdays, a **historic diesel train** choo-choos visitors between Douro towns—from Régua to Pinhão to Tua, then back again (Sat-Sun only, 3 hours round-trip, €43, +351 259 338 135, www. cenarios.pt).

By Car: The region is easy by car. If you're going between Coimbra and the Douro Valley, you'll save time and mileage by coming directly through the mountains (on the A-24 expressway, via Viseu and Lamego), rather than taking the expressway up the coast to Porto and then over.

From Porto, zip on the A-4 expressway to Amarante, then N-101 through the mountains to Mesão Frio (about one hour total). Once in the heart of the Douro, the riverside road follows the north bank from Mesão Frio to Régua in about 30 minutes. From there, you'll cross to the south bank (in the middle of the three bridges) to continue on N-222 into the valley about 30 more minutes to Pinhão (where you'll cross back to reach the town). Everything I've mentioned is no more than about a 10-minute side-trip from the river and the main road. Note that bridges cross the river at Régua, just upstream at Bagaúste, and at Pinhão, but otherwise are scarce.

When passing through Amarante, it's an easy and logical pit stop to detour into the town center to check out the old Roman bridge and impressive church and convent of São Gonçalo.

Tours and Tastings in the Douro Valley

QUINTAS

The main attraction of the Douro Valley is touring the *quintas*, the farms that produce port and table wines. The best *quinta* (KEEN-tah) experiences on this stretch of the Douro are in or near Régua and Pinhão. For both towns, I've noted the best options for non-drivers.

Most *quintas* have an official program: a one-hour tour, followed by a tasting of three or four wines, for about €10. Some have tours at specific times, while others are by prior arrangement only. Ideally, call ahead and ask when you should show up. That said, it's fairly informal—drivers could simply pull into any *quinta* listed in this chapter (or any marked *rota do vinho do Porto*) and ask for a taste. If they're not too busy, you can often get a shorter, less-formal tour even outside of the official times.

Each *quinta* has its own personality. The tours of big companies' *quintas* are slick, but feel like stripped-down versions of the

tours you'll do in the port wine lodges back in Porto (with the happy exception of Quinta do Panascal, where you're set loose in the vineyards). The smaller, independent *quintas* are more intimate, and offer a chance to meet the people who have devoted their

lives to making the best wine they can. At *quintas* operated by big companies, it's fine not to buy. But if a family-run place gives you an in-depth tour, it's polite to buy at least a token bottle. Prices are surprisingly affordable at the source.

GROWING—AND STOMPING—GRAPES IN THE DOURO VALLEY

Port wine can technically only be grown in the Douro Valley, which is characterized by microclimates. A few miles can make a

tremendous difference in terms of temperature, precipitation, humidity, and farming conditions. Even within the same vineyard, each parcel of land has its own characteristics. These subtle changes infuse the grapes with completely different aromas and flavors. Over the years, vintners have learned to micro-

manage their grapes, fine-tuning specific qualities to get the very best port for their conditions.

Near Porto, the Douro has moderate temperatures and a fair amount of precipitation. The vineyards north of Porto are planted with a different grape—Alvarinho—and produce "green wine"

Brits on the Douro: The History of Port

Port is actually a British phenomenon. Because Britain isn't suitable for growing grapes, its citizens traditionally imported wine from France. But during wars with France (17th and 18th centuries), Britain boycotted French wine and looked elsewhere. At that time Portuguese wines often didn't survive the longer sea journey to England.

It's said that the port-making process was invented accidentally by a pair of brothers who fortified the wine with grape brandy to maintain its quality during the long trip. The wine picked up the flavor of the oak, which the English grew to appreciate. The British perfected port production in the succeeding centuries; hence many ports carry British-sounding names (Taylor, Croft, Graham).

In 1703, the Methuen Treaty reduced taxation on Portuguese wines, making port even more popular. In 1756, Portugal's Marquês de Pombal demarcated the Douro region—the third such designation in Europe. From that point on, true "port wine" came only from this region, following specific regulations of production, just as "Champagne" technically refers to wines from a specific region of France. Traditionally, farmers and landowners were Portuguese, while the British bought the wine from them, aged it in Porto, and handled the export business. But that arrangement changed in the late 19th century, when an infestation of an American root insect called phylloxera (which smuggled itself to the Old World in the humid climate of speedy steamboats) devastated the Portuguese—and European—wine industry.

In the Douro Valley, you'll see lasting evidence of the phylloxera infestations in the "dead" terraces, overgrown with weeds and a smattering of olive trees. During the infestations, these particular terraces were treated with harsh chemicals that contaminated the soil, rendering it no longer suitable for grapes. Other terraces were left untouched, as Portuguese vintners simply gave up. Unable to produce usable grapes for over a decade, they sold their land to British companies who were willing to wait until a solution could be found. It was, as phylloxera-resistant American rootstock began to be used throughout Europe. Port production resumed, this time on British-owned land.

Today, Porto and the Douro Valley see many British tourists. Though it's largely undiscovered by Americans, this region is a real hot spot among wine-loving Brits.

(*vinho verde*—Portugal's refreshing light white wine). About 55 miles inland, around Mesão Frio, chains of mountains mark a dramatic change in climate: very hot and dry in summer, with heavy rainfall and extreme cold in winter.

The terrain around the Douro is dominated by sedimentary rocks that have been buried, heated, and deformed into a metamorphic rock called schist *(xisto)*. The easily fractured layers of schist are tilted beneath the soil at an angle, allowing winter rainfall to easily penetrate the earth and build up in underground reserves. The grapevines' roots plunge deep into the ground—up to 30 feet—to reach this water through the long, dry summer.

Building and maintaining the Douro's trademark terraces *(geios)* is expensive, and grapes planted there must be cultivated

by hand. More recently, bigger companies have attempted using larger terraces (called *patamares*) that can be worked by machines, or smoothing out the hillside and planting the vines in vertical rows. Within the demarcated region, farmers are not allowed to irrigate, except with special permission.

Because the crops here are worked mostly by hand, it can be hard to find good workers (especially for pruning, a delicate and skilled task). Most young people from the Douro move to the cities on the coast. To encourage them to stay, the government offers subsidies and other incentives.

To make the finest port, many *quintas* along the Douro still stomp grapes by foot—not because of quaint tradition, but because it's the best way. Machines break the grapes' seeds, releasing too many tannins and resulting in bitter port. But soft soles against stone keep the seeds intact. During harvest time (mid-Sept-early Oct), the grapes are poured into big granite tubs called *lagares*. A team of two dozen stompers line up across from each other, put their arms on each other's shoulders, and march, military-style, to crush the grapes. The stomping can last three to four days, and generally devolves into a party atmosphere—with tourists sometimes joining in...but only later in the evening after the serious work is done.

Port traditionally stays in the Douro Valley for one winter after it's made, as the cold temperatures encourage the wine and brandy to marry. Then it's taken to Porto, where the more humid, mild climate is ideal for aging. For centuries, port could technically only be aged, marketed, and sold in Porto. But this was deregulated in 1987, and now any Douro *quinta* that offers tours can sell its port directly to visitors.

In recent years, vintners have been using their traditional port grapes to make table wines—with great success. These days, most *quintas* offer you tastes not only of port, but of their *vinhos do Douro*, which are gaining international acclaim.

The vineyards along the Douro are traditionally separated by olive trees, many of which produce fine olive oil. The farming demands of olives fit efficiently with those of grapes. There are also almond, orange, apple, and cherry trees, which locals use to make jam.

Peso da Régua

Peso da Régua (PAY-zoo dah RAY-gwah)—or simply Régua, as it's called by locals—is the administrative capital of the Douro Valley. With 22,000 people, Régua feels urban and functional, with modern five- and six-story apartment blocks that seem out of place in these beautiful surroundings. While the town itself isn't worth the trip, the views and access into the surrounding countryside make it worth considering as a home base—or at least a transportation hub.

Orientation to Régua

The core of Régua consists of two bustling streets that run parallel to the Douro. The businesslike upper street, Rua dos Camilos, is lined with workaday shops; the lower, main road—Avenida João Franco—runs just above the scenic river embankment, along a narrow, nicely manicured promenade. Down below is the wider, mostly pedestrianized embankment itself, where pleasure boats come and go. There are three bridges at the east (upriver) end of town.

Tourist Information: Régua's clueless TI is inconveniently located a few blocks up from the river at the west end of town (on Rua da Ferreirinha). The staff at the Douro Museum (and at bigger hotels) are more reliable sources of information.

Arrival in Régua: The **train** station and two recommended hotels are at the eastern edge of the center; buses also stop here. The boat dock is more or less in the middle of town (to reach the train station and hotels, disembark to the right; for the Douro Museum, disembark to the left). **Drivers** can park for free along Avenida João Franco (squeeze between the trees) or on the angled streets leading down to the embankment. There's also a large, free lot at the west end of town (as you approach from Mesão Frio). You have to pay to park along the upper street, Rua dos Camilos.

Tours: A company called **Tremdouro** has a near monopoly on tours here, including a cheesy **tourist train** (€7.50, 1 hour with two stops: mountaintop viewpoint and wine cellar for tasting, departs hourly in season) and river **cruises**. You can choose between a two-hour cruise all the way upriver to Pinhão with a return by train (2/week, €25), or a longer five- to six-hour round-trip lunch cruise to Pinhão and back (daily at 12:00, €65). For details, ask at one of the Tremdouro kiosks (at either end of town along the lower road—Avenida João Franco, +351 254-322-858, www.tremdouro. com). A few other companies, which specialize in longer cruises from Porto, may also run local cruises from Régua, including **Rota do Douro** (www.rotadodouro.pt) and **Tomaz do Douro** (www. tomazdodouro.pt).

Sights and Tastings in and near Régua

Régua's sights are few, and most worthwhile for people without cars (who can't get into the countryside, where time is better spent). Along the upper street (Rua dos Camilos), you can't miss the **Casa do Douro**—the blocky, marble-clad, Fascist-style headquarters of the local port wine industry (ask to see the pretty stained-glass windows inside).

▲Douro Museum (Museu do Douro)
This museum—spanning the lower and upper roads, with a *rabelo* boat permanently moored on its rooftop garden—serves as a sort of cultural center for this little town. It has a restaurant, wine tastings, temporary exhibits, and an endearing permanent exhibit.

Cost and Hours: €6, daily 10:00-18:00, Nov-Feb until 17:30, Rua Marquês de Pombal, +351 254 310 190, www.museudodouro. pt.

Tastings: Each afternoon, the museum offers four different options for sampling five or six port wines. Reserve at least one day in advance (minimum four people). The price varies based on quality of the wines (€5-15, daily 15:00-17:00, +351 254 310 190, geral@museudodouro.pt). They also have a café and wine bar on

Rabelo Boats

Up until the 1970s, when the Douro was tamed by dams, boats called *rabelos* navigated the treacherous waters, carrying port from the hillsides to the cellars of Porto. It was a three-day trip to cover the 50-100 miles. A crew of four loaded the barrels onto the 20-foot boats. For the downstream trip, the captain stood on a platform to spy rocks and shallows ahead, using the long rudder to guide the flat-bottomed boat through whitewater and hairpin turns. It was dangerous work, and the river was once lined with shrines where superstitious sailors prayed.

At Vila Nova de Gaia, they unloaded their cargo—a mere eight barrels, typically—and headed back. For the slow trip upstream, the tall, square sail helped them ride the prevailing westerly winds. Otherwise, they were pulled by ropes up the worst stretches by men or oxen on towpaths that used to line the riverbank.

Nowadays, the Douro is quiet, port is shipped via tanker trucks, and the few remaining *rabelos* are docked by *quintas* for ambience and advertising.

the museum terrace where you can sip port while admiring the vineyards...but with no explanation.

Visiting the Museum: The permanent exhibit, "Douro: Matter and Spirit," explains the landscape, industry, and culture of the Douro Valley. On the ground floor, you'll get a lesson in the region's geology, with a 3-D relief map of the Douro Valley and stuffed specimens of local wildlife. Upstairs, the exhibit delves into local winemaking and the folk culture that goes along with it. At the top of the stairs, the gigantic wall of wine bottles is enough to make any port lover envious.

You'll see models illustrating the construction of *rabelo* boats; traditional costumes and musical instruments; items relating to port production (tools, casks, barrels, decanters, and huge wicker grape-picking baskets that are supported on the forehead); and port wine labels and advertising posters. On one wall, squeeze the bulb attached to each bottle to help train your nose to the various bouquets of port: apple, honey, berry, nut caramel, cinnamon, and so on. The 33-minute film *Giants of Douro* shows the hard work in this land, past and present—showing lots of locals with grape-stained hands.

▲Quinta da Pacheca

Perhaps the most elegant tasting experience I list is perched near the top of the hill across the river from Régua (just under the big Sandeman billboard). You'll drive up the plane-tree-lined driveway to a grand 18th-century manor house nestled in vine-draped hills. Drop by for an impromptu taste in the delightful outdoor wine bar (under a leafy canopy) or call ahead to schedule a one-hour tour of the entire process, including their atmospheric cave. While not one of the more famous labels, Pacheca is upscale and well-respected—making this a nice high-end-feeling option without the impersonal corporate glitz. They also have a fancy hotel (described later).

Cost and Hours: €5 for 4 tastes, €9 tour and tasting, daily 10:00-18:00, Rua do Relógio do Sol 261, +351 254 331 229, www. quintadapacheca.com.

Getting There: It's across the river from Régua and up the hill in Carneiro—cross the bridge, turn right on N-222, and watch for the signs on the right. You'll feel like you're in Sandeman-land until you reach the driveway.

▲Quinta de Marrocos

This is the loosest, most informal *quinta* that I list—casual, traditional, and family-run. It's a great place to sample simple ports while chatting with the folks who made them. You'll wander through the vineyards, check out the stomping and aging rooms, and taste four different ports. They also rent rooms (see "Sleeping in Régua," later).

Cost and Hours: €10, daily 9:00-12:00 & 14:00-18:00, mobile +351 918 828 785, https://golddrink.pt.

Getting There: It's easiest to take a taxi (€10 each way).

▲Quinta da Vallado

Although this *quinta* dates from 1716, they've recently gotten away from their rustic roots and gone in a boldly modern direction—with a new facility stylishly decorated with slate-gray schist and bold lines. They'll take you on a one-hour tour, and then offer a tasting of five types of wines and ports. They also run a fine hotel (see page 410).

Cost and Hours: €15, more for higher-end ports, daily 8:00-24:00, Vilarinho dos Freires, +351 254 318 081, www. quintadovallado.com.

Getting There: Leave Régua at the eastern end of town (under the tall bridge) and follow N-313 up the narrow Corgo River Valley. Immediately after the road crosses the river, watch for signs on the right.

Sleeping in Régua

You have two basic options for sleeping here: Stay in a hotel or *residencial* in town, or sleep at a picturesque *quinta* in the countryside. The in-town hotels are very handy for those using public transportation, but if you've got a car, the *quintas* offer a better value and a more memorable Douro experience. The fancier places serve meals and usually have half-board options (book ahead). If you have a car, get out of town!

If visiting during the grape harvest (mid-Sept–early Oct), book as far ahead as possible. Simpler places charge the same rates year-round; more expensive hotels charge more for weekends and during the busy season (roughly April-Oct).

$$$ Vila Galé Douro, across the river from the town center (about a 20-minute walk), is the most luxurious hotel option within walking distance of Régua. It has 38 stylish rooms (all with river views), an indoor pool, an outdoor terrace with a hot tub, sharp service, and an elegant vibe (air-con, elevator, Lugar dos Varais, Cambres, in village of Lamego, +351 254 780 700, www.vilagale. com, douro.reservas@vilagale.com).

$$ Hotel Régua Douro is big and relatively professional, with a top-floor panoramic breakfast room and 77 business-class, if somewhat, faded rooms—many of them with sweeping river views (air-con, elevator, pool, Avenida Galizia—at the roundabout at the eastern end of town, +351 254 320 700, www.hotelreguadouro.pt, geral@hotelreguadouro.pt).

$ Império Hotel has a convenient, central location in a stark tower a block from the station and across the street from Hotel Régua Douro. Its 33 spartan rooms are a little musty and overlook busy streets, but the price is right (air-con, Rua Vasques Osório 8, +351 254 320 120, www.imperiohotel.com, info@imperiohotel. com).

NEAR RÉGUA

$$$$ The Wine House Hotel, at the recommended Quinta da Pacheca (described earlier), is a classy splurge with 15 rooms filling a meticulously renovated manor house. Or sleep in one of 10 room-sized wine barrels overlooking the estate. The luxurious public spaces—not to mention the stunning vineyard setting—make this a tempting top-end option (air-con, +351 254 331 229,

DOURO VALLEY

www.quintadapacheca.com). For directions, see the winery listing, earlier.

$$$ Quinta da Vallado is two accommodations in one: a sleek, modern, schist-clad design hotel (with eight rooms), and a thoughtfully restored old manor house (with five rooms). The complex, perched on a hill up a little side-valley just northeast of Régua, also has a swimming pool. It's just the place for young urbanites looking for a bit more contemporary sophistication in their rustic Douro Valley experience (air-con, Vilarinho dos Freires, +351 254 318 081, www.quintadovallado.com). For directions, see the winery listing, earlier.

$$ Quinta de Marrocos is a wonderful option if you want to stay on a real-life family farm. The Sequeira family farmhouse operates a simple shop and a family vineyard making good ports and table wines. The four rooms include a rustic living room, where the port's always out. Staying here, with the dogs and farmhands, is a fun, authentic experience—a rare opportunity to spend time with locals who really love what they do (RS%, €25 meals with advance notice, air-con, on N-222 across the river and about 1.5 miles upstream from Régua—about a €10 taxi ride, mobile +351 918 828 785, www.quintademarrocos.com, info@quintademarrocos.com, sisters Rita and Catarina). They also rent a private two-bedroom family-friendly house on their property.

Eating in Régua

$$$$ Castas e Pratos, next to the train station, turned an enormous railway storage facility into the hippest restaurant in this otherwise sleepy town. The interior comes with lounge tunes and low lighting. If the weather is nice, dine in an open-air freight car permanently attached to the restaurant (facing the train tracks). Their mod wine bar has a nice selection of wines by the glass; if you want a bottle, the wine list is as thick as a phone book (restaurant—daily 12:30-15:00 & 19:30-22:30, wine bar—daily 10:30-24:00; Rua José Vasques Osório at train station, +351 254 323 290, www.castasepratos.com).

$$$ A Companhia, a classy dining room on the second floor of the Douro Museum, has a handy €13.50 lunch buffet (daily 12:30-15:00, Rua Marquês de Pombal, +351 254 323 030).

$$ Gato Preto ("Black Cat"), next door to the Douro Museum on the lower street, is classy and affordable (daily 12:00-15:00 & 18:30-22:30, Avenida João Franco, +351 254 313 367).

$ Pastelaria Nacional serves great pastries but also doubles as a restaurant popular with locals. Bubbly Paula and her family pride themselves on customer service and on their regional dishes...and her English is fun (lunch specials, Mon-Sat 12:00-20:30, closed

Sun, on the upper street between the museum and the train station at Rua dos Camilos 86, +351 254 336 231).

Pinhão

Pinhão (PEEN-yow)—known locally as the "heart of the Douro"—feels like a real small town, where locals remain oblivious to the tourists streaming through their streets. The town—with a cobbled main street and a gorgeous deep-in-the-Douro setting—has a certain dirty-fingernails charm. Inside the big,  concrete silos *(balões),* wine used to spend its first winter awaiting shipment downstream to Porto.

Orientation to Pinhão

Pinhão has virtually no sights, but it makes for a handy home base. The town has a train station along the main road (Rua António  Manuel Saraiva), and a boat landing down below on the river. The two *residencials* are across the street from the station, and Vintage House Hotel is just upriver, next to the bridge. The main road rumbles through the middle of town, past the train station and a mix of practical shops and tourist-oriented wine bars. The handiest **ATM** is a block from the train station, on the main street, just past the two *residencials* (exit station to the left, look for CA Bank).

Getting Around: Taxi driver **Manuel Anselmo** speaks some English and is very knowledgeable about local tourism. He can often be found at the train station. A round-trip visit to the recommended Quinta do Panascal costs around €25 (mobile +351 966 192 904, www.taxipinhao.com).

Sights in Pinhão: Unless you arrive on a boat, it's easy to miss the broad and manicured **river embankment** (watch for the steep, downhill road, just west of the train station, near the post office).

DOURO VALLEY

Here you'll find boat docks, a few upscale eateries, parks, fishermen, and some public WCs. It's a pleasant place to simply stroll, with grand views to the vineyards on the opposite banks. At the west end, a modern metal bridge arcs over to another fine embankment for views back on town; if you keep going on this road, you'll reach the Quinta de la Rosa (wine tasting described later).

A popular activity here are **river cruises.** The top option is a round-trip cruise that goes up the river—where no roads go (accessible only by boat or train). It's €10 for a one-hour cruise to a farm and back, or €20 for two hours all the way to the village of Tua (for a port wine tasting) and back. Two fiercely competitive companies both have sales kiosks along the riverfront: **Companhia Turística do Douro** (daily 9:00-19:00, www.ctdouro.com, mobile +351 963 934 951) and **Magnífico Douro** (daily 10:00-18:00, www.magnificodouro.pt, mobile +351 913 129 857).

The **train station** is worth a look even if you arrive by car or boat. It's adorned with modern tiles illustrating the people and traditions of the countryside.

Tastings in and near Pinhão

▲▲Quinta do Panascal

This wonderful *quinta* produces Fonseca—a name familiar to port lovers for its high quality. The affordable, tasty Bin No. 27 is their best-known ruby. It's the only *quinta* that allows you to roam on your own through the terraced vineyards. From the riverside road you'll side-trip up the valley of the Távora River. Venturing up the rough gravel road, you'll feel like you're discovering a special, hidden gem. Yet upon arrival, you'll enjoy the slick efficiency of a corporate producer (Fonseca is owned by Taylor, the port wine giant). Because of its delightfully remote location, and because it gets you out among the grapes, it's among the best *quinta* tours on the Douro.

The tour is self-guided, so there's no wait once you arrive. You'll be given a 30-minute audioguide and set free to wander through the winery, the cellars, and the vineyards—where you can take in the sweeping views (while listening to dry, humorless commentary about the history of port and of the company). Then you'll return to the lodge to watch a 10-minute video—which brings the otherwise still fields to life—while tasting three ports: a dry white, Bin No. 27, and 10-year-old tawny.

Cost and Hours: €10, April-Oct daily 10:00-18:00; Nov-March Mon-Fri 10:00-18:00, Sat-Sun by reservation only; +351 254 732 321, www.fonseca.pt.

Getting There: This place is only accessible by car; it's well-marked off the Régua-Pinhão road (N-222), up a thrilling little side road that follows the Távora River as it branches off from the Douro (closer to Pinhão). Blind curves make this road dangerous for walking, but a taxi ride is a good value for those without cars (figure around €25 round-trip, including some wait time; see recommended driver, earlier).

▲Quinta de la Rosa

This British-owned, family-run *quinta* is proud of its wine and eager to show it off on an in-depth, engaging one-hour tour of the facility with a finale of four tastings. I find this a nice middle ground between big and corporate—and tiny and rustic—it's unpretentious yet rich with tradition. This is perhaps the only family *quinta* that is close enough to do without a car (20-minute hike from Pinhão). Three-course dinners at 19:30, paired with their wines, cost €25 per person; reserve in advance. They also have a hotel (see "Sleeping in and near Pinhão," later).

Cost and Hours: €10, daily at 11:30 and 16:00, one mile downstream from Pinhão, +351 254 732 254, www.quintadelarosa.com.

Getting There: Drivers leave Pinhão to the west (downriver), cross the concrete bridge, turn left and look for the *quinta* on the left side, up the hill. If walking: From the boat landing, cross the blue pedestrian bridge and continue 20 minutes (or take a €6-8 taxi from Pinhão station).

In Town

Pinhão's main street is lined with wine shops, eager to sell you a bottle, a glass, or a taste. Do some window-shopping and take your pick. For something more formal, **Vintage House Hotel**'s lobby wine bar offers expensive, high-end, regularly scheduled Academia do Vinho ("Wine Academy") tastings, usually in the afternoon—call to check the schedule and reserve a spot (€30 tastings, wine shop open daily 10:00-19:00, +351 254 730 230; see hotel listing, later).

Sleeping in and near Pinhão

Your in-town options are a plush splurge hotel or two humble *residencial*s. The *residencial*s are next door to each other, across from the train station. Both operate fine restaurants, and both have riverview rooms that don't cost extra but come with some street noise;

neither has owners who speak English, but each sometimes has an English-speaking son available.

$$$$ Vintage House Hotel is *the* place if you want to splurge on a fancy, formal hotel on the Douro (as opposed to a hillside manor house). It's all class, with a wonderfully atmospheric bar (under tree-trunk rafters), a good restaurant with an over-the-top formal interior and riverside terrace outdoor seating, and a wine shop featuring expensive tastings for aficionados. Each of its 50 rooms has a river view and a terrace or balcony, and elegant tile in the bathroom. The halls are lined with 19th-century photos of the Douro (air-con, elevator, pool, between train station and bridge at Lugar da Ponte, +351 254 730 230, www.vintagehousehotel.com, reservations@vintagehousehotel.com).

$ Hotel Douro offers 14 basic, clean, and bright rooms, many with cute riverview balconies. The halls are nicely tiled, and the communal terrace provides a great, lazy-afternoon view of the river (cash only, air-con, Rua António Manuel Saraiva 39, +351 254 732 404, www.hotel-douro.pt, geral@hotel-douro.pt, Oliveira family).

$ Residencial Ponto Grande is your basic budget choice, with 17 small, simple rooms (cash only, some with air-con, Rua António Manuel Saraiva 41A at Largo da Estação, +351 254 732 456, residencialpontogrande@hotmail.com, Vieira family).

OUTSIDE PINHÃO

$$$ Quinta de la Rosa, a mile downstream of Pinhão, is a riverside winery offering 14 comfortable rooms with light, country-cabana furnishings; all but one overlook the river. Stylish but mellow and a bit ragtag, it's a fine retreat for getting lost in dreamy Douro scenery (ask in advance for the €25 three-course dinner including wine and port; +351 254 732 254, www.quintadelarosa.com, holidays@quintadelarosa.com). For directions, see the tastings listing, earlier.

$$$ Casa do Visconde de Chanceleiros fills a manor house in the village of Chanceleiros, a glorious 15-minute drive through vineyard-covered hills from Pinhão. Stern Ursula and her right-hand woman Adelaide rent 12 rustic, homey rooms scattered over the glorious grounds, with a pristine swimming pool and extravagant views over vineyards, gardens, and the Douro. With a tennis court, hot tub, and sauna, this feels like an exclusive—but not snobby—Old World retreat (air-con, dinner available, +351 254 730 190, www.chanceleiros.com, info@chanceleiros.com).

Getting There: Simply follow the directions to Quinta de la Rosa (see tastings listing, earlier), then keep going past it. The road twists up to Chanceleiros, where you'll find the house on what looks like the main square.

$$$ Casa de Casal de Loivos hovers on a lofty perch above Pinhão, with perhaps the most dramatic views in all of the Douro

DOURO VALLEY

Valley. The warm Sampayo family converted this 17th-century manor house into a six-room hotel with quaintly rustic furnishings and commanding Douro vistas. The family brags that when the BBC filmed a show about the best views in the world, they set up their camera right here (fun family-style dinner—€28/person without wine—reserve ahead, grand-view swimming pool, closed Dec-Feb, +351 254 732 149, www.casadecasaldeloivos.com, casadecasaldeloivos@ip.pt).

Getting There: The house is in the village of Casal de Loivos, atop the mountain overlooking Pinhão. Leaving Pinhão to the west (downriver), first follow signs for *Alijó,* then for *Casal de Loivos,* and wind your way up the mountain roads. Once in town, look for the poorly marked villa on your right (with big iron grates on the windows); if you reach the overlook by the cemetery, you've gone a block too far. If you don't have wheels, catch a taxi from Pinhão's train station (about €10).

Eating in Pinhão

Your choices are limited in this little town. If you're staying at a *quinta* outside of town, dining at your accommodations is a tempting option. Along the main drag, several hardworking restaurants vie for your business; decent choices include the old-school but popular **$$ Residencial Ponto Grande** (at #41, open daily), or the nicely tiled **$$ Bufete Restaurante** (at #13, daily). Down along the riverbank, **$$$ Restaurante Veladouro**—with a tempting menu of pricey grill specialties—is popular (daily, Rua da Praian 3).

PORTUGAL: PAST & PRESENT

Sitting on the fringe of Europe, facing the open Atlantic, Portugal has an epic history that's shaped by the sea. Here's a brief overview.

PREHISTORY TO ROME (2000 BC-AD 500)

Portugal's indigenous race, the Lusiads, was a mix of peoples from many migrations and invasions—Neolithic stone builders (2000 BC), Phoenician traders (1200 BC), northern Celts (700 BC), Greek colonists (700 BC), and Carthaginian conquerors (500 BC).

By the time of Julius Caesar (50 BC), Rome had conquered rebellious Lusitania (Portugal), establishing major cities at Olissipo (Lisbon), Portus Cale (Porto), Conímbriga (near Coimbra), and Ebora (Évora). The Romans brought laws, wine, the Latin language, and Christianity. When Rome's empire fell (AD 476), a northern Germanic tribe called the Sueves invaded (causing havoc in Conímbriga—evidence of which is still visible today), but they were later defeated by Christian Germanic Visigoths ruling distantly from their capital in Toledo.

MUSLIMS VS. CHRISTIANS, AND NATIONHOOD (711-1400)

North African Muslims invaded the Iberian Peninsula, settling in southern Portugal. The Christians retreated to the cold, mountainous north, leaving central Portugal as a buffer zone. During their long rule, the Moors made Iberia a beacon of enlightenment in Dark Age Europe.

But the Christians considered the Moors invaders and infidels, and the remnants of Christian armies in the Iberian Peninsula became the core of the Reconquista. They fought against the Moors, taking back one territory at a time, for eight centuries. Faro was the last Portuguese town to fall, in 1249. Afonso Henriques,

Ten Dates That Shaped Portugal

1128 "Portucale" separates from Castile.

1179 Afonso Henriques (Afonso I) is recognized as the first king of Portugal.

1497 Vasco da Gama sails Portugal into a century of wealth.

1581 King Philip II of Spain inherits the crown of Portugal after King Sebastian dies without an heir.

1640 The Spanish are ousted; the Portuguese gain their independence.

1755 A massive earthquake destroys Lisbon.

1822 Portugal loses Brazil as a colony.

1910 The monarchy is deposed, democracy fails, and repressive military regimes rule.

1974 A left-wing military coup brings democracy.

1986 Portugal joins the European Community (the forerunner of the European Union), boosting the economy.

a popular Christian noble who conquered much Muslim land, was proclaimed king of Portugal (1139), creating one of Europe's first modern nation-states. João I (r. 1385-1433) solidified Portugal's nationhood by repelling a Spanish invasion in 1385, and established his family—the House of Avis—as kings. (For more on the House of Avis dynasty, see page 278.) Romantics prefer the star-crossed tale of João's father, Pedro the Just, and his mistress Inês (see page 297).

THE AGE OF DISCOVERY, SLAVERY, AND INQUISITION (1400-1600)

With royal backing, Portugal built a navy and began exploring the seas using technology the Arabs had left behind. These trips were motivated by spice-trade profit and a desire to Christianize Muslim lands in North Africa. From his base at Cape Sagres—at Portugal's (and Europe's) southwestern corner—Prince Henry the Navigator urged his sailors to go beyond what was then regarded as "the end of the world." Thanks to new maritime inventions—such as the mariner's astrolabe and the caravel—they finally did, slowly making their way down the coast of West Africa. In 1488, Bartolomeu Dias became the first European to sail around the tip of Africa—the Cape of Good Hope. Vasco da Gama followed the same route but continued farther, landing in India in 1498. Suddenly the wealth of all Asia opened up via a fast and cheap sea route. Much to

Typical Church Architecture

History comes to life when you visit a centuries-old church. Even if you wouldn't know your apse from a hole in the ground, learning a few simple terms will enrich your experience. Note that not every church has every feature, and a "cathedral" isn't a type of church architecture, but rather a designation for a church that's a governing center for a local bishop.

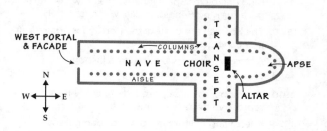

Aisles: Long, generally low-ceilinged arcades that flank the nave

Altar: Raised area with a ceremonial table (often adorned with candles or a crucifix), where the priest prepares and serves the bread and wine for Communion

Apse: Space behind the altar, sometimes bordered with small chapels

Barrel Vault: Continuous round-arched ceiling that resembles an extended upside-down U

Choir: Intimate space reserved for clergy and choir, located within the nave near the high altar and often screened off

Cloister: Covered hallways bordering a square or rectangular open-air courtyard, traditionally where monks and nuns got fresh air

Facade: Exterior of the church's main (west) entrance, usually highly decorated

Groin Vault: Arched ceiling formed where two equal barrel vaults meet at right angles

Narthex: Area (portico or foyer) between the main entry and the nave

Nave: Long central section of the church (running west to east, from the entrance to the altar) where the congregation sits or stands during the service

Transept: One of the two parts forming the "arms" of the cross in a traditional cross-shaped floor plan; runs north-south, perpendicularly crossing the east-west nave

West Portal: Main entry to the church (on the west end, opposite the main altar)

Typical Castle Architecture

Castles were fortified residences for medieval nobles. Castles come in all shapes and sizes, but knowing a few general terms will help you understand them.

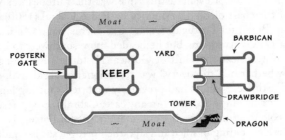

Barbican: Fortifed gatehouse, sometimes a standalone building located outside the main walls

Crenellation: Gap-toothed pattern of stones atop the parapet

Drawbridge: Bridge that could be raised or lowered using counterweights or a chain and winch

Great Hall: Largest room in the castle, serving as throne room, conference center, and dining hall

Hoardings (or Gallery or Brattice): Wooden huts built onto the upper parts of the stone walls; served as watchtowers, living quarters, and fighting platforms

Keep (or Donjon): High, strong stone tower in the center of the complex; the lord's home and refuge of last resort

Loopholes (or Embrasures): Narrow wall slits through which soldiers could shoot arrows

Machicolation: Stone ledge jutting out from the wall, with holes through which soldiers could drop rocks or boiling oil onto wall-scaling enemies below

Moat: Ditch encircling the wall, sometimes filled with water

Parapet: Outer railing of the wall walk

Portcullis: Iron grille that could be lowered across the entrance

Postern Gate: Small, unfortified side or rear entrance; in wartime, became a sally port used to launch surprise attacks or as an escape route

Towers: Square or round structures with crenellated tops or conical roofs serving as lookouts, chapels, living quarters, or the dungeon

Turret: Small lookout tower rising from the top of the wall

Wall Walk (or Allure): Pathway atop the wall where guards could patrol and where soldiers stood to fire at the enemy

Yard (or Bailey): Open courtyard inside the castle walls

the dismay of their competitors in Venice, Portugal's new discoveries caused spice prices to drop to one-fifth of their former market value. For more on Prince Henry the Navigator, see page 197. For more on Portuguese explorations, see page 107.

Another major event at this time was the European exploration of the coast of South America by Pedro Cabral (1500), who claimed Brazil for Portugal. Cabral was on his way to India, following Da Gama's route, but he headed more southwest to bypass rough waters near the Gulf of Guinea. Historians have long debated whether his "discovery" was intentional or accidental, since some Portuguese sailors had previously reported spotting land on the other side of the Atlantic. In any case, Cabral's voyage resulted in the colonization of Brazil—and more riches for Portugal.

Besides trading in spice and silk, the Portuguese also traded in human beings. The Portuguese were the first Europeans to sail to Africa, capture people living there, and bring them back to Europe for sale. In 1482, they built Elmina Castle on the coast of what is now Ghana—the first of many "slave factories" (slave trading posts) that Europeans established in western Africa. The slave trade soon shifted to the New World, where new sugar plantations created a huge demand for cheap labor. Portuguese settlements sprung up in both Guinea and Angola for slavery purposes. Ships would leave Lisbon for West Africa, pick up slaves, and then sail to Brazil, selling their captives to work on plantations and in mines. The ships would return to Portugal loaded with sugar—creating tremendous wealth for the sea captains, slave traders, and merchants.

The Portuguese had a slave-trade monopoly through the 16th century, but England and the Netherlands then began their own slave trade. Historians estimate that, before slavery ended, about 4 million captives were brought from Africa to Brazil—roughly 40 percent of all the slaves brought to the Americas.

Through trade, conquest, and, yes, slavery, tiny Portugal became one of Europe's wealthiest and most powerful nations, with colonies stretching from Brazil to Africa to India to China. The easy money destroyed the traditional economy.

Around this same time, in 1536, the Church launched the Portuguese Inquisition. The main targets were converts of Judaism to Christianity who had been exiled from Spain. Thousands were tried and found guilty of still practicing Judaism and being heretics. Though most punishments ranged from whipping to imprisonment, many innocent people were publicly burned at the stake.

SLOW FADE (1600-1900)

The "Spanish Captivity" (1580-1640) drained Portugal. Late in the 16th century, after the young Portuguese king, Sebastian (Dom Sebastião), died in battle without a direct heir, Portugal's throne

Portuguese Notables

Viriato (d. 139): Legendary warrior who (unsuccessfully) resisted the Roman invasion.

Afonso Henriques, the Conqueror (1095-1185): Renowned Muslim-slayer and first king of a united, Christian nation.

Pedro I, the Just (1320-1367): King and father of João I, famous for his devotion to his murdered mistress/wife, Inês de Castro.

João I, the Good (1358-1433): King who preserved independence from Spain, launched an overseas expansion, fathered Prince Henry the Navigator, and established the House of Avis as the ruling family.

Henry the Navigator (1394-1460): Devout, intellectual sponsor of naval expeditions during the Age of Discovery.

Bartolomeu Dias (1450-1500): Navigator who rounded the tip of Africa in 1488, paving the way for Vasco da Gama.

Vasco da Gama (1460-1524): Explorer who discovered the sea route to India, opening up Asia's wealth.

Pedro Cabral (1467-1520): Explorer who found the sea route to Brazil (1500).

Ferdinand Magellan (1480-1521): Voyager who, sailing for Spain, led the first circumnavigation of the globe (1520).

Manuel I, the Fortunate (r. 1495-1521): Promoter of Vasco da Gama's explorations that made Portugal wealthy. Manueline, the decorative art style of that time, is named for him.

Luís de Camões (1524-1580): Swashbuckling adventurer and poet who captured the heroism of Vasco da Gama in his epic poem, "The Lusiads."

Marquês de Pombal (1699-1782): Controversial chief minister who tried to modernize backward Portugal, regulated the port wine industry, and rebuilt Lisbon after the 1755 quake.

José I, the Reformer (r. 1750-1777): Disinterested king who effectively turned over control of Portugal to the Marquês de Pombal.

Fernando Pessoa (1888-1935): Foremost Portuguese Modernist poet, immortalized in sculpture outside his favorite Lisbon café.

António de Oliveira Salazar (1889-1970): "Portugal's Franco," a dictator who led for four decades, slowly modernizing while preserving rule by the traditional upper classes.

Cristiano Ronaldo (1985-): Prodigiously talented soccer star, and the most famous Portuguese person alive today.

was up for grabs. After a short reign by Sebastian's great-uncle (who died two years after assuming power), the Portuguese throne passed to another distant relative—the Spanish king, Philip II. Philip wanted the two countries to remain separate, and they did under his rule. But his son and grandson—who ruled after him—cared little about Portuguese autonomy, so they imposed new taxes on the Portuguese and forced Portugal's armies to support the Spanish military agenda. After 60 years, the Portuguese nobility had had enough, and when Spanish troops were tied up in the Thirty Years' War, the nobles launched an uprising. One of the leading nobles, the duke of Bragança, was proclaimed king, becoming João IV. Although it's been nearly 400 years, Spain and Portugal continue to have a sibling rivalry—with Spain often acting as the arrogant older brother—though the conflicts now happen on the soccer field rather than the battlefield.

With a false economy, a rigid class system, and the gradual loss of their profitable colonies, Portugal was no match for the rising powers of Spain, England, Holland, and France. The earthquake of 1755 (see page 69) and Napoleon's invasions during the Peninsular War (1808-1814) were devastating. Portugal was a traditional ally of England, and when Napoleon demanded that Portuguese merchants stop trading with England, they refused. Napoleon sent his army through Spain to invade Portugal, where his troops ravaged the countryside. A French coup then placed Napoleon's brother on the Spanish throne, causing a revolt across the Iberian Peninsula. British troops retook Lisbon, and a six-year, back-and-forth struggle eventually ended in Napoleon's defeat.

While the rest of Europe industrialized and democratized, Portugal lingered as an isolated, rural monarchy living off meager wealth from Brazilian gold and sugar. Eventually, the country lost its largest colony in 1822, when Brazil revolted (with the support of the son of the Portuguese king). But Portugal still had a string of colonies across Africa and Asia, including Portuguese Guinea, Angola, Mozambique, Goa, Macau, and Portuguese Timor.

DICTATORSHIP AND DEMOCRACY (1900-2000)

Republican rebels overthrew the king in 1910, founding a republic and abolishing the monarchy, but democracy was slow to establish itself in Portugal's near-medieval class system. During World War I, Portugal joined the Allies, partly to protect its African colonies from the Germans.

The postwar years resulted in political turmoil. A series of military-backed democracies culminated in four decades of António de Oliveira Salazar's "New State," a right-wing regime benefiting the traditional upper classes. For 36 years, the former professor ruled Portugal under an authoritarian regime that banned political parties and independent labor unions. A fascist system of censorship, propaganda, and oppression kept society in order. When opposition arose, the secret police (a.k.a. PIDE—Polícia Internacional e de Defesa do Estado) imprisoned and tortured dissidents. (For more on Salazar, see page 84.)

According to Portuguese historians, Salazar didn't trust Hitler and didn't think the Germans could win World War II. He kept Portugal neutral, even allowing the British to use naval bases in the Azores under an old Anglo-Portuguese treaty. After the war, Portugal was a founding member of NATO—the only dictatorship allowed into the organization at its birth. Salazar wasn't your typical corrupt dictator. As a young man, he considered becoming a priest; as Portugal's leader he continued to be modest, pious, and celibate. Salazar—Europe's longest-serving dictator—ran Portugal until 1968, when he had a stroke and later died.

Salazar's repressive tactics and unpopular wars abroad (trying to hang onto Portugal's colonial empire) sparked the Carnation Revolution of 1974. A little after midnight on April 25, army rebels rolled into Lisbon, and by sunrise the military had taken control from Salazar's successors. They promised to restore citizens' civil liberties and conduct general elections as soon as possible. The coup was nearly bloodless. Residents disobeyed commands to stay in their homes, and instead people flooded the streets in support of the rebels, placing carnations into the barrels of the soldiers' guns as a sign of peace (hence the name "Carnation Revolution"; for more on this, see page 77).

The new regime worked quickly to free Portugal's colonies. Within a few years, Guinea-Bissau, Mozambique, Cape Verde Islands, São Tomé and Principe, and Angola all became independent. After some initial political and economic chaos, Portugal finally adopted democracy. Imagine: In just a dozen years, Portugal went from the isolation of four decades of fascism (when the Salazar dictatorship slogan was "We are proudly alone") to full membership in the European Union (in 1986).

PORTUGAL TODAY: AUSTERITY AND CHALLENGE

The early years of the 21st century were heady days for Portugal. The former backwater was suddenly booming—building superhighways, handing out lavish bonuses to workers, and buying fancy consumer goods from the rest of Europe. Scaffolding was everywhere as the Portuguese scrambled to finish projects funded in part by the European Union.

The EU has worked to bring relatively poor regions (like much of Portugal) up to par with more-developed parts of Europe through matching grants and cheap construction loans. As part of

Portugal Almanac

Official Name: It's República Portuguesa, but locals just say "Portugal."

Population: Nearly 11 million people. Most Portuguese are Roman Catholic (81 percent), with indigenous Mediterranean roots; there are a few black Africans and Brazilians (from former colonies) and some Eastern Europeans.

Latitude and Longitude: 39°N and 8°W (similar latitude to Washington, D.C. or San Francisco).

Area: 57,000 square miles, which includes the Azores and Madeira, two island groups in the Atlantic.

Geography: Portugal is rectangular, 320 miles long and 135 miles wide. (It's roughly the size and shape of Indiana.) The half of the country north of Lisbon is more mountainous, cool, and rainy. The south consists of rolling plains, where it's hot and dry. Portugal has 1,114 miles of coastline (including the Azores and Madeira), much of it sandy beaches.

Rivers: The major rivers, most notably the Rio Tejo (or Tagus River, 600 miles long, spilling into the Atlantic at Lisbon) and the Douro (550 miles long, flowing through wine country, ending at Porto), run east-west from Spain.

Mountains: Serra da Estrela, at 6,500 feet, is the highest point on the mainland (and synonymous with its best cheese), but Portugal's highest peak is Mt. Pico (7,713 feet) in the Azores.

Biggest Cities: Lisbon (the capital, 550,000 in the core, with nearly 3 million in greater Lisbon), Porto (238,000 in the core, with 1.3 million total), and Coimbra and Braga (each with 144,000 in the core).

Economy: The Gross Domestic Product is about $314 billion, and the GDP per capita is around $30,500. Some major money-

the EU, Portugal was considered a low-risk bet for lenders, keeping interest rates artificially low. But with the 2008 banking crisis, money became tight worldwide, and lenders began assessing each country on its individual merits. The risk of lending to Portugal shot up—and so did interest rates.

The economy was floundering, with unemployment around 11 percent (and as high as 26 percent for those under 25 years old). Infrastructure projects—such as plans for a high-speed bullet train from Madrid to Lisbon, an additional runway for Lisbon airport, and superhighway expansion—were put on indefinite hold while investment went into improving tourism services.

In 2011, the EU approved a €78 billion bailout package, but with it came the requirement for strict austerity measures. To enforce these measures, a trio of financial institutions—the European

makers for Portugal are fish (canned sardines), cork, budget clothes and shoes, port wine, and tourism. More than 25 percent of Portugal's foreign trade is with Spain. Still recovering from the Great Recession, Portugal's unemployment hovers around 9 percent. Nine percent of Portuguese people work in agriculture, 67 percent work in service jobs, and 24 percent in industry. The minimum monthly wage is €635, and the average rent is €460.

Government: The prime minister—currently the left-wing António Luis Santos da Costa—is the chief executive, having assumed power as the head of the leading vote-getting party in legislative elections. President Marcelo Rebelo de Sousa commands the military and can dissolve the Parliament when he sees fit (it's rarely done, but he has the power). There are 230 legislators, elected to four-year terms, making up the single-house Assembly. Regionally, Portugal is divided into 18 districts (Lisbon, Coimbra, Porto, etc.).

Flag: The flag is two-fifths green and three-fifths red, united by the Portuguese coat of arms—a shield atop a navigator's armillary sphere.

Soccer: The three most popular teams are Sporting CP Lisbon, Benfica (also from Lisbon), and FC Porto.

The Average *Senhor* and *Senhora*: The average Portuguese is 45 years old and will live 81 years. Two in five Portuguese live near either Lisbon or Porto, and slightly less than two in three own a car.

Commission, European Central Bank, and International Monetary Fund, together referred to as "the troika"—oversaw Portugal's effort to get its economy back on a sustainable track.

These austerity measures included higher road tolls, increased health deductibles (coupled with other health care cutbacks), and new taxes, including a 23 percent tax on all restaurant income. The retirement age was raised from 65 to 66.

Austerity also led to the end of rent control (a remnant of the Salazar period). While necessary, this change spurred a huge spike in rents—causing financial stress for older people, pushing out small shops, and threatening to change the character of traditional neighborhoods.

The country successfully completed the bailout program in 2014. The result: a booming economy, with unemployment drop-

Portugal's "Law 30"

Portugal has one of the more progressive drug policies today. In 2000, the government passed "Law 30," which decriminalized the consumption of all drugs. Although a conservative government replaced the more progressive government that established "Law 30," former opponents agreed that its benefits far outweighed its harms. Now with a center-left government, "Law 30" continues to be the law of the land.

Drug addiction was a major societal concern in Portugal in the late 1990s. A group of experts came together in 1999 to find a solution to the problem. They realized that the "war on drugs" was actually a "war on people." Similar to the US, only about one percent of Portugal's population (100,000 out of 11 million people) was actually using hard drugs.

The goal of "Law 30" was to establish a legal framework for harm reduction. Drug addicts are considered ill, not criminals. Drug use and possession are still illegal, but no longer punishable with jail time. Instead offenders are given treatment, community service, or fines.

A 2010 review of the law studied drug consumption trends from 2001 to 2009. Researchers summed up Portugal's experience this way: "Nothing bad happened." There was no change in actual usage rates, and the big negatives some had predicted, including the expected advent of "drug tourism," didn't materialize (young backpackers didn't start converging on Portugal as the new drug mecca).

Other outcomes of "Law 30" are that Portugal now has fewer people with HIV and more people in treatment. The police like the law because it frees up resources to focus on violent crime. The burden on Portugal's prisons and criminal system has been reduced. And the Portuguese government went from being the enemy of its drug-using population to being its advocate.

ping to eight percent. That may seem high to non-Portuguese, but the country's average unemployment rate since joining the European Union has been around six percent, and current numbers represent a return to pre-2008 trends. Restaurant taxes were dropped from 23 percent back to 13 percent, and investment continues to grow.

Portugal's latest challenge (along with paying off its mountainous debt) is a brain drain. Young people are thirsty for opportunity; the goal of many well-educated millennials is to get out of their parents' house, and then out of the country. Portugal has always had people looking to emigrate—consider the large Portuguese communities in Boston and New Jersey. But over the last several years, 350,000 highly trained young people (out of a population of nearly 11 million) have left the country for more promising careers in lands offering better opportunity. It also remains to be seen how Portugal will deal with the social and economic fallout of the coronavirus pandemic.

Even as Portugal struggles with its contemporary challenges, it remains open and warmly welcoming to outsiders. A visit to today's Portugal lets you personally experience the latest chapter in an epic story.

PRACTICALITIES

This chapter covers the practical skills of European travel: how to get tourist information, pay for things, sightsee efficiently, find good-value accommodations, eat affordably but well, use technology wisely, and get between destinations smoothly. For more information on these topics, see RickSteves.com/travel-tips.

Tourist Information

Portugal's **national tourist office** offers practical information, trip-planning ideas, and downloadable brochures on their website (www.visitportugal.com).

In Portugal, a good first stop in a new city is generally the tourist information office *(posto de turismo)*—abbreviated **TI** in this book. TIs are in business to help you enjoy spending money in their town—which can color their advice—but I still swing by to confirm sightseeing plans, pick up a city map, and get information on public transit, walking tours, special events, and nightlife. Some TIs have information on the entire country or at least the region, so try to get maps and printed information for destinations you'll be visiting later in your trip.

Travel Tips

Travel Advisories: For updated health and safety conditions, including any restrictions for your destination, consult the US State Department's international travel website (www.travel.state.gov).

Emergency and Medical Help: For any emergency service—ambulance, police, or fire—call **112** from a mobile phone or landline (operators typically speak English). If you get sick, do as the locals do and go to a pharmacist for advice. Or ask at your hotel for help—they'll know the nearest medical and emergency services.

ETIAS Registration: The European Union may soon require US and Canadian citizens to register online with the European Travel Information and Authorization System (ETIAS) before entering Portugal and other Schengen Zone countries (quick and easy process). For the latest, check www.etiasvisa.com.

Theft or Loss: To replace a passport, you'll need to go in person to an embassy or consulate (see next). If your credit and debit cards disappear, cancel and replace them (see "Damage Control for Lost Cards," later). File a police report, either on the spot or within a day or two; you'll need it to submit an insurance claim for lost or stolen rail passes or electronics, and it can help with replacing your passport or credit and debit cards. For more information, see RickSteves.com/help.

Embassies and Consulates: US Embassy—dial +351 217 273 300, services by appointment only (Avenida das Forças Armadas, Lisbon, https://pt.usembassy.gov).

Canadian Embassy—dial +351 213 164 600, consular services available Mon-Fri 9:00-12:00 (Avenida da Liberdade 198, third floor, Lisbon, www.canadainternational.gc.ca/portugal).

Avoiding Theft and Scams: Thieves target tourists throughout Portugal, especially in Lisbon and Porto. While hotel rooms are generally safe, thieves snatch purses, pick pockets, and break into cars. Be on guard, especially on the Metro and trolleys, and treat any disturbance around you as a smoke screen for theft. Don't believe any "police officers" looking for counterfeit bills. When traveling by train, keep your luggage in sight.

Time Zones: Though Portugal and Spain are neighbors, Portugal sets its clock one hour earlier than Spain and most of continental Europe. (This is true even during Daylight Saving Time.) Portugal's time zone is the same as Great Britain's: five/eight hours ahead of the East/West coasts of the US. The exceptions are the beginning and end of Daylight Saving Time: Europe "springs forward" the last Sunday in March (two weeks after most

PRACTICALITIES

of North America) and "falls back" the last Sunday in October (one week before North America). For a handy time converter, use the world clock app on your mobile phone or download one (see www.timeanddate.com).

Business Hours: In Portugal, some businesses take a lunch break (usually 12:00-13:30 or 12:30-14:00). Larger shops and museums stay open all day. Banks are generally open Monday through Friday from 8:30 to 15:00. Small shops are often open on Saturday only in the morning and are closed all day Sunday.

Watt's Up? Europe's electrical system is 220 volts, instead of North America's 110 volts. Most electronics (laptops, phones, cameras) and appliances (newer hair dryers, CPAP machines) convert automatically, so you won't need a converter, but you will need an adapter plug with two round prongs, sold inexpensively at travel stores in the US. Avoid bringing older appliances that don't automatically convert voltage; instead, buy a cheap replacement in Europe.

Rip up this book! Turn chapters into mini guidebooks: Break the book's spine and use a utility knife to slice apart chapters, keeping gummy edges intact. Reinforce the chapter spines with clear wide tape; use a heavy-duty stapler; or make or buy a cheap cover (see the Travel Store at RickSteves.com), swapping out chapters as you travel).

Discounts: Discounts for sights are generally not listed in this book. However, seniors (ages 65 and over), youths under 18, and students and teachers with proper identification cards (obtain from www.isic.org) can get discounts at many sights—always ask. Some discounts are available only to European citizens.

Online Translation Tips: Google's Chrome browser instantly translates websites; Translate.google.com and DeepL.com are also handy. The Google Translate app converts spoken English into most European languages (and vice versa) and can also translate text it "reads" with your phone's camera.

Going Green: If you're concerned about the environment, there's plenty you can do to reduce your footprint when traveling. When practical, take a train instead of a flight within Europe, and use public transportation within cities. In hotels, use the "Do Not Disturb" sign to avoid daily linen and towel changes (or hang up your towels to signal you'll reuse them). Bring a reusable shopping tote and refillable water bottle (Portugal's tap water is safe to drink). To find out how Rick Steves' Europe is offsetting carbon emissions with an innovative self-imposed carbon tax, go to RickSteves.com/about-us/climate-smart.

Exchange Rate

1 euro (€) = about $1.20

To convert prices in euros to dollars, add about 20 percent: €20 = about $24, €50 = about $60. Like the dollar, one euro is broken into 100 cents. Coins range from €0.01 to €2, and bills from €5 to €200 (bills over €50 are rarely used).

Check www.oanda.com for the latest exchange rates.

Money

Here's my basic strategy for using money in Europe:

- Upon arrival, head for an ATM at the airport and withdraw some local currency, using a debit card with low international transaction fees.
- In general, pay for bigger expenses with a credit card and use cash for smaller purchases. Use a debit card for cash withdrawals.
- Keep your cards and cash safe in a money belt.

PLASTIC VERSUS CASH

Although credit cards are widely accepted in Europe, cash is sometimes the only way to pay for street food, taxis, tips, and local guides. Some businesses (especially smaller ones, such as B&Bs and mom-and-pop cafés and shops) may charge you extra for using a credit card—or might not accept credit cards at all. Having cash on hand helps you out of a jam if your card randomly doesn't work.

I use my credit card to book and pay for hotel reservations, to buy advance tickets for events or sights, and to cover most other expenses.

WHAT TO BRING

I pack the following and keep it all safe in my money belt.

Debit Card: Use this at ATMs to withdraw local cash.

Credit Card: Handy for bigger transactions (at hotels, shops, restaurants, travel agencies, car-rental agencies, and so on), payment machines, and online purchases.

Backup Card: Some travelers carry a third card (debit or credit; ideally from a different bank), in case one gets lost or simply doesn't work.

A Stash of Cash: I always carry $100-200 in US dollars as a cash backup, which comes in handy in an emergency (for example, if your ATM card gets eaten by the machine).

What NOT to Bring: Resist the urge to buy **euros** before your trip or you'll pay the price in bad stateside exchange rates.

Wait until you arrive to withdraw money. European airports have plenty of ATMs.

BEFORE YOU GO

Use this pre-trip checklist.

Know your cards. US debit cards with a Visa or MasterCard logo will work in any European ATM. As for credit cards, Visa and MasterCard are universal, American Express is less common, and Discover is unknown in Europe.

Know your PIN. Make sure you know the numeric, four-digit PIN for all of your cards, both debit and credit. Request it if you don't have one, as it may be required for some purchases in Europe (see "Using Credit Cards," later), and allow time to receive the information by mail.

Report your travel dates. Let your bank know that you'll be using your debit and credit cards in Europe, and when and where you're headed.

Adjust your ATM withdrawal limit. Find out how much you can take out daily and ask for a higher daily withdrawal limit if you want to get more cash at once. Note that European ATMs will withdraw funds only from checking accounts, not savings accounts.

Ask about fees. For any purchase or withdrawal made with a card, you may be charged a currency conversion fee (1-3 percent) and/or a Visa or MasterCard international transaction fee (less than 1 percent). If you're getting a bad deal, consider getting a new debit or credit card. Reputable no-fee cards include those from Capital One, as well as Charles Schwab debit cards. Most credit unions and some airline loyalty cards have low or no international transaction fees.

IN EUROPE
Using Cash Machines

European cash machines have English-language instructions and work just like they do at home—except they spit out local currency instead of dollars, calculated at the day's standard bank-to-bank rate.

In most places, ATMs are easy to locate—in Portugal look for the *Multibanco* signs (marked with a blue and white *MB* logo). When possible, withdraw cash from a bank-run ATM located just outside the bank.

If your debit card doesn't work, try a lower amount—your request may have exceeded your withdrawal limit or the ATM's

limit (Note that in Portugal, the maximum you can withdraw per transaction at a Multibanco machine is €200). If you still have a problem, try a different ATM or come back later.

Avoid "independent" ATMs, such as Travelex, Euronet, Moneybox, Your Cash, Cardpoint, and Cashzone. These have high fees, can be less secure, and may try to trick users with "dynamic currency conversion" (see next).

Dynamic Currency Conversion

When paying with a credit card, you'll often be asked whether you want to pay in dollars or in the local currency. Always refuse the conversion and choose the local currency. While DCC seems convenient, it comes with a poor exchange rate, and you'll wind up losing money. Many ATMs also offer DCC—again, always select "continue without conversion."

Exchanging Cash

Minimize exchanging money in Europe; it's expensive (you'll generally lose 5-10 percent). In a pinch you can find exchange desks *(casa de câmbio)* at major train stations or airports. Banks generally do not exchange money unless you have an account with them.

Using Credit Cards

US credit cards generally work fine in Europe—with a few exceptions.

European cards use chip-and-PIN technology; most chip cards issued in the US instead require a signature. When presented with a US card, European card readers may generate a receipt for you to sign—or prompt you to enter your PIN. At self-service payment machines (such as transit-ticket kiosks), US cards may not work. In this case, look for a cashier who can process your card manually—or pay in cash.

"Tap to pay" cards and smartphone payment apps work in Europe just as they do in the US, and sidestep chip-and-PIN compatibility issues.

Drivers Beware: Drivers may encounter automated pay points (tollbooths, parking meters, gas pumps, etc.) where US cards are not accepted. Carry cash as a back-up and be prepared to move on to the next gas station if necessary (in some places, gas stations sell prepaid gas cards, which you should be able to purchase with any US card). When approaching a toll plaza, use the "cash" lane.

Security Tips

Pickpockets target tourists. Keep your cash, credit cards, and passport secure in your money belt, and carry only a day's spending money in your front pocket or wallet.

Before inserting your card into an ATM, inspect the front. If anything looks crooked, loose, or damaged, it could be a sign of a card-skimming device. When entering your PIN, carefully block other people's view of the keypad.

Don't use a debit card for purchases. Because a debit card pulls funds directly from your bank account, potential charges incurred by a thief will stay on your account while the fraudulent use is investigated by your bank.

While traveling, to access your accounts online, be sure to use a secure connection (see the "Tips on Internet Security" sidebar, later).

Damage Control for Lost Cards

If you lose your credit or debit card, report the loss immediately to the respective global customer-assistance centers. With a mobile phone, call these 24-hour US numbers collect: Visa (+1 303 967 1096), MasterCard (+1 636 722 7111), and American Express (+1 336 393 1111). From a landline, you can call these US numbers collect by going through a local operator.

You'll need to provide the primary cardholder's identification-verification details (such as birth date, mother's maiden name, or Social Security number). You can generally receive a temporary card within two or three business days in Europe (see RickSteves. com/help for more).

If you report your loss within two days, you typically won't be responsible for unauthorized transactions on your account, although many banks charge a liability fee.

TIPPING

Tipping in Portugal isn't as automatic and generous as it is in the US. For special service, tips are appreciated, but not expected. As in the US, the proper amount depends on your resources, tipping philosophy, and the circumstances, but some general guidelines apply.

Restaurants: At cafés and restaurants, a service charge is included in the price of what you order. If you had good service, it's customary to leave up to 5 percent—or 10 percent for a splurge place. For details on tipping in restaurants, see "Eating," later.

Taxis: For a typical ride, round up your fare a bit (for instance, if the fare is €4.70, pay €5). If the cabbie hauls your bags and zips you to the airport to help you catch your flight, you might want to give a little more.

Services: In general, if someone in the tourism or service industry does a super job for you, a small tip of a euro or two is appropriate...but not required. If you're not sure whether (or how much) to tip, ask a local for advice.

GETTING A VAT REFUND

Wrapped into the purchase price of your Portuguese souvenirs is a Value-Added Tax (VAT, called IVA or *Imposto sobre o Valor Acrescentado* in Portuguese) of about 23 percent. You're entitled to get most of that tax back if you purchase more than €50 (about $60 worth of goods at a store that participates in the VAT-refund scheme. Typically, you must ring up the minimum at a single retailer—you can't add up your purchases from various shops to reach the required amount. (If the store ships the goods to your US home, VAT is not assessed on your purchase.)

Getting your refund is straightforward...and worthwhile if you spend a significant amount.

At the Merchant: Have the merchant completely fill out the refund document (they'll ask for your passport; a photo of your passport usually works). Keep track of the paperwork and your original sales receipt. Note that you're not supposed to use your purchased goods before you leave Europe.

At the Border or Airport: Process your VAT document at your last stop in the European Union (such as at the airport) with the customs agent who deals with VAT refunds. At some airports, you'll have to go to a customs office to get your documents stamped and then to a separate VAT refund service (such as Global Blue or Planet) to process the refund. At other airports, a single VAT desk handles the whole thing. Note that refund services typically extract a 4 percent fee and can refund your money in cash immediately or credit your card. Otherwise, you'll need to mail the stamped refund documents to the address given by the merchant. Allow plenty of extra time at the airport to deal with the VAT refund process.

CUSTOMS FOR AMERICAN SHOPPERS

You can take home $800 worth of items per person duty-free, once every 31 days. Many processed and packaged foods are allowed, including vacuum-packed cheeses, dried herbs, jams, baked goods, candy, chocolate, oil, vinegar, condiments, and honey. Fresh fruits and vegetables and most meats are not allowed, with exceptions for some canned items. As for alcohol, you can bring in one liter duty-free (it can be packed securely in your checked luggage, along with any other liquid-containing items).

To bring alcohol (or liquid-packed foods) in your carry-on bag on your flight home, buy it at a duty-free shop at the airport. You'll increase your odds of getting it onto a connecting flight if it's packaged in a "STEB"—a secure, tamper-evident bag. But stay away from liquids in opaque, ceramic, or metallic containers, which usually cannot be successfully screened (STEB or no STEB).

For details on allowable goods, customs rules, and duty rates, visit http://help.cbp.gov.

Sightseeing

Sightseeing can be hard work. Use these tips to make your visits to Portugal's finest sights meaningful, fun, efficient, and painless.

MAPS AND NAVIGATION TOOLS

A good map is essential for efficient navigation while sightseeing. The maps in this book are concise and simple, designed to help you locate recommended destinations, sights, hotels, and restaurants.

You can also use a mapping app on your mobile device, which provides turn-by-turn directions for walking, driving, and taking public transit. Google Maps, Apple Maps, and CityMaps2Go allow you to download maps for offline use; ideally, download the areas you'll need in advance. For certain features, you'll need to be online—either using Wi-Fi or an international data plan.

PLAN AHEAD

Set up an itinerary that allows you to fit in all your must-see sights. For a one-stop look at opening hours in the big cities—Lisbon and Porto—see this book's "At a Glance" sidebars. Most sights keep stable hours, but you can easily confirm the latest by checking with the TI or visiting museum websites.

Don't put off visiting a must-see sight—you never know when a place will close unexpectedly for a holiday, strike, or restoration. Many museums are closed or have reduced hours at least a few days a year, especially on holidays such as Christmas, New Year's, and Labor Day (May 1). A list of holidays is in the appendix; check for possible closures during your trip. In summer, some sights may stay open late. Off-season hours may be shorter.

Going at the right time helps avoid crowds. This book offers tips on the best times to see specific sights. Try visiting popular sights very early or very late. Evening visits (when possible) are usually peaceful, with fewer crowds. Late morning is usually the worst time to visit a popular sight.

If you plan to hire a local guide, reserve ahead by email. Popular guides can get booked up.

Study up. To get the most out of the sight descriptions in this book, read them before you visit.

RESERVATIONS, ADVANCE TICKETS, AND PASSES

Given how precious your vacation time is, I recommend getting **reservations** for any must-see sight that offers them, such as Sintra's Pena Palace, Moorish Castle, and National Palace in Sintra.

To deal with lines, some popular sights sell **timed-entry tickets** that guarantee admission at a certain time of day (for example, the splendid King João's Library at the University of Coimbra). It's worth giving up some spontaneity to book in advance. While hundreds of tourists sweat in long ticket-buying lines—or arrive to find the sight sold out—those who've booked ahead are assured of getting in. In some cases, getting a ticket in advance simply means buying your ticket earlier on the same day. But for other sights, you may need to book weeks or even months in advance. As soon as you're ready to commit to a certain date, book it.

In Lisbon, the **LisboaCard,** a pass sold at city TIs, covers all public transportation and grants free entry to many museums. It also offers discounts on river cruises, my recommended city tours, many other museums, and sights in Sintra (see page 35).

AT SIGHTS

Here's what you can typically expect:

Entering: You may not be allowed to enter if you arrive too close to closing time. And guards start ushering people out well before the actual closing time, so don't save the best for last.

Many sights have a security check. Allow extra time for these lines. Some sights require you to check day packs and coats. (If you'd rather not check your day pack, try carrying it tucked under your arm like a purse as you enter.)

At churches—which often offer interesting art (usually free) and a cool, welcome seat—a modest dress code (no bare shoulders or shorts) is encouraged though rarely enforced.

Photography: If the museum's photo policy isn't clearly posted, ask a guard. Generally, taking photos without a flash or tripod is allowed. Some sights ban selfie sticks; others ban photos altogether.

Audioguides and Apps: I've produced a free, downloadable audio tour for my Lisbon City Walk; look for the ⌂ in this book. For more on my audio tours, see page 26.

Many sights rent audioguides with recorded descriptions in English. If you bring your own earbuds, you can often enjoy better sound. If you don't mind being tethered to your travel partner, you'll save money by bringing a Y-jack and sharing one audioguide. Museums and sights often offer free apps that you can download (check their websites).

Temporary Exhibits: Museums may show special exhibits in addition to their permanent collection. Some exhibits are included

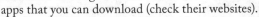

in the entry price, while others come at an extra cost (which you may have to pay even if you don't want to see the exhibit).

Expect Changes: Artwork can be on tour, on loan, out sick, or shifted at the whim of the curator. Pick up a floor plan as you enter and ask museum staff if you can't find a particular item.

Services: Important sights usually have a reasonably priced on-site café or cafeteria (handy and air-conditioned places to rejuvenate during a long visit). The WCs at sights are free and generally clean.

Before Leaving: At the gift shop, scan the postcard rack or thumb through a guidebook to be sure you haven't overlooked something that you'd like to see. Every sight or museum offers more than what is covered in this book. Use the information I provide as an introduction—not the final word.

Sleeping

Extensive and opinionated listings of good-value rooms are a major feature of this book's "Sleeping" sections. Rather than list accommodations scattered throughout a town, I choose hotels in my favorite neighborhoods that are convenient to your sightseeing.

My recommendations run the gamut, from dorm beds to fancy rooms with all the comforts. I like places that are clean, central, relatively quiet at night, reasonably priced, friendly, small enough to have a hands-on owner or manager, and run with a respect for Portuguese traditions. I'm more impressed by a handy location and a fun-loving philosophy than flat-screen TVs and a fancy gym. Most of my recommendations fall short of perfection. But if I can find a place with most of these features, it's a keeper.

Book your accommodations as soon as your itinerary is set, especially if you want to stay at one of my top listings or if you'll be traveling during busy times. See the appendix for a list of major holidays and festivals in Portugal.

Some people make reservations a few days ahead as they travel. This approach fosters spontaneity, and booking sites make it easy to find available rooms, but—especially during busy times—you run the risk of settling for lesser-value accommodations.

RATES AND DEALS

I've categorized my recommended accommodations based on price, indicated with a dollar-sign rating (see sidebar). Room prices can fluctuate significantly with demand and amenities (size, views, room class, and so on), but relative price categories remain constant. Taxes, which can vary from place to place, are generally insignificant (a dollar or two per person, per night).

Room rates are especially volatile at hotels that use "dynamic

PRACTICALITIES

Sleep Code

Hotels in this book are categorized according to the average price of a standard double room with breakfast in high season.

$$$$	**Splurge:** Most rooms over €150
$$$	**Pricier:** €100-150
$$	**Moderate:** €70-100
$	**Budget:** €40-70
¢	**Backpacker:** Under €40
RS%	**Rick Steves discount**

Unless otherwise noted, credit cards are accepted, hotel staff speaks basic English, and free Wi-Fi is available. Comparison-shop by checking prices at several hotels (on each hotel's own website, on a booking site, or by email). For the best deal, *book directly with the hotel*. Ask for a discount if paying in cash; if the listing includes **RS%,** request a Rick Steves discount.

pricing" to set rates. Prices can skyrocket during festivals and conventions, while business hotels can have deep discounts on weekends when demand plummets. Of the many hotels I recommend, it's difficult to say which will be the best value on a given day—until you do your homework.

Booking Direct: Once your dates are set, compare prices at several hotels. You can do this by checking hotel websites and booking sites such as Hotels.com or Booking.com. After you've zeroed in on your choice, book directly with the hotel itself. This increases the chances that the hotelier will be able to accommodate special needs or requests (such as shifting your reservation). And when you book by phone or email, the owner avoids the commission paid to booking sites, giving them wiggle room to offer you a discount, a nicer room, or a free breakfast (if it's not already included).

Getting a Discount: Some hotels extend a discount to those who pay cash or stay longer than three nights. Some accommodations offer a special discount for Rick Steves readers, indicated in this guidebook by the abbreviation "RS%." Discounts vary: Ask for details when you reserve. Generally, to qualify for this discount, you must book direct (not through a booking site), mention this book when you reserve, show the book upon arrival, and sometimes pay cash or stay a certain number of nights. In some cases, you may need to enter a discount code (which I've provided in the listing) in the booking form on the hotel's website. Rick Steves discounts apply to readers with either print or digital books. Understandably, discounts do not apply to promotional rates.

Making Hotel Reservations

Reserve your rooms as soon as you've pinned down your travel dates, particularly for Lisbon. For busy national holidays and religious festivals like the Fátima pilgrimage, it's wise to reserve far in advance (see the appendix).

Requesting a Reservation: For family-run hotels, it's generally best to book your room directly via email or a phone call. For business-class and chain hotels, or if you'd rather book online, reserve directly through the hotel's official website (not a booking website). Most of my recommended hotels take reservations in English.

Here's what the hotelier wants to know:
- Type(s) of room(s) you want and number of guests
- Number of nights you'll stay
- Arrival and departure dates, written European-style as day/month/year (18/06/22 or 18 June 2022)
- Special requests (en suite bathroom, cheapest room, twin beds vs. double bed, quiet room)
- Applicable discounts (such as a Rick Steves discount, cash discount, or promotional rate)

Confirming a Reservation: Most places will request a credit-card number to hold your room. If the hotel's website doesn't have a secure form where you can enter the number directly, share this info via a phone call.

Canceling a Reservation: If you must cancel, it's courteous—and smart—to do so with as much notice as possible, especially for

TYPES OF ACCOMMODATIONS

Hotels

In this book, the price for a double room in a hotel ranges from around $60 (very simple, toilet and shower down the hall) to $300 suites (maximum plumbing and more), with most clustering around $130.

Some hotels can add an extra bed (for a small charge) to turn a double into a triple; some offer larger rooms for four or more people (I call these "family rooms" in my listings). If there's space for an extra cot, they'll cram it in for you. In general, a triple room is cheaper than the cost of a double and a single. Three or four people can economize by requesting one big room.

As a budget alternative in Portugal, I also list several simple, family-run hotels (listed as a *pensão* or *residencial*); they're easy to find, inexpensive, and, when chosen properly, a fun part of the Portuguese cultural experience.

Arrival and Check-In: Hotels and B&Bs are sometimes lo-

From: rick@ricksteves.com
Sent: Today
To: info@hotelcentral.com
Subject: Reservation request for 19-22 July

Dear Hotel Central,

I would like to stay at your hotel. Please let me know if you have a room available and the price for:
• 2 people
• Double bed and en suite bathroom in a quiet room
• Arriving 19 July, departing 22 July (3 nights)

Thank you!
Rick Steves

smaller family-run places. Cancellation policies can be strict; read the fine print before you book. Many discount deals require pre-payment and can be expensive to change or cancel.

Reconfirming Your Reservation: Always call or email to reconfirm your room reservation a few days in advance. For B&Bs or very small hotels, I call again on my arrival day to tell my host what time to expect me (especially important if arriving late—after 17:00).

Phoning: For tips on calling hotels overseas, see page 456.

cated on the higher floors of a multipurpose building with a se-cured door (addresses such as "26-3" indicate a building at #26, on the third floor). In that case, look for your hotel's name on the buttons by the main entrance. When you ring the bell, you'll be buzzed in.

Hotel elevators are common, though small, and some older buildings still lack them. You may have to climb a flight of stairs to reach the elevator (if so, you can ask the front desk for help carrying your bags up).

The EU requires that hotels collect your name, nationality, and ID number. When you check in, the receptionist will normally ask for your passport and may keep it for up to a couple of hours. If you're not comfortable leaving your passport at the desk for a long time, bring a photocopy to give them instead.

If you're arriving in the morning, your room probably won't be ready. Check your bag safely at the hotel and dive right into sightseeing.

In Your Room: Most hotel rooms have a TV, telephone, and free Wi-Fi (although in old buildings with thick walls, the Wi-Fi signal might be available only in the lobby). Simpler places rarely have a room phone.

Breakfast and Meals: Breakfast is generally included (sometimes continental, but often buffet).

Checking Out: While it's customary to pay for your room upon departure, it can be a good idea to settle your bill the day before, when you're not in a hurry and while the manager's in.

Hotelier Help: Hoteliers can be a good source of advice. Most know their city well and can assist you with everything from public transit and airport connections to finding a good restaurant, the nearest launderette, or a late-night pharmacy.

Hotel Hassles: Even at the best places, mechanical breakdowns occur: Sinks leak, hot water turns cold, toilets may gurgle or smell, the Wi-Fi goes out, or the air-conditioning dies when you need it most. Report your concerns clearly and calmly at the front desk.

In Portugal, street noise can be high. You can request a room *com vista* (with a view) or *tranquilo* (quiet), but in most cases, the view comes with street noise. If you find that night noise is a problem (if, for instance, your room is over a nightclub or facing a busy street), ask for a quieter room in the back or on an upper floor.

To guard against theft in your room, keep valuables out of sight. Some rooms come with a safe, and other hotels have safes at the front desk. I've never bothered using one and in a lifetime of travel, I've never had anything stolen from my room.

For more complicated problems, don't expect instant results. Any regulated hotel will have a complaint book *(livro de reclamações)*, which is checked by authorities. A request for this book will generally prompt the hotelier to solve your problem to keep you from writing a complaint. Above all, keep a positive attitude. Remember, you're on vacation. If your hotel is a disappointment, spend more time out enjoying the place you came to see.

Historic Inns

Portugal has luxurious, government-sponsored historic inns. These *pousadas* are often renovated castles, palaces, or monasteries, many with great views and stately at-
mospheres. While full of Old World character, they often are run in a very sterile, bureaucratic way, and can have faded furnishings that are a bit worn for the price range. These are pricey ($250-500 doubles), but can be a good deal for younger people (30

and under) and seniors (55 and over), who often get discounted rates; for details, bonus packages, and family deals, see www.pousadas.pt.

Short-Term Rentals

A short-term rental—whether an apartment, house, or room in a local's home—is an increasingly popular alternative to a guesthouse or hotel, especially if you plan to settle in one location for several nights. For stays longer than a few days, you can usually find a rental that's comparable to—and cheaper than—a hotel room with similar amenities. Plus, you'll get a behind-the-scenes peek into how locals live.

Many places require a minimum stay and have strict cancellation policies. And you're generally on your own: There's no reception desk, breakfast, or daily cleaning service.

Finding Accommodations: Websites such as Airbnb, FlipKey, Booking.com, and the HomeAway family of sites (HomeAway, VRBO, and VacationRentals) let you browse a wide range of properties. Alternatively, rental agencies such as Interhomeusa.com and RentaVilla.com can provide a more personalized service (their curated listings are also more expensive).

Before you commit, be clear on the location. I like to virtually "explore" the neighborhood using Google Street View. Also consider the proximity to public transportation and how well-connected it is with the rest of the city. Ask about amenities (elevator, air-conditioning, laundry, Wi-Fi, parking, etc.). Reviews from previous guests can help identify trouble spots.

Think about the kind of experience you want: Just a key and an affordable bed...or a chance to get to know a local? Some hosts offer self-check-in and minimal interaction; others enjoy interacting with you. Read the description and reviews to help shape your decision.

Confirming and Paying: Many places require you to pay the entire balance before your trip, usually through the listing site. Be wary of owners who want to take your transaction offline; this gives you no recourse if things go awry. Never agree to wire money (a key indicator of a fraudulent transaction).

Apartments or Houses: If you're staying somewhere for several nights, it's worth considering an apartment or rental house (Shorter stays aren't worth the hassle of arranging key pickup, buying groceries, etc.). Apartment or house rentals can be especially

Using Online Services to Your Advantage

From booking services to user reviews, online businesses play a greater role in travelers' planning than ever before. Take advantage of their pluses—and be wise to their downsides.

Booking Sites

Booking websites such as Booking.com and Hotels.com offer one-stop shopping for hotels. While convenient for travelers, they're both a blessing and a curse for small, independent, family-run hotels. Without a presence on these sites, small hotels become almost invisible. But to be listed, a hotel must pay a sizable commission...and promise that its own website won't undercut the price on the booking-service site.

Here's the work-around: Use the big sites to research what's out there, then book direct with the hotel by email or phone, in which case hotel owners are free to give you whatever price they like. Ask for a room without the commission mark-up (or ask for a free breakfast if not included, or a free upgrade). If you do book online, be sure to use the hotel's own website. The price will likely be the same as via a booking site, but your money goes to the hotel, not agency commissions.

As a savvy consumer, remember: When you book with an online booking service, you're adding a middleman who takes roughly 20 percent. To support small, family-run hotels whose world is more difficult than ever, book direct.

Short-Term Rental Sites

Rental juggernaut Airbnb (along with other short-term rental sites) allows travelers to rent rooms and apartments, often providing more value, space, and amenities than a cookie-cutter hotel. Airbnb fans appreciate feeling part of a real neighborhood and getting into a daily routine as "temporary Europeans." Depending on the host, Airbnb can provide an opportunity to get to know a local person, while keeping the money spent on your

cost-effective for groups and families. European apartments, like hotel rooms, tend to be small by US standards. But they often come with laundry facilities and small, equipped kitchens, making it easier and cheaper to dine in.

Rooms in Private Homes *(Quartos):* In touristy resorts—especially beach towns like Nazaré and Salema—you'll typically find locals who've opened up a spare room to make a little money on the side. Usually fairly private and often located in small, apartment-type buildings, a *quarto* (KWAR-too; also known as an *alojamento particular*) is less expensive than a hotel ($45-75 for a double without breakfast). In Nazaré and Salema, you can stumble into town virtually any day (except August weekends) and find countless accommodations in the community.

Critics of Airbnb see it as a threat to "traditional Europe." Landlords can make more money renting to short-stay travelers, driving rents up—and local residents out to more affordable but less charming districts. When those long-term renters go, traditional businesses are replaced by ones that cater to tourists. And the character that made those neighborhoods desirable to the tourists in the first place goes too. Some cities have cracked down, requiring owners to obtain a license and to occupy rental properties part of the year (and staging disruptive "inspections" that inconvenience guests).

As a lover of Europe, I share the worry of those who see residents nudged aside by tourists. But as an advocate for travelers, I appreciate the value and cultural intimacy Airbnb provides.

User Reviews

User-generated review sites and apps such as Yelp and TripAdvisor can give you a consensus of opinions about everything from hotels and restaurants to sights and nightlife. If you scan reviews of a restaurant or hotel and see several complaints about noise or a rotten location, you've gained insight that can help in your decision-making.

But as a guidebook writer, my sense is that there is a big difference between the uncurated information on a review site and the vetted listings in a guidebook. A user-generated review is based on the limited experience of one person, who stayed at just one hotel in a given city and ate at a few restaurants there. A guidebook is the work of a trained researcher who forms a well-developed basis for comparison by visiting many restaurants and hotels year after year.

Both types of information have their place, and in many ways, they're complementary. If something is well reviewed in a guidebook and also gets good online reviews, it's likely a winner.

women hanging out on the streets with rooms to rent. Or just ask around town, at any bar. If you have the nerve to travel without reservations, this is an excellent budget deal. Have fun looking at several places, then hem and haw until the price goes down. Your room is likely to be large and homey, with old-time-elegant furnishings (and the bathroom down the hall). *Quarto* landladies generally speak only a little English, but they're used to dealing with visitors. Given that the boss changes the sheets, people staying several nights are most desirable; one-night stays sometimes cost extra, and in the busy summer months there could be a minimum-night stay.

Renting a room in someone's home is a good option for those

Keep Cool

If you're visiting Portugal in the summer, you'll want an air-conditioned room. Most hotel air-conditioners come with a remote control (like a TV remote) that generally has similar symbols and features: fan icon (click to toggle through wind power, from light to gale); temperature (20 degrees Celsius is comfortable); louver icon (choose steady airflow or waves); snowflake and sunshine icons (cold air or heat, depending on season); and clock ("O" setting: run X hours before turning off; "I" setting: wait X hours to start). When you leave your room for the day, do as the environmentally conscious Europeans do, and turn off the air-conditioning.

traveling alone, as you're more likely to find true single rooms—with just one single bed, and a price to match. These can range from air-mattress-in-living-room basic to plush-B&B-suite posh. While you can't expect your host to also be your tour guide—or even to provide you with much info—some are interested in getting to know the travelers who pass through their home.

Other Options: Swapping homes with a local works for people with an appealing place to offer (don't assume where you live is not interesting to Europeans). Good places to start are HomeExchange.com and LoveHomeSwap.com. To sleep for free, Couchsurfing.com is a vagabond's alternative to Airbnb. It lists millions of outgoing members, who host fellow "surfers" in their homes.

Hostels

A hostel provides cheap beds in dorms where you sleep alongside strangers for under $30 per night. Travelers of any age are welcome if they don't mind dorm-style accommodations and meeting other travelers. Most hostels offer kitchen facilities, guest computers, Wi-Fi, and a self-service laundry. Hostels almost always provide bedding, but the towel's up to you (though you can usually rent one). Family and private rooms are often available.

Independent hostels tend to be easygoing, colorful, and informal (no membership required; www.hostelworld.com). You may pay slightly less by booking direct with the hostel. **Official hostels** are part of Hostelling International (HI) and share an online booking site (www.hihostels.com). HI hostels typically require that you be a member or else pay a bit more per night.

Portugal has plenty of youth hostels, but considering the great bargains on other accommodations, I don't cover many in this book except for the stylish "design hostels" that are a Lisbon specialty. Big, convivial, and professional, these often have private rooms and appeal even to people who would normally choose a hotel (see the Lisbon chapter).

Eating

For listings in this guidebook, I look for restaurants that are convenient to your hotel and sightseeing. When restaurant-hunting, choose a spot filled with locals, not the place with the big neon signs boasting, "We Speak English and Accept Credit Cards." Venturing even a block or two off the main drag leads to higher-quality food for a better price.

The Portuguese meal schedule is slightly later than in the US. Breakfast *(pequeno almoço)* is often just coffee and a sweet roll. Lunch *(almoço)* is served between 12:30 and 14:00, while supper *(jantar)* is from about 19:30 to 21:30. You can eat well in mom-and-pop restaurants for about €10, especially outside Lisbon. All restaurants are smoke-free.

Appetizers Aren't Free: Appetizers (olives, bread, butter, pâtés, and a veritable mini buffet of other tasty temptations) brought to your table before you order are not free. This is common in Portugal as a way to curb your hunger while looking at the menu and waiting for your main dish to arrive. If you don't want them, push them to the side—you won't be charged if you don't eat anything. Simple appetizers usually cost about €1 each, so it won't break the budget—just don't be surprised at extra charges on your bill. And it's smart to be aware of this in unscrupulous, tourist-oriented restaurants, which may use overpriced appetizers to pad the bill.

Portions: Many restaurants save their customers money by portioning their dishes for two people. Menus often list prices for entrées in two columns: *dose* and *meia dose*. A *dose* (DOH-zeh) is generally enough to feed two, while a *meia dose* is a half-portion (plenty for one person). Restaurants have absolutely no problem with diners splitting a single *dose*.

Paying and Tipping: When you want the bill, say, *"A conta, por favor."* Most mom-and-pop restaurateurs will figure the bill in front of you, so everyone agrees on the final amount to be paid.

In nearly all restaurants, service is included—your menu typically will indicate this by noting *serviço incluído*. Still, if you are pleased with the service, it's customary to leave up to 5 percent, or 10 percent for top-notch service or in a fancy place. Leave the tip on the table. It's best to tip in cash, even if you pay with your credit card (there's generally not a place to include a tip on a credit card slip). There's no need to tip if you order food at a counter.

Restaurant Code

Eateries in this book are categorized according to the average cost of a typical main course. Drinks, desserts, and splurge items can raise the price considerably.

$$$$	**Splurge:** Most main courses over €17
$$$	**Pricier:** €12-17
$$	**Moderate:** €7-12
$	**Budget:** Under €7

In Portugal, takeout food is **$**; a basic sit-down eatery is **$$**; a casual but more upscale restaurant is **$$$**; and a swanky splurge is **$$$$**.

RESTAURANT PRICING

I've categorized my recommended eateries based on the average price of a typical main course, indicated with a dollar-sign rating (see sidebar). Obviously, expensive specialties, fine wine, appetizers, and dessert can significantly increase your final bill.

The categories also indicate the personality of a place: **Budget** eateries include street food, takeaway, order-at-the-counter shops, basic cafeterias, and bakeries selling sandwiches. **Moderate** eateries are nice (but not fancy) sit-down restaurants, ideal for a straightforward, fill-the-tank meal. Most of my listings fall in this category—great for a taste of the local cuisine at a reasonable price.

Pricier eateries are a notch up, with more attention paid to the setting, presentation, and (often inventive) cuisine. **Splurge** eateries are dress-up-for-a-special-occasion-swanky—typically with an elegant setting, polished service, and pricey and intricate cuisine.

WHERE AND WHAT TO EAT

For a quick, cheap snack, drop by a bar or café. Bars offer an enticing selection of savory treats on display, such as codfish cakes *(pastéis de bacalhau)*. Sandwiches *(sandes)* are everywhere. Cafés also offer snacks and are usually cheaper than bars. Many cafés double as lunch joints, which locals frequent. If you see a menu written on a paper tablecloth and taped in the window, you can be assured of a quick, home-cooked meal. Just don't expect a fancy presentation (and be willing to share a table with a stranger—don't worry, it makes for great conversation).

Portuguese cuisine is heavy on fish, meat, olive oil, and spices—with many Mediterranean accents. I've described some highlights in the *"Bom apetite!"* sidebar on page 7, and defined some additional menu items below. *Prato do dia* is the daily special.

Seafood: Eat fresh seafood as much as you can in Portugal—except on Monday, when the fish isn't fresh—the fishermen take

Sunday off. *Bacalhau*—codfish that's dried, salted, and then rehydrated—is a Portuguese staple. (Strangely, the codfish aren't found in Portugal's coastal waters, but are fished in the North Atlantic.) The Portuguese also adore *conservas*—canned ("conserved") fish and other seafood, often marinated with olive oil and spices (such as pepper, oregano, tomatoes, fennel, or red pepper). You'll see tinned sardines, mackerel, tuna, salmon, and even octopus. These tend to be less salty or pungent than canned fish back home...give it a

try. The Portuguese also have a knack for decorating the tins with colorful and creative artwork, making a walk through a *conservas* shop a feast for the eyes as well. Aficionados say that the best brand for sardines is Briosa, while Santa Catarina (from the Azores) has the best tuna. Some simple eateries sell cans of fish for you to open up at a table with some fresh bread...a satisfying (and very local) light lunch.

Other Dishes: Popular dishes include *caldo verde* (vegetable soup), *alheira* (smoked sausage made with bread, game, and no pork), and *frango assado* (roast chicken). The African-inspired *piri-piri* sauce—oil infused with hot chilis—is a treat if you like it hot and spicy. Don't confuse *piri-piri* with *pica pau*, a flavorful white-wine sauce with lots of garlic and bay, often served with stewed beef.

Speaking of garlic, Portuguese chefs aren't afraid of that pungent flavor. They also tend to go heavy on the salt, and many dishes come with a fresh, sweet punch of herbs—especially cilantro, parsley, and bay leaf.

Potatoes and greens are popular side dishes. Portugal also has a variety of hearty and delicious rice-based dishes, including *arroz de tomate* (like a tomato risotto), *arroz de pato* (savory rice with roasted duck and chorizo), and the stew-like *arroz de mariscos*. Carbs never went out of style in Portugal—it's common to get both potatoes and rice with a meal.

Colonial Influences: The Portuguese have a special affinity for tropical fruits—thanks both to their own warm-weather outposts (Madeira and the Azores) and their former tropical colonies. You'll see more kiwi, passionfruit, papaya, mango, and guava here than in most of Europe. Fresh-squeezed orange juice (from Algarve-grown fruit) is also very popular...and delicious. Other culinary holdovers from Portugal's colonial days include spicy *piri-piri* sauce (described earlier), palm oil, and the powerful rum-like sugarcane firewater from Cape Verde, called simply *grogue.*

Meat and Seafood

Alheira: Pork-free smoked sausage

Bacalhau: Dried, salted cod that's rehydrated and prepared in many different ways

Bacalhau à Brás: Salt cod, matchstick potatoes, and black olives scrambled with egg

Carne de porco à Alentejana: Stewed pork covered with clams

Conservas: Canned fish, marinated with olive oil and spices

Frango assado: Roast chicken, commonly served with *piri-piri* hot sauce

Percebes: Barnacles

Porco preto: Air-cured ham from *ibérico* pigs

Presunto: Air-cured ham

Sardinhas grelhadas: Fresh sardines, grilled or barbecued

Tripas à modo do Porto: Tripe served Porto-style

Rice, Soups, and Stews

Arroz de mariscos: Rice and mixed seafood stew

Arroz de pato: Duck and chorizo in a rice stew

Caldeirada de peixe: Like *cataplana* (see below), but cooked in a casserole

Caldo verde: "Green" soup of kale and potato puree

Cataplana: Seafood and potatoes cooked in a copper pot

Feijoada: Pork and bean stew

Sopa Alentejana: Garlic soup with a poached egg, cilantro, and bread crumbs

Sopa de mariscos: Shellfish soup

Sopa de peixe: Fish soup

Sandwiches and Snacks

Apertivos: Appetizers

Batatas fritas: Potato chips

Bifana: Pork sandwich

Francesinha ("little French girl"): A sandwich of pork, sausage, and cheese, grilled and topped with more melted cheese and a spicy sauce

Pastéis de bacalhau: Codfish fritters

Petiscos: Portuguese-style tapas—cured meats, cheeses, olives

Prego: Steak sandwich

Sandes de leitão: Suckling-pig sandwich

Tosta mista: Grilled ham and cheese sandwich

Desserts

Arroz doce: Rice pudding with cinnamon

Barriga de freiras ("nuns' belly"): Convent sweet made with egg yolks and sugar

Charcada: Eggy-almond pudding-like dessert

Papo de anjo ("angel's double chin"): Convent sweet made from beaten egg yolks that are baked, then boiled in a sugar syrup

Pastel de nata: Custard tart

Pastel de Santa Clara: Almond and marmalade pastry

Pastel de Tentúgal: Sweet, eggy filling wrapped with puff pastry and dusted with powdered sugar

Pudim: Flan

Queque: Muffin

Salame de chocolate: Dark chocolate and broken cookies rolled into a salami-shaped log that's sliced for serving

PORTUGUESE BEVERAGES
Wine, Beer, and Spirits

Despite its small size, Portugal is among the world's top wine producers—bottling more than 150 million gallons in a good year. And Portuguese wines are cheap, decent, and distinctively fruity.

Vinho verde (VEEN-yoo VAIR-day) is light, refreshing, almost always white, and can be slightly fizzy. This "green wine" is actually golden in color, but "green" (young) in age—picked, made, and drunk within a year. Alvarinho grapes, from the northern Minho region, are low-sugar and high-acid. After the initial fermentation, winemakers introduce a second fermentation, whose byproduct is carbon dioxide—the light fizz. The wines are somewhat bitter alone, but great with meals, especially seafood. The best are from the Monção, Amarante, and Aveleda regions, but the one you'll see on every menu is the perfectly acceptable Casal Garcia.

If you like white *vinho verde*, you might enjoy the harder-to-find red version. It's dark in color, like a cabernet, but still fizzy and light in flavor, like a rosé—a unique combination.

The Dão region also produces fine red wines, mostly from the Mondego Valley between Coimbra, Guarda, and Viseu. They should sit for a year or two in the bottle before drinking.

The Alentejo region (look for bottles labeled "Borba," a major producer) is known for high-quality reds that tend to be full-bodied and fruit-forward; the Alentejo is increasingly producing good

452 Rick Steves Portugal

whites as well. And the Douro Valley—best known as the place where grapes for port are grown—has recently earned an equally strong reputation for its table wines (look for *vinho do Douro*). If you find yourself drowning in choices, simply try a glass of the house wine *(vinho da casa)*.

If you like port wine, what better place to sample it than its birthplace, Port-ugal? (For a crash course on port wine, see page 380.) *Reserva* on the label means it's the best-quality port (and the most expensive). All bottles of port should have a *selo de garantia* (a seal of guarantee) issued by the Port Wine Institute.

Madeira, made from grapes grown in volcanic soil in the Madeira Islands, is fortified and blended (as is port), and usually served as a sweet dessert wine. The English and George Washington both liked it ("Have some Madeira, m'dear"), though today's version is drier and less syrupy. A Madeira called *Sercial* is served chilled (like sherry) with almonds.

The favorite Portuguese spirit is *ginjinha*, a liqueur made with the sour cherry-like *ginja* berry. You'll see shops selling shots on the street (particularly in Óbidos, where it's traditionally sold in tiny, delicate, edible chocolate cups). To take a bottle home, look for the widely available brands Espinheira or Sem Rival; for something a notch better, look for Ginja MSR.

Beer *(cerveja)* is also popular—for a small draft beer, ask for *uma imperial*. You'll see Super Bock in the north, and Sagres in the south—the Bud and Miller of Portugal. Each also produces versions that are dark *(preta)*, nonalcoholic *(sem álcool)*, or both.

Here are some common drinking terms:

Aguardente: Firewater distilled from grape seeds, stems, and skins, with a kick like a mule

Cerveja: Beer

Ginjinha: Sour-cherry liqueur, served at special bars in Lisbon and Óbidos

Grogue: Strong spirits from Cape Verde, derived from sugarcane

Imperial: Small draft beer

Vinho da casa: House wine

Vinho branco: White wine

Vinho tinto: Red wine

Vinho verde: "Green" wine (young, white wine)

Water, Coffee, and Other Nonalcoholic Drinks

Freshly squeezed orange juice *(sumo de laranja)*, mineral water *(água mineral)*, and soft drinks are widely available. When ordering water, fizzy or not, you will be asked, *"Fresco o natural?"* Fresco is chilled, and *natural* is room temperature.

Coffee lovers enjoy a *café*, the very aromatic shot of espresso so popular in Portugal. In Lisbon this is called a *bica*. For an espresso with a little milk (like a *caffè macchiato*), ask for a *café pingado*.

Here are some useful beverage phrases:

Abatanado: Black coffee (but be aware that every café in Portugal has a different take on this; asking for a café Americano might work better to meet your black-coffee expectations)

Água da torneira: Tap water

Água com/sem gás: Water with/without bubbles

Água mineral: Mineral water

Bica: Espresso (Lisbon)

Café: Espresso

Café pingado: Espresso with a little milk, similar to a *caffè macchiato*

Chá: Tea

Fresco: Chilled

Galão: Coffee drink similar to a latte, served in a tall glass and often sweetened

Leite: Milk

Meia de leite: Coffee with warm milk

Natural: Room temperature

Sumo: Juice

Sumo de laranja: Orange juice

Staying Connected

One of the most common questions I hear from travelers is, "How can I stay connected in Europe?" The short answer is: more easily and affordably than you might think.

The simplest solution is to bring your own device—phone, tablet, or laptop—and use it just as you would at home (following the money-saving tips below, such as getting an international plan or connecting to free Wi-Fi whenever possible). Another option is to buy a European SIM card for your US mobile phone. Or you can use European landlines and computers to connect. More details are at RickSteves.com/phoning. For a very practical one-hour lecture covering tech issues for travelers, see RickSteves.com/mobile-travel-skills.

USING YOUR PHONE IN EUROPE

Here are some budget tips and options.

Sign up for an international plan. To stay connected at a lower cost, sign up for an international service plan through your carrier. Most providers offer a simple bundle that includes calling, messaging, and data. Your normal plan may already include international coverage (T-Mobile's does).

Before your trip, research your provider's international rates.

Hurdling the Language Barrier

Many Portuguese people—especially those in the tourist trade and in big cities—speak English. And, in general, the Portuguese speak more English than their Spanish neighbors, since English is required in school. (Their American movies are also subtitled, while the Spanish get their Hollywood flicks dubbed.) But locals will visibly brighten when you know and use some key Portuguese phrases (see "Portuguese Survival Phrases" on page 477). You'll find that doors open more quickly and with more smiles when you can speak a few words of the language.

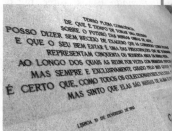

If you speak intermediate Spanish, you'll be able to stumble through newspapers and read road signs, even if you can't pronounce the words (spoken Portuguese sounds like a mix of a Slavic language and Spanish). If you take a Portuguese language course before your trip here, make sure your professor is Portuguese, not Brazilian—the accents are very distinct.

If you're having trouble communicating in Portuguese, try English, French, and Spanish, in that order (because some locals give Spanish speakers the cold shoulder).

For more tips on hurdling the language barrier, consider the *Rick Steves Portuguese Phrase Book* (available at RickSteves.com).

Activate the plan a day or two before you leave, then remember to cancel it when your trip's over.

Use free Wi-Fi whenever possible. Unless you have an unlimited-data plan, save most of your online tasks for Wi-Fi. Most accommodations in Europe offer free Wi-Fi. Many cafés (including Starbucks and McDonald's) offer hotspots for customers; ask for the password when you buy something. You may also find Wi-Fi at TIs, city squares, major museums, public-transit hubs, airports, and aboard trains and buses.

Minimize the use of your cellular network. The best way to make sure you're not accidentally burning through data is to put your device in "airplane" mode (which also disables phone calls and texts), and connect to Wi-Fi networks as needed. When you need to get online but can't find Wi-Fi, simply turn on your cellular network (or turn off airplane mode) just long enough for the task at hand.

Even with an international data plan, wait until you're on Wi-Fi to Skype, download apps, stream videos, or do other megabyte-greedy tasks. Using a navigation app such as Google Maps

How to Dial

Here's how to dial from anywhere in the US or Europe, using the phone number of one of my recommended Lisbon hotels as an example (213 240 990).

From a US Mobile Phone
Phone numbers in this book are presented exactly as you would dial them from a US mobile phone. For international access, press and hold the 0 key until you get a + sign, then dial the country code (351 for Portugal) and phone number.
▸ To call the Lisbon hotel from any location, dial +351 213 240 990.

From a US Landline
Replace + with 011 (US/Canada international access code), then dial the country code (351 for Portugal) and phone number.
▸ To call the Lisbon hotel from your home landline, dial 011 351 213 240 990.

From a European Landline
Replace + with 00 (Europe international access code), then dial the country code (351 for Portugal, 1 for the US) and phone number.
▸ To call the Lisbon hotel from a Spanish landline, dial 00 351 213 240 990.
▸ To call my US office from a Portuguese landline, dial 00 1 425 771 8303.

From One Portuguese Phone to Another
To place a domestic call (from a Portuguese landline or mobile), drop +351 from the phone number.
▸ To call the Lisbon hotel from Porto, dial 213 240 990.

More Dialing Tips
Local Numbers: European phone numbers and area codes can vary in length and spacing, even within the same country. Mobile phones use separate prefixes (for instance, in Portugal, landlines begin with 2, and mobile numbers begin with 9). Some European phone numbers begin with 0; if dialing internationally, drop this 0 (except when calling Italy).

Toll and Toll-Free Calls: It's generally not possible to dial European toll or toll-free numbers from a US mobile or landline (although you can sometimes get through using Skype). Look for a direct-dial number instead.

Calling the US from a US Mobile Phone, While Abroad: Dial +1, area code, and number.

More Phoning Help: See HowToCallAbroad.com.

over a cellular network can require lots of data, so download maps when you're on Wi-Fi, then use the app offline.

Limit automatic updates. By default, your device constantly checks for a data connection and updates app content. Check your device's menu for ways to turn this off, and change your email settings from "auto-retrieve" to "manual" (or from "push" to "fetch").

Use Wi-Fi calling and messaging apps. Skype, WhatsApp, FaceTime, and Google Hangouts are great for making free or low-

Tips on Internet Security

Make sure that your device is running the latest version of its operating system, security software, and apps. Next, ensure that your device and key programs (like email) are password- or passcode-protected. On the road, use only secure, password-protected Wi-Fi. Ask the hotel or café staff for the specific name of their network, and make sure you log on to that exact one.

If you must access your financial info online, use a banking app rather than accessing your account via a browser, and use a cellular connection, not Wi-Fi. Never log on to personal finance sites on a public computer. If you're very concerned, consider subscribing to a VPN (virtual private network).

cost calls or sending texts over Wi-Fi worldwide. Just log on to a Wi-Fi network, then connect with friends or family members who use the same service. If you buy credit in advance, with some services you can call or text anywhere for just pennies.

Buy a European SIM card. If you anticipate making a lot of local calls, need a local phone number, or your provider's international data rates are expensive, consider buying a SIM card in Europe to replace the one in your (unlocked) US phone or tablet. SIM cards are sold at department-store electronics counters, some newsstands, and vending machines (you may need to show your passport). If you need help setting it up, buy one at a mobile-phone shop.

There are generally no roaming charges when using a European SIM card in other EU countries, but confirm when you buy.

WITHOUT A MOBILE PHONE

It's less convenient but possible to travel in Europe without a mobile device. You can make calls from your hotel and check email or get online using public computers.

Most **hotels** charge a fee for placing calls—ask for the rates before you dial. You can use a prepaid international phone card (*cartão telefónico com código pessoal,* usually available at newsstands, tobacco shops, and train stations) to call out from your hotel. Dial the toll-free access number, enter the card's PIN code, then dial the number.

Some hotels have **public computers** in their lobby for guests to use; otherwise you can find them at public libraries (ask your hotelier or the TI for the nearest location). On a European keyboard, use the "Alt Gr" key to the right of the space bar to insert the extra symbol that appears on some keys. Portuguese keyboards are a little different from ours; to type an @ symbol, press the "Alt Gr" key and 2 at the same time. If you can't locate a special character (such as @), simply copy and paste it from a web page.

MAIL

You can mail one package per day to yourself worth up to $200 duty-free from Europe to the US (mark it "personal purchases"). If you're sending a gift to someone, mark it "unsolicited gift." For details, visit www.cbp.gov, select "Travel," and then "Know Before You Go." The Portuguese postal service works fine, but for quick transatlantic delivery (in either direction), consider services such as DHL (www.dhl.com).

Transportation

Figuring out how to get around in Europe is one of your biggest trip decisions. **Cars** work well for two or more traveling together (especially families with small kids), those packing heavy, and those delving into the countryside. **Trains** and **buses** are best for solo travelers, blitz tourists, city-to-city travelers, and those who want to leave the driving to others. Short-hop **flights** within Europe can creatively connect the dots. Just be aware of the potential downside of each option: A car is an expensive headache in any major city; with trains and buses you're at the mercy of a timetable; and flying entails a trek to and from a usually distant airport, and leaves a larger carbon footprint.

If your itinerary mixes cities and countryside, my advice is to connect cities by train (or bus) and to explore rural areas by rental car. Arrange to pick up your car in the last big city you'll visit, then use it to lace together small towns and explore the countryside. For more detailed information on transportation throughout Europe, including trains, flying, buses, renting a car, and driving, see RickSteves.com/transportation.

TRAIN VERSUS BUS

If your trip will cover more of Portugal than just Lisbon, you may need to take a long-distance train or bus, rent a car, or fly. Portugal straggles behind the rest of Europe in train service, but offers excellent bus transportation. Off the main Lisbon-Porto-Coimbra train lines, buses are usually a better bet. In cases where buses and trains serve the same destination, the bus is often more efficient, offering more frequent connections and sometimes a more central station. If schedules are similar, use the maps in this book to determine which station is closest to your hotel.

The best public transportation option is to mix bus and train travel. Always verify bus and train schedules before your departure. To ask for a schedule at an information window, say, *"Horário para* (fill in names of cities), *faz favor.*" (The TI will sometimes have schedules available.) To study train schedules in advance, see www. cp.pt for all domestic and Spain/France routes. Another good resource for train schedules throughout Europe is German Rail's timetable (www.bahn.com).

Departures and arrivals are *partidas* and *chegadas,* respectively. These key Portuguese "fine print" words may also come in handy in your travels: Both *as* and *aos* mean "on"; *de* means "from," as in "from this date to that date"; *só* means "only," as in "only effective on..."; *não* means "not"; and *feriado* means "holiday." On schedules, exceptions are noted, as in this typical qualifier: *"Não se efectua aos sábados, domingos, e feriados oficiais"* ("Not effective on Saturdays, Sundays, and official holidays").

TRAINS *(COMBOIOS)*
The fastest Alfa Pendular and Intercidades trains serve the main Lisbon-Porto line with an occasional extension to Faro or Braga; these trains require seat reservations. Regional and Interregional "milk-run" trains serve most other routes, making lots of stops. On Portuguese train schedules, *diario* means "daily" and *mudança de comboio* means "change trains."

Rail Passes: Because you'll likely use a mix of trains and buses on your trip, a Eurail Portugal Pass doesn't make much sense. Even if your trip extends into Spain, consider that Lisbon-Madrid and Lisbon-San Sebastián trains leave just once a day as an overnight trip (see below). Therefore, many travelers find that flights or buses (not covered by rail passes) are better options for any international route. For information on rail passes, visit RickSteves.com/rail.

Overnight Trains: If you'll be going from Lisbon to Madrid or San Sebastián, check if an overnight train (called the "Lusitânia" and "Surexpreso," respectively) is running and book ahead to ensure you get a berth and/or seat (covered by a Eurail Global Pass, but you must pay for a sleeper reservation).

BUSES *(AUTOCARROS)*
Portugal has several bus companies, sometimes running buses to the same destinations and using the same transfer points. If you have to transfer, make sure to look for a bus with the same name/logo as the company you bought the ticket from. The largest national company is Rede Expressos (covers buses both north and

Portugal's Public Transportation

Legend:
- ------ Rail
- ====== AVE High Speed Rail (Spain)
- - - - - Bus
- .... Boat
- ✈ Airports (Not All Shown)
- O Border Towns

100 Kilometers
100 Miles

To A Coruña · Santiago de Compostela · Lugo

To San Sebastián

Vigo · Ourense · SPAIN

Tui · Valença

To Salamanca

Braga · Guimáres

Porto · Pinhão · Pocinho · Peso da Régua

Aveiro

Atlantic Ocean

PORTUGAL

Pampilhosa · Vilar Formoso · To Salamanca · Fuentes de Oñoro

Figueira da Foz · Coimbra · Guarda · Covilha

Batalha · Valado · Tomar · Fátima

Nazaré · Alcobaça

Óbidos

Entroncamento

Cáceres · To Madrid

Sintra · Cascais · Lisbon · Portalegre · Elvas · Badajoz · Mérida

Setúbal

Évora

SPAIN

Beja

Funcheira

Sagres · Lagos · Tunes · Ayamonte · To Madrid

Salema · Vila Real · Tavira · Faro · Huelva · Sevilla

To Jerez & Cádiz

south of Lisbon, www.rede-expressos.pt). EVA Transportes (www.eva-bus.com) covers some areas south of Lisbon, including the Algarve. Central Portugal is covered by all major bus companies as well as Rodoviária do Tejo (www.rodotejo.pt) and Citi Express (www.citiexpress.eu). You can plan bus trips between cities online, but you should always confirm the schedule in person.

Bus schedules in Portugal are clearly posted at each major

PRACTICALITIES

station. *Directo* is "direct." Slower *ruta* buses make many stops en route. Posted schedules list most, but not all, destinations. If your intended destination isn't listed, check at the ticket/information window for the most complete schedule information. For long trips, your ticket might include an assigned seat.

If the bus station is not central, ask at the TI about travel agencies near your hotel that sell bus tickets. Don't leave a bus station to explore a city without checking your departure options and buying a ticket in advance if necessary (and possible). Bus service on holidays, Saturdays, and especially Sundays can be dismal.

You can (and most likely will be required to) stow your luggage under the bus. For longer rides, give some thought to which side of the bus will get the most sun, and sit on the opposite side. Even if a bus is air-conditioned and has curtains, direct sunlight can still heat up your seat. Long-distance (and most short-distance) buses are nonsmoking. Your ride will likely come with a soundtrack: recorded music (usually American pop), a radio, or sometimes videos. If you prefer silence, bring earplugs.

Drivers and station personnel rarely speak English. Buses usually lack WCs but stop every two hours or so for a 15- to 20-minute break. Ask the driver, "How many minutes here?" *("Quántos minutos aqui?")*. Bus stations have WCs (carry tissue), and cafés offering quick and cheap food.

TAXIS AND RIDE-BOOKING SERVICES

Most European taxis are reliable and cheap. In many cities, two people can travel short distances by cab for little more than the cost of bus or subway tickets. Drivers generally respond kindly to the request, "How much is it to (destination), more or less?" *("Quanto é para Belém, mais ou menos?")* Rounding the fare up to the nearest large coin (maximum of 10 percent) is adequate for a tip. Keep a map in your hand so the cabbie knows (or thinks) you know where you're going. If you like ride-booking services such as Uber, their apps usually work in Europe just like they do in the US: Request a car on your mobile phone (connected to Wi-Fi or data), and the fare is automatically charged to your credit card.

RENTING A CAR

It's cheaper to arrange most car rentals from the US, so research and compare rates before you go. Most of the major US rental agencies (including Avis, Budget, Enterprise, Hertz, and Thrifty) have offices throughout Europe. Also consider the two major Europe-based agencies, Europcar and Sixt. Consolidators, such as Auto Europe (www.autoeurope.com—or the sometimes cheaper www.autoeurope.eu) compare rates at several companies to get you the best deal.

Wherever you book, always read the fine print. Check for add-on charges—such as one-way drop-off fees, airport surcharges, or mandatory insurance policies—that aren't included in the "total price."

Rental Costs and Considerations

Figure on paying roughly $250 for a one-week rental for a basic compact car. Allow extra for supplemental insurance, fuel, tolls, and parking. To save money on fuel, request a diesel car.

Manual vs. Automatic: Almost all rental cars in Europe are manual by default—and cars with a stick shift are generally cheaper. If you need an automatic, reserve one specifically. When selecting a car, don't be tempted by a larger model, as it won't be as maneuverable on narrow, winding roads or when squeezing into tight parking lots.

Age Restrictions: Some rental companies impose minimum and maximum age limits. Young drivers (25 and under) and seniors (69 and up) should check the rental policies and rules section of car rental websites.

Choosing Pick-up/Drop-off Locations: Always check the hours of the locations you choose: Many rental offices close from midday Saturday until Monday morning and, in smaller towns, at lunchtime. When selecting an office, confirm the location on a map. A downtown site might seem more convenient than the airport but could actually be in the suburbs or buried deep in big-city streets. Pedestrianized and one-way streets can make navigation tricky when returning a car at a big-city office or urban train station. Wherever you select, get precise details on the location and allow ample time to find it.

Have the Right License: If you're renting a car in Portugal, bring your driver's license. You're also technically required to have an International Driving Permit—an official translation of your license (sold at AAA offices for about $20 plus the cost of two passport-type photos; see www.aaa.com). How this is enforced varies.

Crossing Borders in a Rental Car: Be warned that international trips—say, picking up in Porto and dropping off in Madrid—while efficient, can be expensive if the rental company assesses a drop-off fee for crossing a border.

Always tell your car-rental company which countries you'll be entering. Some companies levy extra insurance fees for trips taken in certain countries with certain cars (such as BMWs, Mercedes, and convertibles). Double-check with your rental agent that you have all the documentation you need before you drive off.

Via Verde Toll Sensor: To save some hassle paying tolls, rent a "Via Verde" automated toll sensor along with your car (figure about €2/day); at the end of your rental, the car agency will charge your

PRACTICALITIES

credit card for the actual tolls you incur. Be sure the sensor is activated before you leave the rental lot. For more on tolls, see page 465.

Picking Up Your Car: Before driving off in your rental car, check it thoroughly and make sure any damage is noted on your rental agreement. Rental agencies in Europe tend to charge for even minor damage, so be sure to mark everything. Find out how your car's gearshift, lights, turn signals, wipers, radio, and fuel cap function, and know what kind of fuel the car takes (diesel is common in Europe). When you return the car, make sure the agent verifies its condition with you.

Car Insurance Options

When you rent a car in Europe, the price typically includes liability insurance, which covers harm to other cars or motorists—but not the rental car itself. To limit your financial risk in case of damage to the rental, choose one of these options: Buy a Collision Damage Waiver (CDW) with a low or zero deductible from the car-rental company (roughly 30-40 percent extra), get coverage through your credit card (free, but more complicated), or get collision insurance as part of a larger travel-insurance policy.

Basic **CDW** costs $15-30 a day and typically comes with a $1,000-2,000 deductible, reducing but not eliminating your financial responsibility. When you reserve or pick up the car, you'll be offered the chance to "buy down" the deductible to zero (for an additional $10-30/day; this is sometimes called "super CDW" or "zero-deductible coverage").

If you opt for **credit-card coverage,** you must decline all coverage offered by the car-rental company—which means they can place a hold on your card to cover the deductible. In case of damage, it can be time-consuming to resolve the charges. Before relying on this option, quiz your card company about how it works.

If you're already purchasing a **travel-insurance policy** for your trip, adding collision coverage can be an economical option. For example, Travel Guard (www.travelguard.com) sells affordable renter's collision insurance as an add-on to its other policies; it's valid everywhere in Europe except the Republic of Ireland, and some Italian car-rental companies refuse to honor it, as it doesn't cover you in case of theft.

For more on car-rental insurance, see RickSteves.com/cdw.

Navigation Options

If you'll be navigating using your phone or a GPS unit from home, remember to bring a car charger and device mount.

Your Mobile Phone: The mapping app on your phone works fine for navigating Europe's roads. To save on data, most apps allow you to download maps for offline use (do this before you need them,

PRACTICALITIES

Driving in Portugal

100 Kilometers

50 Miles

To Santiago de Compostela

Atlantic Ocean

Porto — Peso da Régua — Pinhão
145m • 3.5h
60m • 1.5h
15m 0.5h
190m • 4h

Salamanca
75m•1.5h
100m•2h
165m•3h
60m•1h

Coimbra
135m•2.75h
Ciudad Rodrigo

55m•1h
240m•4h

PORTUGAL

Nazaré
40m•1h
Fátima
60m•1.h

SPAIN

Óbidos
25m•0.5h
125m•2.5h
80m•1.5h

Sintra
60m•1.25h

315m•5.5h (via Badajoz)
To Madrid

Lisbon
20m•0.5h
90m•2h
Évora

m = miles
h = hours

Note: Your times may vary based on traffic, construction & road conditions.

185m•3h
155m•3h
265m•5h (via Beja)
185m•3h
155m•3h

13m•0.5h
Lagos
Sagres
Salema
13m•0.5h
70m•1.5h
Tavira
100m•1.5h
Sevilla

---

when you have a strong Wi-Fi signal). Some apps—including Google Maps—also have offline route directions, but you'll need mobile data access for current traffic. For more on using a mapping app without burning through data, see "Using Your Phone in Europe," earlier.

GPS Devices: If you want a dedicated GPS unit, consider renting one with your car ($10-30/day, or sometimes included—ask). These units offer real-time turn-by-turn directions and traffic without the data requirements of an app. The unit may come loaded only with maps for its home country; if you need additional maps, ask. Also make sure your device's language is set to English and you know how to use it before you drive off.

Paper Maps and Atlases: Even when navigating primarily with a mobile app or GPS, I always make it a point to have a paper map, ideally a big, detailed regional road map. It's invaluable for getting the big picture, understanding alternate routes, and filling in if my phone runs out of juice. The free maps you get from your car-rental company usually don't have enough detail. It's smart to buy a better map before you go, or pick one up at a local gas station, bookshop, newsstand, or tourist shop.

DRIVING

Drivers in Portugal encounter sparse traffic and very good roads connecting larger cities.

Road Rules: Be aware of typical European road rules; for example, many countries require headlights to be turned on at all times, and nearly all forbid handheld mobile-phone use. In Europe, you're not allowed to turn right on a red light unless there is a sign or signal specifically authorizing it, and on expressways it's illegal to pass drivers on the right. Seat belts are required by law in Portugal. Ask your car-rental company about these rules, or check the "International Travel" section of the US State Department website (www.travel.state.gov, search for your country in the "Learn About Your Destination" box, then click on "Travel and Transportation"). You may be stopped for a routine check by the police (be sure you have your rental paperwork close at hand).

Fuel: Gas and diesel prices are government-controlled and the same everywhere. Gas is around $6.50 a gallon, and diesel is about $5.50. Be careful when filling up: the words are similar for unleaded gas (*gasolina*) and for diesel (*gasóleo*). Some pumps are color-coded: Unleaded pumps are green and labeled "E," while diesel pumps (often yellow or black) are labeled "B." Note that your US credit and debit cards may not work at self-service gas pumps, as well as toll bridges and automated parking garages, even if they have a chip. Be sure to know your credit card's PIN, but just in case, also carry sufficient cash.

STOP AND LEARN THES[E] ROAD SIGNS

Speed Limit (km/hr) — Yield — No Passing — End [of] No Pas[sing] Zon[e]

One Way — Intersection — Main Road — Express[way]

Danger — No Entry — Cars Prohibited — All Vehi[cles] Prohib[ited]

No Through Road — Restrictions No Longer Apply — Yield to Oncoming Traffic — No Stopp[ing]

Parking — No Parking — Customs — Peac[e]

Navigation: On freeways, navigate by direction (*norte* = north, *oeste* = west, *sul* = south, *este* = east). Also, since road numbers can be confusing and inconsistent, navigate by city names. You can pick up a Michelin map in the US or buy one of the good, inexpensive maps available throughout Portugal.

Parking: Parking areas in cities generally have a large white "P" on a blue background. Don't assume it's free—check around for meters or ticketing machines. Signs that say *livre* (free) mean a space is available—not free of charge.

Theft: Choose parking places carefully. Keep your valuables in your hotel room or, if you're between destinations, covered in your trunk. Leave nothing worth stealing in the car, especially overnight. If your car's a hatchback, take the trunk cover off at night so thieves can look in without breaking in. Try to make your car look locally owned by hiding the "tourist-owned" rental-company decals and putting a Portuguese newspaper in your front or back window. Ask your hotelier for advice on parking. In cities, you can park safely but expensively in guarded lots.

Tolls: Almost all Portuguese superhighways are subject to tolls (about €1 per 13 kilometers). There are a variety of ways to pay; for a rundown, see www.portugaltolls.com. Here are the basics:

First off, if renting your car in Portugal, the simplest (and recommended) solution is to get a **Via Verde automated tolling device** from your rental-car company (described in "Renting a Car," earlier). With the Via Verde device, you can pass through tolling plazas using the lanes marked with a green-and-white *V* and the words *Reservada a Aderentes*.

If you'd rather **pay tolls as you go,** be prepared for two different types of tolls: ticket-based or electronic.

The majority of expressways are **manually tolled:** Simply take a ticket as you enter, and pay the toll as you leave (lanes are marked for credit cards or cash).

Other roads—such as the A-22 along the Algarve—are **electronically tolled** using cameras, which identify cars by their license plate as they zip past. Each time you drive under a toll camera, a sign tells you the fee (expect to pay about €10 to cross the entire Algarve coast, which covers the width of southern Portugal).

This electronic toll system offers three payment options, outlined below. To figure out the right option or to estimate your total tolls, start at www.portugaltolls.com (or if picking up your car in Portugal, ask for advice from the rental agency). The entire process is slick and easy.

A **TOLLCard** comes in prepaid amounts (€5, €10, €20, or €40) and is valid for one year. To use it, buy the card online (www.portugaltolls.com) or from the postal service (*Correios* or CTT), then activate it by sending a text message from your mobile phone.

You can check your balance online, plus you'll receive a text message when it runs out (balance is refundable).

TOLL Service is a three-day, €20 prepaid card that includes unlimited travel for those driving a car registered outside Portugal. It's available online, at post offices or at the Porto and Faro airports.

With an **EASYToll** card, your credit card will be charged each time you pass a toll point. You can buy this card online and at certain payment points along the border with Spain. Simply pop your credit card into the machine (which associates your card with your license number) and take your EASYToll card. This covers your car for all toll road use for a month (or until you cancel the account). When leaving the country, be sure to close your account: Go to www.portugaltolls.com, and enter the "identifier number" (located on your EASYToll card) and license plate number. If you don't cancel the account, the next driver can zip around the country on your penny.

FLIGHTS

To compare flights, begin with a travel search engine: Kayak is the top site for flights to and within Europe, easy-to-use Google Flights has price alerts, and Skyscanner includes many inexpensive flights within Europe. To avoid unpleasant surprises, before you book be sure to read the small print about refunds, changes, and the costs for "extras" such as reserving a seat, checking a bag, or printing a boarding pass.

Flights to Europe: Start looking for international flights at least four to six months before your trip, especially for peak-season travel. Depending on your itinerary, it can be efficient and no more expensive to fly into one city and out of another. If your flight requires a connection in Europe, see my hints on navigating Europe's top hub airports at RickSteves.com/hub-airports.

Flights Within Europe: Flying between European cities can be affordable and faster than a long-distance train or bus. Check the cost of a flight on one of Europe's airlines, whether a major carrier or a no-frills outfit like EasyJet or Ryanair. For flights within Portugal, the country's national carrier is **TAP Portugal** (www.flytap.com). For flights between Lisbon and other cities in Europe, also try **Iberia** (www.iberia.com), **Vueling Airlines** (www.vueling.com), **Ryanair** (www.ryanair.com), and **EasyJet** (www.easyjet.com). Be aware that flying with a discount airline can have drawbacks, such as minimal customer service and time-consuming treks to secondary airports.

Flying to the US and Canada: Because security is extra tight for flights to the US, be sure to give yourself plenty of time at the airport (see www.tsa.gov for the latest rules).

Resources from Rick Steves

Begin Your Trip at RickSteves.com

My mobile-friendly **website** is *the* place to explore Europe in preparation for your trip. You'll find thousands of fun articles, videos, and radio interviews; a wealth of money-saving tips for planning your dream trip; travel news dispatches; a video library of travel talks; my travel blog; our latest guidebook updates (RickSteves.com/update); and the free Rick Steves Audio Europe app. You can also follow me on Facebook, Instagram, and Twitter.

Our **Travel Forum** is a well-groomed collection of message boards, where our travel-savvy community answers questions and shares their personal travel experiences—and our well-traveled staff chimes in when they can be helpful (RickSteves.com/forums).

Our **online Travel Store** offers bags and accessories that I've designed to help you travel smarter and lighter. These include my popular carry-on bags (which I live out of four months a year), money belts, totes, toiletries kits, adapters, guidebooks, and planning maps (RickSteves.com/shop).

Our website can also help you find the perfect **rail pass** for your itinerary and your budget, with easy, one-stop shopping for rail passes, seat reservations, and point-to-point tickets (RickSteves.com/rail).

Rick Steves' Tours, Guidebooks, TV Shows, and More

Small Group Tours: Want to travel with greater efficiency and less stress? We offer more than 40 itineraries reaching the best destinations in this book...and beyond. Each year about 30,000 travelers join us on about 1,000 Rick Steves bus tours. You'll enjoy great guides and a fun bunch of travel partners (with small groups of 24 to 28 travelers). You'll find European adventures to fit every vacation length. For all the details, and to get our tour catalog, visit RickSteves.com or call us at 425 608 4217.

Books: This book is just one of many books in my series on European travel, which includes country and city guidebooks, Snapshots (excerpted chapters from bigger guides), Pocket guides (full-color little books on big cities), "Best Of" guidebooks (condensed, full-color country guides), and my budget-travel skills handbook, *Rick Steves Europe Through the Back Door*. A complete list of my titles—including phrase books, cruising guides,

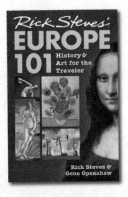

and travelogues on European art, history, and culture—appears near the end of this book.

TV Shows and Travel Talks: My public television series, *Rick Steves' Europe*, covers Europe from top to bottom with over 100 half-hour episodes—and we're working on new shows every year (watch full episodes at my website for free). My free online video library, Rick Steves Classroom Europe, offers a searchable database of short video clips on European history, culture, and geography (Classroom.RickSteves.com). And to raise your travel I.Q., check out the video versions of our popular classes (covering most European countries as well as travel skills, packing smart, cruising, tech for travelers, European art, and travel as a political act—RickSteves.com/travel-talks).

Audio Tours on My Free App: I've produced dozens of free, self-guided audio tours of the top sights in Europe. For those tours and other audio content, get my free **Rick Steves Audio Europe app,** an extensive online library organized by destination. For more on my app, see page 26.

Radio: My weekly public radio show, *Travel with Rick Steves*, features interviews with travel experts from around the world. It airs on 400 public radio stations across the US. An archive of programs) is available at RickSteves.com/radio.

Podcasts: You can enjoy my travel content via several free podcasts. The podcast version of my radio show brings you a weekly, hour-long travel conversation. My other podcasts include a weekly selection of video clips from my public television show, my audio tours of Europe's top sights, and live recordings of my travel classes (RickSteves.com/watch-read-listen/audio/podcasts).

APPENDIX

Holidays and Festivals

This list includes selected festivals in major cities, plus national holidays observed throughout Portugal. Many sights and banks close on national holidays—keep this in mind when planning your itinerary. Before planning a trip around a festival, verify its dates by checking the festival's website or TI sites (www.visitportugal. com). Note that Fátima receives an influx of pilgrims on every 13th from May until October (when the apparitions occurred in 1917). St. Anthony's Day is June 13, but it's celebrated during the entire month of June in Lisbon.

Jan 1	New Year's Day
Feb-March	Carnival (Mardi Gras, a.k.a. Entrudo). Particularly vibrant in Lisbon and Algarve towns, some closures on Shrove Tuesday
Early April	Lisbon Fish & Flavors (*Peixe em Lisboa*, gourmet seafood festival)
Week before Easter	Holy Week (Semana Santa). Religious processions, especially in Óbidos and Porto
Easter weekend (Good Friday-Easter Sunday)	April 2-5, 2021; April 15-18, 2022

April 25	Liberty Day (parades, fireworks)
May 1	Labor Day
Early May	Queima das Fitas, Coimbra ("burning of ribbons," graduation festivities)
May 13	Pilgrimage to Fátima (Peregrinação de Fátima)
June	Festas de Lisboa (series of festivals with celebrations peaking on St. Anthony's Day, Lisbon)
Late spring-early summer	Festival de Sintra (www.festivaldesintra.pt)
June 10	Portuguese National Day (Dia de Camões)
Mid-June	Corpus Christi (religious festival); June 3 in 2021; June 16, 2022
June 13	St. Anthony's Day (Dia de Santo António), Lisbon (dancing, processions)
June 24	St. John's Day (Dia de São João), Porto (fireworks, dancing)
June 29	St. Peter's Day (Dia de São Pedro), Évora (dancing, processions)
Aug 15	Assumption (religious festival)
Sept 8	Our Lady of Nazaré Festival (procession, folk dancing, fairs), Nazaré
Oct 5	Republic Day
Oct 13	Pilgrimage to Fátima (Peregrinação de Fátima)
Nov 1	All Saints Day
Dec 1	Restoration of Independence Day
Dec 8	Feast of the Immaculate Conception
Dec 25	Christmas
Dec 31	New Year's Eve

Books and Films

To learn more about Portugal past and present, check out a few of these books and films.

NONFICTION

The Book of Disquiet (Fernando Pessoa, 1982). This collection of unpublished poetry and thoughts from the great Portuguese writer, Fernando Pessoa, was compiled after they were found in a trunk following his death.

The First Global Village (Martin Page, 2002). Page explores Portugal's profound influence on the rest of the world.

The History of Portugal (James Anderson, 2000). Anderson provides a concise, readable overview of Portuguese history.

The Last Day: Wrath, Ruin, and Reason in the Great Lisbon Earthquake of 1755 (Nicholas Shrady, 2008). The earthquake that leveled Lisbon not only destroyed one of the leading European cities of the time, but also had a lasting effect on the world at large.

Over the Edge of the World: Magellan's Terrifying Circumnavigation of the Globe (Laurence Bergreen, 2003). Magellan's fascinating tale of circumnavigating the globe is told through firsthand accounts.

Portugal: A Companion History (José Hermano Saraiva, 1997). This easily digestible primer on Portugal is accompanied by maps and illustrations.

The Portuguese: A Modern History (Barry Hatton, 2011). Hatton combines information on the country's history, landscape, and culture with anecdotes from his own experience living in Portugal.

The Portuguese Empire, 1415-1808: A World on the Move (A.J.R. Russell-Wood, 1998). Russell-Wood explores the rise and fall of the Portuguese empire.

Prince Henry the Navigator: A Life (Peter Russell, 2000). This biography reveals the man who helped set into motion the Age of Discovery.

Unknown Seas: How Vasco da Gama Opened the East (Ronald Watkins, 2005). Reconstructing journeys from captain's logs, this book explores the expansion of Portuguese trade routes.

FICTION

Baltasar and Blimunda (José Saramago, 1998). Saramago's love story offers a surrealistic reflection on life in 18th-century Portugal.

The Crime of Father Amaro (Jose Maria de Eça de Queirós, 1875). Set in a provincial Portuguese town, this book by the great

19th-century Portuguese novelist highlights the dangers of fanaticism.

Distant Music (Lee Langley, 2003). Catholic Esperança and Jewish Emmanuel have an affair that lasts through six centuries and multiple incarnations; the book also delves into Portugal's maritime empire, Sephardic Jews, and Portuguese immigrants in London.

The Last Kabbalist of Lisbon (Richard Zimler, 1996). The author illuminates the persecution of the Jews in Portugal in the early 1500s.

The Lusiads (Luís de Camões, 1572). Considered a national treasure, Camões' great epic poems of the Renaissance immortalize Portugal's voyages of discovery.

Night Train to Lisbon (Pascal Mercier, 2004). Mercier's international bestseller-turned-2013-film follows the travels of a Swiss professor as he explores the life of a Portuguese doctor during Salazar's dictatorship.

Pereira Declares: A Testimony (Antonio Tabucchi, 1997). Set in Portugal in 1938 during Salazar's fascist government, *Pereira Declares* is the story of the moral resurrection of a newspaper's cautious editor.

A Small Death in Lisbon (Robert Wilson, 2002). In this award-winning thriller, a contemporary police procedural is woven with an espionage story set during World War II, with Portugal's 20th-century history as a backdrop.

FILM AND TV

Amália (2008). This film captures the life of Portugal's beloved fado singer, Amália Rodrigues, who rose from poverty to international fame. (If the film is hard to find, listen to a YouTube clip of her lovely singing.)

The Art of Amália (2000). Interviews with the diva are highlighted in this documentary chronicling her rise to fame.

Capitães de Abril (2000). The story of the 1974 coup that overthrew the right-wing Portuguese dictatorship is told from the perspective of two young army captains.

Letters from Fontainhas (2010). This trio of short films follows three troubled lives in Lisbon.

Pereira Declares (1996). Marcello Mastroianni plays the namesake in this film inspired by the Tabucchi novel mentioned earlier.

The Strange Case of Angelica (2010). Manoel de Oliveira's film about a photographer haunted by a deceased bride is set against the landscape of the Douro Valley.

Conversions and Climate

Numbers and Stumblers

- Europeans write a few of their numbers differently than we do. 1 = 1 , 4 = 4 , 7 = 7 .
- In Europe, dates appear as day/month/year, so Christmas 2021 is 25/12/21.
- Commas are decimal points and decimals commas. A dollar and a half is $1,50, one thousand is 1.000, and there are 5.280 feet in a mile.
- When counting with fingers, start with your thumb. If you hold up your first finger to request one item, you'll probably get two.
- What Americans call the second floor of a building is the first floor in Europe.
- On escalators and moving sidewalks, Europeans keep the left "lane" open for passing. Keep to the right.

Metric Conversions

A **kilogram** equals 1,000 grams (about 2.2 pounds). One hundred **grams** (a common unit at markets) is about a quarter-pound. One **liter** is about a quart, or almost four to a gallon.

A **kilometer** is six-tenths of a mile. To convert kilometers to miles, cut the kilometers in half and add back 10 percent of the original (120 km: 60 + 12 = 72 miles). One **meter** is 39 inches—just over a yard.

1 foot = 0.3 meter	1 square yard = 0.8 square meter
1 yard = 0.9 meter	1 square mile = 2.6 square kilometers
1 mile = 1.6 kilometers	1 ounce = 28 grams
1 centimeter = 0.4 inch	1 quart = 0.95 liter
1 meter = 39.4 inches	1 kilogram = 2.2 pounds
1 kilometer = 0.62 mile	32°F = 0°C

Clothing Sizes

When shopping for clothing, use these US-to-European comparisons as general guidelines (but note that no conversion is perfect).

Women: For pants and dresses, add 32 in Portugal (US 10 = Portuguese 42). For blouses and sweaters, add 8 for most of Europe (US 32 = European 40). For shoes, add 30-31 (US 7 = European 37/38).

Men: For shirts, multiply by 2 and add about 8 (US 15 = European 38). For jackets and suits, add 10. For shoes, add 32-34.

Children: Clothing is sized by height—in centimeters (2.5 cm = 1 inch), so a US size 8 roughly equates to 132-140. For shoes up to size 13, add 16-18, and for sizes 1 and up, add 30-32.

Climate

…erage daily high; second line, average daily low; third
line, … days with some rain. For more detailed weather sta-
tistics for destinations in this book (as well as the rest of the world),
check www.wunderground.com.

	J	F	M	A	M	J	J	A	S	O	N	D
Lisbon												
	57°	59°	63°	67°	71°	77°	81°	82°	79°	72°	63°	58°
	46°	47°	50°	53°	55°	60°	63°	63°	62°	58°	52°	47°
	16	16	17	20	21	25	29	29	24	22	17	16
Faro (Algarve)												
	60°	61°	64°	67°	71°	77°	83°	83°	78°	72°	66°	61°
	48°	49°	52°	55°	58°	64°	67°	68°	65°	60°	55°	50°
	22	21	21	24	27	29	31	31	29	25	22	22

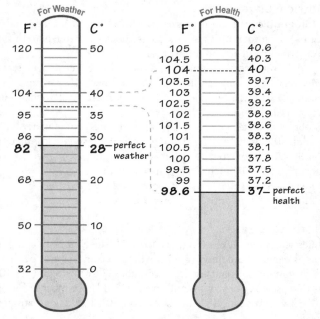

Fahrenheit and Celsius Conversion

Europe takes its temperature using the Celsius scale, while we
opt for Fahrenheit. For a rough conversion from Celsius to
Fahrenheit, double the number and add 30. For weather, remember
that 28°C is 82°F—perfect. For health, 37°C is just right. At a
launderette, 30°C is cold, 40°C is warm (usually the default
setting), 60°C is hot, and 95°C is boiling. Your air-conditioner
should be set at about 20°C.

Packing Checklist

Whether you're traveling for five days or five weeks, you won't need more than this. Pack light to enjoy the sweet freedom of true mobility.

Clothing

- ☐ 5 shirts: long- & short-sleeve
- ☐ 2 pairs pants (or skirts/capris)
- ☐ 1 pair shorts
- ☐ 5 pairs underwear & socks
- ☐ 1 pair walking shoes
- ☐ Sweater or warm layer
- ☐ Rainproof jacket with hood
- ☐ Tie, scarf, belt, and/or hat
- ☐ Swimsuit
- ☐ Sleepwear/loungewear

Money

- ☐ Debit card(s)
- ☐ Credit card(s)
- ☐ Hard cash (US $100-200)
- ☐ Money belt

Documents

- ☐ Passport
- ☐ Tickets & confirmations: flights, hotels, trains, rail pass, car rental, sight entries
- ☐ Driver's license
- ☐ Student ID, hostel card, etc.
- ☐ Photocopies of important documents
- ☐ Insurance details
- ☐ Guidebooks & maps

Toiletries Kit

- ☐ Basics: soap, shampoo, toothbrush, toothpaste, floss, deodorant, sunscreen, brush/comb, etc.
- ☐ Medicines & vitamins
- ☐ First-aid kit
- ☐ Glasses/contacts/sunglasses
- ☐ Sewing kit
- ☐ Packet of tissues (for WC)
- ☐ Earplugs

Electronics

- ☐ Mobile phone
- ☐ Camera & related gear
- ☐ Tablet/ebook reader/laptop
- ☐ Headphones/earbuds
- ☐ Chargers & batteries
- ☐ Phone car charger & mount (or GPS device)
- ☐ Plug adapters

Miscellaneous

- ☐ Daypack
- ☐ Sealable plastic baggies
- ☐ Laundry supplies: soap, laundry bag, clothesline, spot remover
- ☐ Small umbrella
- ☐ Travel alarm/watch
- ☐ Notepad & pen
- ☐ Journal

Optional Extras

- ☐ Second pair of shoes (flip-flops, sandals, tennis shoes, boots)
- ☐ Travel hairdryer
- ☐ Picnic supplies
- ☐ Water bottle
- ☐ Fold-up tote bag
- ☐ Small flashlight
- ☐ Mini binoculars
- ☐ Small towel or washcloth
- ☐ Inflatable pillow/neck rest
- ☐ Tiny lock
- ☐ Address list (to mail postcards)
- ☐ Extra passport photos

APPENDIX

Portuguese Survival Phrases

In the phonetics, nasalized vowels are indicated by an <u>n</u> or <u>w</u>. As you say the vowel, let its sound come through your nose as well as your mouth.

English	Portuguese	Pronunciation
Good day.	*Bom dia.*	bohn **dee**-ah
Do you speak English?	*Fala inglês?*	**fah**-lah een-**glaysh**
Yes. / No.	*Sim. / Não.*	seeng / no<u>w</u>
I (don't) understand.	*(Não) compreendo.*	(no<u>w</u>) koh<u>n</u>-pree-**ayn**-doo
Please.	*Por favor.*	poor fah-**vor**
Thank you. (said by male)	*Obrigado.*	oo-bree-**gah**-doo
Thank you. (said by female)	*Obrigada.*	oo-bree-**gah**-dah
I'm sorry.	*Desculpe.*	dish-**kool**-peh
Excuse me (to pass).	*Com licença.*	koh<u>n</u> li-**sehn**-sah
(No) problem.	*(Não) há problema.*	(no<u>w</u>) ah proo-**blay**-mah
Good.	*Bom.*	boh<u>n</u>
Goodbye.	*Adeus. / Ciao.*	ah-**deh**-oosh / chow
one / two	*um / dois*	oo<u>n</u> / doysh
three / four	*três / quatro*	traysh / **kwah**-troo
five / six	*cinco / seis*	**seeng**-koo / saysh
seven / eight	*sete / oito*	**seh**-teh / **oy**-too
nine / ten	*nove / dez*	**naw**-veh / dehsh
How much is it?	*Quanto é?*	**kwahn**-too eh
Write it?	*Escreva?*	ish-**kray**-vah
Is it free?	*É gratis?*	eh **grah**-teesh
Is it included?	*Está incluido?*	ish-**tah** een-kloo-**ee**-doo
Where can I find / buy...?	*Onde posso encontrar / comprar...?*	**ohn**-deh **paw**-soo ayn-kohn-**trar** / kohn-**prar**
I'd like / We'd like...	*Gostaria / Gostaríamos...*	goosh-tah-**ree**-ah / goosh-tah-**ree**-ah-moosh
...a room.	*...um quarto.*	oo<u>n</u> **kwar**-too
...a ticket to ___.	*...um bilhete para ___.*	oo<u>n</u> beel-**yeh**-teh **pah**-rah ___
Is it possible?	*É possível?*	eh poo-**see**-vehl
Where is...?	*Onde é que é...?*	**ohn**-deh eh keh eh
...the train station	*...a estação de comboio*	ah ish-tah-**sow** deh koh<u>n</u>-**boy**-yoo
...the bus station	*...a terminal de autocarros*	ah tehr-mee-**nahl** deh ow-too-**kah**-roosh
...the tourist information office	*...a posto de turismo*	ah **poh**-stoo deh too-**reez**-moo
...the toilet	*...a casa de banho*	ah **kah**-zah deh **bahn**-yoo
men	*homens*	**aw**-may<u>n</u>sh
women	*mulheres*	mool-**yeh**-rish
left / right	*esquerda / direita*	ish-**kehr**-dah / dee-**ray**-tah
straight	*em frente*	ayn **frayn**-teh
What time does this open / close?	*As que horas é que abre / fecha?*	ahsh keh **aw**-rahsh eh keh **ah**-breh / **feh**-shah
At what time?	*As que horas?*	ahsh keh **aw**-rahsh
Just a moment.	*Um momento.*	oo<u>n</u> moo-**mayn**-too
now / soon / later	*agora / em breve / mais tarde*	ah-**goh**-rah / ayn **bray**-veh / maish **tar**-deh
today / tomorrow	*hoje / amanhã*	**oh**-zheh / ah-ming-**yah**

In a Portuguese Restaurant

English	Portuguese	Pronunciation
I'd like / We'd like...	Gostaria / Gostaríamos...	goosh-tah-**ree**-ah / goosh-tah-**ree**-ah-moosh
...to reserve...	...de reservar...	deh reh-zehr-**var**
...a table for one. / two.	...uma mesa para uma. / duas.	**oo**-mah **may**-zah pah-rah **oo**-mah / **doo**-ahsh
Non-smoking.	Não fumar.	now foo-**mar**
Is this table free?	Esta mesa está livre?	ehsh-tah meh-zah ish-**tah** **lee**-vreh
The menu (in English), please.	A ementa (em inglês) por favor.	ah eh-**mayn**-tah (ay<u>n</u> een-**glaysh**) poor fah-vor
service (not) included	serviço (não) incluído	sehr-**vee**-soo (no<u>w</u>) een-kloo-**ee**-doo
cover charge	coberto	koh-**behr**-too
to go	para fora	**pah**-rah **foh**-rah
with / without	com / sem	koh<u>n</u> / say<u>n</u>
and / or	e / ou	ee / oh
specialty of the house	especialidade da casa	ish-peh-see-ah-lee-**dah**-deh dah **kah**-zah
half portion	meia dose	**may**-ah **doh**-zeh
daily special	prato do dia	**prah**-too doo **dee**-ah
tourist menu	ementa turística	eh-**mayn**-tah too-**reesh**-tee-kah
appetizers	entradas	ay<u>n</u>-**trah**-dahsh
bread / cheese	pão / queijo	pow / **kay**-zhoo
sandwich	sandes	**sahn**-desh
soup / salad	sopa / salada	**soh**-pah / sah-**lah**-dah
meat	carne	**kar**-neh
poultry	aves	**ah**-vish
fish / seafood	peixe / marisco	**pay**-shee / mah-**reesh**-koo
fruit	fruta	**froo**-tah
vegetables	legumes	lay-**goo**-mish
dessert	sobremesa	soo-breh-**may**-zah
tap water	água da torneira	**ah**-gwah dah tor-**nay**-rah
mineral water	água mineral	**ah**-gwah mee-neh-**rahl**
milk	leite	**lay**-teh
(orange) juice	sumo (de laranja)	**soo**-moo (deh lah-**rahn**-zhah)
coffee / tea	café / chá	kah-**feh** / shah
wine	vinho	**veen**-yoo
red / white	tinto / branco	**teen**-too / **brang**-koo
glass / bottle	copo / garrafa	**koh**-poo / gah-**rah**-fah
beer	cerveja	sehr-**vay**-zhah
Cheers!	Saúde!	sah-**oo**-deh
More. / Another.	Mais. / Outro.	maish / **oh**-troo
The same.	O mesmo.	oo **mehsh**-moo
The bill, please.	A conta, por favor.	ah-**kohn**-tah poor fah-**vor**
tip	gorjeta	gor-**zheh**-tah
Delicious!	Delicioso!	deh-lee-see-**oh**-zoo

For many more pages of survival phrases for your trip to Portugal, check out *Rick Steves Portuguese Phrase Book*.

INDEX

MAP INDEX

Explore Europe

At ricksteves.com you can browse through thousands of articles, videos, photos and radio interviews, plus find a wealth of money-saving travel tips for planning your dream trip. And with our mobile-friendly website, you can easily access all this great travel information anywhere you go.

TV Shows

Preview the places you'll visit by watching entire half-hour episodes of *Rick Steves' Europe* (choose from all 100 shows) on-demand, for free.

ur travel dreams into affordable reality

dio Interviews

oy ready access to
k's vast library of radio
rviews covering travel
and cultural insights
t relate specifically to
r Europe travel plans.

avel Forums

rn, ask, share! Our
ine community of
vy travelers is a great
urce for first-time
elers to Europe, as
l as seasoned pros.

Travel News

Subscribe to our free
Travel News e-newsletter,
and get monthly updates
from Rick on what's
happening in Europe.

Classroom Europe

Check out our free resource
for educators with 400+
short video clips from the
Rick Steves' Europe
TV show.

Audio Europe™

Rick's Free Travel App

Get your FREE **Rick Steves Audio Europe**™ app to enjoy…

- Dozens of self-guided tours of Europe's top museums, sights and historic walks

- Hundreds of tracks filled with cultural insights and sightseeing tips from Rick's radio interviews

- All organized into handy geographic playlists

- For Apple and Android

With Rick whispering in your ear, Europe gets even better.

Find out more at **ricksteves.com**

Save time and energy

This guidebook is your independent-travel toolkit. But for all it delivers, it's still up to you to devote the time and energy it takes to manage the preparation and logistics that are essential for a happy trip. If that's a hassle, there's a solution.

Rick Steves Tours

A Rick Steves tour takes you to Europe's most interesting places with great

with minimum stress

guides and small groups. We follow Rick's favorite itineraries, ride in comfy buses, stay in family-run hotels, and bring you intimately close to the Europe you've traveled so far to see. Most importantly, we take away the logistical headaches so you can focus on the fun.

Join the fun

This year we'll take thousands of free-spirited travelers—nearly half of them repeat customers—along with us on 50 different itineraries, from Athens to Istanbul. Is a Rick Steves tour the right fit for your travel dreams?

Find out at ricksteves.com, where you can also check seat availability and sign up. Europe is best experienced with happy travel partners. We hope you can join us.

See our itineraries at ricksteves.com

BEST OF GUIDES

Full-color guides in an easy-to-scan format. Focused on top sights and experiences in the most popular European destinations

Best of England
Best of Europe
Best of France
Best of Germany
Best of Ireland
Best of Italy
Best of Scotland
Best of Spain

COMPREHENSIVE GUIDES

*City, country, and regional gu...
printed on Bible-thin paper. P...
with detailed coverage for a r...
week trip exploring iconic sig...
and venturing off the beaten...*

Amsterdam & the Netherland...
Barcelona
Belgium: Bruges, Brussels,
  Antwerp & Ghent
Berlin
Budapest
Croatia & Slovenia
Eastern Europe
England
Florence & Tuscany
France
Germany
Great Britain
Greece: Athens & the Pelopo...
Iceland
Ireland
Istanbul
Italy
London
Paris
Portugal
Prague & the Czech Republic
Provence & the French Rivier...
Rome
Scandinavia
Scotland
Sicily
Spain
Switzerland
Venice
Vienna, Salzburg & Tirol

HE BEST OF ROME

ne, Italy's capital, is studded with
an remnants and floodlit-fountain
res. From the Vatican to the Colos-
, with crazy traffic in between, Rome
nderful, huge, and exhausting. The
ds, the heat, and the weighty history

of the Eternal City where Caesars walked
can make tourists wilt. Recharge by taking siestas, gelato breaks, and after-dark
walks, strolling from one atmospheric
square to another in the refreshing evening air.

ed *Pantheon*—which
est dome until the
ly 2,000 years old
ty over 1,500).

of Athens in the *Vat-
dies the humanistic
ce.

gladiators fought
nother, entertaining

Complete your library with...

Credits

RESEARCHER
To help update this book, Rick relied on...

Robert Wright

Raised in Memphis, Robert funded his first dream trip to Europe in 1998 by selling his entire *Star Wars* collection—proof that where there's a will, there's a way. He fell in love with Spain and Portugal and constantly returned, all while living for 14 years in Argentina. Robert recently married a *sevillano* and moved to Spain. He continues to enjoy Iberian architecture and loves uncovering forgotten connections between Spain and Portugal's intertwined history.

CONTRIBUTOR
Gene Openshaw

Gene has co-authored more than a dozen *Rick Steves* books, specializing in writing walks and tours of Europe's cities, museums, and cultural sights. He also writes for Rick's public television series, produces audio tours on Europe, and is a regular guest on Rick's public radio show. Outside of the travel world, Gene has co-authored *The Seattle Joke Book*. As a composer, he has written an opera called *Matter,* a violin sonata, and dozens of songs. He lives near Seattle, where he enjoys giving presentations on art and history, and roots for the Mariners in good times and bad.

Acknowledgments

Thanks to Cameron Hewitt for writing the original versions of the Porto and Douro Valley chapters, and to Robert Wright for his contributions over the years. And thank you to Risa Laib for her 25-plus years of dedication to the Rick Steves guidebook series.

Photo Credits

Avalon Travel
Hachette Book Group
1700 Fourth Street
Berkeley, CA 94710

Printed in Canada by Friesens.
11th Edition. First printing March 2021.

ISBN 978-1-64171-376-4

For the latest on Rick's talks, guidebooks, tours, public television series, and public radio
show, contact Rick Steves' Europe, 130 Fourth Avenue North, Edmonds, WA 98020,
425/771-8303, www.ricksteves.com, rick@ricksteves.com.

Rick Steves' Europe
Managing Editor: Jennifer Madison Davis
Assistant Managing Editor: Cathy Lu
Editors: Glenn Eriksen, Suzanne Kotz, Rosie Leutzinger, Jessica Shaw, Carrie Shepherd
Editorial & Production Assistant: Megan Simms
Researcher: Robert Wright
Research Assistance: Rich Earl, Lisa Friend
Contributor: Gene Openshaw
Graphic Content Director: Sandra Hundacker
Maps & Graphics: David C. Hoerlein, Lauren Mills, Mary Rostad
Digital Asset Coordinator: Orin Dubrow

Avalon Travel
Senior Editor and Series Manager: Madhu Prasher
Associate Managing Editors: Jamie Andrade, Sierra Machado
Indexer: Stephen Callahan
Production & Typesetting: Lisi Baldwin, Jane Musser
Cover Design: Kimberly Glyder Design
Maps & Graphics: Kat Bennett, Mike Morgenfeld

COLOR MAPS

Lisbon • Porto • Sintra • Portugal

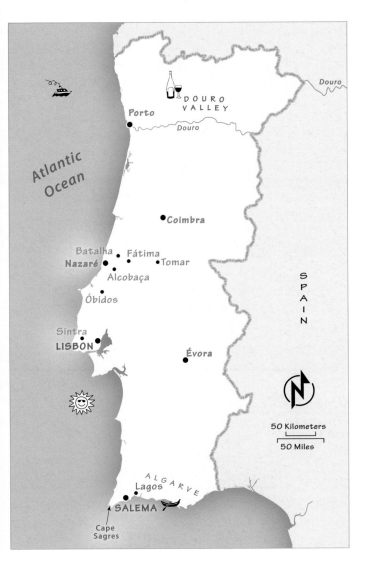

Douro

DOURO VALLEY

Porto

Douro

Atlantic Ocean

Coimbra

Batalha • Fátima
Nazaré • Tomar
Alcobaça

Óbidos

Sintra
LISBON

Évora

S P A I N

50 Kilometers

50 Miles

ALGARVE
Lagos

SALEMA

Cape
Sagres

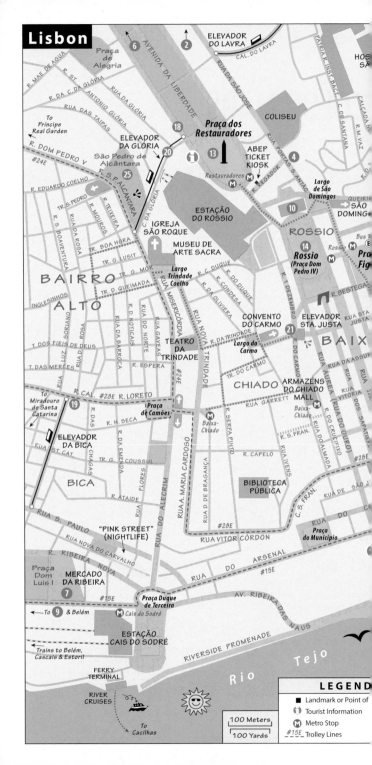

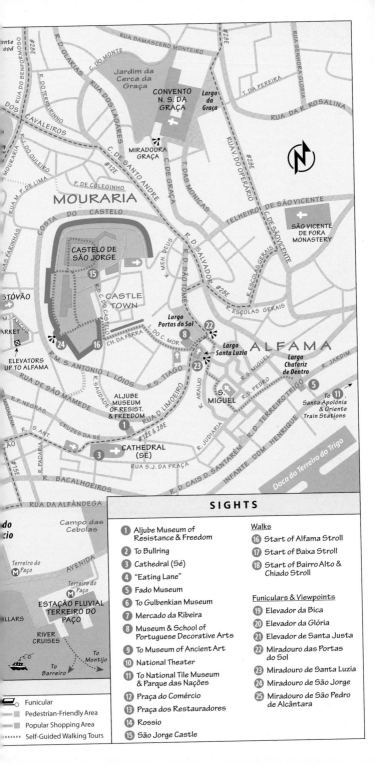

SIGHTS

1 Aljube Museum of Resistance & Freedom
2 To Bullring
3 Cathedral (Sé)
4 "Eating Lane"
5 Fado Museum
6 To Gulbenkian Museum
7 Mercado da Ribeira
8 Museum & School of Portuguese Decorative Arts
9 To Museum of Ancient Art
10 National Theater
11 To National Tile Museum & Parque das Nações
12 Praça do Comércio
13 Praça dos Restauradores
14 Rossio
15 São Jorge Castle

Walks

16 Start of Alfama Stroll
17 Start of Baixa Stroll
18 Start of Bairro Alto & Chiado Stroll

Funiculars & Viewpoints

19 Elevador da Bica
20 Elevador da Glória
21 Elevador de Santa Justa
22 Miradouro das Portas do Sol
23 Miradouro de Santa Luzia
24 Miradouro de São Jorge
25 Miradouro de São Pedro de Alcântara

Porto Center

TRINDADE CHURCH

Praça da Trindade

CITY HALL

RUA DA CONCEICAO

Praça Delgado

Praça de Carlos Alberto

RUA CEUTA

Praça Lencastre

Praça Fernandes

PADARIA RIBEIRO

#22

R. S. TERESA

TOURIGA WINE SHOP

CARMO CHURCH

ARMAZÉNS CUNHAS

RUA DA FÁBRICA

#18

Praça Teixeira

LELLO & IRMÃO BOOKSTORE

CITY

SANTO ANTONIO HOSPITAL

#18 & 22

A VIDA PORT. SHOP

CLÉRIGOS TOWER

Praça da Liberdade

IMPERIA McDONAL

#18

UNIV. OF PORTO

Praça de Lisboa

Aliados

PEDRO IV STATUE

Aliados

Jardim de Cordoaria

R. CAMPO DOS MÁRTIRES DA PÁTRIA

#22

São Bento

SÃO TRA

Largo Amores de Perdição

RUA DE TRÁS

TRANS OFF

CEN

RUA DA VITÓRIA

MISERICÓRDIA CHURCH & MUSEUM

RUA DAS FLORES

RUA MOUZINHO DA SILVEIRA

RUA AFONSO HENRIQUES

RUA C

To Tramway Museum & Foz

RUA BELOMONTE

Largo São Domingos

CALC. VANDOMA

R. C

TOWER

Cathedral Square

PORTO CATHEDRAL

PORT & DOURO WINES INSTITUTE

BORGES MARKET

OLIVA & CO.

RUA SÃO JOÃO NOVO

GRILOS CHURCH

RUA DOM HUGO

METRO LINE

STOCK EXCHANGE PALACE

RUA F. BORGES

Praça Infante

SÃO FRANCISCO

#500

#1

RUA INFANTE DOM HENRIQUE

HOUSE OF HENRY THE NAVIGATOR

PORTOLOGIA

Praça da Ribeira

GUINDAIS FUNICULAR

TO

RUA DE CIMA DO MURO

R. OUT

CAIS DA ESTIVA

CAIS DA RIBEIRA

RIBEIRA

LOWER-BRIDGE (CAR)

To Ponte Arrábida & Atlantic Ocean

RIVER CRUISES

RABELO BOATS

RIVER CRUISES

UPPER BRIDGE (RAIL)

Douro River

RIVER TAXI TO GAIA

VILA NOVA DE GAIA

See detail map

RUA DE FERNANDES TOMAS

TEMPORARY BOLHÃO MARKET

200 Meters
200 Yards

RUA DR. ALVES DA VEIGA

RUA DA ALEGRIA

RUA DE DOM JOÃO IV

To Campo 24 de Agosto
Rede Expresses & Internorte Bus Station

OLD BOLHÃO MARKET (MAY BE CLOSED FOR RENOVATION)

Bolhão

DEPT. STORE

RUA DE SANTA CATARINA

RUA FORMOSA

SHOPPING STREET

RODONORTE BUS STN.

CAFÉ MAJESTIC

RUA DE PASSOS MANUEL

COLISEO DO PORTO

RUA DE SANTO ILDEFONSO

RUA DO MORGADO DE MATEUS

FNAC DEPT. STORE

#22

SAN IDELFONSO CHURCH

RUA ADEIRA

Praça da Batalha

#22

CINEMA

NAT'L THEATER

R. DA AUGUSTO ROSA

RUA HERCULANO

RUA DO DUQUE DE LOULE

AVE. DE RODRIGUES DE FREITAS

To Campanhã Train Station

RUA DAS FONTAINHAS

talha

Vila Nova de Gaia

To Porto Center

100 Meters
100 Yards

RIBEIRA DISTRICT

PONTE LUÍS I

RIVER TAXI

LOWER LEVEL (CAR)

UPPER LEVEL (RAIL)

SERRA DO PILAR MONASTERY

Port Lodges (Tasting)

Douro River

Largo Miguel Bombarda

KOPKE WINE SHOP

AV. D. LEITE

CÁLEM

Jardim do Morro

BOAT TRIPS & RIVER TAXI

Largo Cruz

Cable Car

AVENIDA RAMOS PINTO

RUA 7 PASS.

R. FERN.

SANDEMAN

RUA PILAR

Jardim do Morro

AVENIDA DA REPÚBLICA

FERREIRA

VASQUES DE CARVALHO

QUINTA DE S. EUFÉMIA

RUA COSTA SANTOS

R. CANDIDO DOS REIS

R. GENERAL TORRES

ria Pia, ao João, Freixo Valley

RUA DR. A. GRANJO

R. REI RAMIRO

CROFT

R. BARÃO

RUA RAMADA ALTA

SERRA PINTO

R. AZENHAS

TAYLOR'S

RUA CAMÕES

General Torres

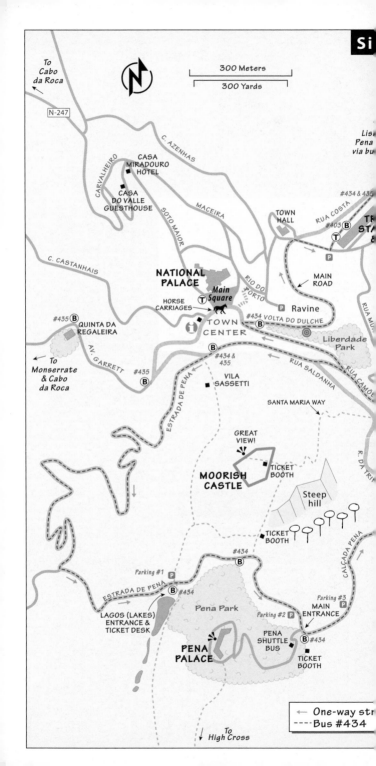

Si

To Cabo da Roca

N-247

To Cabo da Roca

C. AZENHAS

CARVALHEIRO

CASA MIRADOURO HOTEL

CASA DO VALLE GUESTHOUSE

SOTO MAIOR

MACEIRA

Lis
Pena
via bu

TOWN HALL

RUA COSTA

#434 & 435

#403 (B)

TR
STA
&

(T)

P

C. CASTANHAIS

NATIONAL PALACE

Main Square

RIO DO PORTO

(T)

HORSE CARRIAGES

MAIN ROAD

P Ravine

RUA MU

TOWN CENTER

#434 VOLTA DO DULCHE

(B)

Liberdade Park

#455 (B) QUINTA DA REGALEIRA

AV. GARRETT

(i)

(B)

RUA CAMÕE

To Monserrate & Cabo da Roca

#455

#434 & 435

(B)

#435

RUA SALDANHA

ESTRADA DE PENA

VILA SASSETTI

SANTA MARIA WAY

GREAT VIEW!

R. DA TRI

MOORISH CASTLE

TICKET BOOTH

Steep hill

TICKET BOOTH

CALÇADA PENA

#434

(B)

Parking #1 P

ESTRADA DE PENA

(B) #434

Pena Park

Parking #2 P

Parking #3 MAIN ENTRANCE P

LAGOS (LAKES) ENTRANCE & TICKET DESK

PENA SHUTTLE BUS

PENA PALACE

(B) #434

TICKET BOOTH

To High Cross

300 Meters

300 Yards

← One-way str
---- Bus #434

More for your trip!
Maximize the experience with Rick Steves as your guide

Guidebooks
Make side trips smooth and affordable with Rick's Spain and Barcelona guides

Phrase Books
Rely on Rick's Portuguese Phrase Book & Dictionary

Rick's TV Shows
Preview your destinations with a variety of shows covering Portugal

Rick's Audio Europe™ App
Get a free self-guided audio tour for Lisbon

Small Group Tours
Take a lively, low-stress Rick Steves tour of Portugal

For all the details, visit r.icksteves.com